To Jessica -- A great teacher educator!
Cordially,
Gail McCrohon
January 2001

SELF IN THE WORLD

Elementary and Middle School Social Studies

SELF IN THE WORLD

Elementary and Middle School Social Studies

Gail A. McEachron
The College of William and Mary

Boston   Burr Ridge, IL   Dubuque, IA   Madison, WI   New York   San Francisco   St. Louis
Bangkok   Bogotá   Caracas   Lisbon   London   Madrid
Mexico City   Milan   New Delhi   Seoul   Singapore   Sydney   Taipei   Toronto

McGraw-Hill Higher Education

A Division of The **McGraw-Hill** Companies

SELF IN THE WORLD: ELEMENTARY AND MIDDLE SCHOOL SOCIAL STUDIES

Published by McGraw-Hill, an imprint of The McGraw-Hill Companies, Inc., 1221 Avenue of the Americas, New York, NY 10020. Copyright © 2001 by The McGraw-Hill Companies, Inc. All rights reserved. No part of this publication may be reproduced or distributed in any form or by any means, or stored in a database or retrieval system, without the prior written consent of The McGraw-Hill Companies, Inc., including, but not limited to, in any network or other electronic storage or transmission, or broadcast for distance learning.

Some ancillaries, including electronic and print components, may not be available to customers outside the United States.

This book is printed on acid-free paper.

1 2 3 4 5 6 7 8 9 0 QPF/QPF 0 9 8 7 6 5 4 3 2 1 0

ISBN 0–07–239077–8

Vice president and editor-in-chief: *Thalia Dorwick*
Editorial director: *Jane E. Vaicunas*
Sponsoring editor: *Beth Kaufman*
Developmental editor: *Cara Harvey*
Marketing manager: *Daniel M. Loch*
Project manager: *Christine Walker*
Production supervisor: *Kara Kudronowicz*
Coordinator of freelance design: *Michelle M. Meerdink*
Freelance cover designer: *Jamie A. O'Neal*
Cover image: *©Stephen Simpson; FPG International*
Photo research coordinator: *John C. Leland*
Photo research: *Alexandra Truitt & Jerry Marshall*
Supplement coordinator: *Jodi K. Banowetz*
Compositor: *Carlisle Communications, Ltd.*
Typeface: *10/12 Times Roman*
Printer: *Quebecor Printing Book Group/Fairfield, PA*

Library of Congress Cataloging-in-Publication Data
McEachron, Gail A.
 Self in the world : elementary and middle school social studies / Gail A. McEachron.—1st ed.
  p.   cm.
 Includes bibliographical references (p.) and index.
 ISBN 0–07–239077–8
 1. Social sciences—Study and teaching (Elementary)—United States. 2. Social sciences—Study and teaching (Middle school)—United States. I. Title.

 LB1584 .M383   2001
 372.83′044—dc21
                                                    00–033250
                                                      CIP

www.mhhe.com

BRIEF CONTENTS

TABLE OF CONTENTS

PREFACE

Self in the World: Elementary and Middle School Social Studies takes an innovative approach to social studies education. Its underlying theme makes connections between identity formation based on individual characteristics and interests, on the one hand, and social, political, and cultural norms, on the other hand. The significance of this premise is manifested in a variety of ways throughout *Self in the World*. First, *Self in the World* highlights the need to *integrate* social, psychological, and cognitive learning. Second, placing Self as the centerpiece to social learning dramatically challenges traditional social studies frameworks that emphasize the expanding horizons approach. In the *new scope and sequence,* the individual is integrated in learning from kindergarten through eighth grade, not confined to primary levels. At the same time, *Self in the World* addresses national and international dimensions in the primary grades, thereby acknowledging that social learning is not confined to the local community. Third, *Self in the World* not only demonstrates ways to relate to a variety of cultural contexts throughout each grade level, it provides ways that future teachers can incorporate the best *scholarship and practices* that have shaped the social studies field. Future teachers not only learn about best practices in the social studies, they become actively engaged in the material in ways that model effective social studies teaching and incorporate national standards. Each of these unique features is discussed in the following.

✦ INTEGRATING THE INDIVIDUAL IN SOCIETY

Throughout its evolution, social studies has emphasized the study of people and places collectively. This tradition based on the classics, political history, and military history, has influenced the curriculum in significant ways. Less attention has been given to the relationships between one's developing self and one's role in society. *Self in the World* bridges this gap by addressing social, psychological, and cognitive development. The world and more immediate communities are presented as entities with which one has a potential or real psychological connection. Cognitive development is viewed as the growing awareness and knowledge of Self and others as well as one's role in society.

Content from the social science disciplines and humanities is presented in relation to the developmental stages of children and youth. For example, when discussing time and chronology in Chapter 3, a discussion of children's orientations to time and space is given to guide preservice teachers in selecting appropriate subject matter. Unlike texts that present developmental stages in a generic fashion, *Self in the World* ties developmental learning to content in specific disciplines.

In "Professional Discussions and Field Experiences" preservice teachers are given opportunities for active participation as they begin their careers. Contemporary issues and classroom activities are included for students to integrate and apply their college and university learning. The section "Resources: Teacher and Student Materials" provides future teachers with the means to further their education, consult teaching resources, and participate in professional organizations.

Special features actively engage preservice students in the teaching profession. For example, the debate on student-initiated prayer, in Chapter 5, involves students in timely issues and current events. The debate not only provides a great social science model for students to use in the classroom where diverse points of view should be encouraged but also illustrates that the Bill of Rights is a living document. "Case Studies" are another way to integrate learning experiences. In Chapter 7, for example, the schooling experiences of Diane Bradford, a student who has both learning disabilities and gifted characteristics, portray the tough decisions that professionals make when trying to educate the whole child. Case studies model a teaching strategy appropriate to social studies, that is, oral history and interviews, while making teaching realities come alive for preservice students.

✦ SELF IN THE WORLD SCOPE AND SEQUENCE

The generation of educators who will witness the turn of the twentieth century is quite different from educators who lived in the early 1900s when the expanding horizons scope and sequence emerged. Access to the daily lives of people in the far reaches of the globe seemed unusual in the beginning of this century but now has become commonplace through round-the-clock news networks and Internet capabilities. As interdependent relationships have been made more explicit, the assumption that close geographical proximity is more relevant to learning no longer stands. Furthermore, the efforts of social psychologists underscore the dynamic relationship between self-acceptance and the acceptance of others, whether referring to neighbors or people in other countries. Looking ahead to the twenty-first century, it is important to reconceptualize the expanding horizons scope and sequence so that citizenship goals are inclusive of the international community. How world events influence a developing self is a phenomenon that is highlighted in this new scope and sequence.

Self in the World is a scope and sequence that permeates rigid geopolitical boundaries and centers the individual in a way that makes all realms accessible. *Self in the World* builds on the contributions of social studies educators and psychologists, such as John Dewey, Paul Hanna, Hilda Taba, and Jerome Bruner, who have attempted to make the multidimensional context of Self understandable to the elementary and middle school student. The important distinction made by this new configuration is that each of the psychosocial realms of identity can be investigated throughout the elementary and middle school years and beyond. In this way, understanding one's identity and role in the world through connecting spheres is more compatible with human growth and development.

✦ BEST PRACTICE IN SOCIAL STUDIES: ADDRESSING NATIONAL STANDARDS

Certain core ideas in curriculum and instruction are important when developing a social studies program. Core *curriculum* ideas include the history of the field; organizational patterns and scope and sequence; social science disciplines; interdisciplinarity; pluralism; facts, concepts, and generalizations; skill development; and current events. Professional educators continuously build on these core ideas and add further refinement to the efforts of social studies scholars. The *National Standards* featured in this text represent the efforts of many educators whose careers have been devoted to enhancing the social studies curriculum. The *National Standards* and supporting organizations include:

> Curriculum Standards for the Social Studies: Expectations of Excellence;
> National Council for the Social Studies
> National History Standards; National Center for History in the Schools
> National Standards for Civics and Government; Center for Civic Education
> Geography for Life: National Geography Standards; The Geography
> Education Standards Project
> National Content Standards in Economics; National Council on Economic
> Education
> National Standards for Art Education; Consortium of National Arts Education
> Associations

Core *instructional* strategies include direct and indirect instruction, thinking skills, grouping patterns and individualized instruction, objectives and unit preparation, computers and technology, incorporating literature, skill development, and evaluation techniques. Most texts provide students with the *how* and *what* to do but seldom provide lesson plans that demonstrate step-by-step procedures from beginning to end. This text not only provides daily lesson plans but also includes teaching and resource units. In addition, this college-level text makes linkages to K–8 texts as a means to integrate theory and practice. Another unique feature is that the blueprint provided by lesson plans is extended by "Internet Links." Website addresses are included for easy access to additional lesson plans or other pertinent student and teaching resources.

✦ ORGANIZATION

Part I, "The Evolution of Social Studies and Its Future Course," focuses on core curricula in the social studies field. Chapter 1 provides a history of the social studies field and introduces the *Self in the World* scope and sequence. Chapters 2 through 5 spotlight key ideas and concepts in the social science disciplines, including the new categories added by the Social Studies National Standards—Psychology, Ecology, Global Education, and Citizenship. In these chapters, research on children's stages of development appropriate for content is presented. For featured disciplines, linkages to national standards across primary, intermediate, and middle school levels are demonstrated through curricular applications. A matrix entitled "Self in the World

Connections" depicts how classroom practice exemplifies psychosocial identity formation across the expanding horizons. "Resources: Teacher and Student Materials" provides preservice teachers with guidelines for further research in their professional development. "Professional Discussions and Field Experiences" presents topics for college-level discussions and suggested activities for field experiences.

Part II, "Instructional Principles in Teaching Social Studies," addresses classroom practice and salient issues to consider when presenting social studies content. Chapters 6 and 7 present pedagogical principles and contemporary aspects of social foundations that impact on curriculum, primarily cultural pluralism and multicultural education, teaching styles, learning styles, and reflective teaching. In Chapters 8 and 9, preservice teachers are exposed to a variety of skill development exercises for the following topics: concept attainment, time and chronology, maps and globes, cooperative learning, questioning strategies, problem solving and problem-based learning, and creative expression. Evaluating student performance is also presented in Chapter 10, with accompanying case illustrations.

Part III, "Putting It All Together: Unit Development," provides interdisciplinary resource units, teaching units, and literature tied to the reconceptualized scope and sequence *Self in the World.* Chapter 11 provides elements for consideration when developing units, whether one chooses to focus on concepts within a particular discipline such as economics or across disciplines. Illustrative resource units feature literature around the world and survival adventures across time and place. Chapter 12 is an interdisciplinary humanities/social studies unit highlighting artists, artforms, and the importance of designing lessons that foster creative expression. Three appendixes give preservice and experienced teachers useful tools. Appendix A provides excerpts from a variety of national standards resources. Appendix B is a compendium of sample lessons for middle school students. Appendix C is a bibliography of children's literature selections that correspond with popular social studies themes.

✦ FEATURES

Self in the World includes numerous features and pedagogical elements to provide the most comprehensive and engaging learning experience possible.

- Each chapter in Part I includes both *Primary* and *Intermediate Applications* to demonstration how the content discussed can be applied in the classroom.
- The chapters in Part II each contain a *Case Study* that provides a "real-life" application of the materials.
- The text is filled with *figures, tables,* and *student examples* that expand on the content of each chapter.
- Each chapter has *Internet Links*—annotated websites either referred to in the chapter or that will extend learning.
- *Professional Discussions and Field Experiences* appear at the end of each chapter to encourage students to reflect on the reading and their own experiences, and also provide suggested activities they can do with their future students.

- *Resources: Teacher and Student Materials* provides a listing of suggested resources related to the chapter's content.
- *National Standards* are integrated throughout the text. Appendix A provides a listing of pertinent standards for easy reference.
- Appendix B includes a wealth of *Middle School Curriculum Applications.*

✦ FROM "ADVENTURES IN TIME AND PLACE"

In order to provide future teachers with a unique glimpse into the classroom, we have included pieces from the award-winning McGraw-Hill School Division social studies program *Adventures in Time and Place.* These examples include:

Building the Railroad   44
Dictionary of Geographic Words   64
Family and Friends in Japan   98
Citizenship Viewpoints   136
You're a Grand Old Flag   146
Struggling Against Slavery   172
Patriots Fight in the Colonies   175
This is My House   348

✦ ACKNOWLEDGMENTS

My fondness for elementary and middle social studies curriculum and instruction began in the elementary school and continues to expand in higher education. There are many individuals whom I would like to acknowledge for their inspiration in this field. Two teachers stand out in the early years. While attending elementary school in Los Angeles, Mrs. Miyasaki's enthusiasm for all content areas was contagious, and I can still visualize her bulletin board of Children Around the World. When attending Scottsdale High School, Mr. Hathaway taught world history as if he were describing a family event; historical figures became people who could breathe. Moving beyond the core high school subjects of geography and history, undergraduate professors at Arizona State University broadened my understanding of people through anthropology, psychology, and sociology. Eventually, it was Dr. Humphrey's lecture on Plato and the teacher as Philosopher King that provided the final catapult into the field of education.

Appreciating the complexity of human beings was enhanced through graduate work with Kaoru Yamamoto at Arizona State University and O. L. Davis, Jr., at the University of Texas at Austin. Through the inspirational teachings and friendships of Kaoru and O. L., I feel that I have gained a strong foundation in social psychology, a perspective that runs throughout this text. As scholars in their respective fields of education, both continue to influence my thinking as well as the thinking of future educators who enroll in their classes at the University of Colorado and the University of Texas. Through her written works, Hilda Taba has also been a guiding force in my appreciation of social studies curriculum development.

As an associate professor who teaches social studies to graduate and undergraduate students, I have the opportunity to research and teach about social and psychological dimensions of human beings. In addition, by co-coordinating or participating in humanities and social studies institutes for teachers, I have had the benefit of the latest research from colleagues and invited scholars. Many individuals have broadened my perspective about people inside and outside the boundaries of the United States through these summer institutes. Colleagues at the College of William and Mary who have played key roles in the Commonwealth Seminar on East Asia include James Bill (International Studies), Craig Canning (History), Clyde Haulman (Economics), Chonghan Kim (Government), and Tomoko Hamada (Anthropology); colleagues in the Commonwealth Seminar on Latin America include Judith Ewell (History) and George Grayson (Government); colleagues in the Commonwealth Seminar on Europe to the Urals include Brian Blouet (Government/Education) and Alan Ward (Government); support within the School of Education came from John Nagle, Ron Wheeler, and Joyce VanTassel-Baska.

The Colonial Chesapeake Seminar, co-coordinated with Brian Blouet, includes strong representation from colleagues at the College of William and Mary—Robert Gross (American Studies), Thad Tate (History), Katie Bragdon (Anthropology), Gerald Johnson (Geology), Ron Hoffman (Institute for Early American History and Culture), James Axtell (History), David Holmes (Religion), and Joanne Braxton (American Studies).

Colleagues in the six Northern Neck Institutes for Teachers, co-coordinated with Miriam Beckwith, include Dale Hoak (History), John Selby (History), Roger Smith (Government), Brian Blouet (Government/Education), Michael Clark (International Studies), William Hargis (Marine Science), Mark Luckenbach (Marine Science), Dennis Blanton (Archaeology), Colleen Kennedy (English), Deborah Morse (English), Sharon Zuber (English), Kenneth Price (English), Andre Cooper (English), and Norma Day-Vines (Counseling).

The teaching institutes just mentioned, which were designed to advance teachers' knowledge of social studies and the humanities, would not be possible without the participation and financial support from individuals and professionals representing private foundations and public institutions. Funding, grants, and in-kind expenses for one or several of the institutes were given by the Commonwealth of Virginia, the College of William and Mary (Wendy and Emery Reves Center for International Studies and School of Education), Virginia Foundation for the Humanities and Public Policy, Association for the Preservation of Virginia Antiquities, Thomas Jefferson's Poplar Forest, The Mariners' Museum, Hampton University Museum, Colonial Williamsburg Foundation, Yorktown Victory Center, Jamestown Foundation, Smithsonian Institution, Foundation for Historic Christ Church, Jessie Ball duPont Fund, Rouse-Bottom Foundation, Bank of Lancaster, and Chesapeake Bank. Institute speakers representing these organizations include Herman Viola, Cary Carson, Barbara Carson, Pete Pitard, Christy Matthews, Lorena Walsh, Emily James, Mark Wenger, Edward Ayres, Liza Gusler, John Turner, Bill Kelso, Jeanne Zeidler, Sheryl Kingery, Octavia Cubbins, Roger Mudd, and Nathaniel Neblett.

The development of the *Self in the World* theme has been inspired partially by international opportunities to observe public and private schools in the British Isles. Living outside the boundaries of the United States is a great way to become aware of one's cultural blinders and to reexamine one's identity in a global context! The following individuals and organizations have made such mind-opening experiences possible: Don and Ann Nunes, Barbara White, and Andrew Venn, Advanced Studies in England Study Abroad Program, Bath, England; Wynn Humphrey Davies, Gareth Roberts, Iwan Roberts, Colin Baker, Gwilyn T. Jones, Jessica Clapham, John and Della Fazey, the University of Wales at Bangor; and Gordon Mungeam and Nicholas Ward, the British Royal Hospital School, Ipswich, England.

In addition to the individuals, institutions, and foundations who have kept me excited about social studies, graduate students and staff in the School of Education have devoted generous hours of their time to the preparation of this text. Jill Bauserman, Kelly Smith, and Kerry Evans diligently retyped numerous drafts; I'm sure they thought the project just grew and changed with no endpoint. Graduate students Leigh Ann Lynch, Ames Morton-Winter, Mickey Buhl, Katie Savage, Kara Gallagher, Paul Cinoa, Karen Diehl, Amy Winstead, and Stacie Oliver gathered materials, researched topics, surfed the Internet, proofread, and in some cases wrote curricular applications. As future teachers their cheerfulness and positive interest in the ongoing progress of the manuscript kept me returning to it with fresh ideas. Dean Virginia McLaughlin also has been supportive throughout the project, providing extra graduate student support during the summer months.

Educators from Williamsburg/James City County Schools gave generously of their professional expertise. Loretta Hannum has demonstrated strong leadership through her role as a social studies curriculum coordinator. Vicky Pettigo filled an elementary library with such a rich selection of children's literature that bookshelves were added floor to ceiling. Under her direction, Ames Morton-Winter was able to integrate children's literature with the social studies scope and sequence included in this text. Debbie Zanca and Karen Golden kept anecdotal records of children's work so that a range of assessment samples and case studies could be included in Chapter 10. I would also like to acknowledge the hundreds of teachers and student teachers who have allowed me to sit in the back of their classrooms and watch them teach. Seeing the way elementary and middle school students respond to social studies curriculum and instruction has had a tremendous impact on my understanding of best practice.

I would like to give a special thanks to the reviewers who provided feedback on the text during its development. These include:

Wayne Benenson, Illinois State University
Muriel Beckerman, University of Missouri at St. Louis
Bernard R. Brogan, Widener University
Lynn M. Burlbaw, Texas A&M University
George W. Chilcoat, Brigham Young University
Melinda Karnes, State University of New York at Fredonia
Tony Sanchez, Purdue University
Tony L. Talbert, Mississippi State University
Jerry Weiner, Kean College of New Jersey

In addition, I would like to thank the friendly, professional support and dedication given by various staff members at McGraw-Hill: Beth Kaufman, Cara Harvey, Christine Schultz, Michelle Whitaker, Dan Loch, John Leland, and Jodi Banowetz.

Emotional support from family members and friends keeps a long-term project such as this one afloat. My parents, Don and Ann McEachron, have passed on their pioneer spirit and love of people and places. Karen and Mark remind me on a daily basis that living life to the fullest is the best way to be—past, present, and future! Jane Bergquist, Betty Martin, and Joyce VanTassel-Baska are dear friends who do what friends do—share and listen with open hearts, play tennis, and lighten up!

ABOUT THE AUTHOR

Gail McEachron received her bachelor and master's degrees in Elementary Education from Arizona State University. She received her Ph.D. in Curriculum and Instruction from The University of Texas at Austin. She currently teaches courses in social studies and language arts and supervises student teachers at the College of William and Mary.

International education and social psychology are long-standing research interests. Having spent over a year living in England and Wales, Gail has developed a keen interest in comparative and multilingual education. As a recipient of the Borgenicht Peace Research Grant Award, Gail is currently supervising future teachers participating in the Advanced Studies in England Study Abroad Program as they study the needs of elementary minority students in the United States and United Kingdom.

GUIDE TO APPLICATIONS AND INTERNET LINKS

Applications

Primary Applications

Intermediate Applications

Middle School Applications

Internet Links

From McGraw-Hill's *Adventures in Time and Place*

PART I

THE EVOLUTION OF SOCIAL STUDIES AND ITS FUTURE COURSE

P art I explains how social studies has progressed from topics such as good manners and morality that were emphasized during the seventeenth and eighteenth centuries. Not until the end of the nineteenth century had the separation of subject matter into specific categories become the norm. Chapters 1 through 5 describe the evolution of the field of social studies, placing the social science disciplines as the foundation of its knowledge base. As the disciplines are explained in more detail, the notion that subject matter cannot merely be transferred to students without a sensitivity to and an understanding of children's developmental stages is explored. Research tied to the various social science disciplines is presented to help future teachers organize subject matter in a way that corresponds to the student's ability to understand subject matter. The *Self in the World* theme offers a new conceptualization for integrating the rich knowledge base from the social sciences with children's developmental stages.

© Donna Day/Stone

CHAPTER 1

SOCIAL STUDIES

An Evolving and Dynamic Field

Chapter Outline

Social Learning Throughout American
   History

Interdisciplinary Approaches: Social
   Sciences and Humanities

Organizational Patterns: Scope and
   Sequence

Self in the World: A
   Reconceptualization

   Spiral Curriculum

History in Primary Grades

Simultaneous Learning Contexts

Learning About Self and Others

Self in the World

❖ Internet Links

Summary

References

CHAPTER OBJECTIVES

As one who is about to embark upon social studies teaching, you no doubt have many questions about the field itself. If social studies is about the history of the world, how do I select pertinent information for the grade level I will teach? With so many competing ideas about what is considered important in the social sciences and humanities, how do I make my lessons of the past relevant for contemporary and future citizenship? Upon completion of this chapter you will be able to:

1.   Describe how social education has evolved in American elementary and middle school classrooms.
2.   Explain characteristics of best practice in social studies teaching.
3.   Analyze scope and sequence patterns, identifying strengths and weaknesses of each.

If you find people interesting, then you will love teaching social studies! People— their ideas, adventures, inventions, hardships, celebrations—are the heart of the social studies curriculum. From the birth of a baby or the birth of a nation to the death of a life fulfilled or the demise of an entire civilization, social studies is the field through which a teacher explores the gamut of human growth and development. Whether discussing the morning headlines or unearthed treasures that have been traced to people who lived thousands of years ago, a social studies teacher travels with students through time and space exploring the wonders of humanity.

When introducing the topic of social studies it is not unusual to see mixed reactions among students preparing to teach. In some cases, students have fond memories of the activities and projects that they participated in throughout their elementary and middle school years. Reenacting the Boston Tea Party, dramatizing Harriet Tubman's role in the Underground Railroad, inviting friends and family to the school's international festival, or constructing a salt and flour map to scale—these are just a few of the more engaging learning experiences recalled. Other students recount less favorable memories such as reading from the textbook and answering questions at the end of the chapter; memorizing endless lists of names, dates, and places; thinking that all social studies classes were the same, with the exception of the time period; or having only vague memories that social studies was even taught! These are expressions that reflect negatively on social studies curriculum and instruction.

Typically, the distinction between positive and negative experiences is the level of the students' engagement. The positive memories that stayed with students were the ones in which active participation was planned at some point during the topic of study. This is not meant to imply that there were never occasions to review questions at the end of chapters or study important dates and factual information. Most likely, the more stimulating social studies teachers integrated key dates, people, and places with activities that made the time period come alive. Designing social studies curriculum and instruction that reflects sound educational objectives can be a fun and creative process, but one that should be taken very seriously. Learning activities will, it is hoped, motivate students to learn, but motivation should not be an end in itself. Stimulating activities that have no tie into social studies objectives leave students bewildered about the significance of what they are doing.

As a beginning social studies educator you have the benefit of entering a field that has been shaped by social science scholars, classroom teachers, and curriculum developers. Initially, the teaching possibilities may seem limitless and somewhat daunting because a teaching field that includes ancient history to the present is such a vast expanse of time. But as this text unfolds, you will find that the social studies curriculum has an underlying structure that has emerged as educators have kept pace with changes and needs in society. To fully appreciate the learning activities and objectives that have evolved in importance for today's social studies educators, a brief curriculum history is needed. What better way to begin your future career as a social studies educator than through a historical examination of the social studies curriculum itself.

✤ SOCIAL LEARNING THROUGHOUT AMERICAN HISTORY

The social studies curriculum as we know it today is rooted in our nation's educational history. Until the seventeenth century most of American education was informal in nature. The most fundamental education that has been passed down through all generations stems from the socialization process that takes place through role modeling and apprenticeships, the human interactions that have taken place since the beginning of time. The diversity of the American people that is represented by these rich cultural heritages can be likened to a beautiful tapestry wherein students can identify with threads representing their collective ethnic, racial, gender, and class histories. Education about one's surroundings that comes through this socialization process is a less formal learning process in comparison to that in educational institutions.

During the seventeenth century, survival techniques, the production of food, clothing, and shelter, and religious instruction were the primary educational goals. Survival and salvation are two underlying social principles that characterize social learning during this period. The more formal education, reserved primarily for men in the upper classes, was modeled after the western European tradition. For example, under the Old Deluder Satan Act of 1647, Massachusetts towns that exceeded one hundred families were required to employ a teacher of Latin so that students could prepare for entry into Harvard College (Ornstein & Hunkins, 1988).

As the United States attempted to develop its own identity during the eighteenth century, patriotism and principles underlying the Constitution and Bill of Rights characterized what was deemed important for participation in society. One's civic duty was shaped partially by the democratic principles articulated by the Founding Fathers. The significance of these principles for the rights of minorities, women, and other marginalized groups would not be given support until later. The mood in the country turned more to the theme of unification rather than the acknowledgment of the diversity among those who were unified. The popular movement in government contributed to a growing political liberalism that was critical of English traditions. The development of democracy, a strong federal government, and religious freedom influenced educators and curriculum reformers. Thomas Jefferson voiced his goals for formal education by stating that it was a civic concern and that schools should be financed through public support (Jefferson, 1893, pp. 220–229).

In the nineteenth century, states passed laws establishing common schools that became the foundation for public education for elementary students aged 6 to 14. Social learning during this period expanded from religious doctrine to include manners and moral instruction. By 1850, these traditional orientations made room for history and geography. Table 1.1 shows the gradual addition of more and more subjects that we recognize as typical social studies topics—geography, United States history, and Constitution (Cubberly, 1920, p. 756). By the end of the nineteenth century separating subject matter into specific categories had become the norm.

Early in the twentieth century more educators questioned the classical curriculum and the emphasis on drill and rote learning. The pace of immigration, industrialization, and the scientific movement in psychology and education led to more systematic approaches for deciding what and how to teach. John Dewey's *Democracy and Education* put forth a philosophy maintaining that the school was a context in which democracy as a social process could be learned. Dewey's ideas contributed to a shift from describing curriculum in terms of subjects and blocks of time to planning and designing a curriculum that expanded the experiences of children, thereby stimulating intellectual capabilities (Ornstein & Hunkins, 1988, pp. 72–73). This philosophy manifested itself in many of the principles the National Society for the Study of Education (NSSE) outlined in 1927. Harold Rugg, who was chairperson of the NSSE yearbook committee, shifted his efforts in the 1930s and 1940s to the integration of history, geography, civics, and economics—which came to be called "social studies" (Ornstein & Hunkins, 1988, p. 77).

TABLE 1.1

Evolution of the Elementary School Curriculum

1800	1825	1850	1875	1900
Reading	Reading	*Reading*	*Reading*	*Reading*
	Declamation	Declamation	Literary selections	*Literature*
Spelling	*Spelling*	Spelling	*Spelling*	Spelling
Writing	Writing	Writing	*Penmanship*	Writing
Catechism	Good behavior	Conduct	Conduct	Conduct
Bible	Manners and morals	Manners		
Arithmetic	*Arithmetic*	*Mental arithmetic*	*Primary arithmetic*	*Arithmetic*
		Ciphering	*Advanced arithmetic*	
	Bookkeeping	Bookkeeping		
	Grammar	*Grammar*	*Grammar*	Grammar
		Elementary language	Oral language	*Oral language*
	Geography	Geography	Home geography	Home geography
			Text geography	*Text geography*
		U.S. history	U.S. history	History studies
			Constitution	
		Object lessons	Object lessons	Nature study
			Drawing	Drawing
				Music
			Physical exercises	Physical exercises
				Play
	Sewing			Sewing
				Cooking
				Manual training

Note: Italics indicate the most important subjects.

Source: Cubberly, E. P. (1920). *The history of education.* Boston: Houghton Mifflin, p. 756.

CORBIS

While the first half of the twentieth century has been characterized as the birth of the curriculum field in the United States, the second half may be characterized by the refinement of subject matter in specialized fields. Curriculum developers sought to integrate the latest research among social science scholars with the latest research in learning theory. An examination of the lists in Table 1.1 will reveal continuing threads from the nation's social history, e.g., conduct, and novel propositions, e.g., manual training as scholars and curriculum writers attempt to keep pace with changes in their fields and in society. Social development for young people has expanded to encompass "greater sociocultural understanding, an attitude of care and concern, a willingness to participate in social criticism and critical self-reflection, and a commitment to engage in personal actions that serve an increasingly broad number of 'others' " (Houser, 1999, p. 212). Table 1.2 outlines *best practice* curriculum and instruction for social studies educators at the turn of the twentieth century.

TABLE 1.2

Best Practice:
What Exemplary Social Studies Programs Should Include

1. Content that incorporates scholarship from the social science disciplines and the humanities.
2. Facts, concepts, and key ideas from the social sciences and humanities that build bridges between the past, present, and future.
3. Interdisciplinary approaches that integrate the social sciences and humanities.
4. Interdisciplinary approaches that teach across the curriculum, integrating the other core subjects of math, science, and language arts.
5. A global perspective that includes studies of Western and non-Western cultures.
6. An American history that presents a shared culture as well as diversified experiences based on ethnicity, class, gender, exceptionalities, and other cultural distinctions.
7. A study of historical events and famous people balanced with the lives of ordinary individuals and the students' daily lives.
8. Multiple resources and teaching strategies that provide active student participation.
9. Variation in thinking strategies (e.g., creative, problem solving, higher level).
10. Balance among basic knowledge, skills, and values.
11. Access to people and resources from the community.
12. Literature incorporated to weave stories into lessons of the past and future.
13. Current events systematically tied to curriculum and made relevant to students' lives.
14. Evaluation procedures that encompass standardized tests, authentic, and portfolio assessment.
15. An articulated and demonstrated relationship between technology and social learning.
16. Linkages between the social studies curriculum and national, state, and/or local school standards.
17. How social studies content is relevant for participatory citizenship.

Compare the components of best practice with Cubberly's representation of the elementary curriculum in Table 1.1. In what ways have educational goals remained the same? What are their points of departure? As you probably already noted, the social studies components of today reflect a higher degree of specialization tied to the social science disciplines. The core subjects of history, geography, and civics have expanded to include all the social science disciplines and the humanities. In addition, rather than teaching the disciplines in isolation, teachers are encouraged to make linkages within the social sciences and across the content areas. Social studies educators are expected to provide depth in a particular discipline and breadth by integrating material across disciplines. Historical episodes breathe life into the past and provide more in-depth understanding; yet "detailing the vicissitudes of chronological change over large expanses of time remains central to students' understanding of historical context" (VanSledright, 1997, p. 40). You may wonder how so many goals can be met in one subject area, when social studies is only one aspect of the entire school day. As one teacher stated, "We have curricular obesity and everyone wants to add more!" One way elementary and middle school teachers meet this challenge is by creating interdisciplinary lessons, described in the following section.

✦ INTERDISCIPLINARY APPROACHES: SOCIAL SCIENCES AND HUMANITIES

An interdisciplinary lesson allows for the integration of subject matter, yet provides opportunities to make analyses based on concepts from the social science disciplines. In 1966 members of the Social Science Education Consortium published their ideas for organizing social studies content from the disciplines. One of their goals was to present information in a way that incorporates the social science concepts without sounding so academic that students couldn't relate to the material. A shared belief among the participants was that the structures of the disciplines they were developing need not be presented to children, but that learning the structures should be an essential part of teacher education programs. The work that resulted from the Consortium is presented in *Concepts and Structure in the New Social Science Curricula* (Morrissett, 1966). The fundamental ideas, or structures, of economics, political science, sociology, anthropology, and geography developed by the Consortium are presented in the remaining chapters of Part I. Today, roughly thirty-five years later, scholars may modify the figures somewhat, but many of the key concepts are included in each of the knowledge bases for the disciplines. They have continued to make up the core content in social studies and have been consulted throughout the formation of national, state, and local standards projects.

Many social science and humanities concepts overlap from one discipline to the next. By combining concepts that several disciplines address, one can develop a *multi*disciplinary approach. A thematic unit on families, for example, can easily incorporate concepts from history, economics, political science, sociology, anthropology, geography, and psychology. The cluster web in Figure 1.1 illustrates how one topic can tie in concepts from multiple disciplines.

When implementing a multidisciplinary teaching web at the primary level, the teacher may address the sociological concepts shown on the web by having the students graph the frequency of chores in the home. Family structures could be represented by having students make a mobile of the people who live with them. Students could interview the people in their home to compare how educational practices vary from generation to generation. Morin (1997) developed a series of lessons on diverse families through the utilization of software available at most school sites. At the primary level it would not be necessary to tell young children that they are learning sociological concepts. Instead, the instructional sequence might be presented under the heading of "Learning from and Helping Others in the Home." As a teacher plans social studies lessons, however, it is important to be aware of the disciplines that are receiving the greatest attention, and to remember that multidisciplinary teaching maintains the integrity of the discipline. In *New Approaches to and Materials for a Sequential Curriculum of American Society for Grades Five to Twelve,* Ratcliffe (1970) demonstrates how easily social science concepts overlap from one discipline

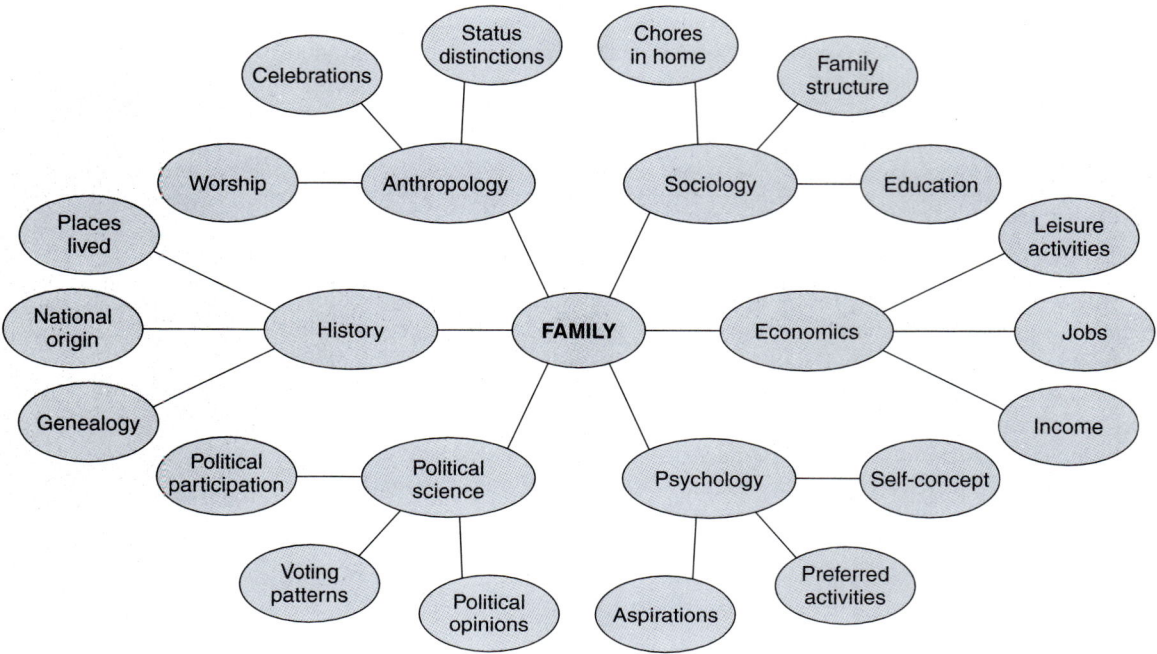

FIGURE 1.1   *Multidisciplinary Teaching Web*

to the next. Additional strategies for developing specific social science concepts are provided in Chapter 8. For now, however, we return to a discussion of how concepts can be combined.

Another way to link ideas and add coherence to a unit of study is to teach across the content areas. Such an *inter*disciplinary approach is more common in the primary grades where teachers are less inclined to use subject-specific language. That is, a first-grade teacher may say that the class will now get ready to learn about farming communities, rather than say "It's time to get ready for social studies," which is commonly heard in upper elementary and middle school classrooms. Figure 1.2 illustrates the components of an instructional unit on farms. Activities integrated across the content areas reinforce skills and knowledge within a theme appropriate for primary students.

*Intra*disciplinary teaching is yet another way to organize curriculum integrating social science concepts within a specific discipline. If a teacher wanted to immerse students in the discipline of economic factors surrounding World War I, for example, the cluster web in Figure 1.3 illustrates such an approach. Middle school students are old enough to focus on the economic conditions such as the depression, government subsidies, natural disasters, and unemployment (Chilcoat, 1998; Sears & Crouch, 1996). To make these economic conditions come alive, teachers can incorporate *Nelda* by Pat Edwards and *Elderberry Thicket* by Joan Zeier to show the impact of the depression on families (National Standards for History, 1994, p. 190).

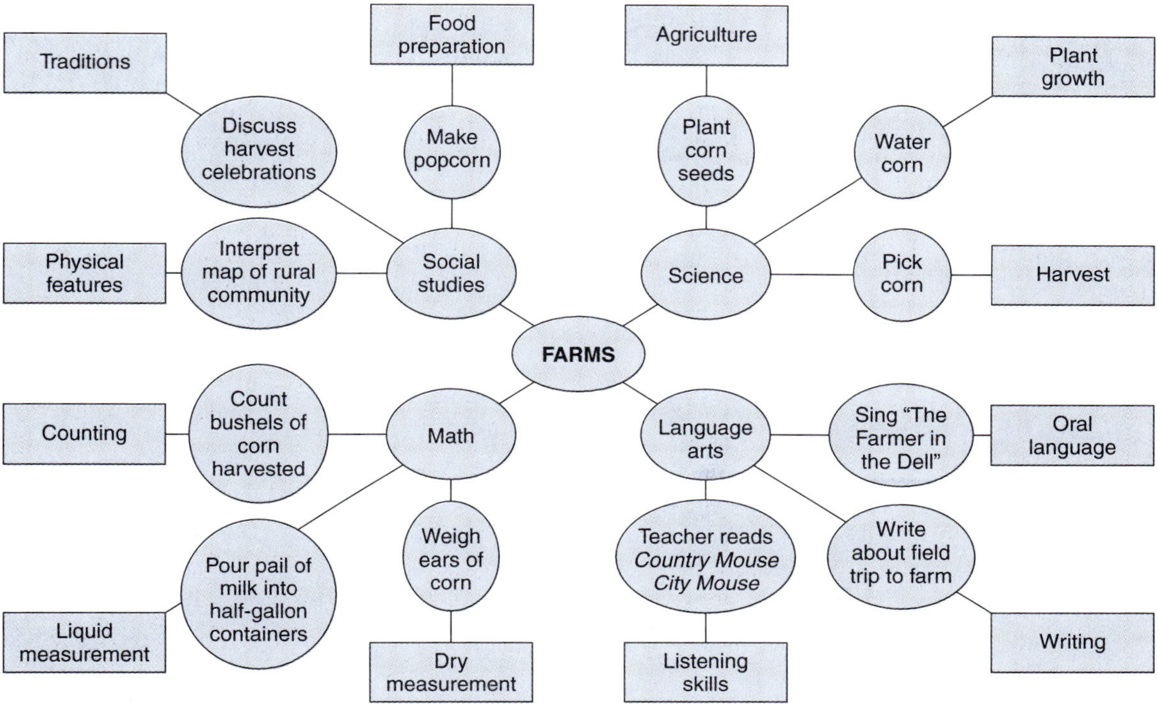

Farms Concept Map

- **Traditions** — Discuss harvest celebrations
- **Food preparation** — Make popcorn
- **Agriculture** — Plant corn seeds
- **Plant growth** — Water corn

- Discuss harvest celebrations — **Social studies**
- Make popcorn — **Social studies**
- **Physical features** — Interpret map of rural community — Social studies
- Plant corn seeds — **Science**
- Water corn — Science
- Science — Pick corn — **Harvest**

- **FARMS**

- **Counting** — Count bushels of corn harvested — **Math**
- Weigh ears of corn — Math
- **Language arts** — Sing "The Farmer in the Dell" — **Oral language**
- Teacher reads *Country Mouse City Mouse* — Language arts
- Write about field trip to farm — Language arts — **Writing**

- **Liquid measurement** — Pour pail of milk into half-gallon containers
- Weigh ears of corn — **Dry measurement**
- Teacher reads *Country Mouse City Mouse* — **Listening skills**

FIGURE 1.2 *Interdisciplinary Teaching Across the Content Areas—Farms*

© Jeff Greenberg/The Image Works

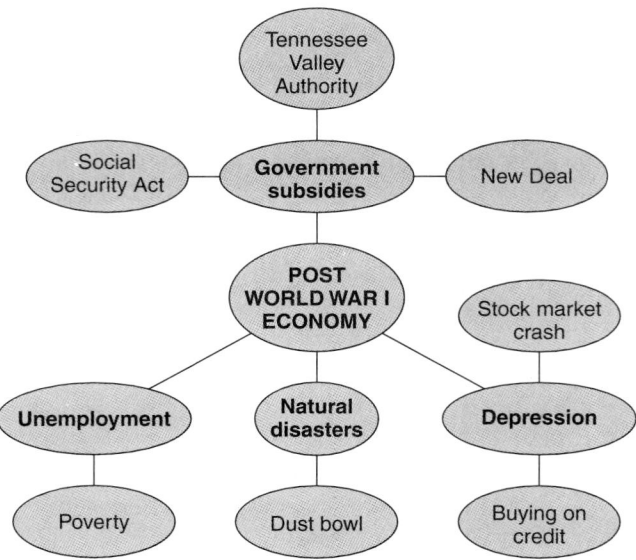

FIGURE 1.3   *Intradisciplinary Teaching Web—U.S. Economy Post World War I*

Interdisciplinary approaches free the teacher to incorporate resources and ideas in creative ways. With national, state, and local standards as guidelines, there is less likelihood that these efforts will create gaps and/or redundancy in the social studies curriculum. In addition to learning about ways to bring focus and cohesion to social studies teaching within specific grade levels, it is important to understand the way the entire curriculum is structured from kindergarten through eighth grade. In the section that follows, organizational patterns demonstrate how educators can represent a variety of disciplines in a way that is consistent with student development.

✦ ORGANIZATIONAL PATTERNS: SCOPE AND SEQUENCE

Curriculum writers attempt to match the content, or *scope,* of what should be taught with the developmental readiness of the students, which influences the *sequence* for when it should be taught. For more than half a century the social studies scope and sequence in Grades K–8 has remained virtually unchanged. A stable framework provides the following advantages to educators in a variety of contexts: (1) members of professional organizations share a common base of understanding, (2) curricular redundancy from one grade level to the next is reduced, (3) publishers use the framework as a basis for textbook and materials production, (4) if students move from one state to another there will be consistency in educational expectations, and (5) the framework is supported through preservice teacher education programs. The current scope and sequence also has certain disadvantages, which will be addressed later in the chapter. For now, however, the long-standing organizational patterns will be described.

TABLE 1.3

Task Force on Scope and Sequence
1984 National Council for the Social Studies

Level	Topic of Study
Kindergarten	Awareness of Self in a Social Setting
Grade 1	The Individual in Primary Social Groups: Understanding **School** and **Family** Life
Grade 2	Meeting Basic Needs in Nearby Social Groups: The **Neighborhood**
Grade 3	Sharing Earth-Space with Others: The **Community**
Grade 4	Human Life in Varied Environments: The Region
Grade 5	People of the Americas: **The United States** and Its Close Neighbors
Grade 6	People and Cultures: The Eastern Hemisphere
Grade 7	A Changing World of Many Nations: A Global View
Grade 8	Building a Strong and Free Nation: The United States

Source: National Council for the Social Studies, Task Force on Scope and Sequence. (1984). In search of a scope and sequence for social studies. *Social Education, 48,* 251. Used by permission.

During the 1930s the following scope and sequence emerged, which proved to be the foundation on which social studies planning would be built for more than half a century (Ornstein & Hunkins, 1988): K–1—Home, Family, School; 2—Neighborhoods, Neighborhood Helpers; 3—Communities; 4—State; 5—The United States; 6—World; 7—American History and Government; 8—Greek and Roman History. As you can see, the scope for the younger grades includes topics that are close in proximity as well as oriented toward the present. For Grades 4 through 8 spatial orientations expand outward, and time periods progress from ancient times to the present and possibly the future. This approach gained wide popularity throughout the United States and received further endorsement through the efforts of Paul Hanna, who in 1963 wrote an article that reinforced the overall logic, calling it the "expanding environments scope and sequence." Throughout the 1970s and 1980s the expanding environments, or expanding horizons, scope and sequence continued and was reaffirmed in 1983 by two National Council for the Social Studies (NCSS, 1984) Task Forces on Scope and Sequence that met to decide its viability for the 1990s. For the most part, the overall scope and sequence remained the same and is listed in Table 1.3, with an accompanying illustration in Figure 1.4. The words in **bold** indicate the continuity between current recommendations and the scope and sequence that emerged nearly seventy years ago.

A comparison of the scope and sequence in the 1930s and the year 2000 reveals minor changes throughout the twentieth century. In the primary grades both scope and sequence remain unchanged with the exception of adding kindergarten and emphasizing regional studies versus state studies in fourth grade. Taken as a whole the scope in Grades 5 through 8 is basically the same, with the exception of a more global perspective, and the sequence shows the study of the United States in eighth grade instead of seventh grade.

A conservative argument that can be made for the reasons the scope and sequence has lasted as long as it has is that there must be some inherent logic to it—

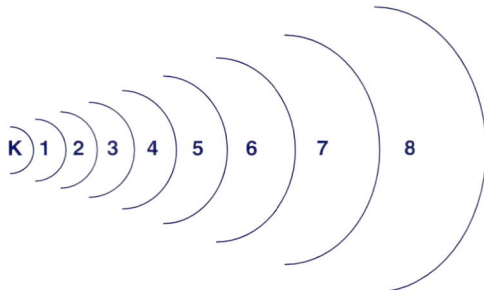

K Self	3 Community	6 Eastern hemisphere
1 School & family	4 Region	7 World of nations
2 Neighborhoods	5 US & neighbors	8 United States

FIGURE 1.4   *National Council for the Social Studies: Scope and Sequence: Expanding Horizons*

SOURCE: Adapted from National Council for the Social Studies Task Force on Scope and Sequence, "In Search of a Scope and Sequence for Social Studies," *Social Education* 48, no. 4 (1984): 249–262.

that's why it continues to the present. There is some truth to this statement as outlined in the advantages listed earlier. The stability allows for predictability and planning for teachers, school districts, and commercial publishers. With the national standards movement under way, curriculum planners at all levels appreciate an organizational framework that brings coherence to the field of social studies. Most of the criticism, however, has not questioned the need for coherence and organization. Those who take issue with the expanding horizons framework are more concerned with its overall conceptualization, the way it portrays social learning. Many critics point out that the expanding horizons approach to understanding other people and societies is not realistic and therefore goes against the grain of cognitive development. We now turn to the nature of these disagreements and the need for alternative frameworks.

✦ SELF IN THE WORLD: A RECONCEPTUALIZATION

Since the 1930s many educators have proposed alternative ways of perceiving social studies curriculum in elementary and middle schools. The critics of the expanding horizons approach often point out that the framework doesn't sufficiently address contemporary needs (Walker & Garcia, 1995). The ideas that have had the greatest potential to modify the current scope and sequence include: (1) the spiral curriculum, (2) the importance of history in the primary grades, (3) simultaneous learning contexts, and (4) learning about self and others. Each of these is presented separately, followed by a reconceptualization of the expanding horizons scope and sequence.

Spiral Curriculum

During the 1950s, social studies researchers such as Florence Stratemeyer (persistent life situations), Alice Miel (democratic citizenship), and Hilda Taba (discovery learning and

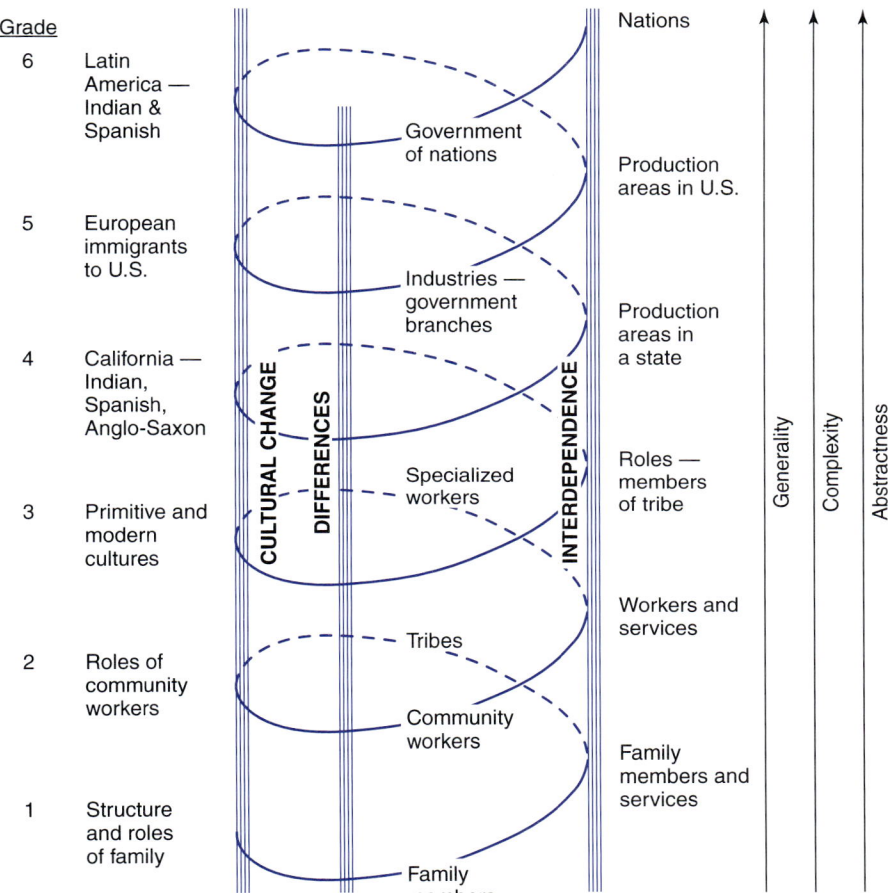

FIGURE 1.5 *The Spiral of Concept Development*

SOURCE: From Teacher's Handbook for Elementary Social Studies by Hilda Taba. ©1967 by Addison-Wesley Publishing Company, Inc. Used by permission of Pearson Learning.

concept formation), "offered attractive alternatives to expanding communities"(Saxe, 1994, p. 163). Of the three, Taba's ideas seem to have had a more lasting impact. Taba devoted a significant part of her career to developing concept attainment strategies. Figure 1.5 illustrates Taba's *spiral curriculum.* The spiral curriculum is different from the expanding horizons scope and sequence because it provides a way to connect the successive "horizons." The spiraling concepts provide threads that run throughout the curriculum beginning as early as kindergarten and going through eighth grade and beyond. Without conceptual themes to add cohesiveness to the scope and sequence, the expanding horizons remain compartmentalized entities in geopolitical space.

To illustrate, Taba (1967) maintains that cognitive learning is enhanced by taking a concept such as *interdependence* and developing it with increasing depth as students progress throughout the grade levels. The concept interdependence is presented in first grade by emphasizing the dynamics with regard to family roles. For second graders, interdependence is demonstrated by focusing on the roles of community and tribal members. As students progress, the concept of interdependence is presented with greater complexity and levels of abstraction as indicated at level six when interdependence takes on global significance.

History in Primary Grades

Of the criticisms targeting the traditional social studies scope and sequence, "none has captured more attention than efforts to bring history into the limelight" particularly in the primary grades (Maxim, 1991, p. 18). While a great deal of this sentiment is voiced by historians, the point is well taken that more substantive content from any social science discipline can and should be included in the early grades. A teacher who is well versed in social science concepts can weave more substantive information into the primary grades (Senesh, 1967). Spending an entire year on the neighborhood or local community underestimates the abilities and interests of primary-aged children.

The premise "History is a story well told" can guide social studies instruction in the primary grades. Concepts from history, sociology, economics, anthropology, psychology, geography, and political science can be integrated into literature, oral histories, or reenactments. Incorporating historical fiction and biography is another effective way to infuse historical information in the primary grades (Mitchell-Powell, 1996; Stewart, 1997). For example, after reading Jean Fritz's story about Columbus, the teacher can trace the voyage of Columbus on the globe and discuss the encounters between the Europeans and the Arawaks without making explicit the fact that they were discussing geography, sociology, economics, anthropology, and political science. However, the teacher should be cognizant of the key concepts that are reinforced, such as exploration, map and globe skills, cross-cultural conflict and accommodation, lifestyle, trade, and power. To provide a sense of educational purpose, the social studies teacher has the professional responsibility of making the linkages with the social science concepts as well as the responsibility of weaving the concepts into an integrated whole or story of the past in a way that is appropriate for the age of the student.

Many of the concerns about putting more history in the primary grades are based on the fear that teachers will be expecting young children to memorize lists of names and dates. On the contrary, curriculum developers are concerned that history is presented with a strong emphasis upon narrative. *Storypath* is one approach that originated in Scotland more than twenty-five years ago. According to Fulwiler and McGuire (1997), the teacher outlines the storyline and then uses key questions to carry the story forward. The curricular illustrations provided demonstrate how historical information evolves through constructivist learning.

Simultaneous Learning Contexts

One position given in support of the expanding horizons scope and sequence is that children might learn better if information about their environment is presented on the basis of physical proximity. That which is proximate to the child has been defined by geopolitical space—family, neighborhood, community, state, nation, world. For an infant, this certainly makes sense. Interaction with the primary caregiver is of prime importance whether the nurturing takes place in the home or on an airplane to Canada. But for a school-aged child the logic of proximity based on geopolitical space breaks down. In the normal course of development children are influenced by all of their surroundings, of which one aspect (or location) may be more salient at any given point in time. For example, the family is always a primary source of influence, but events that are taking place in the community or in an international context may also be foremost on children's minds. For example, to a child who fears for his or her safety on the way to school, the neighborhood is a constant source of concern. To a child who travels regularly outside the boundaries of the United States, the international community is a constant influence on one's view of the world and his or her role in it. These two scenarios point out that the interrelationships between psychological and social learning take place simultaneously in multiple contexts.

A limitation of the expanding horizons approach is that it does not acknowledge the ever-present multiple geographical contexts from one year to the next. Implicit in its organizational structure is that the family is more important in first grade than throughout one's schooling, or that national events are not as relevant in kindergarten through fourth grade as they are in Grades 5 and 8. Furthermore, based on the expanding horizons conception, it is possible that students would not be exposed to cultures beyond North America until the sixth grade. Such a strong nation-centric orientation is inconsistent with our contemporary global interdependence.

With advances in technology and increased mobility, one can no longer assume that social learning proceeds outwardly from experiences close to home. Television and computers bring international events into homes and classrooms; field trips and family vacations expose students to places far from home; children's literature brings magic and adventure from faraway places into the thoughts and dreams of youth. It is erroneous to conceptualize social learning as evolving chronologically in relationship to geopolitical space. Viewing international conflict on Cable Network News, going with Peter Pan to *a faraway place,* and reading Aboriginal folktales create images of time and place that stay with children and youth. Their ability to represent the places spatially on a map or globe or chronologically on a time line is of less importance initially than the world of wonder, fear, and intrigue that constitutes their social learning. In the following section, studies are presented that underscore the important role that a social studies educator can play in educating students about people throughout the globe.

Learning About Self and Others

Attention to cultures outside and inside the boundaries of the United States has been a long-standing tradition in the social studies curriculum. In the 1950s, for example, Kenworthy (1956, p. 7) advanced the notion of a world society and addressed concerns over state sovereignty:

> Such an [international] education would not replace education for local and
> national citizenship. It would refine the loyalty of our citizens to their community
> and their nation within a community of the world. Such an education would not
> denationalize pupils; it would extend their loyal ties to humanity. It would do this

in terms of complementary or supplementary loyalties, adding loyalty to mankind to the already existing emphasis upon loyalty to the family, friendship groups, community, state, and nation.

While Kenworthy increased attention to international education as a component of the social studies curriculum, other educators investigated multicultural relations in the United States, finding that receptivity to and acceptance of others is closely related to acceptance of self (Fey, 1955). During the 1960s social psychologists and international relations scholars began to investigate the relationship between perceptions of self and the acceptance of others inside and outside national boundaries (Clark, 1960; Lambert & Klineberg, 1967; Rosenberg, 1965; Seasholes, 1965; & Williams, 1962). The findings of these studies indicated that psychological states do not develop solely on the basis of inherent characteristics. Rather, ethnocentric attitudes develop in relation to national and social norms (McEachron-Hirsch, 1979).

International and multicultural education will be discussed in more detail in Chapters 4 and 6. The issues raised in this section regarding social learning in relation to self are intended to highlight the need to reconceptualize the expanding horizons scope and sequence. By looking at the expanding horizons illustration, it becomes apparent that there is no intersection between one's psychological development and social, national, and international realms. The only reference to self is at the kindergarten level, not revisited throughout the expanding horizons as the social, national, and international contexts unfold. A new scope and sequence is needed that will conceptualize the interrelationships between one's identity formation and social, national, and international realms of meaning. *Self in the World* is a scope and sequence that offers a synthesis of the expanding horizons and spiral approaches with the addition of self as the anchor for connecting spheres.

Self in the World

Figure 1.6 provides the heretofore missing intersection between one's developing identity (influenced by personal characteristics such as one's ethnicity, gender, class, attributes, interests, and religion, to mention a few) and the social and cultural contexts that interact with these personal characteristics. By graphically representing various aspects of identity in the overall scope and sequence, multicultural aspects of identity are explicitly merged with social and cultural influences, including family, community, state, national, and international orientations. Throughout the course of schooling, the notions of *Self in the World* and the *World in Self* become interchangeable concepts. The scope and sequence is best conceived by acknowledging that students are active learners who come to school representing a myriad of social characteristics and contexts. What they learn about others is dependent upon who they are and how they construct a view of the world around them.

Another way to conceptualize the synthesis between the expanding horizons, spiral curriculum, and self as an overlay is to imagine the expanding horizons existing at each grade level, with the traditional emphasis still intact, as illustrated in Figures 1.7 and 1.8. The bands of color illustrate the presence of traditional grade-level emphases, but featured concepts and key ideas are extended like a spiraling curriculum to the horizons that traditionally were reserved for other grade levels. Even though traditional emphases are in place, the structure allows teachers to integrate realms of experience in

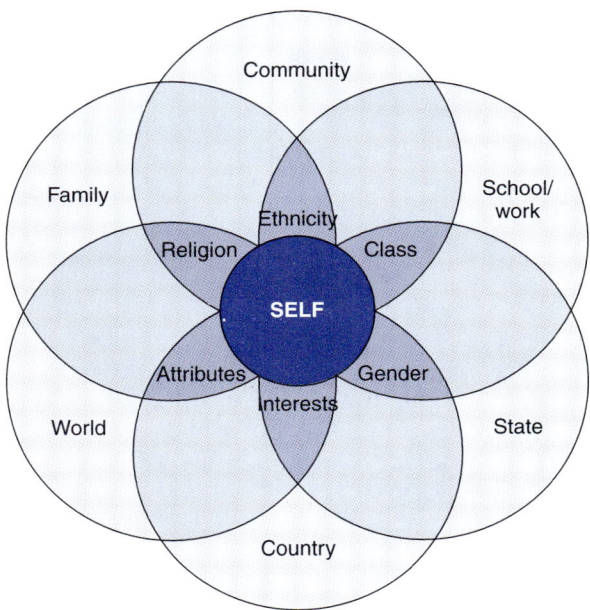

FIGURE 1.6 *Identity Formation in Relation to Social, National, and International Realms of Meaning*

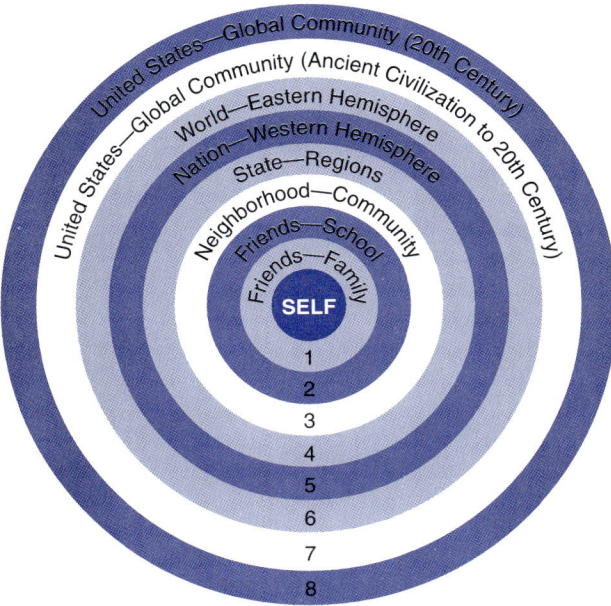

FIGURE 1.7 **Self in the World:** *Elementary and Middle Social Studies Scope and Sequence*

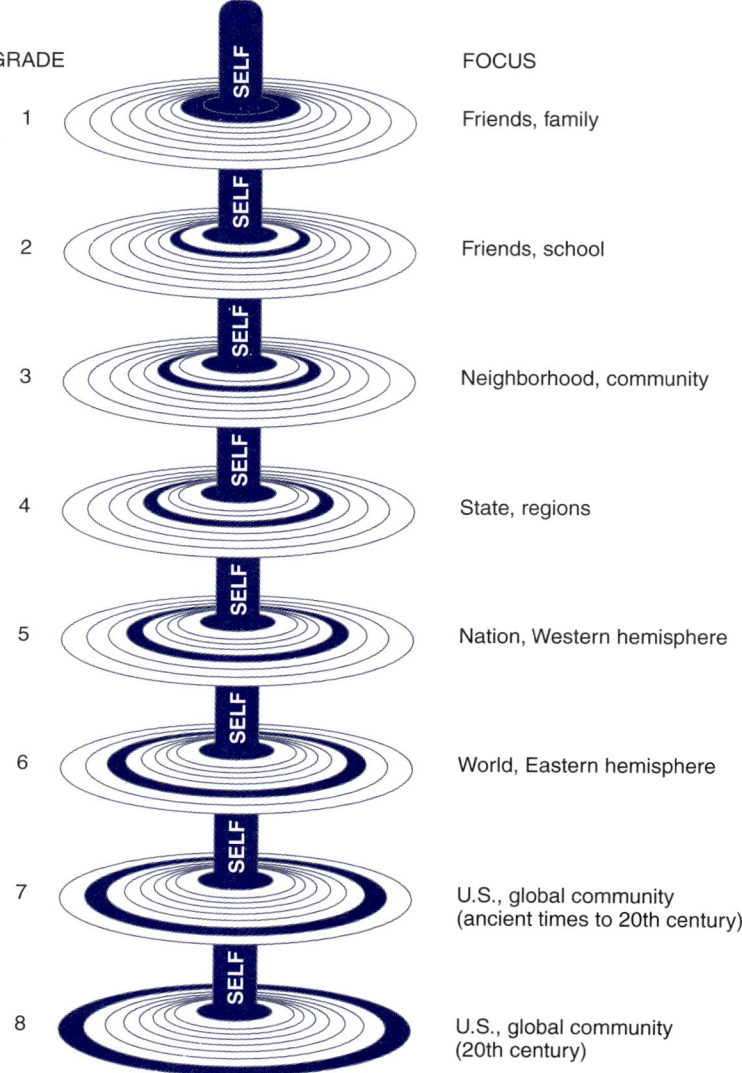

GRADE

FOCUS

Grade	Focus
1	Friends, family
2	Friends, school
3	Neighborhood, community
4	State, regions
5	Nation, Western hemisphere
6	World, Eastern hemisphere
7	U.S., global community (ancient times to 20th century)
8	U.S., global community (20th century)

FIGURE 1.8   **Self in the World:** *A Synthesized Scope and Sequence*

ways that are more natural to the learning process. In the following chapters, a matrix of *Self in the World* learning activities will be presented to illustrate this approach with specific disciplines. Figures 1.7 and 1.8 show this modified version of the expanding horizons and spiral curriculum, emphasizing self as the core and continuous thread. The scope in *Self in the World* is also somewhat different from the National Council for the Social Studies scope, particularly in Grades 7 and 8. *Self in the World* allows for U.S. history to be presented in the context of a global history while distinguishing the modern time period. In Grade 7, U.S. history proceeds from ancient cultures through the nineteenth century. In Grade 8, the twentieth century is emphasized. By designating the twentieth century for eighth grade, students have a greater likelihood of dealing with their more recent history and its relevance for the present and future. Traditionally, U.S. history courses, because they try to cover too many time periods, seldom get beyond World War II. *Self in the World* not only specifies the region of the world to be studied but also offers parameters for time periods at the middle school levels, thereby allowing for greater depth into the modern world.

✣ INTERNET LINKS

INTERNET LINKS

History of Education

http://www.socsci.kun.nl/ped/whp/histeduc/

The History of Education Site.

This is a comprehensive site about the history of education that is maintained by Nijmegen University in the Netherlands. It has a huge collection of links to topics that explore educators, childhood, school (nation-specific school history items), topics in the United States, categories, themes, research, tips, and miscellaneous information. For example, within categories, one can find information on topics such as women's education, higher education, adult and vocational education, special education, and youth activities. Also, interesting topics within themes include thought and theory, psychology, curriculum, religion and schools, and reading/writing. This site also provides access to journals online, discussion lists, research organizations, and conferences around the globe.

INTERNET LINKS

John Dewey

http://www.csupomona.edu/~plin/ls201/dewey1.html

Education and American Democracy—John Dewey.

This website is an excellent resource on the ideas that John Dewey advocated about the social nature of education and his visions for education. Since Dewey believed that the education system should be designed to prepare students to function in a democracy, this site takes a close look at this aspect of his philosophy. The site also provides a score of relevant information about the social environment surrounding education, and the need for and background of democratic education. For anybody interested in the ideas of John Dewey, and their practical application, this site is a must see.

INTERNET LINKS

Interdisciplinary Teaching

http://www.georgetown.edu/crossroads

American Studies Crossroads Project.

This is the website of an international networking and curriculum project built to be a guide to American studies in secondary schools. The four areas of accessibility are curriculum, reference and research, communities, and technology and learning. Of particular interest are the essays on American Studies Pedagogy that can be found in the curriculum section. Within this section of the site is an article on interdisciplinary teaching by Susan Smulyan. "A Multicultural, Interdisciplinary, and Collaborative Curriculum: Discovering Science and Technology Through American History" is a case study on an interdisciplinary teaching project that could be useful in developing lessons of this nature. This site also houses links to other useful teaching resources.

SUMMARY

Social studies has a unique history, one that portrays a continuously evolving field. *Self in the World* offers a contiguous yet dramatically different model for social learning. The model is contiguous in that the expanding horizons model and the spiraling curriculum have been incorporated. *Self in the World* differs from previous curriculum organizations in that it presents the self as a core connecting to all social spheres of influence throughout the kindergarten through eighth grade scope and sequence. The pattern more accurately reflects human growth and development. It is therefore more child centered because it captures the essence of identity formation as a reciprocal interaction between the self and the environment. In addition, by acknowledging individual diversity based on gender, ethnicity, class, religion, attributes, interests, and so on, the intersection between knowledge learned about others and its relevance for oneself and one's role in a social context is made more explicit. Together, students and teachers learn to appreciate knowledge about the world and others as a source of self-growth as well as information needed to learn how to function in society.

The *Self in the World* conceptualization recognizes that the student constructs knowledge based on interaction in a social context. Subject matter is not "out there" in compartmentalized expanding environments, but rather is learned in relation to one's social context and developmental stages. *Self in the World* legitimizes what happens in many classrooms. Teachers start with a curriculum framework provided by national, state, and/or local guidelines. When students and teachers attempt to make the curriculum relevant to their personal lives and social roles, learning and social participation is enhanced.

The *Self in the World* scope and sequence acknowledges the scholarship prevalent in recent decades that gives credence to the notion that knowledge is socially constructed. By combining the spiraling curriculum with the expanding horizons and making the self central, the *Self in the World* model conceptualizes a scope and sequence that is more compatible with contemporary scholarship in social and cognitive learning development. As a future teacher the scope and sequence is designed to assist you in making social studies come alive in ways that are meaningful and relevant to you and your students. A framework is just a blueprint, however. It provides a window to the rich knowledge bases that spring from the social sciences and humanities. This challenge of bringing together theory and practice is where the creative process of curriculum development can flourish!

REFERENCES

Chilcoat, G. W. (1998). Workers' theatre as an inquiry process for exploring social issues of the 1930s. *Social Education, 62* (4), 190–195.

Clark, K. B. (1960). Desegregation: The role of the social sciences. *Teacher's College Record, 62* (1), 16–17.

Cubberly, A. P. (1920). *The history of education.* Boston: Houghton-Mifflin.

Fey, W. (1955). Acceptance by others and its relation to acceptance of self and others: A reevaluation. *Journal of Abnormal and Social Psychology, 50,* 274–276.

Fulwiler, B. R., & McGuire, M. E. (1997). Storypath: Powerful social studies instruction in the primary grades. *Social Studies and the Young Learner, 9* (3), 4–7.

Hanna, P. R. (1963). Revising the social studies: What is needed? *Social Education, 27* (4), 190–196.

Houser, N. O. (1999). Critical literature for the social studies: Challenges and opportunities for the elementary classroom. *Social Education, 63* (4), 212–215.

Jefferson, T. (1893). A bill for the more general diffusion of knowledge. In P. L. Ford (Ed.), *The writings of Thomas Jefferson, Volume II* (pp. 220–229). New York: G. P. Putnam and Sons.

Kenworthy, L. S. (1956). *Introducing children to the world.* New York: Harper and Brothers.

Lambert, W. E., & Klineberg, O. (1967). *Children's views of foreign peoples.* New York: Appleton-Century, Crofts, Irvington.

Maxim, G. (1991). *Social studies and the elementary school child* (4th ed.). New York: Macmillan.

McEachron-Hirsch, G. A. (1979). *International perceptions and curricular strategies of professors of social studies education.* Unpublished doctoral dissertation, The University of Texas at Austin, Austin, Texas.

Mitchell-Powell, B. (1996). Children's literature: Extraordinary aspects of ordinary people and everyday places. *Social Studies and the Young Learner, 8* (3), 18–20, 32.

Morin, J. A. (1997). Software enhancements for a diverse family unit. *Social Studies and the Young Learner, 9* (3), 24–26.

Morrissett, I. (Ed.). (1966). *Concepts and structure in the new social science curricula.* West Lafayette, IN: Social Science Education Consortium, Inc.

National Council for the Social Studies, Task Force on Scope and Sequence. (1984, April). In search of a scope and sequence for social studies. *Social Education, 48,* 251.

Ornstein, A. C., & Hunkins, F. P. (1988). *Curriculum: Foundations, principles, and issues.* Englewood Cliffs, NJ: Prentice Hall.

Ratcliffe, R. H. (1970, July). Social science terms by discipline. In *New approaches to and materials for a sequential curriculum of American society for grades five to twelve* (Vol. 1, pp. 133–135). Washington, DC: U.S. Department of Health, Education and Welfare, Office of Education, Bureau of Research.

Rosenberg, M. (1965). *Society and the adolescent self-image.* Princeton, NJ: Princeton University Press.

Saxe, D. (1994). *Social studies for the elementary teacher.* Boston, MA: Allyn & Bacon.

Saxe, W. (1992). Framing a theory for social studies foundations. *Review of Educational Research, 62* (3), 259–277.

Sears, J. F., & Crouch, F. (Eds.). (1996). A new deal for America. *Social Education, 60* (5), 259–277.

Seasholes, B. (1965). Political socialization of negroes: Image development of self and policy. In W. C. Kvaraceus; J. S. Gibson; F. Patterson; B. Seasholes; J. D. Grambs; *Negro self concept* (pp. 52–90). New York: McGraw-Hill.

Senesh, L. (1967). Organizing a curriculum around social science concepts. In I. Morrissett (Ed.), *Concepts and structure in the new social science curricula* (pp. 21–38). West Lafayette, IN: Social Science Education Consortium, Inc.

Stewart, L. M. (1997). Children's literature: Reading beyond King, Carver, and Tubman. *Social Studies and the Young Learner, 9* (4), 26–27.

Taba, H. (1967). *Teacher's handbook for elementary social studies.* Palo Alto, CA: Addison-Wesley.

VanSledright, B. A. (1997). Can more be less? The depth-breadth dilemma in teaching American history. *Social Education, 61* (1), 38–41.

Walker, A. O., & Garcia, J. (1995). The appropriate ingredients for an effective social studies program: Cultural diversity and conceptual learning. *Social Studies and the Young Learner, 7* (4), 31–32.

Williams, J. E. (1962). Acceptance by others and its relationship to acceptance of self and others: A repeat of Fey's study. *Journal of Abnormal and Social Psychology, 65,* 438–442.

© Mark E. Gibson/Visuals Unlimited

CHAPTER 2

THE LEGACY OF THE PAST

History and Sociology

Chapter Outline

CHAPTER OBJECTIVES

At this stage in your college years you have mastered certain temporal events. You have shaped a career path based on cumulative experiences that occurred mostly in classrooms. As you read this chapter imagine teaching students how their sense of time evolved and influences daily routines. In addition, expand the reflections of your personal history to an understanding of national and global history. What major events and big ideas have you retained? What gaps remain? How does your knowledge of history and society influence your actions today? Upon completion of this chapter you will be able to:

1.   Describe developmental issues relevant to teaching historical time and chronology.

2.   Explain debates within the field of social studies regarding the role of history in relation to other disciplines.

3.   Demonstrate curricular applications of key ideas in history and sociology for various grade levels.

With access to an abundance of resources, a teacher who enjoys history and biographies can make history come alive and encourage students to relate lessons from the past to their daily lives. In this chapter, history and sociology are linked primarily because many of the ideas of the new social historians have had a positive impact on curriculum reform efforts. Incorporating primary resources, conducting oral histories, analyzing diaries, and investigating local history are just a few of the activities supported by the new social historians that lend themselves well to elementary and middle school teaching strategies. Before presenting the linkages between historians and sociologists, however, a discussion of children's conceptual development in time and chronology is provided.

✦ Developmental Issues: Children's Conceptions of Time and Chronology

In the Western world, we have grown accustomed to linear conceptions of time such as twenty-four hours in a day, three hundred sixty-five days in a year, and distinctions between B.C. (before Christ or before the common era) and A.D. (anno domini). Even though various ethnic groups in the United States celebrate non-Western calendar events that reflect their unique cultural heritage, the daily work and school routines of most public institutions are tied to Western traditions. Through socialization young children learn these time and chronology concepts in successive stages of development.

Meerloo (1970) discusses four dimensions of temporal events: biological sense of time, the estimation of time span, the historical sense of time, and the sense of continuity. The historical sense of time involves the classification of different time elements "so that experiences can be placed along a hypothetical time line" (Massad, 1979, p. 7). Since the historical sense of time is emphasized in school settings, the developmental stages in this dimension will be highlighted.

Around the age of 5, when children begin school, the concept of day is understood. More difficult for young children to comprehend is time relative to duration. In *Children in Time and Space,* a father illustrates the confusion surrounding duration through a conversation with his four-year-old son. When told that they would be getting ice cream "later on today" or "in a little while," Jon responded, "No, Dad, today! Let's go today!" (Bauer, 1979, p. 40). Once his father volunteered an association like "after lunch," Jon had a more concrete reference point for marking time. Among 8-year-olds, conversations go beyond references to daily events and reflect concepts about the future. Statements such as "I shall get married," and "I shall be a physician" demonstrate that children can envision plans for the future (Bauer, 1979). From the vague, all-encompassing terms—past, present, future—students begin to learn more precise gradations, for example, milliseconds, light years, and so on, as they approach adolescence.

With older students, abstract time concepts such as the international date line and time zones require careful attention to mathematics. A teacher may erroneously attribute a student's inability to understand time concepts to developmental readiness, when, in fact, the student had not mastered certain mathematical principles. When working with a group of fifth-grade students, I quickly discovered that talking about the time of day in the United States and time 180 degrees on the other side of the globe was a topic of great bewilderment. Through further discussion it became apparent that the students were confusing degrees in a circle with degrees that refer to temperature and climate. They had not yet been taught the formulas for measuring circles. Only when the students had mastered mathematical concepts pertaining to degrees in a circle could they integrate time and space in reference to time zones around the world.

An overemphasis on the conceptual development of time is limited when trying to understand how children think about historical material in the broader context of chronology. Levstik (1986) reminds us "that children's historical understanding proceeds from a subjective involvement in stories of individual lives to a later, more mature level of historical objectivity" (p. 74). For example, a kindergarten teacher said that she had grown more sensitive to the famous people she selected for social studies lessons as a result of children's responses. On President's Day she typically discussed the contributions of George Washington and Abraham Lincoln. After one of her kindergartners asked, "Why are we always talking about all these dead people?," she realized that it would be a good idea to spend some time talking about presidents who were still alive! For at least one kindergartner, the contributions of those in the distant past seemed more elusive than those presidents who were alive and well. In this instance, death, in relation to time and space, was relevant to understanding the past. This doesn't mean, of course, that kindergarten teachers should only talk about the living. Rather, with very young children, teachers need to make more explicit the relevance of people and events from the past to students' lives today.

Once children's developmental stages are better understood, the teacher is in a better position to integrate history with the present and future. As you know, historians emphasize past events and sociologists concentrate more on contemporary social relationships, but together they assist the social studies teacher in making lessons from the past more relevant to students' present and future lives. In the section that follows, interdisciplinary connections are discussed, followed by traditional emphases within each discipline.

✦ LINKAGES BETWEEN HISTORY AND SOCIOLOGY

For over twenty years there has been a long-standing dispute over the validity of different approaches to writing history. Critics of traditional approaches to teaching history have argued that too much attention is given to military history and strategies of war. Lessons emphasize the efforts of those in power, typically an elite group of men, and ignore the lives of women, ethnic minorities, and middle and lower classes of people. Another way of viewing this position is that there is too much emphasis on how history was *made* by small but powerful numbers of people and not enough emphasis upon how history was *lived* by the mass majority of ordinary individuals.

The work of the new social historians who study broad social trends, such as population shifts and the lives of ordinary people, was criticized by scholars whose research emphasizes studies of major political events. As the field expanded to include the voices of women and minorities, some argued that the discipline was becoming too fragmented. In addition, scholarship from the humanities, acknowledging the role of interpretation in the analysis of cultural trends, was incorporated throughout the 1970s, which also expanded the parameters. The debate continued into the 1980s, with scholars arguing that the other was imposing its biases on the rest of the profession.

Among K–12 educators the debate was fueled by tests of historical knowledge. With the publication of *A Nation at Risk,* educators were alarmed by the low performances of American youth on standardized tests and how the test scores reflected on American education in general. E. D. Hirsch, Jr., Diane Ravitch, Chester Finn, and Lynne Cheney were four of the more outspoken critics of social studies education, admonishing teachers for spending too much time on process and not enough time presenting content. Their criticisms not only targeted teaching styles but also pushed for history to be front and center in the schools by de-emphasizing the other social science disciplines.

In 1987, the Bradley Foundation funded the Bradley Commission on History in the Schools, whose purpose was to address how history was taught in American elementary and secondary schools. The Commission recommended in its final report, *Building a History Curriculum: Guidelines for Teaching History in Schools,* that the K–6 social studies curriculum be history centered and that students should have at least four years of history in Grades 7 through 12 (Welton and Mallan, 1992). In 1990, the Bradley Commission on History in Schools became the National Council for History Education. To continue its impact on history teaching, the Council publishes *History Matters,* a newsletter that emphasizes history teaching in the elementary schools.

The history debate continues into the twenty-first century, and it is one that you most likely will participate in as you make decisions about how to define and how to teach history. In fact, it is more accurate to suggest that the history debate includes social and political debate and currently shapes curriculum policy at the national, state, and local levels (Avery & Johnson, 1999; Grant, 1997; Nash, Crabtree, & Dunn, 1997). Within the fields of social studies, opposing points of view by Saxe (1996), Cohen (1996), and Whelan (1996) are presented in *Social Education,* the journal published by the National Council for the Social Studies. As you prepare to enter these debates it is important to have a foundation and knowledge base from which you can critique the arguments. To assist teachers in addressing the question "What is history?," the following definitions have been delineated by Stahl, Hronek, Miller, and Shoemake-Netto (1995, pp. 4–5):

1. History is hard physical evidence, such as records, documents, and artifacts. This concept equates history with the objects and symbols that provide evidence of past occurrences and represent the actions of humans.
2. History is past actualities. This concept equates history with the actual occurrences, thoughts, actions, emotions, statements, and symbol-making activities of humans or those that affected humans of the past.
3. History is non-narrative, discrete information about or from past occurrences and things. This concept equates history with specific, separate bits of information, often mistakenly called facts.

4. History is self-constructed versions of past occurrences that are "in and of the mind." This "history" consists of the constructions, interpretations, and explanations of the past in people's minds.

5. History is a record of one's constructions of the past. This concept equates history to all recorded narratives that report a person's versions of the past, such as lecture notes, test answers, textbooks, trade books, journal articles, conference papers, term papers, theses, dissertations, oral histories, documentaries, and so on.

6. History is a story of past occurrences, people, and things. This concept equates history to a story in the form of a narrative report, not one that meets the literary demands of stories.

Equally compelling in deciding what history is and how it should be taught is to think about how to interpret historical events. Gottschalk (1963) maintains that historians must generalize if they are to say anything of importance. Gottschalk (1963) adds, however, that "historians habitually restrict themselves to 'low-level' generalizations, cautious and limited statements of which they can be reasonably sure . . ." (p. 152). From the six definitions offered by Stahl and his colleagues it is no wonder that historians are cautious about making generalizations. The six broad concepts open the definitions in such a way that history may seem an elusive concept; rather than thinking that there is such a field as history, one is inclined to think that there are instead individual histories. For those who may perceive the breakdown of a former conceptual unity, the words of Norton (1994) capture the opportunity in which educators on all levels may find themselves:

> This brings me to the central irony of the current debate in the humanities, in which many lament the breakdown of a former conceptual unity and the lack of coherence in historical curricula, all supposedly the result of the attempt to integrate new scholarship on women and ethnic minorities into our teaching and research agendas. Precisely the opposite is true, in my opinion: if there is a loss of coherence in our college and high school history courses today, it is because *not enough* is being done to reorient our thinking along the lines suggested by new scholarship, rather than because too *much* is being attempted. (p. 30)

Question number one in the professional discussion section of this chapter gives you an opportunity to pursue this topic in class. At this point, however, the efforts by historians, the new social historians, and sociologists will be highlighted. As you read about the approaches, reflect on whether you think that the curriculum has been enhanced by the new resources previously untapped by historians and sociologists.

History: Key Ideas and Concepts

Even though scholars debate whether or not history can be an objective science, historians utilize approaches that reflect the scientific method of gathering research—identifying a problem, gathering information, observing data, analyzing data, and drawing conclusions. As a part of *The Study and Teaching of Social Science Series,* Henry Steele Commager and Raymond Muessig wrote *The Study and Teaching of History* (1980). Commager addressed key questions posed by historians with the intent of helping students and teachers investigate the past. The perennial questions raised by Commager (Commager & Muessig, 1980) are:

Can history be impartial, can it be objective? Can it divorce itself from the tyranny of the present, of the nation, of the culture? Is the historian a judge—can he [*sic*] in fact avoid that function?—or is he [*sic*] a mere recorder, writing down "what actually happened"? Is it possible ever to know "what actually happened," possible to establish a historical "fact" as one establishes a fact in chemistry or biology? Is there such a thing as historical causation, and can the historian ever know the causes of things? (p. ix)

If one accepts that the *facts* are continuously open to reinterpretation in the present, historical research can be appreciated for its dynamic linkages with contemporary thought. Reinterpreting history encourages students to explain the *why* of history. Looking at "historical content not only in terms of substantive concepts and details, but additionally for indicators of second order understandings such as *cause, motive, evidence,* and *interpretation*" gives history and the teaching of it greater significance (Ashby, Lee, & Dickinson, 1997, p. 17). In addition to the perennial questions raised by Commager, the following organizing concepts assist teachers in developing history curricula.

Continuity and Change

The continuity and change of humans and their environment throughout the life span is one of the bases for historical inquiry. Historians and teachers might examine change in the rise and fall of civilizations, the changing landscape in one's hometown, or the generational differences within families. They also might analyze the diffusion of ideas that takes place throughout the rise and fall of civilizations, the continuity of the landscape despite technological changes to one's hometown, and the continuity of traditions, behaviors, and values from one generation to the next. The concepts of continuity and change can be used as bridges from ancient to contemporary times. For example, a teacher might develop a unit whereby the continuity and change in one's local community is compared with another community or with the same community but during a different time period. One of the goals of social studies teaching is to develop in students an appreciation for the dynamic world in which they live, an appreciation that will help them embrace the changes and continuity in their own lives.

Exploration

Exploration is a natural historical concept because it describes the common behavior of humankind throughout the past (Stavrianos, 1995). Students, and adults, want to know their place of origin whether talking about national origin or place of birth. Social studies textbooks have traditionally spotlighted the positive aspects of European exploration as a means of extolling the virtues of the Western heritage of the United States (Ester, 1997). In recent decades, historians have tempered their interpretations of these explorations and have tried to create a more balanced view of the interaction that took place between those who were exploring and those who were being explored, or in some cases invaded. The *Seeds of Change* (Viola & Margolis, 1991) exhibit at the Smithsonian Institution is a good example of this reinterpretation of history. As a part of the quincentennial exhibition in 1992, which reexamined the significance of Columbus's arrival in what is now North America, the *Seeds of Change* exhibit showed cross-cultural exchanges that took place among several groups of people—Native Americans, African-Americans, Hispanic-Americans, Asian-Americans, and European Americans. Some exchanges were positive and some negative. This exhibit was so popular and well conceptualized for elementary and middle school students and their teachers that Addison-Wesley (Hawke & Davis, 1992) developed curriculum materials to help teachers reeducate students about the significance of Columbus's arrival. It serves as a good model for attempting to balance multiple perspectives surrounding the impact of exploration. *Forces of Change,* a future Smithsonian exhibit, will build on the *Seeds of Change* theme.

Historical Bias

History, according to Commager is not only the past, but the memory of the past. As such it is not only "incomplete, it is also lopsided and biased" (Commager and Muessig, 1980, p. 3). Historical bias, therefore, represents the layers and layers of culture that influence the recorder of history in the present. One is a product of one's past, and the lens through which one looks into the past is glazed with contemporary attitudes and values. Thus, the bias one has looking back in time is similar to the cultural bias one has when examining another culture that is different from one's own. Rather than being ethnocentric one is, in a sense, time-centric.

A popular activity with elementary and middle school students is to stage an event, perhaps a conflict or friendly conversation observable by students. Ask students to write down their version of what happened, addressing the typical news reporting questions of who, what, where, why, and when. Compare interpretations for evidence of historical bias. This is a good lead-in activity to historical research, investigating differences of interpretation for important events. Bringing in a variety of newspapers, representing liberal, conservative, and radical thinking is also a way to illustrate historical bias. The Macmillan/McGraw-Hill Textbook Series for elementary students includes a section entitled "Point-Counterpoint," which provides opposing viewpoints relevant to historical events. They serve as good models for reinforcing the concept of historical bias.

Historical Records

Historical interpretations are limited by the resources and memories available to the historian. Primary resources are original resources such as diaries, census data, speeches, artifacts, and so on. It is common to refer to copies of original resources as primary resources, in classroom situations. But the true primary resource is the original work. Secondary resources are sources that provide commentary on primary resources. This textbook, for example, includes many secondary resources, representing a compilation of ideas from a variety of scholars. A great way to examine primary resources and historical documents is through the National Archives. The National Archives makes historical inquiry more participatory, personal, and accessible by offering a variety of materials that encourage teaching with primary sources at all levels. The gathering of archival material for national collections and local history projects has resulted in a proliferation of materials that constitute the raw data for historical research.

Secondary resources not only provide important information but can be compared for differing viewpoints. Students are often surprised when exposed to resources

© D. Chidester/The Image Works

that have two completely different versions of the "facts." For example, when teaching a group of third graders about the accomplishments of Elizabeth Blackwell, the first woman in the United States to graduate from medical school, they were surprised to find trade books that gave conflicting renditions of the way Dr. Blackwell lost vision in one eye. The third graders wondered, "But how can that be, it says so in a book? I thought if it was printed, it must be true." Bringing in a variety of resources that represent multiple perspectives helps students to understand that our views of the past are limited by the resources available to us, and that given resources often contradict one another.

The New Social History

The new social historians and sociologists have also provided us with refreshing perspectives from which to reconstruct the past and understand the present by examining previously untapped resources. In *Ordinary People and Everyday Life,* Gardner and Adams (1983) compiled the perspectives of several new social historians on topics such as the family; women's history; race, ethnicity, and cultural pluralism; urban and rural life; labor history; and learning social history from artifacts. Stearns (1983) suggested that social history may seem confusing to those accustomed to more conventional modes because of the de-emphasis on familiar landmarks such as biographical sketches of famous people and the importance of dates. Topical expansion has led to an increase in source materials as scholars have turned to census data, police records, wills, worker autobiographies, and diaries of women. The interest in the lives of ordinary people stems, in part, from concern about issues facing contemporary society such as crime and changes in the family. In addition, Stearns (1983) spotlighted the care of children in society by saying "that the history of great ideas must often yield to changes in the way people treat children" (p. 6).

With the expansion of resources social studies teachers are in an enviable yet precarious position. Enviable in that almost any resource is a potential object for classroom inquiry. Precarious in that a teacher must balance the social studies curriculum in such a way that national and global political history does not overshadow social and local history, nor should one's regional and personal history predominate to the extent that a shared national and world history is lost. One of the challenges in grasping the shared cultural history is to include the many voices that constantly reinterpret the meaning of past events (Eshelman, 1997; Lemert, 1993). As more voices are heard in contemporary society, there is greater potential to expand our appreciation of past events (Norton et al., 1998).

As a new millennium begins, historians offer great insights into the kinds of issues that teachers will face as they teach upcoming generations about the legacy of the past and prospects for the future. Stavrianos (1992) argues:

> . . . we have developed the technological capacity to build a new world, but have failed to evolve the social capacity for making it a world worth living in. . . . The fact that the cooperative communalism of our Paleolithic ancestors contributed fundamentally to their survival is obviously relevant to our own current struggle for survival. It teaches us that what has happened in our historic past was not the inevitable result of human genes but rather of human societies, which, being made by humans, can also in the right circumstances be changed by humans. Far from being haunted by imagined genetic defects that drive humans to act inhumanely, we share instead a proud and beneficent Paleolithic heritage and model. Scientists currently are developing what they term "human needs theory" which holds that 'it is simply wrong to claim that human nature is basically individualistic, competitive and aggressive; biologically we are designed to be precisely the opposite. When conflict arises *within* a society, it is almost always because this biologically-based need for bonding among its neighbors is being thwarted by one or another social arrangement.' (pp. 234–235)

Stavrianos maintains that this challenge regarding conflict in social arrangements is a human dilemma that is not unique to our time or society but comes down to values in the most basic sense. He sees parallels between the circumstances in which the great religions arose during the first millennium B.C. and circumstances prevailing today, proposing therefore that the late twentieth century may be viewed as a new axial age.

> Our technological revolution is perhaps deeper, as are also its social repercussions. Its scale is global, rather than being limited to certain regions of Eurasia, and the masses of the people, thanks to modern communications, are activated and assertive to an unprecedented degree. So again, it is unlikely to be happenstance that new religions, new philosophies, new social movements, and new leaders are beginning to crop up on every continent. As in the original axial age, basics are being challenged—governments, isms, traditions, and leaders. In the course of today's axial age, one and all are now on trial. (Stavrianos, 1992, p. 198)

For the social studies teacher, values, in the most basic sense as described by Stavrianos, undergird the majority of social studies lessons (Passe, 1999). Exceptions might be skills-based lessons such as longitude and latitude. Most lessons in history will be about people and cultures and the lifestyles that have emerged since the beginning of civilization. When history is understood as having many definitions or approaches such as those just outlined it is assumed that values will be present throughout, whether they are manifested in the personal narratives of women working in factories during the Industrial Revolution, a speech by Patrick Henry, or eyewitness accounts of historical events. If values are understood as individual preferences about what is good or bad, right or wrong, desirable or undesirable (Curry, Jiobu, & Schwirian, 1999), then lessons from history will by definition depict values. As the twentieth century came to a close, "terms like character education, value training, moral education, transmission of cultural values, and socialization" were used in debates about how values should or should not be taught (Stevens & Allen, 1996, p. 154). Stevens and Allen (1996) maintain that a proper function of teaching public values is providing opportunities to develop an ethical framework for making decisions; such decision making can assist young people with the complex realities of responsible citizenship. In the section that follows, key concepts from sociology are presented and will extend our understanding of ways in which sociologists study contemporary belief systems and social arrangements.

Sociology: Key Ideas and Concepts

The discipline of sociology emerged in the beginning of the nineteenth century and is often traced to the ideas formulated by Auguste Comte. Comte maintained that societies become increasingly scientific as they move through three stages of development—theological, metaphysical, and scientific. The scientific approach may be characterized as positivistic in the assertion that "science, rather than any other type of human understanding, is the path to knowledge" (Macionis, 1987, p. 12). Not all sociologists agree with this position, however, arguing instead that people are creatures of spontaneity and imagination whose behavior cannot always be explained scientifically.

Karl Marx, Emile Durkheim, and Max Weber are also seen as influential in shaping the discipline of sociology. While all were consistent in suggesting that a new social and economic order was emerging as a result of the Industrial Revolution, Marx (1963/1844) sought to liberate workers from poverty, Durkheim (1966/1893) examined the notion of social solidarity, and Weber (1947) maintained that social change could be advanced if tied to rationalization. The debates are provocative and underscore the dynamism that pervades social phenomena. This section outlines how a sociologist takes a broad view of human behavior and social organization, focusing on the social setting of behavior, on the social interaction among people, and on how these factors change through time.

Social Structure

Social structure refers to the underlying pattern that influences relationships in society (Forsyth, 1995). Status, roles, and interactions in groups and institutions are some of the concepts that define social structure. For example, sociologists may be interested in the differences between a person's *ascribed* (i.e., assigned) status and *achieved* status as well as the relationships one has with others based on both forms of status. In elementary and middle school classrooms, role, status, and group inter-action are common themes. Reenacting historical events by having students play the various ethnic, class, and gender roles of individuals who lived during the time pe-riod is popular at all grade levels.

Social Stratification

Social stratification refers to the creation of layers "of people possessing unequal shares of scarce desirables, the most important of which are income, wealth, prestige, and power" (Shepard, 1993, p. 225). Sociologists study census data to investigate the extent of economic inequality in the United States. In elementary and middle school social studies curricula, most of the discussions relative to inequality based on income center on the different classes during the colonial period, inequality due to slavery, the acqui-sition of wealth by entrepreneurs during the industrial period, and the impact of poverty during the depression. Less attention is devoted to layers of stratification in contempo-rary society and the interaction between wealth, gender, and ethnic identity. By con-sulting sociology texts or conducting research utilizing census data and other primary resource material, students and teachers can tie together traditional studies of social stratification with contemporary relationships (Eitzen & Zinn, 1997).

Social Institutions

Sociologists study virtually all institutions that affect people's lives—the family, edu-cational institutions, religious institutions, health care systems, political institutions, and the workplace. Families are examined in terms of their structure, cross-cultural analyses, patterns in the United States, and lifestyle variations. Educational institutions are studied from the perspective of their function in society, educational inequality, and education as transmission of culture. In addition, sociologists ascertain how people worship, take care of their health, work, and govern and the role that institutions fill in meeting these needs. In elementary and middle schools, the study of institutions takes many forms. In the primary grades, the family, school, and community helpers are spot-lighted, reinforcing concepts such as roles and jobs. Many texts and literature for chil-dren provide cross-cultural and structural variation in families. As students progress to middle school greater emphasis is placed on political institutions and economic issues. To date, elementary and middle school social studies curricula have devoted minor cov-erage to health care systems, but as this issue continues to challenge the American peo-ple, we can expect that it will gain more attention. Religion also has been a topic that has been handled delicately given the First Amendment, which reinforces the separa-tion of church and state. However, in 1990 the National Council for the Social Studies developed a position statement to assist educators in teaching *about* religion without ad-vocating a particular religion (Haynes, 1990).

Social Interaction

Sociologists study how people interact with one another to better understand the factors that influence the ways people support one another as well as how anger and conflict is manifested. Five types of social interaction include exchange, cooperation, competition, conflict, and coercion. All of these aspects of social interaction are played out on a daily basis in elementary classrooms. Kohlberg (1979) and Turiel (1983) conducted research with children regarding morality and social conventions that underlie social interactions. Kohlberg suggests that children progress through stages of moral development that increase in complexity. Turiel, a colleague of Kohlberg, argued that children can distinguish between right and wrong (morality) as well as what is considered acceptable (social convention). Their studies help teachers who must continuously address the social interactions that develop positively and sometimes explode in the classroom. Recognizing the various stages and distinctions can provide the teacher with a more informed repertoire from which to help young people develop respect for one another.

Social Change

Sociologists study patterns of change throughout society. Three main theories shape their analyses—functionalism, conflict theory, and symbolic interaction (Curry et al., 1999). In the context of education, functionalism views education as conducive to an orderly and efficient society. Conflict theory views education as perpetuating social inequality. The symbolic interaction perspective views education as interaction in the social setting of the school. Besides analyzing change in educational institutions, sociologists apply these theories to the many changes they study, including urbanization, demographics, socioeconomic status, mobility, inequalities of gender, race and ethnicity, and collective social action, to mention a few.

The scholarship from historians and sociologists continues to inspire curriculum writers and teachers. With more information and resources entering the knowledge base on a daily basis, however, debates ensue as scholars voice their preferences for what is *most* important. Figure 2.1 shows fundamental ideas from the discipline of sociology designed by the Social Science Education Consortium to assist teachers who are developing K–12 curricula (Morrissett, 1967). Although the graphic organizer is not a part of mainstream sociology today, the concepts continue as fundamental ideas. In the next section, curriculum applications illustrate selected concepts from history and sociology.

✦ Curriculum Applications

Key concepts and ideas from history and sociology help students understand their place in contemporary society. Table 2.1 illustrates how historical and sociological principles can be integrated across time and space, thereby modifying the traditional expanding horizons scope and sequence. In a traditional scope and sequence, primary students would not typically address state and national events. Nor would middle school students incorporate genealogical research into world or U.S. history classes. Table 2.1 gives examples of activities relevant to the various realms of experience that students experience simultaneously at all ages. When tied to educational objectives and developed into daily lessons or units of instruction, activities such as these provide alternatives to the traditional scope and sequence. As such they reflect a more integrated approach to social learning.

Self in the World Connections

Illustrations of concepts from history and sociology are presented through lessons at the primary, intermediate, and middle school levels. The primary lesson that follows shows how young children can become actively engaged as researchers learning the heritage

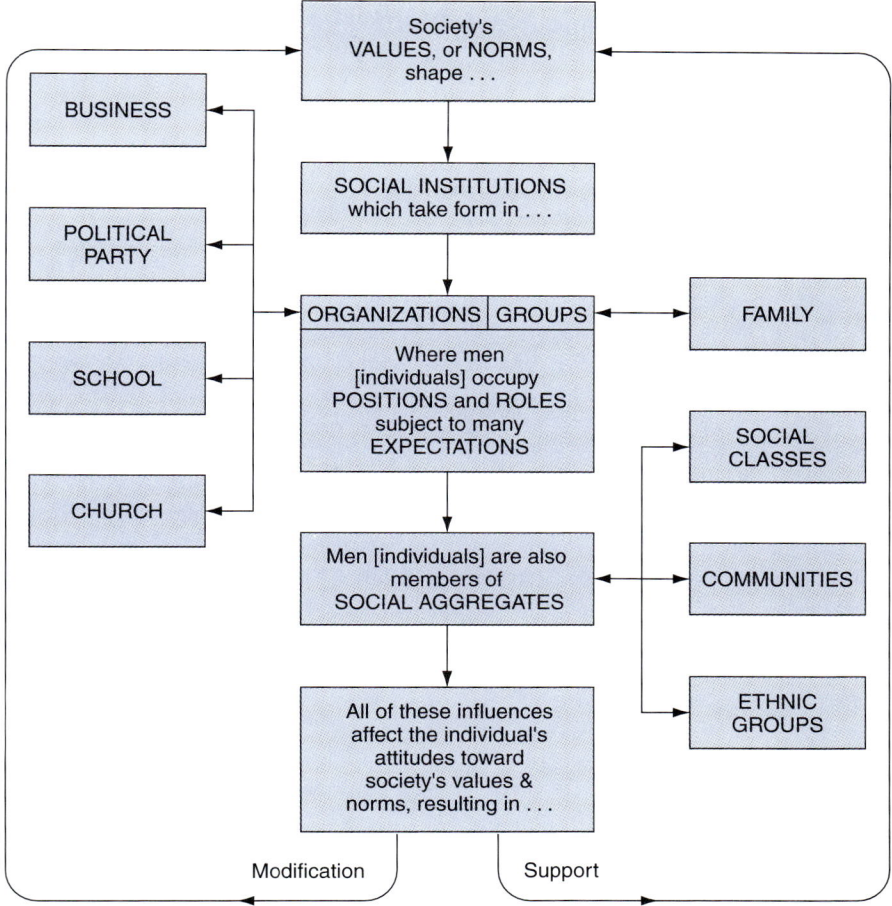

FIGURE 2.1   *Fundamental Ideas of Sociology*

SOURCE: L. Senesh. (1967). Organizing a curriculum around social science concepts, I. Morrissett (Ed.), *Concepts and Structures in the New Social Science Curricula* (New York: Holt, Rinehart & Winston, p. 31). Used by permission of the Social Science Education Consortium.

of people that surround them. The intermediate lesson demonstrates how a textbook can be used as a starting point for historical investigation, then supplemented with primary resources to provide more depth and make history come alive. A middle school lesson on the 1989 events in Tiananmen Square can be found in Appendix B. It provides a model for investigating more recent historical events in a global context.

Each of the lessons also illustrates how curriculum development can be a creative, personalized process. For example, the primary lesson reflects Mrs. Watkins's personal interest in genealogy, an area of curriculum development that provides a natural bridge between the young and old (Hittleman & Hittleman, 1997; Laney, Laney, Wimsatt, & Moseley, 1997). The textbook adaptation lesson was inspired by the fact that the author could obtain an oral history of her grandfather whose life was dramatically affected by the California railroad system. Spears (1999), who conducted oral histories about the civil rights movement, suggests that such an approach offers

TABLE 2.1

Self in the World Connections
Integrating the Self Across Time and Space

	Primary	Intermediate	Middle School
Self	Create and analyze growth charts showing changes in height and weight; study baby picture from birth to current age.	Create a personal time line depicting significant life events, memorable occasions, etc.	Write an autobiography that includes information collected from oral histories of family members. Create book of autobiography complete with maps and pictures of residences.
Family	Conduct oral histories with family members. Bring in oldest object in home and describe its history.	Write essay about how family traditions have been passed down from one generation to the next, e.g., birthdays, holidays, chores, religious instruction, etc.	Create genealogical charts if information is available. Write to genealogical society to gain further information.
Community	Take field trips to historical sites and buildings in one's county. Make a photo history booklet with captions and descriptions.	Establish a community archives at school or a local library. Gather research on local history and store in archives.	Begin a cultural journalism project by subscribing to "Hands On: Cultural Journalism Newsletter" sponsored by the Foxfire fund in Rabun Gap, Georgia.
State	Follow state news throughout the week and create a pictorial time line throughout the classroom.	Visit the State Capitol after researching the event surrounding how it came to be at its present location.	Locate the State Historical Society and visit its archives. Collect research using census data, diaries, or wills. Explain their historical significance for contemporary society.
Nation	When celebrating President's Day, explain the history of the holiday, the importance of Washington and Lincoln and discuss how current president might be remembered.	When studying U.S. history, interview the elderly to find out their firsthand experiences during key historical national events.	Order materials from the National Archives on topics that tie into the curriculum. Examine the primary resources and discuss their historical significance.
World	Bring in products or objects from home that have been made in foreign countries. Locate countries on map and describe how the objects came to the United States.	Research a country that is the place of origin for one's ancestors. Describe the experiences of the group of people who live there.	Compare the histories of two ancient civilizations. Describe the legacies of these cultures and the influence they have on contemporary society.

unique perspectives shaped by the speaker's own experience of an event's legacy. And the middle school lesson was partially inspired by the fact that the student preparing to teach knew someone from China. When lesson design incorporates the personal interests of teachers, both teachers' and students' interests are more engaged in the learning process. As you plan lessons for your coursework or field experiences, be sure to think of ways that you can infuse your own personality and interests. This is part of the creative process that contributes to the art of teaching!

Appendix A shows the National History Standards and the National Standards for the Social Studies. The standards that relate closely to history and sociology are highlighted.

Primary Application: Family/Oral History Project

Lora Watkins, an elementary teacher in Richmond, Virginia, has conducted oral history projects with students throughout her teaching career. A list of questions follows that can be used by students to find out more about their family history or the family history of a good friend. In the primary grades, parents or guardians can read the questions and answer them for their son or daughter. The primary students can recall incidences orally or, if answers are recorded by adults, the classroom teacher or aides can assist students in making a family history booklet that can be illustrated by the children. Writing skills are also developed as students learn how to develop narratives through paragraphs.

MODEL LESSON: FAMILY/ORAL HISTORY PROJECT

All About Mom, Dad, or Significant Other

FIRST PARAGRAPH:

1. What is your full name?
2. Where were you born?
3. When is your birthday?
4. How many brothers and sisters do you have?
5. Are they older or younger than you?
6. Where were you raised?
7. What event during your growing up years stands out in your mind?

SECOND PARAGRAPH:

1. What are the schools you attended?
2. What was your first job?
3. How old were you then?
4. How do you work today? (volunteering, etc.)
5. What do you like about the things you do in your work?

THIRD PARAGRAPH:

Describe Dad/Mom (or significant other, e.g., grandparent, etc., if more appropriate).

FOURTH PARAGRAPH:

1. What is your favorite pastime?
2. What is your favorite book, food, movie, TV show?

LAST PARAGRAPH:

1. What is your best memory so far?
2. What do you want me to remember most about you?

Grandparent Interview

FIRST PARAGRAPH:

1. Where and when were you born?
2. What was happening in the world at that time?
3. Did anything unusual happen to you during your childhood?
4. How many brothers and sisters do you have?

SECOND PARAGRAPH:

1. Tell me something that you remember from your school days.
2. Tell me about your courtship. How did you get engaged? Tell about your wedding, if you had one.

THIRD PARAGRAPH:

1. Tell me about your interesting vacations.
2. What was your career? Did you enjoy it?
3. How did you prepare for your career?
4. Tell me about your hobbies.

FOURTH PARAGRAPH:

1. Describe your children.
2. Tell me something interesting about my mom/dad.
3. How did you encourage my mom/dad?
4. How did your parents encourage you?

LAST PARAGRAPH:

1. What would you like me to remember most about you?
2. How do you want your friends to remember you?

Mom (or Dad) Tells Me About Her (or His) Grandparents

FIRST PARAGRAPH:

1. What was your mom's mother's name?
2. Where and when was she born?
3. Is she still living?

4. When and where did she and your grandfather get married?
5. What was her career?
6. What were her hobbies?
7. What was her personality like?
8. What is your outstanding memory of her?

SECOND PARAGRAPH:

1. What was your grandfather's name?
2. Where and when was he born?
3. Is he still living?
4. What was his career?
5. What were his hobbies?
6. Describe his personality.
7. What event do you remember most about him?

FOURTH PARAGRAPH:

Repeat the same questions for Mom's father's mother.

FIFTH PARAGRAPH:

Repeat the same questions for Mom's father's father.

As you can see, many historical and sociological concepts have been addressed through the interview schedule. Family, tradition, change, personality, education, leisure, generations, norms, and careers are just a few of the ideas explored. The series of interviews meet various elements in the National History Standards, especially (2), (3), and (4) (see Appendix A). For the NCSS standards *Individuals, Groups, and Institutions,* (a), (b), and (f) are reinforced by Mrs. Watkins's genealogy lessons (see Appendix A).

Intermediate Application: Technological Advancement— Railroads

The following lesson plan for intermediate students illustrates how a textbook can be used as a teaching tool that is modified to incorporate the lives of ordinary individuals researched by the classroom teacher or students. The author's 95-year-old grandfather was an inspiration for the adaptation because his family had been positively affected by the railroad industry. The McGraw-Hill text used for this lesson is for fifth graders studying U.S. history. A photo of a Central Pacific crew is shown on page 44. The lesson could also be modified for local history projects that study the railroads.

©Bettman Archive

SOURCE: From *United States: Adventures in Time and Place,* Fifth Grade, Teacher's Multimedia Edition. McGraw-Hill, New York, 2000.

MODEL LESSON: TECHNOLOGICAL ADVANCEMENT—RAILROADS

Level: Fifth   **Time:** One Hour

Topic: An Oral History of the California Railroads

Generalization: Technological advances have a differential impact on individuals and cultural groups.

Objectives:

Knowledge:

   1. Students will name three ways in which railroads affected the U.S. economy and/or individuals around the turn of the century.

From "Building the Railroad," Adventures in Time and Place, Grade 5: United States, Pupil Edition. New York: McGraw-Hill School Division, 2001. Reproduced by permission of the McGraw-Hill Companies.

Brown Brothers

2. Students will describe how the railroads changed the lives of Andrew Carnegie and Edwin Clardy.

Affective:
3. Students will contrast the variable impact $(+/-)$ that technology has based on class structure and ethnicity.

Procedure:

Introduction: Mention that in Chapter 18 (*United States,* McGraw-Hill, 2000), we will talk about the impact of the railroads during the 1800s. Ask: What effect did the railroads have on the Native American tribes? What was the relationship between the "language" of the railroad and the escape of slaves to freedom? Say that today's lesson will examine the effects of the railroad on the immigrants who had come to the United States. Ask students to pay particular attention to the impact of the railroads on individuals as well as the economy.

Content Focus: Take turns reading aloud Chapter 18 in *United States* (2000) about the development of the transcontinental railroad. Discuss the picture of driving the final spike depicted on page 44. Stop periodically to emphasize the following points:

- Transcontinental railroad helped the United States grow but with serious costs.
- Accidents were common on most railroad building jobs.
- Chinese and Irish workers did the most dangerous work.
- The railroads ended the way of life of the Native Americans on the Plains where life had been built up around the buffalo.

Ask students to imagine what it was like for immigrants who worked on the railroad. What kinds of questions would they want to ask someone who lived during that period regarding how they might have been affected by the railroad. List questions on board. Distribute the transcription of Edwin Clardy to students so that they can read along. To make the lesson more interesting, you might ask an elderly man in your community to make an audiotape of the enclosed transcription, so that students could follow along to a human voice. Return to questions on the board, and determine which ones were answered and which questions remain. Ask students to compare the impact of the railroads on Andrew Carnegie, a successful entrepreneur, and Edwin Clardy, a successful working-class person. Emphasize class differences. Students may also want to talk about the vivid descriptions recounted by Edwin Clardy eighty-five years after they were experienced firsthand. A picture of Edwin as a young boy is shown on page 464 in Appendix B. Emphasize how the extensive details about the railroads made a lasting impression.

Closure: Ask each student to write down three ways that railroads affected people in the United States during the late 1800s and early 1900s. Discuss. Ask students if they thought the railroad was a technological advance that contributed positively to all who lived in the United States. Ask them to defend their answers. Emphasize the differential impact on ethnic groups and class levels. Mention that, tomorrow, students will study the ways in which men, women, and children fought to change the oppressive working conditions in factories during the late 1800s and early 1900s.

Evaluation:

Formative: Were students listening attentively? Did they comprehend the text passages? Could they analyze the railroad picture? Could they generate hypothetical questions?

Summative: Students' written responses.

Materials/Resources:

Books: *United States* (McGraw-Hill, 2000, pp. 508–515); oral history audiotape and/or transcription of Edwin Clardy.

AN ORAL HISTORY OF THE CALIFORNIA RAILROADS: INTERVIEW WITH EDWIN CLARDY

MAY 15, 1993 SAN JACINTO, CALIFORNIA
95TH BIRTHDAY, EDWIN JAMES CLARDY, BORN 1898

This segment of the oral history reports the period in Edwin Clardy's life in the early 1900s when making a living on a chicken ranch was difficult for his parents. Their standard of living changed when railroad production expanded job opportunities in Los Angeles. Others present at interview: Margaret (Edwin's wife), Bill Clardy (Edwin's son), Mary Clardy (Edwin's daughter-in-law), Ann McEachron (Edwin's daughter), and Don McEachron (Edwin's son-in-law).

Edwin: We must have moved from there to a chicken ranch in Cyprus. You know where Cyprus is in LA?

Bill: Isn't that Orange County?

Edwin: Yeah. Cyprus [down near Orange]. Between Orange and Pollock and Norwalk. They used to run the red cars from LA down to Santa Ana and they always went by our chicken ranch in Cyprus.

Bill: The red car went right by your chicken ranch?

Edwin: Yes. And we could get on the red car and go to town out by LA or go to Santa Ana on that red car. That was a line that the red cars run on all the time.

Bill: Would it go to Santa Ana or Long Beach?

Edwin: Well, red car lines run all different places out of central Los Angeles. The yellow cars were in central Los Angeles all the time.

Bill: And the LA railways?

Edwin: And the LA railways, yeah.

Bill: What year was that about?

Edwin: Well, we lived on a chicken ranch from . . . ah . . . maybe 1906 to 1908 or 9.

Bill: And the red car was operating that early?

Edwin: Oh yeah, they were all operating all over all the way from—they start building up at 1900 I think it was. Somewhere around 1900.

Ann: What all did you do on the chicken ranch? Did you have to work with the chickens?

Edwin: Well, we had brooders that kept the chickens warm and I probably filled the cans of water that they set in. You turn them upside down and they feed—the water comes out of this can into the saucer around them. They had little chicks in these runs, you know, and they have the brooders.

Margaret: Well, what did you do with all the chickens?

Edwin: They had a man come from somewhere who was in the business of buying up eggs and young chickens.

Mary: Young chickens or baby chicks?

Edwin: Well no . . . he had incubators. I remember the incubators had several sections in it and they were heated by oil lamps to hatch the little chicks. And when they were born out of the eggs, they take the little chicks and put them in runs with a round warm cover where they could go on underneath it. And we had several—4 or 5—of those runs for the little chicks and when they get big enough they put them out in the big pens . . . had several big pens for chicken runs.

Margaret: Well, did you and your mother do all that?

Edwin: Well, yeah.

Ann: Your dad was working?

Edwin: Well no, he had worked on the ranch all the time with the chickens. And we had enough acreage there he planted corn and potatoes and the like. We had an artesian well on the property and it kept flowing water out of the ground and he built a cement frame around the well so that he could raise the water level in that from the ground up. You run that water over into a swimming pool, I guess you'd call it, or a big reservoir, and that filled up and then he took the water from that—run through the orchard or the cornfield and the potato field up that way. And the surface water would be running all the time, you know. It kept running and that would run down the hill, or slope—it was to the back of all the chicken runs and the water had fresh water from the artesian well for all the chickens until down to the river there between them. And the river was, on the low part of the ground in there—whatever it was, I don't know if it was a river or what—but anyway, that's where the water went. And the red line joined our property. It went right by our property on down to Santa Ana and Fortin and Anaheim. So all we could do was walk over there at the back part of our land and flag down a car coming from Santa Ana and they'd stop and pick us up and take us up to LA.

Don: How many years did you say you lived there?

Edwin: About three years I think we lived there.

Don: It sounds great.

Edwin: We moved up to LA again on 24th street about 1909 and then Dad walked the streets for a long time—that was sort of the Depression era.

Bill: 1909?

Edwin:	Yeah. And we were poor of course and moved into this place on 24th street. It had a barnlike place with a shed on the back of the lot and the house was in the front of the lot and it had about I think two bedrooms and a kitchen and dining area in the front of the lot on 24th street. It was a nice house.
Ann:	Why did you move from the chicken ranch? It was not doing well?
Edwin:	Well, I guess they wasn't getting any price from the pullets—or whatever they sold for—young chickens and eggs were probably down and up, feed probably was too much and they couldn't make much money on it.
Margaret:	Was Edith living at home then?
Edwin:	Oh yes, she was. I was only about 7 or 8 then.
Ann:	So did your dad finally get work?
Edwin:	Finally he got work with the Los Angeles railway and the powerhouse. And yellow cars were running then all over in a central location, LA you know. And they had a green line that run from LA down to Redondo Beach and that way. And then another red line run to Venice and Ocean Park and Santa Monica. And I can remember that one time they run two and three cars together from LA to Venice and they had a big wreck on that line coming from Venice up to LA and I think one of those three car trains that they run— the big red cars run together and someway or another and killed a lot of people. And the red line carried people to the outer skirts in different directions. Pasadena and all over, but yellow cars were in a central location. The yellow cars run on a narrow gauge track. The red cars run on a lighter gauge track which was the same as the trains run on. But the yellow cars all had narrow lines. And the trolley wire had to be under the yellow lines so that the trolley would stay straight up there on the yellow cars lines. And the red cars would go on another. They had two lines, two trolley lines I think, and the red car would go on the other line. They were fed by different powerhouses and the yellow cars were fed by other cars. And they all bought their electricity, the city of Los Angeles where they bought their electricity from the Edison Company, so did the red car line.
Mary:	And your dad was in the powerhouse?
Edwin:	He was in the operator and the powerhouse. He worked in the powerhouse on Central Avenue and 6th street [in] LA. And that was an old steam generating plant. A big steam generating plant in this building. They put a rotary converter or, what do you call it, motor generator unit in one section of this steam powerhouse and the steam powerhouse was owned by the gas company at that time. And then he worked in that for a number of years. Of course the railway had substations all around, scattered all around LA. And I guess he still continued to work for them until he retired.

Extension:

Ask students to conduct research for the purpose of investigating the impact that the railroads had on minorities and women. [These extensions will be addressed in Chapter 6.] The oral history of Edwin Clardy combined with text information about the history of the railroads addresses key social studies concepts and ideas. Industrialization, labor, capital, employment, growth, income, class, and technology are key concepts. Important ideas stressed are relevant to the following history standards: Standard (1, B); (2, C); (3, A, D, E) (see Appendix A). For the NCSS standards *Time, Continuity, and Change,* the following are pertinent: (a), (b), (c), (d), (e).

✦ INTERNET LINKS

The preceding lessons explored family while touching on other related topics including tradition, careers, change, and generations. The Internet provides numerous resources for teachers wishing to explore these topics further. Sites include sample lesson plans, activities and background information for all grade levels. The following descriptions are of two examples of sites you may wish to investigate.

INTERNET LINKS
Family

http://www.csun.edu/~vceed009/index.html

Websites and Resources for Teachers.

This site houses a collection of general resources from the Internet for teachers. The resources include lesson plans, background information and interactive activities designed for all grades in all content areas. Included is a page devoted to thematic social studies lesson plans. One of the themes explored is family. These lesson plans are designed for primary grades and include titles such as, "Where We Came From." Family heritage is the focus of this particular lesson. Students discuss with parents their ancestral countries and return to the classroom to research the country that interests them most. Students then share and display the information they gathered. This is just one example of several lessons this site offers that can be easily adapted to fit into any unit on family.

INTERNET LINKS
Genealogy

http://www.execpc.com/~dboals/boals.html

History/Social Studies Websites for K–12 Teachers.

This is another general Internet resource for teachers. Useful educational sites and activities have been organized into several categories including, among others: archaeology, government, religion, genealogy, media, resources for parents, electronic texts, and research. The listings under these categories are extensive. For example, the genealogy page includes hundreds of entries under the following headings: general resources, genealogical societies, national and regional groups, publications and newsletters, ethnic research, guides, tutorials and software, discussion groups, and select family websites. Most of the information presented in these sites is geared toward people searching for family members or tracing their roots. However, teachers could use these sites as a medium for discussing or conducting genealogical research.

The intermediate lesson for this chapter exemplified how a textbook can be used in conjunction with a transcription of an interview with Edwin Clardy. Described in the following is one site that not only will provide great information on California railroads but also will open the door to the abundance of information the Internet provides on national and international railroads.

INTERNET LINKS

Railroads

http://www.ljcds.pvt.k12.ca.us/lower/Railroad/gbial_CArailroad%2FTreashunt.html

Railroad Ho! California or Bust!

This site is extremely useful for both students and teachers. It is designed to answer several specific questions regarding California railroad history such as *What was the significance of the "Golden Spike" ceremony?, Who were the "Big Four"?, Why were they called this and what was the role of each?,* and *What was the role of the Chinese in the building of the Transcontinental Railroad?* Links to other Internet resources are provided to answer these questions. It is this feature that makes this site most useful because the sites that are reached through these links go far beyond answering the one question they were intended to answer. The information gained through these sites is endless, ranging from general information regarding the history of American railroads to more specific information and photos depicting the construction of the transcontinental railroad, the workers involved, and the driving of the last spike. Also included is a site containing resources, activities, and lesson plans for teachers covering California history past to present. The ways in which this site can be used are endless.

SUMMARY

The history debates and research into the way children learn time and chronology have had a positive impact on the teaching of social studies. Key ideas and concepts in history provide a foundation to all other social science disciplines, and sociology in particular provides a contemporary perspective based on the legacy of the past. No longer restricted by the mere memorization of dates and famous battles, students can explore significant historical events from a variety of vantage points. While important historical events and famous leaders should be emphasized, their significance is appreciated further by examining the lives of ordinary individuals who lived in the same time period. A more inclusive approach ensures that many voices are heard through diaries, firsthand accounts, and other primary sources. The excitement that is created when students interpret primary source material appropriate to their level of understanding captures the spirit of studying history. The search for an increased understanding of how people lived in the past provides meaning to one's ongoing quest in the present and future. As a future teacher your opportunities are limitless, ranging from studies of people in the local community to research into the ancient meanings inscribed on the Rosetta Stone. Following the *Self in the World* philosophy, the decisions you make about what is important to teach in relation to institutional guidelines will have an impact on your identity as well as your students. Graham (1991) captures this sentiment in the following remarks:

> . . . I want to explore the proposition that to talk at all about knowledge and the curriculum is inevitably to talk about the self and the manner in which that self makes the flux of experience intelligible. It is in effect to talk about education in its largest sense, whether one conceives education as a developmental process of unfolding or

growth, or as an initiation into worthwhile activities. For if all knowledge begins in self-knowledge, or is a function of self-knowledge, then we cannot be said to truly know something until we have possessed it, made it our own. (p. 3)

The creative process of making connections between theory and practice is truly an opportunity to make knowledge your own. A further challenge is to provide this opportunity to your students, helping them make linkages between subject matter and their own lives.

PROFESSIONAL DISCUSSIONS AND FIELD EXPERIENCES

Discussion Questions

1. Examine three textbook series and report your findings to classmates. Which of the series emphasizes more traditional approaches to teaching history, for example, political and military history? Which of the series reflects the approaches of the new social historians, for example, human interest stories, the lives of ordinary people, activities for local history projects? Do any of the series have what you consider to be an appropriate balance?

2. Bring in family memorabilia such as family trees, genealogical charts, family photo albums, and so on. Share your own family histories with peers. Talk about sensitive issues that arise and how you would need to modify such an activity if conducted in an elementary or middle school. For example, what about students who have very few family memorabilia? What if someone is adopted? What about Jewish-Americans and African-Americans whose ancestral links may have been severed? How do you handle family trees in situations where there has been a divorce and remarriage? How can you include a variety of activities for family or community history projects so that students have choices and are not put in awkward situations?

Field Experiences

1. Initiate a family history or community history project with students. Brainstorm a list of questions that students might choose from to conduct an oral history with parents, grandparents, or people in the community. Encourage students to present their findings to the class and/or compile a booklet of their research.

2. Contact a local nursing home and set up opportunities for intergenerational contacts between students and residents of the nursing home. Activities can be occasional or build more long-term relationships. For example, the elderly can be invited to read stories, participate in craft activities, or contribute their life stories to oral history projects.

3. Visit a county courthouse in your community. Develop a lesson for students based on the information you found, so that they might follow your lead and eventually take a field trip to the courthouse. For example, you might make copies of selected wills of deceased community members. Students can make inferences about the relationships among family members and the lifestyles indicated by the contents in the will. The lesson can be extended further by having students research important national political and historical events that were taking place during the same time period.

RESOURCES: TEACHER AND STUDENT MATERIALS

Articles and Books

Blaustein, R. (1992, September/October). Golden days: An oral history guide. *Gifted Child Today, 15* (5), 15–17.

Carroll, R. (1985, July/August). Exploring the history of a neighborhood: A community project. *The Social Studies, 76* (4), 150–154.

Cerny, J., & Eakle, A. (1985). *Ancestry's guide to research: Case studies in American genealogy.* Salt Lake City, UT: Ancestry.

Croom, E. A. (1983). *Unpuzzling your past: A basic guide to genealogy.* Crozet, VA: Betterway.

Demos, J. (1986). *Past, present, and personal: The family and the life course in American history.* Oxford: Oxford University Press.

Frisch-Ripley, K. (1991). *Unlocking the secrets in old photographs.* Salt Lake City, UT: Ancestry.

Harris, J. J. (1963). *The treatment of religion in elementary school social studies textbooks.* New York: Anti-defamation League of B'Nai B'Rith.

Hawke, S. D., & Davis, J. E. (1992). *Seeds of change: The story of cultural exchange after 1492.* Menlo Park, CA: Addison-Wesley.

Haynes, C. C. (Ed.). (1990). Special section: Taking religion seriously in the social studies. *Social Education, 54* (5), 276–277.

Hickey, M. G. (1991, April/May). And then what happened, Grandpa? Oral history projects in the elementary classroom. *Social Education, 55* (4), 216–217.

Hirschfield, C. (1991, May/June). New worlds from old: An experience in oral history at the elementary school level. *The Social Studies, 82* (3), 110–114.

Hittleman, C. G., & Hittleman, D. R. (1997). Bringing grandparents into social studies: A unit of study. *Social Studies and the Young Learner, 10* (2), P1–P4.

Horwedel, D. M. (1988, March). Write women back into history: Creative ways to recognize women's accomplishments in your history lessons year-round. *Instructor, 97* (7), 26–28.

Kohlberg, L. (1979). *Measuring moral judgment.* Worcester, MA: Clark University Press.

Laney, J. D., Laney, J. L., Wimsatt, T. J., & Moseley, P. A. (1997). Youngster, Oldster: Aging education in the primary grades. *Social Studies and the Young Learner, 9* (4), 4–9.

Leinwand, G. (1978). *Teaching of world history.* Bulletin No. 54. Washington, DC: National Council for the Social Studies.

Monk, L. R. (1994). *Ordinary Americans: U.S. history through the eyes of everyday people.* Alexandria, VA: Close-Up.

Olson, M., & Hatcher, B. A. (1982). Cultural journalism: A bridge to the past. *Language Arts, 59* (1), 46–50.

Perschbacher, R. (1984). An application of reminiscence in an activity setting. *The Gerontologist, 24* (4), 343–345.

Reep, B., & Early, P. (1988). Grandpals: This program narrows the distance between young and old. *The Executive Educator, 17,* 26.

Ritchie, D. A. (1994, Winter). Teaching the Cold War through oral history. *Magazine of History,* 10–12.

Schamel, W. B., & West, J. (1991). "A date which will live in infamy": The first typed draft of Franklin D. Roosevelt's war address. *Social Education, 55* (7), 467–470.

Schwartz, D. (1990). "Who will tell them after we're gone?": Reflections of teaching the holocaust. *The History Teacher, 23* (2), 95–110.

Sears, A., & Bidlake, G. (1991, July/August). The senior citizen's tea: A connecting point for oral history in the elementary school. *The Social Studies, 82* (4), 133–135.

Spears, E. (1999). Will the circle be unbroken? Using oral histories to tell the story of the civil rights movement. *Social Education, 63* (4), 198–206.

Turiel, E. (1983). *The development of social knowledge.* Cambridge: Cambridge University Press.

(2000). *United States,* Fifth Grade Textbook. New York: McGraw-Hill School Division.

Wigginton, B. E. (Ed.). (1972). *The foxfire book: Hog dressing; log cabin building; mountain crafts and foods; planting by the signs; snake lore, hunting tales, faith healing; moonshining; and other affairs of plain living.* New York: Anchor.

Winkler, K. J. (1989). Dispute over validity of historical approaches pits traditionalists against advocates of new methods. *The Chronicle of Higher Education,* January 11, A4-5, A7.

Wolfman, I. (1991). *Do people grow on family trees? Genealogy for kids and other beginners.* New York: Workman.

Organizations

American Association for State and Local History
530 Church St., Ste. 600
Nashville, TN 37218
(601) 225–2971

American Historical Association
400 A St., S.E.
Washington, DC 20003
(202) 554–2422

Association for the Study of African-American Life and History
7961 Eastern Ave., Ste. 301
Silver Spring, MD 20910
(301) 587–5900

The Atlantic Council of the United States
910 17th St., N.W., Ste. 1000
Washington, DC 20006
(202) 778–4964

National Association for Asian and Pacific American Education
c/o ARC Associates
1212 Broadway, Ste. 400
Oakland, CA 94612
(510) 834–9455

National Council for History Education
c/o Elaine Wrisley Reed
26915 Westwood Rd., Ste. B-2
Westlake, OH 44145-4657
(216) 835–1776

Oral History Association
P.O. Box 3968
Albuquerque, NM 87190-3968
(505) 277–8213

Organization of American Historians
112 N. Bryan St.
Bloomington, IN 47408
(812) 855–7311

Organization of History Teachers
University of Chicago Laboratory School
1362 E. 59th St.
Chicago, IL 60637
(312) 702–0588

Western History Association
University of New Mexico
1080 Mesa Vista Hall
Albuquerque, NM 87131
(505) 277–5234

World History Association
Marilynn Hitchens
720 Josephine
Denver, CO 80206
(303) 312–1615

REFERENCES

Ashby, R., Lee, P., & Dickinson, A. (1997). How children explain the "why" of history: The Chata research project on teaching history. *Social Education, 61* (1), 17–21.

Avery, P. G., & Johnson, T. (1999). How newspapers framed the U.S. history standards debate. *Social Education, 63* (4), 220–224.

Banks, J. A. (1990). *Teaching strategies for the social studies.* New York: Longman.

Bauer, D. H. (1979). As children see it. In K. E. Yamamoto (Ed.), *Children in time and space* (pp. 83–114). New York: Teachers College Press.

Cheney, L. V. (1987). *American memory: A report on the humanities in the nations' public schools.* Washington, DC: National Endowment for the Humanities.

Cohen, R. (1996). Moving beyond the name games: The conservative attack on the U.S. history standards. *Social Education, 60* (1), 49–54.

Commager, H. S., & Muessig, R. (1980). *The study and teaching of history.* Columbus, OH: Merrill.

Curry, T., Jiobu, R., & Schwirian, K. (1999). *Sociology for the twenty-first century.* Upper Saddle River, NJ: Prentice-Hall.

Dellios, H. (1994, October 30). Battle over history may prove itself historic. *Chicago Tribune,* 1 & 4.

Diggins, J. P. (1994, November 19). Historical blindness. *The New York Times,* 23.

Durkheim, E. (1966). *The division of labor in society.* New York: Free Press. (Original work published 1893)

Eitzen, D. S., & Zinn, M. B. (1997). *Social problems* (7th ed.). Boston: Allyn & Bacon.

Educational Materials from the National Archives. (n.d.). Washington, DC: National Archives.

Eshelman, J. R. (1997). *The family.* Boston: Allyn & Bacon.

Ester, A. (1997). *The western world: A narrative history Prehistory to Present* (2nd ed.). Upper Saddle River, NJ: Prentice-Hall.

Forsyth, D. R. (1995). *Our social world.* Pacific Grove, CA: Brooks/Cole.

Gardner, J. B., & Adams, G. R. (Eds.). (1983). *Ordinary people and everyday life.* Nashville, TN: The American Association for State and Local History.

Gluck, C. (1994, November 14). History according to whom? *The New York Times,* 23.

Gottschalk, L. (Ed.). (1963). *Generalization in the writing of history.* Chicago: The University of Chicago Press.

Graham, R. J. (1991). *Reading and writing the self: autobiography in education and the curriculum.* New York: Teachers College Press.

Grant, S. G. (1997). Appeasing the right, missing the point? Reading the New York State social studies framework. *Social Education, 61* (2), 102–106.

Hakim, J. (1993). *A history of U.S.* Oxford: Oxford University Press.

Hawke, S. D., & Davis, J. E. (1992). *Seeds of change: The story of cultural exchange after 1942.* New York: Addison-Wesley.

Haynes, C. C. (Ed.). (1990). Special section: Taking religion seriously in the social studies. *Social Education, 54* (5), 276–277.

History-Social Science Framework. (1988). Sacramento, CA: California State Department of Education.

Lemert, C. (Ed.). (1993). *Social theory: The multicultural and classical readings.* Boulder, CO: Westview Press.

Leo, J. (1994, November 14). The hijacking of American history. *U.S. News & World Report,* p. 36.

Levstik, L. S. (1986). Teaching history: A definitional and developmental dilemma. In V. A. Atwood (Ed.), *Elementary school social studies: Research as a guide to practice.* (pp. 68–84). Bulletin No. 79. Washington, DC: National Council for the Social Studies.

Macionis, J. J. (1987). *Sociology.* Englewood Cliffs, NJ: Prentice-Hall.

Marx, K. (1963). Estranged labour-economic and philosophic manuscripts of 1844. In C. Wright Mills (Ed.), *Images of man.* New York: George Braziller. (Original work published 1844)

Massad, C. E. (1979). Time and space in space and time. In K. E. Yamamoto (Ed.), *Children in time and space.* New York: Teachers College Press.

Meerloo, J. A. (1970). *Along the fourth dimension: Man's sense of time and history.* New York: John Day.

Morrissett, I. (Ed.). (1967). *Concepts and structure in the new social science curricula.* West Lafayette, IN: Social Science Education Consortium, Inc.

Nash, G., Crabtree, C., & Dunn, R. E. (1997). *History on trial: Culture wars and the teaching of the past.* New York: Knopf.

National Center for History in the Schools. (1994). *Fact sheet.* Los Angeles, CA: Author.

National Standards for United States History, Grades 5–12, 1994. University of California, Los Angeles.

Norton, M. B., Katzman, D., Escott, P., Chudacoff, H., Paterson, T., & Tuttle, W. (1998). *A people and a nation: A history of the US. Vol. II since 1865* (5th ed.). Boston: Houghton Mifflin.

Norton, M. B. (1994). Rethinking American history textbooks. In L. Kramer, D. Reid, & W. L. Barney (Eds.), *Learning history in America* (pp. 25–33). Minneapolis: University of Minnesota Press.

Passe, J. (1999). The value of teaching values. *Social Education, 63* (2), 124–125.

Ravitch, D., & Finn, C. E. (1987). *What do our 17-year-olds know?* New York: Harper & Row.

Saxe, D. W. (1996). The national history standards: Time for common sense. *Social Education, 60* (1), 44–48.

Shepard, J. M. (1993). *Sociology.* St. Paul, MN: West.

Stahl, R. J., Hronek, P., Miller, N., & Shoemake-Netto, B. R. (1995). *Doorways to thinking: Decision-making episodes for the study of history and the humanities.* Tucson, AZ: Zephyr Press.

Stavrianos, L. S. (1992). *Lifelines from our past: A new world history.* New York: M. E. Sharpe.

Stavrianos, L. S. (1995). *The world to 1500: A global history* (6th ed.). Englewood Cliffs, NJ: Prentice-Hall.

Stearns, P. N. (1983). The new social history: An overview. In J. B. Gardner & G. R. Adams (Eds.), *Ordinary people and everyday life* (pp. 3–21). Nashville, TN: The American Association for State and Local History.

Stevens, R. L., & Allen, M. G. (1996). Teaching public values: Three instructional approaches. *Social Education, 60* (3), 155–158.

Thomas, J. U.S. panel's history model looks beyond old Europe. (1994, November 11). *The New York Times,* A1 and A14.

Viola, H., & Margolis, C. (1991). *Seeds of change.* Washington, DC: Smithsonian Institution.

Weber, M. (1947). *The theory of social and political organization.* Trans. A. M. Henderson & Talcott Parsons. New York: Oxford University Press.

Welton, D. A., & Mallan, J. T. (1992). *Children and their world: Strategies for teaching social studies.* Boston: Houghton Mifflin.

Whelan, M. (1996). Right for the wrong reasons: National history standards. *Social Education, 60* (1), 55–57.

Yamamoto, K. (Ed.). (1979). *Children in time and space.* New York: Teachers College Press.

© Will Hart/PhotoEdit

CHAPTER 3

READING THE LANDSCAPE

Geography, Economics, and Ecology

Chapter Outline

CHAPTER OBJECTIVES

As you think about places where you have lived, visited, and studied, near and far, no doubt you are in awe of the tremendous cultural differences that have emerged based on geography, material resources, and belief systems. Unraveling the ways in which humans have shaped and been shaped by their environment is an exciting endeavor. As you read this chapter think about how you will prepare students to make decisions about their local environment with a view toward global implications for the twenty-first century. Given recent changes in world economies and domestic policies, such as welfare and health care, what economic principles will you teach that will allow for critical thinking to solve ongoing and future economic challenges? Upon completion of this chapter you will be able to:

1. Describe developmental issues relevant to children's conceptions of space and material culture.

2.   Identify linkages between geographic, economic, and ecological principles and their relevance for teaching elementary and middle school students.
3.   Demonstrate curricular applications of key ideas in geography, economics, and ecology.

S canning the natural environment, we immediately see the changes that have been brought about by the efforts of human beings. Humans not only have altered the natural environment through such projects as redirecting river flow, cutting passages through mountains, and so on, but also have utilized natural resources in such a way that new forms of material objects have been added to the landscape. From the early days of creating primitive tools from animal bones to futuristic notions of celestial space stations, men and women have shaped and been shaped by their environment.

In this chapter, geography, economics, and ecology have been linked to reflect the natural relationship between the environment and the creation of material culture. Material culture represents the artifacts and ideas created by people and the human relationships that emerge in relation to these artifacts and resources. Because material goods and human resources are explained in terms of location and exchange, two concepts tied to the geographic concept of place, geographers and economists are inextricably linked. Their studies provide valuable insights into ecological principles. Before discussing how geography, economies, and ecology are relevant to the social studies curriculum, children's orientations to the environment will be presented.

✦ DEVELOPMENTAL ISSUES: CHILDREN'S CONCEPTIONS OF SPACE AND MATERIAL CULTURE

Take a moment to sketch a map of your house and the neighborhood you lived in as a young child. By the age of 4 children already have developed mental images of their surroundings based on daily interactions. Scholarly assessment of the ability to reproduce these mental images in the form of maps or drawings is an untapped area for future research, but an area that is readily accessible in classroom settings. In informal ways, I have investigated mental maps by asking third-grade students and preservice students such as yourselves to re-create maps of the earliest neighborhoods they lived in. Both groups created maps that included their house in relation to places where they played, shopped, or visited friends. When third graders were asked to complete the same task, they also came up with maps that make a statement about their relationship to surroundings and activities in their neighborhood. Figures 3.1 to 3.3 show the third-graders' maps. How does your map compare with theirs?

What do the mental maps of early childhood memories constructed by adults and children tell us about developmental stages of spatial orientations? First, a child's orientation to space is a function of the activities that take place in those spaces. For example, your mental maps probably represent several activities recalled even though you may not have visited the neighborhood in years. Riding in a stroller across the railroad tracks to get coffee ice cream, not being allowed to play in the open field behind the

FIGURE 3.1   *A Third Grader's Map*

FIGURE 3.2   *A Third Grader's Map*

FIGURE 3.3   *A Third Grader's Map*

house, and swinging on a friend's swingset are a few of the reminisces from my mental map. Second, the mental maps say less about the frequency of the activity than the poignancy of the memory. That is, there may have been "more traveled paths" in those earlier days, but the images that remain most likely represent more memorable occasions, both positive and negative. Third, the mental maps represent spatial orientations based on relative location. Since precise locations (absolute location using longitude and latitude) are learned in more formal educational settings, the relative locations reflect natural orientations to one's surroundings. In other words, children's experiential mental maps precede knowledge of constructed maps. It is certainly possible to construct a map based on expectations or planned exploration, but the distinguishing characteristics of the memory maps are revealed by the fact that applying relative location concepts are as natural as learning to walk. The process exemplifies one's developing sense of adaptation to surroundings using geographic and material boundaries.

The common use of landmarks to denote location becomes obvious when, for example, someone asks for directions by street names. We are sometimes hard-pressed to generate the names of streets that we pass hundreds of times because, more likely, we "turn at the fire station" or "by the large oak tree" that we see rather than look for the name written on a street sign. For most of the elementary and middle school years, students use these more informal spatial orientations. Gradually, through the process of schooling, children learn more precise orientations to their surroundings through social studies skill development, traditionally map and globe skills. The importance of these mental maps as a foundation for more sophisticated geographic understanding is stated in *Geography for Life* (1994):

Students should be encouraged to develop and update their mental maps to ensure that they continue to have essential knowledge of place location, place characteristics, and other information that will assist them in personal decision-making and in establishing a broad-based perception of Earth from a local to a global perspective. (p. 66)

Geographic literacy depends on one's knowledge of maps and globes. In the early sixties, Joyce (1964) investigated the reasonable placement of map and globe skills based on developmental levels. Table 3.1 provides selected expectations for map and globe skill development in Grades 1 through 6. The grade level distributions have been reflected in subsequent textbooks, curriculum guides, and the *K–6 Geography: Themes, key ideas, and learning opportunities* (1987). Current social studies texts offer a wide range of support for teaching geographic content. An example is shown from McGraw-Hill's Second Grade, Student's Edition textbook, "*Dictionary of Geographic Words.*"

What can be said about the attention given developmental awareness of the social relationships that arise relative to place and material culture, in other words the interrelationships between geographic and economic principles?

Most of the research on the development of economic learning has focused on children's ability to grasp economic concepts. Less attention has been devoted to students' understanding of the social relationships that emerge in relation to material culture. A partial explanation for this lack of research is because the study of social relationships in relation to material culture is a relatively young field (Gardner & Adams, 1983). A second reason is that an analysis of social interaction is based more on inferential data. Hypothesizing about human interaction surrounding material objects hundreds of years in the past requires abstract reasoning. When looking at pictures of people, young children can certainly describe who is doing what with specific goods and services, but the more abstract dynamics related to power are typically beyond their grasp. For these two reasons, research on economic development in young children has concentrated on the acquisition of more concrete economic concepts.

The development of economic reasoning has been tied closely to Piaget's stages of cognitive development. Kourilsky (1985) and Schug and Birkey (1985) suggest that economic learning is tied to the physical characteristics of objects or processes when children are in the preoperational stages (ages 2–7), emerging reasoning during the concrete operational stage (ages 7–11), and a reflective level of economic reasoning during the formal operational level (ages 11–16). Attention to the stages of development provides guidelines for knowing when to introduce economic concepts in meaningful ways. For example, teachers deal with scarce resources in the classroom on a regular basis; for example, not enough construction paper, not enough time to complete a given task, not enough computers, and so on. Teachers can utilize these occasions to reinforce economic principles such as needs, wants, and scarcity (Schug & Armento, 1985).

In addition to developmental stages influencing the acquisition of economic understanding, Schug and Birkey (1985) found that economic thinking varies somewhat by concept and may depend on students' experiences. When students have firsthand experiences with economic decision making, their understanding is obviously enhanced. Jahoda investigated the influence of firsthand experiences on economic understanding by comparing children's explanations of *profit* in the countries of Scotland, England, Holland, and Zimbabwe. The Zimbabwe children had a greater grasp of the concept, a finding that Jahoda (1983) attributed to their experience with trading activities.

Dictionary of GEOGRAPHIC WORDS

HILL Land that is higher than the land around it, but lower than a mountain.

PENINSULA Land that has water on three sides.

PLAIN Flat land.

LAKE Body of water with land all around it.

ISLAND Land that has water all around it.

R8

From "Dictionary of Geographic Words," Adventures in Time and Place, Grade 2, Pupil Edition. New York: McGraw-Hill School Division, 2001. Reproduced by permission of the McGraw-Hill Companies

TABLE 3.1

Representative List of Map and Globe Skills for Grades 1–6

Grade	Representative Map and Globe Skills
Grade 1	Uses such relative terms in indicating direction as *this way, that way; to the right, to the left; in front of, in back of;* etc.
	Understands that in the early morning the sun is first seen in the east, appears to be nearly overhead at noon, and is last seen in the west during the late afternoon.
	Uses relative terms in expressing distance: *short, long, near, far, nearby, far away,* etc.
	Distinguishes between land and water masses on maps and globes; recognizes that there is more water than land on the earth's surface.
	Describes the location of his [*sic*] home in relation to such natural and man-made features of his [*sic*] environment as sidewalks, streets, hills, railroad tracks, streams, ponds, wooded areas, etc.
	Watches a stream and notes the direction in which water flows; discovers that water tends to flow from higher to lower levels.
	Uses pictures, drawings, films, or aerial photographs to identify familiar places in and around his [*sic*] local community.
	Representative Map and Globe Skills
Grade 2	Finds wind direction by observing the effects of wind on weather vanes, trees, flags, puddles, lakes, etc.
	Uses the terms *north* and *south* to show he [sic] knows that *north* is in the direction of the north pole and that *south* is in the direction of the south pole.
	Using a globe, discovers that north-south lines extend from pole to pole.
	Compares the actual length of a city block with a block as shown on a map.
	Recognizes that long distances on the ground can be represented by short distances on a map.
	Studies different sized maps of his [*sic*] classroom showing the same area and objects; recognizes that the same area can be represented by maps of different sizes.
	Tells why large-scale maps of his [*sic*] neighborhood tend to be more accurate than small-scale maps.
	Constructs a map of his [*sic*] neighborhood, showing the location of familiar places and then indicates on this map the routes he [*sic*] takes in going from his [*sic*] home to these places.
	Constructs floor maps of his [*sic*] home neighborhood and local community by using models, drawings, and photographs depicting features of the landscape.
	Representative Map and Globe Skills
Grade 3	Explains that when he [*sic*] locates any one direction (north, south, east, or west), he [*sic*] can then locate the other directions.
	Finds direction by observing shadows.
	Uses the terms *up* and *down* to show he knows that *up* is the direction away from the center of the earth and that *down* is the direction toward the center of the earth.
	Using a globe, demonstrates how it is possible to travel toward the north or south poles from any other points on the earth.
	Locates the continents and ocean basins on maps and globes; discovers that the size and shape of continents and ocean basins is shown differently on maps and globes.
	Using a world map and a globe, locates North America, the United States, his [*sic*] home state, and home town.

Continued

TABLE 3.1 (continued)

Representative List of Map and Globe Skills for Grades 1–6

Grade	Representative Map and Globe Skills (continued)
Grade 3	Using a street map of his local community, locates his [*sic*] home neighborhood, his [*sic*] home, and other familiar places. Using a globe and a world map, locates countries, continents, and bodies of water studied in class. Identifies features of the terrain which impede or facilitate travel in his [*sic*] home neighborhood and local community. Using maps, recognizes semipictorial symbols which depict rivers, lakes, coastlines, islands, mountains, roads, cities, railroads, etc.

Representative Map and Globe Skills

Grade	
Grade 4	Using a globe, discovers that east-west lines are parallel to the equator, parallel to each other, and encircle the earth. Orients street maps of his [*sic*] local community to aerial photographs of the same area. When comparing different kinds of maps, notes that north is not always at the top of the map—it depends on the location of the north pole. (For example, north would lie at the top of a mercator projection, but would lie at the center of a polar projection. Locates north, south, east, west, northeast, northwest, southeast, and southwest on maps and globes. Using a globe, locates the four hemispheres and the equator. Using a map of the world, locates the equator, the poles, rivers, lakes, islands, peninsulas, the Arctic and Antarctic Circles, and north-south and east-west lines. Using maps, locates important cities, countries, and continents studied in relation to the poles, equator, and Arctic and Antarctic Circles; discovers interrelationships among location and climate, weather and terrain. Using maps, locates important cities, countries, and continents studied in class; discovers interrelationships that exist among location and commerce, transportation routes, etc. Using maps, identifies more complex semipictorial symbols which depict falls and rapids, deltas, dams, canals, deserts, swamps, etc. Compares different kinds of maps with regard to the use of color, discovers that color may be used to designate elevations of land or the depth of water, to represent political boundaries, and to show rainfall, population, temperature, and other similar data. Reads a map and infers the relationships suggested by the data shown. (For example, the factors determining the location of cities, manufacturing centers, crop and livestock production, political boundaries, recreation facilities, etc.)

Representative Map and Globe Skills

Grade	
Grade 5	Reads a compass to find directions. Estimates, then measures, the dimensions of his [*sic*] classroom; draws a floor plan of the classroom to scale, with all measurements in inches. Estimates, then measures, the dimensions of his [*sic*] schoolyard; draws a map of the schoolyard to scale, with all measurements in feet or yards. Estimates, then computes, ground distances between the same two points on maps of identical areas, but of different scale. Compares the results. Estimates, then computes, air distances between various places on the globe, using the great circle routes.

	Estimates, then computes, amount of time needed in traveling between locations shown on a road map with regard to the mode of transportation used, such as walking, riding a bicycle, riding in a car, riding in an airplane, etc.
	Using the equator as a point of reference, locates the low, high, and middle latitudes on a globe and world map.
	Uses a number-and-letter grid for locating places on a road map.
	Locates time zones on maps and globes; explains how time at any given moment will vary from zone to zone.
	Recognizes the differences between various map projections, and notes the distortion involved in any representation of the earth, other than that of a globe.
	Reads merged relief maps showing altitude and slope of terrain, as indicated by gradual shading or merging of colors.
Grade	**Representative Map and Globe Skills**
Grade 6	Constructs maps of his [*sic*] local community by laying out directional lines with the aid of a compass.
	Uses north-south and east-west lines in locating directions on maps and globes.
	Estimates, then measures, distances around his [*sic*] home neighborhood; draws a map of the neighborhood to scale, with all measurements in yards, blocks, or miles.
	Estimates, then computes, ground distances between the same two points on a globe, using latitude as a basis for measurement.
	When given the latitude and longitude of a place, he [*sic*] can show its approximate location on a map or globe.
	Reads distribution maps containing data relative to rainfall, crop production, population, transportation facilities, etc.; understands the use of dots, lines, and shading.

SOURCE: Excerpt from *Teaching social studies in the elementary and middle schools.* Copyright © 1979 by William W. Joyce and Janet E. Alleman–Brooks, adapted by permission of Harcourt, Inc.

Seefeldt (1989) reviewed several major studies in economics education for primary and elementary-aged children. Of the studies reviewed, several generalizations emerged. When placed in a context that was familiar to students, economic principles—for example, travel and communication, labor, needs and wants—were more easily grasped. More difficult concepts to present to young children are supply and demand, social implications of unemployment, and competition as a foundation of capitalism (Brown, 1968; Darrin, 1968; Larkin & Shaver, 1969; Robinson and Spodek, 1965; Senesh, 1960).

The Joint Council on Economic Education has played a significant role in articulating how economic principles can be infused in the elementary curriculum through its Developmental Economic Education Program for Schools (Walstad & Soper, 1991; Walstad & Watts, 1985). In *Part II: Strategies for Teaching Economics, Primary Level (Grades 1–3),* Davidson (1977) underscores the notion that if economics is "presented within their experience realm, children can gain valuable insights into basic economic concepts and relationships" (p. 1). For example, the concept of scarcity is manifested in a young child's decision about how to use free time. Also, the use of simulations has been popular in economics education because they are close to real-life experiences, they encourage active participation, and they include actual decision making on the part of students (Kourilsky, 1974).

In Chapter 7 you will learn more about Diane Bradford, a student who has both gifted characteristics and learning disabilities. Relaying her experiences with economic principles reveals how crucial it is to make abstract concepts relevant to a student's everyday experiences. Diane had difficulty with computation, a skill that is reinforced when teaching the value of coins and other forms of money. Her fourth-grade teacher in a suburban school district outside Washington, D.C., believed in interdisciplinary teaching and the use of simulations. As a part of an instructional sequence in social studies, Ms. Barnes implemented a simulation on the marketplace. Students could assume a role they were comfortable with such as grocery store checker, banker, producer, consumer, and so on. At first, Diane had no interest in a role such as checker or banker because she knew that math would be involved. However, the excitement of being a banker in charge of all that money outweighed the reluctance to count it! Soon Diane was motivated by the interaction and exchange with customers who would come to the bank, and she tackled the initial difficulties of differentiating between dollars, quarters, dimes, nickels, and pennies. The role playing and interpersonal interaction no doubt alleviated feelings of embarrassment and lack of confidence that may have been manifested in more competitive, large-group lessons. The simulation provided an opportunity to build on her strengths (leadership characteristics and social skills) while addressing computation learning difficulties.

The marketplace simulation illustrates a good match between student needs and economic curriculum goals. It also exemplifies the interaction between geographic, economic, and ecological principles and extensions into the other disciplines. The geographic principles indicating where products sold in the marketplace originate (farms, factories, forests, food-processing plants, manufacturing, artisans, etc.) and how they were affected by such issues as climate, transportation, and land use correspond to both spatial and ecological perspectives.

In addition to viewing economic goods and services based on their value and how they were produced, teachers can lead students to more abstract economic reasoning such as how social interactions are influenced by their value. Demonstrating how social interaction influences the exchange of goods and services is a dynamic principle that exemplifies concepts shared by historians, geographers, psychologists, sociologists, economists, and political scientists. An illustration will make these principles more explicit.

Cary and Barbara Carson are American Studies scholars who have investigated the role of material culture throughout history. While giving a presentation, "Material Culture: Landscape, Structure, and Artifacts" to a group of social studies teachers, Barbara Carson sparked an interesting brainstorming session about the nature of social interaction surrounding the silver pitcher that was presented in her slide program. Moving beyond the material aspects of silver, where it comes from, and how much the pitcher may have cost in Colonial America in the 1700s, she probed the teachers' understanding of the cultural context in which the silver pitcher functioned. She asked: How would the pitcher be viewed by the silversmith who made it? What meaning did it have to the slave who polished it? What thoughts were going through the mind of the woman who was planning to use the silver pitcher in the dinner party that evening? What negotiations took place when the "master" of the house purchased the pitcher? A silver pitcher analyzed in this light becomes much more complex in comparison to analyses such as its material value and composition. The interdisciplinary concepts brought to the forefront of such a conversation through a teacher's questioning strategies can include social status, power, material culture, goods and services, labor, property, exchange, productivity, and so on.

The social dynamics that center around one object, in this case the silver pitcher, reflect complex community relationships. On a global scale social dynamics are equally complex. Consider, for example, the ecological issues surrounding the production of coffee, sugar, and cotton. To peasant farmers in El Salvador, being displaced by large landowners who cater to foreign markets has adverse consequences. No longer able to be subsistence farmers, they are forced to take only seasonal work, which often leaves them poor and malnourished. The ecological balance for humans creates a geographic irony according to Stoddard, Wishart, and Blouet (1989), who state that "regions where a larger share of the population is engaged in agriculture are the areas where malnutrition is most common" (p. 278).

Demonstrating how geography, economics, and the balance of human life are interrelated makes the study of these disciplines more relevant and interesting to students. Given the dramatic impact of such issues, ecological principles have been added to the 1994 list of National Standards for the Social Studies. In the next section, we examine some of the key concepts in geography, economics, and ecology.

✦ How Humans Shape and Are Shaped by Their Environment

Economics and geography are complementary disciplines just as geography and history or history and sociology complement each other. Taken together, geography and economics help to explain the interrelationships among people within a family, neighborhood, or throughout the globe. Geographers use two organizing themes to study these relationships—the spatial perspective and the ecological perspective. Economists focus on how people produce and exchange goods and services to fulfill needs for food, shelter, transportation, and recreation (*Geography for Life,* 1994). A summary of key ideas from geography, ecology and economics follows.

Geography and Ecology: Key Ideas and Concepts

Geographers typically view natural and human-made phenomena from either a spatial or ecological perspective (Stoddard et al., 1989). The spatial perspective analyzes why the landscapes people create are arranged the way they are. For example, investigations of productivity, consumption, and how goods are moved typically begins with the location of these economic activities. To pursue questions of where these activities take place the spatial perspective often incorporates maps for analysis. Hence, a major focus of geography is the geometry of the earth's surface, map projections (cartography), and the precise location of places (Banks, 1990). Once location is determined, geographers attempt to understand the reasons behind such locations.

The ecological perspective seeks to explain how people interact with the natural environment (Johnson, 1998; Smith, 1996). Since the time of the ancient Greeks "the reciprocal relationship between people and the natural environment, each affecting and being affected by the other, has been at the forefront of geographical investigation . . ." (Stoddard et al., 1989, p. 6). Subfields within the ecological perspective reflect attempts to explain many interacting phenomena between humans and the environment—physical geography or the earth science tradition; regional geography or the area studies tradition; cultural geography or the human-land tradition;

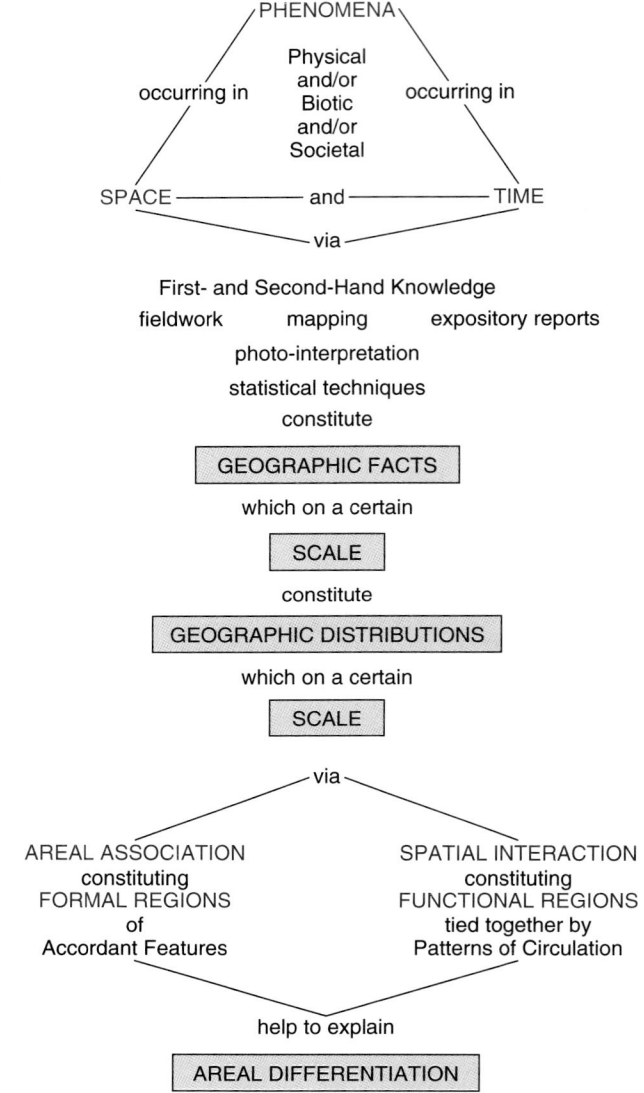

FIGURE 3.4   *Fundamental Ideas of Geography*

SOURCE: L. Senesh. Organizing a curriculum around social science concepts, in I. Morrissett (Ed.), *Concepts and structures in the new social science curricula* (New York: Holt, Rinehart, & Winston, 1967). Used by permission of the Social Science Education Consortium.

and historical geography (Banks, 1990). Geographers attempt ultimately to maximize geographic understanding by integrating or synthesizing the spatial and ecological perspectives (Stoddard et al., 1989). Since the 1960s educators have worked with social science scholars to identify fundamental geographic ideas that should be taught to elementary and middle school students. The efforts of the Social Science Education Consortium to depict these key ideas are presented in Figure 3.4. Key concepts

© Elizabeth Crews

and ideas articulated more recently by geographers and educators in the development of the National Geography Standards are presented in the following and in the "Resources: Teacher and Student Materials" section at the end of this chapter.

The World in Spatial Terms

Geographic literacy depends on a person's ability to "describe and analyze the spatial organization of people, places, and environments on Earth's surface" (*Geography for Life,* 1994). Examples of physical phenomena include topography, bodies of water, climate, and vegetation, whereas human elements may include population distribution, channels of trade, transportation networks, and the spread of disease. Geographers first describe spatial patterns by breaking them into more simple components—points, lines, areas, and volumes—then describe the relationships between these elements using concepts such as location, distance, direction, density, and arrangement.

Map and globe skills offer many opportunities for the social studies teacher to address spatial concepts. Probably all of you remember locating population centers on maps, using map pencils to color special purpose maps, or locating places on the globe using longitude and latitude. These classroom activities continue in popularity today with the support of attractive desk maps from publishers such as Nystrom and Glencoe. More modern mapping techniques are made possible through Radarsat satellite images, which can image areas beneath heavy clouds and on the dark side of the earth. "The technical name for interpreting satellite images and aerial photographs is *remote sensing*" (Kirman, 1999, p. 167).

Because mental maps are readily accessible and closely tied to experience, the social studies teacher has an ever-present classroom resource that can be tapped for spatial awareness. The Geography Standards give mental maps more prominence because of their distinguishing characteristics. Mental maps (a) are a personal mix of both objective knowledge and subjective perceptions, (b) are used by people throughout their lives, (c) represent ever-changing summaries of spatial knowledge, and (d) indicate how well people know the spatial characteristics of places (*Geography for Life,* 1994).

Places and Regions

Geographers study how places and regions influence people and vice versa (Knox & Marston, 1998). A person's identity is shaped by having a sense of place. To say one is a Texan, Californian, or Virginian signals where one lives. But often when people move and still have an affinity for where they lived before, they might say "I am a Texan through and through" or "I am a Californian at heart" or "My roots are in Virginia." A recent ad for attracting visitors to North Carolina stated, "You can leave North Carolina, but North Carolina will never leave you." These sentiments capture the emotional impact of place on personal identity. Regional affiliations are defined by a number of different criteria, ranging from physical characteristics such as coastlines and mountain ranges to such allegiances as athletic teams.

The National Geography Standards describe three kinds of regions—formal, functional, and perceptual. A formal region is characterized by a shared human property such as language, religion, or the presence of certain physical features such as climate or a form of vegetation. Functional regions are organized around a focal point such as communication or transportation systems and metropolitan areas. Perceptual regions encompass shared human feelings and attitudes. For example, regions in the United States such as southern California, Dixie, and the upper Midwest may bring forth certain images, and in some cases, stereotypes (*Geography for Life,* 1994). Social studies exploration units on topics such as the Oregon Trail and Lewis and Clark expeditions incorporate the study of formal, functional, and perceptual regions (Holt, 1998).

Physical Systems

Physical systems refer to processes that modify the earth's physical features and ecosystems on the earth's surface (Strahler & Strahler, 1997). Geographers group physical processes into four categories (*Geography for Life,* 1994):

> those operating in the atmosphere (i.e., climate and meteorology), those operating in the lithosphere (e.g., plate tectonics, erosion, and soil formation), those operating in the hydrosphere (e.g., the circulation of the oceans and the hydrologic cycle), and those operating in the biosphere (e.g., plant and animal communities and ecosystems).

A change in one ecosystem can affect others; for example, when developers consider draining marshlands to improve the natural environment. Yet such actions could have detrimental effects on wildlife and groundwater systems (Stoddard et al., 1989). Many of the emphases in physical systems lend themselves nicely to teaching across the content areas, especially with physical science. For example, recycling and conservation units incorporate concepts relevant to physical systems in geography and physical science.

Human Systems

Humans disperse throughout the earth creating a myriad of patterns. Geographers investigate these population distributions on the basis of historical migratory patterns, environmental factors, and existing services such as education and economic opportunities, to mention just a few. Belief systems are another aspect of human systems as a subcategory for geographical analysis. Religion, customs, language, values, and worldviews that are shared create patterns of lifestyle that can be represented geographically.

Human growth patterns indicate the "differential effects of past events, such as wars, disease, famine, improved sanitation, and vaccination programs, on birth- and death rates and gender" (*Geography for Life,* 1994, p. 79). The study of human systems provides many opportunities for interdisciplinary teaching. History, sociology, political science, economics, and anthropology are social science disciplines that address patterns of human growth and interaction. Some scholars estimate that as many as 100 million people inhabited the Americas at the end of the fifteenth century, compared with 18 million by 1750, as a result of disease and conflict from European exploration (Stoddard et al., 1989). The legacy of these historical events offers many opportunities for social studies educators. Given the rich diversity of human systems in the United States, students in the classroom can become active geographers in researching their own life stories as well as members of their community. Predictions from the U.S. Census Bureau project that the U.S. population will increase from the 248 million recorded in the 1990 census to 275 million in the year 2000, 347 million in 2030, and 394 million in 2050 (Rong, 1998).

Environment and Society

As humans interact with society the environment around them changes. Some of the changes are intentional, but there are also unintended differences. Irrigation systems and dams can alter the flow of water, creating both local and regional changes. Or large-scale global changes result, for example, when there is a depletion of the ozone layer by chlorofluorocarbons. Geographers point out the need for students to understand the relationship between population growth, urbanization, and the stresses brought to the environment as a result of certain lifestyles and human expectations. *Sim City* is a computer simulation that illustrates the interaction between these concepts. Helping students recognize these relationships will assist them in identifying roles that they can perform to protect the environment.

The Uses of Geography

Geographic analyses help to interpret historical events, present phenomena, and plan for future events. Geographers and historians share the belief "that the human story must be told within the context of three intertwined points of view—space, environment, and chronology" (*Geography for Life,* 1994, p. 101). The notion of time zones, for example, emerged in response to technological advances, specifically railroads, that made it possible to move at a rapid rate around the globe. Learning to analyze space and the environment in a given cultural context increases one's geographic literacy, thus making it possible to make more informed personal decisions about work, home, and participation in a global community.

© Gale Zucker/Stock Boston

Economics: Key Ideas and Concepts

As with most fields there is ongoing debate about emphases within the discipline and economics is no exception (Field, 1987; Henderson, 1995). Colander and Brenner (1992) take a critical look at the field in an attempt to explore their assumption that economics education is not succeeding. Brenner (1992) maintains that one can look at the scientific approach to economics "not as an activity where abstract theories and facts are being confronted, but as an everyday business where considerations of wealth, status, reputation, and broader issues intermingle with strictly scientific ones" (p. 11). These healthy debates will most likely strengthen the discipline, but in the meantime elementary teachers should forge ahead to do their part in support of economic awareness. Thus, basic organizing themes, however imperfect, will be presented as a means to help teachers in selecting economic concepts and principles.

Economists divide their discipline into two branches—microeconomics and macroeconomics. Microeconomics focuses on smaller economic units such as firms, households, and individuals, and macroeconomics examines the economy as a whole, for example, rates of unemployment, inflation, and balance of trade (Baumol & Blinder, 1997; Mankiw, 1997, 1998; Stiglitz, 1993a, 1993b). The science of economics is based on the premise that the distribution of resources in an economy is tied to the choices that humans make. Scarcity plays a major role in these choices because resources are limited but wants can be unlimited. Economists organize their field of study around four questions: What is produced, and in what quantities? How are goods produced? For whom are these goods produced? Who makes economic decisions, and by what process? (Stiglitz, 1993b, p. 11). An explanation of these questions follows.

What Is Produced, and in What Quantities?

Supply and demand are concepts that partially explain what is produced and in what quantities. Production patterns change over time as a result of changes in lifestyle, the availability of natural resources, production patterns, and trade. What is produced in the United States and in what quantities is largely determined by the private interaction of firms and consumers with some governmental influence. Determining why the prices of certain products increase or decrease is a central question to economists.

In the early grades the question of what is produced takes several forms. Defining basic concepts such as *product, work, consume, cost, value, goods, services,* and *natural resources* lays a foundation for further understanding of productivity. The natural resources, goods, and services provided by the local community and state are common economic topics in the primary grades. National productivity is presented in fourth and fifth grades when students often identify the state and regional origins of certain products. The volume of goods produced is represented through graphs and charts in the upper elementary and middle school levels.

How Are These Goods Produced?

Goods are produced by hand, through simple machines, or highly computerized technology. Goods may be produced from beginning to end by one person or through assembly-line techniques. Production for a car or tennis shoe, for example, may start in a country other than the United States and receive the finishing touches in a U.S. factory. Economists study the effects of technology on the labor market, investigating the relationship between laborsaving devices and employment patterns. More modern equipment may cost more but require less labor, for example. Firms determine how goods are produced through the influence of government, "which sets regulations and enacts laws that affect everything from the overall organization of firms to the ways they interact with their employees and customers" (Stiglitz, 1993b, p. 11).

Addressing the question of how goods are produced takes many forms in elementary and middle school classrooms. In the early grades teachers may simulate textile production with hand looms made out of construction paper and string, or make peanut butter sandwiches using an assembly-line technique. *Barnyard Economics,* a play about economic decision making, is a creative way to use children's theater to teach *opportunity cost, production of goods, productive resources,* and *services* (Shotick & Walsko, 1997). Throughout the elementary and middle school grades inventors and their inventions are spotlighted. Interdisciplinary connections can be made in science by having students make their own inventions or construct simple machines. The effects of technology and production techniques on the labor market are topics that receive greater attention in the upper elementary grades, especially when studying the Industrial Revolution and labor laws.

For Whom Are These Goods Produced?

Distributing goods and services is a notion that involves consumer economics. The question of who consumes the goods produced depends on both values and wants as well as the ability to purchase goods and services. Typically, those who have higher incomes can purchase more. But this relationship is very complex and leads to additional questions outlined by Stiglitz (1993b, p. 11): *What determines the differences in income and wages? What is the role of luck? of education? of inheritance? of savings? of experience and hard work?* How these questions are addressed depends on the kind of economy that exists in a particular locale. The United States is characterized by a mixed economy, which means that there is a mix between public (governmental) and private decision making.

In the elementary and middle school classrooms the distribution of goods is presented in several ways. In the primary classroom, family economics and marketplace simulations are used to demonstrate both barter systems and the exchange of U.S. currency. In some cases, classroom management procedures employ token economies and often give tangible rewards that can be exchanged for objects or designated activities. In Richmond, Virginia, local banks set up temporary offices in school cafeterias once a month to reinforce banking concepts. "Overseen by the PTA, children bring in their account books and money, and make their deposits" (Coleman, 1995). Marketplace simulations, fund-raising activities, studies of the depression, the impact of the Industrial Revolution, and the impact of technology are common economic topics included in the social studies curriculum. In middle schools stock market games are popular because they engage students actively over a period of weeks while teaching them about financial markets (Cox, 1997). Global studies at the middle school level provide opportunities to discuss the global marketplace, economic interdependence, and the environment (Salvatore, 1998; Schug & Shaw, 1997; Schug & Western, 1997). Eichengreen's (1987) discussion of macroeconomics and history provides helpful analyses of additional historical events that lend themselves well to teaching economic concepts and principles.

Who Makes Economic Decisions, and by What Process?

Economic decision making usually involves both the government and the private sector. Economists study the balance or relationship between both. In a centrally planned economy most of the economic decisions are made by the government, as in the Soviet Union prior to 1988. When there is a combination between governmental and private decision making, a mixed economy exists, as in the United States. Studying economic decision-making processes in other countries usually doesn't take place until the middle school years when there is a greater focus on global studies. Current events are one way, at the upper elementary and middle school levels, to address who makes decisions affecting the economy, as in governmental intervention in the number of imported cars, and the economic impact of the Environmental Protection Agency in regulating how products should be designed.

Whether taking a microeconomics or macroeconomics approach, elementary and middle school teachers are challenged to provide fundamental understanding of key economic concepts and principles. Continuing debates among scholars within the field of economics make this challenge more exciting. Debate centers around three main issues: the appropriate model for the economy, how to interpret data to make predictions about the economy, and policy decisions based on value conflict. The efforts of the Social Science Education Consortium are presented in Figure 3.5 to demonstrate one way to graphically organize key concepts and ideas in economics. In addition, *The National Content Standards in Economics* (1997) presents twenty broad economic content standards to assist teachers.

✦ CURRICULUM APPLICATIONS

The curriculum applications in this chapter feature ways in which concepts in geography, economics, and ecology can be addressed in many environmental contexts from kindergarten through eighth grade. First, Table 3.2 presents a sampling of activities across grade levels. This table is followed by more comprehensive plans for two levels. They include a primary lesson on map interpretation in a first-grade classroom and an intermediate lesson, "The International Arctic Project" developed by the National Geographic Society. A middle school lesson on the North American Free Trade Agreement is in Appendix B. The first lesson develops spatial concepts and the second and third integrate geographic, economic, and ecological principles. The National Geography Standards, the National Social Studies Standards, and National Content Standards in Economics are listed in Appendix A, highlighting the geography, economics, and environmental themes.

Primary Application: Reading Maps to Find Classroom Treasures

"Reading Maps to Find Classroom Treasures" is a mapping exercise taught by the author to a group of first graders. As a guest speaker, the author wanted to present a lesson that was educationally sound, of course, but since her son was in the class, there was additional pressure to ensure that students wouldn't be bored! A treasure hunt seemed the best way to get the students engaged from the start. As you view the videotape and examine the lesson plan you will discover that its basic structure has many of the characteristics of the Madeline Hunter teaching model. Madeline Hunter (1984) identified nine steps to include in a lesson as follows:

Anticipatory Set: elicits attending behavior
Objective and Its Purpose: teacher informs student what he/she will be able to do at end of instruction and why it is important
Input: teacher presents information
Modeling: demonstration of expectations
Check for Understanding: teacher checks for students' possession of information
Guided Practice: student performs part of task to assess clarification
Independent Practice: student practices without teacher
Closure: activities tied to objectives; wrap-up; review
Evaluation: homework, demonstration of competence

See if you can identify these components as you watch the videotape, keeping in mind that they may not occur in the same order as listed. In addition, of the four key concepts presented—symbol, route, pathway, map key—which ones do you think the children understood? Are there any that will require more reinforcement or reteaching? What did you observe to make such inferences?

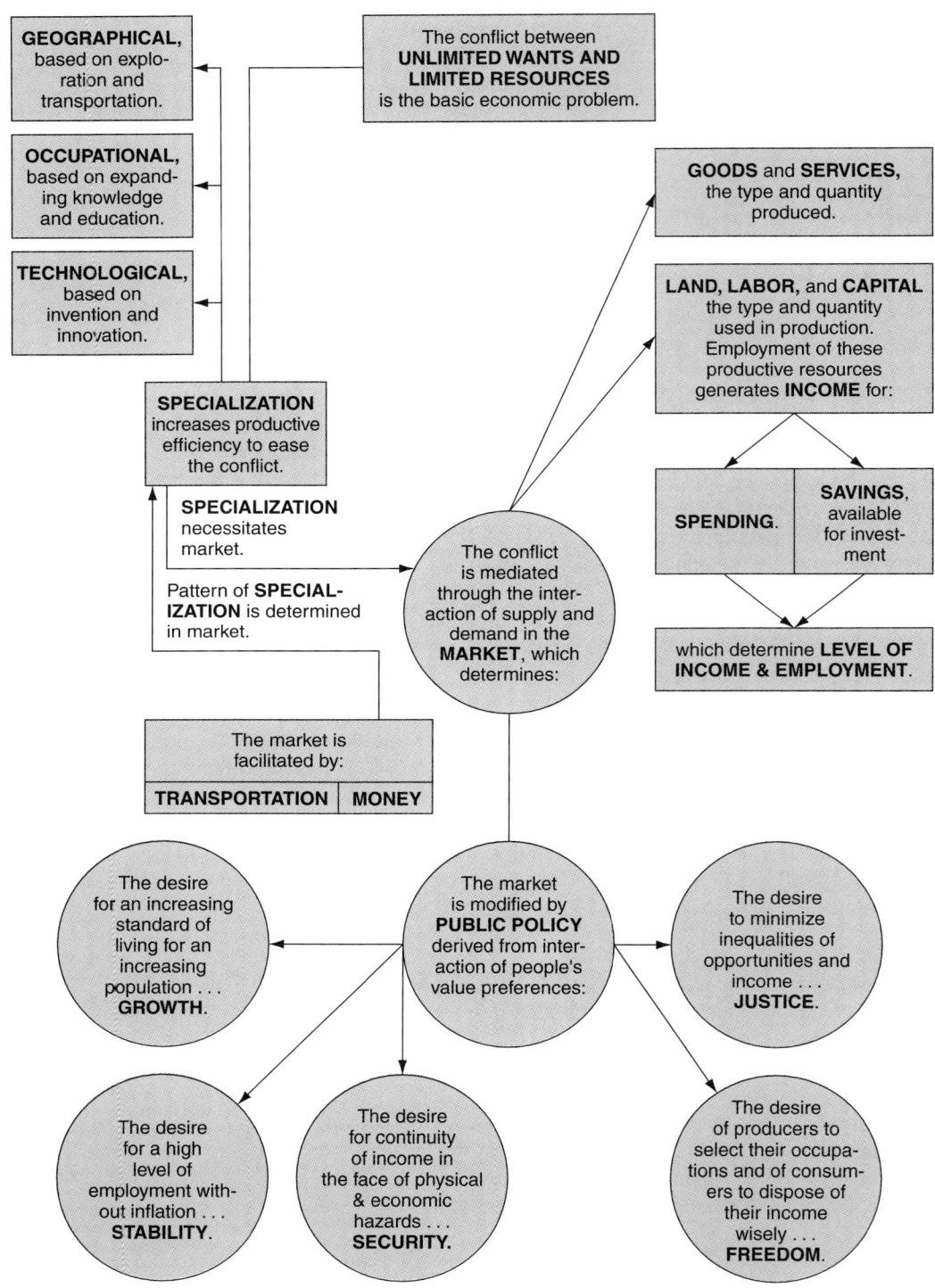

FIGURE 3.5 *Fundamental Ideas of Economics*

SOURCE: L. Senesh. Organizing a curriculum around social science concepts, in I. Morrissett (Ed.), *Concepts and structures in the new social science curricula* (New York: Holt, Rinehart, & Winston, 1967). Used by permission of the Social Science Education Consortium.

TABLE 3.2

Self in the World Connections
Establishing a Sense of Place and Productivity

	Primary	Intermediate	Middle School
Self	Lay down on long sheet of butcher paper and have teacher trace around body. Color in and hang up "body maps" in classroom.	Using DeLorme Mapping: Street Atlas USA computer program, have students locate all residences where they have lived.	Write an essay providing an imaginary description of what your place of residence looked like prior to the building of the house, apartment, etc.
Family	List needs and wants of family members; design map of room in one's house or backyard.	Students' families are given imaginary $500 community service award; plan with family how it should be spent; plot an imaginary week-long family vacation, indicating overnight stays and total mileage.	Establish recycling program in family, estimate savings to the environment; draw map of route parent or guardian takes to work (to scale).
Community	Take field trip to grocery store where students can identify nutritional needs from four main food groups; use "left" and "right" for practicing directions on desk maps of school.	Create a marketplace within the classroom; use compasses and written cardinal directions to locate designated places while walking throughout the neighborhood.	Create a salt and flour map of community to scale; interview manager of local drugstore to determine supply and demand patterns of specific products.
State	Use pictorial map symbols to locate natural resources on state map.	Identify an important industry in the state; imagine that the business burns down; research the economic impact on state, community, employees, etc. Brainstorm how the business will recover.	Determine the monetary amount of a natural resource produced by state and exported to other states; create an elevation map for the state.
Nation	Sing "This Land Is Your Land," locating the states mentioned on U.S. map; collect canned goods and distribute to U.S. citizens who have experienced recent natural disaster.	Research statistics on national employment patterns; create a special purpose map indicating national employment patterns.	Describe how the Federal Reserve works; create a map and explain the weather patterns across the nation for one week.
World	Have students bring objects from home that were made in other countries; locate origin on globe.	Compare U.S. international import/export patterns with language and cultural patterns found in U.S. and foreign countries.	Identify countries with whom the U.S. is a major trade partner. Investigate the effects of El Niño throughout globe.

MODEL LESSON: READING MAPS TO FIND CLASSROOM TREASURES

Level: First Grade   **Time:** One Hour

Topic: Map Skills

Standards:

National Geography Standards: The World in Spatial Terms #1.
National Social Studies Standards: People, Places, and Environments (b).

Concepts: Symbol, route, pathway, map key.

Objectives:

1. Identify and use map symbols as pictures that stand for something real on the earth.
2. Identify color or patterns used symbolically.
3. Interpret classroom map to locate hidden treasures.
4. Complete map keys.

Procedure:

Introduction: Tell students that a map is a picture of a place and that it helps us find or locate people, places, or things. Talk about treasure maps that many explorers followed, in some cases hoping to find gold. Tell students that they will be finding hidden treasures (hold up gelt, for example) if they can interpret (figure out) a map of their classroom.

Content Focus: Circulate one map to each student and place classroom map on overhead projector (model attached). Select individual students to locate object or desk in room and then point to the same object *symbol* (small drawing of a real thing) on the overhead transparency. Ask students at their desks to point to the objects on their maps. Ask all students to point to where they are sitting; *check for understanding;* ask them to color desk black.

Select one student to walk to a specified place in the room. This step *models* what selected students will be asked to do. Draw the pathway or route that was taken on the overhead transparency. Tell students that the map not only includes recognizable furniture or places where students sit, but now tells directions for finding certain places or objects in the room. Emphasize the importance of maps for these purposes: for example, locating where one is and finding other objects or places in relation to one's location.

Tell class that the teacher is now going to draw a *route,* or *pathway* (provide definitions, e.g., *input:* a way to get from one place to another), on the overhead and a representative from each group of tables will see if they can follow the map to find a hidden treasure (e.g., *guided practice*). The other children in the group can help the representative "explorer" if they think he/she is not going the right way. When all students have treasures, divide them up and let children eat the candy.

On board, teach students how to make a *map key* (a picture of symbols that tells where things are located on a map). On classroom map, students will already have their desk colored in black. Ask them to color the teacher's desk red and the reading table blue. Demonstrate how to make a map key on board and ask students to draw one on the reverse side of their classroom maps. This step provides students with independent practice.

Closure: Review vocabulary learned in lesson. What is a symbol? What is a map? What is a route or pathway? Why do we need maps? Ask students to give examples of when we would need a map. What would be the greatest treasure you would like to find, if someone gave you a treasure map?

Evaluation:

Formative:

Individuals: Check to see if students can locate their desks on individual maps.
Small groups: Can groups interpret map to locate hidden treasures?
Group: Can students define map, symbol, route/pathway and state purpose of maps?

Summative:

Individuals: Classroom maps with desk location; map keys

Materials and Resources:

Classroom maps and markers or crayons for each student; overhead transparency of classroom map; overhead projector; gelt or other candy treasure.

Extensions:

Ask each group to hide an object and draw a route on their map. Exchange maps among groups and have them interpret maps and find hidden objects.

This map lesson for primary students introduces the concepts *map, route, pathway,* and *symbol.* It reinforces national standards in geography (The World in

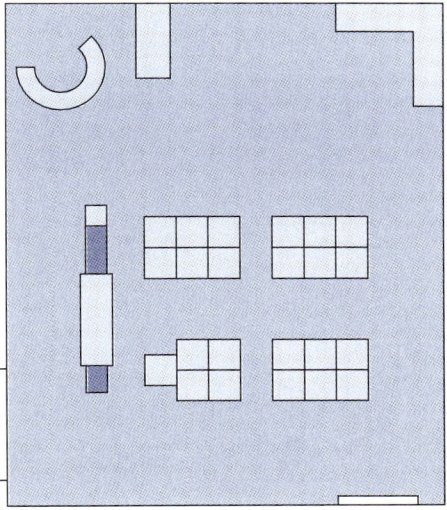

Sample classroom map

Spatial Terms #1) and social studies (People, Places and Environments, b). From the videotape you have probably observed that certain concepts were grasped more easily, while others, for example, *symbol,* still remain somewhat vague and abstract. It is rare to accomplish mastery when concepts are being introduced for the first time. Additional mapping activities are needed to reinforce these new terms and ideas.

NATIONAL
GEOGRAPHIC
SOCIETY

GEOGRAPHY EDUCATION DIVISION

January 27, 1995

Dear Teacher-Consultant:

I am writing to tell you of an exciting project. Beginning March 5, renowned polar explorer Will Steger will lead an international team of women and men on a historic trek across the Arctic Ocean. In a four-month journey, the researchers and explorers of the International Arctic Project will travel by dogsled and specially designed canoe-sled across more than 2,000 miles of solid and broken sea ice from Russia to Canada via the North Pole in the first surface crossing of the region by dogsled in a single season. The purpose of the expedition is to educate people on the environmental issues that are critical to the Arctic today—particularly the problem of transboundary pollution—and to draw attention to the region's critical role in the global environment.

There are several opportunities for you to involve your classes in this unique project. If you have access to the Internet computer network, your students can communicate with the International Arctic Project Expedition team, as well as with scientists and fellow students via ECONET. Scholastic Network, on America Online, will post expedition reports daily, conduct live on-line "chats" with the team members and other Arctic experts, and provide extensive background resources. A Listserv will provide daily reports, and a telephone information line (1-900-976-POLE) will give periodic updates on the team's progress. Additional materials, including a tracking map and resource guide, will be available in early February.

To further the impact of project, National Geographic Television will produce several short videos featuring expedition team members for its EXPLORER series, and NATIONAL GEOGRAPHIC magazine will also pursue a story on the expedition. The International Arctic Project team will send messages to participants in all National Geographic Kids Network units from February through the end of this school year.

If you are interested in following the International Arctic Project, you can obtain more information about the daily expedition on-line reports and printed materials by contacting:

> Education Director
> International Arctic Project
> 413 Wacouta Street, #200
> St. Paul, MN 55101
> Fax: 612-293-0137
> e-mail: arcproject@aol.com

I encourage you to take advantage of this wonderful opportunity to join Will Steger and his team.

Sincerely,

Robert E. Dulli
Director, Geography Education Program

1145 17th Street N.W., Washington, D.C. 20036-4688   Telephone: (202) 775-6701   Fax: (202) 429-5701
Cable Address: NatGeoSoc, Washington   ♻ Recycled-content paper

INTERNATIONAL ARCTIC PROJECT
Expedition Route

Intermediate Application: International Arctic Project

The intermediate lesson designed by the National Geographic Society's Geography Education Division is included as a sample of the kinds of lessons the Society provides teachers periodically. They distribute such announcements as a service to educators. The International Arctic Project has several exciting features. It is history in the making! How often do students get to be involved in an expedition in progress? To extend the lesson, exploration across the Arctic Ocean can be compared with other kinds of exploration, such as crossing the Atlantic or travel to the moon. Another innovative feature of the program is that students can access the information through the computer network ECONET, in conjunction with scientists and other students. Thus, interdisciplinary global networks are activated. Finally, transboundary pollution, an important ecological issue, is presented to students through a real-life, history-in-the-making activity.

Through the exciting National Geographic Expedition students address several national geography and social studies standards. In geography key ideas relevant to *Places and Regions* and *Physical Systems* are reinforced. In addition, NCSS standards for *Global Connections,* (d) and (e), are pertinent to Will Steger's exploration across the Arctic Ocean. The use of America Online also reinforces innovative communication networks. Also, look for other similar opportunities at nationalgeographic.com.

✦ INTERNET LINKS

The Internet provides many sites that house an abundance of mapping activities and information for students and teachers. A few sites are presented here.

INTERNET LINKS

Mapping

Lycos Road Map

http://www.proximus.com/lycos/

Map Blast!

http://mapblast.com/

Both of these sites allow students to "create" maps for themselves. For example, in Map Blast the student can enter any street address to produce a street map. The student can zoom out from this detailed street map to produce a smaller-scale map of the areas that include lakes, rivers, highways, state boundaries, etc. This kind of activity not only is fun for students but also gives them hands-on experience in working with maps and map symbols.

INTERNET LINKS

Mapping

http://www.nationalgeographic.com/resources/ngo/maps/atlas/namerica/usofamm.html

National Geographic Map Machine Atlas.

Clickable maps on this site provide general information on states and countries throughout the world. The address provided above will lead directly to a map of the United States. By clicking on any state, a student or teacher will be able to learn more about that particular state.

INTERNET LINKS

Mapping

http://www.usgs.gov/education/learnweb/

USGS Maps.

This site is a great resource on mapping at Grades K–12. It provides teaching "packets" for different grade levels.

K–3:   Map Adventures. In this packet, lessons focus on visualizing objects from different perspectives and understanding and using maps.

5–8:   What Do Maps Show? Lessons in this packet are designed to focus on the following themes: location, place, relationships, movement, and regions.

7–12:   Exploring Maps. In these lessons, students learn basic map-reading and mapmaking skills.

SUMMARY

Adults have a profound sense of the interdependent nature of geographic, economic, and ecological principles operating in the world. Through education and the media we are informed of natural disasters, the effects of global warming, deforestation, and people's efforts to improve their ways of life and belief systems. The majority of adults work in both paid and nonpaid work roles and are therefore affecting the economic system in which they live. Elementary-aged children, on the other hand, have limited awareness of spatial and temporal concepts. A teacher plays an important role in helping young children "situate" themselves in time and place, building on the time period and community in which they live, yet helping them identify webs of interdependence among wider human and ecological systems.

One of the tenets undergirding the *Self in the World* orientation is the assumption that knowledge of the world is filtered through one's knowledge and appreciation of one's own culture. This belief embraces the philosophies of Dewey (1938) and Vygotsky (1978, 1987) whose works are currently referred to as social constructivism. Social constructivism views learning as a process during which "agent, activity, and the world mutually constitute each other" (Lave & Wenger, 1991, p. 33). Consider, for example, the question raised by Prasch (1995) when discussing international trade: "If the primary goal of a free trade policy is to raise the profit rate—and if it is the case that the only way to accomplish this is to lower the wage rate—is it the case that . . . free trade is potentially detrimental to the interests of labor?" (p. 71). Economics, geography, and ecology provide us with tools to tackle these complex and challenging questions for which there are no easy answers. Research in these fields helps to place individual identity, needs, and wants in an international context.

PROFESSIONAL DISCUSSIONS AND FIELD EXPERIENCES

Discussion Questions

1. Compare and contrast the state level of spending on education for each of the fifty states. Investigate the standardized achievement test scores for each of the states as well. Is there a relationship? That is, are the achievement levels higher in those states where the government spending is higher? Are they lower? How do you account for the variation, if any?

2. Create a mental map of your childhood home, going back to the earliest memory of a specific locale. Share with peers the significance of your map and the experiences associated with the various landmarks. Discuss the benefits of such an exercise when implemented in elementary and middle school classrooms. How does such an exercise contribute to geographic literacy?

3. In small groups, design a map of your college or university campus without the use of actual maps. Typically, students get into animated discussions about the location of buildings that they have passed many times. Relate this experience to what elementary and middle school students are often asked to do, for example, design a map of their schoolgrounds, classroom, and so on. Having experienced this firsthand, how will you prepare students to work cooperatively and resolve disagreements? What geographic concepts are developed through this activity?

Field Experiences

1. With primary students take a walking tour of the neighborhood. Use disposable cameras and take pictures of houses and buildings along the way. Record the order in which you take the pictures as you pass the structures. After developing film, provide each student with a photo. Ask each student to draw the building. Create a map of the walking tour and attach each student's picture at the appropriate place.

2. Set up a marketplace in the classroom for fourth or fifth graders. Assign roles to each student (e.g., worker, farmer, consumer, banker, artisan, caregiver, etc.). Simulate what happens to a product from the time it is produced to the time it is purchased and consumed. For example, follow an ear of corn from the farm to the dinner table including processes such as growth, harvest, transportation to grocery warehouse, to market, purchase by consumer, preparation for dinner, consumption by student. Or follow the path of an ear of corn to the classroom and make popcorn for students to eat! Other possibilities: milk to ice cream, peanuts to peanut butter, berries to cobbler, wheat to bread, water to soft drink.

3. Involve middle school students in a fund-raising activity such as a car wash. Help them organize it and make sure that all purchases are recorded so that profits (hopefully) can be accurately computed. Let them decide how the profits will be spent. Popular activities for spending profits may include a pizza party, trip to the movies, or charitable donation.

Resources: Teacher and Student Materials

Berti, A. E. (1992). Acquisition of the profit concept by third-grade children. *Contemporary Educational Psychology, 17* (3), 293–299.

Bosshardt, W., & Watts, M. (1994). Instructor effects in economics in elementary and junior high schools. *Journal of Economic Education, 25* (3), 195–211.

Carr, F. M. (1994). Enhancing K–12 economic education with contemporary information resources. *ERIC Clearing House, 67* (6), 348–353.

Chicola, N. A., & English, E. B. (1996). The child's world: Geography around the home. *Social Studies and the Young Learner, 9* (1), P5–P8.

Cox, A. C. (1997). Using the stock market game in the social studies classroom. *Social Education, 61* (6), 347–350.

Dalgaard, B. R. (1994). Economics in the social studies. *International Journal of Social Education, 8* (3), 35–39.

Day, H. R. (1991). *Economics and entrepreneurship: Operating a classroom business in the elementary and middle school.* Indianapolis, IN: Indiana State Department of Education. ERIC #346 012.

Dewey, J. (1944). *Democracy and education.* New York: Free Press. (Originally published, 1916)

Dictionary of geographic words, in J. A. Banks, B. K. Beyer, G. Contreras, J. Craven, G. Ladson-Billings, M. A. McFarland, & W. C. Parker, (2001). *People together: Adventures in time and place,* Grade Two Pupil Edition, p. R8. New York: McGraw-Hill School Division.

Diem, R. A. (Ed.). (1999). Preservation and change: Dilemmas facing Costa Rica and Mexico. *Social Education, 63* (2), 65–128.

Economics Association's Primary Economics Awareness Working Group. (1991). Economic awareness in primary education. *Economics, 27* (116), 171–174.

Freese, J. R. (1997). Using the National Geography Standards to integrate children's social studies. *Social Studies and the Young Learner, 10* (2), 22–24.

Hallows, K., & Becker, W. (1994). What works and what doesn't: A practitioner's guide to research findings in economic education. *International Journal of Social Education, 8* (3), 87–95.

Handley, L. M. (Ed.). (1994). Global economics, curriculum concerns. *Social Studies and the Young Learner, 6* (4), 17–18.

Holt, P. W. (1998). The Oregon Trail: Wyoming students construct a CD-ROM. *Social Education, 62* (1), 41–45.

K–6 Geography: Themes, key ideas, and learning opportunities. (1987). Indiana, PA: National Council for Geographic Education, Indiana University of Pennsylvania, 15705.

Kirman, J. M. (1999). Radarsat satellite images: A new geography tool for upper elementary classrooms. *Social Education, 63* (3), 167–169.

Kourilsky, M. (1993, April). *An integrated teacher education model for enhanced economic literacy of primary teachers.* Paper presented at the Annual Meeting of the American Educational Research Association, Atlanta, GA. (ERIC No. ED 360 287).

Laney, J. D. (1993). Economics for elementary school students: Research-supported principles of teaching and learning that guide classroom practice. *Social Studies, 84* (3), 99–103.

Laney, J. D., Moseley, P. A., & Crossland, R. B. (1991, November). *The effect of economics instruction on economic reasoning: A comparison of verbal, imaginal, and integrated teaching-learning strategies.* Paper presented at the Annual Meeting of the National Council for the Social Studies, Washington, DC. (ERIC No. ED 355 137).

Lockledge, A. (1991). Some lesson plans for economic geography in the elementary classroom. *Journal of Geography, 90* (6), 295–297.

Lynn, K. (1992). *Teacher use of economics and cultural geography for a middle school social studies class: Planning a trip to Kenya and Tanzania.* (ERIC No. ED 356 987).

Miller, S. L. (1994). Conceptualizing global economic education. *International Journal of Social Education, 8* (3), 49–85.

Morgan, J. C. (1991). Using "Econ and Me" to teach economics to children in primary grades. *Social Studies, 82* (5), 195–197.

National Content Standards in Economics. (1997). Washington, DC: National Council on Economic Education.

North Carolina State Department of Public Instruction. (1993). *Exploring life skills: Middle grades exploratory vocational and technical education.* Raleigh, NC: Author. (ERIC No. ED 361 476).

Pahl, R. H. (Ed.). (1992, November/December). Special section: From Buttonwood to Silicon: A bicentennial look at the New York stock exchange. *The Social Studies, 83* (6), 236–252.

Radford, R. (1992). Young investors. *Social Studies, 83* (6), 241–243.

Rong, X. L. (1998). The new immigration: Challenges facing social studies professionals. *Social Education, 62* (7), 393–399.

Rong, X. L., & Hickey, G. M. (Eds.). (1998). Social studies and the new immigration. *Social Education, 62* (7), 393–399.

Schoenfeld, D. (1992). Project business: The bridge between business and education. *Social Studies, 83* (4), 148–151.

Schug, M. C. (1994). How children learn economics. *International Journal of Social Education, 8* (3), 25–34.

Schug, M. C., & Shaw, J. S. (1997). The economics of saving endangered species: A teaching activity. *Social Education, 61* (6), 334–336.

Schug, M. C., & Western, R. D. (1997). Introduction: An economic perspective on protecting the environment. *Social Education, 61* (6), 329–330.

Shotick, J. A., & Walsko, G. (1997). Using children's theater to teach economics. *Social Studies and the Young Learner, 9* (3), 11–13.

Smith, R. F. (1994). Economic education: Forward to the basics. *International Journal of Social Education, 8* (3), 40–48.

Valentine, G. P. (1994). Economics for grades K–9. *Social Studies, 85* (5), 218–221.

VanCleaf, D. W., & Sesow, F. W. (1993). Investigating ghost towns: Activities for upper elementary and middle school students. *Social Studies, 84* (1), 37–41.

REFERENCES

Banks, J. A. (1990). *Teaching strategies for the social studies.* New York: Longman.

Baumol, W. J., & Blinder, A. S. (1997). *Microeconomics: Principles and policy* (7th ed.). Fort Worth, TX: Dryden Press/Harcourt Brace College.

Brenner, R. (1992). Making sense out of nonsense: Economics in context. In D. Colander & R. Brenner (Eds.). *Educating economists* (pp. 11–48). Ann Arbor, MI: The University of Michigan Press.

Brown, H. (1968). *Basic economic concepts taught in public elementary schools at Louisiana 1967–1968.* Unpublished doctoral dissertation, University of Louisiana.

Colander, D., & Brenner, R. (Eds.). (1992). *Educating economists.* Ann Arbor, MI: The University of Michigan Press.

Coleman, J. (1995, May 30). Should child's money be tied to chores? *Richmond Times-Dispatch,* p. D4.

Darrin, G. (1968). *Economics in the elementary school curriculum: Study of the District of Columbia laboratory schools.* Unpublished doctoral dissertation, University of Maryland.

Dewey, J. (1938). *Education and experience.* New York: Collier Books.

Davidson, D. G. (1977). *Part II: Strategies for teaching economics, Primary level (Grades 1–3).* New York: Joint Council on Economic Education.

Eichengreen, B. (1987). Macroeconomics and history. In A. J. Field (Ed.), *The future of economic history* (pp. 43–90). Boston: Kluwer-Nijhoff.

Field, A. J. (Ed.). (1987). *The future of economic history.* Boston: Kluwer-Nijhoff.

Gardner, J. B., & Adams, G. R. (Eds.). (1983). *Ordinary people and everyday life.* Nashville, TN: American Association for State and Local History.

Geography for Life: National Geography Standards. (1994). Washington, DC: National Geographic Research and Exploration.

Henderson, J. P. (Ed.). (1995). *The state of the history of economics.* New York: Routledge.

Hunter, M. (1984). Knowing teaching and supervising. In P. L. Hosford (Ed.), *Using what we know about teaching* (pp. 175–176). Alexandria, VA: Association of Supervision and Curriculum Development.

Jahoda, G. (1983). European "lag" in the development of an economic concept: A study in Zimbabwe. *British Journal of Developmental Psychology, 1,* 113–120.

Johnson, G. D. (1998). *The living world.* New York: McGraw-Hill.

Joyce, W. W. (1964). *The development and grade placement of map and globe skills in the elementary social studies program.* Unpublished doctoral dissertation, Northwestern University, Evanston, IL.

Joyce, W. W., & Alleman-Brooks, J. E. (1979). *Teaching social studies in the elementary and middle schools.* New York: Holt, Rinehart & Winston.

Knox, P. L., & Marston, S. A. (1998). *Places and regions in global context: Human geography.* Upper Saddle River, NJ: Prentice-Hall.

Kourilsky, M. L. (1974). *Beyond simulation: The mini-approach to instruction in economics and other social sciences.* Los Angeles, CA: Educational Resource Associates.

Kourilsky, M. L. (1985). *Children's use of cost-benefit analysis: Developmental or nonexistent?* Paper presented at the annual meeting of the American Educational Research Association, Chicago, IL.

Larkin, A., & Shaver, J. (1969). Economics learning in grade one: The USA assessment studies. *Social Education, 33,* 958–963.

Lave, J., & Wenger, E. (1991). *Situated learning: Legitimate peripheral participation.* Cambridge: Cambridge University Press.

Mankiw, N. G. (1997). *Principles of microeconomics.* Fort Worth, TX: Dryden Press/Harcourt Brace College.

Mankiw, N. G. (1998). *Principles of macroeconomics.* Fort Worth, TX: Dryden Press/Harcourt Brace College.

Prasch, R. E. (1995). International trade, machinery, and the remuneration of labor. In J. P. Henderson (Ed.), *The state of the history of economics* (pp. 68–80). New York: Routledge.

Robinson, H., & Spodek, B. (1965). *New directions in the kindergarten.* New York: Teachers College Press.

Salvatore, D. (1998). *International economics* (6th ed.). Upper Saddle River, NJ: Prentice-Hall.

Schug, M. C., & Armento, B. J. (1985). Teaching economics to children. In M. C. Schug (Ed.), *Economics in the school curriculum, K–12.* (pp. 33–43). Washington, DC: Joint Council on Economic Education and National Education Association.

Schug, M. C., & Birkey, C. J. (1985). *The development of children's economic reasoning.* Presented at the meeting of the American Educational Research Association, Chicago, IL.

Seefeldt, C. (1989). *Social studies for the preschool-primary child.* Columbus, OH: Merrill.

Senesh, L. (1960). The organic curriculum: A new experiment in economic education. *The Counselor, 20,* 43–56.

Smith, R. L. (1996). *Ecology and field biology* (5th ed.). New York: HarperCollins College Publishers.

Stiglitz, J. E. (1993a). *Principles of macro-economics.* New York: Norton.

Stiglitz, J. E. (1993b). *Principles of micro-economics.* New York: Norton.

Stoddard, R. H., Wishart, D. J., & Blouet, B. W. (1989). *Human geography: People, places, and cultures.* Englewood Cliffs, NJ: Prentice-Hall.

Strahler, A., & Strahler, A. (1997). *Physical geography: Science and systems of the human environment.* New York: John Wiley & Sons.

Vygotsky, L. S. (1978). *Mind in society.* Cambridge, MA: Harvard University Press.

Vygotsky, L. S. (1987). Thinking and speech. In R. W. Rieber & A. S. Carton (Eds.), *The collected works of L. S. Vygotsky, Volume 1: Problems of general psychology.* Trans. N. Minick. New York: Plenum. pp. 375–384.

Walstad, W. B., & Soper, J. C. (Eds.). (1991). *Effective economic education in the schools.* Washington, DC: Joint Council on Economic Education and National Education Association.

Walstad, W., & Watts, M. (1985). The current status of economics in the K–12 curriculum. In M. C. Schug (Ed.), *Economics in the school curriculum, K–12.* (pp. 8–20). Washington, DC: Joint Council on Economic Education and National Education Association.

CHAPTER 4

IDENTITY FORMATION IN CULTURAL CONTEXT

Psychology, Anthropology, and Global Education

Chapter Outline

CHAPTER OBJECTIVES

Those who have reflected on the questions of how they have developed into the person they are have wrestled with the same questions pursued by psychologists and anthropologists. To what extent have I been shaped by the parents or guardians who raised me? In what ways have I shaped my identity by actively pursuing alternative paths to those intended by others in my immediate surroundings? What if I was raised in a culture on the other side of the world? How would my identity and views of the world differ? As you read this chapter, reflect on these questions regarding your own identity. In addition, think about your role as a potential "significant other" in the lives of your future students. How will you shape their identity? In what ways will your identity be shaped by your students and fellow teachers? Upon completion of this chapter you will be able to:

1.   Differentiate between the implicit and explicit ways that principles from anthropology, psychology, and global education manifest themselves in the social studies curriculum.

2.   Demonstrate curricular applications of key ideas in anthropology, psychology, and global education.
3.   Reflect on ways in which principles of identity formation will operate simultaneously for both you and your students in the classroom context.

Anthropology, psychology, and global education are combined in Chapter 4 because all address the interaction between cultural context and identity formation. Anthropology, on the one hand, looks holistically at human beings and the way culture influences identity. Psychology, on the other hand, places more emphasis on individuals and their perceptions of environmental influences. Both fields, anthropology and psychology, are linked with global education because how individuals view themselves and others is an underlying principle that affects cultural interaction around the world. Wlodkowski and Ginsberg (1995, p. 11) express this relationship clearly when they say that culture is a dynamic and changing concept for each of us: Our cultural identities are constantly evolving or changing, and, consequently, values, customs, and orientations are equally fluid.

✦ DEVELOPMENTAL ISSUES: GLOBAL EDUCATION

Given the interdependent world in which we live, it is difficult to imagine isolationist attitudes in the recent past. Through the media young people view cultures and events around the world with almost as much frequency as exposure to local cultural events. Exposure through media accounts is helpful in providing timely information and history as it is being made, but in-depth understanding of the cultures around the world often lags behind. Social studies is the logical place in which this depth can be provided. However, the underlying attitudes that are conveyed in the process can sometimes cause more harm than good when strong biases are expressed. As seen in the following excerpt, attention to global education through the social studies curriculum has come a long way since the nineteenth century. In *Old Textbooks,* Nietz (1961) cites the jingoistic tendencies of a textbook published in 1840:

> The European or Caucasian is the most noble of the five races of men. It excels all others in learning and the arts, and includes the most powerful nations of ancient and modern times. The most valuable institutions of society, and the most important and useful inventions, have originated with the people of this race. (p. 216)

Developmental issues in this chapter focus on the way in which children and youth have been socialized to view peoples around the globe. Strong cultural messages have been portrayed that hold certain cultural groups in higher esteem than others. By understanding this history, you will be in a better position to reflect on your own attitudes and beliefs as you think about the manner in which you present the study of cultural groups, globally and within the boundaries of the United States. Gordon (1964, p. 33) explains the importance of understanding the complexity of social interaction within all communities, whether local or global: Culture and social structure are obviously closely related and in a constant state of dynamic interaction, for it is the norms and values of the society that, for the most part, determine the nature of the social groupings and social relationships that its members will create. Moving beyond the earlier jingoistic sentiments identified by Nietz, a survey of twentieth-century practices will be reviewed.

In the beginning of the twentieth century, international events influenced educators' efforts to change ethnocentric attitudes toward people in other countries. After World War I, pleas that the school curriculum stress peace and international understanding were common. During the interwar period and World War II, international education was often viewed as integrally linked with the works of international organizations and with the building of a stable world society (Butts, 1969). However, during the cold war years, international education in elementary and middle schools slowed despite the continued growth of international studies in colleges and universities.

Leonard Kenworthy stands out as one who was not constrained by the cold war sentiment during the 1950s. In *Introducing Children to the World,* Kenworthy (1956) called on educators to advance the notion of a world society and attempted to address the perceived dilemma of state sovereignty:

> Such an [international] education would not replace education for local and national citizenship. It would refine the loyalty of our citizens to their community and their nation within a community of the pupils; it would extend their loyal ties to humanity. It would do this in terms of complementary or supplementary loyalties, adding loyalty to mankind to the already existing emphasis upon loyalty to the family, friendship groups, community, state, and nation. (p. 7)

During the late sixties and early seventies international curriculum programs were influenced by the International Education Act that Congress passed in 1966. In proposing the Act to Congress, President Johnson helped to establish an international philosophy for education by saying:

> International education cannot be the work of one country. It is the responsibility and promise of all nations. It calls for free exchange and full collaboration. We expect to receive as much as we give, to learn as well as to teach. (Taylor, 1969, p. 172)

This sentiment was perhaps a turning point in the political rhetoric for international education. Throughout the cold war years, political leadership advanced the notion of learning more about "foreign" nations because of the potential role of influence the United States might have. The International Education Act proposed ways in which resources and governmental programs could be used for education. Several curriculum programs for elementary and middle schools emerged during this time, including: *Social Studies Curriculum Materials Data Book* (1971), *International Education Resources* (1972), *The World: Context for Teaching in the Elementary School* (King, 1971), and *Toward a Mankind School: An Adventure in Humanistic Education* (Goodlad, 1971).

Another factor that has contributed to the increased popularity of international and global education over the past twenty years is the changing attitudes of educators and teacher educators. As more teacher educators have become interested in global issues, future teachers have been made aware of ways to modify the traditional nation-centric scope and sequence (McEachron-Hirsch, 1979). The interest spawned additional curriculum projects and institutes such as The Center for Global Futures at Ball State University and the Center for Teaching International Relations at The University of Denver. Additional international education organizations and study abroad programs are listed at the end of this chapter.

A beginning teacher has many opportunities to get involved in international and global education. As you become more knowledgeable about the ways of life of cultures around the world, your students will benefit (Palmer, 1997; Rourke & Boyer, 1998). To assist teachers in the area of civic education, Patrick (1996) discusses the international role of democracy conceptualized by three waves:

> The first wave, rooted in the American and French revolutions, flowered from 1828–1926. There was a second, short wave between 1943–1962. And the world took notice of a dramatic, global resurgence of democracy during the 1980s and 1990s, which has been dubbed the third wave by Samuel Huntington. (p. 414)

Patrick notes the weaknesses in civil society development in third-wave democracies throughout the world. The following deficiencies are important issues that you will no doubt explore when taking a global approach to social studies: dependence on external sources for funding, inadequate distribution of information and communication technologies, low levels of social capital, ethnic and sectarian divisions, and insufficient security for constitutional rights to freedom of speech, press, assembly, and associations (Patrick, 1996, p. 415). Additional teaching suggestions are provided in the following articles in the journal *Social Education:* "The World Around Us: Global Education" (1996) and "Global Education: Challenges, Cultures, and Connections" (Collins, Czarra, & Smith, 1998). Topics include NATO expansion, population and development issues, landmines, human rights, and fighting stereotypes. Both issues include Internet linkages and teaching resources. In addition, educators are exploring the possibilities of creating certain components of the school curricula by using an international team of curriculum developers (Parker, Ninomiya, & Cogan, 1999).

International education requires the increased awareness among social studies educators of their own worldviews as well as knowledge of how these views are communicated to students. Try the following projective technique as a means to discover more about your perceptions of the world. It is an exercise the author has utilized in researching children's and adults' views of the world (McEachron-Hirsch, 1979). First, list twenty-five nations including the United States that come to mind, almost in terms of free association. Next, on round stickers, place the names of the nations you have identified and make an arrangement of the nations inside a large circle representing the globe. Group the nations in any way you choose. Share the results and the reasons for the groupings with peers. Be sure to do this before reading the next paragraph!

What did you discover about your own views of the world in addition to those of your peers. Among the individuals who participated in the author's research, interesting worldviews emerged, demonstrating a variety of cognitive and psychological attachments. The influence of history, economics, political ideology, religion, cultural heritage, and current events played important roles in shaping their perceptions. This earlier research was expanded with both American and Japanese college students (Yamamoto, Davis, & McEachron-Hirsch, 1983; Yamamoto & McEachron-Hirsch, 1985). The underlying patterns that emerged were *we, they,* and *others* configurations. The *we* cluster represented the countries of Europe, apparently regarded as friendly and familiar; the *they* cluster represented nations that were in the news, often reporting problematic issues; the *others* cluster were nations that stayed on the periphery of one's awareness. Among the younger children as well as adults, the nations that often remained remote were island nations, geographically small nations, African and South American nations, and nations whose political and religious orientations were in contrast with the dominant ideologies in the United States.

One of the earliest studies of school teachers' opinions of ethnic and racial groups was published by Emory Bogardus in 1925 (Bogardus, 1925). Kleg and Yamamoto (1993) utilized essentially the same instrument as Bogardus (one that measures social distance) to investigate the views of teachers nearly seventy years later. Optimistically speaking, they discovered a decrease in social distance over the seven decades. However, Kleg and Yamamoto (1998) also identified a similar pattern of affiliation over time:

> In other words, through all the social changes over the aftermath of the First World War, the Great Depression, the Second World War, the Korean War, the struggle for equal rights, the space exploration, the Vietnam War, the collapse of the Communist block, the Persian Gulf War, and many other upheavals, those who had earlier enjoyed a higher level of permissible intimacy stayed the more preferred. This cluster included the peoples of the British Isles, French, Dutch, Scandinavians, and Germans. In the same vein, those who had been more distanced in the 1920s were still the less preferred in the 1990s. This cluster included Arabs, Turks, Orientals, Mexicans, and African-Americans. It appears that certain perceived physical features continue to function as the signal for negative social attitudes. In that sense, there may be little that is different even in the allegedly smaller world of the 21st century. (pp. 186–187)

Given these patterns, teachers have a unique opportunity to address these research findings. The first step is to assess one's own beliefs and take stock of necessary next steps. It is healthy to recognize that one's views of others require continuous reflection and reexamination. Through this process, knowledge gaps can be identified and assessed in terms of the ability to educate students about a variety of cultural groups. Anthropology, psychology, and global education are crucial to our understanding of identity formation, perceptions of self, and perceptions of others, from the college student in the desk next to us, the stranger on the other side of the globe, or the elementary student who looks to us for leadership.

✦ THE INDIVIDUAL IN RELATION TO OTHERS

Anthropologists have provided us with rich analyses of collective identities through interpretations of ethnic, tribal, national, and gender relationships. At the same time psychologists have attempted to explain identity in terms of a reciprocal relationship between the individual and others. The impact of these scholarly efforts on curricula is both implicit and explicit. One could argue that anthropological concepts have always been addressed in social studies because anthropology is about people and cultures, and social studies is about people and cultures.

Psychology is another discipline that is treated as germane to social studies, but whose concepts such as motivation, learning, and behavior may be perceived

Family and Friends in Japan

こんにちは

UNITED STATES

JAPAN

Konnichiwa! That means "hello." My name is Miko Ota. I live in Japan.

This is my family. We love and care for one another. My grandfather and grandmother live with us.

From "Family and Friends in Japan," Adventures in Time and Place, Grade 1, Pupil Edition. New York: McGraw-Hill School Division, 2001. Reproduced by permission of the McGraw-Hill Companies.

I walk to school with my friends. We follow rules to keep us safe. We wear yellow hats to school. Drivers see us when we cross streets.

Children in Japan work very hard in school. I like reading and writing.

Sayonara! Goodbye!

さようなら

1. Miko is part of which groups?

2. How is Miko's life like yours? How is it different?

65

as pervasive in the school environment. Since the National Council Social Studies Standards designated *Individual Development and Identity* as a separate area of focus in 1994, psychological principles and their implications for social studies instruction have been made more explicit. Selected lessons from past curricula emphasizing social psychology will be presented in this chapter. The McGraw-Hill first-grade text on pages 97 and 98 illustrates how textbook publishers currently provide cross-cultural comparisons of identity formation. Future curriculum materials will most likely emerge as a result of NCSS adding a separate category *Individual Development and Identity*. Take advantage of these fresh opportunities to innovate within the field of social studies. In the sections that follow, key ideas and concepts from anthropology and psychology are presented followed by curricular applications.

Anthropology: Key Ideas and Concepts

Anthropology is a field of study that is characterized by its holistic approach to understanding human beings. Anthropology attempts to generalize about humans through comparative analyses as well as in-depth analyses of a particular culture. Whiteford and Friedl (1992) offer useful distinctions between anthropology and other social science disciplines. They point out that whereas historians focus on past events and attempt to explain why events happened, anthropologists seek to make generalizations from such explanations. An important distinction between anthropology and sociology is that sociology is more concerned with contemporary society, whereas anthropology is a comparative discipline that focuses on all societies, past and present. Another difference in emphasis between sociology and anthropology is that sociologists tend to be more interested in quantitative data; anthropologists are more concerned with qualitative data. The field of anthropology has grown into many subareas of study. Four broad areas of specialization are described next: physical anthropology, archaeology, anthropological linguistics, and cultural anthropology.

Physical Anthropology

Physical anthropology emerged from two major lines of scholarly research. Around 1860 people were concerned with biological evolution, studies that looked at the similarities between humans and other primates. Another area of study during this time period was the concept of race, which was manifested in the various disciplines of biology, botany, and zoology. Scholars became interested in physical appearances, which resulted in attempts to classify humanity into races and explain their origins. Today anthropologists continue to investigate inherited biological features. Branches within physical anthropology include paleontology, comparative human biology, primatology, anthropological genetics, human growth, and body types (Jurmain, Nelson, Kilgore, & Trevathan, 1997).

Social studies and science lessons in elementary and middle schools address certain aspects of physical anthropology. In the primary grades, teachers often show pictures of all kinds of people and ask children to point out similarities and differences in physical characteristics and the actions of people. At the middle school

© David J. Sams/Stock Boston

levels, science lessons include the study of genetics. Students often compare their own genetic characteristics and those of family members with classmates. When teaching genetics in this manner, teachers should be sensitive to students who live in families that do not include biological parents.

Archaeology

Archaeology studies the past, often focusing on the period before people kept written records (Hayden, 1993; Renfrew & Bahn 1996). Archaeologists distinguish between prehistoric archaeology, which is the study of extinct cultures that left no written records, and historic archaeology, which investigates groups for whom there are written materials to accompany archaeological evidence (Whiteford & Friedl, 1992). Archaeologists typically make inventories of objects found at a given site, noting the frequency of occurring objects, how they were made, and so on. The meaning given to the object by the person using it, however, cannot be known to us. Nevertheless, archaeologists make inferences about the way of life of the people who made and used the objects. Hickey (1997) demonstrates this technique through the use of a Family Artifact Report, yielding great family stories about bloomers, bell bottoms, and hula hoops.

Archaeological approaches are often emulated by classroom teachers. Primary and elementary teachers sometimes simulate an archaeological "dig" by burying objects such as bones and pottery somewhere on the school grounds. Students conduct their field work by digging at the site, perhaps marking the location of objects, then making inferences about the culture who used the object (Hightshoe, 1997; Yell, 1998). Barry Beyer (1979) developed a curriculum around such an exercise using artifacts from the town of Kiev and presented it in his book *Teaching Thinking in Social Studies,* which emphasizes inquiry learning. Another popular activity is to have students design their own archaeological or "time capsule" and bury it on the school grounds. Students enjoy selecting objects for the capsule and hypothesizing about the message the object will send to whomever opens the capsule hundreds or thousands of years into the future.

Anthropological Linguistics

Anthropological linguists investigate the relationship between language and cultural behavior (Yule, 1996). Several areas of specialization fall within the rubric of anthropological linguistics. One is the study of the origin of language; a second subgroup is *sociolinguistics,* which is the role that language plays in social behavior; and a third area is the study of *folk categories,* or the units of meaning manifested in a culture's language system.

There are at least two ways of thinking about the ramifications of anthropological linguistics in a social studies curriculum context. In some instances, teachers who present the study of other cultures may be knowledgeable in the language of that culture and will share their expertise with students. Occasionally, texts or trade books provide activities for learning basic words in a different language or learning to write a different language, for example, Chinese characters or Indian symbol writing. Cross-cultural literature translated into English is another way to expose students to the different worldviews of other cultures. Another way to think about the importance of anthropological linguistics is by being sensitive to the unique language systems each student brings to the classroom (Feinberg & Morencia, 1998). Many educators and linguists are investigating the relationship between the meaning that language and social interaction has in relation to achievement and classroom behaviors (Gollnick & Chinn, 1994).

Cultural Anthropology

Cultural anthropologists compare cultures from different times and places to understand more about human life (Hannerz, 1996). The two main branches of cultural anthropology are prehistoric archaeology and ethnology, both emphasizing the study of learned social traits rather than biological features.

> Prehistoric archaeology extends the sample of human behavior beyond the bounds of historic time, while ethnology, which is the description of the world's living cultures and the building of generalizations about human nature by comparing those cultures, provides us with a more representative sample by including the lifeways of groups in every part of the globe. (Taylor, 1988, p. 7)

Anthropologists in the United States make further distinctions within the field of cultural anthropology: ethnology and ethnography. Ethnology emphasizes the comparative study of cultural groups, whereas ethnography is a description of one culture. Thus, an ethnological study might be based on two or more ethnographies. Describing and comparing cultures is a difficult task for anyone because, as one anthropologist stated, "putting something from another cultural context into the concepts and words available in the English language is not always possible" (Whiteford & Friedl, 1992, pp. 16–17). Anthropologists continue to examine their roles as ethnographers, refining and redefining roles. For example, distinctions are made between roles such as the "contract ethnographer" and the "ethnographic evaluator" whose roles go beyond description, analysis, and interpretation in order to have an impact on policy decision making (Reed, 1997).

There have been several noteworthy social studies curriculum development projects in the area of cultural anthropology, most of these reaching their hiatus in the 1970s. They include *The Human Relations Area Files, The University of Georgia Anthropology Curriculum,* and *Man: A Course of Study (MACOS).* Each of these is described in greater detail in the curriculum section that follows. Their combined efforts reflect the support that social studies educators and funding gave to the field of anthropology, support that has not been matched in contemporary times. Nevertheless, in classrooms throughout the United States, teachers continue to illuminate anthropological concepts and the diverse ways in which humans create meaning. For example, as a part of their study of Asian societies, sixth-grade teachers asked students to explore mask making in conjunction with coming-of-age ceremonies (Singer et al., 1998). Their research explored the universal ways in which young people mark transformations in their lives. Figure 4.1 is an example of efforts by members of the Social Science Education Consortium to organize the field for classroom teachers.

Psychology: Key Ideas and Concepts

Because most teacher education programs include courses in theories of development, you are probably familiar with psychological principles as they relate to learning (Ormod, 1995). Therefore, this section highlights only a few. Many Western educational psychology texts separate major theories of learning into behaviorism and cognitive field theories (Duran, Guillory, & Villanueva, 1990). Others divide cognitive field theories into cognitive-developmental and phenomenological-humanistic theories. Because the three divisions have had a differential impact on curriculum development, each is presented.

Behaviorism

Behaviorism emphasizes conditioning behavior by providing environmental stimuli as reinforcers for a desired response. Ivan Pavlov, John B. Watson, Karl S. Lashley, and B. F. Skinner have had a pervasive influence upon behaviorist theories (Benjafield, 1996). Skinner, perhaps more than the others, attempted to apply his theories to classroom situations. Proponents of behaviorist approaches emphasize

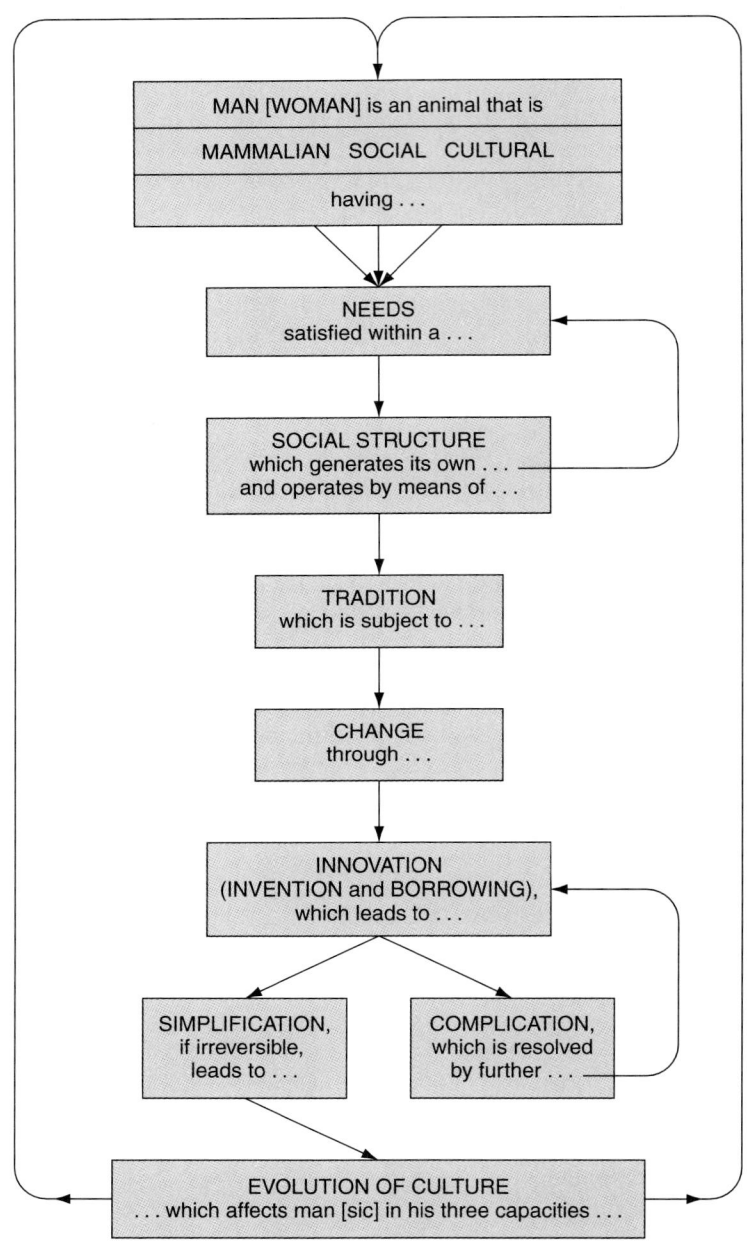

FIGURE 4.1   *Fundamental Ideas of Anthropology*

SOURCE: L. Senesh. Organizing a curriculum around social science concepts, in I. Morrissett (Ed.), *Concepts and structures in the new social science curricula* (New York: Holt, Rinehart, & Winston, 1967), p. 33. Used by permission of the Social Science Education Consortium.

conditioning behavior through reinforcement and altering the environment to shape desired responses from the learner. Critics maintain that behaviorist approaches foster mechanical learning, whereby the student is a recipient of knowledge through drill and practice, rather than one who learns in relation to developmental needs.

Cognitive-Developmental Theories

Most cognitive theorists maintain that growth and development occur in progressive stages (Hollin, 1995; Ornstein & Hunkins, 1988). They classify human growth and development as *cognitive, social, psychological,* and *physical.* The theories of Dewey (1938), Piaget (1948), Bruner (1963), and Vygotsky (1986) have had particular relevance for understanding developmental stages of elementary and middle school students. For Piaget, assimilation, accommodation, and equilibration are the three cognitive processes that form the basis of growth; for Dewey, the three processes are situation, interaction, and continuity; for Bruner, the three learning modes are enactive, iconic, and symbolic; for Vygotsky, understanding and cognition emerges through social and cultural contexts.

Bruner is one theorist who applied his theories of thinking and cognitive development to social studies curriculum development. His curriculum, *Man: A Course of Study (MACOS),* reflects his work on intuitive thinking and the three modes of learning he identified—enactive, iconic, and symbolic. A description of *MACOS* is provided later in this chapter. Vygotsky (1986) has influenced the thinking and curriculum development approaches of educators primarily through the traditions of cognitive constructivism and social constructivism. Scheurman (1998) describes the role of the teacher supported by the tradition of cognitive constructivism as a facilitator who challenges students by promoting disequilibrium with discrepant objects and events, guiding students through problem-solving activities, and monitoring reflective thinking *after* discoveries. Scheurman describes the role of the teacher supported by social constructivist theory as a collaborator who participates with students as they construct reality by eliciting and adapting to student (mis)conceptions, engaging in open-ended inquiries, and by guiding self and students to authentic resources and procedures. Scheurman and Yell (1998) edit a series of curriculum applications of constructivist thinking in *Social Education,* listed at the end of this chapter.

Critics of the cognitive-developmental theories argue that some interpretations are narrowly defined. They maintain that developmental theories create rigid stages that have difficulty explaining exceptions based on age and transitions from one stage to the next. Proponents of cognitive-developmental theories argue that this area in psychology has been the main source of educational innovation and reform for more than thirty years.

Phenomenological-Humanistic Theories

Phenomenology emphasizes the total organism or person. Phenomenologist ideas find their roots in the field theories that developed from Gestalt psychologists during

© Elizabeth Crews/Stock Boston

the 1930s and 1940s; for example, Kurt Koffka, Kurt Lewin, and Kurt Goldstein (Benjafield, 1996). The field theorists maintain that one's perception is derived from meaning given to a field or context. One's behavior is influenced by this "field-ground" relationship. Phenomenology is also influenced by existentialist philosophy, both emphasizing the study of immediate life experiences as one's reality. For phenomenologists, what one does and the extent to which one learns is closely tied to one's view of self. Humanistic education, which became a dominant force in education in the 1960s, fell into two camps, one focuses on developing positive self-concept, and the other centers on building interpersonal skills. Humanistic theorists include Rollo May, Abraham Maslow, Carl Rogers, and George Kelly.

Proponents of phenomenological-humanistic theories argue that the development of the emotional and cognitive aspects of the child should be central to notions of human growth and development inside and outside the classroom. Questions about the extent to which one can understand the influence of feelings and perceptions on behavior and learning are continuously raised by critics of phenomenological-humanistic approaches. Few comprehensive curricula have been developed to apply these principles to educational settings. A. S. Neil's (1960) Summerhill school in Great Britain is perhaps a viable prototype of an educational program based on the tenets of humanistic psychology. Classroom teachers respond to the ever-changing moods and emotions of students on a daily basis. In recent years, addressing sensitive issues and emotional concerns has come under the purview of guidance counselors whose role for systematically dealing with inter-personal issues has been legitimized.

Theories of learning provide teachers with a variety of models for under-standing how best to support a classroom environment conducive to learning. Per-haps, you have already identified with one particular learning theory over another and you are beginning to formulate teaching behaviors that reinforce your prefer-ences. It is useful to keep in mind, however, that teaching is a dynamic process and that principles of all theories can be identified simultaneously in most classrooms. Because they are manifested in implicit ways theoriest don't always agree about what they see, even if they observe the same lesson! In the following sections, cur-riculum applications will be presented to make more explicit the psychological prin-ciples from three branches of psychology.

Science Research Associations (Lippit, Fox, & Schaible, 1969) developed one of the few curriculum programs featuring social-psychological principles for upper elementary students. The curricula is organized around the following themes: learn-ing to use social science, discovering differences, friendly and unfriendly behavior, being and becoming, individuals and groups, and deciding and doing. One of the les-sons, "Six Years of Silence," is featured in the "Curriculum Applications" section. It includes psychological principles that would allow a teacher to discuss behaviorism, cognitive-developmental theories, and phenomenology.

✦ CURRICULUM APPLICATIONS

Key ideas from anthropology, psychology, and global education are evident at all grade levels and play an important role in the way individuals learn about themselves and others. Table 4.1 illustrates activities that reinforce the reciprocal way in which the student shapes and is shaped by his or her culture.

Self in the World Connections

The curriculum applications in this section include "My Family and the Berenstain Bears," a lesson for second graders, and "Six Years of Silence," a lesson for fourth and fifth graders. "Alberta Clardy: Elderly Identity in a Youth Culture," a lesson for seventh and eighth graders, is included in Appendix B. "My Family and the Beren-stain Bears," illustrates how peers try to influence a second-grader's beliefs of right and wrong. This lesson reinforces anthropological principles of learning from others and psychological principles of being strong against peer pressure. "Six Years of Si-lence" shows fourth and fifth graders how children learn in atypical ways. Modified from an earlier version published by Science Research Associates, the revised lesson uses psychological principles to interpret the progress made by a 6-year-old girl whose mother was without speech and hearing capabilities. "Alberta Clardy: Elderly Identity in a Youth Culture" provides students with an opportunity to analyze a diary kept by a woman from ages 76 to 85. The lesson encourages students to examine the relationship between their views of the elderly and American culture that caters to youth.

Self in the World Connections
Tradition and Growth across the Life Span

	Primary	Intermediate	Middle School
Self	Make a mobile of objects that represent self—interests, activities, etc.	Prepare coat of arms or mandala depicting heritage and interests.	Write an autobiographical essay. Keep a journal for one month; upon reflection, report to class what you learned about yourself.
Family	Make stick puppets of people who live in household. Act out recent shared activity of family members.	Bring a personal object from each family member to school. Imagine that peers discovered objects in archaeological dig. What inferences do they make about specific families?	Share family photo album or favorite family recipes. Combine recipes into classroom cookbook and sell as a school fundraising activity.
Community	Study different examples of communication used throughout community, e.g., braille, sign language, foreign languages, etc.	Compare and contrast various structures for places of worship throughout the community. Research the history and meaning of architectural styles.	Visit community centers that cater to different ages, e.g., nursery schools, assisted living for the elderly. Report to class an assessment of needs for the various age groups.
State	Identify the state symbols, e.g., motto, flower, bird, animal, etc. Find out why and how they were selected.	Find out the fastest-growing cultural group in your state. Study why it is growing faster than other cultural groups.	Investigate state policies regarding the education and housing of juvenile delinquents. Invite a guest speaker from such an agency to speak to your class.
Nation	Learn about Smokey the Bear as a symbol of protecting the natural environment in our country's national parks.	Read an autobiography of a famous American. Describe how you think the American wants to be remembered.	Discuss a key educational or health care issue in class. Develop a list of concerns and/or recommendations. Prepare letter of explanation and send with concerns to a representative in Congress.
World	Examine international symbols used by the airlines and postal carriers.	Research the history of Esperanto and discuss its lack of popularity as an international language.	Through the Internet, search the history of one of your family names. Locate the names and addresses of others with same name throughout the globe.

Primary Application: My Family and the Berenstain Bears

MODEL LESSON:
MY FAMILY AND THE BERENSTAIN BEARS

Level: Second   **Time:** One Hour

Topic: Making Choices

Standards: National Council Social Studies Standards

Culture: e. identify and describe ways family, groups, and community
                influence the individual's daily life and personal choices.

Individual Development and Identity: (e, f, and g; see Appendix A)

Objectives:

1. After listening to the teacher read *The Berenstain Bears and the In-Crowd,*
   students will discuss ways to respond to peer pressure.
2. Using puppets, students will act out peer pressure and appropriate ways to
   respond to it.

Procedure:

Introduction: Tell students that they will listen to a book about how friends can
sometimes make others do things that may not be the right thing to do. Read Berenstain book about Sister Bear wanting to be accepted by the in-crowd and trying to ride
Brother Bear's bicycle that was too big.

Content Focus: With students, clarify the issue that Sister Bear faces. Encourage students to share similar instances that they may have experienced that relate to the issue of wanting to fit in but wanting to be unique or special. On chart paper, list the
many different ways in which the issues were resolved by Sister Bear or solicit ideas
from students. Emphasize that making good decisions sometimes means standing
apart from a group of peers.

    Using stick puppets, have students act out three scenes from the Berenstain book
or from experiences offered by students. The scenes should be (1) Cause, (2) Effect,
and (3) Solution. Stick puppets can be made by having students draw faces on circles
of construction paper glued to popsicle sticks.

Closure: Students act out their puppet shows in pairs or threesomes for the rest of the
class or for parents. At the end of each presentation a student can state the solution to
peer pressure.

Evaluation:

Formative: Students' listening skills during story time; students' ability to relate to story
through discussion; students' cooperation with peers during puppet presentations.

Summative: Puppet presentations; list of ideas on chart paper.

Materials and Resources:

Construction paper; popsicle sticks, Berenstain book.

Berenstain S., & Berenstain, J. (1989). *The Berenstain Bears and the In-Crowd.* New York:
    Random House.

Background Information:

This story is about a new girl cub who is showing off her two-wheeler and putting down Sister Bear and Lizzy by excluding them and making fun of Sister Bear's clothing. At first, they try to fit in but eventually they return to what they do well and win the Double-Dutch jump rope tournament. Additional situations that student may act out with stick puppets include: taking school supplies out of another student's desk without asking permission upon encouragement from peers; telling friend that he/she can't play with your group at recess upon encouragement from peers; stopping at a friend's house on the way home from school instead of going directly home, upon encouragement from peers.

Through stories that children can relate to such as *The Berenstain Bears and the In-Crowd,* national standards relevant to anthropology and psychology are addressed. The NCSS standards include: *Culture* (e) and *Individual Development and Identity* (e), (f), and (g) (see Appendix A). Social studies concepts relevant to anthropology and psychology include: family leadership, peer pressure, and groups.

Intermediate Application: Six Years of Silence

 MODEL LESSON:
SIX YEARS OF SILENCE

Level: Fourth/Fifth   **Time:** Two Hours
Topic: Influences on Learning
Standards: National Council Social Studies Standards

Culture:	c. describe ways in which **language,** stories, folktales, music, and artistic creations serve as expressions of culture and influence behavior of people living in a particular culture;
Individual Development and Identity:	d. relate such factors as physical endowment and capabilities, learning, motivation, personality, perception, and behavior to individual development.

Objective: Students will apply principles of learning to a case study of Isabelle.

Procedure:

Introduction: Ask students to recall and share memories they may have about learning to read or ride a bicycle. Did it seem difficult? Did it happen naturally and easily? More difficult to recall is the experience of learning how to speak. Ask students if their parents or guardians told them what their first word was? Explain that since speech begins during the toddler years and typically precedes reading, it is more difficult to remember the process. However, there are many similarities in learning how to read and learning how to speak. The process is tied to ways in which children learn from other people—parents, guardians, family members, friends, and teachers. Today's lesson will describe principles of learning and apply them to the story of a girl named Isabelle who was found unable to speak after being raised by her mother who could neither speak nor hear.

Content Focus: Ask students to take turns reading aloud the case illustration "Six Years of Silence." [Students may prefer to read passage silently.] Ask them to think about how Isabelle changed from the time she began working with Dr. Mason. When they have finished, ask students to share their feelings about Isabelle and her relationships with her mother and Dr. Mason. Possible discussion starters may be: Why did she act the way she did when she first came to the hospital? What made her change?

Divide students into three groups and ask each group to analyze how and what Isabelle learned from her mother and how and what she learned from Dr. Mason. Students will record their responses on a worksheet. Group roles should be assigned—recorder, facilitator, respondents.

Closure: In a large group, have students report their group findings. On board or chart-paper, the teacher or students will record responses. See main ideas in Background Information to reinforce key concepts and principles of learning if not provided by students (e.g., motivation, reinforcement). Close by saying that many psychological principles have emerged to help us understand the learning process. The wide range of possible explanations provides parents, educators, and other professionals with multiple perspectives that help us understand the mysteries of the learning process.

Evaluation:

Formative: Student responses to case illustration

Summative: Group worksheets indicating application of psychological principles

Extensions:

Recommend that students might read the story of Helen Keller and her nurse, Ann Sullivan.

Materials and Resources:

Board; worksheet; book

Lippitt, R., Fox, R., & Schaible, L. (1969). Six years of silence. In *Social science laboratory units* (pp. 61–64). Chicago, IL: Science Research Associates, Inc.

Background Information:

The case study about Isabelle illustrates how learning took place for a human being in a concentrated way. For most people learning to speak takes place in surroundings where adults both speak and hear. Given Isabelle's history, speech evolved outside the primary family unit. Key learning principles to emphasize for fourth and fifth graders are how Dr. Mason tried to motivate and reinforce Isabelle's successive steps toward increasing her vocabulary and communication with others. (Key concepts: **Motivate**—induce, influence, persuade; **reinforce**—strengthen, support.)

It is also important to identify the different kinds of behaviors learned from caregivers. We don't know very much about the mother, but she clearly had a system of communication with Isabelle.

Behaviors learned from mother include:

- croaking noises
- an individualized sign language and a trusting relationship

Behaviors learned from Dr. Mason in laboratory setting include:

- speech
- a trusting relationship

Approaches taken by Dr. Mason that contributed to learning:

- establishing friendship and atmosphere of trust (e.g., did not approach directly)
- offered interesting objects (e.g., ticking watch, ring, doll)

- responded to Isabelle's interests with language (e.g., when Isabelle pointed to doll's eye, Dr. Mason said "eye")
- praised Isabelle when she spoke

The following information serves as background information for the teacher. There are three quotes from Skinner, Vygotsky, and Rogers. Behaviorist principles such as attempting to set up a positive environment for learning through trust and reinforcement follow from Skinner's quote. Vygotsky's quote emphasizes the strong relationship between teacher and student, where there is mutual give-and-take. For Rogers, the relationships with teacher, peers, and Isabelle's desire to grow in certain directions can be emphasized.

Psychological Principles That May Be Attributed to Theorists

Behaviorism

Skinner, B. F. (1971). *Beyond freedom and dignity.* New York: Knopf, pp. 149, 150, 167.

> "We need to design contingencies under which students acquire behavior useful to them and their culture—contingencies that do not have troublesome byproducts. . . ."
>
> *Excerpts from "Six Years of Silence" That Reflected Skinner's Psychological Principles of Behaviorism*—Acquiring useful behaviors to act upon the environment. " 'Top it—'at's mine;" "Please," "I'm sorry," "I love you Dr. Mason."

Cognitive Developmental

Vygotsky, L. (1986). *Thought and language.* Cambridge, MA: MIT Press. Translation by Alex Kozulin, p. xxxi.

> "Studying the development of thought and speech in childhood, we found that the process of their development depends not so much on the changes within these two functions, but rather on changes in the primary relations between them . . ."
>
> *Excerpts from "Six Years of Silence" That Reflect Vygotsky's Psychological Principles of Cognitive Development*—Isabelle initiates and Dr. Mason provides new information.
> Isabelle pointed to the doll's eye, Dr. Mason said, "Eye, eye—the doll's eye."

Humanism

Rogers, C. (1983). *Freedom to learn for the eighties.* Columbus, OH: Merrill, p. 20.

> "Let me define a bit more precisely the elements that are involved in such significant or experiential learning. *It has a quality of personal involvement*—the whole person in both feeling and cognitive aspects being *in* the learning event. . . . She knows whether it is meeting her need, whether it leads toward what she *wants* to know, whether it illuminates the dark area of ignorance she is experiencing."
>
> *Excerpts from "Six Years of Silence" That Reflect Rogers' Humanism*
> "Isabelle was delighted with the sound she made."

Six Years of Silence

When Isabelle was brought to the hospital, she acted more like an animal than a human being. Her eyes were wild and full of fear. She made strange croaking noises instead of talking. Her legs were deformed and badly bowed.

Isabelle was angry and lonely. She cried for hours at a time. For two days, she would eat nothing but a few sips of milk and a cookie or two.

What were the causes of her strange behavior? Why was she so different from other 6-year-olds?

Since birth, Isabelle had lived in a small, dark room with her mother, who was a deaf-mute. They didn't talk; they used a crude kind of sign language. Isabelle had never learned to speak because no one had ever spoken to her.

In those first weeks at the hospital, Dr. Marie K. Mason worked hard to make friends with Isabelle. Dr. Mason was a social scientist who helped people with speech and hearing problems. Another doctor at the hospital operated on Isabelle's legs. Lack of sunshine, fresh air, and proper food had caused her bowed legs. After the operation Isabelle walked more easily because she could place her feet flat on the floor.

Some of the doctors who worked with Dr. Mason thought Isabelle would never be able to talk. Dr. Mason disagreed. But she knew one of the hardest things would be to win Isabelle's trust.

At first Dr. Mason did not approach Isabelle directly. When the doctor came into the ward, she talked and played with another girl. But she was watching Isabelle out of the corner of her eye. Eventually Isabelle became used to the doctor.

One day Dr. Mason held her wristwatch to Isabelle's ear so that she could hear the ticking. After a moment Isabelle was curious enough to stretch out her hand. She touched Dr. Mason's watch with her finger. Then she noticed the doctor's ring. Isabelle took Dr. Mason's hand and held the ring finger close to her ear. Then she looked puzzled. She seemed to have noticed that the ring did not tick like the watch. Dr. Mason shook her head as if to say that the ring made no sound. Then she held the watch up to Isabelle's ear again. Dr. Mason smiled warmly and gently patted Isabelle's hand. Then she left the room.

When Dr. Mason returned the next day, she brought a toy wristwatch, a ring, and a doll for Isabelle. She seemed interested in the doll, so Dr. Mason handed it to her. Isabelle smiled and quickly pulled off the doll's stocking.

When Isabelle pointed to the doll's eye, Dr. Mason said, "Eye, eye—the doll's eye." A moment later she pointed to the doll's nose and said, "Nose, nose—the doll's nose." Then Dr. Mason touched Isabelle's nose gently and said, "Nose, nose."

Isabelle seemed amused, but she did not attempt to repeat the words. She seemed happier, though. And it was obvious that she was responding to the care and affection given her.

Dr. Mason still could not tell for sure whether Isabelle understood much. Each time she saw Isabelle pick up a toy, she repeated the name of the object several times. After a week had passed, Dr. Mason showed Isabelle a ball. "Here is a ball, Isabelle."

Dr. Mason leaned closer and whispered in Isabelle's ear: "Ball, ball—say ball, Isabelle, ball . . . lll." Unexpectedly Isabelle said, "buh . . . buh." Isabelle was delighted with the sound she had made. Dr. Mason was thrilled. She praised Isabelle warmly. Then she said "car" for Isabelle to repeat. Isabelle said "ahhh" for car.

It was a joyous day at the hospital.

Three months later Isabelle could say simple sentences like "I love my baby" and "That's my baby," "Open your eye" and "Close your eyes." She was learning quickly.

When another girl tried to take one of her toys, Isabelle said, " 'Top it—'at's mine." A month later Isabelle even told Dr. Mason to say "Please" when she asked Isabelle to hand her something. Isabelle also said "I'm sorry" when she accidentally hurt another child's finger. Then Isabelle said, "I love you, Dr. Mason."

Isabelle's rapid progress continued. By the end of a year she could read many printed words and sentences. She could write some words, count to twenty, and do addition. She could even sing and retell a story she had heard.

After two years in her new environment Isabelle had learned things that most children learn in six years! She had a good sense of humor and she liked to tease. She asked many questions and learned even more.

Many social scientists have been interested in Isabelle's history. What do you think made the greater difference in Isabelle's case—heredity or environment? Doctors and scientists don't always agree.

Some think that the change in Isabelle's environment was responsible for the great progress she made. Others think that the early communication between Isabelle and her mother was an important factor, even though it was only sign language.

The doctors who said Isabelle would never learn to speak thought that she had not *inherited* enough intelligence. She proved their prediction wrong.

Isabelle's recovery indicates that both environment and heredity played important roles. She could not have learned without inherited intelligence. Yet the new environment was needed to make her learning possible.

Source: Lippitt, R., Fox, R., & Schaible, L. (1969). *Social science laboratory units.* Chicago: Science Research Associates.

By reading the case study of Isabelle, students see how a change in learning conditions brings about growth. National standards addressed include NCSS *Culture* (c) and *Individual Development and Identity* (d). Social studies concepts in the field of psychology that are relevant include behavior, change, drives, environment, growth, interaction, motivation, needs, wants, reinforcement, and socialization.

G R O U P   W O R K S H E E T

How and What Isabelle Learned

Recorder: _____

Facilitator: _____

Respondents: _____

From her mother:	
What	How

From Dr. Mason:	
What	How

| Unknowns | Questions |

Group Worksheet—Answers

How and What Isabelle Learned

Recorder: _____

Facilitator: _____

Respondents: _____

From her mother:

What	How
a. croaking noises	a. case study didn't say
b. individualized sign language	b. maybe mother modeled signs

---

From Dr. Mason:

What	How
a. speech	a. modeling; reinforcement
b. trusting relationship	b. at first did not approach directly gradually increased interaction when Isabelle was receptive

Unknowns	Questions
a. Why Isabelle was fearful, angry and cried.	a. Was she afraid of her new surroundings?
	b. Was she sad to have been taken away from her mother?
	c. Had she been mistreated by her mother?

✦ INTERNET LINKS

The intermediate lesson "Six Years of Silence" looked at different theories of learning as they related to the case study of Isabelle. It is not often that the field of psychology gets such attention at the primary or intermediate levels. Many Internet sites provide general psychological information as well as more specific information on topics such as peer pressure.

 INTERNET LINKS

Psychology

http://www.tiac.net/biz/drmike/Current.shtml

Current Topics in Psychology.

This site is put together by clinical psychologist Dr. Michael Fenichel. It is a compilation of websites, articles, and research tools in the field of psychology. In the area of adolescent mental health Dr. Fenichel has included many resources involving self-esteem and peer pressure. These topics are addressed in articles, Internet activities, and short stories. For example, an article from the University of Nebraska-Lincoln provides "down-to-earth information about peer pressure," an interactive Teen Advice site is included, and a page called Courageous Kids presents stories written by kids ages 9 to 13 that illustrates how courage helps us through personal difficulty. These resources have great potential for both teacher and student in that they can provide background information and ideas for lesson plans and activities.

Global education is also a main focus of this chapter. The Internet provides great opportunities for teachers to open up their classrooms to the world.

 ## INTERNET LINKS

Global Education

http://www.peacecorps.gov/www/dp/wws1.html

World Wise Schools.

This is a very good resource for global educators. It provides lesson plans, teacher guides, and videos for teachers. Lesson plans are included for Grades 3 to 12. Lessons are based on specific Peace Corps host countries and support the National Geography Standards. Titles of some of the lessons for Grades 3 to 5 include:

> Geography: Amazing Maize (Lesotho), Find the Treasure (Honduras), and Street Map of Dakar (Senegal)
> Language Arts: King of Sedo (Senegal), Let's Play (Nepal), and A Clever Idea (Honduras)
> Science: Tropical Rain Forests (Honduras), Water and Rain (Lesotho), and "Aleluya" (Paraguay)

Also included in this site are letters from volunteers and interviews with volunteers that have been incorporated in lesson plans, photographs of the landscape and peoples of different countries, information about how to get returned Peace Corps volunteers to speak in your class, or how to correspond with a present volunteer.

Finally, this site includes links to other global education resources and contains the addresses, telephone numbers, e-mail addresses, and/or Web addresses of over forty different organizations dedicated to global education. Organizations include: Childreach, The American Forum for Global Education, Choices for the 21st Century, GlobaLearn, National Geographic Kids Network, Umbrella Project, and World Eagle.

 ## INTERNET LINKS

Global Education

http://www.gsn.org/index.html

Global Schoolnet Foundation: Linking Kids Around the World.

This is a good resource for parents, teachers, and students interested in global education. This site connects classroom teachers around the world, provides interesting collaborative projects, opportunities for professional development, and houses many other educational articles, resources, and tools. Teachers are given the opportunity to join existing projects such as "Outside Our Windows." This is a project designed for students ages 5 to 10. Participating classes read one of the books suggested on the website. Then they brainstorm a list of characteristics of their town/city and take a picture of their community. The picture and its description are scanned into the computer and sent to the project coordinator who then posts all received photos on the Web. Teachers can use these pictures in any way they like. Suggestions given include: choose two pictures and make a Venn diagram comparing and contrasting the two communities; categorize the pictures as urban, suburban, and rural; or calculate the distance between two communities. Teachers are encouraged to create and post their own project ideas. All projects are arranged according to age level and subject area and are free to join.

SUMMARY

In this chapter, global education and the disciplines of anthropology and psychology have been linked to illustrate how identity formation takes place in an international context. Ethnicity, class, gender, cultural identification, and one's sense of efficacy are influenced by one's national identity (Morgen, 1989). According to Ahmed and Shore (1995), "as ethnicity has become central to geopolitical conflict, anthropological expertise has become highly relevant and even practical as 'culture' (understood in terms of history, language, religion or class) lies at the heart of ethnic identification" (p. 31). As a young person learns about the world and develops an identity, his or her options for adult roles are presented through the social studies curriculum and the cultural lens of the teacher in addition to many other influential adults. The *Self in the World* framework encourages the teacher to think globally and equip young people with the knowledge that by studying cultures throughout their community, nation, and world, they will have the potential to develop a greater appreciation of who they are, what they believe in, and an appreciation for the beliefs of others. According to Abbs (1976), the teacher who utilizes autobiographical reflection to recreate his or her past is in a better position to draw self and world together. A teacher who contemplates this relationship can reveal to students "the intimate relationship between being and knowing, between existence and education, between self and culture"(Abbs, 1976, p. 148).

PROFESSIONAL DISCUSSIONS AND FIELD EXPERIENCES

Discussion Questions

1. Yamamoto, Soliman, Parsons, and Davis (1987) found that one of the most stressful life events for children in the United States is being retained in school. Discuss why you think this is so and identify values in the U.S. culture and our educational institutions that would reinforce such concerns.
2. Anthropology and psychology are two disciplines that have not enjoyed the attention that some of the other social science disciplines have received in curriculum development. Discuss why you think this may be so.

3. Think of a time when you may have been in a cultural context that was different from the "culture comfort" you had been used to: for example, travel to a different country, visiting a different church, having a conversation with someone from a different culture. Describe the nature of the exchange: for example, what you learned about yourself or the other person's culture and how you felt about the communication.

Field Experiences

1. Visit a local museum and make arrangements for students to take a field trip there. Design a list of questions for students to investigate while visiting the museum. To make the experience more motivational, the activity can be set up in the form of a scavenger hunt. Emphasize anthropological concepts.

2. Organize a group of upper elementary students to "bury some artifacts" at a designated location on the schoolgrounds or close to the school. Arrange for the upper elementary students to take primary students on an archaeological dig at this sight. Encourage the primary students to ask the older students about the objects and their meaning. Upper elementary students should have had experience doing such an activity before they repeat it for the younger students.

3. To find out more about the students with whom you are working, administer an interest inventory or incomplete sentences. Samples are provided in the following lists.

Interest Inventory

What do you like to do when you have extra time of your own?
What do you like to play best?
What is your favorite work?
What things do you like to do in school?
What things don't you like to do in school?
What kind of music do your prefer?
What are your favorite records?
What are your favorite TV programs?
How much TV do you watch each day?
What are your favorite movies?
What kind of newspapers and magazines do you like?
Name a place you would like to visit.
What was the best part of the summer?
What three wishes would you make if you knew that they would come true?
What are you really great at doing?

Incomplete Sentences

I often wish I could . . .
My parent/guardian sometimes . . .
I am afraid when . . .
I feel bad when . . .
The worst thing a person can do is . . .
I get excited when . . .
I hate . . .
Most people don't know that I . . .
I like people who . . .
I feel proud when . . .

I get mad when . . .
I like to dream about . . .
I wish my family would . . .
I do not like people who . . .
I am happy when . . .
I love . . .
Someday I will . . .
I wish . . .
Someday I would most like to be like . . .
If I were an inventor, someday I would invent . . .
I wish I were _____ years old, because then I could . . .
Children would be better off if . . .

RESOURCES: TEACHER AND STUDENT MATERIALS

Journal Articles

Brook, D. L. (Ed.). (1997). Perspectives on sub-saharan Africa. *Social Education, 61* (7), 368–441.

Collins, H. T., Czarra, F. R., & Smith, A. F. (Eds.). (1998). Global education: Challenges, cultures, and connections. *Social Education, 62* (5), 241–320.

Feinberg, R. C., & Morencia, C. C. (1998). Bilingual education: An overview. *Social Education, 62* (7), 427–431.

Hickey, M. G. (1997). Bloomers, bell bottoms, and hula hoops: Artifact collections aid children's historical interpretation. *Social Education, 61* (5), 293–299.

Hightshoe, S. (1997). Sifting through the sands of time: A simulated archaeological dig. *Social Studies and the Young Learner, 9* (3), 28–30.

Parker, W. C., Ninomiya, A., & Cogan, J. (1999, Summer). Educating world citizens: Toward multinational curriculum development. *American Educational Research Journal, 36* (2), 117–145.

Patrick, J. J. (1996). Civil society in democracy's third wave: Implications for civic education. *Social Education, 60* (7), 414–417.

Scheurman, G. (1998). From behaviorist to constructivist teaching. *Social Education, 62* (1), 6–9.

Scheurman, G., & Yell, M. M. (Eds.). (1998). Constructing knowledge in social studies. *Social Education, 62* (1).

Simpson, M. (Ed.). (1996). The world around us: Global education. *Social Education, 60* (7), 386–459.

Singer, A., Gurton, L., Horowitz, A., Hunte, S., Broomfield, P., & Thomas, J. (1998). Coming of age ceremonies: A mask project. *Middle Level Learning: Supplement to Social Education,* No. 3, M14–M15.

Yell, M. M. (1998). The time before history: Thinking like an archaeologist. *Social Education, 62* (1), 27–31.

Curricula

- Lippitt, R., Fox, R., & Schaible, L. (1969). *Social science laboratory units.* Chicago, IL: Science Research Associates. Seven interdisciplinary units that reinforce principles in social psychology were developed by scientists and educators at the University of Michigan, Ann Arbor. The seven sections on human behavior can be taught in discussion sessions, with a small group of teachers or by individual teachers. The topics for intermediate students include: Learning to Use Social Science, Discovering Differences, Friendly and Unfriendly Behavior, Being and Becoming, Individuals and Groups, Deciding and Doing, and Influencing Each Other.

- *University of Georgia Curriculum.* The University of Georgia Anthropology Curriculum features archaeological principles for primary and elementary students. Students are placed in the role of anthropologists who are actively engaged in field research.

- *Man: A Course of Study (MACOS).* Developed in the 1960s, MACOS features the instructional theories of psychologist Jerome Bruner. The MACOS curriculum uses three questions as guiding themes: What is human about human beings? How did they get that way? How can they be made more so? The questions are pursued through tool making, language, social organization, the management of the prolonged childhood of humans, and the desire for humans to explain their world.

- Shirts, R. G. (1976). *Rafá Rafá: A cross culture simulation.* Del Mar, CA: Simile II. Rafá Rafá is a cross-cultural simulation whereby students are divided into two groups—the Alpha Culture and the Beta Culture. People "in the Alpha Culture are fun loving, superstitious, honor their elders, and enjoy touching one another. People in the Beta Culture are hard working, businesslike, foreign speaking, and do not like to be close to one another" (Shirts, 1976, p. 5). The simulation is intended to raise student awareness of issues one may encounter when interacting with people from different lifestyles.

Organizations

The American Forum: Education in a Global Age
45 John Street, Suite 1200
New York, New York 10038

The Alliance for Education in Global and International Studies (AEGIS)

The Center for Teaching International Relations
The University of Denver
Denver, CO

The Council on International Educational Exchange
205 East 42nd Street
New York, New York 10017

Educators for Social Responsibility
The International Council on Education for Teaching (ICET)
Kappa Delta Pi, An International Education Organization

References

Ahmed, A. S., & Shore, C. N. (Eds). (1995). *The future of anthropology.* London: Athlone.

Abbs, P. (1976). *Root and blossom: Essays on the philosophy, practice and politics of English teaching.* London: Heinemann.

Benjafield, J. G. (1996). *A history of psychology.* Boston: Allyn & Bacon.

Beyer, B. (1979). *Teaching thinking in social studies.* Columbus, OH: Merrill.

Bloom, B. S. (1956). *Taxonomy of educational objectives: Handbook I. Cognitive domain.* New York: Longman.

Bogardus, E. S. (1925). Measuring social distance. *Journal of Applied Sociology, 9,* 299–308.

Bruner, J. (1959). *The process of education.* Cambridge, MA: Harvard University Press.

Bruner, J. (1963). *Toward a theory of instruction.* Cambridge, MA: Harvard University Press.

Butts, R. F. (1969). America's role in international education: A perspective on thirty years. In H. G. Shane (Ed.), *The United States and international education.* (pp. 3–45). Chicago, IL: National Society for the Study of Education.

Conant, J. B. (1951). *Science and common sense.* New Haven, CT: Yale University Press.

Cowgill, D. O., & Holmes, L. D. (Eds.). (1972). *Aging and modernization.* New York: Appleton-Century-Crofts.

Dewey, J. (1938). *Experience and education.* New York: Macmillan.

Duran, E., Guillory, B., & Villanueva, M. (1990). Third and fourth world concerns: Toward a liberation psychology. In G. Stricker, E. Davis-Russell, E. Bourg, E. Duran, W. R. Hammond, J. McHolland, K. Polite, and B. E. Vaughn (Eds.), *Toward ethnic diversification in psychology education and training.* (pp. 211–217). Washington, DC: American Psychological Association.

Educating Americans for tomorrow's world: State initiatives in international education. (1987). Washington, DC: National Governor's Association.

Gagne, R. M. (1985). *The conditions of learning* (4th ed.). New York: Holt, Rinehart & Winston.

Gollnick, D. M., & Chinn, P. C. (1994). *Multicultural education in a pluralistic society* (4th ed.). New York: Merrill.

Gordon, M. M. (1964). *Assimilation in American life, the role of race, religion and national origins.* New York: Oxford University Press.

Goodlad, J. (1971). *Toward a mankind school: An adventure in humanistic education.* Los Angeles, CA: University of California Laboratory School.

Guilford, J. (1967). *The nature of human intelligence.* New York: McGraw-Hill.

Hannerz, U. (1996). *Transactional connections: Culture, people, places.* London: Routledge.

Hayden, B. (1993). *Archaeology: The science of once and future things.* New York: W. H. Freeman.

Hollin, C. (Ed.). (1995). *Contemporary psychology.* London: Taylor & Francis.

International education resources. (1972). Washington, DC: Institute of International Studies.

Jurmain, R., Nelson, H., Kilgore, L., & Trevathan, W. (1997). *Introduction to physical anthropology* (7th ed.). Belmont, CA: Wadsworth.

Kenworthy, L. S. (1956). *Introducing children to the world.* New York: Harper & Brothers.

King, E. (1971). *The world: Context for teaching in the elementary school.* Dubuque, IA: Brown.

Kleg, M., & Yamamoto, K. (1998). As the world turns: Ethno-racial distances after 70 years. *The Social Science Journal, 35* (2), 183–190.

Lipman, M. (1984, September). The cultivation of reasoning through philosophy. *Educational Leadership, 42* (1), 51–56.

Lippitt, R., Fox, R., & Schaible, L. (1969). *Social science laboratory units.* Chicago, IL: Science Research Associates.

Maslow, A. (1962). *Toward a psychology of being.* New York: Van Nostrand Reinhold.

Matthews, C. (1993). Beyond self-esteem. In G. McEachron-Hirsch (Ed.), *Student self-esteem: Integrating the self* (pp. 37–56). Lancaster, PA: Technomic.

McEachron-Hirsch, G. A. (1979). *International perceptions and curricular strategies of professors of social studies education.* Unpublished doctoral dissertation, The University of Texas at Austin.

McEachron-Hirsch, G. A. (1993). *Student self-esteem: Integrating the self.* Lancaster, PA: Technomic.

Miller, J. P., & Seller, W. (1985). *Curriculum perspectives and practice.* New York: Longman.

Morgen, S. (Ed.). (1989). *Gender and anthropology: Critical reviews for research and teaching.* Washington, DC: American Anthropological Association.

Neil, A. (1960). *Summerhill: A radical approach to child rearing.* New York: Hart.

Nietz, J. A. (1961). *Old textbooks.* Pittsburgh, PA: University of Pittsburgh Press.

Ormod, J. E. (1995). *Human learning* (2nd ed.). Englewood Cliffs, NJ: Prentice-Hall.

Ornstein, A. C., & Hunkins, F. P. (1988). *Curriculum: Foundations, principles, and issues.* Englewood Cliffs, NJ: Prentice-Hall.

Palmer, M. (1997). *Comparative politics: Political economy, political culture, and political interdependence.* Itasca, IL: Peacock FE Publishers.

Piaget, J. (1948). *Judgment and reasoning in the child.* New York: Harcourt Brace.

Reed, M. C. (Ed.). (1997). *Practicing anthropology in a postmodern world: lessons and insights from federal contract research.* Napa Bulletin No. 17. Arlington, VA: National Association for the Practice of Anthropology.

Renfrew, C., & Bahn, P. (1996). *Archaeology theories, methods, and practice.* London: Thames and Hudson.

Rogers, C. (1983). *Freedom to learn for the 1980s* (2nd ed.). Columbus, OH: Merrill.

Rourke, J. T., & Boyer, M. A. (1998). *World politics: International politics of the world stage, Brief* (2nd ed.). New York: McGraw-Hill.

Shirts, R. G. (1976). *Rafá Rafá: A cross culture simulation.* Del Mar, CA: Simile II.

Skinner, B. F. (1971). *Beyond freedom and dignity.* New York: Knopf.

Social studies curriculum materials data book. (1971). Boulder, CO: Social Science Education Consortium.

Sternberg, R. (1986, Summer). Intelligence, wisdom, and creativity. *Educational Psychologist, 21,* 175–190.

Sternberg, R. (1984, September). How can we teach intelligence? *Educational Leadership, 42* (1), 38–48.

Stricker, G. Davis-Russell, E., Bourg, E., Duran, E., Hammond, W. R., McHolland, J., Polite, K., & Vaughn B. E. (1990). *Toward ethnic diversification in psychology education and training.* Washington, DC: American Psychological Association.

Taylor, H. (1969). *The world as teacher.* New York: Doubleday.

Taylor, R. B. (1988). *Cultural ways: A concise introduction to cultural anthropology* (3rd ed.). Prospect Heights, IL: Waveland.

Torrance, E. P. (1965). *Rewarding creative behavior.* Englewood Cliffs, NJ: Prentice-Hall.

VanTassel-Baska, J. (1993). Developing self-concept in gifted individuals. In G. McEachron-Hirsch (Ed.), *Student self-esteem: Integrating the self.* (pp. 311–344). Lancaster, PA: Technomic.

Vygotsky, L. (1986). *Thought and language.* Trans. Alex Kozulin. Cambridge, MA: MIT Press.

Walther-Thomas, C. (1993). Self-esteem and students with special needs. In G. McEachron-Hirsch (Ed.), *Student self-esteem: Integrating the self.* (pp. 281–309). Lancaster, PA: Technomic.

Whiteford, M. B., & Friedl, J. (1992). *The human portrait: Introduction to cultural anthropology* (3rd ed.). Englewood Cliffs, NJ: Prentice-Hall.

Wlodkowski, R. J., & Ginsberg, M. B. (1995). *Diversity and motivation: Culturally responsive teaching.* San Francisco: Jossey-Bass.

Yamamoto, K., Davis, O. L., & McEachron-Hirsch, G. A. (1983). International perceptions across the sea: Patterns in Japanese Young Adults. *International Journal of Intercultural Relations, 7,* 69–78.

Yamamoto, K., & McEachron, G. (1977). *Mirror, mirror on the wall: A curricular unit on the self-concept for teachers-to-be.* Austin, TX: Texan House.

Yamamoto, K., & McEachron-Hirsch, G. A. (1985). Patterns of international perceptions in young adults. *Texas Tech Journal of Education, 12* (1), 7–18.

Yamamoto, K., Soliman, A., Parsons, J., & Davis, O. (1987). Voices in unison: Stressful events in the lives of children in six countries. *Journal of Child Psychology and Psychiatry, 28* (6), 855–864.

Yule, G. (1996). *The study of language* (2nd ed.). New York: Cambridge University Press.

© Bill Bachmann/The Image Works

CHAPTER 5

PARTICIPATION IN A CHANGING SOCIETY

Political Science and Citizenship

Chapter Outline

CHAPTER OBJECTIVES

There is great variation among preservice teachers regarding their recollections of political discussions in the home and school. Some remember few, if any, while others recall animated or heated discussions about political events. What memories of political family discussions do you have? How have these earlier discussions influenced your current political views? Reflecting on your own political biases, have you considered how you will be objective when discussing political viewpoints with elementary and middle school students? How will you foster a climate that establishes respect for democratic processes? Upon completion of this chapter you will be able to:

1. Explain the development of political knowledge and attitudes in children.

2. Identify social studies trends for incorporating citizenship and political science concepts.
3. Demonstrate curriculum applications of key ideas and concepts in political science and citizenship.

In Chapter 1 Cubberly's evolving elementary curriculum depicted "constitution" as a new addition to the list of most important subjects for 1875. Prior to that time, what we thought of as social studies subject areas included only U.S. history and geography. The inclusion of "constitution" may be viewed as a precursor to what the curriculum in the twenty-first century refers to as political science and citizenship. All emphasize principles of governance, the role that citizens play in shaping government, and the impact of governmental structures upon individual citizens. Chapter 5 discusses how principles of government, political science, and civics are presented to students in elementary and middle schools based on appropriate developmental stages.

✤ DEVELOPMENTAL ISSUES: CITIZENSHIP AND GEOPOLITICAL ATTACHMENT

As college students, you have already assumed a variety of citizenship roles, thus making you participants in the political process. Activities such as voting, demonstrations, signing petitions, paying taxes, following traffic codes, and volunteering in civic organizations are just a few of the more obvious political roles. Choosing not to participate in these activities also may be considered a political decision. To children and youth in kindergarten through eighth grade, political roles and their meaning vary considerably from adults. The differences may be due to developmental stages, societal influences, or, of course, curricular emphases.

The research presented by Hess and Torney (1967) in *The Development of Political Attitudes in Children* provides useful analyses of preadult political socialization. Hess and Torney maintain that acquisition of political information and attitudes proceeds rapidly during the elementary and middle school years and that the primary agents of socialization are the family and school. In their study of second through eighth graders, Hess and Torney found that younger children think of political objects in terms of "good" and "bad" and the more complex orientations are only partially conceived by eighth grade. The variation they discovered, based on the developmental stages of children, signals potential grade level emphases for the social studies curriculum.

The following excerpt of a conversation with a second-grade boy demonstrates how national symbols exist as objects for attachment (Hess & Torney, 1967, p. 28):

> **What is a nation?**
> A nation is a state isn't it? Certain places in it that are important.
> **Can you name a nation?**
> Washington, New York.
> **You see the flag up there? What does the flag mean?**
> Well, I don't quite know. It just stands up there, and you say something to it. We put our hands over our heart and say the Pledge of Allegiance to the flag.

What does it mean when you pledge allegiance?
Well, we're pledging to the flag.
What do you pledge to the flag?
To give us freedom.
What does the flag stand for?
It stands for freedom and for peace.

The pairing of abstract terms such as freedom and liberty to concrete objects is also illustrated by another second-grade boy who said that if the Statue of Liberty was gone, "there wouldn't be any liberty" (Hess & Torney, 1967, p. 29).

As children get older, political attachment to the nation-state acquires different cognitive emphases. For example, when asked why they preferred being American to other nationalities, older children made statements emphasizing ideological features such as "freedom" and "democracy" while placing less emphasis on concrete aspects of country. In response to the question "What is freedom?" a fifth-grader responded (Hess & Torney, 1967):

Well, to be free, you could vote any way you want. Like Khrushchev makes
everybody vote for him, because he uses force. And in America, in a free country,
you can do whatever you want. Free speech, I guess that's what it means. (p. 30)

By the time students reach eighth grade, the nation-state is viewed as part of a larger network of countries. Hess and Torney (1967, p. 30) found that when students were asked "Who does most to keep peace in the world: the United States or the United Nations?" second graders overwhelmingly responded "the United States," whereas eighth graders decidedly responded "the United Nations."

The research findings by Hess and Torney illustrate that students' political information is a reflection of developmental stages and that significant increases in substantive information take place between the fourth and fifth grades. Given their findings, it is tempting to conclude that younger children are just not ready to grasp substantive information about political ideas. However, such a generalization is potentially limiting to the development of a challenging social studies curriculum. It is quite possible, for example, that some of the differences reported by Hess and Torney are not solely due to developmental stages, but rather a combination of developmental stages and the presence or absence of deliberate political concept development via the social studies curriculum. One of the limitations of the Hess and Torney investigation is that they did not conduct an extensive analysis of the political information that was presented either through textbooks, teacher-directed lessons, or other sources of information. Since the primary grades typically emphasize family, neighborhood, and community, it is feasible that the concepts Hess and Torney discovered in the older grades weren't taught in the younger grades.

The overemphasis on developmental stages to the detriment of appreciating contextual influences on political cognition is a research question also pursued by Gustav Jahoda. Jahoda's investigations of children's geopolitical orientations called into question Piaget's suggestion that an understanding of spatial relations preceded an understanding of nationality relations: "Piaget and Weil asked children to draw circles representing Geneva and Switzerland, the critical issue being whether they showed one as enclosed by the other, or drew them side by side" (Jahoda, 1964, p. 1082). Jahoda asked children to arrange squares and circles that represented

Britain, England, Scotland, and Glasgow to see if they could grasp spatial relations. Jahoda surmised that a major flaw in Piaget's treatment of nationality relations is that

> He [Piaget] regarded children's failure to handle these correctly as being due to an inability to make logical class inclusions before the age of about 10 or 11; but there is evidence that many children are capable of dealing with part-whole relations at a much earlier age [e.g., apples are fruit, potatoes are vegetables, etc.]. (1964, p. 1092)

The studies by Piaget and Weil (1951) and Jahoda (1963, 1964) alert the classroom teacher to the importance of: (1) representing geopolitical boundaries as concretely as possible, (2) demonstrating part-whole relationships visually, for example, neighborhood, community, city, state, nation, world, and (3) developing geopolitical space through concept attainment lessons. For further study of children's political orientations and knowledge of geopolitical space see Torney-Purta's (1991) review of research, "Cross-National Research in Social Studies."

Before a classroom teacher can provide direct instruction, however, it is important to diagnose students' developmental stages with regard to spatial orientations. What follows are samples of the seminal research by Jahoda in Figure 5.1 as well as recent applications in Figures 5.2 to 5.4 by students enrolled in social studies methods courses. The education students gathered the information as a part of their fieldwork assignment. Since students were assigned to a variety of grade levels, they selected the geopolitical concepts that were emphasized at their particular grade level. They were free to identify the shapes as well as what they represented.

After examining the various geopolitical spatial representations from kindergarten through fourth grade, what inferences can you make about developmental stages and knowledge? What we still don't know from these informal data collections is what formal instruction has taken place in the classroom for each of these students. Be sure to ask the teachers you work with how they have taught geopolitical space and their corresponding concepts. In the section that follows, you are presented with an overview of some of the main concepts addressed by social scientists and social studies educators as children progress from rudimentary notions of political space to abstract principles of liberty and citizenship.

✦ POLITICAL SCIENCE AND SOCIAL STUDIES TRADITIONS

Political Science: Key Ideas and Concepts

Nearly thirty years ago, Yale political scientist Robert Dahl said that "twenty-five centuries of dedicated study of politics have naturally produced a good many highly plausible but, unfortunately, contradictory hypotheses, each strongly supported by common sense, that can be argued till Doomsday." In his book *Modern Political Analysis,* Dahl (1970), outlines a small number of basic concepts and ideas to provide the reader with a foundation from which to build greater competence in political analysis. This section attempts to do just that—equip the beginning teacher with a foundation on which to build a greater knowledge base of political ideas to

Pieces provided to children: Largest square = Britain; second largest square = England; third largest square = Scotland; circle = Glasgow.

In Jahoda's study, the youngest children (6 and 7-year olds) typically placed the pieces side-by-side or occasionally overlapped them. The most frequent misconception was represented by placing the disc between the two white squares, suggesting that the children did not grasp the notion of spatial inclusion.

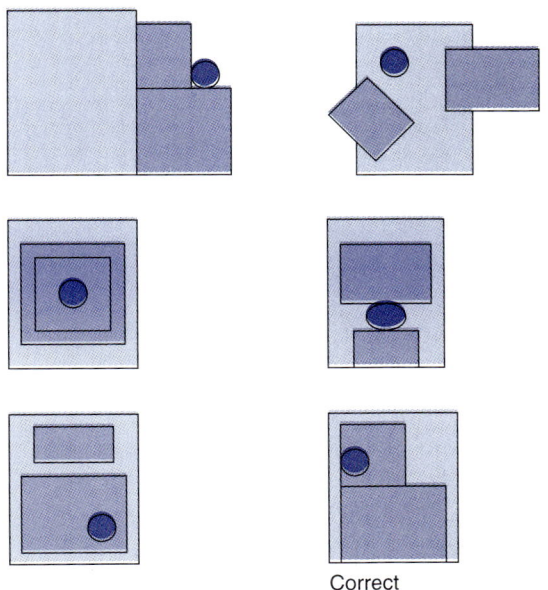

Correct

FIGURE 5.1 *Developmental Stages and Spatial Orientation*

SOURCE: Adapted from G. Jahoda. The development of children's ideas about country and nationality, *British Journal of Educational Psychology, 33* (1963): 54. Reproduced with permission from the British Journal of Psychology, © The British Psychological Society.

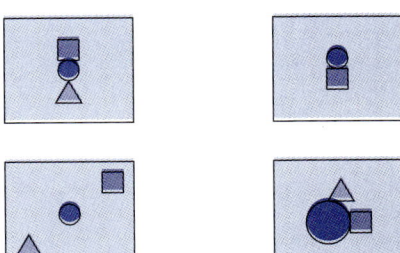

FIGURE 5.2 *Students' Field Studies in Spatial Orientation* Roxana Cornejo gave kindergarten students the following pieces: Rectangle = Virginia; circle = Williamsburg; square = house; triangle = school.

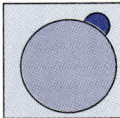

"The circle is the earth and the little circle is the sun coming up and the square is the picture frame."

"Virginia is next to the Williamsburg, the United States is in the World."

"The circles go next to each other and the squares go next to each other."

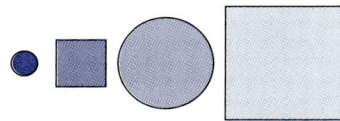

"Williamsburg goes next to Virginia because they rhyme. You say Williamsburg, Virginia. Then the United States comes next and then the Earth."

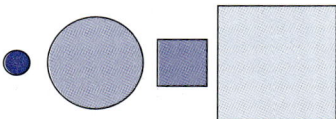

"Williamsburg is closer than the United States. Virginia is far away and the World is the farthest away."

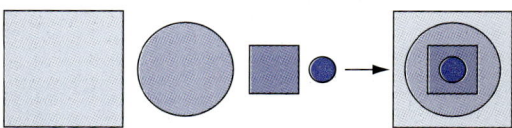

"The United States is in the world, Virginia is in the United States and Williamsburg is in Virginia."

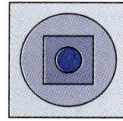

"Williamsburg is in Virginia, Virginia is in the United States, the United States is in the World."

FIGURE 5.3 *Students' Field Studies in Spatial Orientation* Christy Frandsen gave first graders these pieces: Large square = World; large circle = USA; medium square = Virginia; small circle = Williamsburg. Children's explanations are shown below their arrangements.

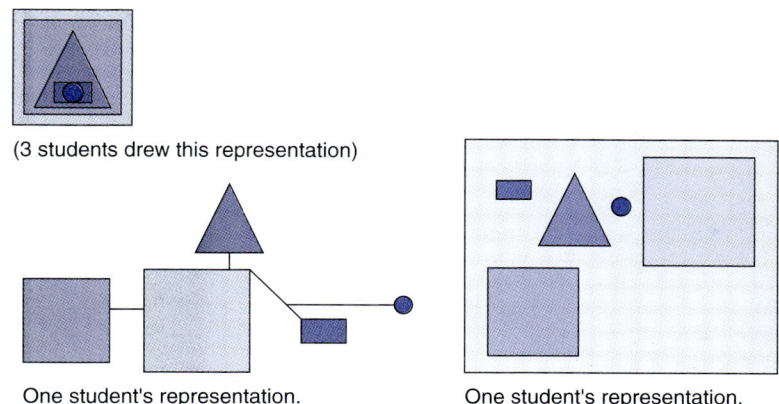

(3 students drew this representation)

One student's representation.   One student's representation.

FIGURE 5.4   *Students' Field Studies in Spatial Orientation*   Beth Vachet gave fourth
graders the following pieces: Large square = world; medium square = North America;
triangle = United States; rectangle = Virginia; circle = Williamsburg.

incorporate in the social studies curriculum. The knowledge base includes bases of
politics, ideology, political systems, and the social context of politics (Squire, Lindsay, Covington, & Smith, 1997).

Bases of Politics

Political science in the United States can be characterized by at least three distinct approaches: traditional, behavioral, and postbehavioral. According to Roskin, Cord,
Medeiros, and Jones (1994), *traditional* politics "encompasses a wide range of approaches, ranging from the philosophical and ethical to the institutional and power-
oriented," (p. 15). In the 1950s, *behaviorists* were heavily influenced by the empirical
approaches of scholars in the field of psychology and turned to studies that incorporate
statistics via elections, voting patterns, and public opinion surveys. In the late 1960s,
younger political scientists questioned previous approaches, arguing that behaviorists
were predisposed to the status quo. Roskin and colleagues (1994) point out that these
postbehaviorists were concerned with the big questions of politics and the possibility
of change and that their approach can be seen as a synthesis of traditional and behavioral approaches. For the social studies teacher, it is important to recognize that all three
approaches are viable and may be represented through most political science departments in higher education. In addition, these basic scholarly approaches continue to influence the development of textbooks and curriculum materials. The following section
presents key ideas and major concepts in political science and citizenship.

Ideology

The term *ideology* means the analysis of ideas and was first used by Antoine Louis
Claude Destutt Compte de Tracy in 1796 (Freeman, 1994, p. 171). Before the six-
teenth century, political ideology and theory is referred to as *classical* and *medieval*,
drawing heavily on the Greeks and Christianity through the works of St. Augustine

© Bob Daemmrich/The Image Works

and St. Thomas Aquinas. Political scientists maintain that the transition from classical and medieval political philosophy to modern political theory is marked by three significant changes (Gamble, Irwin, Redenius, & Weber, 1987):

1. The state developed into a temporal, secular, centralized, national, territorial phenomenon unknown in the earlier eras.
2. Whereas the medieval world was otherworldly and concerned with salvation, the modern world was concerned with the here and now.
3. Modern liberal democratic political theory assumes that the people rather than a monarch, a privileged class, or an established church are the sole source of political legitimacy. (pp. 62–63)

As a result of these changes, contemporary ideologies such as liberalism, conservatism, capitalism, socialism, communism, and fascism have emerged in public discourse. Since these ideologies "are particularistic definitions of the path to the good and the just society," the modern world continues to be plagued by the differences among them (Gamble et al., 1987, p. 63). Middle and upper elementary textbooks present the various political ideologies in general terms, but more in-depth analysis is reserved for high school and college courses. For example, terms such as liberalism, conservatism, capitalism, socialism, communism, and fascism can be found more explicitly in fifth- through eighth-grade textbooks.

Political Systems

As the research by Jahoda cited earlier in this chapter indicated, political entities are vague concepts to children, and their meaning develops gradually with increased knowledge and maturity. However, one cannot assume that the distinctions among adults are without confusion either. In a study I conducted, social studies educators were asked to list twenty-five nations. In two cases, professors named nations as well as the continents of Africa and South America! If the *continents* had been pointed out by the researcher, the participants surely would have been amused by their selection errors. However, the errors illustrate more about the vagueness of our culture's understanding of the continents of Africa and South America than perhaps the ability of the participants to distinguish between nations and continents (McEachron-Hirsch, 1979). Think about the distinctions between city, county, state, and nation. Would you be able to provide clear definitions to an elementary student?

In the primary grades, attachment to the nation-state takes place through a variety of political socialization efforts. The Pledge of Allegiance and celebration of presidents' birthdays, typically George Washington and Abraham Lincoln, are activities designed to instill patriotism and attachment to one's homeland. One of the challenges for elementary teachers in the third through fifth grades is helping students distinguish between city, county, state, and nation-state. Depending on district emphases, fourth graders either study regions in the United States or focus on the state in which they live. Fifth grade is the first year that historical emphasis is placed on the United States, and the constitutional efforts of the Founding Fathers are spotlighted. In Grades 7 and 8 the social studies curricula devotes greater attention to political institutions and civic life. The most common topics presented in the social studies curriculum include: *legislative* institutions; *executive* institutions and leadership; *judicial* institutions and legal process; and the *bureaucracy.* To date, however, more attention has been given to executive, judicial, and legislative institutions. When studying Clinton's executive roles, Luckowski and Lopach (1999) demonstrated that by "using an issues-centered approach to teaching impeachment, teachers would help students to focus on the historical and constitutional context and avoid the more salacious details of the Clinton scandal" (pp. 106–107).

The Social Context of Politics

Political scientists are interested in how and why individuals participate in the political process as well as the factors that may impede their participation. According to Gamble and colleagues (1987, p. 95), "people's attitudes, values, and beliefs are the key determinants of political behavior, [therefore] the factors that shape those attitudes, values, and beliefs are" important subjects to explore. Political socialization, public opinion, and electoral behavior are primary sources for understanding the nature of political participation. The dynamic relationship between political learning and participation across the life cycle is shown in Figure 5.5 (Hague, Harrop, & Breslin, 1992, p. 149). As you can see, the importance of the role of the elementary and middle school teacher for increasing political knowledge is illustrated by the surge of learning during late childhood.

Political socialization is the process by which individuals learn about the political system and the political culture in which they live. Political scientists offer two interpretations of the political socialization process (Dye & Zeigler, 1996).

> The "liberal" view of socialization sees it as a natural process through which
> culture is passed on across the generations, mainly through the family. By contrast
> "radicals" view socialization as a deliberate and ongoing process of class
> indoctrination carried out through the media. (Hague et al., 1992, p. 154)

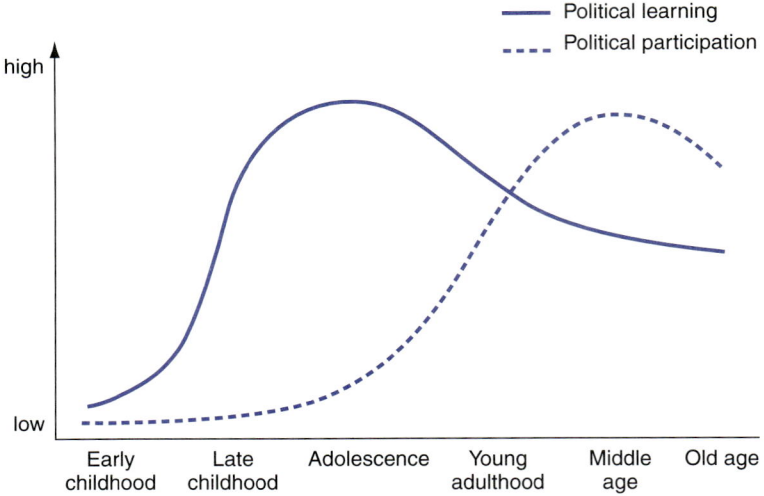

FIGURE 5.5   *Political Learning and Participation Across the Life Cycle: The Liberal View*

SOURCE: R. Hague, M. Harrop, & S. Breslin. *Political science: A comparative introduction* (New York: St. Martin's Press, 1992), p. 149. Copyright © 1993 by Bedford/St. Martin's, Inc. From: Political Science: A Comparative Introduction By: Hague, Harrop & Breslin. Reprinted with permission of Bedford/St. Martin's Press, Inc.

The dissonance characterized by these opposing views is often expressed by students in teacher preparation courses. Some students are frustrated by classroom rituals such as the Pledge of Allegiance, arguing that this is merely a form of indoctrination. Others see this as a developmentally appropriate way to instill a sense of identity with and attachment to the student's homeland. What is your position? Through the discussion questions at the end of this chapter, perhaps there will be an opportunity for you to discuss these viewpoints in class.

Public opinion is another important topic in the social context of politics. In *Introduction to Political Science,* Gamble and colleagues (1987) define public opinion as "an aggregate of individual attitudes and beliefs shared by some part of a political community"; whether expressed orally or in writing, it:

> is a vital form of political participation in a democracy and can be made known through the various types of interest group activity such as lobbying and mass propaganda, through electoral activity in support of a candidate or a party, or in ways that manifest either support for, or opposition to, existing or potential public policies. (p. 102)

Public opinion surveys usually ask citizens their views on contemporary issues.

Voting is another way in which citizens participate in the political process. The decline in the number of people voting in presidential elections concerns politicians and political scientists (Zuckerman, 1991). There is speculation about this decline, and the following list summarizes the reasons by Gamble and colleagues (1987):

Voter participation has declined because . . .

1.   certain groups are alienated from the system
2.   [there] is a sense of cynicism about politics and politicians

3. the average citizen fails to see any direct impact of political decisions on their lives except in the negative form of income taxes withheld from their paychecks

4. large numbers of citizens are basically satisfied with the system as it is

5. for most people, politics is not one of their primary interests (pp. 108–109)

In addition, the political scientists maintain that those who are inclined to vote are individuals from the upper socioeconomic classes who strongly identify with one of the major parties, professional people, and those with many years of education. Given this profile of American voters, Gamble and colleagues conclude that political participation, as represented by the voting behavior of citizens, is an elitist activity. These patterns create special challenges for the social studies teacher. Do you think that an important goal for teachers is to increase the number and range of voters? McGraw-Hill tackled this timely issue by challenging third graders to reflect on three Americans' viewpoints about voting patterns (see pages 136 and 137).

In elementary and middle school classrooms, it is common for teachers to hold mock elections, especially during presidential election years. When public opinion polls are included in the simulation, students are more fully engaged in the activities that adults exercise as participants in the political process. When the mock election precedes election day, the school election results are good predictors of the voting patterns of adults in the school community because children and youth typically vote the way their parents do! These activities are highly motivational to students and, it is hoped, will inspire them to participate in the real political process as adults.

What role will you play to address some of the concerns raised above by Gamble and colleagues? Discussion question number 2 at the end of this chapter offers an

© Michael Newman/PhotoEdit

CITIZENSHIP

VIEWPOINTS

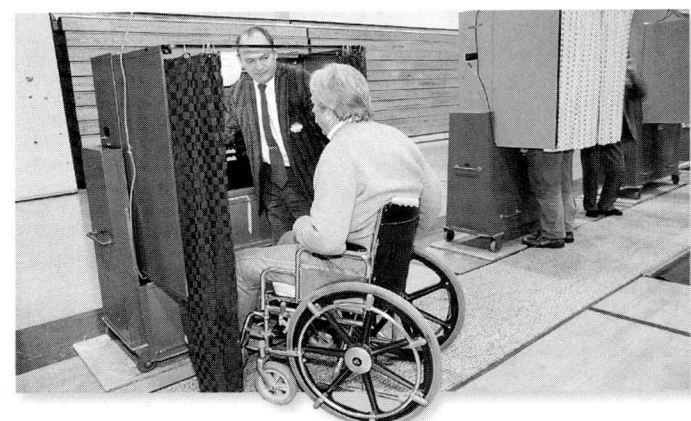

Citizens of the United States vote in booths like this one.

Should voting be required?

United States citizens 18 years or older have the right to vote. In most states voters must also register before their first election and any time they move. To register means giving proof of your citizenship and address.

Although United States citizens have the right to vote, many don't use this right. In our country only five out of ten people vote.

Some people suggest that citizens should be made to vote. Suzanne Hee's viewpoint on the next page expresses this idea. Others like Debbie Macon believe that it is best not to vote if you are not informed. Still others, like Joel Rosch, say that voting should be made easier. If Election Day was a national holiday, for example, people would find it easier to vote.

Consider the viewpoints at right, then answer the questions that follow.

198

Three DIFFERENT Viewpoints

 SUZANNE HEE
Researcher, Santa Monica, California
Excerpt from Interview, 1997

I think voting should be required. Voting should be what each citizen gives back to society for all that he or she receives from society. I think it is very important for people to know about the issues that affect them and have a say on those issues. I don't think people realize that their votes count.

"... voting should be required."

 DEBBIE MACON
Community Leader, West Bloomfield, Michigan
Excerpt from Interview, 1997

I believe that every citizen should be encouraged to vote, but not required. In our country freedom of choice is as important as the right to vote. Many times people don't vote because they feel they don't have enough information. If people have enough information, they will vote on their own without forcing them.

"... freedom of choice ..."

JOEL ROSCH
Teacher, Raleigh, North Carolina
Excerpt from Interview, 1997

Forcing people to vote is a good idea, but there have to be certain conditions. People should not have to take time off from their jobs. Instead, voting should take place when people have time off. Democracy involves not only rights but responsibilities. If we are going to live in a democracy, going out to vote is a small price to pay.

"... not only rights but responsibilities."

BUILDING CITIZENSHIP

1. What is the viewpoint of each person?
2. How are they alike? In what ways are they different?
3. What other opinions might people have on this issue?

SHARING VIEWPOINTS

Discuss what you agree or disagree with in these and other viewpoints. Be sure to give reasons to support your opinions. Then as a class try to write one statement about which you can all agree.

199

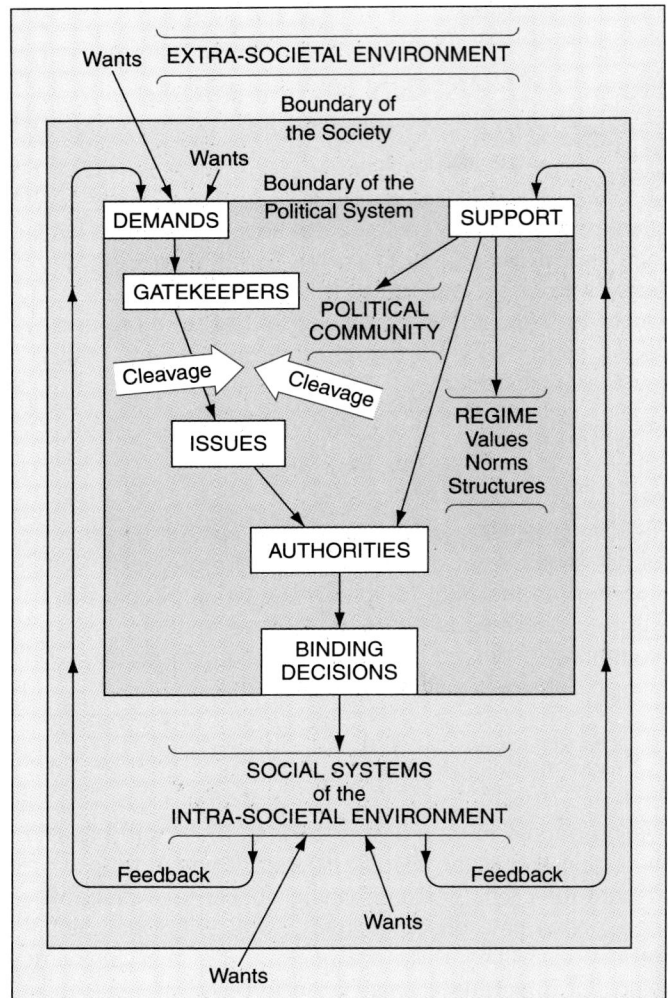

FIGURE 5.6   *Systems Analysis of Political Life*

SOURCE: L. Senesh. Organizing a curriculum around social science concepts, in I. Morrissett (Ed.), *Concepts and structures in the new social science curricula* (New York: Holt, Rinehart, & Winston, 1967), p. 29. Used by permission of the Social Science Education Consortium.

opportunity for you and your classmates to reflect on issues related to voter apathy. There are also curricular applications of political party platforms for presidential elections. Additional suggestions by the Social Science Education Consortium to organize key ideas and concepts in political life are represented in Figure 5.6.

Citizenship and Social Studies Education

In Chapters 2 through 4, social science disciplines were linked together for purposes of discussion. In this chapter citizenship is linked with a traditional social science discipline—political science. In addition, there are National Social Studies Standards, which treat political science and civics separately. It is important, however, to discuss how citizenship has been a more pervasive theme throughout the social studies curriculum, regardless of whether one is talking about political science, civics, or government.

The causal connection between formal education and the creation of good citizens can be traced to the educational writings of Dewey ([1916] 1966) and Merriam (1931, 1934), who both followed the tradition of Enlightenment theorists John Locke and John Stuart Mill. Niemi and Junn (1998) explain this connection as follows:

> Common among these perspectives is the argument that education has transcendent importance in the development of the qualities essential to citizenship in a democratic polity. This emphasis on the responsibility of American schools to teach the facts and principles of American democracy to the largest group of new and emerging citizens . . . continues unabated in contemporary American politics. The call for education to alleviate political as well as social and economic ills is a familiar refrain of politicians and policymakers alike, . . . by business leaders who call for training programs to prepare the next generation for an increasingly technologically advanced workplace, and by academics, reformers, and politicians who call for greater civic knowledge and participation as an antidote to collective ennui and growing political cynicism. (p. 2)

In *Defining the Social Studies,* Barr, Barth, and Shermis (1977) outline three traditions that they maintain characterize citizenship education. In attempting to delineate three traditions, they demonstrate emphases that may seem to have different underlying goals, but the primary goal they all share is citizenship. The three traditions are social studies taught as: citizenship transmission, social science, and reflective inquiry.

The *citizenship transmission* position views citizenship education as teaching about people and society while instilling a sense of loyalty to society. Usually, social studies lessons that reflect this position encourage students to respect and support democratic principles. Citizenship education via the *social science* position emerges from identifying the concepts, problems, processes within a discipline. This form of citizenship defines knowledge as a means for understanding the real world. Scholars who support this position argue that "the knowledge gained through social science inquiry will lead students to a better quality of participation in civic life" (Barr et al., 1977, p. 79). From the standpoint of the *reflective inquiry* position, a good citizen needs to know a body of personally tested insight. In educational discourse, insight refers to knowledge gained through firsthand experience and personal inquiries. Based on experience, weighing evidence, and developing reason, it is assumed that students will be able to make better informed decisions as active citizens.

Twenty years ago the efforts by Barr et al. were applauded because they helped to clarify citizenship constructs within the social studies. Yet even then critics argued that it was not possible to "homogenize" the three philosophic traditions. Shirley Engle, for example, maintained that the transmission and social science "positivism" are conservative positions designed to maintain the status quo, whereas reflective inquiry and social criticism (not addressed by any of the traditions) reflects theoretical constructs that are more dynamic and call for social change (Barr et al., 1977, p. 103). Jean Fair (Barr et al., 1977, p. 107) criticizes the three positions because they do not address the meaning of cultural pluralism and how to adapt social studies education for a variety of cultural groups. The issues raised by Fair continue to be the subject of debate today. They will be discussed in more detail in Chapter 6, but for now, it is important to recognize the three traditions as competing and overlapping models offered by Barr et al. as a way to understand a dynamic and politically sensitive field. Extending the desire for coherence, some of today's social studies educators view the national standards movement as an attempt to bring organization to the field and the entire K–12 social studies curriculum.

Think about citizenship education for the twenty-first century. What are the important issues that should be addressed to ensure that students become active participants in the political process? What are important political issues that affect teachers in the workplace? The ongoing debate on student-initiated prayer and religious activities is one source of controversy that affects the political charge of the classroom teacher. Can you think of others? Look at the following debate forum and discuss the implications for your role as a classroom teacher and as a potential debate that students might hold in class at the upper elementary level.

In recent years, the issue of prayer in schools has received widespread publicity. The issue has sparked public debate about whether or not prayer in school constitutes a violation of the First Amendment. The debates center around interpretation of the free exercise clause and the establishment clause, both components of the First Amendment. The debate also has opened discussion about the appropriateness of using school buildings for student religious organizations. As states develop policies to guide teachers and administrators, their legal advisers draw on some of the cases in the debate forum that follows. Where do you stand on the issue of student-initiated prayer and religious activities and how will you respond to parental and student inquiries? Examine the following debate to help clarify or expand your position.

> First Amendment: *Congress shall make no law respecting an establishment of religion, or prohibiting the free exercise thereof; or abridging the freedom of speech, or of the press; or the right of the people peaceably to assemble, and to petition the government for a redress of grievances.*

✦ Debate Forum: Student-Initiated Prayer and Religious Activities

PRO Student-Initiated Prayer or Religious Activities

Cantwell v. Connecticut, Connecticut (1940). In *Cantwell v. Connecticut* the Supreme Court "already established that the free exercise clause of the First Amendment was applicable to the states via the Fourteenth Amendment" (Long, 1990, p. 33). This free exercise clause "guarantees all citizens of the United States the rights of free exercise and religion as well as freedom of speech and the right to peaceful assembly"(Baron & Bishop, 1991, p. 29). The Supreme Court used this case as a precedent in *Wisconsin v. Yoder.*

Wisconsin v. Yoder, Wisconsin (1972). When Wisconsin attempted to enforce the school attendance law requiring all children to remain in school until the age of 16, the Amish communities in the area refused to send their children beyond the eighth grade and were thus convicted for violating the law. When the case eventually reached the Supreme Court, a unanimous decision, siding with the Amish, excused them from the school attendance law, citing it as an "unconstitutional violation of the free exercise of religion clause contained in the First Amendment" (Long, 1990, p. 33). The Justices agreed that the state lacked a compelling reason to keep the Amish students in school since such exposure to "worldly" interests would directly affect the unique lifestyle practiced by the Amish people, especially since the Amish children were "privy to alternative vocational training" (Long, 1990, p. 33).

Widmar v. Vincent, Pennsylvania (1981). The Supreme Court ruled "that a public university that allowed student groups a public forum could not prohibit religious groups from meeting without violating their free speech and equal protection rights as guaranteed under the first and fourteenth amendments" (Baron & Bishop, 1991, p. 29). The court ruled that allowing the groups to meet did not violate any prong of the Lemon test. Such a ruling "opened the door for many student groups and clubs that previously had been denied the right to conduct their meetings in public schools and universities" (Baron & Bishop, 1991, p. 29).

Bender v. Williamsport Area School District, Pennsylvania (1986). Students in the Williamsport schools wanted to create an extracurricular religion club, which the schools refused to allow. The students then sued the school and the court, citing *Widmar v. Vincent* as a precedent, the court ruled in favor of the students, allowing them the prayer club on the grounds that the school violated the students' right to free speech. The court additionally held that high school students were mature enough "not to mistake the school's permission as an endorsement" (Rossow, 1987, p. 39). The school appealed, and the previous court's decision agreeing to the students' right to free speech, but not religious speech, was reversed. The appellate court also disagreed with the judgment of student maturity, citing instead that students in high school were extremely impressionable and might mistake permission for endorsement. The case went to the Supreme Court, which reversed the appellate court's ruling based on technicalities faulting the way in which the case was appealed. Thus, the Supreme Court's decision reinstated the original district court ruling, which is still in effect, permitting the extracurricular religion club to meet. Currently, the issue remains unresolved between the interpretations of the Equal Access law. Appellate courts continue to find prayer clubs illegal while Congress, through the Equal Access Act, directs school boards to permit students to form religious groups under certain circumstances.

Board of Education of Westside Community School v. Mergens, Nebraska (1990). The students of Westside Community School wanted to form a religious club but the school board refused to permit them. The federal district court agreed with the school board's ban so the students then appealed the decision in the 8th Circuit Court of Appeals. They, in turn, reversed the district court ruling, determining "first, that banning the student group from meeting in a public high school would be in direct violation of the Equal Access Act, and second, that the Equal Access Act itself withstood all three prongs of the Lemon test [see *Lemon v. Kurtzman* in the following] and was not in violation of the establishment clause." The Supreme Court concurred on June 4, 1990.

CON Student-Initiated Prayer or Religious Activities

Engel v. Vitale, New York (1962). Parents of ten students sued when schools started the day reciting the Regents Prayer, claiming it violated the establishment clause of the First Amendment. Even though students could remain silent or be excused if they opposed the prayer, the United States Supreme Court reversed the previous rulings made by the New York Supreme Court and Court of Appeals, citing that "recitation of such prayer was wholly inconsistent with establishment of religion clause of Constitution" (Siler, 1990, p. 38). Furthermore, the fact that the teachers were involved made it appear as if the schools financed a religious exercise (Siler, 1990, p. 39).

Abington v. Schempp, Pennsylvania (1963). The Supreme Court ruled that Bible readings to start the day at school were unconstitutional. This decision, as well as the previous year's ruling and many others, made it clear that the court wished to "keep religious activities out of the public schools" (Baron & Bishop, 1991, p. 29).

Lemon v. Kurtzman (1971). Because of the entanglement begun by the previous two cases and the contradictory nature of the establishment clause and the free exercise clause, the court created a test [called the Lemon test] in this case to "determine the constitutionality of statutes and government policies. To avoid violating the establishment clause, under that test, a statute of policy must (1) have secular legislative purpose, (2) have a principal effect that neither advances nor inhibits religion, and (3) must not foster excessive government entanglement with religion" (Baron & Bishop, 1991, p. 29). Following this case, the three-prong test, as it is known, was used with many cases involving student religious groups and their interest in using public facilities to hold their meetings.

Johnson v. Huntington Beach Union High School District, California (1977). Using the three-prong test the California Court of Appeals ruled that the students' desire to hold a Bible study group in a public school would "foster excessive government entanglement in religion" (Baron & Bishop, 1991, p. 29).

Wallace v. Jaffree, Alabama (1983). In 1981 an attorney challenged the law permitting a moment of silence in the schools. The law was struck down by the Supreme Court in 1983.

Mozert v. Hawkins, Tennessee (1987). Parents in Hawkins county complained that the basal readers their children were studying offended their fundamentalist rights because the stories that "portrayed the modern role of men and women were too 'favorable . . . about the women's rights movement' "; they criticized other stories like the *Wizard of Oz* because they encouraged "the imagination 'beyond the limitation of scriptural authority'." When the parents withheld their children from participating in the reading class, the children were "dismissed from school," causing the parents to sue demanding an alternative text be used. The district court threw out the case in 1984, but the parents appealed; at that point the judge "proposed they 'opt out' of reading class," thus leaving the schools vulnerable to any sect that felt offended in the schools to follow the same path. "In August, 1987, the appeals court reversed the lower court ruling declaring that 'the requirement that public school students study a basal reader series does not create an unconstitutional burden under the free exercise clause' " (Adler, 1988, pp. 20–21).

Smith v. Commissioners, Alabama (1987). Parents of pupils in the public schools sued for allowing certain books be read in the school asserting that they promoted " 'secular humanism,' " also referred to as " 'anti-Christian and anti-American,' " according to the fundamentalist readings of the Bible. The judge presiding over the district court agreed with the parents and ordered the removal of the books. However, the circuit court overturned the decision, ruling that " 'the message conveyed by these textbooks with regard to theistic religion is one of neutrality; the textbooks neither endorse theistic religion as a system of belief, nor discredit it' " (Adler, 1988, p. 22).

The debate about religious activities illustrates how many decisions about the nature of government and the allocation of power are embodied in laws. For additional classroom applications of law-related education, see Gallo's (1996) middle school lesson on the establishment of religion and Eden and Ryan's (1999) examination of affirmative action. Strum and Shmidman (1969) suggest that political science evolved as a method for evaluating and choosing the best possible system that would help human beings as they struggled for power to make decisions about the welfare of themselves and their families. Furthermore, "since laws are an expression of a society's values, social change—an alteration in the environment that creates values—usually precedes legal change" (p. 6). In contemporary political arenas we have witnessed the significance of this statement with regard to human rights, a term that has evolved to represent a broad range of freedoms, including religious freedom.

In *Human Rights and Education,* Tarrow (1987, p. 8) discusses the important role that educators play in addressing educational rights of all citizens. Thus, studying the Magna Carta, the Statute of Religious Freedom, the Declaration of Independence, the Covenant of the League of Nations, and The Universal Declaration of Human Rights has relevance not only for understanding political issues in the global arena but in understanding the teacher's role as an agent of political socialization. Children internalize nationalistic identifications and international orientations as they formulate a worldview based on their nation's history of alignment with other nations (McEachron-Hirsch & Hirsch, 1990). Unlike the teacher's role, which tends to foster loyalty and identification to the nation-state, attachment to the international domain is more selective and, therefore, more disconnected (McEachron-Hirsch & Hirsch, 1990). Traditionally, this has been the result of national sovereignty as noted by Becker (1973):

> As long as the framework for international education is based on the notion that education, like military power, is but a means to achieve national ambitions, progress in building better cross-cultural and global relations among people and nations is likely to be incidental and haphazard. Education viewed solely as a matter of getting ahead is divisive at local, national and international levels. The need is to devise a system that educates all comers, rich and poor, foreign and domestic, to full humanity. (p. 106)

Weissbrodt (1988) maintains that one way to redirect political socialization from a competitive nationalism orientation to cooperative internationalism is to focus on international human rights. He pointed out that while most political, religious, philosophical, and economic ideologies are tied to a particular tribe, group, nation or group of nations, human rights represents an idea that is growing in world-wide acceptance. McEachron-Hirsch and Hirsch (1990) develop this notion by building on Schaar's term "covenanted patriotism." In *Learning to Live Together: Political Socialization and the Formation of International Identity,* McEachron-Hirsch and Hirsch (1990) suggest innovative ways that teachers can foster international identification, "guided by and directed toward the international mission established in international human rights covenants" (p. 382).

✦ CURRICULUM APPLICATIONS

Political science and civics curriculum applications for primary, intermediate, and middle school students are included in this section. Table 5.1 gives a sampling of activities across grade levels. This chart is followed by more comprehensive plans for three levels. The primary applications include a list of selected teaching suggestions from Carol Seefeldt's (1989) *Social Studies for the Preschool-Primary Child.* The intermediate application is in the form of an outline for developing a three-week instructional sequence on presidential elections in the fall of an election year and was prepared by the author and Herbert Hirsch, Professor of Political Science, Virginia Commonwealth University. The middle school teaching unit on Congressional Elections, in Appendix B, is designed for eighth-grade students and was prepared by Michael Buhl who was enrolled in a social studies methods course. Mickey had no previous teaching experience, and the social studies course was one of the first he had taken as a part of his certification program. As you can see from the unit, Mickey did a great job utilizing his previous knowledge and transferring it to an appropriate curriculum development format. You can do the same.

See Appendix A for the National Social Studies Standards featuring concepts in government.

Primary Applications: Understanding the Flag; Political Participation

Seefeldt (1989) suggests that primary teachers use common everyday experiences (a) to emphasize the purposes of rules, laws, and government, (b) to explain community services the government provides, and (c) to help children build meaningful associations with political symbols. Following is a selected list of activities to help children develop their political and civic awareness (Seefeldt, 1989, pp. 231–232).

Understanding the Flag

- American Flag: Ask the "Veterans of Foreign Wars, American Legion, or other patriotic group to demonstrate the proper ways of handling and caring for the flag" [and the history behind these techniques].

TABLE 5.1

Self in the World Connections
Integrating the Self with Others Across Geopolitical Space

	Primary	**Intermediate**	**Middle School**
Self	Let students make decisions about participation in groups or alone.	Ask students to vote on a classroom issue.	Students could design and circulate a political participation survey/self-assessment.
Family	Students identify how they work in cooperation with family members.	Investigate how to start recycling program for family.	Interview parent(s)/guardian(s) about their political views.
Community	Study community helpers; invite speaker to classroom.	Study city and county history and the roles of individuals in city and county offices.	Create a newsletter to inform classmates and local community about student positions on civic issues.
State	Make models of capitol buildings.	Examine the political history of the state; perform reenactment of significant even.	Identify what elected officials are doing on specific statewide civic issues.
Nation	Say pledge to flag; sing patriotic songs; celebrate birthdays of national heroes.	Prepare videotape of news conference regarding national issue.	Civics; current events; elections.
World	Write to a pen pal; discuss current events.	Participate in disaster relief efforts.	Research human rights issues in another country.

- Classroom Flag: Encourage children to design various classroom flags that mean time to come in, time to clean up, storytime, and so on.
- Reserve saying the pledge for special days—Earth Day; Lincoln's, Washington's, or Martin Luther King's birthday; Flag Day—so that children learn that the pledge has special meaning and importance.
- Invite a Scout troop to the class to demonstrate their flag ceremony and recite the Pledge of Allegiance. The Scouts might explain the meaning of their actions and tell what the flag means to them.
- Sing patriotic songs, or read poems or stories about the flag that may be more meaningful to young children. "This Land is Your Land," "Yankee Doodle," and "Flag of America" are examples of songs children enjoy and can understand." For example, the illustrations for George Cohan's "You're a Grand Old Flag," shown on pages 146 and 147, would certainly inspire students and teachers to sing in the context of discussing the key concepts tied to the song—such as *peace, freedom,* and *bravery.*

209

Political Participation

Seefeldt distinguishes between democratic decisions that young children can make for themselves and decisions that adults need to make for them. Understanding these differences helps children learn civic roles and build a sense of political efficacy necessary for future political participation.

Seefeldt (1989, pp. 232–233) offers the following categories:

Decision Making

- Voting to make Jell-O or pudding (each child makes his/her choice)
- Choosing selected games to play, separately
- Choosing selected games to play based on the will of the majority
- Establishing rules for woodworking, block building, use of bathrooms

Rules Made for Children by Adults

- Fire drill procedures
- Traffic laws
- Rules for riding the bus
- Rules at home [such as bedtimes, table manners, phone manners]

Seefeldt (1989) underscores the value of discussing the purpose of rules and procedures for getting along in a group and maintains that children should "have the responsibility to follow the rules, to make rules that are needed for living within a group, to change those that no longer function to protect them and others, and to adjust the rules to fit changing situations" (p. 234). This approach encourages critical thinking versus blind obedience to systems of authority.

National Council for the Social Studies Standards for *Civic Ideals and Practices* are (b), (j); *Power, Authority, and Governance* are (a), (b). National Standards for Civics and Government are (I.A.X), (I.C.X), (I.E.X). Concepts addressed in political science and citizenship include: behavior, citizenship, decision making, governmental community services, rules.

Intermediate Application: Cast Your Vote!

 MODEL LESSON: CAST YOUR VOTE!

THREE-WEEK OUTLINE FOR TEACHING ABOUT PRESIDENTIAL ELECTIONS WITH HERBERT HIRSCH

Week One: History of United States Presidential Elections
Week Two: Stages of Presidential Elections
Week Three: Elections: Victory and Defeat

HISTORY

A.   *Overview.* Provide narrative about presidential elections in U.S. history. Include an explanation of the Constitutional Convention and what it said about how the president should be elected. Include pictures of different presidents and events associated with their campaign for office.

B.   *Political parties.* Present the differences and similarities between the Republican and Democratic parties. This will consist largely of historical case studies of the most important and interesting elections. Provide pictures of the candidates and their campaign material. These might include campaign songs, posters, buttons, mottoes, cartoons, and so on. Elections to be examined may include the following:

1789   George Washington and John Adams. The first election that began to establish the precedents.

1800   Jefferson and Adams. The first election in which there was a real contest between two political parties and two candidates.

1828   Andrew Jackson and John Quincy Adams. The election of Andrew Jackson and the growing importance of the "common man."

1856   James Buchanan and John C. Fremont. The election that saw the emergence of the Republican Party.

1860   Abraham Lincoln and Stephen Douglas. The election of Lincoln that also illustrates the importance of third parties.

1876   Samuel Tilden and Rutherford B. Hayes. The famous "disputed election," which is important because it demonstrates what happens if neither candidate receives a majority in the electoral college and the House of Representatives has to choose the president.

1912   Woodrow Wilson, Theodore Roosevelt, William Taft, and Eugene Debs. The election of Wilson, which shows the importance of third parties and also demonstrates what happens if one of the two major parties splits its vote and becomes divided by ideological conflict.

1932   Franklin Roosevelt and Herbert Hoover. The election of Franklin Roosevelt and the emergence of the "Roosevelt Coalition."

1960   John Kennedy and Richard Nixon. The election of John Kennedy. The first Catholic to become president. This election also shows the importance of the modern system of primary elections.

1964   Lyndon Johnson and Barry Goldwater. One of the clearest examples of ideological differences between candidates.

1968   Hubert Humphrey and Richard Nixon. This election shows the importance of third parties (George Wallace) as well as showing what happens when ideological conflict splits a party.

1972   Richard Nixon and George McGovern. A second example of ideological differences between candidates.

1976   Jimmy Carter and Gerald Ford. The election of Jimmy Carter. The use of a new symbolism—the "outsider" or nonpolitician.

1980   Jimmy Carter and Ronald Reagan. Brought in social issues (e.g., crime, drugs) and perception that social fabric of America was falling apart; strong defense; balancing budget.

1984   Ronald Reagan and Walter Mondale. When Mondale talked about raising taxes, the American public was strongly opposed.

1988   George Bush and Michael Dukakis. Bush perpetuated negative images of liberalism, which fostered his success.

1992   George Bush and Bill Clinton. Clinton shifted Democrats to middle of the road; focused on domestic issues. Bush criticized for raising taxes after saying earlier, "Read my lips, no new taxes." H. Ross Perot took votes away from both Clinton and Bush.

1996   Bill Clinton and Robert Dole. Clinton shifted emphasis from domestic to for-
        eign policy. Clinton adopted Republican issues such as welfare reform and
        anticrime and turned them into Democratic issues.

C.   *Minorities, women and third parties in presidential elections.* Minority groups and
women have always been underrepresented in presidential elections. There has never
been a woman or minority president. Yet minorities and women have been important
voting blocs, and there have been minority and women candidates. For example, not
many people know that the first woman presidential candidate was Victoria Woodhull.
She ran for the presidency in 1872. Minorities have also run for the presidency. In 1968
Dick Gregory ran on the Freedom and Peace and New party tickets.

Third parties have also been important. In some cases they have taken enough votes
away from one of the two major parties to cause the defeat of that party. In examining
third parties the teacher can refer back to several of the elections mentioned previously,
especially 1860, 1912, 1968, and 1992. This section could also include lists of interesting facts about the presidents.

STUDENT ACTIVITIES: HISTORY

A.   Students should vote for a candidate in upcoming presidential election. It is important that they vote on the first day of the unit. During the last week of the unit they
will vote again and comparisons of voting before and after information is presented
will be made to exemplify voting behaviors.
B.   Students can make political cartoons fashioned after some of the ideas presented
in class.
C.   Instructions for making "election booklets" can be provided so that students will
have a complete summary of daily lessons that they can share with family and friends.

STAGES OF PRESIDENTIAL ELECTIONS

Candidates for the presidency generally pass through the following four stages in order to win the office.

A.   *Positioning.* This stage involves the candidate gaining exposure in the media;
that is, demonstrating that he or she has the "right" personality, that he or she has the
makings of a president, that he or she is photogenic. In short, it involves the prospective candidate making a name for himself or herself and getting to be known by the
public—getting publicity. It is important in this stage that the candidate get to know
important people and people who have money to contribute to the campaign.
B.   *Primaries.* This is the stage during which the candidates attempt to secure delegates to the national party nominating conventions. The first primary is usually held
in New Hampshire and attracts most of the major candidates. After New Hampshire
the candidates may run in twenty or thirty primaries. The goal here is to pick the primaries that will make the candidates look most favorable in comparison to the others. Examples can be drawn from the elections in 1960 and 1976.
C.   *The national party nominating conventions.* This is one of the most colorful and
interesting events in the campaign. Balloons, decorations, "spontaneous demonstrations," confetti and bands, campaign songs, and signs with the names of all the states
are everywhere. Politicians give picturesque speeches extolling the virtues of their

candidate and party and pointing out the shortcomings of their opponents. Meetings of committees are held to plan the party platform and to decide how to go about electing their candidate.

D. *Campaign.* At this stage, the nominees of the two parties have been chosen by the conventions and the candidates now crisscross the country giving speeches, meeting different groups of people and generally trying to get elected. How they do it, how they use television, how the campaign is planned, who runs it, and so on, are interesting stories.

STUDENT ACTIVITIES: STAGES OF PRESIDENTIAL ELECTIONS

A. Students may be organized into party caucuses to choose delegates to the national party nominating conventions.

B. Students can hold a mininational party nominating convention. As noted in the content outline, this is one of the most colorful and interesting events and should be one of the highlights. Students can decorate the classroom to look like a convention hall. Balloons, red, white and blue crepe paper, confetti, and so on, should be used. Students can make nominating speeches for their candidates. After each nominating speech a "spontaneous demonstration" is held, complete with bands and marchers. Students also can hold committee meetings to plan the party platform. They can make the signs that identify the different states.

C. The class may be divided into two, three, or more different parties to engage in the campaign. Possibly other classrooms can be designated as Republicans and Democrats if teachers present unit at same time. The students can make campaign buttons, posters, bumper stickers and all the paraphernalia of a political campaign.

ELECTION AND VICTORY OR DEFEAT

A. *Voting and how it is accomplished.* Different methods of voting—machines, punch card ballots, and paper ballots—can be examined. Teacher explains how the different types of ballots might affect the outcome of the election as well as how people go about registering to vote. A copy of the county voting roll (a list of registered voters) should be secured from the county clerk. The discussion should also include what happens when people go door-to-door to persuade others to vote for their candidate. Sample ballots are usually available in newspapers or from the county clerk or League of Women Voters.

B. *Guest speaker.* A representative from the League of Women Voters or a candidate for office can be invited to explain and answer questions about the voting process.

C. *Voting patterns/Tally results.* Compare votes with the votes students cast on the first day of unit. Compare with voting patterns of parents and general public. Why do people vote as they do? What determines how a person will vote, and whether they will vote? Could students identify what may have influenced their vote during the campaign and election? Discuss what happens if election is close—refer to election of 1876.

D. *Evaluation and celebration.* The unit may be concluded by having an inaugural speech and ceremony followed by an inaugural ball and party. An inaugural ceremony is a great way to culminate the election unit. The winning candidate may be sworn in by the Chief Justice of the U.S. Supreme Court, and an inaugural ball or party can provide an opportunity for parents, teachers, and students to celebrate the election of their new president.

Student Activities: Election and Victory or Defeat

A.   Students can be presented with sample ballots. They can also be shown how voting machines and punch card ballots work. Students may role-play handing out pamphlets and going door-to-door to persuade others to support their candidate. They could also role-play phone calls usually made by party workers to try to persuade people to "get out and vote" for their candidate.

B.   Students or teachers might write to the national party headquarters asking for information, or they could take a field trip to the local headquarters of one or both of the parties. The field trip can demonstrate how the campaign apparatus works and is an opportunity to collect information about the parties and candidates. Speakers from the League of Women Voters or other service organizations may be asked to talk to the class and bring with them examples of ballots and scorecards that students might use on the day of the election.

NCSS Standards for *Civic Ideals and Practices* include (e), (f), (g), (h). Standards for Government and Civics include (III.B.X), (V. A.X). Concepts addressed by this voting unit are political parties, primaries, minority, social/political process, vote, leadership, democracy, public opinion, and presidential elections.

✦ Internet Links

Citizenship is a common theme found in the primary, intermediate, and middle school lessons of this chapter. Many Internet sites have been created to aid in teaching citizenship. *World Desk* (Boe, Graubort, & Cappo, 1996) is another great source of websites for government and geography.

Internet Links

General Teacher Resource

http://www.education-world.com

Education World.

This search engine is for educational websites only and therefore is an excellent online resource guide for educators. Anything and everything an educator might want to know can be easily located by searching the database of 56,000-plus sites. For the purposes of this chapter, the keyword *citizenship* was plugged in. Numerous interesting sites appeared, two of which are described next.

INTERNET LINKS

Citizenship

http://www.education-world.com/a_curr/curr008.shtml

Teaching Citizenship's Five Themes.

This site is constructed in conjunction with *Weekly Reader* and helps to develop K–6 students' understanding of five themes of citizenship: honesty, compassion, respect, responsibility, and courage. These themes are explored by providing teachers with various activities for different grade levels.

Links to other citizenship sites are provided as well. One addresses the theme of citizenship by allowing students to write a letter (on the computer) to a *Weekly Reader* character who is faced with a problem involving one of the themes. Students have access to past problems and student responses.

Other interesting links include: National Standards for Civics and Government, Welcome to the White House for Kids, and Citizenship Books and Activities: 13 Terrific New Titles and What to Do With Them.

INTERNET LINKS

Citizenship

http://civnet.org

Civnet: International Resource for Civic Education and Civil Society.

This site is a teaching resource center that provides a library of teaching materials and a directory of other useful civic organizations. Teaching materials include lesson plans, textbooks, and access to the National Standards for Civics and Government. Lesson plans are categorized by grade levels and examples of titles include: "Why do we need a government?," "How can citizens participate?," and "What are the possible consequences of privacy?"

SUMMARY

Political science and citizenship are essential components of social studies because they focus on the importance of government and laws designed to support human rights. The fact that humans have rights that need to be protected is an idea that has evolved and continues to be examined in a global context. This chapter has provided research on children's developing attachment to multiple realms of geopolitical space and corresponding leaders, underscoring the role that teachers can play as agents of political socialization. The *Self in the World* orientation is manifested in children's developing political attitudes as we have seen from this body of research. Loyalty to one's own culture and nation-state

The Civic Education of the American Teacher. (1983, November/December), *Journal of Teacher Education. 34* (6), 3–41.

Clark, T. (1990, September/October). Participation in democratic citizenship education. *The Social Studies, 81* (5), 206–208.

Dolenga, J. (1992, September). CAAPS off to kids! *Educational Leadership, 50* (1), 70–71.

is instilled through patriotic traditions such as the Pledge of Allegiance and the celebration of national holidays. As children get older these attachments become more differentiated as students analyze political issues in greater complexity; for example, religious

Eden, J. M., & Ryan, J. P. (1999). Affirmative action: Contentious ideas and controversial practices. *Social Education, 63* (2), 110–115.

Eveslage, T. (1990, October). The unfulfilled promise of citizenship education. *Social Education, 54* (6), 359–360.

Fontana, L. A., & Mehlinger, H. D. (1981). *Citizenship education.* Washington, DC: National School Boards Association.

Ganz, R. (1981, October). Social studies teachers as political participants. *Social Education, 45* (6), 408–411.

Harvey, K. (1996). Teaching about human rights and American Indians. *Social Studies and the Young Learner, 8* (4), 6–10.

Miljeteig-Olssen, P. (1992, April/May). Children's participation: Giving children the opportunity to develop into active and responsible members of society. *Social Education, 83* (3), 216.

Mitchell-Powell, B. (1996). Children's literature: Moral, social, and civic issues in the classroom. *Social Studies and the Young Learner, 8* (4), 21–22.

O'Brien, E. (1999). We must integrate human rights into the social studies. *Social Education, 63* (3), 171–176.

Palonsky, S. B. (1987). Political socialization in elementary schools. *The Elementary School Journal, 87* (5), 492–505.

Parker, W. C. (Ed.). (1989, October). Participatory citizenship. *Social Education, 53* (6), 353–370.

Pereira, C. (1988, February). Educating for citizenship in the elementary grades. *Phi Delta Kappan, 69* (6), 429–431.

Peters, M. M., & Bjorklun, E. C. (1996). Torts and tales: Teaching about personal injury law in the primary grades. *Social Studies and the Young Learner, 8* (4), P5–P8.

Porter, P. H. (1996). Teacher's resources: Moral, social, and civic issues—Conflict resolution in the peaceable classroom. *Social Studies and the Young Learner, 8* (4), 23–25.

Proctor, D. R., & Hass, M. E. (1990, November). *A handbook of school-based community projects for student participation.* Presentation at annual meeting of the National Council for the Social Studies. Anaheim, CA.

Seefeldt, C. (1989, Spring). Perspectives on the pledge of allegiance. *Childhood Education, 65* (3), 131–132.

Sesow, F. W., & VanCleaf, D. (1988). *Social studies and youth organizations: Partners in the development of civic responsibility and action.* Based on paper presented at National Council for the Social Studies. (ERIC No. ED 299 221)

Solovitch-Haynes, S. (1996). Street-smart second graders navigate the political process. *Social Studies and the Young Learner, 8* (4), 4–5.

Totten, S. (1999). The scourge of genocide: Issues facing humanity today and tomorrow. *Social Education, 63* (2), 116–121.

Woyach, R. B. (1992). Leadership in civic education. ERIC No. ED 351 270.

Organizations

American Bar Association Special Committee on Youth Education for Citizenship (YEFC), 1155 East 60th Street, Chicago, IL 60637, (312) 947–3960.

American Civil Liberties Union, 125 Broad Street, New York, NY 10004-2400.

Association for Supervision and Curriculum Development (ASCD), 225 North Washington Street, Alexandria, VA 22314, (703) 549–9110.

The Bill of Rights Educational Program, 5000 Park Street North, St. Petersburg, FL 33709.

Center for Citizenship Education, 1100 Seventeenth Street, N.W., Suite 1000, Washington, DC 20036, (202) 466–2822.

The Center for Civic Education, 5146 Douglas Fir Road, Calabasas, CA 90005.

Citizenship Development Program, The Mershon Center, Ohio State University, 199 West 10th Avenue, Columbus, OH 43201, (614) 422–1681.

Citizenship Education Clearing House (CECH), University of Missouri-St. Louis; 312 Marillac Hall, 8001 Natural Bridge Road; St. Louis, MO 63121, (314) 516–6820.

Citizenship Education, Development Division, Research for Better Schools, Inc. (RBS), 444 North Third Street, Philadelphia, PA 19123, (215) 574–9300.

Close-Up Foundation, 1055 Thomas Jefferson Street, N.W., Washington, DC 20007, (202) 342–8700.

Commission on the Bi-Centennial of the United States Constitution, 808 Seventeenth Street, Washington, DC 20006.

The Constitutional Rights Foundation, 601 South Kingsley Drive, Los Angeles, CA 90005.

C-SPAN in the Classroom, 444 North Capitol Street, N.W., Washington, DC 20001.

Effective Participation in Government Program, Box 632, Fayetteville, NY 13066.

First Amendment Congress, Graduate School of Public Affairs, University of Colorado at Denver, 1445 Market Street, Suite 320, Denver, CO 80202.

First Liberty Institute, George Mason University, Robinson Hall #3307, 4400 University Drive, Fairfax, VA 22030.

Future Problem Solving Program, P.O. Box 98, 115 West Main Street, Aberdeen, NC 28315.

Future Systems, Inc. (FSI), Suite 207, 1422 West Lake Street, Minneapolis, MN 55408, (612) 822–3181.

Global Perspectives in Education, Inc. (GPE), 218 East 18th Street, New York, NY 10003, (212) 475–0850.

The Great Decisions Program, The Foreign Policy Association, 1900 M Street, N.W., Washington, DC 20036.

The Jefferson Foundation, 1529 Eighteenth Street, N.W., Washington, DC 20036.

National Council for the Social Studies (NCSS), 3615 Wisconsin Avenue, N.W., Washington, DC 20016, (202) 966–7840.

National Issues Forum in the Classroom, 100 Commons Road, Dayton, OH 45459.

National Street Law Institute, 605 G Street, N.W., Washington, DC 20001, (202) 624–8217.

Phi Alpha Delta Public Service Center, Suite 325E, Bethesda, MD 20814.

A Presidential Classroom for Young Americans, 441 North Lee Street, Alexandria, VA 22314-2346.

Resources for Just Communities, Harvard Graduate School of Education, Larson Hall, 315 Appian Way, Cambridge, MA 02138, (617) 495–3546.

Social Science Education Consortium, Inc. (SSEC), 855 Broadway, Boulder, CO 80302, (303) 492–8124.

Social Studies Development Center (SSDC), Indiana University, 513 North Park, Bloomington, IN 47405, (812) 337–3838.

Speak for Yourself, 625 4th Avenue South, Minneapolis, MN 55415.

The Study Circles in the Resources Center, Choices Education Project, Center for Foreign Policy Development, Box 1948, Brown University, Providence, RI 02912.

REFERENCES

Adler, M. N. (1988). The politics of censorship. *PS: Political Science and Politics, 21* (1), 18–24.

Almond, G., & Verba, S. (1963). *The civic culture.* Princeton, NJ: Princeton University Press.

Baron, M. A., & Bishop, H. L. (1991). Come one, come all. *The American School Board Journal, 178* (3), 29–30.

Barr, R. D., Barth, J. L., & Shermis, S. S. (1977). *Defining the social studies,* Bulletin 51. Arlington, VA: National Council for the Social Studies.

Becker, J. M. (1973). International and cross-cultural experiences. In G. Henderson (Ed.), *Education for peace: Focus on mankind.* (pp. 101–124). Washington, DC: Association for Supervision and Curriculum Development.

Boe, T., Graubort, C. B., & Cappo, M. (1996). *World desk: A student handbook for the internet.* Santa Cruz, CA: Learning in Motion.

Civic Achievement Award Program. (1987). Arlington, VA: Close-Up Foundation.

CIVITAS: A Framework for Civic Education. (1990). Calabasas, CA: Center for Civic Education.

Dahl, R. A. (1970). *Modern political analysis.* Englewood Cliffs, NJ: Prentice-Hall.

Danziger, J. N. (1994). *Understanding the political world.* New York: Longman.

Dewey, J. [1916] (1966). *Democracy and education.* New York: Free Press.

Dye, T., & Zeigler, H. (1996). *The irony of democracy: An uncommon introduction to American politics* (10th ed.). Orlando, FL: Harcourt Brace College.

Freeman, D. A. (1994). *Political concepts.* Dubuque, IA: Kendall/Hunt.

Ethridge, M. E., & Handelman, H. (1994). *Politics in a changing world.* New York: St. Martin's Press.

Evans, J. M., & Brueckner, M. M. (1990). *Elementary social studies: Teaching for today and tomorrow.* Boston, MA: Allyn & Bacon.

Gallo, M. (1996). Controversial issues in practice. *Social Education, 60* (1), C1–C4.

Gamble, J. K., Jr., Irwin, Z. T., Redenius, C. M., & Weber, J. W. (1987). *Introduction to political science.* Englewood Cliffs, NJ: Prentice-Hall.

Hague, R., Harrop, M., & Breslin, S. (1992). *Political science: A comparative introduction.* New York: St. Martin's Press.

Hess, R. D., & Torney, J. V. (1967). *The development of political attitudes in children.* Chicago, IL: Aldine.

Jahoda, G. (1963). The development of children's ideas about country and nationality. *British Journal of Educational Psychology, 33,* 47–60.

Jahoda, G. (1964). Children's concepts of nationality: A critical study of Piaget's stages. *Child Development, 35,* 1081–1082.

Long, G. P. (1990). Understanding religious freedom through courtroom simulation. *OAH Magazine of History, 5* (1), 31–34.

Luckowski, J. A., & Lopach, J. J. (1999). Teaching presidential impeachment, *Social Education, 63* (2), 106–109.

McEachron-Hirsch, G. (1979). *International perceptions and curricular strategies among social studies educators.* Unpublished doctoral dissertation, The University of Texas at Austin, Austin, TX.

McEachron-Hirsch, G., & Hirsch, H. (1990). Learning to live together: Political socialization and the formation of international identity. *International Journal of Group Tension, 20* (4), 369–390.

Merriam, C. E. (1931). *The making of citizens: A comparative study of methods of civic training.* Chicago: University of Chicago Press.

Merriam, C. E. (1934). *Civic education in the United States.* New York: Scribner's.

Niemi, R. G., & Junn, J. (1998). *Civic education: What makes students learn.* New Haven, CT: Yale University Press.

Piaget, J., & Weil, A. M. (1951). The development in children of the idea of the homeland and of relations with other countries. *International Social Science Bulletin, III,* 561–578.

Roskin, M. G., Cord, R. L., Medeiros, J. A., & Jones, W. S. (1994). *Political science, an introduction.* Englewood Cliffs, NJ: Prentice-Hall.

Rossow, L. F. (1987). Conflicting directives from Congress and the courts put you in the hot seat. *The American School Board Journal, 174* (2), 38–39.

Seefeldt, C. (1989). *Social studies for the preschool-primary child.* Columbus, OH: Merrill.

Shively, W. P. (1995). *Power and choice, an introduction to political science.* New York: McGraw-Hill.

Siler, C. (1990). The establishment clause: Teaching first amendment rights using primary sources. *OAH Magazine of History, 5* (1), 35–39.

Squire, P., Lindsay, J., Covington, C., & Smith, E. (1997). *Dynamics of democracy.* Madison, WI: Brown & Benchmark.

Strum, P., & Shmidman, M. (1969). *On studying political science.* Pacific Palisades, CA: Goodyear Publishing.

Tarrow, N. B. (Ed.). (1987). *Human rights and education.* New York: Pergamon Press.

Torney-Purta, J. (1991). Cross-national research in social studies. In J. P. Shaver, *Handbook of research on social studies teaching and learning* (pp. 591–601). New York: Macmillan.

Weissbrodt, D. (1988). Human rights: An historical perspective. In P. Davies (Ed.), *Human rights* (pp. 1–20). New York: Routledge.

Wellek, A. (Editorial Adviser, 4th Edition). (1991). *The encyclopedic dictionary of American government.* Guilford, CT: Duskin.

Zuckerman, A. S. (1991). *Doing political science: An introduction to political analysis.* San Francisco, CA: Westview Press.

PART II

Instructional Principles in Teaching Social Studies

In Part I we examined the history of the social studies field and its origins in the social science disciplines. Each of the core subject areas—language arts, science, math, and social studies—can trace its knowledge base to the arts and science disciplines. It is important for a beginning teacher to have an appreciation of these knowledge bases and how they evolved. Such information will enable the novice to weigh whether the latest educational innovations and reformist notions are truly innovations or merely new slogans embracing traditional approaches. But a strong grounding in knowing *what* to teach is only part of the challenge in making decisions about social studies. Building a strong curriculum requires not only a strong grounding in the knowledge base but also attention to the social and developmental characteristics of students. According to Ladson-Billings (1990, 22) "teachers work within three dimensions: their conception of themselves and others, their knowledge, and their classrooms' social structure." In Part II we address the conception of students in the social and psychological context of the classroom, examining their cultural and developmental needs and how they can be addressed through a variety of instructional approaches.

CORBIS

CHAPTER 6

THE SIGNIFICANCE OF HISTORICAL EVENTS IN A PLURALISTIC SOCIETY

Chapter Outline

CHAPTER OBJECTIVES

As a teacher, you will play a major role in selecting content, instructional strategies, and a classroom environment that will educate students. The decisions you make will be influenced by many factors. Your interests, values, and education; the interests, abilities, and motivation of your students and their parents or caregivers; and the institutional and community expectations where you work are the primary influences.

Given the range of multicultural opportunities experienced by students preparing to teach, it is common for them to express the following concern: "How can I relate to the cultural needs of all of my students?" Another related question phrased more tentatively is, "I'm only familiar with my own cultural experiences, how can I teach and be sensitive to another person's cultural background?" And "Why am I held responsible for the bad deeds my ancestral cultural group did hundreds of years ago?" is a more defensively phrased question. These challenging questions lead swiftly to discussions of our pluralistic society and how diversity is presented in the social studies curriculum. Upon completion of this chapter you will be able to:

1. Describe historical influences on the defense of individual freedom and diversity in an American culture that strives to uphold a societal core.
2. Explain how the tenets of societal unity and diversity have been analyzed in the context of curriculum and instruction.
3. Identify strategies for creating a balance between unity and diversity based on your personal reflections.

The United States is a country that is rich in diversity. Yet only in recent years has the diversity been written about by a diverse population. That is, the voices of people of color, women, the elderly, special populations, and the poor have found their way into educational discourse as they have attained the skills of writing and communication to speak for themselves. Until this time, marginalized groups were studied and written about largely by people outside their realm of experience. On a positive note, scholarship, research, literature, and art—essentially the culture as a whole—has been enriched by the expansion of educational opportunities. At the same time, our schools may be systematically perpetuating practices that impede educational achievement for certain groups as a result of inattention to cultural differences. In this chapter, we examine the complex relationship between schools and society and the challenge that faces each teacher as he or she attempts to meet the diverse needs of individual students.

Debates about pluralism and a common culture can be traced to events that shaped the relationships among people during precolonial times. Pluralism as we know it today was not a highly esteemed value among the people who came together during the fifteenth century. How then did the concept emerge given the legacy of the age of exploration, and how can educators address diversity in the United States without alienating one cultural group from another? That is, how can a shared history of the United States be presented in such a way that the differential impact of historical events on various cultural groups and individuals is honored? According to Sleeter and Grant (1994) *multicultural education* refers "to educational practices directed toward race, culture, language, social class, gender, and disability, although in selecting the term we do not imply that race is the primary form of social inequality that needs to be addressed" (p. 33). To understand recent reforms and scholarship in multicultural education it is helpful to trace the origins of the terms *pluribus, unum, assimilation, melting pot, cultural pluralism,* and the more recent slogan *political correctness.* From there a discussion of scholarship on multicultural education will be presented.

✦ Cultural Pluralism and Multicultural Education

According to Cortes (1994), two values that have often been at odds with each other throughout U.S. history are *pluribus* and *unum*. *Pluribus* signifies "the defense of individual freedom and societal diversity," whereas *unum* signifies "upholding the societal core" (Cortes, 1994, p. 6). Cortes points out that, on the one hand, extremist views of pluribus can result in societal disintegration, while on the other hand, unum extremism can lead to the oppression of individual liberties. For example, not allowing a person of one race to marry someone from another race may be an extreme measure to maintain racial distinctions for the purpose of pluralism, although it is debatable because scholars disagree as to whether there is such a thing as a pure race. Extreme emphasis on unum can be oppressive if, for example, individuals are forced by public policies to deny their beliefs or traditions. Religion and language are two areas where pluribus and unum have continued to spark debate in educational circles since the beginning of public instruction (Greer, 1972; Haynes, 1990; Porter, 1990; Regoli, 1992).

In *Ordinary People and Everyday Life* (Gardner & Adams, 1983), Howard Rabinowitz presents three theories about the interaction between a host society and minority groups. These terms are often used interchangeably in educational discourse even though their intended meanings are quite distinct. According to Rabinowitz (1983), *assimilation* is the process by which "foreign or racial outsiders [to those in power] become 'Americanized' " (p. 25). Rabinowitz maintains that the oldest view of assimilation is the *melting pot,* which suggests that a new race would emerge as generations of mixed ancestry would evolve. A second view of the melting pot theory is that cultural differences would melt away as people became Americanized. Rabinowitz (1983) suggests that the immigration laws of the 1920s reflected this position because a doctrine of Anglo conformity emerged "which held that more recent newcomers had nothing to add to the values, virtues, institutions, and behavior of old-stock Americans" (p. 26). This interpretation implies a form of negating the cultural experiences that existed prior to arrival in the United States.

Cultural pluralism is the third model of assimilation that is more popular today. During the 1920s, Horace Kallen coined the term, which he argued should represent the process whereby ethnic groups retain their own language, religion, schools, clubs, history, customs, food, and other aspects of culture. Kallen saw cultural pluralism as compatible with national unity and felt that the "American creed" guaranteed equality *and* diversity. Kallen's model has been likened to the metaphor of an orchestra, whose meaning was later reflected in Carl Degler's use of the term *salad bowl.* That is, "the constituent elements retain their special character, but blend together to form something greater than the sum of the parts" (Rabinowitz, 1983, p. 27). The work by Rabinowitz, Kallen, and Degler represents scholarship among social historians that has shaped our views about what it means to have a diverse cultural heritage. Although cultural pluralism has undergone several reinterpretations since the 1920s, the term is generally used today to describe how members of American society respond to diverse ethnic and racial groups.

The civil rights movement and social science scholars heightened sensitivity to the limitations of educational practices that overemphasized homogeneous values and nation-centric approaches. Reforms in the social studies curriculum sought to infuse information about the variety of cultural groups within and outside the United

States. Visually, textbooks reflected greater attention to members of ethnic groups, women, and people with special physical needs. That is, the graphic material depicted greater diversity. Whether or not substantive changes were made is still a topic of debate (Tetreault, 1987). In addition to curricular modifications, the roles of teachers in diverse classroom settings were addressed. To illustrate some of these modifications, a brief overview of selected curricular and instructional strategies that have contributed to the field of multicultural education is presented next.

During the eighties, educational systems were under attack by critics who argued that not enough time was spent teaching content; too much time was wasted on teaching processes and skills (Cheney, 1987; Hirsch, 1987; Ravitch, 1985). Media attention shifted public attention to *what* was taught or, at least, should be taught. These criticisms, which were highly publicized, provided a supportive context for those who advocated teaching about a common or shared American culture. E. D. Hirsch's (1987) *Cultural Literacy: What Every American Needs to Know* was a prototype of books in support of a common base of information. Hirsch argued that cultural literacy is developed through the retention of factual information, and he developed specific lists and outlines of facts appropriate for various grade levels. Based on Cortes's discussion of pluribus and unum, Hirsch's approach would be characterized as supportive of the unum principle because he proposed a common curriculum for all students.

Multicultural curriculum reform efforts have been criticized in varying degrees, partially as a result of scholars' predilection toward pluribus or unum principles. In recent years the term *political correctness* has emerged as a pejorative label applied to issues of cultural pluralism. Efforts to include the voices of women, minorities, the disabled, and the elderly have been labeled *politically correct,* which implies that such inclusions are unnecessary or controversial. Simonson and Walker (1988) argue that such efforts represent support for *multi*cultural literacy. In many cases, the criticisms against the infusion of diverse perspectives reflect what Cortes referred to as extreme unum positions. As these ongoing debates continue, teachers and curriculum specialists are faced with the challenge of striking an appropriate balance between the pluribus and unum principles.

Scholars such as Banks and Banks (1989, 1991, 1994), Sleeter and Grant (1994), Tetreault (1987), Gollnick and Chinn (1998), and Garcia (1994) have developed systematic approaches for analyzing curriculum materials and teaching practices to ascertain the extent to which people of color, women, people from various socioeconomic levels, and people with special needs are included. Their analyses go beyond notions of political correctness by providing teachers with frameworks for determining whether the inclusion of multiple perspectives is superficial or tied to historical contexts and social action in a more integrated fashion. These efforts have come under the rubric of *multicultural education,* a term that implies the need for changing traditional curriculum materials and instructional practices. In defining the nature of multicultural education, Banks (1989) claims that it is an ongoing process whose goals will never be fully realized, so "we should work continually to increase educational equality for all students" (p. 3).

Grelle and Metzger (1996) discuss the importance of having a balanced perspective that will move us beyond a *socialization versus multiculturalism* debate to a position that embraces both commitment and critique. They cite Arthur Schlesinger as a liberal who accuses multiculturalism of "sowing seeds of division between

Americans by concentrating too much on what divides them rather than on what unites them" (Grelle & Metzger, 1996, p. 151). Further criticism of multiculturalism comes from William Bennett, who accuses multiculturalism of "undermining the task of citizenship education by concentrating too much on the shortcomings rather than the accomplishments of traditional American values, virtues, and institutions" (p. 151). Grelle and Metzger suggest that despite these arguments, more valid sources for social devisiveness can be found in "the inequitable distribution of power and resources along the lines of class, race, gender, and ethnicity that multiculturalism has in part sought to address" (p. 151). They view multiculturalism as part of a broader movement that seeks to address these inequities.

Teaching in a multicultural classroom requires sensitivity to cultural differences and similarities and is particularly challenging for new teachers who have not lived in multicultural environments (Fuchs, Fuchs, Mathes, & Simmons, 1997; Swearingen, 1996; Wade, 1998). Student-to-student relationships and adult-to-student relationships in school settings are very crucial factors in understanding teacher-student expectations for academic achievement and personal efficacy. The article "Dos and Don'ts for Teachers in Multicultural Settings" (Dawson, 1974) illustrates the sentiment that seventies' educators hoped would guide *classroom behaviors.* More than twenty years later, these principles in Table 6.1 still provide useful guidelines.

TABLE 6.1

Dos and Don'ts for Teachers in Multicultural Settings

Dos	Don'ts
Do use the same scientific approach to gain background information on the culture of multiethnic groups as you would to tackle a complicated course in science, mathematics, or any subject area in which you might be deficient.	Don't rely on elementary school textbooks, teachers' guides, and brief essays to become informed on minorities. Research and resources will be needed.
Do engage in systematic study of the disciplines that provide insight into the cultural heritage, political struggle, contributions, and present-day problems of minority groups.	Don't use ignorance as an excuse for not having any insight into the problems and culture of Blacks, Chicanos, Native Americans, Puerto Ricans, Asian-Americans, and other minorities.
Do try to develop sincere personal relationships with minorities. *You can't teach strangers!* Don't give up because *one* Black or other minority person rejects your efforts. All groups have sincere individuals who welcome honest, warm relationships with members of another race. Seek out those who will accept or tolerate you. This coping skill is one that minorities have always used.	Don't rely on the "expert" judgment of *one minority person* for the answer to all the complicated racial and social problems of his/her people. For example, Blacks, Mexicans, Indians, and Puerto Ricans hold various political views on all issues.
Do recognize that there are often more differences within a group than between two groups. If we recognize diversity among races, we must also recognize diversity within groups.	Don't be fooled by popular slogans and propaganda intended to raise the national consciousness of an oppressed people.

(Continued)

TABLE 6.1 (Continued)

Dos and Don'ts for Teachers in Multicultural Settings

Dos	Don'ts
Do remember that there are many ways to gain insight into a group. Visit their churches, homes, communities; read widely and listen to various segments of the group.	Don't get carried away with the "save the world concept." Most minorities have their own savior.
Do remember that no one approach and no one answer will assist you in meeting the educational needs of all children in a multicultural society.	Don't be afraid to learn from those who are more familiar with the mores and cultures than you.
Do select instructional materials that are accurate and free of stereotypes.	Don't assume that you have all the answers for solving the other person's problems. It is almost impossible for an outsider to be an expert on the culture of another group.
Do remember that there is a positive relationship between teacher expectation and academic progress.	Don't assume that all minority group children are culturally deprived.
Do provide an opportunity for minority group boys and girls and children from the mainstream to interact in a positive intellectual setting on a continuous basis.	Don't develop a fatalistic attitude about the progress of minority group pupils.
Do use a variety of materials and especially those that utilize positive, true-to-life experiences.	Don't resegregate pupils through tracking and ability grouping gimmicks.
Do provide some structure and direction to children who have unstructured lives, primarily children of the poor.	Don't give up when minority group pupils seem to hate school.
Do expose all children to a wide variety of literature as a part of your cultural sensitivity program.	Don't assume that minorities are the only pupils who should have multicultural instructional materials. Children in the mainstream can be culturally deprived in terms of their knowledge and understanding of other people and their own heritage.
*Do remember that in spite of the fact that ethnic groups often share many common problems, their specific needs are diverse.	Don't go around asking parents and children personal questions in the name of research. Why must they divulge their suffering? It is obvious.
*Do utilize the rich resources within your own classroom among various cultural groups.	Don't get hung up on grade designation when sharing literature that provides insight into the cultural heritage of a people.
Do remember that human understanding is a lifetime endeavor. You must continue to study and provide meaningful experiences for your pupils.	*Don't try to be cool by using the vernacular of a particular racial group.
*Do remember to be honest with yourself. If you can't adjust to children from multicultural homes, get out of the classroom.	Don't make minority children feel ashamed of their language, dress, or traditions.

*Helpful suggestions of "Dos and Don'ts" were made by Delores Fitzgerald and Robin Kovats of St. Paul the Apostle School and Raven Oas Burvard of Columbia School, both in New York City.

SOURCE: Dawson, M. E. (1974). *Are there unwelcome guests in your classroom?* Washington, DC: Association for Childhood Education International.

During the 1970s, educators such as Apple (1979), Freire (1970), and Illich (1971) wrote about the inequities in society and the influence of political power on social relationships. Their theories highlighted the roles of teachers and students as agents of change. Building on the work of these reconceptualists (Ornstein & Hunkins, 1988), particularly Freire, Giroux (1988, 1998) advances the notion of cultural politics. For Giroux (1998), social transformation stems from discourse that can arise "from universities, from peasant communities, from workers councils, or from within various social movements. . . . What brings them together is a mutual respect forged in criticism and the need to struggle against all forms of domination" (p. 52).

✦ PLURALISM AND UNITY IN CURRICULUM AND INSTRUCTION

Pluralism and unity in curriculum and instruction refers to the challenges faced by classroom teachers as they attempt to treat each student as an individual, yet create a sense of acceptance and belonging for the class as a whole. This requires the diplomatic skills of members of the United Nations! Elementary students want and need to feel accepted and treated equally in terms of their right to an education. At the same time, teachers recognize that differences based on religion, gender, ethnicity, race, exceptionalities, language, abilities, and class require adapting curriculum and instruction. This section discusses curriculum reform efforts in selected areas, primarily ethnicity, gender, class, and exceptionalities.

Analyses of Ethnicity and Curricular Reform

James Banks (1988) suggests that multicultural *curriculum* reform since the 1960s can be characterized by four different approaches: the contributions approach, the ethnic additive approach, the transformation approach, and the decision-making/social action approach.

Contributions Approach

In the *contributions approach,* ethnic heroes, holidays, and discrete cultural elements are infused into the mainstream curriculum. Although easy to do, the contributions approach is limited because it remains an "appendage to the main story of the development of the nation and to the core curriculum in the language arts, the social studies, the arts, and to other subject areas" (Banks, 1988, p. 1). Another weakness of the contributions approach according to Banks is that it often trivializes "ethnic cultures, the study of their strange and exotic characteristics, and the reinforcement of stereotypes and misconceptions" (p. 1).

Additive Approach

The *additive approach* is similar to the contributions approach in that the mainstream curriculum remains intact, and books, activities, or special thematic units are typically added without substantive curricular changes.

© Will Hart/PhotoEdit

Transformation Approach

The *transformation approach* changes the underlying assumptions of the curriculum by infusing various perspectives from ethnic groups in such a way that the complexity of U.S. society is addressed. Banks suggests that when studying the American Revolution, for example, the ideas of Anglo Revolutionaries, Anglo Loyalists, Afro-Americans, Indians, and the British should be represented. In the transformation approach the emphasis is on "how the common U.S. culture and society emerged from a complex synthesis and interaction of the diverse cultural elements that originated within the various cultural, racial, ethnic, and religious groups that make up American society" (Banks, 1988, p. 2).

Decision-Making/Social Action Approach

The *decision-making/social action approach* builds on the transformation approach by encouraging students to take action and make decisions about a particular issue. For example, a real issue such as prejudice and discrimination in the school is a topic that students discuss and come up with a plan of action for combatting its presence. The underlying goal of the decision-making/social action approach is to empower students and give them a sense of political efficacy. Banks points out that teachers who are seeking to make their curricula more multicultural gradually incorporate the transformation and social action approaches. Examining key Supreme Court decisions on affirmative action and assessing or taking action to influence school policy is one way in which students can have an impact on their community. Eden and Ryan (1999) report the approaches taken by several educational institutions.

In *Multiethnic Education: Theory and Practice,* Banks (1994) expands on his four analyses of curriculum reform by incorporating more recent research and recasting the four approaches into five dimensions: *content integration, knowledge construction, prejudice reduction, equitable pedagogy,* and *empowering school culture and social structure.* Ogbu (1990, 1991, 1994) also has investigated the interaction between school culture and ethnic identity and performance. His studies advance our understanding of the differential impact that schooling has on various ethnic groups as well as the differential ways in which members of ethnic groups respond to school culture. Ogbu's work encourages teachers to scrutinize their perceptions of minorities more closely; for example, using a comparative perspective to investigate further the legacy of immigrant versus involuntary minorities. Building on Ogbu's research, O'Connor (1997) found that the attitudes and perceptions of subordinate populations "are more than a reflex of their historical and social positioning" (p. 624). O'Connor demonstrates that selected African-Americans in her study not only had insightful recognition of their collective heritage as an oppressed minority, and skepticism regarding the chances for individual upward mobility, but also may have been disposed toward taking political action as a result of their insights.

The resistance of minorities toward those exercising various forms of power over them has taken many forms throughout American history. For an example of how one fifth-grade textbook addresses the rebellious ways in which African-Americans fought for freedom and maintained personal dignity in the context of oppression, see page 172.

For inspirational stories of youth ranging in age from 9 to adulthood who dared to make a difference in their communities, see *It's Our World, Too! Stories of Young People Who Are Making a Difference* (Hoose, 1993). These nonfictional accounts report the strength of character among young people as they *take a stand* (against racism, sexism, and inner city crime); *reach out to others* (including the homeless, elderly, and those who have been victims of car accidents); *heal the earth* (preserving rainforest land, protecting dolphins); and *create a safer future* (building a statue for peace in the birthplace of the atom bomb, using autobiography of a Cambodian taken from his family to build hope for other refugees). Hoose follows these biographical sketches with step-by-step procedures written *to* children, encouraging them to take action in their schools and communities.

Analyses of Gender and Curricular Reform

Tetreault (1987) developed a system for analyzing ways in which women and gender issues are presented in the social studies curriculum. Tetreault has applied these *phases* to textbooks and other curriculum materials, concluding that there is a long way to go to improve the quality of curriculum materials. One of the observations she has made is that curriculum materials may include more pictures of women but that the pictures are seldom supported with substantive information. The histories typically remain male defined. Following is a condensed version of Tetreault's phases: male-defined history, contribution history, bifocal history, histories of women, and histories of gender.

STRUGGLING AGAINST SLAVERY

Most enslaved workers were brought from the present-day countries of Ghana and Nigeria in West Africa. They spoke different languages and had different cultures. The major ethnic groups from Nigeria were the Hausa (HOW sah) and the Yoruba (YOH ru bah). The Ashanti (uh SHAHN tee) and the Fante (FAHN tee) came from Ghana.

To keep them from communicating with each other, slave traders and slave owners separated captives who spoke the same language. As Captain William Smith wrote in 1744, "By having some of every sort on board, there will be no more likelihood of their succeeding in a plot." Still, enslaved people found ways to communicate with each other. In fact, some African words that they used, such as *banana* and *boss*, became part of the English language.

Rebellion

Captives showed their anger toward the slave owner in different ways. Many enslaved people refused to work. "They often die before they can be conquer'd *[forced to work]*," wrote one Englishman visiting the colonies.

Other captives worked slowly or purposely broke tools. Still others escaped. Escaping captives were hunted down. When caught, they were usually beaten, whipped, and sometimes killed. Even so, many kept trying to escape.

One thing the planters feared most was rebellion. When they got the chance, some captives were willing to die for their freedom. In many rebellions enslaved people organized raids, burned houses, and killed people. In the Stono Rebellion of 1739, a captive named Cato led a rebellion in which 30 colonists of South Carolina were killed. To stop the rebellions the planters strengthened the slave codes.

Stratford Hall (below left) in Virginia was built with the help of enslaved African workers. Most enslaved Africans had little time to create artwork, such as this sculpture from the eighteenth century (below).

240

Textbooks can help students understand minorities' acts of resistance against oppression.

SOURCE: From "Struggling Against Slavery," Adventures in Time and Place, Grade 5: United States, Pupil Edition. New York: McGraw-Hill School Division, 2001. Reproduced by permission of the McGraw-Hill Companies.

Male-Defined History

The absence of women is not noted. There is no consciousness that the male expe-rience is a "particular knowledge" selected from a wider universe of possible knowl-edge and experience. It is valued, emphasized, and viewed as the knowledge most worth having.

Contribution History

Women are added into history, but the content and notions of historical significance are not challenged. There is a search for missing women according to a male norm of greatness, excellence, or humanness. Women are considered as exceptional, deviant, or "other."

Bifocal History

Human experience is conceptualized primarily in dualist categories: male and fe-male; private and public; agency and communion. Efforts to include women lead to the insight that the traditional content, structure, and methodology of the disciplines are more appropriate to the male experience.

Histories of Women

A pluralistic conception of women emerges that acknowledges diversity and recog-nizes that variables other than gender shape women's lives—for example, race, eth-nicity, and social class. Women's experience is analyzed within the social, cultural, historical, political, and economic contexts.

Histories of Gender

A multifocal, relational, gender-balanced perspective is sought that weaves together women's and men's experiences into multilayered composites of human experience. At this stage, scholars are conscious of particularity, while at the same time identify-ing common denominators of experience. They must begin to define what binds to-gether and what separates the various segments of humanity.

In addition to Tetreault's phases for analyzing curriculum, McIntosh (1983) identified five similar phases. There are striking similarities between the two, despite the reverse order of their appearance in the journal *Social Education.* Tetreault's work appeared in 1987; McIntosh's work was cited in 1997 (Crocco, 1997). McIntosh's five phases of curricular revision include: womanless history; woman in history; woman as problem, anomaly, or absence; woman as history; and history redefined to include us all. Crocco (1997) illustrates how the categories developed by McIntosh can be applied to various historical periods. In addition, she provides useful refer-ences for teachers and students at all levels.

The American Association of University Women (AAUW) compiled data from various studies that assessed differential achievement patterns in boys and girls. Their reports *How Schools Shortchange Girls* (AAUW, 1992) and *Girls in the Middle* (1996) provide valuable information for understanding the impact of curriculum content and interpersonal dynamics on achievement. For example, a

National Assessment of Educational Progress (NAEP) survey revealed that the performance of boys and girls varied according to the type of reading exercise:

> Boys did as well as girls on the expository passages and were most disadvantaged relative to girls in the literary passages. This is consistent with the finding that boys read more nonfiction than girls, and girls read more fiction than boys. This is also consistent with the finding that boys do slightly better than girls on other NAEP tests in subjects requiring good skills in expository reading and writing: civics, history, and geography. . . . If, as some suggest, boys regard fiction as more "feminine," any advantage girls experience relative to boys in the NAEP may reflect culturally defined biases against boys' reading certain kinds of material. (AAUW, 1992, p. 23)

These findings suggest that social studies teachers should be sensitive to the kinds of reading material they present. If civics, history, and geography are emphasized through expository reading with minor attention to historical fiction and other kinds of literature, then female students may be somewhat at a disadvantage in terms of interest and motivation. Conversely, an overemphasis on fiction may adversely affect boys. This is assuming that these differences will in fact exist among your students, and this is a big assumption. Just as the gap has narrowed in mathematics achievement levels as girls have been encouraged to take higher levels of math, so too have the gaps in verbal skills. Researchers who compared earlier studies of verbal abilities with more recent research concluded that there are no differences "in American culture, in the standard ways that verbal ability" is measured (AAUW, 1992, p. 22).

There are many positive examples of ways in which educators have developed lessons to erase the absence of women in social studies curricula. In *The Finding a Way Project* teachers are taught creative and innovative strategies for encouraging girls of all racial and ethnic backgrounds in the area of geography (Cruz & Prorok, 1997). Categories of work studied in relation to rural and urban women in Kenya include: productive work, reproductive work, support networks, kin work, and status-enhancing work. Levstik (1997) discusses perspectival history as another way to represent the voices of female historical figures. Perspectival history removes the protection of an *official story* and "suggests that children learn to challenge assumptions, ask sometimes uncomfortable questions, demand support for assertions, and develop supportable interpretations of the past" (Levstik, 1997, p. 50). Some textbooks have made great progress in including the roles and accomplishments of women in their accounts of history, considering the absence of women in earlier editions. See, for example, the excerpt from McGraw-Hill's fifth-grade text featured on page 175.

Additional sources for studying women in various ethnic, racial, class, religious, and international groups are listed in the Reference section at the end of this chapter (Crocco, 1995; Labbo, 1997; Pflepsen & Vokes, 1996; Reese, 1996). In addition, for inspiration regarding "engaged pedagogy," consult Bell Hooks (1998), who discusses her passion as a feminist scholar and teacher in *Ecstasy: Teaching and Learning Without Limits.* Hooks views critical thinking as the primary element that brings about change and encourages teachers to challenge the status quo despite the negative consequences that may ensue.

PATRIOTS FIGHT IN THE COLONIES

Patriots like George Rogers Clark and John Paul Jones led the Americans to victories over the British. Other men and women also played important roles in the fight for independence.

Benedict Arnold Turns Traitor

As a Patriot commander, Benedict Arnold had helped the Americans win at Fort Ticonderoga and Saratoga. In 1778, however, Arnold married a woman from a Loyalist family. He lived a life of luxury and was soon in debt.

In 1780 Washington gave Arnold command of West Point, a key fort on New York's Hudson River. In exchange for money, Arnold planned to tell the British about West Point's defenses. When the Americans found out, Arnold escaped and became an officer in the British army. Many British soldiers,

Patriot women who fought the British included Mary Ludwig Hays (left), Nancy Hart (top), and Deborah Sampson (above), who is disguised as a man.

however, never fully trusted him. Today, a "Benedict Arnold" has come to mean a traitor to one's country.

Supporting the Soldiers

Fortunately there were many Americans who helped the Continental Army. Mary Ludwig Hays went with her husband to the battlefield. Because she brought pitchers of water to the thirsty soldiers during battles, she was called "Molly Pitcher." She also helped load cannons and even took up her husband's gun when he was wounded.

Some women like Deborah Sampson disguised themselves as men and fought

330

Textbooks are doing a much better job of covering the accomplishments and roles of women in history.

SOURCE: From "Patriots Fight in the Colonies," Adventures in Time and Place, Grade 5: United States, Pupil Edition. New York: McGraw-Hill School Division, 2001. Reproduced by permission of the McGraw-Hill Companies.

Analyses of Class and Curricular Reform

Gollnick and Chinn (1998) and Stronge (1992) have identified special needs of children in lower socioeconomic levels and homeless children. These children typically have no spokespersons who are organized politically to effect change. Following is a summary of some of the issues that educators can address for curriculum reform and interpersonal responsiveness (Gollnick & Chinn, 1994, pp. 69–70):

1. The curriculum and textbooks focus on the values and experiences of a middle-class society. They highlight the heroes of our capitalist system and emphasize the importance of developing the skills to earn an income to enable students to soon own the home, the car, and the furniture and appliances that have become the symbols of middle-class living.
2. The curriculum often ignores the history and heroes of the labor struggle in this country.
3. The inequities based on the income and wealth of one's family are usually neither described nor discussed.
4. The knowledge and skills that students from dissimilar socioeconomic levels learn to survive in their community environments are not valued by teachers and a system with a middle-class orientation.
5. When studying historical or current events, teachers should examine the event from the perspective of those in poverty as well as from the perspective of our country's leaders.
6. Instruction should show that not all persons share equally in material things in this country, but that all persons have potential to be developed.
7. Teachers should be attentive to health and hygienic needs of the poor, ensuring that resources are available so that they are not rejected by peers.

SOURCE: Multicultural Education in a Pluralistic Society by Gollnick, Chinn, © 1994. Adapted by permission of Prentice-Hall, Inc. Upper Saddle River, NJ.

The humanities provide sensitive ways to deal with some of these issues with young people. Examining art is a stimulating and subtle way to direct student attention to material culture and its relationship to people's socioeconomic levels. Lessons that emphasize "language and communication skills, personal biographies, art, poetry, dance, drama, literature, psychology, ethics, religion, and other aesthetic, humanistic, and spiritual subject matter comprise a good part of the reconstructionist curriculum" (Ornstein & Hunkins, 1988, p. 44). Children's literature offers human interest stories. For example, selections such as *Ellis Island: New Hope in a New Land* (Jacobs, 1990), *Children of the Dust Bowl: The True Story of the School at Weedpatch Camp* (Stanley, 1992), *The Whispering Cloth: A Refugee's Story* (Shea, 1995), *Appalachia: The Voices of Sleeping Birds* (Rylant, 1991), *Brother Can You Spare a Dime? The Great Depression 1929–1933* (Meltzer, 1969), and *If You Traveled on the Underground Railroad* (Levine, 1988) are books that reveal the human quest for a better life. Additional books about homelessness, child laborers, the role of working-class immigrants in economic development, diversity more generally, and the use of these books in social studies classrooms can be found in reviews by Alter (1995), Hoffbauer and Prenn (1996), Pallante and Shively (1999), and Lamme (1998).

© Topham/The Image Works

Addressing the immediate needs of students in the classroom who may lack basic resources also requires sensitivity to feelings of pride and social awareness. A teacher in one of my classes shared a very humane approach to providing food and clothing to children in need. She had a box that was filled with all kinds of objects—toys, books, nutritious snacks, and clothing. The opportunity to select objects from the box was based on such performances as completing work and demonstrating appropriate behavior. She noted that the children who needed the food and clothing often selected those items without feeling any stigma since the decision was entirely their choice.

Analyses of Special Needs and Curricular Reform

Determining ways to provide services for students with special needs requires a great deal of sensitivity juxtaposed with proactive efforts. After reviewing a series of studies conducted with students who had a variety of exceptionalities, Fuchs et al. (1997) suggest "that many teachers create homogeneity by eliminating difficult-to-teach students from consciousness" (p. 177). Their study spotlights the need to vary instruction based on various categories of students: learning disabled, average achieving, high achieving, gifted, talented, and low performing (regardless of ability levels). This requires grouping at designated times during the school day or week. The advantages of various grouping strategies along with the latest efforts for inclusion strategies is reviewed in this section.

Heward and Orlansky (2000) point out that educators have debated the merits of labeling, arguing on the one hand that labels are important for obtaining special services for exceptional students. Others maintain that labels result in the exclusion of minorities and exceptional students from the mainstream of educational opportunity. Following is a listing of the pros and cons of labeling that Heward and Orlansky (2000) designed primarily for students with exceptionalities. However, with modifications, the logic in their explanations is applicable to other groups.

Possible Advantages of Labeling

1. Categories can relate diagnosis to specific treatment.
2. Labeling may lead to a protective response in which nonlabeled children accept certain behaviors of their handicapped [or other exceptionalities] peers more fully than they would accept those same behaviors in normal children.
3. Labeling helps professionals communicate with one another and to classify and assess research findings.
4. Funding of special education [and gifted] programs is often based on specific categories of exceptionality.
5. Labels allow special-interest groups to promote specific programs and to spur legislative action.
6. Labeling helps make the special needs of exceptional children more visible in the public eye. (Heward & Orlansky, 2000, p. 13)

Possible Disadvantages of Labeling

1. Labels usually focus on negative aspects of the child, causing others to think about the child only in terms of inadequacies or defects. [Converse true for gifted/high achievers]
2. Labels may cause other people to react to and hold low expectations of a child based on the label, resulting in a self-fulfilling prophecy. [Gifted students often feel they need to excel at everything]
3. Labels that describe a child's performance deficit often mistakenly acquire the role of explanatory constructs (e.g., "Sherry acts that way because she is emotionally disturbed.").
4. Labels used to classify children in special education emphasize that learning problems are primarily the result of something wrong within the child, thereby reducing the likelihood of examining instructional variables as the cause of performance deficits.
5. A label may help cause a child to develop a poor self-concept.
6. Labels may lead peers to reject or ridicule the labeled child.
7. Labels have a certain permanence about them. Once labeled as *retarded* or *learning disabled,* a child has difficulty ever achieving the status of being just like the other kids.
8. Labels often provide a basis for keeping students out of the regular classroom.
9. A disproportionate number of students from culturally diverse groups have been inaccurately labeled *handicapped.*
10. The classification of exceptional children requires the expenditure of much professional and student time that could be better spent in planning and delivering instruction. (Heward & Orlansky, 2000, pp. 13–14)

SOURCE: Exceptional Children: An Introduction to Special Education, Sixth Edition. By Heward, William L. © 2000. Reprinted by permission of Prentice-Hall, Inc., Upper Saddle River, NJ.

As a result of the inclusion movement in special education, more than 70 percent of students with learning disabilities, mild mental handicaps, and behavior disorders are educated in the general education setting. The impetus for this movement came from Public Law 94-142, passed in 1975, mandating that students with disabilities be provided services in the least restrictive environment. Determining the least restrictive environment requires an understanding of the various service alternatives, including instruction through the general classroom, a consultant, an itinerant teacher, resource room, special class, special day school, or residential school (Mercer, 1997). According to Walther-Thomas, Korinek, McLaughlin, and Williams (2000), regular and special education teachers who want to see their students succeed have common goals; these aims include the development of caring relationships, a sense of belonging, and holistic and flexible learning opportunities. In *Collaboration for Inclusive Education,* Walther-Thomas et al. provide helpful suggestions to classroom practitioners who would like to develop programs for students with disabilities and other at-risk students. They present strategies for assistance teaming, collaborative consultation, and coteaching as well as student-based structures such as peer tutoring and cooperative learning to enhance academic and social progress.

Exceptionalities require curriculum differentiation for activities common in a social studies classroom. McCoy (1998) and Mercer (1997) offer helpful suggestions to teachers who recognize the need to make adaptations in reading material, projects, and writing assignments for students with learning problems. With traditional emphasis on the text in many classrooms, it is important to follow effective reading strategies such as activating prior knowledge, setting a purpose for reading, discussing title and subheadings, analyzing pictures, and asking questions as advance organizers. For projects, McCoy suggests providing checklists as a guide to organize task for completion, because a project that unfolds at varying rates can seem overwhelming by the open nature of the tasks. For writing assignments McCoy suggests that key vocabulary terms be listed in a prominent place in the classroom so that children will have a ready reference point for correct spelling.

The passage of PL 94-142 and the resulting funds appropriated for its implementation raised awareness about the importance of responding to individual needs of learners characterized by exceptionalities. VanTassel-Baska (1994) illustrates the opportunities for meeting the needs of gifted students in *Comprehensive Curriculum for Gifted Learners.* In a chapter devoted to social studies curriculum for the gifted, VanTassel-Baska and Feldhusen (1994) offer the following as key social studies goals for gifted programs:

1. To develop critical thought and the spirit of inquiry
2. To understand and develop a world cultures view
3. To appreciate the interrelationship of social science disciplines and institutions
4. To gain knowledge of significant developments in human history and the social systems of which they are a part
5. To develop research, discussion, and thinking skills
6. To develop skill in writing and project activities in the social studies domain (p. 168)

VanTassel-Baska suggests that the most practical approach for meeting the needs of gifted students may be through the development of specialized units of study for gifted students to pursue within the context of the regular classroom or with more explicit guidance from a resource teacher. However, VanTassel-Baska (1994) encourages more flexible grouping strategies, maintaining that "it would be preferable for the gifted to have an instructional grouping in the social studies areas throughout the elementary grades" (p. 185).

The case study of Diane Bradford (VanTassel-Baska, 1992) in Chapter 7 will offer additional guidance for curriculum adaptations when working with students with exceptionalities. Diane is both learning disabled and gifted, presenting many challenges for teachers, peers, and family members. For additional case studies consult *Exceptional Lives: Special Education in Today's Schools* (Turnbull, Turnbull, Shank, & Leal, 1999) and Negron and Ricklin (1996), who tie their case study approach to social studies. Curtis (1991) also discusses instructional approaches for students at risk and with disabilities. The role of the school in either perpetuating stereotypes or opening the doors to many opportunities based on an appreciation for diversity is one that cannot be underestimated. To fully appreciate the importance of a multicultural classroom, it is important to appreciate the diversity of the student population and how students construct their own identities given the many options presented to them through culture. The following case study personalizes the discussion of cultural learning styles that will follow.

✦ CASE STUDY: ANTHONY E. WRIGHT

Bruner (1990) discusses the importance of individuals constructing their own identities and views of the world in *Acts of Meaning*. He argues that classical sociological approaches that define groups on the basis of social class, roles, and so on, need to be balanced by the social, political, and psychological distinctions that people make in their daily lives. Rosenberg (1979) supports this notion by maintaining that "one cannot assume a direct conversion of social identity evaluation into self-evaluation . . . [but] one can assume that people *respond* in various ways to the social evaluation of their identity elements" (p. 13). In other words, when a teacher is faced with a group of students for the first time, names and physical characteristics may generate certain cultural assumptions and stereotypes. But as Rosenberg points out, these assumptions may be all too typical reactions to the traditional ways in which our culture has defined groups. The goal for the teacher then becomes getting beyond these social stereotypes and finding out how each student constructs his or her own identity based on many contexts of social interaction, including the classroom.

The following case illustration demonstrates the individual challenge of constructing an identity in a society that places a great deal of emphasis on ethnic classifications. While attending a teacher's institute conducted by the staff of Facing History and Ourselves (Strom & Parsons, 1982) the case illustration was distributed as a catalyst for discussing the danger of labels. As you read "Little Boxes," an essay addressing the difficulties in identifying simple ethnic characteristics, think about your own cultural values and stereotypes. Do the incidences described characterize some of your experiences?

LITTLE BOXES

Racial/Ethnic Definitions, U.S. Government

American Indian or Alaskan Native: A person having origins in any of the original
people of North America, and who maintains cultural identification through tribal
affiliation or community recognition.

Asian or Pacific Islander: A person having origins in any of the original peoples of the
Far East, Southeast Asia, the Indian subcontinent, or the Pacific Islands. This area
includes, for example, China, India, Japan, Korea, the Philippine Islands, Samoa,
and Vietnam.

Black Non-Hispanic: A person having origins in any of the Black racial groups of
Africa (except those of Hispanic origin).

Hispanic: A person of Mexican, Puerto Rican, Cuban, Central or South American, or
other Spanish culture or origin, regardless of race.

White Non-Hispanic: A person having origins in any of the original peoples of Europe,
North Africa, or in the Middle East.

Little Boxes: "How would you describe yourself? (please check one)." . . . Little boxes
and circles [on forms and surveys] bring up an issue for me that threatens my identity. Who am
I? Unlike many others, I cannot answer that question easily when it comes to ethnicity. My
mother is Hispanic (for those who consider South American as Hispanic) with an Asian father
and my father is white with English and Irish roots. What does that make me? My identity already gets lost when my mother becomes a "Latino" instead of an "Ecuadorean." The cultures
of Puerto Rico and Argentina are distinct, even though they are both "Hispanic." The same applies to White, Asian, Native American, or Black, all vague terms trying to classify cultures
that have sometimes greater disparities inside the classification than with other cultures. Yet I
can't even be classified by these excessively broad terms.

My classification problem doesn't stop with my ethnicity. My father is a blue-collar
worker, yet the technical work he does is much more than manual labor. My family, through
our sweat, brains, and savings, have managed to live comfortably. We no longer can really be
classified as poor or lower class, but we really aren't middle class. Also, in my childhood my
parents became disillusioned with the Catholic religion and stopped going to church. They
gave me the option of going or not, but I was lazy and opted to stay in bed late on Sunday morn-
ings. Right now I don't even know if I am agnostic, atheist, or something else, like transcen-
dentalist. I just don't fit into categories nicely.

My biggest conflict of identity comes from another source: education. In the seventh grade,
I was placed in a prep school from P.S. 61. The only similarity between the two institutions is that
they are both in the Bronx, yet one is a block away from Charlotte Street, a nationally known symbol of urban decay, while the other is in one of the wealthiest sections of New York City. Prep for
Prep, a program for disadvantaged students that starts in the fifth grade, worked with me for four-
teen months, bringing me up to the private school level academically and preparing me socially,
but still, the transition was rough. Even in my senior year, I felt like I really did not fit in with the
prep school culture. Yet I am totally separated from my neighborhood. My home happens to be
situated there, and I might go to the corner bodega for milk and bananas, or walk to the subway
station, but that is the extent of my contact with my neighborhood. I regret this, but when more
than half the teenagers are high school dropouts, and drugs are becoming a major industry there,
there is no place for me. Prep for Prep was where I would "hang out" if not at my high school; it

took the place of my neighborhood and has been a valuable cushion. At high school, I was separate from the mainstream majority, but still an inextricable part of it, and so I worked there and put my effort into making it a better place.

For a while, I desperately wanted to fit into a category in order to be accepted. Everywhere I went I felt out of place. When I go into the neighborhood restaurant to ask for "arroz y pollo," my awkward Spanish and gringo accent makes the lady at the counter go in the back for someone who knows English, even though I think I know enough Spanish to survive a conversation. When I was little, and had short straight black hair, I appeared to be one of the few Asians in my school and was tagged with the stereotype. I went to Ecuador to visit relatives, and they could not agree about whether I was Latino or gringo. When the little boxes appeared on the Achievements, I marked Hispanic even though I had doubts on the subject. At first sight, I can pass as white, and my last name will assure that I will not be persecuted as someone who is dark and has "Rodriguez" as his last name. I chose Hispanic because I most identified with it, because of my Puerto Rican neighborhood that I grew up in, and my mother; putting just "Hispanic," "White," or "Asian," I felt as if I was neglecting a very essential side of me, and lying in the process. I now put "Other" in those little boxes, and when possible indicate exactly what I am.

I realize now the problem is not with me but with the identification system. The words "Black," "White," "Hispanic," "Asian," and "Native American" describe more than one would expect. They describe genealogy, appearance, and culture, all very distinct things, which most people associate as one; but there exists many exceptions, like the person who grows up in the Black inner city and adopts that culture, but is white by birth; or the Puerto Rican immigrant with blue eyes and blond hair. Religion can also obscure definitions, as is the case in Israel recently with the label "Jewish," which can be race, culture, or religion, and the definition of being Jewish by birth. The classifications especially get confused when appearance affects the culture, as with non-White cultures due to discrimination. Defining what is "culture" and the specifics also confuses the issue. For example, it can be argued that almost every American, regardless of race (genealogy), is at least to some degree of the white culture, the "norm" in this country. With more culturally and racially mixed people like myself entering society, these classifications have to be addressed and defined.

My mixture helps me look to issues and ideas from more than one viewpoint, and I like that. Racial, economic, social, and religious topics can be looked upon with a special type of objectivity that I feel is unique. I am not objective: I am subjective with more than one bias, so I can see both sides of an argument between a black militant and white conservative, a tenant and a landlord, or a Protestant and a Catholic. I will usually side with the underdog, but it is necessary to understand opposing viewpoints in order to take a position. This diversity of self that I have, I enjoy, despite the confusion caused by a society so complex that sweeping generalizations are made. I cannot and don't deserve to be generalized or classified, just like anybody else. My background and position have affected me, but I dislike trying to be treated from that information. I am Anthony E. Wright, and the rest of the information about me should come from what I write, what I say and how I act. Nothing else.

SOURCE: The Case of Anthony Wright, 1990. *Point of View.* Amherst College: Amherst, MA.

Anthony's poignant reflections highlight the paradox inherent in social classifications. Although he said, "I chose Hispanic because I most identified with it," others, like the lady in the Spanish restaurant and his Ecuadorian relatives, were doubtful. Based on diverse cultural experiences, some of which were open to choice, Anthony constructed an identity that was truly his own. Given the circumstances into which he was born, his life could have taken many different paths. Today, classrooms are filled with students like Anthony. Their mixed cultural heritage provides them with many opportunities to choose and shape their own identity. Attempting to understand how students perceive themselves and potential opportunities in society is a complex challenge facing teachers, but one of the most important. Encouraging students to tell their own stories is a powerful means of affirming the lives of students and informing others. Egan (1998) is a valuable source for investigating further *Teaching as Story Telling.*

The federal government has been collecting racial data in many forms for more than two hundred years. The first formal standards for racial and ethnic data reporting developed during the 1970s. As the demographic complexity of the United States has continued to increase, individuals have become increasingly frustrated when faced with forms that do not provide adequate ways to reflect their ethnic and racial identity. Since 1993 the Office of Management and Budget (OMB) has been reviewing the "standards for collecting, analyzing, and reporting all government data which depicted racial and ethnic backgrounds" (Davis-VanAtta, Arnold, & Lyddon, 1998). The ongoing efforts surrounding this issue can be reviewed through the OMB website: http://www.whitehouse.gov/WH/EOP/OMB/html/fedreg/Ombdir15.html. The site has a time line of procedures developed since 1974 as well as projections for the year 2003 when all current and new federal data collection and reporting must comply with revised OMB regulations.

It is clear from Anthony's case illustration and the efforts of the OMB that government and civic organizations can influence the manner in which individuals are asked to define themselves. In addition, scholars who have studied cultural diversity provide useful typologies of individual constructions of ethnic identity. Arthur Mann (1979), for example, identifies four groups, each responding differently to cultural heritage. Members of the first group, called "total identifiers," live within their ethnic group and adopt the same customs and traditions of their ancestors. Rabinowitz (1983) suggests that Mexican-Americans are the closest contemporary group that approximates this kind of identity because immigration is a continuing process and their homeland is so close.

"Partial identifiers" still regard ethnic attachment and their cultural heritage as important but not all-inclusive. This group has undergone partial acculturation but keeps primary group contacts, typically family, alive, particularly "with respect to associational, religious, and recreational activities, or with marriage partners" (Mann, 1979, p. 40). Members of the third group, "disaffiliates," choose to deviate from their cultural heritage. They typically form a separate group and establish their own values and traditions. Disaffiliates are not tied by common ancestry, and their numbers tend to increase in relation to the attainment of a college education. The fourth group identified by Mann is called "hybrids," those of mixed ancestry who are unable to identify themselves with a singular heritage. Based on this definition, one wonders if "hybrids" are fast becoming the norm in the United States.

Mann's typology spotlights the complexity involved in classifying a person. His four categories, for example, do not create distinct groups. To illustrate, it is possible to apply three categories to Anthony Wright's identity. Anthony may be considered a "partial identifier" because he keeps alive family contacts with both his father and his mother who both have diverse heritages representing four ethnic groups. Anthony may also be considered a "disaffiliate" because he doesn't belong to a particular religious group and has also stepped out of his family's traditional educational institutions. With his mixed ancestry, Anthony also fits the "hybrid" category. There are many additional bases for operationalizing Mann's labels embedded in Anthony's story.

In my college classes we try to use the labels to see if they give insight into how we identify ourselves. We soon realize that we are not terribly different from Anthony in that in some ways we identify strongly with aspects of our family's cultural heritage but in many other ways we have changed or adapted various beliefs and practices. If time allows, you might try this in your social studies class.

After reviewing the evolution of terms such as cultural pluralism, melting pot, and typologies for ethnic identification, the following quote by Rabinowitz (1983) captures the complexity of multicultural issues that will remain with us into the twenty-first century:

> In the end, a critical matter for debate will be whose responsibility it is to further ethnic identification and what form that identification should take. Is it the job of the family and the ethnic community, or is it the responsibility of the public sector, through its schools, museums, preservation societies, and governments? . . . I think that, in this regard, John Higham's concept of a system of "pluralistic integration" provides some guidelines. Such a system would "uphold the validity of a common culture, to which all individuals have access, while sustaining the efforts of minorities to preserve and enhance their own integrity." The key to such a dual commitment would be the distinction between "nuclei" and "boundaries." Boundaries would be understood to be permeable; ethnic nuclei would be respected as enduring centers of social action. Thus, "Both integration and ethnic cohesion are recognized as worthy goals, which different individuals will accept in different degrees." . . . The problem is that it will not always be self-evident where the nucleus ends and the boundaries begin; but, of course, this gets at the whole issue of American nationality or identity and the rights of minorities. (pp. 41–42)

The issue of American nationality or identity and the rights of minorities is, again, tied to achieving a balance between *pluribus* and *unum*. In school settings, educators have addressed this polarity in a variety of ways. One dilemma is the use of labels based on exceptionalities, whether these exceptionalities refer to gender, race, class, or learning needs. The section that follows represents the efforts of educators to make generalizations about groups of students. As you read their analyses, think critically about their usefulness in working with the wide range of diversity that characterizes many of today's classrooms.

✦ CULTURAL LEARNING STYLES

Being alert to individual identities helps to prevent stereotyping. Yet as we saw in the dos and don'ts in multicultural settings (refer back to Table 6.1), there is value in understanding intergroup differences and similarities based on cultural backgrounds. Such knowledge can lead to what Banks refers to as *equitable pedagogy,* the modification of teaching to ensure the needs of diverse students. To instill a commitment to academic achievement, a teacher "must affirm those behaviors needed to demonstrate achievement in the larger academic community, while simultaneously understanding the cultural- and learning-style diversity that the minority [or diverse] student brings to the learning environment" (Howard, 1987, p. 13). We will now turn to some of the generalizations that have emerged regarding cultural- and learning-style diversity. I use the term *generalizations* loosely because the empirical base that supports these generalizations is in its formative stages.

Examine Table 6.2, which presents Halverson's (1979) cultural learning styles for child-adult relations, child-child relations, and cognitive styles for the following groups—Mexican-Americans, traditional females, Native Americans, blacks, and whites. Granted, we could immediately argue about the categories themselves, but Halverson is making an attempt to understand cultural patterns. As you examine the table, keep in mind the following. First, the table addresses the frequently raised question, "How can I relate to the cultural needs of all my students?" Second, remember that more differences occur within a group than between groups. And finally, more research in classroom situations is needed to substantiate the claims that follow. Also, ask yourself, "Do these generalizations add to my understanding of different cultural groups, or do they increase my stereotypes of different cultural groups?"

The generalizations cited by Halverson provide a variety of ways to attempt to explain cultural differences. However, as you can see there is uneven treatment even in Halverson's attempt to cross ethnicity and class. For example, upper-class whites in urban settings are not compared with upper-class blacks in urban settings, and so on with other classes and ethnic groups. Returning to the sentiment advanced by Anthony in "Little Boxes," it is erroneous to make assumptions about cultural and learning styles based on someone's physical appearance or surname. For who is to know whether a student may fit more of a "hybrid" orientation according to Mann (or a "hybrid" about certain beliefs or practices but a "total identifier" about others). To ensure that many learning styles are addressed without pigeonholing specific students, a teacher should plan social studies lessons that cater to many kinds of learning. In so doing, students will identify with certain approaches while being challenged to learn different cultural orientations and world views.

The Internet is helpful to teachers and administrators who address multicultural issues in the classroom and school community. Multicultural Pavilion (http://curry.edschool.Virginia.edu/go/multicultural/) is one site that can be reached through Education World (http://www.education-world.com/awards/past/r0897-14.shtml). The site includes teaching activities, archives, book reviews, research organizations, and an online discussion forum.

The Clearinghouse for Multicultural/Bilingual Education is another useful source, located at http://www.weber.edu/mbe/htmls/mbe.html. It includes a variety of biographical information about women, people from a variety of ethnic groups, study books in Spanish for children and adolescents, and grant competitions to mention a few listings. (See more information in the "Internet Links" section.) Tiedt and Tiedt (1990) offer additional ideas in *Multicultural Teaching: A Handbook of Activities, Information, and Resources.* Another helpful source is *American History Through Multicultural Literature* (Edwards, 1995).

Just as there are many cultural backgrounds to consider when designing curriculum, a teacher should also be aware of the idea of multiple styles of learning. Learning styles will be discussed in more detail in Chapter 7. The ones popularized by Howard Gardner (1983, 1999) are applied in the curriculum strategies section later in this chapter; they include the following multiple intelligences: linguistic, musical, logical-mathematical, spatial, bodily kinesthetic, intrapersonal, interpersonal, and naturalistic. Gardner (1999) is working on a ninth intelligence, which he refers to as

TABLE 6.2

Cultural Learning Styles

Questions About Values, Beliefs, and Behavior	Selected Cultural Patterns of Racial/Ethnic and Sex Groups	Suggested Classroom Instructional Strategies
Child-Adult Relations		
1. Does the child obey the adult or must respect be earned?	*Low-income Urban Black* Respect is earned by adult relating to child as an individual. Child responds to shame and to avoidance of physical punishment. Child may openly confront adult if respect is not earned.	Teacher needs to earn respect by relating to students personally.
	Traditional Native American Leaders chosen by community and will stay as long as community accepts them. Older adults seen as wise.	Teacher can gain respect if he/she demonstrates acceptable behavior. Older teachers may easily gain more respect.
	Traditional Mexican-American Respect is given to adult if adult demonstrates approved values such as contributing to community.	Same as above.
	Middle-class White Respect is earned. Boys allowed more open disagreement; girls not encouraged to be aggressive, and disagreement more passive and hidden. Child responds to guilt, withdrawal of love, and external rewards.	Teacher may need to encourage children away from external rewards such as grades in order to be self-directed.
2. Does the child seek a relationship with the adult that is friendly and personal or formal and task-oriented?	*Traditional Mexican-American* Child seeks friendly and personal adult relationships.	Teachers need to arrange instructional time so that they can work with students in a small group and in individualized situations where personal feelings and experiences can be shared. Since assistance to others is given freely without asking for it and is highly valued, teachers need to be sensitive to the need for help. Older students also need to experience working in a more formal and task-oriented situation.

Questions About Values, Beliefs, and Behavior	Selected Cultural Patterns of Racial/Ethnic and Sex Groups	Suggested Classroom Instructional Strategies
Child-Adult Relations		
	Middle-class White Child functions in relationship that is somewhat formal and task-oriented.	Child can try working independently of teacher; interactions with teacher can focus on task at hand. Child working alone should not be perceived as rejecting teacher or other children.
3. Is the child encouraged to disagree or challenge the adult on ideas, or is disagreement seen as disrespectful?	*Traditional Native American* Respect shown to adult does not allow disagreement. Adult perceived as wise, particularly if old.	Teacher should avoid placing student in a position that encourages him/her to disagree. Teacher who perceives self as an equal to students may find student doesn't share that opinion. Student may be unsure how to act in this situation.
	Middle-class White Child is encouraged to challenge adult on opinions.	Teacher can play "devil's advocate" to stimulate independent thinking.
Child-Child Relations		
4. How do boys and girls interact with each other?	*Traditional Mexican-American* Physical contact and discussion of sex are not sanctioned between adolescent boys and girls.	Human relations and physical education activities that encourage physical contact between boys and girls should be avoided so that girls are not placed in a position where school encourages them to violate their self-respect.
5. Does the child work well with children who are older, younger, and/or the same age.	*Low-income Urban Black* Children are frequently partially cared for by older siblings. After about age 6, children relate mostly to peers.	Cross-age tutoring and multiage classrooms can be used effectively.

(Continued)

TABLE 6.2 (Continued)

Cultural Learning Styles

Questions About Values, Beliefs, and Behavior	Selected Cultural Patterns of Racial/Ethnic and Sex Groups	Suggested Classroom Instructional Strategies
Child-Child Relations		
6. Does the child work well independently or cooperatively with other students?	*Low-income Urban Black and Traditional Mexican-American* Children are encouraged to help siblings, particularly younger ones. Families tend to be large and may include cousins. Competition discouraged. Peer groups tend to be strong and give members support.	Small-group situations where students cooperate, tutoring, and paired learning are encouraged. Where peer groups are strong, it may be helpful to maintain existing peer group as instructional group in classroom. Students may need more practice working by themselves.
	Traditional Native Americans Individual competition or demonstration achievement in front of a group discouraged. Competition appropriate in sports with teams.	Same as above.
	Middle-class White Male Working independently is highly valued.	Students can learn when working by themselves and may need skill development in working cooperatively.
	Traditional Female Girls are not encouraged to problem-solve independently. Friendliness and ability to get along with others valued, so conflict and disagreement are frequently hidden.	Female students may need skill development in facing independent tasks and in reducing test anxiety.
7. How is status achieved?	*Traditional Mexican-American* Working for the benefit of family and community and assisting others are highly valued.	Small-group situations where students can cooperate. Tutoring and paired learning are encouraged. If competition with others is used, even those who excel may not want to participate in outshining their peers. Students need practice working in competitive situations, such as timed tests, so that they can also do well in these situations.

Questions About Values, Beliefs, and Behavior	Selected Cultural Patterns of Racial/Ethnic and Sex Groups	Suggested Classroom Instructional Strategies
Child-Child Relations		
	Low-income Urban Black Rivalry and competition are discouraged in augmented families, and working for benefit of family is emphasized. Status is also given for one's communicative style.	Teacher should avoid embarrassing student in front of peers. Direct confrontation better handled privately with students.
	Traditional Native American Persona should be developed in many spheres of life including spiritual, bodily, and artistic ability, not only marketable skills. Dignity in front of peers highly valued.	Teacher should develop program to facilitate holistic development.
	Middle-class White Male Achievement and being the best highly valued in academic and athletic areas.	Students will respond to competitive situations where they can excel. If they perceive they cannot compete, they may give up. Relying on competition is questionable since only those who feel comfortable in succeeding may respond. Status for working cooperatively needs to be encouraged.
	Traditional Female Physical appearance and friendliness valued. Academic achievement negatively valued as girls approach adolescence since this is seen as unfeminine, particularly in science and math. Approval from males is often negatively related to academic success.	Female students need to overcome fear of rejection for excellence. They may need opportunities to compete only with other females. They also need to be encouraged to use their abilities when working with male students.

(Continued)

T A B L E   6 . 2   (Continued)

Cultural Learning Styles

Questions About Values, Beliefs, and Behavior	Selected Cultural Patterns of Racial/Ethnic and Sex Groups	Suggested Classroom Instructional Strategies
Child-Child Relations		
8. Does the student become more involved in the task or social surroundings?	*Traditional Female, Traditional Mexican-American, and Low-income Urban Black* Child is sensitive to feelings of others. "Soul" (empathic [sic] understanding), the ability to participate in the feelings of others or the capacity to interject one's own emotions into a situation to be able to analyze subjectively all the nuances of feelings in that situation, is valued among low-income urban blacks.	Teacher needs to allow time for students to relate personally to each other before working together; tasks may not be completed successfully unless human relations have been attended to.
9. Is the child more analytic or global in problem solving? Analytic: Field independent, gives attention to parts and details; abstract thinking, spatial ability, and analytic problem-solving skills; inductive thinking or forming generalizations. Global: Field sensitive or field dependent, gives attention to the whole contextual field; holistic thinking.	*Traditional Native American, Traditional Mexican-American, Traditional Female, and Low-income Urban Black* Global style. Holistic thinking is encouraged. Ways of knowing can include subjective and intuitive approaches. Artistic as well as intellectual pursuits are encouraged. Analytic areas such as math and science are discouraged for females.	Uses personalized and holistic approaches. Concepts presented in humanized story form ("S" is a snake); analogies instead of dictionary definitions. May need to develop analytic style.
	Middle-class White Male Analytic style. Encouraged from young age to think abstractly. Emotions should not enter into thinking; thought should be logical, empirical.	Learns well from graphs, charts, formulas. May need to develop holistic approach to conceptual style.

existential. In the section that follows, the author attempts to demonstrate through a topical outline of a unit on the railroad industry how a teacher might approach curriculum development in a way that ensures a balance between pluribus and unum.

✦ Guidelines for Curriculum and Instruction

Returning to the frequently expressed concern raised by students preparing to teach, "How can I relate to the cultural needs of all my students?," this section provides a framework for addressing the *big picture;* that is, designing curriculum that allows for many voices and perspectives, yet looks for aspects of a shared human culture as well. No one can be all things to all people; however, most people can be open to multiple perspectives and actively seek them out. As you look for ways to organize curriculum and instruction, the following guidelines may serve as a useful checklist. The framework is divided into two parts: The Big Picture—Curriculum Guidelines; and The Big Picture—Instructional Guidelines. Curriculum guidelines primarily address thoroughness and significance of historical information and conceptual linkages. Instructional guidelines examine pedagogical principles and ways to group students. After presenting the two parts, a curriculum application will illustrate the integration of both parts.

The Big Picture—Curriculum Guidelines

Historical Context

1. What were the major events in the designated time period?
2. If focusing on an event, what were the circumstances leading up to the event?
3. Who were the key players during the time period/event? Include famous people from variety of perspectives, for example, class, gender, ethnicity, elderly, other marginalized groups.
4. What were the lives of ordinary people like during the time period or time of the event? Include ordinary people from variety of perspectives, for example, class, gender, ethnicity, elderly, other marginalized groups.
5. What were the multiple perspectives surrounding the event/period?
6. How did society and individual lifestyles change during the time period or as a result of the event?
7. How did the event or time period maintain the status quo for society or individual lifestyles?
8. What events in other parts of the world had an impact on event or events during the time period?
9. In the context of American history, how did the ideals of the Founding Fathers weather the passage of time and change? Did the ideals favor certain groups of people? Why were there no Founding Fathers of color or Founding Mothers?
10. In the context of world history, what impact did the events/time period have in the international community?
11. What is the legacy of the events under study for conditions in society today?
12. What aspects of this legacy would you want to change or keep the same?
13. How would you go about changing the legacy or keeping the legacy alive?

Conceptual Themes

1. What key concepts illustrated by the historical case illustration are relevant for historical events in different time periods?
2. How can those concepts be illustrated across time periods in the United States?
3. How can those concepts be illustrated across cultural groups?
4. How can those concepts be illustrated in relation to cultures outside the boundaries of the United States?
5. How can the key concepts be made relevant to the lives of students today?

The Big Picture—Instructional Guidelines

Grouping Strategies

1. Do social studies lessons allow for variation in grouping strategies? Large group, small group, and individual activities?

Large Group
- Large-group settings favor active participation for those who are more outspoken and assertive in projecting their ideas.
- Large-group settings may not be supportive to those for whom a competitive atmosphere stifles their willingness to participate.
- Large-group discussions add an element of cohesiveness to the "whole," for example, the entire class

Small Groups
- Small-group settings maximize participation by creating more informal arrangements and multiplying the opportunities for students to respond to questions or learning tasks.
- Small groups shift the locus of control from the authority figure (as in large-group settings) to peers; students have greater opportunities to facilitate discussion or develop shared ownership for task completion.
- Small-group settings can be either homogeneously (similar criteria) or heterogeneously (varied criteria) grouped. Criteria for grouping can be based on interests, achievement, ability, self-selections, or random assignment. When grouping strategies create divisions based on gender, class, or ethnicity, the teacher must be cognizant of flexible grouping so that stereotyping is not perpetuated based on these classifications.
- Small-group arrangements may make students curious about what is going on in the other groups; there may be a need for closure in the large group by having students share the ideas or activities they pursued in small groups.
- Small-group settings build interpersonal skills such as sharing, taking turns, compromise, leadership, negotiation, and problem solving.

Individual Learning Settings
- Students have opportunities to think and create on their own; they have complete ownership for their own performance or creation.
- Students may feel in competition with peers in that their performance will be compared to others.

Curriculum and Instruction Outline

Using the preceding guidelines, it is possible to prepare a comprehensive outline on a particular topic, in this instance, the American railroad industry. You may recall the Family/Oral History application in Chapter 2. In that lesson an oral history of Edwin Clardy, an "ordinary" middle-class American whose family benefited from the California railroad industry, was presented to strike a balance with the typical emphasis upon famous people in textbooks. As a stand-alone lesson it met the objective of trying to demonstrate not only how history was *made* by famous people, but how it was *lived* by ordinary people. In both cases, however, Edwin Clardy and Andrew Carnegie were white males. Now we have an opportunity to expand on our initial introduction by elaborating on the railroads' impact on people of color and women, as well as the impact of people of color and women on the railroads. In addition, the significance of the railroad industry upon American culture in general is addressed with a view to the future. In other words, the legacy of the railroads for all Americans is examined. The illustration that follows should demonstrate a difference between political correctness and curriculum that is multicultural. It strives to be comprehensive as opposed to symbolically representative in the sense that Banks defines the contributions approach to cultural diversity.

The American Railroads: A Transformation
The Big Picture—Curriculum Guidelines
Historical Context

I.   History of the Railroad, 1830–1930
    A. Transcontinental Connections
        1. Power Sources
            a. Andrew Carnegie, Entrepreneur
            b. The Big Four, Businessmen (Stanford, Crocker, Huntington, Hopkins)
            c. Theodore Judah, Engineer
        2. Industrial Progress
            a. Central and Union Pacific
                (1) Promontory Point, Utah (May, 1869)
            b. Safety Factors
        3. Political Activity
            a. Pacific Rail Act; July 1, 1862
            b. *Plessy v. Ferguson* (1896)
    B. Impact on American Lives
        1. Job Opportunities
            a. Men's Roles
                (1) European Immigrants (Irish, Dutch, Poles, Germans)
                (2) Chinese Immigrants
                (3) African Americans
                (4) Mexican Nationals
            b. Women's Roles
                (1) The Harvey Girls
                (2) Kate Shelley's Heroic Act

        2. Native Americans
           a. "Bad-Medicine Wagons"
           b. Treaty of Medicine Lodge
        3. Transportation/Communication Networks
           a. Wider Distribution of Manufactured Goods
           b. Enhanced Mail Service
    C. Social Transformation
        1. Political Participation
           a. American Railway Union; Eugene Debs
           b. Brotherhood of Sleeping Car Porters
              (1) First all-Black union
           c. Chinese Six Companies
        2. Popular Culture
           a. Literature
              (1) Casey Jones and John Henry
           b. Music
              (1) Wallace Saunders (Black musician who sang railroad ballads)
        3. International Time
           a. Time Zones
           b. International Calendar
II.   Contemporary Transportation Issues
    A. Trains
        1. Competition With Automobiles & Airplanes
           a. Decline in passenger service
           b. Governmental airline subsidies
    B. Future Possibilities
        1. Transcontinental Trains
           a. Passenger
           b. Cargo
        2. Improved Designs
           a. Commuter Trains
              (1) National Railroad Passenger Corporation (Amtrak)
           b. English/French Chunnel (Fetherson, 1997); Japanese Bullet
           c. Trains in the Twenty-First Century

Conceptual Themes

Several themes emerge from a history of the railroads spanning a hundred-year period from 1830 to 1930. Depending on teacher and student interest, one or several of the following themes might be developed as threads tying the lessons together:

Unifying a Continent: Urban and Rural Development Coast to Coast
Westward Expansion Versus Eastern Invasion
Industrialization and Railroad Technology
Americans Vying for a Place in a Changing Society

    For example, to develop the theme of Urban and Rural Development, concepts from geography, economics, and sociology can be integrated. If the theme of Westward Expansion Versus Eastern Invasion were emphasized, the relationships between the Native Americans and all other ethnic groups would be represented as opposing forces, with some exceptions. Industrialization and Railroad Technology would allow for in-depth analyses of the great inventions and technological advances that characterized the nineteenth century, as well as provide opportunities to examine conditions in factories and other areas of the workplace. The focus on Americans Vying for a Place in a Changing Society might emphasize the impact of the railroads upon the lives of individuals and subgroups throughout society based on ethnicity, gender, and class. How individuals transformed society and how social opportunities transformed the lives of individuals could be developed through biographies, literature, and the humanities.

Cross-cultural international comparisons can be made by studying the impact of the railroad industry in other countries. The *Orient Express* would be a colorful way to investigate the impact in Europe and East Asia. The importance of the railroads to the lives of students today can come alive by field trips to local train depots, some of which have been converted to shopping malls and museums. Investigating the train folklore in one's hometown can generate interesting stories about landmarks that may be familiar to students. Identifying a specific transportation problem in one's local community and asking students to invent a solution by using the train industry in some way will also generate creative problem-solving skills.

The Big Picture—Instructional Guidelines

A teacher can structure student activities in a variety of ways. Some may be done as a large group, such as singing songs or listening to music. Others may be developed through small-group projects such as having students set up an actual train set, run it, and explain its historical significance. Independent investigations can take the form of research projects that are written to be shared, kept private, or given orally to the rest of the class. The number of activities that students could do are endless. With learning styles in mind, the following list offers just a few suggestions.

Learning Styles and Grouping Strategies

Linguistic: With peers, read *Across America on an Emigrant Train,* by Jim Murphy. The book re-creates the journey taken by Robert Louis Stevenson in 1879, when he traveled from Scotland to California to be with the woman he loved. Students can identify real-life accounts of train experiences based on Stevenson's journal entries.

Musical: Investigate the history and significance of railroad songs. If they are able, students can perform the songs by singing or playing them on their instrument of choice.

Logico-mathematical: Research the development of international time zones. Investigate how mathematicians developed the system when the railroad brought people closer together, thereby creating more efficient communication networks.

Spatial: Design an international train system, identifying the population centers that will be served. Explain how it will operate and how long it will take to get from one place to the next. What will have to happen to make such a system viable?

Bodily kinesthetic: Set up a train in the classroom. Explain to the class the historical significance of the train, for example, when it was invented and so on.

Intrapersonal: Independently investigate a topic relevant to the railroad industry such as working conditions, ethnic conflict, women's roles, political movements, the kinds of trains, geographical barriers, use of explosives, casualties when building the railroad and so on.

Interpersonal: In pairs or a small group, visit the local history society and conduct an oral history of someone who is knowledgeable about the railroad industry in your local community.

Naturalistic: Investigate the sites where dynamite was used to create a pathway through a mountainous or hilly area for a railroad. Study the layout of the land and the engineers' decisions. Could there have been an alternate route that would have reduced the necessity to alter the natural landscape?

At this point, you may be excited about the possibilities of exploring a topic in more depth than is typically provided in textbooks. In fact, the original textbook lesson from which this unit outline emerged devoted only several paragraphs to the railroad industry. How then is it possible to pursue such a topic in the ways that have been outlined and still cover the expected nine-month scope and sequence? The *depth* versus *coverage* dilemma is one that is constantly on the minds of teachers. It is not possible to go into depth on every national, state, or local standard. Deciding which topics to pursue is often one of the creative advantages that teachers have. Curriculum focus is shaped by national, state, local, district, and schoolwide programs, but in most cases the individual teacher has many opportunities to be innovative and resourceful. The art of teaching refers not only to those teaching moments in the classroom. Many artistic endeavors take place in the design stage of curriculum development. A curriculum that demonstrates the greatest fit among national, state, and local standards would certainly be the most defensible.

✦ Reflections on Practice

In a recent social studies class I asked my students if they felt the Big Picture framework was a useful tool to a beginning teacher. As a class the students had researched the Colonial Period and developed five-day units at various grade levels. While no one student could possibly cover the Big Picture in five hours of instruction, collectively the twenty-two students addressed a significant portion of the items on the Big Picture list. Of course, when the collective units were combined, the total hours of instruction amounted to 110 hours, far more than any one elementary teacher would spend on this period in history. To do so at the rate of one hour per day would take twenty-two weeks—more than half the school year! The students made many good observations about the Big Picture and multicultural teaching more generally in the discussion that ensued. Their comments centered around time limitations, curriculum constraints, and the cultural context under study, as far as limitations go. For strengths of the Big Picture, students identified its usefulness as a tool for planning instruction, developing student projects, and examining scope and sequence for the school year. Each of these is discussed separately.

Strengths
Tool for Planning Instruction
The Big Picture serves as a planning tool in that a more comprehensive approach is obtained through its structure. By keeping the framework in mind a teacher is less

likely to be sidetracked into spending a great deal of time on less significant events or areas of interest.

Developing Student Projects

If the designated direct instruction time is insufficient for addressing some of the points in the Big Picture, it is possible to include them in student projects or research assignments. This also may allow students to gain more depth on topics of personal interest.

Examining Scope and Sequence

Sometimes a specific instructional sequence or unit will exclude certain groups of people. It is therefore important to examine whether certain groups are systematically left out across the curriculum from kindergarten through the eighth grade. How are they included? In an integrated fashion or at the contribution level, according to Banks? Thus, one strength of the Big Picture framework is its usefulness in looking at the entire scope and sequence in social studies as individual units are prepared.

Limitations

Time Limitations

Depth versus coverage is a dilemma for teachers planning instruction when so little time is allotted to specific historical periods, topics, or social studies in general. To continue the Colonial period as an illustration, students expressed frustration at conducting more in-depth research on a topic that didn't always generate even treatment across ethnic groups. Resources on medicinal practices of settlers were more plentiful than medicinal customs of African-Americans or Native Americans, for example. Other African-American and Native American customs such as messages sent through spirituals and folktales were developed, but an equivalency of time allotment across topics was not possible, nor was it necessarily desirable.

Curriculum Restraints and Cultural Context

Certain topics on historical periods included for a particular grade level by their general scope may exclude certain groups. When addressing the *big picture* for the Colonial Period, for example, it is readily apparent that Asian-Americans receive minor attention, if any. When this situation arises there may be a logical explanation. There are few specific references to Asian individuals because not many lived on the East Coast during that period. As a major ethnic group there is some recognition that Asian-Americans migrated across the Bering Strait when discussing life before the European explorers, so linkages between Asian-Americans and Native Americans can be made. What is perhaps just as important is whether or not Asian-Americans are discussed in the social studies curriculum in other periods. If a group such as Asian-Americans are left out in other periods as well, then either the omissions reflect insufficient research on Asian-Americans or there is perhaps a built-in bias within the overall curriculum framework that excludes Asian-Americans.

✦ INTERNET LINKS

INTERNET LINKS

Multicultural Education

http://aace.virginia.edu/go/multicultural/home.html

Multicultural Pavilion.

This site provides "resources and dialogues for educators, students, and activists." The teachers' corner, the international project, awareness activities, research and inquiry, the online discussion board, Voices! Intercultural poetry and prose, multiculturalism and the arts, multiculturalism and the Internet, and multicultural paths to other sites are the features of the Multicultural Pavilion. These elements can all play a useful part in a multicultural classroom. For example, the teachers' corners provides teachers with feature articles just for them, a toolbox of ideas to use in the classroom, links to other teaching resources, and an online archive box.

INTERNET LINKS

Multicultural Education

http://www.eastern.edu:80/publications/emme

Electronic Magazine on Multicultural Education.

EMME is an online magazine that explores different aspects of multiculturalism and diversity within each issue. It exposes the reader to little-known details and provides a basis to build one's own ideas about multiculturalism. The current issue being explored by the publication is "understanding one's own culture through cultural narration." *EMME* is published quarterly, and each issue contains instructional ideas, reviews of resources, thematic articles, an open forum (for writings that are beyond, yet related to, the current theme), and essays for and by scholars, teachers, and students.

INTERNET LINKS

Multicultural Education

http://gilligan.esu7.k12.ne.us/~esu7web/resources/multi.html

Check the Nebraska Slate!!

This site provides five main areas to explore: Internet integration ideas; professional support resources; events; curriculum links; and connections, communications, and collaborations. A very helpful link, found under curriculum, is the multicultural link. This gives a listing of project links that a teacher can use in the classroom for multicultural education. The projects are broken down into general categories as follows: culture, diversity, immigration, languages, multicultural education links, and multicultural organizations. This page also provides links to other resources and contacts pertaining to literature and publishing, museums and exhibits, and online archives. Unique to this site are the links that are ethnicity-specific, which include African-American, Asian-American, Hispanic/Latino-American, and Native American links.

SUMMARY

As you strive for the *big picture* with a desire to capture the significance of historical events in a pluralistic society, there is no easy formula. Nor does the existence of a national scope and sequence; national, state, and local standards; or commercial texts and trade books suffice for curriculum development. Teaching for cultural pluralism requires an awareness of one's own knowledge gaps regarding other cultures as well as one's own cultural biases. Elementary teachers are not usually expected to be specialized in cultures throughout the globe. Yet our school population will most likely reflect a global heritage. If one is committed to teaching for a pluralistic society, then educating oneself becomes part of the process.

The *Self in the World* orientation emphasizes identity development in relation to knowledge about the world. As we have seen in this chapter, the relationship of the individual to the widening circles of social identity (i.e., race, ethnicity, class, gender, and exceptionalities) involves both the need to be unique as well as the need to be accepted as a member of the classroom, community, state, nation, and world. In the United States and other Western societies the self is seen as developing both independently and as a member of various groups, whereas in some Eastern societies the boundaries of the self are perceived as more fluid and integrated with the larger community. As ethnic collective movements have strengthened around the world, the trend toward active multiculturalism has replaced the more laissez-faire attitude toward cultural differences (Moghaddam, 1998). The teacher can play a crucial role in supporting the multicultural "notion that a sense of security and positive in-group identity will lead to open and accepting attitudes toward out-groups" (Moghaddam, 1998, p. 508). I join Brake, Walker, and Walker (1995) in challenging you to reflect on your own cultural heritage and its potential for influencing others. Their sentiment expressed in the context of working with individuals who conduct business in the international community is pertinent for educators who are trying to understand the relationship between *self* and the rest of the *world:*

> It [their book] challenges individuals to learn more about multicultural interactions while stepping back introspectively and defining their own cultural heritage, regardless of nationality. The journey, like any other, will have its twists and turns, and the traveler will change and grow along the route. We trust that by accepting the challenges of the multicultural . . . world, the reader will discover new areas of personal and professional development, areas that stimulate creativity, productivity, and enhanced human understanding and collaboration (p. ix).

PROFESSIONAL DISCUSSIONS
AND FIELD EXPERIENCES

Professional Discussions

1. Think about your own multicultural background in comparison to Anthony E. Wright. Do you have a mixed cultural heritage? Or is it more homogeneous? Given the way government forms specify certain categories, Anglo students often consider themselves homogeneous. But often when they think about cultural influences either through birth or guardians, a rich cultural diversity emerges. Many of you will resemble Anthony Wright while others may have a diverse combination of Anglo influences—French, Scottish, Irish, German, and so on. Still others will have a combination of Anglo, Hispanic, Asian, and/or African heritage. By sharing this exercise as a class you will be able to appreciate that the heritage of most Americans is a rich mixture of cultural backgrounds. For more information about how the government struggles with forms designed to provide demographic characteristics, see the following website: http://www.whitehouse.gov/WH/EOP/OMB/html/fedreg/Ombdir15.html

2. Reflect on the way in which your gender identity was formed through selective choices you made and the influences of others. Think of significant male/female roles as modeled or discussed in the homes where you grew up. In what ways were they traditional; that is, did females assume responsibility for the children and domestic sphere while males spent most of their time in the public sphere? How were the roles different from this dichotomy? In what ways were roles shared, both traditional and nontraditional? Were there significant others inside and outside the family or home who challenged your thinking about gender expectations? Share these experiences with your classmates.

Field Experiences

1. How would you describe the cultural and socioeconomic background of the students you have observed in a classroom setting? In addition, are there students who are given services for a variety of needs, such as exceptionalities, special education, gifted, language, religion, free-meals, and so on? Ask a teacher in the building to describe the advantages and/or limitations of these programs. Does the teacher have recommendations for improvement? In what ways?

2. Assuming that recess and lunchroom activities are free time and not overly structured by school policy, observe the patterns of interaction among students. Do the boys and girls play together or separately? Do children of various ethnic backgrounds congregate? Or do lunchroom and playground patterns reflect a mix across gender and ethnicity? How do you interpret these patterns? Do you think that children's playtime and lunchtime activities should be socially regulated by teachers and administrators? If so, in what ways? If not, why not?

REFERENCES

Alter, G. (Ed.). (1995). Diverse learners in the social studies classroom. *Social Studies and the Young Learner, 7* (4), 1–32.

American Association of University Women. (1992). *How schools shortchange girls.* Washington, DC: National Education Association.

American Association of University Women. (1996). *Girls in the middle.* Washington, DC: National Education Association.

American Heritage. (Eds.). (1960). *Railroads in the days of steam.* New York: Author.

Apple, M. W. (1979). *Ideology and curriculum.* Boston: Routledge & Kegan Paul.

Banks, J. A. (1988). Approaches to multicultural curriculum reform. *Multicultural Leader, 1* (2), 1–3.

Banks, J. A. (1989). Multicultural education: Characteristics and goals. In J. A. Banks & C. A. Banks (Eds.), *Multicultural education: Issues and perspectives* (pp. 2–26). Boston: Allyn & Bacon.

Banks, J. A. (1991). Multicultural education: Its effects on students' racial and gender role attitudes. In Shaver, J. P. (Ed.), *Handbook of research on social studies teaching and learning* (pp. 459–469). New York: Macmillan.

Banks, J. A. (1994). *Multiethnic education: Theory and practice.* Boston: Allyn & Bacon.

Brake, T., Walker, D. M., & Walker, T. (1995). *Doing business internationally: The guide to cross-cultural success.* New York: McGraw-Hill.

Bruner, J. (1990). *Acts of meaning.* Cambridge, MA: Harvard University Press.

Cheney, L. V. (1987). *American memory: A report on the humanities in the nation's public schools.* Washington, DC: National Endowment for the Humanities.

Clearinghouse for Multicultural/Bilingual Education. Available online: www.weber.edu/mbe/htmls/mbe.html.

Cortes, C. E. (1994, Winter). Limits to *pluribus,* limits to *unum:* Unity, diversity, and the great American balancing act. *Pi Kappa Phi Journal, 6*–8.

Crocco, M. S. (Ed.). (1995). Breaking the chains: The 75th anniversary of women's suffrage. *Social Education, 59* (5), 252–314.

Crocco, M. S. (1997). Making time for women's history . . . When your survey course is already filled to overflowing. *Social Education, 61* (1), 32–37.

Cruz, B. C., & Prorok, C. V. (1997). "Women at work": Incorporating gender into a geography lesson. *Social Education, 61* (7), 385–389.

Curtis, C. K. (1991). Social studies for students at-risk and with disabilities. In J. P. Shaver (Ed.), *Handbook of research on social studies teaching and learning* (pp. 157–174). New York: Macmillan.

Davis-Van Atta, D., Arnold, C., & Lyddon, J. W. (1998). *Air alert #6—New federal standards for racial and ethnic data collection and reporting.* Washington, DC: Office of Management and Budget.

Dawson, M. E. (1974). *Are there unwelcome guests in your classroom?* Washington, DC: Association for Childhood Education International.

Dilts, J. D. (1993). *The Great Road: The building of the Baltimore and Ohio, the nation's first railroad, 1828–1853.* Stanford, CA: Stanford University Press.

Eden, J. M., & Ryan, J. P. (1999). Affirmative action: Contentious ideas and controversial practices. *Social Education, 63* (2), 110–115.

Edwards, G. (1995). *American history through multicultural literature.* Torrance, CA: Frank Schaffer Publications.

Egan, K. (1998). *Teaching as story telling.* London, Ontario: The Althouse Press.

Fetherston, D. (1997). *Chunnel: The amazing story of the undersea crossing of the English Channel.* New York: Random House.

Fisher, L. E. (1992). *Tracks across America: The story of the American railroad 1825–1900.* New York: Holiday House.

Fraser, M. A. (1993). *Ten-mile day and the building of the transcontinental railroad.* New York: Holt.

Freire, P. (1970). *Pedagogy of the oppressed.* New York: Herder & Herder.

Fuchs, D., Fuchs, L. S., Mathes, P. G., & Simmons, D. C. (1997). Peer-assisted learning strategies: Making classrooms more responsive to diversity. *American Educational Research Journal, 34* (1), 174–206.

Garcia, E. (1994). *Understanding and meeting the challenge of student cultural diversity.* Boston: Houghton Mifflin.

Gardner, H. (1983). *Frames of mind: The theory of multiple intelligences.* New York: Basic Books.

Gardner, H. (1999). *Intelligence reframed: Multiple perspectives for the 21st century.* New York: Basic Books.

Gardner, J. B., & Adams, G. R. (1983). *Ordinary people and everyday life.* Nashville, TN: The American Association for State and Local History.

Giroux, H. A. (1988). *Teachers as intellectuals: Toward a critical pedagogy of learning.* Westport, CT: Bergin & Garvey.

Giroux, H. A. (1998). Culture, power and transformation in the work of Paulo Freire. Reprinted in F. Schultz (Ed.), *Notable selections in education* (pp. 43–52). Guilford, CT: Dushkin/McGraw-Hill.

Gollnick, D. M., & Chinn, P. C. (1998). *Multicultural education in a pluralistic society.* New York: Merrill.

Gorski, P. (1998, August 6). Multicultural Pavilion. Available online: curry.edschool.-Virginia.edu/go/multicultural.

Greer, C. (1972). *The great school legend.* New York: Viking.

Grelle, B., & Metzger, D. (1996). Beyond socialization and multiculturalism: Rethinking the task of citizenship education in a pluralistic society. *Social Education, 60* (3), 147–151.

Halverson, C. (1979). Individual and cultural determinants of self-directed learning ability: Straddling an instructional dilemma. In D. Della-dora & L. J. Blanchard (Eds.), *Moving toward self-directed learning* (pp. 000–000). Alexandria, VA: Association for Supervision and Curriculum Development.

Haynes, C. C. (1990). Taking religion seriously in the social studies. *Social Education, 54* (5), 276–277.

Heward, W. L., & Orlansky, M. D. (2000). *Exceptional children: An introductory survey of special education* (6th ed.). Columbus, OH: Merrill.

Heward, W. L., & Orlansky, M. D. (1989). Educational equality for exceptional students. In J. A. Banks & C. A. Banks (Eds.), *Multicultural education: Issues and perspectives* (pp. 231–250). Boston: Allyn & Bacon.

Hirsch, E. D. (1987). *Cultural literacy: What every American needs to know.* Boston: Houghton Mifflin.

Hoffbauer, D., & Prenn, M. (1996). A place to call one's own: Choosing books about homelessness. *Social Education, 60* (3), 167–169.

Holbrook, S. H. (1960). *The golden age of railroads.* New York: Random House.

Hooks, B. (1998). Ecstacy: Teaching and learning without limits. In F. Schultz (Ed.), *Sources: Notable selections in education* (pp. 229–232). Guilford, CT: Dushkin/McGraw-Hill.

Hoose, P. (1993). *It's our world, too! Stories of young people who are making a difference.* Boston: Little, Brown.

Howard, B. C. (1987). *Learning to persist, persisting to learn.* Washington, DC: The Mid-Atlantic Center for Race Equity.

Illich, I. (1971). *Deschooling society.* New York: Harper & Row.

Jacobs, W. (1990). *Ellis Island: New hope in a new land.* New York: Charles Scribner.

Jensen, O. (1975). *The American Heritage history of railroads in America.* New York: American Heritage.

Labbo, L. D. (1997). "Off the shelf": Resources for celebrating the lives of African American women. *Social Studies and the Young Learner, 9* (3), 21–23.

Ladson-Billings, G. (1990). Culturally relevant teaching: Effective instruction for black students. *College Board Review, 155,* 20–25.

Lamme, L. L. (1998). Child laborers in children's literature. *Teaching and Learning Social Studies in the Middle Grades/Social Education, Social Education,* Special Issue, M15–M16.

Levine, E. (1988). *If you traveled on the Underground Railroad.* New York: Scholastic.

Levstik, L. S. (1997). "Any history is someone's history": Listening to multiple voices from the past. *Social Education, 61* (1), 48–51.

Mann, A. (1979). *The one and the many: Reflections on the American identity.* Chicago: University of Chicago Press.

McCoy, K. (1998). Strategies for teaching social studies. In E. L. Meyen, G. A. Vergason, & R. J. Whelan, *Educating students with mild disabilities* (pp. 207–236). Denver, CO: Love Publishing.

McEachron-Hirsch, G. A. (1993). *Student self-esteem: Integrating the self.* Lancaster, PA: Technomic.

McIntosh, P. (1983). *Interactive phases of curricular re-vision: A feminist perspective.* Working paper No. 124. Wellesley, MA: Wellesley College Center for Research on Women.

Meltzer, M. (1969). *Brother can you spare a dime? The Great Depression 1929–1933.* New York: Alfred A. Knopf.

Mercer, C. D. (1997). *Students with learning disabilities.* Englewood Cliffs, NJ: Prentice-Hall.

Moghaddam, F. M. (1998). *Social psychology: Exploring universals across cultures.* New York: W. H. Freeman.

Multicultural Pavilion. *Education World* Available online: education-world.com/awards/past/r0897-14.shtml.

Murphy, J. (1993). *Across America on an emigrant train.* New York: Clarion.

Negron, E., & Ricklin, L. P. (1996). Meeting the needs of diverse learners in the social studies classroom through collaborative methods of instruction. *Social Studies and the Young Learner, 9* (2), 27–29.

O'Connor, C. (1997). Dispositions toward (collective) struggle and educational resilience in the inner city: A case analysis of six African-American high school students. *American Educational Research Journal, 34* (4), 593–629.

Ogbu, J. U. (1990). Overcoming racial barriers to equal access. In J. Goodlad & P. Keating (Eds.), *Access to knowledge* (pp. 59–90). New York: The College Board.

Ogbu, J. U. (1991). Immigrant and involuntary minorities in comparative perspective. In J. Ogbu & M. Gibson (Eds.), *Minority status and schooling: A comparative study of immigrant and involuntary minorities* (pp. 3–36). New York: Garland.

Ogbu, J. U. (1994). Racial stratification and education in the United States: Why inequality persists. *Teachers College Record, 96* (2), 264–298.

Ogburn, C. (1977). *Railroads: The great American adventure.* Washington, DC: The National Geographic Society.

Ornstein, A. C., & Hunkins, F. P. (1988). *Curriculum: Foundations, principles, and issues.* Englewood Cliffs, NJ: Prentice-Hall.

Pallante, M. I., & Shively, C. (1999). My brother and I: Brickyard laborers in an Ohio town. *Middle Level Learning, Social Education,* Issue 5, M10–M13.

Patton, M. M. (1996). Where do you live when you don't have a house? *Social Studies and the Young Learner, 8* (4), 14–15.

Pflepsen, A., & Vokes, S. (Eds.). (1996). Meeting ordinary and extraordinary women worldwide: A delegation of the girls International forum travels to China. *Social Studies and the Young Learner, 8* (3), 30–32.

Porter, R. P. (1990). *Forked tongue: The politics of bilingual education.* New York: Basic.

Rabinowitz, H. N. (1983). Race, ethnicity, and cultural pluralism in American history. In J. Gardner & G. Adams, *Ordinary people and everyday life* (pp. 23–49). Nashville, TN: The American Association for State and Local History.

Ravitch, D. (1985). *The schools we deserve.* New York: Basic.

Reese, L. (1996). Bringing Beijing home . . . and into the classroom. *Social Education, 60* (7), 410–413.

Regoli, M. (Ed.). (1992). Teaching and learning about religion. *Magazine of History.* Bloomington, IN: Organization of American Historians.

Rosenberg, M. (1979). *Conceiving the self.* New York: Basic.

Rylant, C. (1991). *Appalachia: The voices of sleeping birds.* San Diego: Harcourt Brace Jovanovich.

Shea, P. (1995). *The whispering cloth: A refugee's story.* Honesdale, PA: Boyds Mills Press.

Simonson, R., & Walker, S. (Eds.). (1988). *Multicultural literacy: Opening the American mind.* St. Paul, MN: Graywolf Press.

Simpson, M. (Ed.). (1996). The world around us: Global education. *Social Education, 60* (7), 386–459.

Sleeter, C. E., & Grant, C. A. (1994). *Making choices for multicultural education.* New York: Merrill.

Snow, R. (1978). *The iron road: A portrait of American railroading.* New York: Four Winds Press.

Stanley, J. (1992). *Children of the dust bowl: The true story of the school at Weedpatch Camp.* New York: Crown.

Strom, M. S., & Parsons, W. S. (1982). *Facing history and ourselves: Holocaust and human behavior.* Watertown, MA: International Educations.

Stronge, J. H. (Ed.). (1992). *Educating homeless children and adolescents: Evaluating policy and practice.* Newbury Park, CA: Sage.

Swearingen, J. A. (1996). Promoting tolerance in preservice teachers. *Social Education, 60* (3), 152–154.

Tetreault, M. K. (1987, March). Rethinking women, gender, and the social studies. *Social Education, 51* (3), 172–173.

Tetreault, M. K. (1989). Integrating content about women and gender into the curriculum. In J. A. Banks & C. M. Banks (Eds.), *Multicultural education* (pp. 124–144). Boston: Allyn & Bacon.

Tiedt, I. M., & Tiedt, P. (1990). *Multicultural teaching: A handbook of activities, information, and resources.* Boston: Allyn & Bacon.

Turnbull, A., Turnbull, R., Shank, M., & Leal, D. (1999). *Exceptional lives: Special education in today's schools.* Columbus, OH: Merrill.

Tuttle, L. (1994). *A multicultural portrait of the railroads.* New York: Marshall Cavendish.

VanTassel-Baska, J. (1992). *Planning effective curriculum for gifted learners.* Denver, CO: Love Publishing.

VanTassel-Baska, J. (1994). *Comprehensive curriculum for gifted learners.* Boston: Allyn & Bacon.

VanTassel-Baska, J., & Feldhusen, J. Social studies curriculum for the gifted. In J. VanTassel-Baska (1994). *Comprehensive curriculum for gifted learners* (pp. 166–195). Boston: Allyn & Bacon.

Wade, R. (1998). Brick walls and breakthroughs: Talking about diversity with white teacher education students. *Social Education, 62* (2), 84–87.

Walther-Thomas, C., Korinek, L., McLaughlin, V. L., & Williams, B. T. (2000). *Collaboration for inclusive education: Developing successful programs.* Boston: Allyn & Bacon.

© Elizabeth Crews

CHAPTER 7

TEACHING AND LEARNING STYLES

Reflections on Social Interaction in the Classroom

Chapter Outline

Reflective Teaching

Reflecting on the Technical and Practical

Reflection in Action

Reflection as Critical Inquiry

Learning Styles

Teaching Styles

Direct Instruction: Teacher As Disseminator of Information

Lecture

Guided Discussion

Storytelling

Demonstrations

Tutorials

Indirect Instruction: Teacher As Facilitator and Resource

Inquiry and Discovery

Computers

Role Playing and Simulations

Learning Centers

Field Trips

❖ **Case Study: Diane Bradford**

Diane: Challenge and Competence

Individualizing Curriculum Through Collaboration

❖ **Internet Links**

Summary

Professional Discussions and Field Experiences

References

CHAPTER OBJECTIVES

As a student teacher you have preconceived notions of how you will perform in the classroom setting. For example, one student intern liked to design activities for children to work in small groups so that he could talk with them on a more informal basis. Another student teacher preferred large-group instruction where she could have greater control over class discussions and interaction. But what about the preferred learning styles of students? What if your preferred teaching style appears to be a good match for some students while others show signs of boredom or disruption? Do you feel inclined to hold fast to initial convictions based on a set of values and educational program, or do you think you will make adjustments along the way? Answering this question is more complex than reflecting on whether you are confident or ambivalent about beginning, as it hints at a certain paradox regarding professional growth. Upon completion of this chapter, you will be able to:

1.   Explain the relationship between reflective teaching and professional growth.
2.   Identify a wide range of learning and teaching styles and explain their significance for instructional strategies.
3.   Explain a process for individualizing instruction through consultation with students, parents, peers, and other professionals.

In Chapter 6 we looked at the way in which society influences student relationships, curriculum, and instruction, and how these elements in turn influence society. Returning to Ladson-Billings's (1990) statement that "teachers work within three dimensions: their conception of themselves and others, their knowledge, and their classrooms' social structure," (p. 22) we will now address educators' conceptions of self and others. By examining teaching and learning styles, we gain insights into classroom dynamics. Despite initial preferences, beginning teachers soon learn that their teaching styles develop into more complex arrangements as they reflect on the dynamic exchanges between teachers and students. This chapter examines the nature of this interplay. A case study of Diane Bradford is presented to illustrate how she, her parents, and professionals made decisions about teaching and learning based on individual needs.

✦ REFLECTIVE TEACHING

Students preparing to teach often identify the student teaching experience as the most challenging and informative experience of their teacher preparation program. One of the reasons they give is that learning theories and methods of teaching specific content areas come together in an integrated fashion. This integration is not necessarily one that is free of chaos and confusion by any stretch of the imagination. But it is one that brings together theory and practice with live specimens—students. The ability to apply what has been learned through a process of reflection and decision making is the *rite of passage* that transforms interns into novice teachers.

Reflective teaching is a process whereby teachers illuminate their capabilities as professionals. It is a process where teachers analyze the art and science of teaching in a way that empowers them to make a difference. Reflective teaching is a way to understand the demands and rewards of teaching in order to contribute to growth and mastery teaching. Ideals such as reflective teaching or critical thinking require an openness to interpretations by practitioners. The analysis, reflection, and decision making that go into teaching is the hard work that teachers find exhausting yet gratifying. Through a review of literature, Adler (1994) identified three traditions on reflective teaching: (1) reflecting on the technical and practical, (2) reflection in action, and (3) reflection as critical inquiry.

Reflecting on the Technical and Practical

The technique of *reflecting on the technical and practical* refers to a strategy whereby in-service teachers peer-teach in a laboratory setting, then reflect on technical aspects

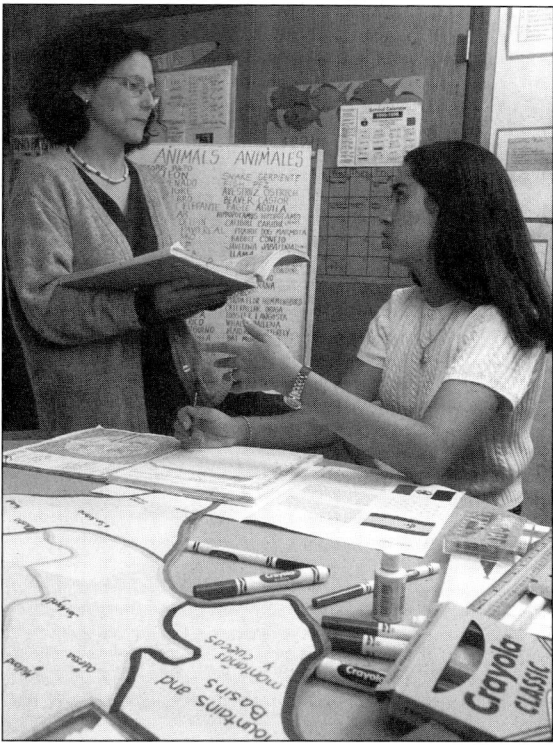

© Bob Daemmrich/The Image Works

of lesson design and implementation. Having used a variation of this model in my social studies methods class, it is evident that students gain a variety of insights from the experience. Here's how it works. In a small group of peers, in-service teachers plan, then teach a social studies lesson that they expect to teach to elementary or middle school students during their field placement. Being able to "pilot" the lesson provides them with opportunities to reflect upon time management, their use of audio-visual materials, content focus, and clarity. With peers simulating a student audience, questions arise that may not have been anticipated and these questions allow the pre-service teacher to think through how he or she will answer such questions posed in the *real* classroom. The feedback from peers also represents a modified version of peer coaching. Peer coaching is a practice used by experienced teachers whereby they plan, implement, and provide feedback to each other for the purpose of improving their teaching effectiveness (Henderson, 1992).

Reflection in Action

The second model, *reflection in action* (Schön, 1983, 1987), describes the reflective practitioner as one who is capable of thinking and acting in the face of uncertainty and conflict. Schön maintains that *knowledge in action, tacit knowledge,* and *reflection in action* are key elements for reflection. All elements spotlight the expertise that is developed based on professional experience. That is, reflection in action is knowledge constructed or reconstructed from practice. From working with preservice teachers, reflection in action manifests itself in both the peer-teaching experiences as well as throughout student teaching. When asking students to describe their performance, they often remark that once they got into the lesson they could see that certain intended activities "just weren't going to work." Students often say, "Well, I had to scrap that idea and go back to the drawing board." Sometimes preservice teachers monitor and adjust on their feet, depending on the circumstances. At other times, they say explicitly to their students, "We're going to leave this and go on to something else." Initially disconcerting, novice teachers soon realize that responding to students and adjusting plans requires this openness to reflection in action.

Reflection as Critical Inquiry

The model of *reflection as critical inquiry* goes beyond technical proficiency and context-specific decision making. While inclusive of these aspects of reflective inquiry, Zeichner and Liston (1987) suggest that teachers need to become transformers of the teaching/learning process by considering the ethical and political consequences of their actions on human beings. This requires an examination of teaching practices in a broader cultural context and is often the more difficult arena in which to identify significant change. A recent experience of a student teacher illustrates this challenge. In our social studies class, we had discussed the importance of the hidden curriculum that can discriminate against girls. For example, we noted a tendency for boys to be more vocal in classroom discussions. When the student teacher was discussing this observation with her cooperating teacher, the cooperating teacher said it was a concern to her as well and that she hoped she had a proper balance. They agreed to have the student teacher tally the number of times the cooperating teacher called on boys and girls. Despite the teacher's best intentions, she did in fact call on more boys than girls, thus reinforcing the hidden curriculum of passive learning on the part of girls and greater attention-getting behaviors on the part of boys. From that point on, both student and teacher actively sought ways to change this pattern. They included more small-group activities that assigned roles to members of groups so that boys and girls wouldn't be in a position to compete for or acquiesce to task assignments. In addition, they called on girls regardless of whether or not their hands were raised. Reflection as critical inquiry underscores the need to examine long-range consequences when transforming the role of educational institutions in a broader cultural context.

Colleges and universities are giving greater credence to reflective teaching as a significant aspect of teacher preparation. Bridging theory and practice is the salient feature of this area of professional development. Table 7.1 summarizes various levels of reflective teaching as outlined by Linda Valli (1992). The taxonomy places technical rationality on a continuum with reflective practice, suggesting that all levels are worthwhile but that the higher levels require greater depth and challenge in bringing about significant change. Reflective teaching is tantamount to making informed decisions about the relationship between one's teaching styles and students' learning styles.

TABLE 7.1

Levels of Reflective Teaching

	Level	Quality of Reflection	Content for Reflection
Reflective Practice	6. critical	problematizing the goals and purposes of schooling in light of justice and other ethical criteria	social and political dimensions of schooling
	5. personalistic	hearing one's own voice	personal growth relational issues
	4. deliberative	weighing competing claims and viewpoints	a range of teaching concerns
	3. reflection-in-action	contextualizing claims and viewpoints	personal teaching performance
Technical Rationality	2. technical decision making	matching performance to external guidelines	generic instruction and management behaviors derived from research on teaching
	1. behavioral	not applicable	generic instruction and management behaviors derived from research on teaching*

*At the behavioral level, this is prescribed, not reflective content.

Source: Valli, L. (1992). *Reflective teacher education: Cases and critiques.* Albany: State University of New York Press. Reprinted by permission of the State University of New York Press © 1992, State University of New York. All rights reserved.

✣ LEARNING STYLES

As a part of your teacher preparation you have probably taken a learning theories course. In this section you will see selected examples of the way in which learning theories affect teachers' decisions regarding curriculum and instruction. By this time in your role as a student, you probably have a fairly good idea of your preferred learning style. But perhaps you have never thought about it in a systematic way. When you have a homework assignment or need to study for a test, do you like to gather a group or do you prefer to isolate yourself for solitary concentration? When you are in a classroom situation, do you prefer to listen to a lecture or discuss ideas in small-group settings? Would you rather read a book or watch a video? Work in the morning or late in the evening? Do your preferences change when the subject matter changes? That is, do you prefer doing math homework alone but social studies assignments in a group? Your preferences may be related to your preferred learning style.

Dunn and Dunn (1978) studied adults and children and derived eighteen elements that relate to learning styles. They fall into four broad categories. *Environmental elements* include sound, light, temperature, and physical design. *Emotionality elements* include motivation, persistence, responsibility, and the need for structure or flexibility. *Physical needs* include perceptual strengths (sight, sound, touch), intake (food, drink), time of day (morning, afternoon), and mobility (need to move around, ability to sit still). *Sociological preferences* include works best alone, works

TABLE 7.2

Learning Style Inventory

1.	Time	When is the student most alert? In the early morning, at lunchtime, in the afternoon, in the evening, at night?
2.	Schedule	What is the student's attention span? Continuous, irregular, short bursts of concentrated effort, forgetting periods, etc.?
3.	Amount of Sound	What level of noise can the student tolerate? Absolute quiet, a murmur, distant sound, high level of conversation?
4.	Type of Sound	What type of sound produces a positive reaction? Music, conversation, laughter, working groups?
5.	Type of Work Group	How does the student work best? Alone, with one person, with a small task group, in a large team, a combination?
6.	Amount of Pressure	What kind of pressure (if any) does the student need? Relaxed, slight, moderate, extreme?
7.	Type of Pressure and Motivation	What helps to motivate this student? Self, teacher expectation, deadline, rewards, recognition of achievement, internalized interest, etc.?
8.	Place	Where does the student work best? Home, school, learning centers, library media corner?
9.	Physical Environment and Conditions	Floor, carpet, reclining, sitting, desk, temperature, table lighting, type of clothing, food?
10.	Type of Assignments	On which type of assignments does the student thrive? Contracts, totally self-directed projects, teacher-selected tasks, etc.?
11.	Perceptual Strengths and Styles	How does the student learn most easily? Visual materials, sound recording, printed media, tactile experiences, kinesthetic activities, multimedia packages, combination of these?
12.	Type of Structure and Evaluation	What type of structure suits this student most of the time? Strict, flexible, self-starting, continuous, occasional, time-line expectations, terminal assessment, etc.?

Source: Rita and Kenneth Dunn, *Practical Approaches to Individualizing Instruction* (© 1972, Parker Publishing Co., Inc., West Nyack, New York), pp. 29–30.

best with peers, works best paired with someone else and works best with adults. The Dunns suggest that teachers ask students to respond to a learning style inventory such as the one listed in Table 7.2 so that they can individualize instruction accordingly.

Howard Gardner's eight types of intelligence have been translated to ways of thinking about learning styles. Gardner maintains that American culture has had a limited view of intelligence, emphasizing verbal and reasoning abilities at the expense of other forms of intelligence. He suggests that all individuals have the various types of intelligence, which are tied to different neurological systems. Some may be more fully developed than others, but all students have the potential to develop the eight intelligences in varying degrees. Gardner's views encourage teachers to be more open-minded about the range of intelligence in young people so that these dimensions can be identified and nurtured. Based on Gardner's theory, a teacher should attempt to recognize the various aspects of intelligence in students and plan lessons which will cultivate the eight areas. Following are the eight types of intelligence identified by Gardner (1983, 1999; Gardner, Kornhaber, & Wake, 1996):

1. *Linguistic intelligence:* auditory and oral aspects of language that relate to word meaning, order syntax, and inflections
2. *Musical intelligence:* sensitivity to rhythm, pitch, and timbre of music
3. *Logical-mathematical intelligence:* ability to perform actions with objects and understand relations among actions
4. *Spatial intelligence:* capacity to perceive and re-create forms in the physical world
5. *Bodily kinesthetic intelligence:* ability to use body in skilled ways, either expressively or athletically
6. *Intrapersonal intelligence:* ability to assess one's own feelings and emotions
7. *Interpersonal intelligence:* ability to assess the feelings and moods of others
8. *Naturalistic intelligence* ability to identify and classify patterns in nature

Gardner continues to develop his theory and, at the writing of this book, is considering a ninth intelligence, *existential intelligence.*

Scholars continue to research the relationship between learning styles, teaching styles, and academic achievement. Reflection versus impulsivity, field dependence versus field independence (e.g., working with others or alone), conceptual development, and locus of control (e.g., the degree of self-directed behavior) are the more observable factors that have been investigated (Hunt, 1968; Yando & Kagan, 1968). Interest inventories, questionnaires, and observation may provide the teacher with information about preferred learning styles, but achievement motivation may be influenced by a host of factors not accessible to these diagnostic tools. In *Student Self-Esteem: Integrating the Self* (McEachron-Hirsch, 1993) scholars found that the desire to achieve was tied to global images of self, not merely highly specialized images of a learning style. Their findings underscore the importance of viewing learning style classifications in a broader context. Encouraging students to do well in school is much more complex than creating a match between an instructional strategy and preferred learning styles. In addition to expectations, academic achievement is tied to family, peers, perceptions of self, and social perceptions of cultural groups. When reflecting on specific learning styles, it is always healthy to examine the wide range of social factors influencing academic performance. The same holds true for teaching styles, to which we now turn.

✦ TEACHING STYLES

Beginning student teachers' preferred teaching styles usually develop into wider repertoires through additional years of experience. Traditional images of teachers typically include the teacher at the front of the class facing an "audience" of students who are taking notes (Joseph & Burnaford, 1994). Although transmitting information is still appropriate today, educators have expanded teaching roles to include direct and indirect instruction. This section examines the variety of roles open to teachers. Even though the subsections are entitled *direct* and *indirect* instruction, it is useful to keep in mind that teaching roles often change from one mode to another within a given lesson.

Direct Instruction: Teacher As Disseminator of Information

Direct instruction refers to a more formalized role of the teacher as a disseminator of information. This can take many forms—lecture, storytelling, guided discussion, demonstration, reenactment, and tutorial, to mention a few. Elementary and middle school teachers recognize that the lecture style of teaching should be used in limited ways due to the developmental stages of students. Primary-age children do not have the attention spans to listen to expository presentations for extended periods of time. Likewise, upper elementary students begin to *tune out* if lectures are not motivational. The challenge for you is to determine when it is appropriate to relay information and how it can be done to hold student attention.

Lecture

There are times when the most efficient and practical way to present information is through a *lecture* format. Imagine for example, that you are a seventh-grade teacher who is starting an in-depth unit on the Depression and you need to review the events in the 1920s to provide a common base of information. One way is to plan a twenty-minute presentation that is carefully organized with a beginning, middle, and end. The beginning may include the purpose and objective of your talk. The middle, or content focus, might include key events in the twenties. To maintain student interest, include audiovisual materials such as music and pictures from the Roaring Twenties. Or you might provide an outline on an overhead transparency that has broad categories listed, with the expectation that students will fill in details from the lecture. This helps focus students' attention and communicates that even though the information is a review leading up to a major unit, the information is as important as the events of the 1930s. The end could be a summary of key ideas that will set the scene for what will ensue in the 1930s. At the end of this lecture format, a list of key questions can set up the next phase of the class, which would be a guided discussion. With a little creativity, lectures do not need to be stuffy or boring.

Guided Discussion

Guided discussion is a modified form of direct instruction because the teacher is in control of where he or she wants the discussion to go. The kinds of questions asked determine the nature and mood of the discussion. For example, if the teacher is asking a lot of *convergent* questions, students will be responding with answers that are based on recalling information. "What important federation of craft unions was created in the U.S. in 1886?" is a convergent question because the American Federation of Labor is the one answer. If the teacher is asking *divergent* questions, the questions are more open-ended; thus, the student responses will have greater variation. "What distinguishes modern artists from impressionists?" is a divergent question because several characteristics can be presented.

How a teacher asks questions also influences the flow of the discussion. For example, if the teacher asks nondesignated questions, he or she typically responds to students who either raise their hands or call out the answers. A designated question is one that is asked of a specific student and is often a way to bring students into the discussion who don't necessarily volunteer responses. The kinds of questions posed by the teacher dictate both the content of the discussion and who participates. Questioning strategies as a means to elicit different levels of thinking will be discussed in more detail in Chapter 9.

Storytelling

Storytelling is a way to present information in an expository fashion that is motivational to younger children. Telling children facts about historical events can sometimes be dry, but when a teacher reviews the information and weaves it into a story, the children hear history come alive and will listen for longer periods of time. If the teacher dresses up as a figure in history, and reenacts biographical anecdotes or significant events, children will be mesmerized by hearing history in first person. Another way that history can come alive is through literature. More trade books of the historical fiction genre are available for young children. While reading such stories audiovisual aids such as flannel board pieces can help to illustrate the story in a more dynamic way.

Joy Hakim writes history texts with the intent to make history interesting to children and youth. Her series relies heavily on feedback from students who are the age of the intended audience. For example, they review her writing and use the following symbols—G, UC, B—to indicate *good, unclear,* and *boring.* During an age where teachers compete with video productions, it is necessary to achieve the delicate balance between motivation through a story well told and the search for historical accuracy. An important word of caution—the teacher needs to be very critical and continue to conduct research to ensure that the history depicted by trade books is factually correct. According to Barton (1997) one of the limitations of using a narrative style is that children may think of the past as *too much* like a story, that is, that historical developments proceeded in a linear fashion. Barton suggests that children need guidance because "they do not automatically recognize that many things were going on simultaneously, or that different groups of people were having different experiences" (p. 16).

Demonstrations

Demonstrations are additional ways to spark interest in a particular phase of history or contemporary event. For example, showing students how an astrolabe works or demonstrating the use of a loom used by the Navajo Indians allows students to go back in time, albeit somewhat vicariously. Bringing in a spectrophotometer, a modern instrument that compares light rays, is a way to connect human innovations of the past with contemporary technological inventions. Allowing students to *use* antiquated as well as modern inventions after they have been demonstrated is even more effective.

Of course, it is not always feasible to bring ancient artifacts or expensive technology into the classroom and demonstrate their use. Creative elementary and middle school teachers often find ways to design activities that incorporate renditions of the actual artifacts. For example, primary students can card wool, make looms the size of geoboards, or weave construction paper mats to relate to the process of Navajo weaving. Intermediate students can gather leaves and berries from the natural environment, make dyes, color wool, and spin yarn. Middle school students can compare the design patterns of Navajo rugs with those of Peruvian blankets with the purpose of deriving the meaning generated from each culture. The varied student activities are extensions of the initial teacher demonstration. With careful planning, the teacher can simulate workmanship and other creative processes without trivializing the cultural experience across time and space.

Tutorials

Tutorials, or one-on-one instruction, are another form of direct instruction. There are many occasions when tutorials are necessary. A student may embark on a special area of inquiry and the teacher will want to personalize instruction in a way that relates to the student's interests. In this context, direct instruction comes in the form of challenging the student by offering ideas, suggestions, or raising questions. There are also times when students need individualized instruction because there are gaps in their understanding of a certain concept or they have quickly mastered a concept and are ready to move on for greater depth or new material. In these instances teachers use direct instruction to reteach material not previously understood or to move students forward so that their learning progresses.

As you can see, direct instruction takes many forms. Whereas traditional images depict teachers in a lecture mode, this section has demonstrated that a variety of options are available to teachers who want to impart knowledge in interesting ways.

Indirect Instruction: Teacher As Facilitator and Resource

Indirect instruction also requires careful planning and resourcefulness on the part of the teacher. During indirect instruction, the teacher provides students with access to information through inquiry or discovery activities, research, learning centers, computers, simulations, role playing, or field trips, to mention a few. In all instances, students are actively engaged in learning that the teacher has organized. The more active role of the teacher takes place behind the scenes as he or she previews sites for field trips, selects computer programs, designs learning centers, provides a structure for student learning exercises, conducts research, and evaluates student performance.

Working with and observing students as they perform their learning tasks is another important aspect of indirect teaching. To an untrained eye, the teacher who is monitoring the work of students as they progress through these activities may appear to be "not teaching." On the contrary, indirect teaching highlights the importance of planning activities that involve students in more active ways, while the teacher monitors and assesses growth and achievement. Indirect teaching can be effective only when students are actively engaged in learning tasks. This requires planning and close supervision on the part of the teachers. A few examples of indirect instruction are described next.

Inquiry and Discovery

Hilda Taba (1962) and Jerome Bruner (1959) popularized inquiry learning. They advocated the importance of developing content and methods that lead to conceptual learning and have wide transfer value. There is a great deal of overlap between discovery learning and inquiry. Bruner maintains that discovery and inquiry learning "takes place when students are not presented with subject matter in its final form, when subject matter is not organized by the teacher but the students themselves" (Ornstein & Hunkins, 1988, p. 102). Taba contrasted discovery learning with traditional learning (i.e., direct instruction), arguing that in the former context students might discover through exploring the concrete, for example, but in the latter instance, verbal information is transmitted to the learner through the teacher. Both inquiry and discovery learning incorporate aspects of the scientific method. In conjunction with the teacher:

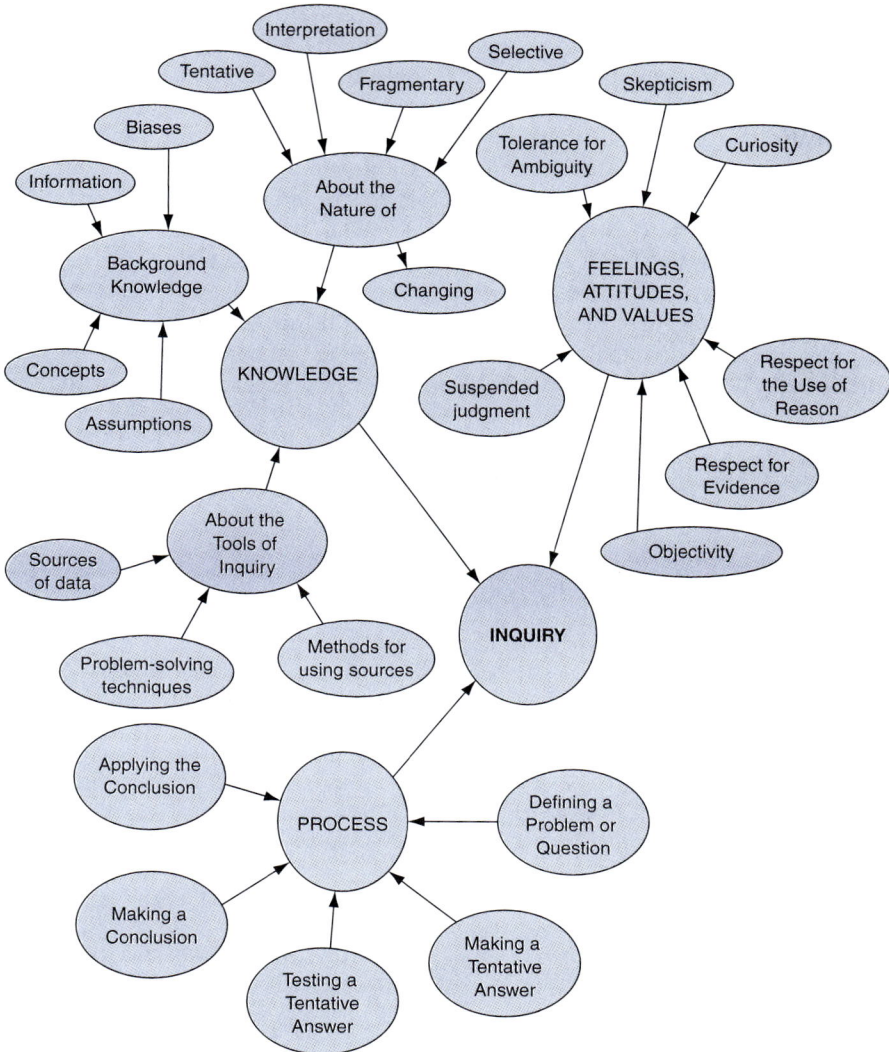

FIGURE 7.1   *The Nature of Inquiry*

SOURCE: Teaching Thinking in Social Studies by Beyer, © 1979. Reprinted by permission of Prentice-Hall, Inc., Upper Saddle River, NJ.

1. Students identify a problem or issue for exploration.
2. Students formulate a hypothesis.
3. Students collect and analyze data to research hypothesis.
4. Students formulate generalizations based upon collected data.

While this condensed four-step process seems rather simplistic, the kinds of thinking and learning that take place during the process are multifaceted. Beyer (1979, p. 29) charts the variety of student responses that emerge throughout inquiry and discovery activities in Figure 7.1.

When students are conducting inquiry it is important that the teacher develop a mechanism for retrieving the many kinds of learning that take place. That is, once inquiry begins student investigation branches in several directions simultaneously. As the search unfolds, students discover tremendous amounts of information, some directly related to the hypothesis, others leading off on tangents. Frustration may set in unless the teacher stresses that the tangential information is not irrelevant. Rather, it is important as a significant aspect of conducting research and discovering new ideas. Many students return to the classroom excited about interesting facts that evolved from the initial inquiry. These exciting facts expand their minds and interests and often lead to further research projects. They are a legitimate part of the research process.

The following guide was developed as a checklist for teachers to self-evaluate their responsiveness to inquiry and discovery teaching. You may find it helpful when making classroom observations during your field experiences in addition to your future teaching endeavors.

CHECK YOUR INQUIRY

Teaching Technique

Mary Sugrue and Jo A. Sweeny

As a teacher, are you concerned with helping your pupils become better thinkers? Do you want students to gain in their ability to utilize knowledge independently and effectively? If so, you may find this checklist of classroom behaviors helpful to you [see Table 7.3].

Read each described classroom behavior carefully; then ask yourself: When my classroom is in normal operation, does the behavior described occur regularly, frequently, sometimes, or seldom? Check the space which you think best describes the normal operation of your classroom. When you have finished, give yourself four points for each item marked "regularly"; three points for "frequently"; two for "sometimes"; and one for "seldom." Fifty points or less means lots of room for improvement; 51–85, you're coming along; 86–110, you're better than most; 111–136, you've mastered inquiry techniques.

Don't be discouraged if you didn't score as well as you wished. Fill out the checklist again a month from now and see how much you've improved.

Source: Today's Education/NEA Journal 58 (May 1969): 43–44. Used by permission.

TABLE 7.3

Am I an Inquiry Teacher?

As Planner:	Regularly	Frequently	Sometimes	Seldom
I focus on lessons involving exploration of significant ideas, concepts, or problem areas that can be investigated at many levels of sophistication	_____	_____	_____	_____
I prepare for a broad range of alternative ideas and values which the students may raise related to a central topic	_____	_____	_____	_____

	Regularly	Frequently	Sometimes	Seldom
I select materials and learning experiences to stimulate student curiosity and support student investigation	_____	_____	_____	_____
Skill-building exercises are tied directly to ongoing learning where they can be utilized and applied	_____	_____	_____	_____
As Introducer:				
My introductory lessons present some problem, question, contradiction, or unknown element that will maximize student thinking	_____	_____	_____	_____
My aim is for students to react freely to the introductory stimulus with little direction from me	_____	_____	_____	_____
I encourage many different responses to a given introductory stimulus and am prepared to deal with alternative patterns of exploration	_____	_____	_____	_____
As Questioner and Inquiry Sustainer:				
The students talk more than I do	_____	_____	_____	_____
Students are free to discuss and interchange their ideas	_____	_____	_____	_____
When I talk, I "question" not "tell"	_____	_____	_____	_____
I consciously use the ideas students have raised and base my statements and questions on their ideas	_____	_____	_____	_____
I redirect student questions in such a way that students are encouraged to arrive at their own answers	_____	_____	_____	_____
My questions are intended to lead the pupils to explore, explain, support, and evaluate their ideas	_____	_____	_____	_____
I encourage the students to evaluate the adequacy of grounds provided for statements made by them or others	_____	_____	_____	_____
Students gain understanding and practice in logical and scientific processes of acquiring, validating, and using knowledge	_____	_____	_____	_____

(Continued)

T A B L E   7 . 3   (Continued)

Am I an Inquiry Teacher?

As Questioner and Inquiry Sustainer:	Regularly	Frequently	Sometimes	Seldom
My questions lead the students to test the validity of their ideas in a broad context of experience	_____	_____	_____	_____
I encourage students to move from examination of particular cases to more generalized concepts and understandings	_____	_____	_____	_____
As Manager:				
I emphasize learning and the use of ideas, rather than managerial functions, such as discipline and record keeping	_____	_____	_____	_____
I allow for flexible seating, student movement, and maximum student use of materials and resources	_____	_____	_____	_____
Class dialogue is conducted in an orderly fashion that emphasizes courtesy and willingness to listen to each person's ideas	_____	_____	_____	_____
Students are actively involved in the planning and maintenance of the total classroom environment	_____	_____	_____	_____
I foster balanced participation by encouraging the more reticent students to take an active role in classroom activities	_____	_____	_____	_____
As Rewarder:				
I encourage and reward the free exchange and testing of ideas	_____	_____	_____	_____
I emphasize the internal rewards that spring from the successful pursuit of one's own ideas	_____	_____	_____	_____
I avoid criticizing or judging ideas offered by students	_____	_____	_____	_____
Each student's contribution is considered legitimate and important	_____	_____	_____	_____
I evaluate students on growth in many aspects of the learning experience, rather than simply on the basis of facts acquired	_____	_____	_____	_____

As Value Investigator:	**Regularly**	**Frequently**	**Sometimes**	**Seldom**
I emphasize that concepts, social issues, policy decisions, attitudes, and values are legitimate areas for discussion	_____	_____	_____	_____
All topics are critically examined, not "taught" as closed issues with a single "right" solution	_____	_____	_____	_____
Use of unfounded, emotionally charged language is minimized in discussing attitudes and values	_____	_____	_____	_____
I encourage the students to explore the implications of holding alternative value and policy positions	_____	_____	_____	_____
I make the student aware of personal and social bases for diversity in attitudes, values, policies	_____	_____	_____	_____
I encourage the students to arrive at value and policy positions of their own that they understand and can defend	_____	_____	_____	_____

Over thirty years later the principles of social inquiry listed in the preceding are most relevant for today's classroom. One modification to the checklist developed by Sugrue and Sweeny is the inclusion of technology as a source of social inquiry. For example, Garofalo, Bennett, and Mason (1999) discuss how graphing calculators, most often used in math classrooms, can help students broaden their social inquiry skills. Through data plotting, students can analyze climate patterns and locations and evaluate multiple perspectives. Graphing calculators can also be used to interpret political polls through statistical analyses. Garofalo, Bennett, and Mason underscore the opportunities for collaboration among teachers across content areas.

Computers

Educating students to be technologically literate is an important goal of social studies teaching. Computers have made it possible for students to access information about people and places from all corners of the world. The Internet makes the notion of bringing the world into the classroom a reality. Not only is it possible to download information, global communication is possible through direct contact with people via Internet capabilities. For example, 11- to 13-year-old students in New York City and New Zealand participated in a five-year project via faxes, videotaping, e-mail, and *plain old letter writing*. The teachers wanted the students to describe their cultures to one another in their own words. Through the exchanges students learned about the cultural resurgence of the Maori of New Zealand, to value their own multicultural

PhotoDisc

backgrounds, and how to investigate ways in which cultures and subcultures pass down cultural values (Schnell & Schur, 1999, p. 75).

Educational institutions at all levels are racing to keep abreast of computer technology in the workplace. There is a tremendous range of resources across levels. Probably more than any other subject area, computer literacy cannot be correlated with age levels. In other words, some students in the primary levels may know more about computer technology than some university professors because the students have been educated by teachers, family members, or friends. Schools can play an important role in closing these gaps if teachers receive support through training programs and resource allocations. In this section an overview of computer-assisted instruction is provided, followed by a list of computer information sources.

Information technology (IT) can take many forms in elementary and middle school classrooms. Skill development, drill and practice, simulations, tutorials, and database problem solving are some of the more prevalent approaches. Word-processing programs are common in the early grades and teach basic skills such as keyboarding to build a foundation for long-term computer literacy. More sophisticated skill-building activities introduced in the upper elementary grades include the use of spreadsheets. After students learn how to enter data in rows and columns, they can then retrieve and chart the data, thus helping them with the important research skill of categorizing and organizing information. Appleworks and Microsoft® Works are integrated programs that combine word processing and spreadsheets. Lotus® 1-2-3 and Microsoft® Excel are additional spreadsheet packages.

Drill-and-practice exercises, whether on or off the computer, are typically very dry. However, a computer can provide immediate reinforcement in ways that may be more motivational to students than using flashcards or workbooks. For students who may become frustrated by writing exercises, drill-and-practice exercises on the computer may be preferred because they use a multiple-choice response format. Locating places using longitude and latitude and learning the states and their capitals are typical drill-and-practice social studies exercises available on computers (Welton & Mallon, 1992). Tutorials are another way in which computer programs simplify information by arranging it in step-by-step sequences. Many of these tutorials are available through Internet capabilities, cited at the end of this section.

Computers generate stimulating social studies lessons via database problem solving. Students can enter large amounts of data, from diary entries to demographic information about the world's population. Diary analysis can generate insights into the everyday lives of ordinary and famous people. Students might ask, "How did the daily activities of William Byrd's life change after the death of his wife?" The diaries of William Byrd reveal a great deal about the life of a man who left a record in shorthand. Spanning more than thirty years of his life, the diaries may not have been intended for public scrutiny. One might ask students, "What are the social ethics of diary analysis?"

Demographic investigations can yield information ranging from human rights violations to birth and death rates throughout the globe. By raising the question "Is there a relationship between forms of government and the number of human rights violations?" students may develop numerous hypotheses about political systems. CompuServe and PC Globe are programs that have multifaceted database programs. Scholastic has data files for U.S. history, U.S. government, and world geography. CD-ROMs also contain vast amounts of information and are less expensive than printed forms.

Computer simulations are another popular tool used to teach social studies. *The Oregon Trail, Where in America is Carmen San Diego?, Lemonade Stand,* and *Maya Quest* are just a few of the programs that allow students to imagine social and economic conditions. Most of the simulations are designed for upper elementary students. *Sim City* is one I recently observed seventh graders "playing." Although it may have seemed like play to them, they were learning the complex interrelationships between city planning and the impact of human beings on land use. Students had to make timely decisions about neighborhood growth in relation to the depletion of natural resources. They quickly learned that there is a much more dynamic impact on land use and property based on human settlement patterns.

Computers offer many exciting alternatives to teachers and students. Yet there are a few issues that require further attention. Teacher preparation and in-service programs are hard-pressed to keep pace with the latest technology. Many educators question the quality of the software purchases that are expensive but end up being underutilized due to equipment that is in disrepair. These limitations have more to do with inadequate maintenance procedures rather than the intended use of computers. Additional concerns are related to the ways in which computer packages are integrated into the curriculum. Many teachers welcome computer labs, which offer opportunities for students to preview software, but they are frustrated by the add-on nature of programs. More time and coordination is needed to integrate the programs with curricular goals. Nevertheless, the benefits of computers appear to outweigh the drawbacks. Once these concerns are addressed, students and teachers will be able to access information and analyze it in ways that build bridges between the classroom and the rest of the world. For further information about computer-based education you can consult the following sources. Additional website sources are listed in the Reference section of this chapter.

- *Classroom Computer Learning.* Intentional Educations Inc., 341 Mt. Auburn Street, Watertown, MA 02172
- *The Computing Teacher.* International Council for Computers in Education, University of Oregon, 1878 Agate Street, Eugene, OR 97403-1923
- *Educational Products Information Exchange.* P.O. Box 620, Stony Brook, NY 11790
- *Educator's Handbook and Software Directory.* Vital Information, Inc., 7899 Mastin Drive, Overland Park, KS 66204
- *Electronic Education.* Suite 220, 1311 Executive Center Drive, Tallahassee, FL 32301
- *Electronic Learning.* 2280 Arbor Boulevard, Dayton OH 45439
- *Microcomputer Software and Information for Teachers.* Northwest Regional Education Lab, 300 SW 6th Avenue, Portland, OR 97204
- *Minnesota Education Computing Corporation.* 3490 Lexington Avenue North, St. Paul, MN 55126
- *School Microwave Directory.* Dresden Associates, P.O. Box 246, Dresden, ME 04342
- *Softswap* (for exchanging original programs). San Mateo County Office of Education, 333 Main Street, Redwood City, CA 94063
- *Sources for Courses.* TALMIS, 115 N. Oak Park Avenue, Oak Park, IL 60301
- *Swift's Directory of Educational Software.* Sterling Swift Publishing Co., 1600 Fortview Road, Austin, TX 78704

Role Playing and Simulations

Role playing and simulations are two creative ways to teach indirectly. Both allow students to put themselves in imaginary situations that either re-create past events or perform social encounters that could happen in the present or future. The benefits of role playing and simulations include opportunities for students to:

1. Assume a character quite unlike oneself.
2. Develop an appreciation for the social contexts in which people live.
3. Develop an appreciation for someone else's point of view.
4. Plan and perform for classmates, teachers, and parents.
5. Compare one's life with others across time and space.
6. Participate in an activity that is expressive.

Role playing can range from very informal and impromptu acts to highly structured situations. Primary students might act out the exchange of money between a cashier and customer. More elaborate role-playing activities would be singing and acting out the motions to "The Wheels on the Bus." Intermediate students may role-play *Paul Revere's Ride* and middle school students might reenact speeches given at the first woman's conference in Seneca Falls in 1848. More elaborate upper elementary role playing would include creating a way to demonstrate how a bill becomes law or performing a mock trial at the House of Burgesses.

Simulations help students understand how others may have responded in different time periods or social situations. *Rafá Rafá* (Shirts, 1976), for example, is a simulation that creates scenarios for two distinct cultural groups who encounter each other for the first time. Their behaviors and language are entirely different, and they, therefore, need to decode meaning from actions and sounds. From these *hypothetical* cultural encounters, teachers and students become more sensitized for understanding another culture.

One of the drawbacks of simulations is that they are "gamelike," even though this quality is what makes them motivational and engaging to students. Like reenactments, role playing, and storytelling, there is risk for distorting history. Therefore, it is always a good idea to discuss the limitations of simulations with students before and after their use. With older students it would be a challenge to see if they could create a simulation. As a part of a unit of study, groups of students could conduct extensive research, then design a simulation with the understanding that peers and teachers would critique the interpretation for historical accuracy.

Selecting simulations requires careful scrutiny on the part of teachers and curriculum coordinators. Sharon Muir (1980) published a useful guide, *Simulation Games for Elementary Social Studies,* in *Social Education.* "AskERIC" is an Internet source of simulations on topics such as voting and the American Revolution (http://www.ericir.syr.edu/Virtual/Lessons/Social_St/US_history/USH0003.html). Key questions for analysis when previewing a selection might include: Does the simulation reflect careful research? Are the lives of people portrayed in realistic ways, or are cultural traditions trivialized? Is enough information provided to students, or are the roles expected to be filled extemporaneously? Are the goals and objectives clearly stated? Does the simulation add to a broader unit of study or is it being used as a filler? Are the social studies generalizations and key concepts explicitly stated? Although simulations are a great way to teach in an indirect manner, one must ensure that the simulation is not so indirect as to send confusing or unintended messages to students.

Learning Centers

Learning centers have been a mainstay of elementary and middle school classrooms for years. In a nineteenth-century one-room schoolhouse, a table with a rock collection constituted a learning or interest center. Today, computers are popular learning centers. Indirect teaching through learning centers was quite popular in the 1970s. Having had an opportunity to do an internship in the British Primary Schools during this time, I and fellow students from Arizona State University were filled with enthusiasm about implementing the more indirect style of teaching observed in Great Britain. Learning centers and open education were perceived as innovations in teaching at that time. Even though this status has faded over the past twenty years, learning center strategies have made significant contributions to variation in classroom instruction. This section describes the purposes, kinds and components of learning center approaches.

One of the purposes of a learning center is to provide students with self-directed experiences. When a student is engaged in learning center activities, he or she is exploring, analyzing, reading, computing, building, writing, measuring, or conducting various other tasks. Often students work independently, in pairs, or occasionally in small groups. In working with others, students have the added opportunity to plan and negotiate learning tasks with peers. A related purpose of learning centers is to engage students in self-directed activities so that the teacher can observe student learning and provide individualized instruction where needed. Often, while students are participating in learning center activities, the teacher has opportunities to provide direct instruction to students through tutorials or small-group instruction. In this latter situation, an observer might see direct and indirect instruction taking place simultaneously.

There are many different kinds of learning centers. The following list describes some that you may have already seen in practice or participated in when you were in elementary or middle school.

1. **Display.** A display table or display case presents artifacts, materials, student projects, and the like, for student viewing. Teachers may leave such viewings open-ended and informal, or they may ask that students examine and record specific information.

2. **Computer.** Computers are found within the classroom or in a computer lab. Those located in the classroom are usually used as students finish other work or on a rotational basis to include all students. Computer labs are sometimes set aside for weekly classes similar to the format of art, music, and physical education.

3. **Research Center.** Teachers often set up research centers in the classroom where they display materials and books that supplement traditional resources such as textbooks. Given thematic units such as Indigenous Populations or Inventions, students also add their own resources to the center. Inquiry questions often lead students to these centers or are generated by the center.

4. **Activity Center.** Learning centers can be designed to complete specific tasks. For example, students may measure distances on maps, locate places using longitude and latitude, or prepare salt and flour maps. Students may create a panoramic display of significant events in their community's history.

5. **Working Bulletin Boards.** Bulletin boards can be transformed to learning centers. By designing an activity on the bulletin board, students have another place for indirect instruction. Self-checking answer flaps are motivational devices that can provide immediate reinforcement.

Most of the learning centers just described require space, which is at a premium. But teachers have always been creative when it comes to maximizing limited resources. For example, learning centers suspended from the ceiling, posted on the sides of file cabinets, or stored in tote trays or file folders are just some of the ways that centers can fit into crowded classrooms.

Even though learning centers have great variation in style, you should be aware of certain shared characteristics to maximize their effectiveness. Since one of the benefits to learning centers is that students are self-sufficient, instructions should be clearly posted or explained in advance. Many logistical problems arise when directions are unclear and students from several learning centers need assistance from one teacher at the same time. It is also important to have a system for recording the performances of students at the learning centers. Being accountable for the learning that takes place through these indirect approaches is necessary for students to appreciate that the knowledge they gain through their efforts is valued in the same way that the knowledge imparted directly from the teacher is valued.

Another important consideration is the amount of time it takes to design and create learning centers. Whether gathering artifacts for displays, previewing software, or constructing a three-paneled backdrop, all centers require extensive preparation outside of the daily teaching routine. Therefore, it is important to design center materials so that they can be revitalized on a regular basis or stored easily for future use. For example, if you wanted students to work on their map and globe skills on a weekly basis throughout a large part of the school year, there are timesaving devices that a beginning teacher should know. If learning *scale* is one of a variety of map and globe objectives, you may not want to design the entire learning center, complete with motivational visuals, around the topic of *scale*. Instead, consider making an attractive learning center with the theme of map and globe skills or a more appealing title like "Finding Your Place in the World." For a couple of weeks, scale might be the theme of the activities. Later, the map and globe skills activity might change to time zones or interpreting weather maps, and so on. In this manner, you would not be starting from scratch each time you wanted to prepare learning center activities; rather, you would be revitalizing the basic theme of map and globe skills.

Field Trips

When students recall social studies experiences they had in elementary or middle school, field trips usually generate fond memories. When I ask my students to share their memories, it is evident that one's historical knowledge is tied closely to the part of the United States where they went to school. Students from Texas remember the Alamo and where Kennedy was assassinated; Virginians recall Jamestown, Yorktown, and Colonial Williamsburg, and so on. I remember seeing the ships in Los Angeles Harbor as a first grader and making tugboats when we returned to school. Field trips are a great way to move from a classroom context of learning about something *out there* to learning while *being there*. Being at a historical site allows students to visualize what life was like and to learn about the people who lived there from docents or other knowledgeable professionals.

In addition to historical sites, students gain firsthand knowledge of the workplace by visiting factories, harbors, kitchens, assembly lines, hospitals, and fire stations. Many industries include student tours as a normal part of their operations. Smaller businesses generally welcome visits by classrooms if teachers have explained what they want the students to observe, as long as production can continue smoothly. Primary students can learn how cookies and bread are made at the local bakeries. Free samples at the end of the tour are a special treat! On a recent visit to the Zapata Haynie, a menhaden fishing industry in the Chesapeake Bay, the manager and owner, Steve Jones, was happy to inform teachers of field trip opportunities. Through this exchange we discussed the kind of job training that was needed by the schools' vocational education programs. Such two-way exchanges are good ways to build community ties and develop mutual goals.

Field trips require thorough planning to be effective. When field trips take place in the local community, the teacher can make preliminary contacts. Occasionally, a class may take long bus trips to visit a site for the first time. In these instances, teachers can write to the location in advance and receive materials that he or she can then use in preparation for the excursion. At the local level the following suggestions are useful steps when preparing for the actual visit.

Prior to Field Trip

1. Contact the location to determine if there are organized tours for students. Ask whether the organization or institution has materials they send that prepare students for the visit.
2. When possible, visit the location, take notes, and observe specific sources of information that are most relevant to the unit of study.
3. Prepare an Observation Guide that students can take with them to record pertinent information. Be careful not to overstructure the Guide or students will lose the freedom to explore the site.
4. Prepare students for the field trip by ensuring that the visit fits into a particular unit of study. Ask them to make predictions about what they might see and generate questions regarding their expectations.
5. Organize the logistics of transportation and meals: for example, permission slips, bag lunches, admission fees, departure and arrival times and locations, chaperons, behavioral expectations on bus, buddy systems, and so on.

Field Trip

6. If students have been thoroughly prepared and have sufficient background knowledge to appreciate what they are seeing, questions should be forthcoming in a natural way. Encourage students to ask questions. Docents appreciate students who are well prepared. Remind students, when appropriate, to complete their Observation Guide.

Post Field Trip

7. Discuss knowledge gained from field trip. Check Observation Guide. Assess which questions raised by students were addressed by the visit and which ones require further research. Extend the field trip into additional activities such as art, writing, and other forms of creative expression.
8. When appropriate, students can write thank-you notes to staff at sponsoring site, as well as to chaperons.

Field trips signify an excursion for students to learn more about their community. Yet field trips can also be a time when students can have an impact on the community. Some communities have set up regular visits between students and the residents of nursing homes, for example. Planned activities such as reading, playing music, or art projects are ways in which generations can join together informally, followed by more task-oriented visits when mutually desirable. Sometimes these experiences lead to more structured opportunities such as conducting oral histories. Both students and residents are enriched by the chance to talk with each other, especially since these generations may have limited involvement if students don't live close to grandparents and vice versa. Additional ways in which field trips are designed for students to have an impact on the community include philanthropic projects like painting homeless shelters, beautifying the neighborhood by planting trees, and cleaning polluted areas.

The Internet offers a new vehicle for taking a field trip—the virtual field trip. A virtual field trip can help students prepare for the actual field trip, or it can provide a simulated field trip to a place that may not be logistically possible to visit. Bellan and Scheurman (1998) demonstrate how they have utilized the virtual site of Ft. Snelling Historic Site in St. Paul, Minnesota, to prepare for the actual field trip as well as extend the learning once they return to the classroom. Their article in *Social Education* also provides additional sites for virtual trip adventures.

As you reflect on the many different teaching and learning styles, it may become obvious that direct and indirect teaching take place simultaneously throughout the course of a student's school day. There are varying degrees to which direct and indirect teaching take place, depending on the teacher's preferred styles, student learning styles, and instructional guidelines from the administration. In the case study that follows, you will see how teaching and learning styles, motivation, abilities, and curricula is integrated through the experiences of an elementary student, Diane Bradford. The purpose of the case study is to demonstrate how one student's needs are met through collaboration among professionals, parents, and the student. It also spotlights the hard work and commitment required on the part of the team to match student needs with the classroom environment. Commentary by the educators who conducted the case study demonstrates the challenge of curriculum integration and individualizing instruction.

✦ CASE STUDY: DIANE BRADFORD

Diane Bradford is a gifted student with a learning disability whose needs came to my attention and that of colleagues several years ago. In a project involving educators with expertise in school psychology, special education, gifted education, and curriculum and instruction, a curriculum plan was developed to illustrate collaborative planning for students with special needs. Excerpts from the project are presented here to illustrate child-centered curriculum development across content areas. For a more elaborate discussion of the collaborative process with child-study teams, see *Planning Effective Curriculum for Gifted Learners* (VanTassel-Baska, 1992).

Diane: Challenge and Competence

Diane was selected for child study because she expressed a variety of behaviors, sometimes charming, sometimes difficult. Based on certain classification schemes in gifted and special education programs, Diane would qualify for both services. Because of her frustration with schoolwork and the perceived discrepancy between her ability and performance in the classroom, Diane was referred for special education testing. In the classroom Diane showed difficulty with reading, handwriting, and organization skills, such as following directions.

Background information revealed that Diane lived with her biological parents in a large metropolitan area in the eastern United States; she has a sister five years older. Her Caucasian parents were both professionally employed. Her father earned a bachelor's degree in political science and a law degree and currently holds a prominent governmental position. Diane's mother earned a bachelor's degree in education and has worked part-time as a teacher, model, and clothing representative until the year of the case study, when she took a full-time position as admissions director of a private secondary school. The family is active in athletic, volunteer, church, and political organizations.

As a young child, Diane was characterized by her mother as fitful in sleep patterns, intense, and exhibiting high energy levels. She showed early signs of physical agility and precocious motor development. Health problems centered on ear infections (otitis media) and allergies. Diane was also characterized by her mother as a defiant child at home and an aggressive, easily frustrated child at school. Beginning in third grade, Diane began taking Ritalin daily and, as a result, attentional and emotional concerns had been somewhat alleviated.

A special education report qualified Diane for special education services as a learning disabled student, with an IEP program that addressed visual-motor integration problems, remedial reading, reduction of workload in the classroom, and peer support. She met weekly with a learning disabilities specialist and a speech therapist. Diane had not been referred to a gifted program, partially due to the difficulty she had experienced with schoolwork and partially due to an IQ-based cutoff score for gifted programs at a level beyond her tested functioning. On a WISC-R, her performance score was 105 and her verbal score was 124, yielding a combined IQ score of 118, and placing her at the 88th percentile on the test. Such a disparity between performance and verbal scores could suggest a learning disability; yet it also reflects a strength in verbal areas not discerned from the global IQ score. In Diane's school division, students must score at 140 or above on a global IQ measure to receive gifted services.

Strong abilities were demonstrated, however, in several areas. Outside the classroom she was actively involved in sports activities in which she competed at a high level of achievement. She had exemplary performances within her age group on a local swim team and competed as a third grader at an international swimming competition. In addition, Diane held a local record in running on a recreational track team.

Diane exhibited social and leadership strengths as well. When teachers felt that certain competencies had been achieved after instruction with the special educator and that it was no longer necessary to leave her regular classroom, Diane insisted on continuing with the class so she could perform the leading role in a play that was in progress. Somehow, through finesse and persuasion, Diane managed to continue leaving the regular class to continue her role in special education for reasons that appear to be socially motivated. Diane's experience in a social studies simulation in the regular classroom provided further insights into her social capabilities. As "store manager," Diane quickly mastered her responsibilities as a link in the exchange of goods and services and performed admirably in this complex role.

Diane showed some evidence of low self-esteem, indicating to her parents that she thinks of herself as "stupid" and that other students don't like her. Her older sister was identified for the gifted program several years ago and evidences more classic "gifted behaviors," such as high test performance, early literacy development, and ease in mastering school subjects. The presence of a highly successful and achieving sibling may also affect Diane's self-perception. Yet, social-emotional assessment from observations, interview, and projective data does not reveal any serious emotional concerns.

There are indications that Diane tends to possess very high self-expectations and ambitions but may not always possess the internal resources to meet those goals. A sense of frustration and disappointment may result when goals are not attained, and this may further impact upon her self-esteem. She appears to derive a great deal of satisfaction from her athletic endeavors, and this seems to give her a sense of accomplishment. Overall, Diane appears to enjoy school but is aware of her difficulties in the classroom. Even so, she seems to maintain her motivation for academic success in the face of obstacles.

In educational terms, Diane would likely be diagnosed as gifted learning disabled based on the behaviors she demonstrates in various settings. Yet, as is the case with most special populations of gifted learners—those with handicaps, cultural diversity, low income—educational contexts have trouble accommodating the discrepancy pattern of functioning they represent. This pattern is characterized by some easily identifiable variables that cut across those populations, including a peak and valley profile of behavior, underachievement, problems in normalized social environments, and atypical family dynamics, many times exacerbated by the child's behavior.

Individualizing Curriculum Through Collaboration

The team of specialists in curriculum, gifted, special education, and school psychology met over a series of months to devise recommendations for Diane. They addressed psychological theories, developmental stages, and teaching and learning styles. Table 7.4 summarizes their curriculum and instructional recommendations, personalized to Diane's individual needs.

The case illustration of Diane Bradford illustrates the integrated way in which psychological theories, developmental stages, and teaching and learning styles manifest themselves in the teacher/learner relationship. For example, behaviorist influences across areas of expertise are more apparent in the recommendations, characterized by self-regulating behavior, teaching study and organizational skills, diagnostic-prescriptive models, and computer applications that provide immediate reinforcement on an individualized basis without peer competition. Cognitive developmental awareness is reflected in recommendations that underscore the importance of simulations, role playing, hands-on materials and projects, problem-solving strategies, literature-based reading, and thematic curricular approaches. Phenomenological theoretical aspects manifest themselves by an awareness of the need to balance in-school and out-of-school experiences to benefit the "whole" child, through the following: building self-esteem by reading to younger children, developing recognition for athletic strengths, providing support for strengths in the arts and social leadership, encouraging horseback riding activities for organizational skills and relaxation, and addressing issues such as ceasing Ritalin use and sibling rivalry in a family context. Attention to learning styles also emerged across areas of expertise in curriculum, special education, gifted education, and school psychology. Diane would not be viewed as comfortable in competitive academic contexts when speed in recall of information from print material or mathematical solutions were presented. Athletic competition based on speed in running or swimming or competition that is demonstrated through social negotiation and leadership are contexts that Diane would probably relish. Thus, interpersonal and intrapersonal learning styles vary based on the social and academic context. Visual and auditory experiences are beneficial to Diane, whereas visual processing difficulties manifested through decoding print material spotlight the need to enhance Diane's comfort level with being a linguistic learner. Given Diane's preference for social interaction with peers, she would also be considered a learner who favored a field-dependent learning style.

TABLE 7.4

Interventions for Diane Bradford and Her Family

Discipline	Specific Intervention
General Education	Simulations
	Hands-on approaches
	Role playing (creative dramatics)
	Problem-solving strategies
	Small groups (by task, role, and interest area)
	Instructional grouping in math; individualization in reading
	Avoidance of competition in basic academics
	Athletic program
	Reading to younger children as a way to build self-esteem
	Use of computer for skill development in math and reading
	Self-regulation of behavior
Special Education	Teaching specific learning strategies and study skills such as decoding (e.g., DISSECT program), test-taking, and mnemonics
	Teaching organizational strategies (time and materials)
	Focus on research skills (library skills)
	Development of social skills (leadership/followership)
	Development of self-control and self-management
	Planning for future learning
	Use of alternative media/modes for instruction (video, audio, computer)
Gifted Education	Literature-based reading program (based on interest level and book selection geared to gifted population)
	Diagnostic-prescriptive model in basic reading skill development
	Cooperative learning model in mathematics, focusing on the use of: challenging problems, real-life problems (challenge of the unknown), and spatial/visualization techniques
	Special project approach in teaching science and social science
	Thematic curriculum
	Strong emphasis on the arts and providing aesthetic experiences in art, music, dance, dramatic interpretation, debate, and speech
	Emphasis on oral expression as an alternative mode
	Development of creative thinking and critical thinking skills
	Co-curricular activities such as theatre, athletics, and art programs
	Diane to "try out" in a program for gifted learners, based on thinking skills and project work
	Regular classroom placement consideration in cluster groups for most curriculum areas
Psychological/Family Systems View	Ways to develop more positive self-esteem
	Self-control and self-management techniques
	Coping and compensation strategies
	Elimination or reduction of drug dependency with counseling

Source: Van Tassel-Baska, J. (1992). Planning effective curriculum for gifted learners. Denver, Co: Love Publishing.

Diane has shown us how complex individual needs are! The collaborative efforts of colleagues took weeks of interviewing, diagnosing, researching, discussing, and planning—all for one student. You can see what a challenge it is to individualize instruction and how important it is to be eclectic when applying learning theories. Multiplying these efforts twenty-five to thirty times, which represents the typical number of students in an elementary or middle school classroom, presents incredible challenges for the classroom teacher. You would be very fortunate indeed if you were able to devise an individualized plan for each student that could be updated on a weekly basis. These are important goals, but require long-range planning across the school year. If a teacher plans variety in instructional strategies (e.g., collaborative learning, direct and indirect instruction, computer-assisted instruction, etc.), many learning styles can be tapped and supported. It is also the task of the teacher to develop strengths in nonpreferred learning styles to encourage breadth in learning. For often, children and youth come to school with preferred learning styles, but leave with a wider repertoire because teachers have varied teaching strategies. Not only can the social studies teacher expand student awareness of a rich diverse cultural history of the United States and world, he or she can develop an appreciation for the diverse backgrounds, talents, and learning preferences of peers.

As previously stated, Diane Bradford was a fourth-grade student at the time the case study was conducted. Since that time she has continued to struggle with schoolwork and has maintained her commitment to swimming. In fact, she has received a full college scholarship based on her swimming ability and hopes to qualify for the Olympic team in the year 2000. To prepare for such an honor it was necessary to discontinue taking Ritalin. While initially there was a drop in her overall performance as a sophomore in high school, she succeeded in stabilizing her schoolwork. With the continued support of teachers, coaches, and parents, Diane has worked hard to develop the strengths she has always had and to develop and improve the areas that have been constant challenges. As educators, we can learn a lot from Diane's winning Olympic attitude!

✦ INTERNET LINKS

INTERNET LINKS

Teaching Styles and Multiple Intelligences

http://www.interserf.net/mcken/teacher.htm

Innovative Teaching

This is a dynamic site for teachers, and teaching needs. It provides ideas for lessons and projects for various subjects, links to virtual field trips, webquests, newsgroups, inventors and inventions, cutting-edge information in the field of education, and much more. This site always has a featured unit for teachers to explore, whether the topic is presidents or frontiers integration, or so on. Another plus for this site is the extensive look at multiple intelligence and how to approach MI. For example, the page on MI lists Gardner's MI criteria, it gives several overviews of the multiple intelligence idea, and also provides links to several activities that are relevant to the enhancement of each of the different intelligences.

INTERNET LINKS

Learning Styles

http://www.geocities.com/CollegePark/Union/2106/

The NC Education Place

This is an all-inclusive site for teachers. The site explores issues that are of interest to educators, including professional development, and also classroom issues. The site includes a page that looks specifically at different learning styles. This page explores the basics of learning styles, and the four modalities. This page also gives attention to small-group techniques and implementation. Other assets to the learning styles link are the recommended reading list, which provides books that would be a valuable resource to any teacher wanting to learn different approaches to the learner, and also a complete list of links to other sites about learning styles.

INTERNET LINKS

Discovery Learning

http://www.ils.nwu.edu/~e_for_/nodes/I-M-INTRO-ZOOMER-pg.html

Engines for Education

This site is guided by the questions that are raised. The pages that were set up for educators supply a unique perspective on discovery, or natural, learning. The pages for educators begin with four guiding questions: What do the kids think?, The Problem Today, The Course of Tomorrow, and Teach Thyself. For example, if the question "What do the kids think?" is chosen, a brief article pops up that explains a child's view of the classroom and at the end of the article, more questions pertaining to the topic are supplied so that the person viewing the page controls the direction that is taken. It is very insightful and interesting to take a look at school from a different angle.

SUMMARY

We began this chapter with a discussion of reflective teaching and closed with the successful account of Diane Bradford's winning attitude. Diane's case illustration underscored the many variables that a teacher may reflect on as his or her relationship unfolds with each student. Yes, many of the issues surrounding Diane's needs were tied to family background and interaction, and to a certain extent, not entirely within the realm of a teacher's control. Yet the decisions that teachers and other professionals made on Diane's behalf reveal a sensitivity toward creating a comfortable fit between individual needs, academic performance, abilities, learning styles, and teaching styles. The documentation and recommendations may seem overwhelming to a beginning teacher, but if you start with anecdotal records for each student at the beginning of the year, it is very realistic to expect that over the course of nine months, similar plans can be created for each student. By enlisting the support of family members, mutual expectations and goals can be developed with the students' best interests in mind.

PROFESSIONAL DISCUSSIONS AND FIELD EXPERIENCES

Professional Discussion

1. The educational standards movement has rekindled discussions about the relationship between an emphasis on the acquisition and assessment of subject matter and the trend away from inquiry teaching. Use the inquiry guide in this chapter as a basis for interviewing a teacher about his or her attitudes toward inquiry teaching. Determine the extent to which the teacher values inquiry teaching and whether or not the standards movement has had an impact on the frequency of inquiry approaches. Share these findings with peers and discuss the implications for your own teaching roles.

2. There are case studies throughout Part II. Perhaps you will be asked to conduct a case study of one of the students you are observing. Before embarking on such a journey it is helpful to discuss some of the forthcoming challenges. Will your interpretations be based on a wealth of resources or limited by privacy issues? Will you have the benefit of perspectives from teachers, parents, and students? Will you be able to make recommendations for instruction and see the effects of implementation strategies? As you talk about these issues, keep in mind that each case is likely to be complex (Stake, 1995) and that changes will be gradual.

Field Experiences

1. After observing at least two teachers over a period of weeks, describe their teaching styles. Does the teacher seem to prefer one particular style over another as evidenced by the amount of time devoted to each? That is, do you see more large-group, small-group, or independent activities designed for students? More direct or indirect instruction? Are their discipline styles different? In what ways? Of the two you have observed, do you identify with one over the other? In what ways do you think you will be different from both?

2. Develop an informal checklist, utilizing the categories developed by Dunn and Dunn or Gardner. Select at least two students for observation, and use the checklist to analyze student learning styles. Be sure to observe the students in a variety of settings (e.g., different subject areas, art, music, physical education, etc.). Were you able to identify preferred learning styles as evidenced by student participation and enthusiasm? What are the implications of your findings for your own teaching?

REFERENCES

Adler, S. (1994). Reflective practice and teacher education. In Ross, E. W. (Ed.), *Reflective practice in social studies* (pp. 51–58). Washington, DC: National Council for the Social Studies.

Barton, K. C. (1997). History—It can be elementary: An overview of elementary students' understanding of history. *Social Education, 61* (1), 13–16.

Bellan, J. M., & Scheurman, G. (1998). Actual and virtual reality: Making the most of field trips. *Social Education, 62* (1), 35–40.

Beyer, B. (1979). *Teaching thinking in social studies.* Columbus, OH: Charles Merrill.

Bruner, J. S. (1959). *The process of education.* Cambridge, MA: Harvard University Press.

Chapin, J. R., & Messick, R. G. (1989). *Elementary social studies: A practical guide.* New York: Longman.

Cruikshank, D. R. (1987). *Reflective teaching: The preparation of students of teaching.* Reston, VA: Association of Teacher Educators.

Diem, R. A. (1999). Exploring development issues on the internet. *Social Education, 63* (2), 92–93.

Dunn, R., & Dunn, K. (1978). *Teaching students through their individual learning styles: A practical approach.* Reston, VA: Reston Publishing.

Eby, J. W. (1992). *Reflective planning, teaching, and evaluation for the elementary school.* New York: Macmillan.

Foster, S. J., & Hoge, J. D. (1997). Surfing for social studies software: A practical guide to locating and selecting resources on the internet. *Social Studies and the Young Learner, 9* (4), 28–32.

Fox, R. (1994). American Revolution simulation. *AskERIC Lesson Plan,* #AELP-USH0003. Available online: ericir.syr.edu/Virtual/Lessons/Social_St/US_history/USH0003.html.

Gardner, H. (1983). *Frames of mind.* New York: Basic Books.

Gardner, H., Kornhaber, M., & Wake, W. (1996). *Intelligence: Multiple perspectives.* Fort Worth, TX: Harcourt Brace.

Gardner, H. (1999). *Intelligence reframed: Multiple perspectives for the 21st century.* New York: Basic Books.

Garofalo, J., Bennett, C., & Mason, C. (1999). Plotting and analyzing: Graphing calculators for social inquiry. *Social Education, 63* (2), 101–104.

Hakim, J. (1994). *War, terrible war.* New York: Oxford University Press.

Henderson, J. G. (1992). Reflective teaching: Becoming an inquiring educator. New York: Macmillan.

Hennings, D. G., Hennings, G., & Banich, S. F. (1989). *Today's elementary social studies.* Prospect Heights, IL: Waveland Press.

Hess, R. D., & Torney, J. V. (1967). *The development of political attitudes in children.* Chicago: Aldine.

Hunt, D. E. (1968). *From psychology theory to educational practice: implementation of a matching model.* Washington, DC: Educational Research Information Center, U.S. Office of Education. (ERIC No. ED 068 438)

Hunter, M. (1984). Knowing teaching and supervising. In P. L. Hosford (Ed.), *Using what we know about teaching* (pp. 175–176). Alexandria, VA: Association of Supervision and Curriculum Development.

Jenne, J. T. (1994). Why teacher research? In Ross, E. W. (Ed.). *Reflective practice in social studies* (pp. 59–68). Washington, DC: National Council for the Social Studies.

Joseph, P. B., & Burnaford, G. E. (1994). *Images of schoolteachers in twentieth century America.* New York: St. Martin's Press.

Kohlberg, L., & Ladson-Billings, G. (1990). Culturally relevant teaching: Effective instruction for black students. *College Board Review,* 155, 20–25.

Kranning, A., & Ehman, L. (1999). Help! I'm lost in cyberspace! *Social Education, 63* (3), 152–156.

Ladson-Billings, G. (1990). Culturally relevant teaching: Effective instruction for black students. *College Board Review,* 155, 20–25.

Leeman, W. P. (1999). American history websites for use in secondary schools. *Social Education, 63* (3), 144–150.

McEachron-Hirsch, G. (Ed.). (1993). *Student self-esteem: Integrating the self.* Lancaster, PA: Technomic Publishers.

Muir, S. P. (1980). Simulation games for elementary social studies. *Social Education, 44,* 35–39, 76.

Olwell, R. B. (1999). John Kay's Civil War: A multimedia internet project for middle school social studies. *Social Education, 63* (3), 134–138.

Ornstein, A. C., & Hunkins, F. P. (1988). *Curriculum: Foundations, principles, and issues.* Englewood Cliffs, NJ: Prentice-Hall.

Peck, K. L. (1994). Voting simulation. *AskERIC Lesson Plan,* #AELP-GOV0049. Available online: ericir.syr.edu/Virtual/Lessons/Social_St/Government/GOV0049.html.

Robinson, F. P. (1970). *Effective study.* New York: Harper & Row.

Ross, E. W. (1994). *Reflective practice in social studies.* Washington, DC: National Council for the Social Studies.

Savage, T. V., & Armstrong, D. G. (1992). *Effective teaching in elementary social studies.* New York: Macmillan.

Schön, D. A. (1983). *The reflective practitioner: How professionals think in action.* New York: Basic Books.

Schön, D. A. (1987). *Educating the reflective practitioner: Toward a new design for teaching and learning in the professions.* San Francisco: Jossey-Bass.

Schnell, C., & Schur, J. B. (1999). Learning across cultures: From New York City to Rotorua. *Social Education, 63* (2), 75–79.

Shirts, R. G. (1976). *Rafá Rafá: A cross culture simulation.* Del Mar, CA: Simile II.

Skinner, B. F. (1953). *Science and human behavior.* New York: Macmillan.

Skinner, B. F. (1954, Spring). The science of learning and the art of teaching. *Harvard Educational Review, 24* (2) 86–97.

Stake, R. E. (1995). *The art of case study research.* Beverly Hills, CA: Sage.

Sugrue, M., & Sweeny, J. A. (1969). Check your inquiry-teaching technique. *Today's Education/NEA Journal, 58,* 43–44.

Taba, H. (1962). *Curriculum development: Theory and practice.* New York: Harcourt Brace.

Tyler, R. W. (1949). *Basic principles of curriculum and instruction.* Chicago: University of Chicago Press.

Valli, L. (1992). Afterward. In *Reflective teacher education: Cases and critiques.* (pp. 213–225). Albany: State University of New York Press.

VanTassel-Baska, J. (1992). *Planning effective curriculum for gifted learners.* Denver, CO: Love Publishing.

Weaver, J. (1994). Science role plays. *AskERIC Lesson Plans,* #AELP-SPS0006. Available online: ericir.syr.edu/Virtual/Lessons/Science/Process_skills/SPS0006.html.

Welton, D. A., & Mallon, J. T. (1992). *Children and their world: Strategies for teaching social studies.* Boston: Houghton Mifflin.

Willis, A. (1999). Content-rich commercial websites. *Social Education, 63* (3), 157–159.

Yando, R. M., & Kagan, J. (1968). The effect of teacher tempo on the child. *Child Development, 39,* 27.

Zeichner, K. M., & Liston, D. P. (1987). Teaching student teachers to reflect. *Harvard Educational Review, 57* (1), 23–48.

© Elizabeth Crews

CHAPTER 8

SKILL DEVELOPMENT IN CHILDREN AND YOUTH

Chapter Outline

CHAPTER OBJECTIVES

Reading a map, taking one's turn in a conversational setting, and observing global interdependence in action are skills that have become natural to most of us. But to students, these and many other skills need to be taught explicitly in elementary and middle school classrooms. Skill development requires that teachers break down a process into its component parts. As you read this chapter, think about the importance of language, its relation to the visual or material world as well as its use in conversing with others. Can you generate ways to teach the meaning of concepts when dictionary definitions leave students bewildered? Are you an acute observer of classroom dynamics, one who recognizes the persuasive or sometimes bullying tactics among students? Upon completion of this chapter students will be able to:

1. Explain at least five different strategies for teaching concepts.
2. Differentiate appropriate levels of skill development for teaching about time, chronology, maps, and globes.
3. Identify cooperative learning strategies, citing research for appropriate grouping patterns.

S kill development makes entry into the world of cultures more accessible. That is, lessons that focus on concept attainment, map and globe skills, time and chronology, and social interaction such as cooperative learning will give students tools for learning about the world around them. This chapter discusses each of the skills and provides a variety of teaching suggestions for their development.

❖ CONCEPT ATTAINMENT

In Chapter 1 we saw how social science concepts could be discussed in an interdisciplinary context. In this section, we examine how concept teaching is much more complex than providing the name of the concept and its definition. Concept *attainment* as a skill emphasizes the student's mastery of a concept. It is helpful to differentiate between a concept, fact, and data. A *concept* is an idea that has relatable features. *Needs, role,* and *power* fit this definition. *Data,* by contrast, is an unorganized sum total of information. For example, data may include all known phenomena relevant to changes in climate. A daily list of temperatures for a specific location represents data. *Facts* are selected elements of data. "London, Chicago, and Los Angeles are densely populated cities" is a statement of fact.

Bruner, Goodnow, and Austin (1956) identified three kinds of concepts: conjunctive, disjunctive, and relational. In a *conjunctive* concept all of the defining characteristics of the concept must be present in order to be a proper example. For example, there are four equal sides in a square. Or taxes are (a) a class of payments, (b) levied according to law, and (c) paid to the government. When explaining *disjunctive* concepts it is not always necessary for all defining attributes to be present. Either/or characteristics are permissible. For example, it is possible to be a citizen of the United States if one's parents are born in the United States, or by passing an exam, or if one is born in the United States. It is not necessary for all these conditions to be present simultaneously. *Relational* concepts are defined by attributes that bear a specific relationship to one another as in the case of population density or per capita income.

Concepts also can be classified according to levels of abstractness. Concrete examples are easier to explain and illustrate. Islands and lakes are easily illustrated with pictures or by drawing them on the board. Gross national product can be defined as "the total monetary value of all final goods and services produced in a country during one year" (Stein, 1988, pp. 582–583). As concepts reach higher levels of abstraction they are more difficult to define and illustrate. Interdependence and liberty, for example, require precise definitions, a variety of examples, and identification of relationships. Interdependence may be defined as "a state of being dependent upon one another." Its relevance may be catered to curricular goals at various grade levels. That is, a third-grade teacher may talk about the interdependence of community helpers, whereas a sixth-grade teacher may discuss the interdependence among nations.

Concepts can be value laden or value neutral. Typically, value-neutral concepts such as *product, income,* and *peninsula* do not arouse animated discussions. However, if these topics lead to discussions of *scarcity, poverty,* and *manifest destiny,* more value-laden issues might arise. In a social studies class, one should keep in mind that many terms can quickly lead to values lessons, either intentionally or unintentionally. Whether the values relate to differences in customs or points of view regarding justice, it is shortsighted to think that a social studies class can or should avoid values. Being aware of levels of abstractness and value ladenness can make you better prepared for values discussions.

To ensure deeper levels of conceptual understanding, a variety of approaches can be taken; these include (1) providing definitions, (2) structural comparisons, (3) listing, grouping, classifying, (4) providing examples and nonexamples, and (5) graphic organizers. Even though they are discussed separately here, the approaches may be used interchangeably within the same lesson.

Definitions

In using a textbook you will often find words in bold that introduce new terms or concepts. It is useful to separate those words that can be simply defined and those that are of a more general or conceptual nature. Concept attainment lessons should be developed around those concepts that require more than a dictionary definition. The decision about which concepts require development is based more on the students' levels of understanding rather than the word itself. For example, when introducing the term *island* to a primary student, the teacher may provide a definition and show many examples. For an intermediate student, a dictionary definition may be sufficient for reinforcement because one can assume that the concept was taught in the primary grades. A more challenging concept for an intermediate student would be *delta* or *atoll*. Concepts *island, delta,* or *atoll* are concrete, but since they are being introduced for the first time it would be appropriate to provide several examples and illustrations. Giving demonstrations, using analogies, and providing antonyms and synonyms are additional ways to define concepts.

Structural Comparisons

Comparing and contrasting various aspects of culture is fundamental practice in the social studies curriculum. Ellis (1995, p. 137) characterizes one such approach as *structural comparison.* The illustration developed by Ellis, shown in Table 8.1, gives contrasting information about two different cultures. The exercise reinforces the concepts of cultural similarities and cultural differences. Structural comparisons also can be used to compare and contrast different aspects of transportation, technology, material culture, and so on.

Listing, Grouping, Labeling

This approach to concept attainment was developed by Hilda Taba. As you can see from Table 8.2, Taba draws concepts from the students in an inductive fashion. When teaching inductively, the teacher gives several examples or situations, and the students identify a label or concept. By contrast, when teaching deductively, a definition is introduced and examples are provided to illustrate the concept. There are greater chances of a variety of conceptual understanding when a lesson is designed inductively. There is also the chance that the students will not provide the concept the teacher desires. One of the great benefits of teaching inductively is the opportunity for the teacher to understand the concepts as seen by the students, based on their levels of development and experience. From this foundation the teacher can then build additional conceptual understanding.

Examples/Nonexamples

For concepts that can be easily contrasted, the examples/nonexamples strategy is helpful to students. Primary students who are introduced to natural resources for the first time need to see trees, water, and coal in contrast to human-made tools and artifacts

    TABLE 8.1

Structural Comparison of China and Japan

Characteristic	China	Japan
Size	Large (larger than U.S.)	Small (smaller than CA)
Population	1,000,000,000; 4/5 rural	1,000,000,000; urbanized
Income	Poor	Wealthy
Landscape	Varied (plains, mts., valleys)	Mountainous
Ethnicity	Homogeneous (some minorities)	Homogeneous
Economy	Socialist, centralized	Capitalist, private
Minerals	Good (iron, coal, oil)	Poor
Cities	Large cities in east (Beijing, capital)	Urbanized (Tokyo, capital)
Climate	Varied, extreme; dry to wet; hot to cold	Somewhat varied, subtropical south; cold winter north
Empire	Several possessions	None
Agriculture	Rice south; wheat north	Rice
Soils	Fertile in river valleys	Mountainous, poor
Culture	Ancient (5,000+ years)	Ancient (offshoot of China)
Military	World's largest army	Self-defense force
Education	High value	High value (high level of formal education)
Rivers	Great rivers (Yellow, Yangtze)	No major rivers
Manufacturing	Weapons, steel, heavy machinery, bicycles	Steel, autos, electronics for world markets
National Goals	Industrialization, birth control, food supply, education	Education, expanded markets, agriculture, new capital

Source: Ellis, Arthur K. *Teaching and Learning: Elementary Social Studies* (5th ed.) Copyright © 1995 by Allyn & Bacon. Reprinted/adapted by permission.

    TABLE 8.2

Concept Formation

Overt Activity	Covert Mental Operations	Eliciting Questions
1. Enumeration and listing	Differentiation	What did you see? hear? note?
2. Grouping	Identifying common properties, abstracting	What belongs together? On what criterion?
3. Labeling, categorizing	Determining the hierarchical order of items. Super- and sub-ordination.	How would you call these groups? What belongs under what?

Source: Taba, H. (1967). *Teacher's Handbook for Elementary Social Studies.* Palo Alto, CA: Addison-Wesley Publishing Co., p. 92.

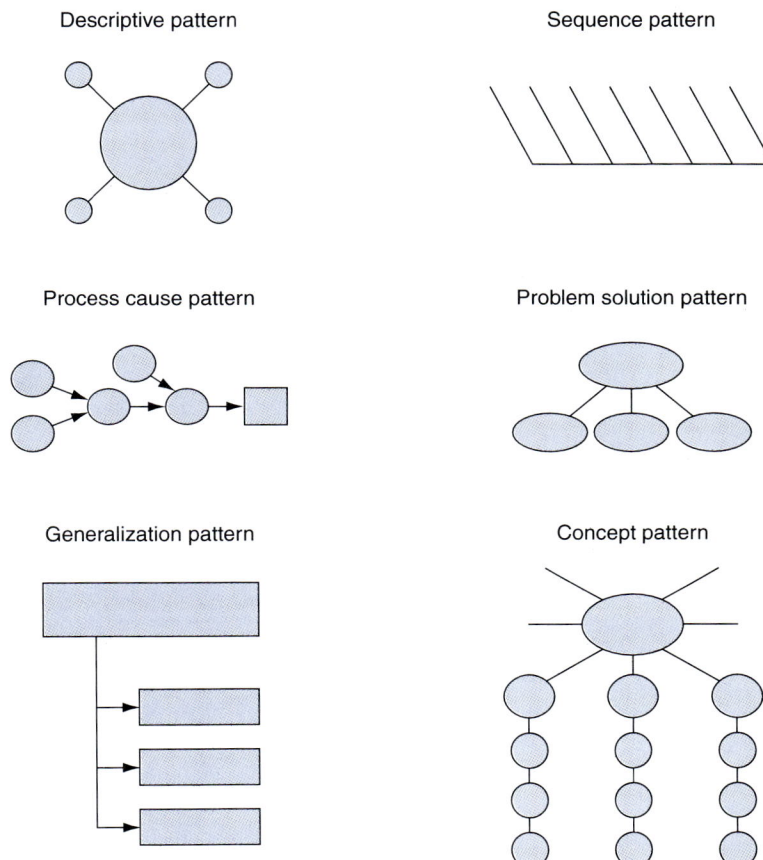

Descriptive pattern

Sequence pattern

Process cause pattern

Problem solution pattern

Generalization pattern

Concept pattern

FIGURE 8.1 *Graphic Organizers*

SOURCE: Marzano, R. (1992). Cultivating thinking in English. Urbana, IL: National Council of Teachers of English. Copyright 1992 by the National Council of Teachers of English. Reprinted with permission.

such as machinery, manufactured clothing, bowls, and so on. A fifth-grade teacher used the examples/nonexamples technique to distinguish between the Union and Confederate states. Venn diagrams also can be used to reinforce examples and nonexamples, especially when there are overlapping areas. One student teacher wanted her third graders to identify which artifacts were used during the Colonial Period and which would be used in modern times. She soon discovered that the grouping didn't break logically into two sets; instead there were certain items, such as wooden spoons, that belonged in both time periods. Venn diagrams and other graphic organizers help students classify and organize information.

Graphic Organizers

A graphic organizer is a way to organize information in a diagram and has particular appeal to the visual learner. Marzano (1992) describes a variety of ways to do concept mapping for which adaptations have been made in Figure 8.1. Originally designed for

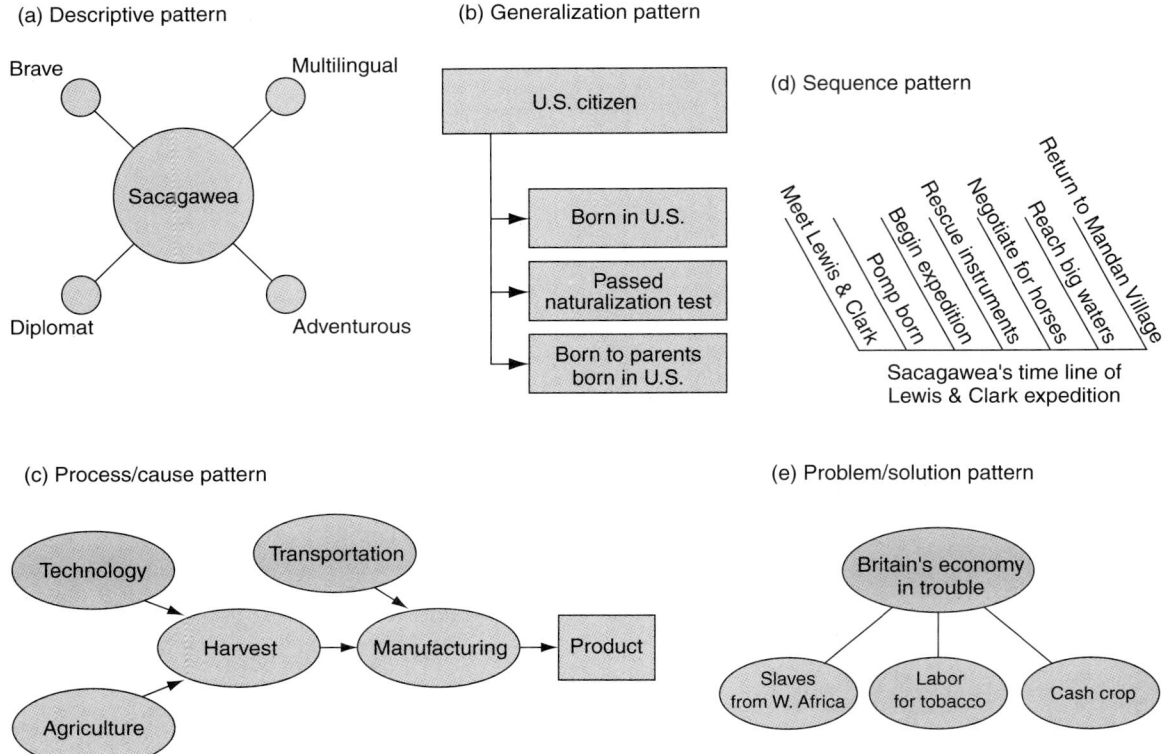

FIGURE 8.2   *Sample of Graphic Organizers Adapted to Social Studies*

use in cultivating thinking in English, the graphic organizers can be adapted to social studies as shown in the applications (see Figure 8.2) that follow. For additional background regarding the theories underlying concept development consult Martorella (1991).

✦ TIME AND CHRONOLOGY

Time and chronology concepts follow a logical sequence throughout the elementary and middle school social studies classes. The calendar is an important tool for teaching time in primary classrooms. Note in the classrooms that you observe that the calendar is quite large and in a prominent position. Most primary teachers refer to it on a daily basis. Some may place a large "X" or sticker on the days of the month that have passed. Other symbols such as holidays and birthdays are also marked. Teachers emphasize the days of the week and sometimes ask the children to count the number of days that have passed throughout the month. Primary teachers occasionally extend the notion of counting beyond just the month and place the total number of school days that have passed around the walls in the room. By the end of the school year the children are counting in the hundreds.

(f) Concept pattern

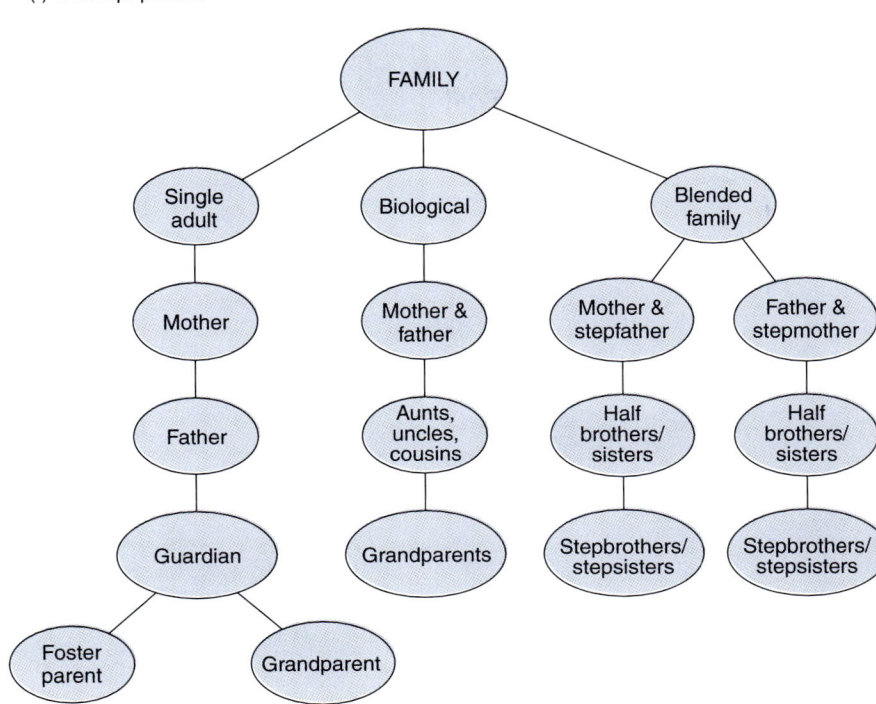

FIGURE 8.2   *Sample of Graphic Organizers Adapted to Social Studies (continued)*

As students progress to Grades 4 and 5, the curriculum introduces language like centuries, B.C. and A.D. A new concept for them is the realization that dates which begin with 18 such as 1850, 1865, and so on, are not referring to the eighteenth century. Work with time lines helps to make the centuries more explicit. Exercises that ask how long ago 1500 B.C. was make students more aware of the fact that civilizations have been in existence much longer than two thousand years, a mistake often made because students erroneously assume that recorded history is as old as the date of the current year.

Upper elementary students can grasp more challenging time and chronology concepts. Middle school students can explore worldwide travel conditions by studying time zones. Donovan (1985) designed a group activity that utilizes a variety of resources and skills (maps and globe, time zones, atlases, almanacs). Following the lines of a detective story, students solve the mystery whodunit.

Middle school students can collect data about population patterns in their region or community. Predictions about how an area might change as a result of population growth or decline could be added to a time line of community events. After computing the rate of growth, students then make predictions about the future. The information can be translated onto population maps of the future. Interviews

© Elizabeth Crews

with members of community councils would expose students to ways in which community planning operates. Interdisciplinary connections with the sciences could easily be made with topics such as conservation and land use. Studying the refurbishing or depletion of natural resources over time provides stimulating findings that might motivate students to take action to protect their local environment. For additional research studies that provide insight into selecting appropriate teaching strategies for time and chronology, consult Downey and Levstik (1991).

✦ MAP AND GLOBE SKILLS

"If you don't know where you are, you can't know where you're going!" is a popular quote among geographers. The sentiment is a succinct rationale for teaching map and globe skills to elementary and middle school students. In a sense, teaching students to locate where they are is a first step in enabling them to explore the rest of the world. Learning spatial orientation from kindergarten through eighth grade follows a logical pattern based on children's developmental stages. The notion that the globe is a model of the earth is a challenging concept for primary students. Using model cars along with real cars to illustrate the concept of *model* is a beginning step in comparing the globe to earth. With older students the globe presents challenges at different levels of abstraction. For example, a lesson proposed by Ludwig (1991) poses the questions, "How much water flows in a specific

© Charles Gupton/Stock Boston

stream during a 24-hour period?" and "How many people could live from the water?" This exercise requires estimates of stream depth, width, speed of flow, and knowledge of human water use in order to analyze the global balance between nature and humans.

Map and globe skills can be divided into several main categories: symbols, mental maps, scale, distance, location, orientation and direction, and map projections. The first of the National Geography Standards, *The World in Spatial Terms,* provides objectives for Grades K–4 and 5–8 to assist teachers in determining which map and globe skills are appropriate for the various grade levels. Additional resources at the end of this chapter will also provide guidance. The geography section in Chapter 3 also provides Internet sites. In *Teaching Map Skills: An Inductive Approach* (Anderson, 1986) suggests using the mnemonic device of TOADSIGs (Table 8.3) as a way to think holistically about the important elements of maps. Following is an overview of the important categories on maps and globes accompanied by a sampling of activities.

Symbols

Symbols are used by mapmakers to condense large amounts of information about various territories into a small amount of space. A symbol is a sign, picture, or other representational object of something that is real. The lesson in Chapter 3, "Reading Maps to Find Classroom Treasures," introduced the concept *symbol* to first graders by using

8.1   SYMBOLIZATION

Map symbols are the "words" in a graphic language, the vehicles that carry messages about a place or the relationships between places. A map symbol can resemble the thing it represents or be an abstraction of it. Some map symbols have been used in roughly similar ways by many people for a long time; these symbols have become parts of a standard language of maps. Other symbols must be defined when they are used, which is one purpose of a map legend. Graphic symbols are able to represent many different kinds of data because symbols can vary in many ways:

Spatial Extent (the dimensionality of a symbol)

1. *Point symbols* (dots, graduated circles, letters, icons, pie graphs) are used to mark the locations of things, to depict quantities that were measured at particular places or within certain areas, or to summarize the characteristics of a surrounding area.
2. *Line symbols* (lines, dot strings, flowlines, contours, color bands) are used to mark the locations of rivers, highways, or other linear features, to enclose or separate areas, to show the shape of a landform or other surface, to point out the connections between places, or to clarify a map layout.
3. *Area symbols* (shading, coloring, crosshatching, or dot patterns) are used to indicate regions that are uniform, to identify areas that have common traits, and to separate parts of a map layout (especially to identify the surrounding country or other important part of an area).

Abstractness (the representative nature of a symbol)

1. *Iconic symbols* are pictoral, with shapes and/or colors that map readers are likely to associate with the things being mapped.
2. *Linguistic symbols* are letters that are usually associated with the mapped phenomena in the language of the map reader.
3. *Abstract symbols* are geometric shapes that have been arbitrarily selected to represent the phenomena being mapped.

Traits (other characteristics of map symbols)

1. *Shape*—distinctiveness of form or outline
2. *Size*—dimensional extent of the inked area
3. *Complexity*—amount of detail in the boundary
4. *Value*—light reflected from the surface
5. *Color hue*—red, orange, green, purple, etc.
6. *Color chroma*—gray, weak, or intense color
7. *Pattern*—arrangement of marks in an area
8. *Orientation*—arrangement with respect to border
9. *Association*—connection with other symbols

Source: Gersmehl, P. J. (1991). *The language of maps.* Indiana, PA: National Council for Geographic Education. Used by permission.

TABLE 8.3

Map Elements

T	=	Title	:	What, where, and when
O	=	Orientation	:	Directions
D	=	Date	:	When map was made
A	=	Author	:	Who made the map
L	=	Legend	:	What the symbols mean
S	=	Scale	:	What the map distance is
I	=	Index	:	Map address of places
G	=	Grid	:	Locates places on a map
s	=	source	:	Of map information

Source: Anderson, J. (1986). *Teaching map skills: An inductive approach.* National Council for Geographic Education. Macomb, IL: Western Illinois University. Used by permission.

objects they could see in their surroundings and transposing them using shapes and colors. Shapes and colors are the most basic symbolic forms introduced to primary students. Typically, they learn that water is blue and landmasses (continents) are green or a variety of colors.

Gradually, the symbols become more elaborate, and by the time students complete eighth grade they most likely will have been exposed to the range of symbols as described by Gersmehl (1991, p. 105) in Box 8.1.

Mental Maps

Mental maps are formed from impressions and personal experiences relevant to our physical surroundings. We also may have images based on what we have read or seen through the media, never having been to the places. Encouraging students to recognize that they have a "head full of maps" (Anderson, 1986) is a way to build confidence in their familiarity with map skills. Pictures, prose, aerial photographs, statements, or anything that permits a person to visualize where things are located is a mental map. One of my daughter's most traumatic kindergarten experiences was the day she was asked to escort a fellow classmate to the library. She had no problem taking her friend *to* the library, but her mental map became jumbled on the return trip to the classroom. Lost in the hallway, she broke into tears until a teacher could point her in the right direction.

Kindergartners' verbal statements reveal a great deal about their mental maps. Often their most frequently used descriptors are, "You go this way . . . that way" as they point in certain directions. Building on these mental maps, teachers can introduce the use of more specific terminology such as to the *right* or the *left*. Chapter 3 revealed pictorial maps prepared by third graders based on mental maps of their neighborhoods. When presenting this lesson, I was impressed by the similarities of the results and reminded once again of the importance of finding out what students are visualizing so that teachers can relate to their developmental stages. Besides revealing developmental stages about spatial orientations, mental maps are sources of perceptual information regarding cultural orientations.

8.2 MENTAL MAPPING

Preview of Main Ideas

We all form impressions and images of our physical surroundings—even of places we've never been. These impressions are what geographers call our *mental maps*. Geographers are interested in the concept of mental maps and how they are developed. Understanding the way people view different regions can help experts understand and predict how the land may be used and, among other uses, what patterns of migration may be expected. This lesson uses mental maps to explore student perceptions of different regions of the United States. The teaching level is grades 7–12.

The geographical themes are place, location, human/environment interactions, movement, and regions.

Connection with the Curriculum

United States and world history are filled with examples of regional suspicions, misconceptions, and antagonisms. World conflict and cooperation, topics commonly studied in world geography, are influenced by the perceptions that people of different nations have of each other. The geographic and research tools applied in this lesson are useful in all social studies contexts.

Materials

- One copy of the handout Where Would You Like to Live? for each student
- One outline map of the United States for each student, and one map for each group.
- Colored pencils or markers
- Calculators (optional)
- Classroom atlases (optional)
- Overhead projector (optional)

Objectives

Students are expected to:

- Understand the concept of mental mapping
- Construct maps using their own mental maps of places where they would like to live

Suggestions for Teaching the Lesson

Opening the Lesson

All of us have images of different regions of the world that we have developed through a variety of processes. These processes are usually a mix of factual data, incomplete information, and personal bias or subconscious prejudices. This lesson explores these mental images, or *mental maps*. No one has a totally accurate image of the world, so there is no completely accurate mental map, although people's mental maps of their own immediate environment tend to be more realistic than those of places they've never visited.

Ask students to share their images of some places in the United States or elsewhere in the world. What mental pictures come to mind at the mention of the South, New England, the Pacific Northwest, or a region in your state? What mental pictures come to mind at the mention of Canada, China, Germany, Japan, and Nigeria? Are the images positive or negative? How were they developed?

Ask students where in the United States they would most like to live. Ask where they would least like to live. Explore the reasons they hold these views of different regions of the country. Explain that the images and perceptions they hold are part of their unique mental maps of the United States. Each person has a different mental map, but common patterns emerge when images of various regions are combined and mapped.

Tell students that they will explore mental maps by following this sequence of activities.

- They will ask a research question: Where in the United States do students in the class most want to live?
- They will collect data.
- They will analyze the data by using maps.

Developing the Lesson

Distribute Handout #1—Where Would You Like to Live? Have students rank the states and the District of Columbia using the scale at the top of the worksheet. Tell students how to use the ranking scale. (For example, a ranking of number 1 means the student would *never* want to live there. A ranking of number 5 means the student would *really* like to live there. A ranking of number 3 means the student doesn't have strong feelings one way or another.)

Personal Preferences Have students map their own preferences. Divide the states into four or five groupings from lowest to highest. Assign each group a color. A color gradation from light (for the group of lowest rated states) to dark (for the group of highest rated states) should result in an easy-to-read map. Color each state with the appropriate color.

Discuss the personal preference maps by asking students:

- Why would you like to live in the states that you rated highly?
- How did you decide that certain states are undesirable?
- Did you rate neighboring states more highly than more distant states? Why?
- What experience or information did you use to arrive at your decision? (Answers may include previous travel, books, short stories, TV programs, locations of friends or relatives, discussions with adults.)
- What kinds of additional information concerning each of the states would help you to make a more intelligent decision on where you would like to live?
- Do you think you will eventually move to one of the states you prefer? What are some of the forces that "push" people out of a home state? What are some "pull" factors that attract people to other states?

Class Preferences Calculate the average ranking for each state by adding each student's ranking for each state. Then divide each state's total by the number of students in the class to get the average ranking for each state.

List the states in order of preference. It might help to organize the data in a table.

(continued)

Have students create a class-preference map using data groupings similar to those they used for their personal-preference maps. Students may want to produce the preference map on an overhead transparency, using marking pens so that the entire class can see it. It could also be produced on a large-scale map for display on a bulletin board or classroom wall.

Help students analyze the class-preference map by asking:

- Which states were rated high? Which were rated low? Were the residential preferences for California, Colorado, and Florida high or low? Why?
- Identify regions that have similar preference values. What reasons can students give for these similarities?
- What patterns, if any, are apparent on the map?
- What generalizations can be made about the residential-preference patterns?
- What factors affect the development of mental maps?

Concluding the Lesson

Ask students: What is the effect of distance on residential preference and mental images of places? What conclusions can they draw about the residential-preference patterns of the class?

If it appears that students' mental maps are based on unreliable data or on biases, suggest they research their top-rated and bottom-rated states to see if their impressions hold up.

Ask students to suggest some practical applications for the information they have elicited. (For example, guidance counselors might seek more information on colleges or job opportunities in the highly rated states.)

Ask students how tourist bureaus might use this information to attract people to visit a state.

Extending the Lesson

Some of the questions and generalizations in this lesson may be restated in the form of hypotheses. Have students hypothesize about the relationship between residential preferences and per capita income in each state. Then have them consider recreational and cultural opportunities, crime rates, employment options, and living costs. To investigate the appeal of specific cities or metropolitan areas in the United States, students might enjoy looking at the *Places Rated Almanac,* by Rick Boyer and David Savageau (New York: Rand McNally, 1985).

Expand the survey by asking students to poll other students, relatives, or friends.

Arrange for a class in another area of the country to complete this lesson, then exchange results.

Assessing Student Learning

Ask students to describe factors that affect the development of mental maps.

Additional Reading

Clay, G. (1980). *Close-up: How to read the American city.* Chicago: University of Chicago Press.

Lynch, K. (1960). *The image of the city.* Cambridge, MA: MIT Press.

Where Would You Like to Live?

Rank the states and the District of Columbia using this preference scale.

1	2	3	4	5
Very Undesirable	**Undesirable**	**No Opinion**	**Desirable**	**Very Desirable**

Alabama	Montana
Alaska	Nebraska
Arizona	Nevada
Arkansas	New Hampshire
California	New Jersey
Colorado	New Mexico
Connecticut	New York
Delaware	North Carolina
District of Columbia	North Dakota
Florida	Ohio
Georgia	Oklahoma
Hawaii	Oregon
Idaho	Pennsylvania
Illinois	Rhode Island
Indiana	South Carolina
Iowa	South Dakota
Kansas	Tennessee
Kentucky	Texas
Louisiana	Utah
Maine	Vermont
Maryland	Virginia
Massachusetts	Washington
Michigan	West Virginia
Minnesota	Wisconsin
Mississippi	Wyoming
Missouri	

SOURCE: Ludwig, G. (1991). Maps and Mathematics: Bringing Geography into Your Classroom. Washington, DC: National Geographic Society. Reprinted by permission.

The upper elementary "Mental Mapping" exercise provided in Box 8.2 (Ludwig, 1991, pp. 144–147) depicts mental maps of residential preferences. By asking students where in the United States they would like to live, it is possible to generate data that leads to discussions of regional characteristics such as recreational opportunities, crime rates, and cost of living. As the lesson points out, geographers are interested in the mental maps that people create and the implications of these maps for understanding how people respond to their environment. Although geographers have been interested in mental maps for some time, their value in K–12 education has only recently been highlighted. The second National Geography Standard (*Geography for Life,* 1994) specifies that students will "use mental maps to organize information about people, places, and environments in a spatial context," so it is likely that social studies textbooks and other resource materials will be incorporating more information about mental maps in the future.

Scale and Distance

Map scale is the concept used to convert measurements from map units to ground units. This relationship can be expressed with respect to either linear or areal measurement. Linear measurement is expressed with a word statement, a fraction, or a graphic scale (Ludwig, 1991). Saying that "three inches are equal to one mile" is a common linear phrase. A fraction or ratio is an easier way to describe scale, as in 1:40,000, which means one inch is equal to 40,000 miles. Graphic scales are typically represented by a *bar scale,* which looks like a ruler printed on the map. When map users are interested in the size of an area in terms of acres or square miles, areal scale is more practical than linear scale.

Explanations of scale to students may initially sound confusing. Especially when teachers start out with the notion that the ratio is larger in a small scale map. The following description may help:

> *Small scale* maps result when map distance is small relative to ground distance—
> that is, when the scale ratio is large; on *large scale* maps, the map-ground ratio is
> small. Since map distance is always stated in the numerator of the RF
> [representative fraction] as 1, it follows that the smaller the denominator (the
> closer to a 1 to 1 ratio), the larger the scale will be. Thus, a map scale of 1:20,000
> is twice as large as a scale of 1:40,000. If that sounds backwards, remember that
> the RF is a fraction, and 1/2, after all, is larger than 1/4. (Ludwig, 1991, p. 415)

The comparison by Anderson (1986, p. 18) in Figure 8.3 should help to clarify this abstract notion.

Like any new concept, mastery comes from repeated applications. By providing students with many activities that require their use of scale, they will become more comfortable. One popular technique used with primary students is the grid system. One teacher asked her first graders to draw a picture of an animal, reminding them of their favorite pets or stuffed animals. The teacher then showed students how to impose a grid on top of their drawings. With an enlarged grid students made very large animals by transferring the image one square at a time. In addition to teaching the concept of scale, the resulting drawings made a very warm and friendly atmosphere for primary students when displayed in the classroom.

Two additional popular ways to teach scale are with the opaque projector and a pantograph. Opaque projectors, which seem to be from the dinosaur era compared with other technological additions to the classroom, are machines that project an image from a book, magazine, photograph, or drawing onto the wall. When butcher paper is posted on the wall, students can trace the image and then figure out the difference in scale using the original. A pantograph is another device which holds a pencil or chalk in two places; when an image is traced using one pencil, the other pencil enlarges or reduces the image simultaneously.

For eighth graders who have had basic algebra, scale can be changed using mathematical formulas. A sample problem from *Maps and Mathematics: Bringing Geography into Your Classroom* (Ludwig, 1991, p. 416) follows:

> Problem 2. On one map, with a scale of 1:100,000, the distance between two cities
> is .7 cm. On a second map, the distance between the same two points is .5 cm.
> What is the scale of the second map?

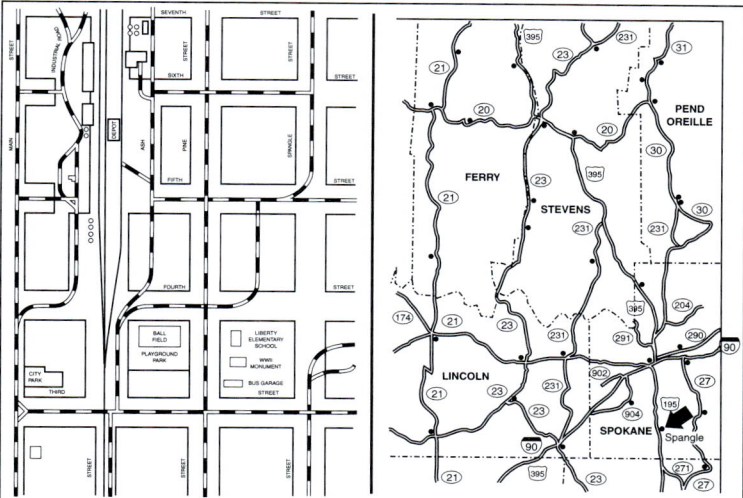

FIGURE 8.3   *Comparison of Small-Scale and Large-Scale Maps*   Small-scale maps have much less detail than large-scale ones. Streets and even buildings can be shown on a large-scale (approximately 1:4800) map of Spangle, Washington (left); whereas on a small-scale (approximately 1:2000000) map of Washington State (right), Spangle is just a dot. Source: City map, Spangle (1969) and Washington State Department of Transportation map (1981).

SOURCE: J. Anderson, *Teaching map skills: An inductive approach* (Macomb, IL: National Western Illinois University, Council for Geographic Education, 1986), p.18. Used by permission.

The solution involves equating distance on the first map to distance on the second. Answer:

$$(.5 \text{ cm}) (X) = .7 \text{ cm} (100{,}000)$$
$$.5X = 70{,}000$$
$$X = 70{,}000 \, / \, .5$$
$$X = 140{,}000$$

Distance and scale go hand in hand when teaching map skills. Distance concepts may be thought about in several ways, *relative, physical* and *functional.* Relative distance states a relationship between places based on proximity. Physical distance assumes a close relationship between map and ground distance. Functional distance takes into consideration the expense, time, and energy expended to get from one place to another. Students can look at simple maps to determine relative sizes of rooms and relative distances between points. Direct observation is encouraged to compare map representation with real spaces. With young children, aerial photos can be used to describe distance between features. For example, students might count the number of houses between selected features. From these exercises using relative distances, students can progress to the use of scale for greater accuracy in determining physical distances. Creating lessons where students plan a trip using several means

© Jacksonville Journal Courier/The Image Works

of transportation is a challenging way to integrate the use of relative, physical, and functional distances. For example, making arrangements to take a field trip from Chicago to Mexico City using planes, boats, trains, taxis, and cars emulates a real-life situation where several distance concepts are used simultaneously. Since there are no right or wrong answers, doing the exercise in groups yields a variety of possibilities.

Location, Orientation, and Direction

Many exercises reinforce students' knowledge of location, orientation, and direction. Lines of longitude and latitude or more basic grid systems are popular tools used with intermediate students. Large floor maps help primary students orient themselves by using their entire bodies. For example, children can stand on a map of the United States while the teacher asks them to face North, South, East, or West. To a student standing on Pennsylvania, the teacher can ask, "Which state is closer, New Mexico or Mississippi?" In *Teaching Map Skills: An Inductive Approach,* Anderson (1986) provides upper elementary teachers with a good model for teaching orientation utilizing the compass rose.

Absolute and relative location are two concepts that Mau (1999) focused on in a literature-based social studies lesson for middle school students. Using excerpts from the journal of Robinson Crusoe by Daniel Defoe, Mau (1999, p. M3) addressed the following objectives during her instructional sequence:

Objectives:
- to use map skills to discover places on Crusoe's voyages based on absolute and relative location
- to use mapmaking skills to chart Crusoe's island

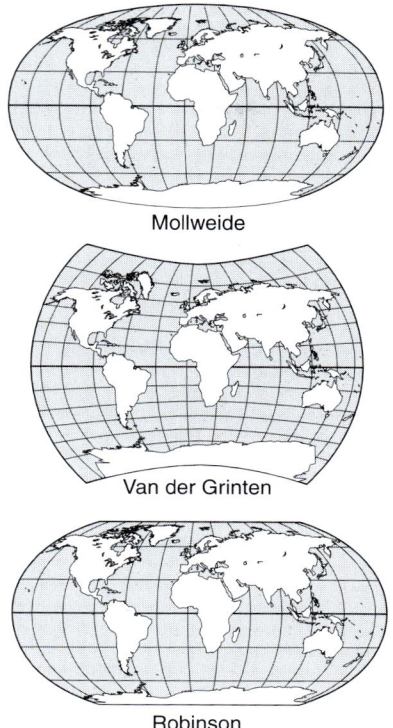

Mollweide

Van der Grinten

Robinson

FIGURE 8.4   *Map Projections*

SOURCE: The Geography Education Standards Project (1994). Geography for Life: The National Geography Standards, 1994, p. 145. Washington, DC: National Geographic Society. Used by permission.

- to analyze what Crusoe needed to survive on the island given the resources provided by the environment
- to evaluate how Crusoe's survival was affected by his attitude, experience, and the tools available to him
- to invent other possible responses to Crusoe's situation

Map Projections

Naturally, a globe is a more accurate representation of the earth than a map. Students need to be aware that when the round earth is projected onto a flat map, distortions occur. For over fifty years the National Geographic Society used the 1922 Van der Griten projection depicted in Figure 8.4 (*Geography for Life,* 1994). The Van der Griten map represents more accurately the shapes of landmasses but distorts their relative size. Prior to this time the Mollweide (Figure 8.4) developed in 1805 was used. It is characterized by the distortion of shape but relative accuracy with regard to size of landmasses. The Robinson projection (Figure 8.4) is a compromise between size and shape and was adopted by the National Geographic Society in 1989. By examining Greenland and the

Antarctic in the three projections you can see the distortions more explicitly. As of 2000, the National Geographic Society has adopted the Winkel Tripel projection that avoids the compression of polar areas.

In addition to pointing out the accuracy of map projections it is fun for students to think about map projections in relation to worldviews. For example, the common use of the Van der Griten, Mollweide, and Robinson projections reinforces the visual prominence of countries emanating from the equator as the central focal area. By contrast, the view of the world would be radically different if, for example, Australia were placed in the center, which probably more accurately reflects how Australians perceive themselves in relation to the rest of the world. Teachers and students can discuss how the world may be perceived differently among cultures based on their location in the world and the effects of climatic conditions.

✛ COOPERATIVE LEARNING

The skills we have been discussing thus far in Chapter 8 pertain to ways of acquiring knowledge. In addition to cognitive learning, teachers can foster social skills through cooperative learning. One of the purposes of cooperative learning is for students to realize that people need to work and learn together. Employment depends on cooperative skills in the workplace. Throughout direct instruction students learn to wait their turn to respond, listen to teachers and peers, and retain information. Cooperative learning reinforces these same skills but emphasizes learning and negotiation with peers, typically in a small-group format or with another person. There are many kinds of cooperative learning formats with the common goal that students work together on projects or to solve problems, rather than in individual competition. However, a competitive element can be introduced with cooperative learning when groups compete with one another.

Cooperative ventures may be structured by having students assume specific roles. A group of four might have a recorder, discussant, encourager, and reporter. The discussant facilitates conversation, the encourager reinforces the ideas put forth by others, the recorder writes down the ideas, and the reporter shares the group's work with the larger group. One of the advantages of assigning roles is to maximize the participation for each member of the group. Rotating the roles ensures that members broaden their interaction skills. It is possible, however, that you may want to assign a task to a group and let the members figure out on their own how they might tackle the assignment. After a few group sessions the teacher might bring the small groups together and help them analyze how they were functioning. The following questions help students become more aware of their social dynamics:

1. How were the expressed ideas received? Did members of the group laugh at or put down others' ideas? Did people feel that peers listened to their ideas?
2. Did one person dominate the discussion? Did a natural leader emerge based on knowledge of the subject or based on assertiveness?
3. Did members of the group try to get others off-task? If so, how and what was the response of other members of the group?
4. Would you say that your group worked together well? How might working relationships be improved?

Reflecting on collaboration during group work is productive for large-group analysis as well. Miller (1997) discusses the role that class meetings can play in creating a sense of classroom cohesiveness, another important factor for collaboration. Miller selects provocative topics to encourage student participation—making fun of others, individual differences, and endangered animals. Students learn to be receptive to the views of others and resolve differences through open discussion. According to Miller (1997), "students develop a sense of ownership and responsibility for their roles as functioning members of the classroom society" (p. 20).

Educators have refined several cooperative learning strategies. *Jigsaw,* originally designed by Aronson (1978) gives each group member a task that contributes to the overall group task or problem. Completion of the task depends on individual performances. *Student Teams Achievement Decisions* (STAD) emphasizes that each member of the team is responsible for each other's learning (Slavin, 1983). The group is not finished unless all members have been quizzed to indicate mastery of the task at hand. Team scores are based on improved scores of individual students. Additional cooperative learning strategies are available in *Cooperative Learning: Theory, Research, and Practice* (Slavin, 1990).

Ability levels are a consideration when constructing cooperative groups. In a group where there are a wide range of ability levels, the teacher should be sensitive to the kinds of roles assigned within the group so that each member can make valuable contributions. In cooperative groups where the dynamics are free-flowing for an extended period of time, students below grade level may feel overshadowed by students who are above grade level. Conversely, above grade level students may feel as if they are carrying the responsibility for those who are working below grade level. Kulik and Kulik (1982) found that there were more positive results when students were grouped by average and above-average, or average and below-average abilities. When there was a range of below-average, average, and above-average students, the results were counterproductive to cooperative learning goals. When the purpose of cooperative learning is to instill an appreciation for the contributions of others, it is important to monitor individual performances within the groups.

Johnson and Johnson (1989) cite research findings that support cooperative learning. They maintain that students are more motivated to learn and that they enjoy school more when there are opportunities for cooperative learning. In addition, students develop more positive attitudes toward themselves and others regardless of individual differences. Johnson and Johnson also cite higher achievement, better retention, and growth in moral and cognitive reasoning. Since the 1980s cooperative learning has become a more dynamic alternative to individual competition in the classroom.

Gay's (1991) review of research indicates that many ethnic minority students prefer to learn in a group context. Some of the strategies that Gay identified included connaration[1] of stories by native Hawaiian children, choral response patterns by Native American students, group assistance in task performance among some Hispanics, and the call-response patterns among African-American children. With continued research educators will be able to refine the conditions under which students may benefit from both competitive and cooperative learning environments.

---

[1]Connaration: several students deliver speech forms together.

✦ Case Study: County Formation in Seventeenth-Century Virginia

One lesson designed by the author and taught in Mr. Thompson's fourth-grade classroom integrates several topics presented in this chapter—time and chronology, map and globe skills, and cooperative learning. The lesson plan is extensive and spans at least three days, so for purposes of illustration, excerpts tied to topics in this chapter will be highlighted.

Fourth-grade social studies often features state history along with regional features of the continental United States. In Virginia, the early settlement of the colonists provides an opportunity to explore the relationships between colonists, Native Americans, and African-Americans. By starting with an examination of primary documents, specifically maps representing the formation of counties, fourth-grade students were able to hypothesize about the impact of the settlements on the various ethnic groups. Skill development in time and chronology, maps and globes, and cooperative learning are outlined in the following. After students formulated hypotheses, secondary resource material was provided to affirm or reject initial hypotheses. This approach utilizes the inquiry approach discussed in Chapter 7.

Time and Chronology

Students were divided into five groups. Each group was given two maps as follows:

Group One	Map 1: Native American Tribes	Map 2: Virginia Counties 1634–40
Group Two	Map 2: Virginia Counties 1634–40	Map 3: Virginia Counties 1641–50
Group Three	Map 3: Virginia Counties 1641–50	Map 4: Virginia Counties 1651–60
Group Four	Map 4: Virginia Counties 1651–60	Map 5: Virginia Counties 1661–70
Group Five	Map 5: Virginia Counties 1661–70	Map 6: Virginia Counties 1691–1700

Once each group was given two maps, students were asked to hypothesize about the events that brought about the differences from one map to the next. This exercise addressed the following Virginia Standard of Learning (4.1): The student will explain the impact of geographic factors in the expansion and development of Virginia, with emphasis on (a) the location of American Indians, various European settlers, and African slaves; and (b) the location and growth of cities in relation to the Atlantic Ocean, the Chesapeake Bay, major rivers, the fall line/fall zone, and the Shenandoah Valley. Once the initial hypotheses were formulated, each group placed one map above a time line mounted in the hallway outside the classroom. Underneath the time line, the students posted their hypotheses generated on the first day of the instructional sequence. Selected hypotheses are as follows:

Map 1 to Map 2: Because the Virginia Company gave land to settlers who stayed more than seven years (around 1611), the ability to own property influenced the development of land boundaries.

Map 2 to Map 3: Accawmack County changed its name to Northampton County because Indians were driven off by the settlers and they no longer occupied the territory.

Map 3 to Map 4: Horrible hurricane ripped through the mouth of the Chesapeake Bay destroying tobacco crops so settlers moved further North.

Map 4 to Map 5: Because of religious differences, people on one side of the
Rappahannock River disagreed with people on the other side. Because of
these neighboring feuds Rappahannock County divided into Richmond and
Essex Counties.

Map and Globe Skills

On the second day students were given resource material pertinent to the time period
spanned by their maps. The resources were selected so that information about
colonists, Native Americans, and African-Americans would be available. Students
were asked to read the information and record the information on a research log, underneath their hypotheses. Their original predications were either affirmed or rejected, or in the some cases, maintained without knowledge to support the position
one way or the other. With the new information, students discussed the relevance to
the map changes once again. The new information was posted on the time line under
their hypotheses as "research." Some of the findings are listed as follows:

> **Map 1 to Map 2: From "Grevious Crimes of Pyracie and Murther"**
> Tobacco had been established as a staple crop for export. "[I]nterdiction of Virginia
> shipping on the high seas and the wilinginess of English mariners . . . who were
> occasionally given to dabbling in piracy, were problems that threatened to spread
> eventually to the very sands of the tidewater itself . . . And, on the seas as in the
> undefended colonial frontier environment of the Chesapeake, lawlessness and the
> constant threat of attack by a host of assailants was the price to be paid for planting
> the seeds of the empire" (Shomette, 1985, pp. 7–11).
>
> **From *A Share of Honor***
> . . . authority in Indian society did not belong to men alone. Succession among
> Virginia Indians was matrilineal: Political power was inherited through the mother
> rather than the father, and females were eligible to become rulers . . . [Queen
> Appamatuck] reinforced her authority as rulers often did and in ways that
> Englishmen readily understood—by regal dress, by a dignified bearing, and by
> keeping her distance. In the Indians' own language, this formidable woman was a
> *werowance,* the highest authority in her tribe. Among Virginia Indians, for women
> to hold such positions was not unusual, and the English, fresh from the reign of
> Elizabeth I (1558–1603), knew a queen when they saw one. What was more
> difficult for them to grasp was the importance of Indian women in the texture of
> everyday life . . . [W]hen the English were desperate for food, she supplied them
> with corn. By 1611, however, she was alarmed. Launching an aggressive policy of
> expansion, the English began carving out plantations on her tribal territory. The
> queen of the Appamatuck decided to resist. She began by inviting fourteen
> colonists to a party. When the men arrived, they were ambushed and everyone was
> killed. Reprisal was immediate. An English detachment attacked her town, burned
> it, and killed everyone they could find, including women and children. The queen
> herself was shot, probably fatally, as she tried to escape. (Lebstock, 1984, p. 13)

With the support of historical accounts, the maps had greater significance to the students. The knowledge they gained reinforced both national and state standards. At the
national level, the National Geography Standards (*Geography for Life,* 1994, p. 115)
for *Places and Regions* state that students will: Identify and describe a variety of regions that result from spatial patterns of human activity or human characteristics

(e.g., political regions, population regions, economic regions, language or other regions). A second Virginia standard (4.3) addressed by the mapping activity states: The student will explain the economic, social, and political life of the Virginia colony, with emphasis on (a) its political and economic relationship to England and other nations; (b) characteristics and contributions of various groups of people.

Cooperative Learning

By structuring the cooperative learning, Mr. Thompson's class benefited in several ways. First, generating hypotheses in small groups involved many more student ideas than would have been generated in a large-group setting. In addition, students learn important social skills by listening to and supporting the ideas of others. There were approximately five students in five groups, and over the course of three days, each member of the group was responsible for several of the following tasks since the tasks rotated from one day to the next: recording, brainstorming, reading supplementary resources, displaying information on timeline, and reporting to large group. Second, by distributing different maps to each group, it was possible to cover a greater time span. If each group had been expected to analyze all six maps, roughly fifteen hours would have been needed to complete the assignment. Devoting this amount of depth to seventeenth-century maps would be difficult to justify given fourth-grade curriculum expectations. By allowing each group to go into depth on one set of maps and share the results with the large group, the research and map interpretations could be shared. Students were expected to take notes and study the finished time line to ensure that they grasped the significance of the changes among colonists, Native Americans, and African-Americans. In addition to assessing the knowledge gained, Mr. Thompson asked each group to rate their performance as a team. As always, some teams worked more efficiently than others, but for fourth graders these skills are certainly in their formative stages.

✦ INTERNET LINKS

INTERNET LINKS

Cooperative Learning

http://www.sherm.com/

Sherman Consulting—Cooperative Education

Link to *Inclusive Education,* and you won't be disappointed with the information that can be found under skills and strategies. The section about cooperative learning is insightful and includes ideas for planning group work, evaluating group work, classroom rules for group work, teaching cooperative learning to others, and techniques such as paired heads, jigsaw, and learning centers.

INTERNET LINKS

Map and Globe Skills/Time Skills

http://members.aol.com/bowermanb/101.html

Geography World

This is an "everything geography" site. The links are arranged in categories that include all aspects of human geography and physical geography, games using geography, news and quizzes for geography teachers, and educational media. The link for map and globe skills contains an extensive list of resources for students, including: calculating world distances, history of mapmaking, clickable maps, how to make a map, several world atlases, and much more. Another exciting link is for time, which includes such topics as: time units explained, the source for days, how calendars are constructed, how to save time, and many other time-related activities. This site makes geography easy.

INTERNET LINKS

Cooperative Learning

http://www.atozteacherstuff.com

A to Z Teacher Stuff

This is a complete site of teacher resources that includes ideas for lesson plans, a thematic units index, teacher tips, book activities, and contests for all levels of teachers. The site also provides a page which takes a close look at cooperative learning. For example, this page includes answers to the questions of why teachers should use cooperative learning, what are the basics of cooperative learning, and how to use cooperative learning in the classroom. There are links to numerous cooperative learning activities and lessons, a cooperative learning lesson plan index (with links to lessons for all subjects), and archives for collaborative/cooperative learning lessons.

SUMMARY

By organizing lessons with attention to skill development, social studies teaching can be made more manageable for students. Concept attainment lessons foster conceptual understanding. Map and globe skills provide the tools to place the study of people and cultures in time and place. Time and chronology lessons equip students with the skills to understand historical context. Cooperative learning instills in students a sense of social responsibility. When taught in isolation, skills can seem irrelevant to students. But when incorporated into lessons that involve people and cultures, their meaning and usefulness are enhanced.

The skills lessons in this chapter assist elementary students in becoming active participants in the world around them. The *Self in the World* orientation emphasizes learning that helps students understand themselves and their role in the world better. Conceptual understanding, rather than rote learning, builds confidence in one's ability to learn because knowledge is constructed and developed in context. Map and globe skills enable students to navigate the world beyond their neighborhood and community. Developing conceptions of time and chronology allows children to travel backward and forward in time to appreciate global events and how they have influenced their views of the world. Cooperative learning in a classroom setting fosters in children an appreciation for the interdependence of human beings.

At no other time in history have these skills been as crucial for future generations. In ancient times, according to Stavrianos (1992) population increases were relatively slow and partially accommodated:

> . . . the Indians migrated southeast into the Ganges valley, and the Chinese south into the Yangtze valley and beyond. Western Europeans of medieval times migrated eastward in large numbers into the underpopulated lands of central and eastern Europe. More spectacular yet was the tidal wave of Europeans who flooded into the "empty" lands of the Americas and Oceania. Today, however, when world population increase far outstrips any in the past, no more "empty" territories remain. (pp. 154–155)

Stavrianos reminds us of the significance of coalescing the skill development presented in this chapter. With the current global demographic trend, future generations will need these skills to address the social and ecological challenges brought about by unprecedented population growth.

PROFESSIONAL DISCUSSIONS AND FIELD EXPERIENCES

Professional Discussions

1. In recent years as the study of ancient cultures has been introduced at earlier grade levels, teachers have raised important questions about the appropriateness of such study when young children have such a limited understanding of the notion "a generation ago," much less "thousands of years ago." Do you think that the study of ancient civilizations is appropriate in the primary grades? If so, why? If not, why not? A more fundamental question relevant to this discussion is, "Is the ability to learn about different ways of life dependent on a child's ability to grasp the concept of time during which the people lived?" Defend your answer.

2. The lesson on county formation in Virginia is important as both a lesson in American history as well as a regional history of Virginia. Investigate the historical maps that are pertinent to your local community. Often they are available in state museums, archives, and public libraries. What inferences can you make about changes over time? Share the maps you have discovered, or describe them if you were unable to make copies, with your classmates and brainstorm ways to develop lessons across grade levels.

Field Experiences

1. If possible, plan an activity that requires group cooperation. For example, provide students with baggies filled with equal parts of salt and flour. Ask students to mix them together and add enough water to make a salt and flour map of an imaginary island. Specify geographic features to be included such as mountains, rivers, lakes, and peninsulas. Decide if you would like to structure the activities by assigning specific roles to each student. Or ask them to divide the activities among themselves. Observe the way in which the students work together. Did they cooperate and share responsibility in a friendly manner? Were there students who were somewhat domineering? How would you adjust the lesson if you were to teach it again?

2. Collectively report to class the many ways in which time and chronology is depicted visually in the classrooms in which you observe. Calendars, time lines, clocks, visual marking of time such as pictures of the physical changes of chicks once they have hatched, or the changes in children's pictures from the time they were toddlers to their current age are just some of the many illustrations you might find. Share with the class the teaching activities that reinforce time and chronology

REFERENCES

Anderson, J. (1986). *Teaching map skills: An inductive approach.* National Council for Geographic Education. Macomb, IL: Western Illinois University.

Aronson, E. (1978). *The jigsaw classroom.* Beverly Hills, CA: Sage.

Batt, M. (1988). *The complete guide to creative watercolor.* Fort Lauderdale, FL: Creative Art Publications.

Bellanca, J., & Fogarty, R. (1991). *Blueprints for thinking in the cooperative classroom* (2nd ed.). Palatine, IL: Skylight Publishing.

Bruner, J. S., Goodnow, J. J., & Austin, G. A. (1956). *A study of thinking.* New York: Wiley.

Donovan, M. (1985). Research challenges. Carthage, IL: Good Apple, Inc.

Downey, M. T., & Levstik, L. S. (1991). Teaching and learning history. In J. P. Shaver (Ed.), *Handbook of research on social studies teaching and learning* (pp. 400–410). New York: Macmillan.

Ellis, A. K. (1995). *Teaching and learning elementary social studies* (5th ed.). Boston: Allyn & Bacon.

Gallagher, J. J. (1995). Perceptions of educational reform by educators representing middle schools, cooperative learning, and gifted education. *Gifted Child Quarterly 39* (2), 66–76.

Gay, G. (1991). Culturally diverse students and social studies. In Shaver, J. P., *Handbook of research on social studies teaching and learning* (pp. 144–156). New York: Macmillan.

Geography for Life: National Geography Standards 1994. (1994). Washington, DC: National Geographic Research and Exploration.

Gersmehl, P. J. (1991). *The language of maps.* Indiana, PA: National Council for Geographic Education.

Gustafson, M. H., & Meagher, L. Y. (1993). America's youngest citizens: Close up for grades 1–8. *Social Studies, 84* (5), 213–217.

Heatwole, C. (1993). Which way is Mecca? *Journal of Geography 93* (6), 267–269.

Holt, L. (1993). *Cooperative learning in action.* Columbus, OH: National Middle School Association.

Hubbard, R. (1993). Time will tell (Teachers Notebook). *Language Arts, 70* (7), 574–582.

Jarolimek, J. (1990). *Social studies in elementary education.* New York: Macmillan.

Johnson, D. W., & Johnson, R. T. (1989). *Cooperation and competition: Theory and research.* Edina, MN: Interaction Book Co.

Johnson, J., Carlson, S., Kastl, J., & Kastl, R. (1992). Developing conceptual thinking: The concept attainment model. *Clearing House, 66* (2), 117–121.

Kulik, C. C., & Kulik, J. A. (1982). Effects of ability grouping on secondary school students: A meta-analysis of evaluation findings. *American Educational Research Journal, 19* (3), 415–428.

Levstik, L. S., & Barton, K. C. (1994, April). *They still use some of their past: Historical salience in elementary children's chronological thinking.* Paper presented at the annual meeting of the American Educational Research Association, New Orleans, LA.

Ludwig, G. (1991). *Maps and Mathematics: Bringing Geography into Your Classroom.* Washington, DC: National Geographic Society.

Martorella, P. H. (1991). Knowledge and concept development in social studies. In J. P. Shaver (Ed.), *Handbook of research on social studies teaching and learning* (pp. 370–384). New York: Macmillan.

Marzano, R. (1992). *Cultivating thinking in English.* Urbana, IL: National Council of Teachers of English.

Mau, D. K. (1999). Shipwreck: Using literature and student imagination to teach geography. *Middle Level Learning.* Issue 5. Supplement to National Council for the Social Studies Publications. Washington, DC: National Council for the Social Studies.

Michaelis, J. U. (1992). *Social studies for children* (10th ed.). Boston: Allyn & Bacon.

Miller, F. (1997). A class meetings approach to classroom cohesiveness. *Social Studies and the Young Learner, 9* (3), 18–20.

A nation divided. (1989, January/February). The Education Center, Inc. The Mailbox.

Platten, M. (1991, March). *Teaching concepts and skills of thinking simultaneously.* Paper presented at the annual conference of the National Art Education Association, Atlanta, GA.

Sidler, J. L. (1992). *Pilot projects in portfolio and performance-based assessment. 1991–1992 progress report.* Philadelphia, PA: Research for Better Schools, Inc.

Slavin, R. E. (1983). *Cooperative learning.* New York: Longman.

Slavin, R. E. (1990). *Cooperative learning: Theory, research, and practice.* Needham Heights, MA: Allyn & Bacon.

Slavin, R. E. (1993). Ability grouping in the middle grades: Achievement effects and alternatives. *Elementary-School Journal 93,* (5), 535–552.

Stavrianos, L. S. (1992). *Lifelines from our past: A new world history.* New York: M. E. Sharpe.

Stein, J. (1988). *The random house college dictionary revised edition.* New York: Random House.

Wineburg, M. S. (1995, April). *The process of peer coaching in the implementation of cooperative learning structures.* Paper presented at the annual meeting of the American Educational Research Association, San Francisco, CA.

© Michael Newman/PhotoEdit

CHAPTER 9

ENGAGING STUDENT THINKING, KNOWLEDGE, AND CREATIVE EXPRESSION

Chapter Outline

CHAPTER OBJECTIVES

Most beginning teachers aspire to be dynamic and motivational in the classroom. But it's a rare person who can be charismatic two hundred days a year! One key to success is putting the spotlight on students, engaging them in ways that keep them motivated to learn. How will you maximize student participation so that it's not always the same handful of students responding? How will you ensure that students are challenged to think for themselves and move beyond the recall of important names and dates in history? What will you do to stimulate creative expression and problem-solving approaches when teaching social studies? Upon completion of this chapter you will be able to:

1. Design questions and activities that increase student participation and encourage critical thinking skills.
2. Develop learning tasks that allow students to solve problems.
3. Establish a classroom environment and learning activities that foster creative expression.

S cholarship in the past fifty years has expanded our understanding of how students think, solve problems, and express their own ideas. Cognitive developmentalists have contributed to this growth by emphasizing that learning and teaching is a reciprocal process between the student and his or her surrounding world. The traditional learning metaphor of the student as an empty vessel to be filled by information imparted from the teacher is limited and outdated. This notion ignores more recent research that acknowledges how students construct their own learning based on an interaction between their internal motivations, interests, and abilities and the experiences and ideas to which they are exposed (Brooks & Brooks, 1993). A more fitting metaphor would be that of a live oak, which starts as a seed and adds many different paths of branches and leaves that bend and turn in a variety of directions. Or another apt image is the chambered nautilus that builds chamber upon chamber while traversing and digesting the ocean bounty. This chapter explores the implications of these theories on the pedagogical principles of questioning strategies, thinking, problem solving, and creative expression.

✦ QUESTIONING STRATEGIES AND THINKING SKILLS

Asking students questions is a natural part of the ebb and flow of classroom interaction. But question asking can truly be an art. Most of you can recall those moments in your schooling experience when a teacher would ask a question and several reactions would be set in motion: the same hands shooting up immediately, the hope that you wouldn't be called on, the skill of avoiding eye contact with the teacher when you didn't know the answer, and, of course, relief when you did know the correct answer. Naturally, no one wants to show ignorance, but the overemphasis on having the right answer can undermine a positive learning environment. Research on questioning strategies has expanded the way we think about posing questions (Beyer, 1991; Hunkins, 1995; Wilen & White, 1991). Some of these methods are presented in this chapter to help you develop a range of questioning styles.

Questioning Patterns

The typical questioning pattern between teachers and students is: teacher asks question, student responds, teacher gives some kind of reinforcement (positive, negative, or neutral), then the teacher proceeds with another question or statement (see Figure 9.1). Some teachers give a lot of praise, some may give negative responses, while others may be more neutral by nodding or calling on another student. The atmosphere created by the reinforcement style of the teacher is unique to each classroom. For example, just because a teacher doesn't give a great deal of praise doesn't mean that the atmosphere is negative. Depending on the teacher and students, an abundance of praise can appear to be patronizing or insincere. On the other hand, teachers who tend to emphasize the negative may inhibit students or may be unintentionally encouraging negative behaviors. Greater understanding of reinforcement patterns can be gained by consulting the books on classroom management listed at the end of this chapter. For our purposes, however, questioning strategies are examined with regard to social interaction and thought processes.

There are techniques that a teacher can use to break the typical pattern characterized by Figure 9.1. When asking a question, a teacher can create a discussion pattern as

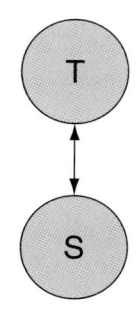

FIGURE 9.1
Typical Questioning Pattern

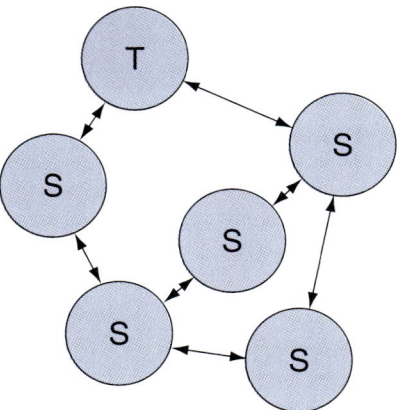

FIGURE 9.2   *Discussion Pattern*

depicted in Figure 9.2. One way to do this would be to ask a question, invite a student's response, then redirect the same question to another student using one of the following phrases, "How would you have answered that question?," "Do you have a different perspective on the same question?," "Does anyone else agree or disagree?," or "What is another way to answer the same question?" These follow-up questions generate more student ideas than if only one student answered. The teacher also can invite students into the role of providing reinforcement or building on the ideas of fellow students by offering the following questions: "What do you think about Daniel's comparison between the Greeks and the Incas?," "In what ways do your ideas about the future of the rainforest differ from Kathy's?," or "How have Asha's statements changed the way we think about India?" By using these phrases, the teacher forges links between and among students and encourages greater respect for their contributions.

In addition to analyzing questions for their impact on social dynamics and participation, educators have investigated how questioning patterns influence thinking patterns. Convergent questions elicit responses that are usually right or wrong answers. Examples of convergent questions are: What is the capital of Colorado? Who developed the Universal Declaration of Human Rights? How does a bill become law? The questions require that students recall previously studied information. The thought processes involve listening or reading about the events, perhaps studying written materials or notes, and retrieving the information from memory. Divergent questions elicit different kinds of thinking. A divergent question is more open-ended and can generate a variety of responses. Sometimes divergent questions have no right or wrong answers. Examples of divergent questions are: If the Civil War had been won by the South, how might the course of American history have been altered? How would you have handled the events surrounding the Bay of Pigs? What do you think the American people should do about the Equal Rights Amendment? Responses to these questions require students to recall background information about the events or issues and propose fresh ideas for either reconstructing history, altering the course of history, or proposing future actions. The thought processes allow for originality, problem solving, and creativity. In Box 9.1, Williams (1967) offers twenty-one strategies to assist teachers in developing productive-divergent thinking or action.

9.1   TEACHING STRATEGIES TO EXTEND PRODUCTIVE-DIVERGENT THINKING

Today's teachers frequently hear about the need for creativity—the use of divergent and creative elements of productive thinking. To diverge thoughts as producing new ideas, responses, or products, a person draws on stored knowledge to make new associations; these result primarily from inferences, implications, assumptions, or applications based on learned information. How can children be helped to acquire knowledge in such a way that they may draw on it readily?

This article presents a plan for achieving this goal. No drastic innovations are needed in curriculum or practice that innovative teachers are not already implicitly doing.

To aid teachers in experimenting with ways to use the twenty-one strategies of teaching—or tools that teachers can apply to all learning situations—the following illustrations assist in producing various behaviors essential for productive-divergent thinking or action:

1. *Use paradoxes.* A paradox is an inconsistency between the things people hold as true and the way they act. In exploring the problems of poverty, have pupils consider proverbs such as "Hard work will solve any problem"; in science, "Touching a toad causes warts." Sensitize students to evaluate in terms of what really exists versus what people think is true.

2. *Use analogies.* Point out how new information, facts, or principles can be derived from looking at similar settings. Flight of birds—flight of airplanes; principles of sonar—ability of bats to use reflected sound; shape of fishes—submarine design.

3. *Sensing deficiencies or unknowns.* Think about what humans do not know instead of what is known. Look for gaps, missing information, unknowns, inconsistencies in knowledge. List things that "bother" people, things people need, things wrong with something—the puzzles of nature, human nature, the world.

4. *What if? In what other ways?* Point out how one thing leads to another. What if all people were alike? What if no one paid taxes? What if there were no gravity on earth?

5. *Provocative questioning.* Encourage depth comprehension rather than factual recall. How much? Why? How would you? How else? Sensitize to question *asking* as well as to answer finding.

6. *List attributes of things or qualities.* Mentally take apart product or process and think about using its parts—new and unusual uses for common things; variation in uses of processes.

7. *Explore the mystery of things.* In natural, physical, and social sciences, have students deduce each step in their discovery they should apply or verify. Conduct "brainstorming" sessions about the mystery of events, phenomena, or people.

8. *Encourage original answers.* Allow for answers different from the ones in the book through an "idea bee" where unusual responses are sought.

9. *Learning to expect and accept the necessity for change.* Parallel change in nature to human change—humans adjust to a changing environment *plus* people change their environment.

10. *Teach about rigidities, fixation, and habits.* Show how lives and functions of people and machines have been habit-bound. Jet propulsion, known since

Chinese historical times before Christ, has only been recently applied in the last two decades; mineral wealth of the seas, known since early Phoenician times, only now being explored for "harvesting."

11. *Teach the skills of search.* Ways in which people seek truth. Historical search—how someone else sought or solved. Descriptive search—describe, compare, contrast several methods; trial-error. Controlled research—experimental observations. Showing *how* it is done is often as important as what is done.

12. *Build self-directed learning situations.* Lead the situation to a definite point, stop, let the student be puzzled, involved, challenged; nonsupply of "pat" answers.

13. *Provide for use of intuition or "hunches" as educated guesses.* Ask students to write, tell, or dramatize feelings or guesses about something. Use examples where "hunches" paid off—Edison, G. Washington Carver, Goodyear, Marconi, Salk, etc.

14. *Teach processes of invention and innovation.* Irritating problem, past knowledge for proposed attack, sustained effort, hard work, attempts and trials, meticulous recording of steps, findings, conclusions. Edison said, "I have found 99 ways of *not* doing thus-and-so."

15. *Serendipity—capitalizing on failures, mistakes, and accidents leading to development of worthwhile things.* Early efforts of men and women in flight; astronauts' death through accident; insulation of electric wires through previous dangers. Mistakes are the least proof of effort—one must *learn* through mistakes.

16. *Study lives of creative individuals.* Their personal lives; their interaction with other people; their products. Show how personal or social *discomfort* or deep concern fosters creative behavior. (Society for Prevention of Cruelty of Animals; child labor laws; unions; polio vaccines, etc.)

17. *Encourage new thinking based on stored knowledge.* Encourage combination of known ideas to form new associations—better ways to improve traffic safety, public health, delinquency control.

18. *Teach for cause and effect in different combinations.* Evaluate answers or solutions in terms of "Yes, but what if. . . ?" to refute or verify consequences or implications.

19. *Alertness to unexpected responses, ideas or solutions.* Evaluation in terms of relevancy rather than "snap judgment" or rejection.

20. *Develop skills of reading creatively.* Point out difference between reading as an information-acquiring process and one that leads to an idea formulation and development. Provide opportunities for scanning, rearranging, synthesizing information.

21. *Develop skills for perceiving through all senses.* Help students listen for information that leads to other things rather than only that which was heard in the original presentation. Draw attention to shapes, colors, textures, sounds, contrasts, similarities, differences.

Source: Williams, F. E. (1967). *Teaching strategies to extend productive-divergent thinking.* Adapted mimeographed handout from Williams, Director of Creativity and National Schools Project. St. Paul, MN: Macalester College.

Critical thinking approaches have expanded tremendously since the sixties. Wilen and Phillips (1995) propose a metacognitive approach to teach critical thinking skills. In the context of critical thinking, "metacognition refers to what a learner knows about his or her thinking processes (conscious awareness) and the ability to control these processes by planning, choosing, and monitoring"(Wilen & Phillips, 1995, p. 135). They offer useful teaching suggestions about the components of the metacognitive process (awareness and action) as well as a systematic approach for its implementation (e.g., explanation by the teacher, modeling by the teacher, modeling by the learner). Additional critical thinking strategies developed for elementary and middle school students include infusion (Wright, 1995), and anthropological approaches to gender issues (Schur, 1995); both are presented in a special issue of *Social Education.* In addition, the Just Think Foundation, found on the Internet, stimulates critical thinking about popular media for the purpose of gaining a better understanding of society (http://www.justthinking.-org/justthinkingeneral.html). The Center for Critical Thinking, sponsored by five nonprofit organizations can be located at http://www.sonoma.edu/cthink/default.html. AskERIC is another source for critical thinking strategies (http://-ericir.syr.edu/Virtual/Lessons/Interdisciplinary/INT0013.html).

Bloom's Taxonomy

Benjamin Bloom (1956) developed taxonomies for the cognitive and affective domains that teachers have found useful in developing questions and learning activities. The cognitive domain is represented by six levels of thinking as shown in Box 9.2 (Milner & Milner, 1993). The first two levels emphasize the recall and comprehension of information and the four additional levels spotlight more divergent thinking skills.

Bloom's Taxonomy is helpful when constructing higher-level questions, and perhaps more important, for planning activities. From working with the taxonomy over the years, I have found that there is quite a distinction between the two processes. Posing questions from the various levels is not a sufficient step for ensuring that thinking is occurring at the designated level. A group of student teachers taperecorded a lesson during which they asked questions using each level of the taxonomy. The student teachers then transcribed the audiotapes and analyzed student thinking generated by the questions. They discovered that merely posing a higher-level question did not guarantee student thinking at that level. Sometimes the response to the question proved to be at a lower level according to the taxonomy. In other cases, students responded to lower-level questioning with questions that revealed more complex thinking often missed by the student teachers because they were expecting answers on a lower level.

Based on the findings of student teachers it became apparent that applying the taxonomy to verbal questions was a beginning step in addressing Bloom's levels of thinking. More useful is the application of the taxonomy to learning tasks. By designing activities that retrieve higher-level thinking processes, the teacher will have more confidence in his or her ability to stimulate more complex thinking. The middle school lesson (McEachron-Hirsch, 1992) developed from the videotape *The In-*

9.2   BLOOM'S TAXONOMY

1. *Knowledge:* the ability to recognize or recall previously learned information and processes. Knowledge is usually defined more broadly; here it merely involves remembering information.
2. *Comprehension:* the ability to understand what is being communicated, but at a basic level. The student knows the meaning of information or ideas, but may not necessarily be able to relate it or apply it to other material or see its implications.
3. *Application:* the ability to use learned knowledge in particular and concrete situations. The student can apply rules, principles, concepts in new and appropriate contexts.
4. *Analysis:* the ability to break down information into its component parts.
5. *Synthesis:* the ability to put together elements or parts so as to form a whole. The student arranges and combines pieces to form a pattern or structure that was not clearly evident before.
6. *Evaluation:* the ability to judge the value of materials, methods, or ideas for a given purpose. This represents the highest level of intellectual functioning and is difficult for even the brightest students.

Source: Bridging English by Milner/Milner, © 1993. Reprinted by permission of Prentice-Hall, Inc., Upper Saddle River, NJ.

cas Remembered (Jarvis, 1986) demonstrates how activities can ensure performances at higher levels of Bloom's Taxonomy. The lesson begins by viewing a videotape that explains the history of the Incas. While students watch the video they are asked to complete a listening guide that highlights pertinent information needed for subsequent activities. The information gained from the videotape and questions on the listening guide reinforce the Knowledge and Comprehension levels of Bloom's Taxonomy. Establishing a strong knowledge base provides a foundation for higher levels of thinking. Sometimes beginning teachers think that Bloom's higher levels should be emphasized. But as they soon discover, without a strong knowledge base the higher-level questioning is weakened because there is not enough information upon which to build.

Once students are knowledgeable about the Incas' ancient civilization they are in a position to compare the Incas with the Greeks. This lesson assumes that students have already studied the ancient Greek civilization, a typical sixth-grade topic in social studies. The next task you see in the lesson plan is a structural comparison between the two civilizations, focusing on the concepts of medicine, government, language, religion, economics, and the arts. This activity corresponds to the Analysis level of Bloom's Taxonomy. Students are asked to identify ways in which the two ancient civilizations are alike and different.

FIGURE 9.3   *Two World Views of Western Culture*

Extending an idea originating in *The Age of Western Expansion* series (Educational Research Council of America, 1975) that compared Greco-Roman and Judeo-Christian worldviews, students were asked to imagine that the successful settlements in what is now called the United States were the Incas from the South rather than the English from Europe. How would life be different today? What would be a worldview and slogan expressed by the Incas? What symbols would be prominent? This activity corresponds to Bloom's Synthesis level because the development of an all-encompassing slogan and worldview requires a holistic examination of the culture as presented through the videotape. See Figures 9.3, 9.4, and 9.5.

The Application and Evaluation levels can easily be incorporated into this lesson on ancient Incan civilization. At the Application level students might build a model of the Incan village, reproducing the trapezoidal arch used in Incan architecture. The Evaluation level could be addressed in several ways. When simulating this lesson with college students I have asked which aspects of Incan culture would ben-

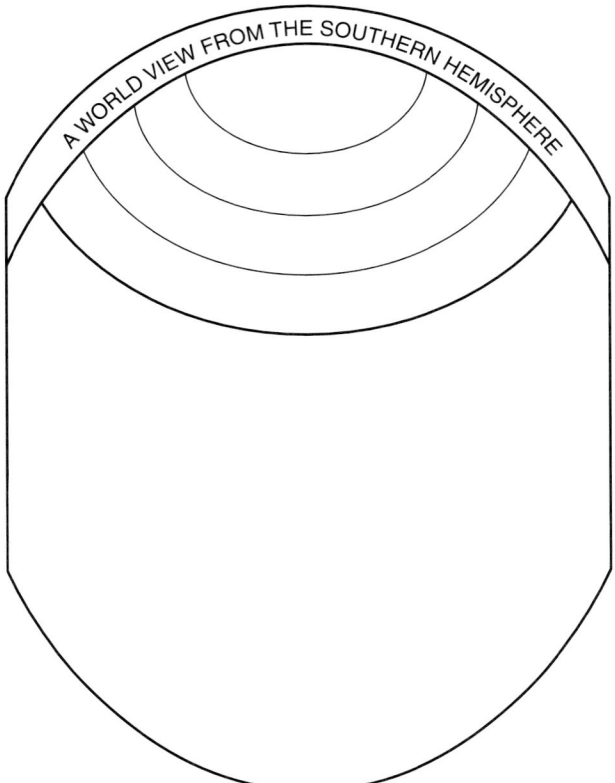

FIGURE 9.4   *A World View from the Southern Hemisphere*

efit what is now American culture if the Incas had arrived and settled instead of the English. These questions ask students to make a personal judgment about what they have learned.

Recalling our earlier discussion regarding the limitations of using Bloom's Taxonomy for only verbal exchanges, the lesson on Incas demonstrates how to exercise greater control in attaining the desired thinking levels. By planning tasks and developing evaluation instruments that assess student performance, there is a greater likelihood that the questioning strategies will generate higher levels of thinking. That is, the listening guide documents the recall of information, the compare and contrast form records analytical thinking, and the worldview slogans and symbols verify a synthesis of ideas. By taking Bloom's Taxonomy and constructing activities that allow for greater *time on higher-level tasks,* the desired levels of thinking may be attained. Laney, Laney, Wimsatt, and Moseley (1997) demonstrate this principle in their curriculum applications for primary students. In a unit on aging education they demonstrate how guiding questions could be addressed through student activities at each level of Bloom's Taxonomy.

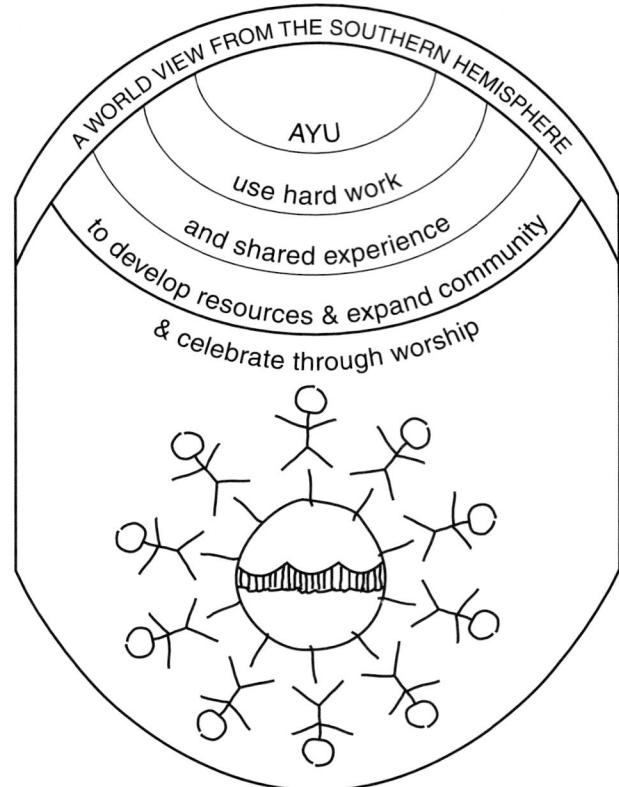

FIGURE 9.5   *A World View from the Southern Hemisphere—A Student Response*

Intermediate Application: Questioning Strategies

MODEL LESSON:
"THE INCAS REMEMBERED"

REPORTED IN VIRGINIA GEOGRAPHER
(MCEACHRON-HIRSCH, 1992)

Level: 6–8   **Time:** 2 Hours/2 Days

Purpose:

The purpose of this lesson is threefold:

1. To internationalize a curriculum that emphasizes Western cultures
2. To involve students in a guided discussion
3. To stimulate higher levels of thinking by asking students to:
   a. compare/contrast two cultures
   b. synthesize what they know about Incas so they can imagine how life would be different if we (U.S.) were settled by the Incas

c. derive generalizations about Incan contributions to a Southern Hemisphere worldview

Objectives:

1. Students will compare and contrast the ancient Incas and the Greco-Roman civilizations
2. Students will formulate generalizations about contributions of the Incas to the United States, recasting history based on the assumption that European settlers went to India and not the West Indies

Concepts: (defined previously; applied in this lesson)

legend, technology, politics, work, worship, arts, medicine, resources, communication

Procedure:

Introduction: Talk about the tendency to focus on our Western heritage, for example, studying ancient Greek and Roman civilizations (e.g., Chinese, Egyptian, Aztec, Myan) and *Incan,* which will be examined today. Ask students to look for any differences and similarities between the Greek/Roman civilizations and the Incas when showing video.

Content Focus: Pass out viewing guide to be completed while watching video; show video, *The Incas Remembered.* In pairs, have students fill out any missing information. On board or overhead, display table (see handout). Call on students to provide differences and similarities between ancient civilizations. See attached sample. Tie exercise together by discussing the fact that leadership, hierarchical structures, the economy, military strength, art, philosophical and religious expression all flourished before demise that came from greed, power, and territorial conquest.

Ask students to imagine that the European settlers never came to what is now the United States. Imagine instead that Incas traveled by boat through the many rivers, heading northward, crossing through what is now the Caribbean, further northward until coming to what is now Jamestown, but instead calling it Mini Machu Picchu.

> How would Virginia be different today?
> What would our architecture look like?
> Would William and Mary be here?
> Would you be here? If so, what would you be doing? If not, why not?
> How would life be different?

Divide students into groups of three. Show them pictures of political buildings in Washington D.C., as well as comparisons with ancient Greece and Rome. Pass out model of Greco-Roman and Judeo-Christian worldviews. Discuss; then show the students the blank form and ask them to fill in generalizations, reflecting the Southern Hemispheric heritage. Let students draw a picture depicting some aspect of how our cultural heritage would be altered.

Closure: Share generalizations about pictures. Discuss the importance of historical events in solidifying contemporary ideologies and lifestyles. Underscore the notion that relationships among people from different cultures can be enhanced when there is knowledge and understanding of respective cultures and their history.

Evaluation:

Formative: Viewing guides; written generalizations and pictures

Summative: Listening Guide, Comparing/Contrasting Ancient Civilizations, Worldview from Southern Hemisphere

Materials/Resources:

Video—*The Incas Remembered*
Table written on board or overhead
The Age of Western Expansion (Educational Research Council of America, 1975)
Handout—"Worldview from the Southern Hemisphere"

LISTENING GUIDE TO THE INCAS REMEMBERED

1. From childhood the Incas are trained to expand their:
   a. horizons   b. *memories*   c. friendships

2. "Towantan Suyo" means "the four ___*corners*___ of the world," and its splendor matches any ancient civilization whose ruins you might see in Spain, Greece, and Babylon.

3. There are three interpretations regarding how the Incas came to what is now Peru; list them
   a. Bering Straight *people traveled from Asia, across strait to South America*
   b. Vera Cocha *God created men/women in his own image; would return one day*
   c. Inti (Sun god) *built empire where golden staff disappears in the earth*

4. ___*Ayu*___ is a term referring to a cooperative family unit.

5. Labor hours are divided among three constituents; they are
   a. ___*state*___
   b. ___*priest*___
   c. ___*ayu (family group)*___

6. Three strategies developed by the Incas helped them to cultivate the land; these were:
   a. ___*terracing*___
   b. ___*guano*___
   c. ___*irrigation*___

7. Thor Heyerdahl imported Incas to help him make ___*reed boats*___ .

8. Two developments in the Inca civilization helped them expand their communication networks. One technique developed from natural resources and facilitated travel: ___*bridges*___ . Another was comprised of young relay runners called ___*cheskies*___. The young runners brought back ___*news*___ and ___*supplies*___ to the royalty.

9. ___*Laziness*___ was considered a crime, often punished by death.

10. True/False. ___*False*___ Because ancient Incas abused the fermented corn beer, chewing coca leaves was instituted.

11. To the Incas, public celebration was thought to be less dangerous than private ___*shame*___ .

12. The __alpaca__, __llama__, and __vicuna__ were animals considered valuable to the Incas and utilized in a fashion similar to the way that the American Indian survived from the bison.

13. __Yustas__ were selected because of their beauty and purity of lineage; their primary purposes in life were to __weave__ and bear only the offspring of royalty. If they failed to keep their vows, they were buried alive and their lovers were hanged.

14. The most treasured metal was __gold__.

15. Work quotas, called "mita," were met by:
    a. __farming__
    b. __weaving__
    c. __going to war__

16. After making a conquest, the Incas:
    a. *assimilated the people and their ideas into societal ranks*
    b. incorporated the people as slaves

17. The Incas developed the architectural feat of the trapezoidal arch to reduce damage from __earthquakes__.

18. What kind of surgery was repeated in modern times using the tools developed by the Incas? __brain__

19. The Incas used a system of record keeping that is similar to the decimal system and is characterized by __tying knots__.

20. For nearly two and a half centuries the Incas ruled nearly half of South America, ranging from northern __Ecuador__ to southern __Chile__.

21. The Incas offer several interpretations of the fall of their ancient civilization; list them:
    a. __prophecy; invaders would return from across the ocean__
    b. __greed between two brothers__

COMPARING/CONTRASTING ANCIENT CIVILIZATIONS

Greeks/Romans	Topics	Incas
Similarities		*Differences*
	Politics	
	Work	
	Worship	
	Legends	
	Technology	
	Arts	
	Medicine	
	Resources	
	Communication	

✦ PROBLEM SOLVING AND PROBLEM-BASED LEARNING

Problem solving and problem-based learning can be viewed as a constructivist approach to learning (Boyce, 1996). *Problem solving* as a thinking strategy is an idea not new to the social studies curriculum. In practice, students are given a task by the teacher and asked to solve the problem individually or in a group. The problem can require one class period to complete or may take days, following an inquiry model or more direct instruction. *Problem-based learning* is a relatively new term to the social studies curriculum, having come through the ranks of math and science traditions, with origins in the field of medicine. Yet the process has most of the characteristics of inquiry and discovery learning, mainstays of social studies traditions. Problem-based learning implies that the students are given a broad issue or situation and they are responsible for defining the parameters of investigation. Problem solving, on the other hand, can be a problem posed by the teacher. In both cases, however, the teacher facilitates throughout the problem-solving process.

Perhaps a few illustrations will make the differences more apparent. At the primary level, for example, teachers can provide problem-solving opportunities by asking students to think of different ways they might get to school if traditional paths are blocked (e.g., roadway covered with snow, car is out of gas, bus is not working, train is being repaired, etc.). Thinking of these transportation alternatives, or even ways to access school assignments (e.g., Internet capabilities, friends, closed-circuit television) generates many problem-solving ideas. Problem solving at the intermediate and middle school levels can be more elaborate. Students might be presented with a nat-

© J. Kirk Condyles/Impact Visuals

ural disaster scenario, such as how their community would respond to an earthquake or hurricane. What would they do if fires broke out or if the water supply was cut off?

Like problem solving, problem-based learning fosters creative and higher-level thinking skills. In problem-based learning, defining the problem lies more with the students than the teacher. Proponents of problem-based learning advocate presenting students with "ill-structured" problems that they explore while defining ways to tackle the issues (O'Neil, 1992; Savoie & Hughes, 1994). Working on the problems may take weeks, whereas most classroom problems are set up so that they can be "solved" during a few class periods. Typically, problem solving and problem-based learning are collaborative processes so that the ideas of many can be shared.

With the exception of one field tested science curricula (O'Neil, 1992), most of the examples of problem-based learning in social studies are at the high school level. Pahl (1995) applies the six-hat strategy, adapted from De Bono (1985), at the secondary level, but as you can see from the following categories, the applications at the elementary and middle school levels are limitless. Pahl (1995) suggests using inexpensive colored-paper party hats for each of the following five student groups (the teacher wears the blue hat symbolizing direction given to the process):

> **White Hats:** These students are to present the known facts concerning the problem under review by the class. Just the facts, and only the facts.
> **Red Hats:** These students describe only their raw emotions and feelings concerning the problem, as well as the raw emotions of others involved in the issue at hand. The Red Hats need not be concerned with facts, just emotions.
> **Yellow Hats:** These students analyze the situation and describe the logical negative consequences or events surrounding the issue being discussed. For example—what was a tragic or bad consequence of this problem?
> **Black Hats:** These students are the opposite of the Yellow Hats in that they must analyze and describe the logical positive consequences or events surrounding the issue. For example, what are the good consequences of this problem?
> **Green Hats:** These students leave the facts and their emotions aside and think creatively about the problem, employing different ways of looking at this issue or hypothesizing about future consequences related to the issue. What are some ways to think of this problem that no one has ever thought of before? What are some possible future consequences of the issue? (p. 154)

As you can see from the process developed by DeBono and applied by Pahl, a wide range of skills are addressed cooperatively throughout the problem-solving process—developing a knowledge base, expressing human emotion and values, generating analysis and logic, and stimulating creative thought.

Examples of problem-based learning for elementary students have been developed for the study of colonial history. The Center for Problem-Based Learning created a seventeenth-century challenge for students in American Studies. The scenario is described in Box 9.3 (Stepien & Gallagher, 1993).

As you can see, curriculum and instruction unfolds as students build on their ideas. The teacher serves as a catalyst for introducing new questions to keep the process going. Stepien (1994) also emphasizes that "reasoning is characterized by a reiterative process involving observation, hypothesis, inquiry, critical thinking and conclusion (decision). Assessment is an authentic companion to the problem and the process" (p. 1). For a more

9.3 AMERICAN STUDIES

[Students] in the role of directors of the Virginia colony are requested to explain to the King what they are going to do about the fact that colonial Virginia has not produced revenue for the last three years. Under a heading of "What do we know?" on the chalkboard, the students begin to list facts about the settlement of Virginia recalled from previous contact with American history. Not much help here! The teacher starts a new section: "What do we need to know?" The board begins to fill up quickly: Don't we have a charter with the King? What did we promise? What do we get from the Crown in return? Are there other colonies in the New World? How well are they doing? What are they doing to make a profit? Is there contact with natives? What is the contact like? What is life in Virginia like? As the questions are collected, the teacher prompts new lines of thought: "What are you thinking about? Have you got a hunch about something?" Hypotheses are written on a third section of the board. As the ideas are listed, the teacher probes for the type of information that will help the students decide whether a hypothesis is true, false, or needs refinement.

At the close of each class period, the students agree on which questions should be considered before the next class meeting. The assignment of questions is completed and students decide whether their textbooks or materials in the library are the best resources to consult.

After a few days, a second letter arrives in class. A member of the King's inner circle warns the directors that the King is becoming extremely concerned. The source suggests the directors must do something—and soon! The students must now use what they know, even if it is incomplete or contains conflicting data, to decide on the nature of their problem. After an acceptable problem statement has been crafted, the students turn their attention to solutions.

detailed explanation of problem-based learning, Stepien (1994) has prepared a planning booklet for the design of instructional materials, available through the Center for Problem-Based Learning, the Illinois Mathematics and Science Academy, Aurora, Illinois 60506-1039. In addition, AskERIC has a website entitled "Problem-Solving—A Part of Everyday Thinking" for Grades 4 to 12 (http://ericir.syr.edu/Virtual/Lessons/-Interdisciplinary/INT0057.html). Stepien's ten-step process is outlined as follows:

Planning Step No. 1   Finding a Situation with Potential
Planning Step No. 2   Constructing the Situation; Identifying the Role
Planning Step No. 3   Mapping Your Problem
Planning Step No. 4   Defining the Problem
Planning Step No. 5   Highlighting Outcomes
Planning Step No. 6   Building a Program Log
Planning Step No. 7   The Synthesizing Performance
Planning Step No. 8   Where Will Information Come From?

Planning Step No. 9   The Instructional Schedule
Planning Step No. 10   The Coaching Plan

Controversial Issues and Violence

Once you are comfortable with a process to encourage problem solving and problem-based learning, the topics will arise naturally from the time period, historical event, or significant issue. Controversial issues are natural sources for problem solving and problem-based learning because they are multifaceted and often include value conflicts. Violence is certainly a controversial and timely topic because school violence increased dramatically as the twentieth century came to a close. Violence in relation to television viewing (Hepburn, 1997), gun control laws (Watkins, 1997), motivational factors of youth (Croddy, 1997), urban life (Russell, 1997), prevention (Hess, 1997; Pereira & Rodriguez, 1997), unowned places and times (Astor, Meyer, & Behre, 1999), and constitutional protection from unreasonable search and seizure (Arbetman & Perry, 1997; Rothwell, 1997) are just a few of the important issues of concern to educators, parents, and youth. Problem solving ways to make communities safe from violence is a teaching opportunity that is not too advanced for elementary and middle school students. Because young people are surrounded by violence either directly or through popular culture, adults are in a position to model proactive stances against violence (see Kelly [1997] for a description of the experiences of a student teacher working in an alternative program for juvenile offenders in New Jersey). Addressing violence issues through the social studies curriculum, literature (Banaszak & Banaszak, 1997; Russell, 1997), and conflict resolution (Alter, 1996), demonstrates to young people that teachers care about their safety. For a more extensive discussion of controversial issues and instructional materials for the twenty-first century, see "Teaching Controversial Issues" (Rossi, 1996a).

✦ CREATIVE EXPRESSION

Along with thinking skills, questioning strategies, problem solving, and problem-based learning, cognition develops through creative learning. Creativity exists in any discipline or content area; for that matter, it can emerge in any context, in or outside of school. In this section, we examine creative expression, traditionally linked with the arts and humanities, to understand how it can be fostered throughout the social studies curriculum. There are many opportunities for creative expression in the area of social studies. Designing an imaginary civilization, creating scenarios between the Hopis and Navajos, simulating the marketplace, and writing a letter to one's representative in Congress are all ways that students express their creativity. Setting up a classroom environment that allows creativity to emerge in both directed and nondirected ways is crucial and requires an appreciation of the creative process.

In 1961, E. Paul Torrance, "The Creativity Man," outlined five principles that he said would foster creativity, and they still hold true today (Millar, 1995, pp. 77–78):

1. Be respectful of unusual questions, but tell children only what they cannot learn for themselves. Teach them the skills for inquiry and how to sustain a question, to toss it back and forth, to refine it and to accept the questioning mood without the need for ready-made answers from parent or teacher.

© Edouard Berne/Stone

2. Be respectful of unusual ideas and thinking.
3. Show children their ideas have value.
4. Provide opportunities for self-initiated learning and give credit for it. A mark of the highly creative individual is his self-starting ability.
5. Provide for a period of non-evaluated practice or learning. We do not have to evaluate everything. ("Gifted Children," 1961, p. A16)

Being mindful of these principles also helps to counteract the more widespread cultural forces that may impede creativity. Torrance (Millar, 1995) suggests that American and Canadian cultures have "stiflers" to the creative process, which include:

- Success orientation or a preoccupation with prevention of failure.
- Contemporary pressure on the individual to conform.
- The "curiosity killed the cat" philosophy, which discourages questioning.
- Cultural tradition that has made sensitivity a feminine value and independence a masculine one.
- Belief that any divergence from behavioral norms is an indication of something abnormal or unhealthy.
- The culturally inspired tradition that one is supposed to hate work and love play.

Torrance's "stiflers" are provocative and deserve further illumination because they point out truisms about our culture that are manifested in classroom settings even when teachers have the best intentions to foster creativity. I hope that, by addressing each separately, you will be able to identify and waylay similar "stiflers" as you teach.

Success Orientation

Most classroom environments stress mastery of skills and the acquisition of knowledge. Mastery and acquisition is measured by performances on tasks, quizzes, tests, and so on. This atmosphere is a viable reality and one to be valued and maintained. Yet having certain achievement standards implies an endpoint that one is trying to reach, and the inability of reaching this point signals failure. The climate needed for creativity to flow can be in sharp contrast to an atmosphere of success orientation. When children are given materials to "play with" or experiment with in an unstructured way, they have natural opportunities to create. In other words, when the urge to create is viewed as a natural human phenomenon, adults need merely to present children and youth with stimulating materials that will set the process in motion. An illustration may help you see how this works in a classroom.

Puppetry is a great way for elementary students to express themselves, whether they are acting out literature selections or role-playing the interaction between people to illustrate events in history. A structured way to encourage this expressiveness is to provide students with scripts that can be memorized. The performance itself can be exciting to the puppeteers and audience and provides opportunities for retelling history and oral language development. One way to make the experience more creative is to provide students with a wide range of materials from which to create puppets with a puppet show in mind. As students make their puppets, they are talking and creating characters as they work; the characters and the script emerge together. Whether the performance is tied to language arts or social studies, the creative elements blossom because *unstructured time is planned into the lesson.* Although it may seem ironic that a teacher *plans* for *unstructured time,* it is important to recognize this as a deliberate goal when setting the stage for creativity.

Pressure to Conform

The school environment places a great deal of emphasis on conformism, especially when the typical number of students in a given class exceeds twenty. Raising hands, not calling out of turn, turning in papers in a designated box, placing a heading on the paper in a specific way—all are procedures that require students to conform to classroom rules. And yes, these procedures are important to prevent chaos over logistical details. But when is spontaneity encouraged? Off-the-wall remarks? Random thoughts? Ideas that are not fully developed?

When teaching *artforms* (Chapter 12) to elementary students, we were faced with the realization that students were receiving contradictory messages about creativity. For example, when giving biographical sketches of each artist, I thought I had emphasized how each one sought to be different, a necessary aspect of the urge to create, which led to the development of each artist's unique style. After a demonstration of the artist's unique style, the students were free to experiment on their own. While two boys were painting the skulls popularized by Georgia O'Keeffe, one said to the other, "You can't put that earring on the skull!," which made the other boy hesitate with embarrassment. Somewhere along the way, we hadn't stressed that students were being exposed to a variety of artforms but that they didn't need to feel that they had to replicate the artist's style. Not enough time for random experimentation and creativity had been built into the curriculum. This anecdote reminds me of so many classroom instances where creative thoughts emerge when we are either preoccupied with the *planned* curriculum or when we are concerned that acknowledgment of the creative thought may violate another classroom protocol, such as behavior that is off-task. This limitation is similar to Torrance's point that deviation from behavioral norms is viewed as unhealthy.

"Curiosity Killed the Cat" Philosophy

"Are there any questions?" the teacher asks one minute before it's time to change classes and students are packing their books. We're all guilty of this. Filling the class with so much activity and information, the question becomes rhetorical because there just isn't time to get into substantive questions. Besides allowing more time throughout classroom activities there are additional ways to encourage questioning. Setting a genuine tone that values questions is one way. Statements such as "There is no such thing as a stupid question," or "Don't be afraid to make mistakes; if you don't fall on your face occasionally you won't do anything interesting or different," transmit an openness toward receiving any and all kinds of questions. Risk-taking behavior and creativity go hand in hand.

A shoebox covered with butcher paper and decorated with question marks is a simple way to encourage questions that arise from reticent students who may not want to compete with the eager students who never run out of questions. The box also allows for questions after thoughts have been mulled over or questions that emerge after classroom activities have ended. Retrieving questions and bringing them back to the class sends a strong message that questions are a valued part of learning and time will be set aside to address them. Naturally, inquiry and discovery learning, discussed elsewhere in this book, are ways to inspire creativity through curiosity.

Feminine and Masculine Values

How often we hear that women and girls are the peacemakers, the nurturers. This role requires sensitivity, good listening, and receptivity. The traditional role of men and boys, on the other hand, is espoused as one of conquest and adventure, a role that requires a *take charge* attitude, decisiveness, and authority. Torrance helps us see this polarity when he suggests that these cultural stereotypes impede creativity. Encouraging all students to be sensitive to the ideas of others and the world around them would certainly contribute to seeing things in novel ways. By the same token, that take-charge, or authoritative, attitude can only help students pursue their endeavors when creativity is set in motion. A teacher who wants to foster creativity should therefore instill in both boys and girls a sensitivity to explore and observe the world around them while at the same time instill the sense that they can make a difference in the world.

Hate Work and Love Play

We definitely send mixed messages to students regarding the dichotomy between work and play. On the one hand, adults advance the notion that students should pursue jobs that are satisfying, jobs that they will enjoy because they are naturally suited for them. Yet a gap seems to exist between understanding job satisfaction and taking pride in school efforts. Despite Dewey's philosophy that the classroom is a microcosm of society and classroom exchanges should be valued for themselves, as opposed to being viewed as a stepping-stone for future endeavors, students often feel that the classroom is something to be endured while recess and after-school activities are viewed as fun and relaxation. If teachers can empower students to take responsibility for their learning and to view this responsibility as necessary for lifelong learning and job satisfaction, perhaps they will narrow the gap. Of course, ensuring that learning activities are motivational and tied to students' interests and levels of development are half the battle!

Despite the "stiflers" embedded in our culture, Torrance offers teachers a variety of approaches to foster creativity in students. According to Torrance (Millar, 1995, pp. 353–357), learning activities should enable students to:

- Produce and consider many alternatives. (Or: Think of lots and different kinds of ideas.)
- Be original. (Or: Be inventive!)
- Elaborate. (Or: Add some extras.)
- Highlight the essence. (Or: Get to the heart of the matter.)
- Keep open. (Or: Don't take the easiest way out.)
- Be aware of emotions. (Or: Know and express your feelings.)
- Put your ideas in context. (Or: Get the big picture.)
- Combine and synthesize. (Or: Get it together.)
- Visualize it richly and colorfully. (Or: See things in all their splendor.)

- Fantasize. (Or: Use your imagination.)
- Enrich imagery. (Or: Feel it, smell it, touch it, taste it, hear it.)
- Have an unusual visual perspective. (Or: Seeing things from a different angle.)
- Have an internal visual perspective. (Or: Don't judge a book by its cover!)
- Breakthrough—extend the boundaries. (Or: Break habit thinking.)
- Have a sense of humor. (Or: Laugh a little.)
- Decentrism—glimpse infinity. (Or: Get out your crystal ball.)

The work by Torrance has inspired many educators to value the search for creative opportunities in the classroom. Starko (1995) reviews scholarship in creativity and provides many teaching suggestions in *Creativity in the Classroom*. Divergent thinking strategies, brainstorming, SCAMPER, attribute listing, morphological synthesis, lateral thinking, metaphors and analogies, visualization, and creative dramatics are just a few of the strategies Starko describes. The reference section at the end of this chapter provides additional resources for creative teaching suggestions. In addition, the Internet site "Future Problem-Solving Program," whose founder is Paul Torrance, provides materials to help students learn *how* to think, not *what* to think (http://www.fpsp.org/overview.html).

✦ CASE STUDY: PULLMAN STRIKE OF 1894

The U.S. Department of Education provides federal funds for educational projects in a variety of areas. The Javits Grant Program is designated for programs that enhance learning for at-risk gifted students. Through the leadership of Joyce VanTassel-Baska, who has been the recipient of several Javits grants, Lisa Kaenzig and I (Kaenzig, 2000) had an opportunity to develop a social studies curriculum for at-risk gifted students. There were many overarching goals, but the ones featured in this case illustration are those that pertain to (a) critical thinking and reasoning skills, and (b) student participation in small-group and entire-class settings.

During the brainstorming phase of unit planning, we faced the challenge of addressing state and national standards in a way that would make history come alive. The designated standards delineated the structures and functions of national, state, and local governments and the division of powers among them. Rather than teaching these principles of government in isolation, we felt that the events surrounding the Pullman Strike of 1894 demonstrated the interdependent operations of local, state, and national governments. After a brief description of the story line created by Lisa Kaenzig, a breakdown of critical thinking and reasoning skills, and strategies to increase student participation, will be provided.

The Event

The major historical background needed for this unit is an understanding of the importance of the railroad to the westward expansion of the United States and the transportation of goods that shaped the Industrial Revolution. The Homestead Act, passed by Congress in May of 1862, offered 160 public acres of land to anyone who agreed to cultivate it for five years and build a home. This Act greatly helped the country's westward expansion, but at the same time, more power was obtained by the railroad owners who bought much of the land without fulfilling requirements of the Act. In 1862, another important law was passed by the Congress, the Pacific Railroad Act, which fostered competition between two different railroads (one representing the South and the other, the North) to see who could build the lines more quickly. Most of the workers on the railroad were immigrants from China and Western Europe. On May 2, 1869, the two lines met at Promontory Point, Utah. This building of the railroad lines resulted in fast transportation for millions of new Americans who wanted to settle or travel to the West. The country was growing exponentially in the mid to late 1800s and growing pains were imminent for new immigrants who came to the United States willingly, for African-Americans who were struggling for freedom, and for Native Americans who perceived this Westward Expansion as an Eastern Invasion.

The period of 1870 to 1900 marked the period of the development of the industrial United States. The Industrial Revolution resulted in a move away from the majority of Americans as independent shopkeepers and artisans to workers who relied on wages from big companies. Due to this decrease in autonomy, workers felt that they needed to organize into groups in order to have some power against the big corporations. These organized groups of workers were called labor unions.

The Supreme Court and the Congress were very much in favor of big business at this time in history, and much of the legislation of the time helped many of the "robber barons" build large corporations by setting up trusts. For example, many small business owners felt that the railroads had too much power and therefore could charge high prices for shipping goods. In 1886, the Supreme Court ruled in *Illinois v. Wabash, St. Louis, and Pacific Railroads* that states could not legislate railroad rates because only the Congress had the power to regulate interstate commerce. In 1887, the Congress passed the Interstate Commerce Act, which attempted to limit the power of the railroads to charge unfair prices. This Act also established the Interstate Commerce Commission, which was charged with supervising the rates and investigating complaints.

Many Americans were complaining in the 1880s that the corporations had too much power. In response to this public concern, the Congress passed the Sherman Antitrust Act in 1890, an attempt to outlaw monopolies. However, the companies found loopholes and continued to gain power.

A recession occurred across the country in the 1890s. This recession led to the Panic of 1893 where many companies were cutting wages. The Pullman Palace Car Company, which manufactured railroad cars, was cutting the wages of its employees while refusing to reduce the rents of employees who were required to live in the company town of Pullman, Illinois. This unfairness led workers to protest. At this time, unions were beginning to organize in order to promote the rights of workers. There were different types of unions. Some unions were specialized so that many of the workers of the same company might be in different unions (e.g., seamstresses were in one type of union while engineers were in a different union). However, the American Railway Union (ARU) was started so that railroad workers would have more power by all being part of the same union.

The Pullman Strike of 1894 was an important labor dispute in U.S. history. On May 11, 1894, the workers of the Pullman Palace Car Company in Chicago went on strike to protest wage cuts and the firing of union representatives. The workers sought support from their union, the ARU led by Eugene Debs. On June 26, 1894, the ARU called a boycott of all Pullman railway cars. Within days, 50,000 rail workers complied and railroad traffic out of Chicago came to a halt. When the railroad owners asked the state government to send in the state militia, the governor of Illinois, Jon Peter Altgeld, refused. So the companies called on the federal government to intervene, and Attorney General Richard Olney (also a director of the Burlington and Santa Fe railroads) obtained a blanket court injunction on July 2. On July 4 (what irony here!), President Cleveland dispatched federal troops to Chicago. The government's action broke the strike, and the boycott collapsed. The basis of the federal government's claim was that the trains were carrying cars filled with the U.S. mail (which the Pullman Company had cleverly attached by adding mail cars in the midst of the strike as a smart strategy). The federal government, in its role as the regulator of interstate commerce, would not allow the unions to disrupt a federal service to the American people. There was rioting and lives were lost. Debs and three other officials of the union were jailed for disobeying the president's injunction. Governor Altgeld, and the mayor of Chicago, Steven Hopkins, did not want the federal government to intervene in an issue that the governor and the mayor felt was one for the State of Illinois to deal with. The mayor and governor felt that the local authorities could have handled the strike situation without federal intervention.

Fostering Critical Thinking

From the preceding story line one can see the complex and dynamic ways in which the lives of Americans were shaped by decisions made at the local, state, and national levels. As college students, you have a sufficient background in American history and government to know how the various levels of government operate. But to an upper elementary and middle school student, understanding the interdependence and powers assigned to each level of government is in its beginning stages. The Pullman Strike and surrounding events are a provocative way to analyze government, business, and labor, but to do so requires having a knowledge base in each of the three areas. For example, consider asking students the following questions and analyze how the questions ask students to move beyond mere recall of the historical events just outlined. Critical thinking is required to explain the interrelationships among levels of government, business, and labor.

Key Questions

1.   Many of the workers of the Pullman Palace Car Company who went on strike did not make high wages. Do you think they should have risked losing their jobs to strike? Explain your answer. (This requires an understanding of the beliefs of workers regarding the protections provided by membership in labor unions; support was not uniform from union to union; the historian Ray Ginger, [1975] maintains that so few unions organized and suggests that individuals were more willing to "go it alone" given the opportunities of American life; critical thinking about the role of labor unions in American life today is a logical extension of this discussion.)

2.   Describe the actions taken after the Pullman Strike and take a position defending the rate regulations or criticizing actions taken by the government to regulate rates. (A position defending the regulations requires an

appreciation for the individual rights of workers and consumers; a position criticizing actions taken by the government would cite such information as the United States operating on the principles of capitalism, e.g., supply and demand influence market prices, against government interference.)

3. On what basis did Governor Altgeld and Mayor Hopkins take the position that the Pullman Strike should be dealt with by State of Illinois government officials? On what basis did the federal government take the position that federal troops could end the boycott? Which level of government had authority in this instance? Explain how and why? (Knowledge of rights designated by the Constitution is necessary for this analysis; also the way in which the doctrine of laissez-faire was applied selectively during this period of time; e.g., the shift in the balance of power away from agriculture and toward commercial-industrial interests was evidenced by federal agencies giving considerable aid to railroads while farmers struggled.)

4. Investigate the number of states in the United States where it is illegal to be a member of a labor union. Do you think this is unconstitutional? Why or why not? (This requires critical thinking while interpreting the U.S. Constitution and state constitutions.)

5. Point/Counterpoint: Child Labor Laws. Defend two positions. The first position is an argument in favor of allowing children to work. There are cultures that support the working roles of children, particularly in family-owned businesses, and these cultures maintain that compulsory education laws intervene in the rights of parents to decide what constitutes appropriate educational experiences. The second position is an argument against allowing children to work before the age of 16. This position maintains that formal education in the United States should be decided upon at the state level and that all families should follow the state system of education. (These positions require an understanding of the child labor laws and compulsory education laws.)

Critical thinking about the Pullman Strike, as indicated by the preceding five questions, necessitates that students be taught knowledge in the following categories. Knowledge in one category is insufficient for addressing the complexity of the issues. That is, for critical thinking to take place students need to have a foundation of how the branches of government function in relation to business and labor. Thus, critical thinking is enhanced by interdisciplinary teaching strategies from the fields of history, political science, economics, and sociology.

Government	Business	Labor	Biography
Constitution	Laissez-faire	Working conditions	George Pullman
Executive branch	Capitalism	Workers' rights	Eugene Debs
Legislative branch	Mass production	Union formation	Jennie Curtis
Judicial branch	"Invisible hand"	Collective bargaining	Grover Cleveland

Case study illustrations provide a way to integrate concepts from the various disciplines so that historical events are seen as representing many diverse points of view. To help students organize key issues surrounding historical events, the steps outlined by Farris and Cooper (1997) are quite useful. Farris and Cooper suggest that the questions work well with younger children when applied to literature selections such as *The Little Red Hen.*

The Case Study Method

Step 1: Review the facts of the case.
What happened in this story?
Who is involved?
What facts are important?
Is there any information missing that would be helpful?
Why did the people act the way they did?

Step 2: State the issue in the form of a question.
This step raises the level of abstraction.
The teacher may need to frame the issue.
Is it a legal, ethical, or policy issue?

Step 3: Discuss the arguments.
What are the arguments for and against each side?
What alternative courses of action are there?
What would be the consequences for each alternative?

Step 4: Make a decision.
What is your decision in this case?
What is your stand on the issue we posed?
What are your reasons for taking this position? (Farris & Cooper, 1997)

✦ INTERNET LINKS

INTERNET LINKS

Creativity

http://www.ozemail.com/au/caveman/creative/index2.html

Creativity Web

This site was designed as a resource guide to enhancing creativity and innovation in students. The creativity basics help an individual discover what creativity is, if that individual could be considered creative, what obstacles an individual must overcome to be creative, and activities to improve creativity. Ten creative quick starts are ideas to enhance creative thinking. The techniques list several links to sites that explain different methods for improving creativity. Also included in the children's corner are methods to employ in a classroom or at home to enhance and achieve peak creative performance in children.

INTERNET LINKS

Problem Solving

http://www.fpsp.org

Future Problem-Solving Program

This program was developed by Paul Torrance in 1974 to help students develop their creativity and problem-solving abilities. This site provides an explanation of his program, the criteria that he hopes each learner can achieve by becoming a good problem solver, and the six-step foundation for problem solving. The site also provides links to units that can be used in classrooms as tools to enhance problem solving and creativity, such as: women in the workplace, freedom, natural disasters, and low gravity sports. The site also provides information on how students can become involved in the program, competitively or noncompetitively, on the local level.

SUMMARY

Teaching strategies that foster critical thinking, higher-level thinking, problem solving, and creative thinking engage students in active ways. As we have seen in this chapter, such approaches encourage students to think for themselves, thus building confidence, knowledge, and a sense of efficacy in the world around them. Some of the most memorable elementary social studies lessons recalled by college students are the ones that reflect these approaches: for example, building model communities that required students to problem-solve in small groups; creative stimulation when presented with the challenge to design a radio broadcast program for current events; critical analyses when asked to reflect on the differences and similarities among Islam, Christianity, and Judaism. The fact that these experiences have stayed with them over the years demonstrates the lasting impact of knowledge generated when students have ownership of their learning and an opportunity to pursue topics in depth.

The curriculum applications presented in this chapter reinforce the *Self in the World* orientation in several ways. Activities that ask students to imagine how their world would be different if key historical events were altered in some way gives them an appreciation for the legacy of the past and also challenges them to reflect on personal values that they may take for granted. The case illustration also demonstrates the complexity of the relationships among various levels of government, an interdependence that is appreciated when actual events are analyzed in depth. Whether designing activities that require students to think critically about the past or designing activities that present creative opportunities for students to chart new territories, the teacher plays a key role in helping students participate in as well as shape the world around them.

PROFESSIONAL DISCUSSIONS AND FIELD EXPERIENCES

Professional Discussions

1. Torrance pointed out how conformism is a stifler to creativity. Ironically, some school districts have argued for school uniforms as a way to "redirect" student attention to more creative and academic thinking in the school environment. School administrators maintain that students are less distracted by the competition brought about by American popular culture, which emphasizes fad and fashion. What are your thoughts on this issue? What are the advantages and disadvantages of school uniforms? What factors would you identify in the

ethos of a school that would contribute positively toward creative thinking? What are the stiflers to creativity?

2. Think of activities that, when given a choice, you prefer to avoid—perhaps programming the VCR to record at a certain time, sewing a button on a shirt, changing the oil in your car, cooking more than a one-course meal, creating a watercolor painting, or writing fiction. Are there other tasks that you can add to this list for which you typically find someone else to do, or pay to have someone do for you? Depending on the extent to which you would like to explore these *anxieties,* attempt to do one of the items on the list that you typically avoid. Share with classmates the attitudes and feelings you had while performing tasks that are not your favorite or that you simply dislike. I have fond memories of changing a tire on the interstate as a police officer read the manual. He had informed me that police officers were not supposed to change tires. Such empowerment I felt when it was over! As you reflect on these feelings, imagine what many students experience when asked to perform in ways that are not familiar, or ways that are inconsistent with their preferred ways to learn. In what ways can you foster an environment that encourages creativity and exploring the unknown? In what ways can you demonstrate empathy with your students?

Field Experiences

1. Make arrangements to observe a class during which the teacher will be asking a lot of questions. Record the questions asked as well as the students' responses. This exchange goes rapidly so try to record the main ideas rather than a verbatim account. Classify the questions into Bloom's Taxonomy. Describe any patterns you discover. Analyze the nature of the students' responses. It is not unusual to categorize a question on one level and discover that the student response reflects thinking that is at quite a different level from the teacher's intention. How would you describe the relationship between the question asked and the student response? Were there questions asked that didn't fit into Bloom's Taxonomy? How would you categorize them? Which questions were open-ended and elicited a variety of responses? Which ones were convergent and required correct answers? What do you feel are the greatest challenges in constructing questions that require critical thinking?

2. Ask students to share concerns they may have regarding their school or local community. Safety issues are becoming an increasing concern, whether pertaining to the bus (e.g., loading and unloading at the primary levels), or peer intimidation and bullying at the upper elementary level. Related to safety are the rising number of violent acts perpetuated on school grounds. Other issues might include language support. With permission from the classroom teacher, set up the concerns in the form of a problem-based learning exercise, using Stepien's ten-step approach.

REFERENCES

Alter, G. T. (1996). Violence in society, war in the world: Preventing and resolving conflict. *Social Studies and the Young Learner, 8* (4), 26–28.

Arbetman, L., & Perry, M. (1997). Search and seizure: The meaning of the fourth amendment today. *Social Education, 61* (5), 273–276.

Astor, R. A., Meyer, H. A., & Behre, W. J. (1999). Unowned places and times: Maps and interviews about violence in high schools. *American Educational Research Journal, 36* (1), 3–42.

Banaszak, R. A., & Banaszak, M. K. (1997). Trade books for reducing violence. *Social Education, 61* (5), 270–271.

Beyer, B. K. (1991). *Teaching thinking skills: A handbook for elementary school teachers.* Boston: Allyn & Bacon.

Bloom, B. S. (1956). *Taxonomy of educational objectives; The classification of educational goals.* New York: David McKay.

Boyce, L. N. (1996). Problem-based learning literature review. Center for Gifted Education, The College of William and Mary, Williamsburg, VA, February draft paper.

Brooks, J. G., & Brooks, M. B. (1993). *The case for constructivists' classrooms.* Alexandria, VA: Association for Supervision and Curriculum Development.

Cohen, J. J. (1993). *Handbook of school based interventions: Resolving student problems and promoting healthy educational environments.* San Francisco: Jossey-Bass.

Croddy, M. (1997). Violence redux: A brief legal and historical perspective on youth violence. *Social Education, 61* (5), 258–264.

Curwin, R., & Mendler, A. N. (1988). *Discipline with dignity.* Alexandria, VA: Association for Supervision and Curriculum Development.

DeBono, E. (1985). *Six thinking hats.* Boston: Little, Brown.

Educational Research Council of America. (1975). *The age of western expansion.* Boston: Allyn & Bacon.

Evertson, C. M., Emmer, E. T., Clements, B. S., Sanford, J. P., & Worsham, M. E. (1994). *Classroom management for elementary teachers* (2nd ed). Boston: Allyn & Bacon.

Farris, P. J., & Cooper, S. M. (1997). *Elementary and middle school social studies.* Boston, MA: McGraw-Hill.

Froyen, L. A. (1993). *Classroom management: The reflective teacher-leader.* New York: Macmillan.

Gallo, M. (1996). Controversial issues in practice. *Social Education, 60* (1), C1–C4.

Garcia, O. (1994). Problem solving—A part of everyday thinking. *AskERIC Lesson Plans,* #AELP-INT0057. Available online: ericir.syr.edu/Virtual/Lessons/Interdisciplinary/INT0057.html.

Ginott, H. (1972). *Teacher and child.* New York: Macmillan.

Glasser, W. (1993). *The quality school teacher.* New York: Harper Perennial.

Henderson, J. G. (1992). *Reflective teaching.* New York: Macmillan.

Hepburn, M. A. (1997). TV violence: A medium's effects under scrutiny. *Social Education, 61* (5), 244–249.

Hess, D. (1997). Violence prevention and service learning. *Social Education, 61* (5), 279–281.

Hillman, B. W. (1981). *Teaching with confidence: How to get off the classroom wall.* Springfield, IL: Charles C Thomas.

Holbrook, D. (1994). *Creativity and popular culture.* Cranbury, NJ: Associated University Presses.

Hunkins, F. P. (1995). *Teaching thinking through effective questioning* (2nd ed.). Norwood, MA: Christopher-Gordon.

Jarvis, P. (Producer and Director). (1986). *The Incas remembered.* [videotape]. (Available from Creative Projects Inc.)

Johnson, D. W., & Johnson, R. T. (1991). *Learning together and alone* (3rd ed.). Englewood Cliffs, NJ: Prentice-Hall.

Jones, V. F., & Jones, L. S. (1986). *Comprehensive classroom management: creating positive learning environments.* Boston: Allyn & Bacon.

Just Think Foundation. Available online: www.justthink.org/justthinkgeneral.html.

Kaenzig, L. (2000). The road to the White House: The American system of representational democracy in action. Williamsburg, VA: Center for Gifted Education, Project Phoenix (funded by United States Department of Education Grant #321211).

Kellough, R. D. (1994). *A resource guide for teaching: K–12.* New York: Merrill.

Kelly, J. P. (1997). Experiences in a juvenile justice system. *Social Education, 61* (5), 268–269.

Laney, J. D., Laney, J. L., Wimsatt, T. J., & Moseley, P. A. (1997). "Youngster, Oldster": Aging education in the primary grades. *Social Studies and the Young Learner, 9* (4), 4–9.

Larrivee, B. (1992). *Strategies for effective classroom management: Creating collaborative climate: Leader's guide to facilitate learning experiences.* Boston: Allyn & Bacon.

Levin, J., & Nolan, J. F. (1991). *Principles of classroom management: A hierarchical approach.* Englewood Cliffs, NJ: Prentice-Hall.

Lockwood, A. L. (1996). Controversial issues: The teacher's crucial role. *Social Education, 60* (1), 28–31.

McBee, R. H. (1996). Can controversial issues be taught in the early grades? The answer is yes! *Social Education, 60* (1), 38–41.

McEachron-Hirsch, G. (1992). Comparing and contrasting western and non-western ancient civilizations: 500 years after they were connected by Columbus. *Virginia Geographer, 24* (1), 11–15.

Menke, D. J., & Pressley, M. (1994). Elaborative interrogation: Using "Why" questions to enhance the learning from text. *Journal of Reading, 37* (8), 642–645.

Millar, G. W. (1995). *E. Paul Torrance: "The creativity man."* Norwood, NJ: Ablex.

Milner, J. O., & Milner, L. F. M. (1993). *Bridging English.* New York: Merrill.

Olmstead, T. S. (1994). Critical thinking strategies. *AskERIC Lesson Plans,* #AELP-INT0013. Available online: ericir.syr.edu/Virtual/Lessons/Interdisciplinary/INT0013.html.

Olsen, D. G. (1995). "Less" can be "more" in the promotion of thinking. *Social Education, 59* (3), 130–134.

O'Neil, J. (1992). Rx for better thinkers: Problem-based learning. *Update, 34* (6), 1–5, Association for Supervision and Curriculum Development, Alexandria, Virginia.

Pahl, R. H. (1995). Six-hat social studies. *Social Education, 59* (3), 154–157.

Pereira, C., & Rodriguez, K. (1997). Linking violence prevention and good social studies: Research and development. *Social Education, 61* (5), 282–287.

Rauschenbach, J. (1994). Checking for student understanding—four techniques. *Journal of Physical Education, Recreation, and Dance, 64* (4), 60–63.

Rief, S. F. (1993). *How to reach and teach ADD/ADHD children: Practical techniques, strategies, and interventions for helping children with attention problems and hyperactivity.* New York: Center for Applied Research in Education.

Rossi, J. A. (Ed.). (1996a). Teaching controversial issues. *Social Education, 60* (1), 1–64.

Rossi, J. A. (1996b). Creating strategies and conditions for civil discourse about controversial issues. *Social Education, 60* (1), 15–21.

Rothwell, J. T. (1997). What is justice for juveniles? *Social Education, 61* (5), 265–267.

Russell, C. (1997). Book review: *fist, stick, knife, gun* by Geoffrey Canada. *Social Education, 61* (5), 272.

Sabatino, D. A. (1983). *Discipline and behavioral management: A handbook of tactics, strategies, and programs.* Rockville, MD: Aspen System.

Savoie, J. M., & Hughes, A. S. (1994). Problem-based learning as classroom solution. *Educational Leadership, 52* (3), 54–57.

Schur, J. B. (1995). Students as social science researchers: Gender issues in the classroom. *Social Education, 59* (3), 144–147.

Soley, M. (1996). If it's controversial, why teach it? *Social Education, 60* (1), 9–14.

Starko, A. J. (1995). *Creativity in the classroom.* New York: Longman.

Stepien, W. J. (1994). Designing problem-based instructional materials. Geneva, IL: Human Learning Resources.

Stepien, W. J., & Gallagher, S. (1993). Problem-based learning: As authentic as it gets. *Educational Leadership, 50* (7), 25–28.

The Center for Critical Thinking. Available online: www.sonoma.edu/cthink/default.html.

Tompkins, J., & Tompkins-McGill, P. L. (1993). *Surviving in schools in the 1990s: A strategic management of school environments.* Lanham, MD: University Press of America.

Torrance, E. P. (1998, August 6). Future problem-solving program: Opening doors to the future. Available online: www.fpsp.org/overview.html.

Wang, M. C. (1992). *Adapting education strategies: Building on diversity.* Baltimore, MD: Brookes.

Watkins, C. (1997). Gun control: The debate and public policy. *Social Education, 61* (5), 250–257.

Wilen, W. W., & Phillips, J. A. (1995). Teaching critical thinking: A metacognitive approach. *Social Education, 59* (3), 135–138.

Wilen, W. W., & White, J. J. (1991). Interaction and discourse in social studies classrooms. In J. P. Shaver (Ed.), *Handbook of research on social studies teaching and learning.* (pp. 483–495). New York: Macmillan.

Williams, F. E. (1967). *Teaching strategies to extend productive-divergent thinking.* Adapted mimeographed handout from Williams, Director of Creativity and National Schools Project. St. Paul, MN: Macalester College.

Wright, I. (1995). Making critical thinking possible: Options for teachers. *Social Education, 59* (3), 139–143.

Young, K. A. (1994). *Constructing buildings, bridges, and minds: Building an integrated curriculum through social studies.* Portsmouth, NH: Heinemann.

CHAPTER 10

EVALUATING STUDENT PERFORMANCE

Chapter Outline

Formative Evaluation

   Smiley Faces

   Graffiti

   Videotapes

   Checking for Understanding

   Anecdotal Records

   Self-Checking

Summative Evaluation

   Checklists

   Worksheets

   Quizzes

   Tests

   Pretests

Standardized Tests

Portfolios and Authentic Assessment

Conferences

   Teacher/Student Conference

   Parent/Teacher Conference

   Home Visits

❖ **Case Studies: Kindergarten and Sixth Grade**

❖ **Internet Links**

Summary

Professional Discussions and Field Experiences

References

CHAPTER OBJECTIVES

Imagine that you are into your first nine weeks of teaching and parent-teacher conferences are next week. You know that you have worked hard since the school year began and that students have learned a great deal. How will you document student progress so that you have evidence of the learning that has taken place? How will you inform students of their progress on a regular basis? What records will you share with parents? Upon completion of this chapter you will be able to:

1. Delineate techniques for gathering formative and summative evaluation.
2. Differentiate between standardized tests and portfolio and authentic assessment.
3. Describe effective approaches for conducting student and parent conferences.
4. Analyze case illustrations to determine the range of student performances within classrooms.

When the topic of evaluation is introduced to preservice teachers, it is not unusual for them to say, "Not much evaluation goes on in the primary grades because students are still developing and formal testing is therefore unnecessary." Or "It's useless to have students memorize dates and places for the purpose of giving them back on a test." Occasionally a student will say, "If the emphasis in social studies is on inquiry and discovery, it's not possible to evaluate students because they would all be in different places." All these statements raise valid concerns regarding the necessity and context for evaluation in social studies. However, if you accept the assumption that evaluation is an integral part of teaching, the question is not whether to evaluate, but what form of evaluation is appropriate at each stage of the learning process. This chapter delineates the many kinds of evaluation and appropriate contexts for their use. Formative and summative evaluation, portfolios and authentic assessment, standardized tests, and conferences are addressed, followed by case illustrations of evaluation at the primary and middle school levels.

✦ FORMATIVE EVALUATION

Formative evaluation takes place throughout a lesson or learning activity during both direct and indirect instruction. Teachers use formative evaluation techniques when a lesson is ongoing. For example, during direct instruction, a teacher can observe students to see if they are paying attention, responding to questions (correctly or incorrectly), interested in the topic, confused or bewildered, and so on. A teacher uses formative evaluation as a kind of gauge of the learning climate in the classroom. Formative evaluation takes place in indirect ways as the teacher monitors seatwork, small-group interaction, or when students are working on individual projects. When the teacher circulates in the classroom to observe students as they work, formative evaluation is taking place.

You may ask, "What is the benefit of formative evaluation if it exists only in the teacher's mind?" The high number of classroom transactions teachers encounter makes it impossible to record every evaluative or diagnostic observation throughout the course of one day, or even one hour. Typically, students in elementary and middle school classrooms are doing several things simultaneously, especially when flexible grouping patterns are utilized. But if you listen to teachers as they plan ahead, formative evaluation is an integral part of the process. Statements such as "I really lost the students during the discussion of the Statute of Religious Freedom" or "Students got so involved in planning how to beautify their playground that we never finished talking about Rachel Carson's work in conservation" reveal how teachers monitor and adjust their perceptions of teaching based on the reaction of students. Despite its seeming elusive quality, formative evaluation is inherent to the art of teaching.

There are ways to make formative evaluation more systematically retrievable. With a little imagination, techniques are easy to design and provide useful feedback for students and teachers. When evaluation instruments are made more available to students, they can broaden their understanding and comfort with the evaluation process. Instead of being viewed as the formal test that will determine whether or not they pass or fail, evaluation becomes a way to gain and give feedback on a regular basis. Giving students opportunities to evaluate the teacher is another way to communicate an openness toward feedback as a means to change one's performance.

1.   Field trip to the farm:

2.   Field trip to the factory:

3.   Creating a mural showing
     how corn gets to the market:

4.   Having an assembly line to
     make pizza:

5.   Hearing a guest speaker
     talk about 4-H Club:

6.   Writing a class letter
     to the City Manager:

FIGURE 10.1   *A Feedback Form on "Farms and Cities" Unit for Primary Grades*

Smiley Faces

In the primary grades a teacher might pass out the smiley faces shown in Figure 10.1 and ask children to place an X on the one that represents their feelings about the social studies learning activities they did during a unit on "Farms and Cities."

Graffiti

An effective technique to gain feedback about a unit from intermediate and middle school students is graffiti. A student teacher posted butcher paper on the back of her learning center after she had finished a two-week unit. She asked students to write whatever they wanted about the unit, especially what they liked and didn't like. The students liked the graffiti idea and wrote compliments along with constructive comments, which proved to be valuable feedback for the student teacher. They also broadened their perspectives by seeing the comments made by peers.

Videotapes

One way to supplement written feedback is the use of videotapes. Viewing a videotape gives feedback that may otherwise have been missed during instruction. At the end of the "Artforms" unit (Chapter 12), students remarked that if they never did *Gyotaku* (fish printing) again it would be no great loss! When viewing the videotape of the fish printing lesson, however, I observed students who were captivated by the experience of bathing the fish to remove the mucous membrane prior to dousing with ink for the printing phase. Adjectives such as *slimy, scaly, slippery, gross, prickly,* and *sharp* emerged from smiling faces even though they were moaning and groaning throughout. Sometimes a teacher may choose to repeat an activity when the students were so engaged, despite their complaints!

Checking for Understanding

This term popularized by Madeline Hunter identifies a wide range of techniques. Many primary teachers ask students for *thumbs up* or *thumbs down* to indicate whether or not they agree with an observation or statement of fact. For variation, they might ask students to *tap their noses* or *pat their heads*. This technique is also a way to ensure that students are paying attention because they are asked to respond to the reactions of their classmates. At the intermediate and middle school levels, individually or in pairs, students can be given erasable boards; if they disagree with peers, they can write a different response on the board and hold it up. When done in small groups, this strategy is a popular form of review for a quiz or test. At any level the teacher can ask a question and ask each student to provide an anonymous written response. Once collected, the teacher can determine the extent to which concepts or ideas have been mastered.

Anecdotal Records

A 5-inch × 7-inch card for each student is an easy way to start an anecdotal record system. Placing the cards in alphabetical order in a card file, the teacher can pull a student's card out if something noteworthy happened on a particular day. By recording the date with a brief statement, the teacher has a record of student performance. For example, one teacher noted that Suzanne was not participating with her friends as they reviewed Studs Terkel's photos of people during the Depression. The statement provided a record and alerted the teacher to observe Suzanne in other situations to see if this was a typical pattern of social relationships. In this example, the student's behavior prompted the teacher to make a notation. Another way in which the anecdotal cards are useful is that they can point out the students whose behavior does not get the attention of the teacher. That is, if the teacher looks through the card file and realizes that there are no remarks for particular students, this will point out the need to pay more attention to those students who might otherwise be somewhat invisible. By scanning the anecdotal records, important feedback is also obtained about the perceptions of teachers toward their students. If a teacher is recording only negative statements, then that should be a clue to look for more positive performances or to address the predominance of negative observations. Enlisting students in this approach to formative evaluation encourages shared responsibility.

Self-Checking

At any stage of the learning process students can rate their own performances and levels of understanding. If journals are an integral part of the curriculum, students may record areas that they find confusing, interesting, too easy, or boring. Students can also be asked to reflect on their performance by indicating whether they put forth their best effort, average effort, or poor effort. There may be times when the teacher would ask for the information to be shared, or it may be kept as a private record.

✦ SUMMATIVE EVALUATION

Summative evaluation determines what has been learned upon completion of a unit of study or sequence of learning activities. Summative evaluation may assess knowledge, skills, concepts, processes, and values. Since best practice in social studies

TABLE 10.1			
Map and Globe Skills			
	M	**G**	**R**
1. Locates and names landmasses.	✓		
2. Locates and names oceans.		✓	
3. Calls the seven landmasses "continents."	✓		
4. Names the seven continents.	✓		
5. Locates and names the Atlantic and Pacific Oceans.	✓		
6. Locates and names the North and South Poles.			✓
7. Identifies a map and a globe.	✓		

M = Mastery; G = General Knowledge; R = Needs Reteaching.

teaching addresses the wide range of competencies indicated in Chapter 1, summative evaluation should reflect this range. Checklists, worksheets, quizzes, and tests are common ways to obtain summative evaluation. Summative evaluation can be administered to individuals or groups. It is particularly useful for assessing individual performances because formative evaluation typically surveys performances during whole-class instruction. Examples of summative evaluation follow.

Checklists

Imagine that map and globe skills have been an ongoing part of social studies in your primary classroom. You have reinforced certain objectives and want to determine which students have reached mastery. Working with students on a one-to-one basis, you can ask questions that reflect performance outcomes on the checklist in Table 10.1.

Ellis (1995) shows an example of a skills checklist appropriate for use with inquiry units in Table 10.2. The thoroughness of the checklist illustrates the complexity of inquiry lessons and the importance of evaluating the process as well as learning outcomes.

Worksheets

You have probably completed many worksheets throughout your schooling experience. A worksheet is a page or series of pages on which students record their thoughts, record data, answer questions, perform exercises, or organize projects, to mention just a few of the many possibilities. Worksheets are a way to structure learning activities and provide students and teachers with a written record of the learning or activities that have taken place. Worksheets are such a mainstay of elementary and middle school classrooms that many schools ask teachers to provide their own paper to cut down on copying costs. This volume, however, may suggest an overuse of worksheets. Thus, it is important to view worksheets as one among many forms of evaluation.

TABLE 10.2

Checklist—Skills Checklist Suitable for Use in Inquiry Units

	Attacks problem in rational manner			Organizes data			Gathers information				Grasps geographic principles				
	Sets up hypothesis	Tests hypothesis against data	Identifies questions for study	Differentiates data	Categorizes data	Generalizes from data	Studies pictures	Uses maps and globes	Listens to stories	Handles artifacts	Knows cardinal directions	Identifies land and water forms	Uses map symbols to represent reality	Compares distances to known distances	TOTAL
Maddy A.	/	/	/	/	/	/	X	X	X	X					14
Tim A.	/	/	/	/	/	/	/	/	/	/					7
Jenny B.	X	X	X	X	X	/	X	X	X	X		X			23
Lara C.	/	/	/	/	/	/	X	X	/	/					13
Josh C.	/	/	X	/	/	/	X	X	/	/					12
Ted E.	X	X	/	X	X	X	X	X	X	X					25
Shanda G.	/	/	/	/	/	/	X	X	X	/					15
Natasha J.	X	/	/	/	/	/	X	X	X	X					18
Derek L.	/	/	/	/	/	/	X	X	X	/					15
Sook M.	/	/	/	/	/	/	X	X	/	X					14
Me Lin N.	X	/	/	/	/	/	X	X	X	X		/			20
Kinta N.	/	/	/	/	/	/	X	X	/	/		/			13
Orca O.	/	/	/	/	/	/	/	/	/	/					5
Dana P.	/	/	/	/	/	/	X	X	/	/					13
William R.	/	/	/	/	/	/	/	/	/	/					7
Matthew R.	X	X	/	X	X	X	X	X	X	/		/			24
Cash R.	/	/	/	/	/	/	/	/	/	/					6
Brandy S.	X	/	/	/	X	/	X	X	X	/					16
River T.	/	/	/	/	/	/	X	X	X	/		/			11
Reg T.	X	/	/	/	/	/	X	X	X	/	X	/	/	/	22
Luanda W.	/	/	/	/	/	/	X	X	X	X					16
CLASS TOTAL	22	20	28	22	25	22	35	30	36	34	11	15	2	6	

No evidence ☐ 0 points

Some evidence ◹ 1 point

Good evidence ⊠ 2 points

Source: From Ellis, Arthur K., Teaching and Learning: Elementary Social Studies (5th ed.). Copyright © 1995 by Allyn & Bacon. Reprinted/adapted by permission.

When studying county formation in Virginia, worksheets A and B (see the following) were developed so that the teacher could evaluate what students had learned from their discussions and reading materials. Worksheets on the Incas in Chapter 9 illustrated ways to evaluate levels of questioning and thinking skills.

E X E R C I S E   9 . 1

County Formation Worksheet A

Write at least one hypothesis for the changes made from one map to the next. After discussing hypotheses in class, research county formation and record information derived in space provided.

Change: Map 1 (Native American Tribes) to Map 2 (1634–40)
Hypothesis:

_____

_____

_____

_____

Research:

_____

_____

_____

_____

Change: Map 2 (1634–40) to Map 3 (1641–50)
Hypothesis:

_____

_____

_____

_____

Research:

_____

_____

_____

_____

Change: Map 3 (1641–50) to Map 4 (1651–60)
Hypothesis:

_____

_____

_____

_____

Research:

_____

_____

_____

_____

E X E R C I S E   9 . 2

County Formation Worksheet B

Describe how the county boundary changes reflect social, political, and economic changes upon various groups of people.

Change/Impact		
Map	**Social/Political**	**Economic**
1 to 2 Colonists African-Americans Native Americans		
1 to 2 Colonists African-Americans Native Americans		
1 to 2 Colonists African-Americans Native Americans		

Quizzes

A quiz is an assessment of performance that takes place after smaller segments of learning. That is, in contrast with a test, which implies a more comprehensive assessment, the quiz may be given after a homework assignment, at the end of a presentation, before proceeding to newer concepts, and so on. *Pop quizzes,* as you are aware, are unannounced quizzes designed to keep students active in their learning. If students know there will be an occasional pop quiz, chances are they will not procrastinate with their studies. The format of quizzes follow test format but are usually shorter.

Tests

Objective and essay tests are the most commonplace. Objective tests include true-false, multiple-choice, and matching and are usually easy to score. Students have mixed reactions to objective tests. Some feel relief that they can have information provided and select or "guess" the right answer. Others find objective tests confusing because they may have more difficulty eliminating responses that are "partially" correct but may not be the best answer or the one that the teacher had intended. From the teacher's standpoint, objective tests require more time in construction to ensure validity. Conducting an item analysis of test questions is a way to get feedback for refining tests should they be repeated from one year or class to the next. Many resources are available to assist teachers in constructing valid tests, some of which are listed at the end of this chapter.

Essay tests allow for more original thought and organization on the part of the student. They can be structured in such a way that students are asked to address specific information to support their argument, or they can be designed so that there is not one right answer. Instead the student is asked to state a position and defend it. Essay tests are relatively easy to develop but require a great deal of time to grade. It is a good idea to provide students with both essay and objective tests for the reasons previously mentioned. Some students prefer objective tests, whereas others prefer the opportunity to express themselves freely in an essay. By providing a combination the teacher is responsive to different learning styles.

Pretests

When beginning a unit of study, it is useful to administer a pretest for several reasons. First, it will tell you if there are students who already know the material you plan to present. If this is the case, you can modify exercises for those who may need depth or entirely new material. Second, the pretest may tell you information that students may have that could be incorporated into the lessons. For example, if students have visited or lived in places you plan to discuss, they can share their experiences and resources. Third, a pretest can serve as an advance organizer for students. From completing the pretest, they receive an orientation to the forthcoming unit. Fourth, the pretest can be compared with a posttest to demonstrate performance gains.

Regardless of whether you are using formative or summative evaluation, it is important that the information you derive reflects knowledge, higher-level thinking, creativity, skills, and processes. Because traditional teaching emphasizes the recall of information, traditional evaluation instruments reflect the same. Evaluation techniques need

Artforms Pretest/Posttest

Record your answers on a separate sheet of paper.

Art Appreciation

1. Do you think creativity is something one is born with, is developed throughout one's lifetime, or is some combination of both? Explain your answer.
2. Do you think that you are creative? If so, in what way? If not, why not?
3. Can you remember when you became interested in art? If so, describe when or how.
4. Describe art classes you have had other than in school.
5. Is there an artist and/or particular style of art that you admire or prefer? Please explain.
6. When studying an artist, do you think that it is possible to appreciate his or her artform if you do not like the way he or she led his/her life? Explain.

Art History

7. Name three necessary ingredients in a solar painting.
8. Describe a nonobjective painting.
9. What do you call a painting that shows several sides of an object?
10. Name one of Picasso's painting periods.
11. Name a word used by both musicians and artists when referring to a composition.
12. What color in a painting would describe a soft soothing melody?
13. Name two artforms used in the medieval period.
14. How were books made before the printing press was invented? Who made them?
15. What were the artists called who first started painting the effects of sunlight and shadows out of doors?
16. Name one of the artists in the period in question number fifteen and describe his/her brush strokes.
17. Who was the American who was invited to join the French Impressionist group? What was the main subject matter of her painting?
18. Name the artform that contains symbols and geometric shapes that can have meaning in *your personal* life.
19. In what country did gyotaku originate?
20. Name one purpose of fish printing.
21. Name a contemporary artist who combined the artform of quiltmaking with her painting.
22. What is a triptych and how was it used?
23. Why was it necessary for monks to copy manuscripts?
24. What is the difference between abstract and nonobjective art?
25. Name an artist who often painted abstract scenes and skulls in the Southwest.
26. In what way did Mary Cassatt use her art to stage a political protest?
27. What are some of life's challenges addressed through folktales and fantasy?
28. What artform did the Russian artist Fabergé create?
29. What is the significance of a universal system of symbols?
30. How were mandalas used by the Navajo Indians?

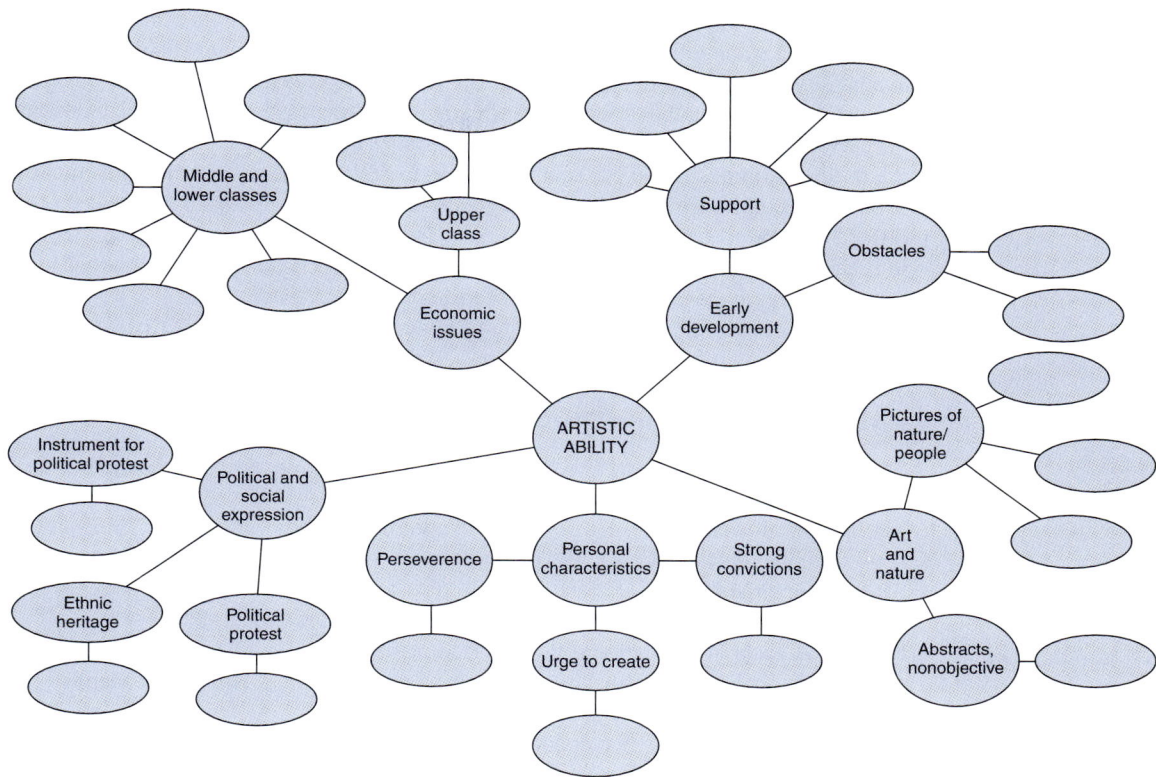

FIGURE 10.2   *Social Foundations of Artistic Ability*

to keep pace with the research gains made in more diverse and complex understandings of cognition. If your teaching has included attention to higher-level thinking, creativity, skills, and processes along with the transmission of knowledge, evaluation instruments that reflect this range will be easy to construct. More difficult will be the attempt to assess this range of learning activities if they have not been included in your objectives.

The evaluation instruments designed for the *Artforms* unit (Chapter 12) also are included here to illustrate a pretest/posttest (Table 10.3), and web, "Social Foundations of Artistic Ability" (Figure 10.2), which when combined include objective and essay questions, creative assessments, and higher level thinking skills.

✦ STANDARDIZED TESTS

Most standardized tests that have social studies components give a measure of student performance in relation to a national sample. This information can be useful in comparing student performance in a local context with student performance throughout the United States. Standardized tests are *norm-referenced* tests, which means that one student's score is compared with a larger sampling of students of the same grade and age who live throughout the United States. The factors most affecting the performance on these standardized tests include the extent to which the teacher taught information presented in the standardized test, the performance levels of individual students, and the availability of community, school, family, resources. Given these factors, teachers should recognize that the groups from which the students were randomly selected may have a range in achievement from two to four grades below or two to four grades above the norm (Jarolimek, 1990). It is unrealistic to expect that all students in a given class should reflect the norm; some will be higher while others lower. Norm-referenced tests differ from *criterion-referenced* tests because the latter are developed to assess mastery in relation to a set of learning objectives. School districts can arrange to contract with test publishers to develop large-scale criterion-referenced tests.

The following list is provided should you want to investigate further the kinds of social studies information that is assessed through standardized tests (Jarolimek, 1990, pp. 416–417). Most of the information emphasizes knowledge rather than values and attitudes in the affective domain.

Stanford Achievement Test, The Psychological Corporation, 757 Third Avenue, New York, NY 10017

Methropolitan Achievement Tests, The Psychological Corporation, 757 Third Avenue, New York, NY 10017

SRA Achievement Series, Science Research Associates, Inc., 155 North Wacker Drive, Chicago, IL 60606

Sequential Tests of Educational Progress: Social Studies, Level 4, Grades 4–6, Addison-Wesley Publishing Company, Inc., 2725 Sand Hill Road, Menlo Park, CA 94025

Iowa Test of Basic Skills, Riverside Publishing Company, 1919 South Highland Avenue, Lombard, IL 60148

California Achievement Tests, CTB/McGraw-Hill, Del Monte Research Park, Monterey, CA 93940

The preceding standardized tests have been measuring achievement for many years. A more recent entrant into U.S. history and geography testing is the National Assessment of Educational Progress (NAEP). The ongoing NAEP project samples students for age groups 9, 13, and 17. Performance standards for these age groups include *Basic*—partial mastery; *Proficient*—solid academic performance that demonstrates competency in challenging subject matter; and *Advanced*—superior performance. Table 10.4 outlines the NAEP (1994) performance levels for U.S. history.

The NAEP (U.S. Department of Education, 1994) report also notes differences based on subgroups as indicated in the following:

- U.S. history scores at all grades were higher for students whose parents had more education.
- At Grade 12, males scored higher than females in U.S. history. No differences between males and females in average scores were evident at Grades 4 and 8.
- At Grades 4, 8, and 12, white and Asian students had significantly higher U.S. history scores than did black or Hispanic students.
- Fourth-, eighth-, and twelfth-grade students attending non-public schools displayed higher U.S. history scores than did their counterparts attending public schools. (p. v)

TABLE 10.4

1994 National Assessment of Educational Progress
U.S. History

Grade Level	*Performance Standard Percentage*		
	Basic	**Proficient**	**Advanced**
4	64	17	1–2
8	61	14	1–2
12	43	11	1–2

Source: From "1994 National Assessment of Educational Progress in U.S. History". Reprinted with permission of the National Assessment Governing Board.

During a time when there is a great deal of debate about establishing national tests in each subject area, it is likely that additional assessment measures will evolve from the national standards movement. The following five groups have already had an impact in articulating what the social studies curriculum should emphasize: History Standards Project, Geography Standards Project, National Council for Economics Education, Center for Civic Education, and the National Council for the Social Studies. Excerpts from these sources are included in Appendix A.

The Internet is a valuable resource for multiple ways to assess students. The ERIC Clearinghouse on Assessment and Evaluation can be located through the ERIC home page at http://ericae.net/main.htm. The Alternative Assessment Database is also useful to teachers, school districts, and assessment developers who are looking for new ways to assess student growth (http://cresst96.cse.ucla.edu/database.htm).

✦ PORTFOLIOS AND AUTHENTIC ASSESSMENT

Portfolios and authentic assessment refer to the practice of personalizing evaluation measures to a wide range of student performances. In simple language, these terms mean utilizing many resources for assessing academic, personal, and social gains. Teachers have always done this in varying degrees. In some circles, the formalized terms *portfolio* and *authentic assessment* have entered educational discourse as a way to make stronger statements about the importance of these evaluation measures. In a context where educational debate places certain practices in competition with each other, standardized tests and authentic assessment are no exceptions. When proclaimed as *the only* way to understand student performance as an outcry against standardized testing, an unnecessary polarization emerges. When taken together, standardized tests and authentic assessment provide information about education in both a local and national context. Ross (1996, p. 162) summarizes the benefits of portfolio assessments; they

- illustrate the actual work of students,
- illustrate student growth and learning over time,
- enhance teacher and student involvement in evaluation,

- promote student reflection and self-assessment, and
- provide opportunities for student choice and decision making regarding the construction and evaluation of portfolios.

Examples of authentic assessment are scattered throughout this book. Authentic assessment is tied to the curriculum materials teachers use or have developed. Often commercial materials may include worksheets, quizzes, or tests. If they are administered to assess what was taught, they become part of the authentic assessment package. Or a teacher may develop a test and worksheets to accompany a unit that utilized lessons from many resources. Research projects, historical reenactments, the construction of technological inventions, and artwork are creative sources for authentic assessment. When evaluation instruments such as these reflect the curriculum that transpired, they are authentic assessment. *Authentic assessment* implies that the evaluation procedures were planned for the curriculum materials that were taught rather than that measures were externally imposed and had minor relevance to student needs.

Alleman and Brophy (1998) challenge teachers to use a social constructivist model when planning assessment. Since key strategies in the social studies classroom include discussion and cooperative learning, student behaviors during these sessions should be assessed for the purpose of demonstrating how students can improve their social interaction skills. The following student behaviors are worthy of assessment: helps define the issues, sticks to the topic, is an interested and willing listener, considers ideas contrary to own, synthesizes information presented by peers, generalizes when appropriate, and arrives at conclusions that produce new meaning (Alleman & Brophy, 1998, p. 32). By assessing the dynamics of student interaction, teachers demonstrate that they value discourse as a primary learning strategy.

Portfolio assessment includes authentic assessment. A portfolio is a collection of work. Portfolios may be a compilation of student work and materials in three-ring notebooks, accordian files, file folders, boxes, or crates. Some teachers prefer to set up portfolios that hold polished student work, eventually to be shared with parents during conferences. Other teachers include selections of student work in varying stages of completion. Some samples of work may be returned to for further development. Others may be left in their incomplete state. Portfolios may include both authentic assessment and standardized tests. However, to many educators the term *portfolio* implies authentic assessment only.

✦ CONFERENCES

How many of you can remember a conference with one of your teachers? It is a rare occasion but quite powerful. Conferences held between teacher and student or between teacher, student, and parent can be very productive, if they are personal, direct, and candid. When conducted in a professional manner, the student will walk away feeling as if he or she was truly understood. If handled in an insensitive manner, the student, parent, or teacher may feel disappointment. The key to an effective conference is *balanced sharing*. Balanced sharing occurs when teacher, student, and parent can identify areas of strength and areas that require further growth. Communicating this balance takes skill, compassion, and practice.

Teacher/Student Conference

A conference between student and teacher can address both formative and summative evaluation. To prepare for the conference, the student should know in advance when the conference will take place, its purpose, and how he or she should prepare. When the conference is targeted upon a particular skill, a particular performance on a project, and/or an overall grade, the student should come to the conference prepared to volunteer perceptions about performance. If possible, it is helpful to provide the student with a self-rating form that can be a springboard for discussion. Table 10.5 illustrates a form where both teacher and student assessment can be recorded. To begin the conference, the teacher should start out informally, for example, asking the students how the weekend went, how their favorite pet is, and so on. The teacher should then focus the discussion by saying that the purpose of the conference is to discuss strengths and areas for improvement. This sets a very professional, businesslike, yet caring tone, in that the student will feel that the conference will have positive elements as well as constructive feedback. Once the information is shared it is a good idea to summarize the conference in written form, again to ensure balance. Often, no matter how carefully the teacher has constructed the conference, the student may remember only the positive or only the constructive. By the same token, a teacher may *think* he or she is participating in a balanced conference, but because the constructive feedback is such an emotional issue, it may either be presented in an *overkill* or *understated* manner. The written form provides documentation that can be revisited in an objective manner.

Parent/Teacher Conference

Building a positive rapport with parents is key to having a successful school year. Establishing open communication about one's son or daughter helps to establish a team effort versus an adversarial relationship. Many of the components of the student/teacher conference are applicable to the parent/teacher conference. To summarize:

1. Establish a purpose for the conference.
2. Clarify how parents and teacher should prepare for the conference.
3. Begin the conference with informal conversation.
4. State that the purpose of the conference is to identify performance strengths and areas for improvement.
5. Start out with the positive (show samples of work, share comments from anecdotal records, etc.).
6. Encourage shared perceptions.
7. Discuss areas that need improvement (show samples of work, share comments from anecdotal records, etc.).
8. Set performance goals.
9. When appropriate, provide a brief written summary of the conference.

The logistics of a parent/teacher conference play a large part in determining its success. It is nearly impossible to accomplish the preceding nine steps when conferences are scheduled at fifteen-minute intervals. If you allow for a mere five minutes of informal conversation, only ten minutes are left for the other eight steps. If there has been thorough preparation for the conversation from both parties, ten minutes is

TABLE 10.5

Teacher and Student Assessment

How Am I Doing?

Student _____   Class _____

Study Habits	Student	Teacher
Completes Assignments on Time		
Homework Is Thorough		
Keeps Up with Reading Material		
Investigates Variety of Resources		
Knowledge		
Knows the Events Leading to the Revolutionary War		
Knows the Roles of Six Key Men and Women		
Can Explain Different Views of Rebels and Tories		
Can Explain Key Postwar Events		
Application		
Writing Project (First Draft; Revised; Typed Final)		
Creative Expression (Diorama; Map; Narrative; Artifact)		
Shared Work with Peers		
Interviewed Member of the Community		
Overall Strengths:		
Areas for Improvement:		

V = Very Well; A = Average; N = Needs Improvement

not enough time to pursue the issues in depth—to the point that the teacher and the parent feel that they have reached a team effort and commitment. The major drawback in having limited time is that a teacher will feel compelled to zero in on areas that need improvement, thereby missing the balance needed for a parent to feel that the teacher really understands his or her child.

However, many schools follow this tight scheduling for conferences; therefore, if it looks as if the pattern is institutionalized, a letter home to parents describing the steps that will be followed may help structure the time more efficiently. More desirable would be parent/teacher conferences that are staggered throughout the school year. This allows greater flexibility for time management. If a school automatically schedules parent/teacher conferences on Election Day and other days throughout the school year, the teacher might still use these short periods of time for follow-up on the previously scheduled, more thorough conferences. You will be amazed at the positive impact that time devoted to conferencing will have on your classroom climate.

Home Visits

Linda Sidebottom has been teaching elementary school for nearly thirty years. Recently, she shared her attitudes about the importance of home visits. At the beginning of each school year, Ms. Sidebottom makes a point to go to the homes of each of the students in her class. Within one class the homes may range from a shelter with no indoor plumbing to a five-bedroom house with a swimming pool. She keeps the visit strictly social, explaining to parents that she merely wants to get acquainted and share the kinds of activities and learning that will be taking place throughout the school year. Ms. Sidebottom says that most of the students like to show her their pets, hobbies, favorite stuffed animals or toys, or trophies and awards they have earned for various sporting or other recreational events. Having begun this practice late in her teaching career, Ms. Sidebottom says she wishes she had been doing it all along because she can see the positive effects it has in opening up the communication between home and school.

✦ Case Studies: Kindergarten and Sixth Grade

Two classroom teachers, Ms. Zanca and Ms. Golden, were most helpful in providing samples of student work that represent a range of performance levels. Until now we have discussed ways of looking at individual student performances. One of the most difficult tasks you will have as a beginning teacher is developing a frame of reference from which to make determinations about student performances that can be identified as *on, above,* or *below* grade level. With experience you will be able to recognize patterns within your classroom and make judgments about how to encourage individual growth.

Kindergarten: Timothy, Janice, and Diane

Debbie Zanca is a kindergarten teacher whose formative and summative evaluation techniques are tied to classroom experiences that often integrate science, math, language arts, and social studies. In kindergarten children exhibit a wide range of abilities based on their experiences prior to entering school. This range is illustrated in the samples of work that follow (see Figures 10.3–10.5). After taking a field trip to a Living Museum, children were asked to record their observations and draw pictures of what they saw. Recognizing the importance of support and encouragement in their beginning stages of formal schooling, Ms. Zanca encourages children to record their thoughts without emphasizing correct spelling.

    Timothy drew a picture of a snake and dictated his sentence to Ms. Zanca as follows: *We saw a snake.* **Janice** drew a picture of a bat, a deer, and a fox and wrote: *I like the deer. I like the baby bat. I like the raccoon. I like the eagle. I like the fox.* **Diane** liked all the animals she saw and drew a bat, sun, bee, deer, fish, fox, and perhaps

FIGURE 10.3 *Timothy's Picture*

FIGURE 10.4 *Janice's Picture*

the beaver. She dictated the following sentences: *I like the foxes, the otters, the eagle, the deer, the dinosaur, the beaver, the bees, the owl, the bat and the sun and the fish. I like them all.* From Timothy to Diane you can see a range from being able to decipher about one word out of four to being able to read thirty words with three spelling errors. A shared activity such as a field trip is a great way to generate a range of stu-

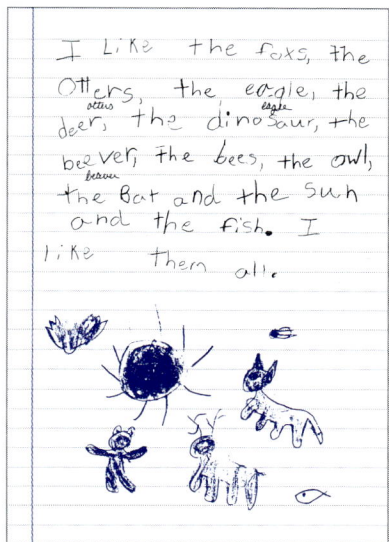

I LiKe the foxs, the
Otters, the eagle, the
deer, the dinosaur, the
beever, the bees, the owl,
the Bat and the Sun
and the fish. I
like them all.

FIGURE 10.5   *Diane's Picture*

dent outcomes. Given the variety of responses, how will you continue to vary class-room activities to address individual needs?

Sixth Grade: Richard, Sharon, and Trey

Karen Golden is a sixth-grade social studies teacher who is faced with the challenge of evaluating students who have a range of abilities and dispositions. She has se-lected three for the purpose of sharing decisions regarding formative and summative evaluation: Richard, who is performing below grade level; Sharon, a B/C student who occasionally performs A-level work; and Trey, for whom As seem to come eas-ily. Formative assessments include peer interaction, responses during large group in-struction, general observations, and conversations with parents. Summative evalua-tion for each student is presented in the form of tests, homework assignments, worksheets, and a booklet of geographic terms. By examining the same summative instruments for three different students, the range of performances becomes more explicit.

     Richard has difficulty concentrating and takes Ritalin as a means to help him focus, although he is not learning disabled. He has good peer relations, is well ac-cepted, and is very personable. Through formative evaluation Ms. Golden has iden-tified certain performance patterns. Richard is often quiet, and if he doesn't under-stand, he acts confused. Richard seldom participates in class. When called on directly, he often doesn't know where the rest of the class is and won't even try. His response will be dead silence. When working in small groups, Richard needs an adult to be sitting with him to accomplish anything; he can do very little independ-ently. When working with peers, chances are good that he will do nothing and peers

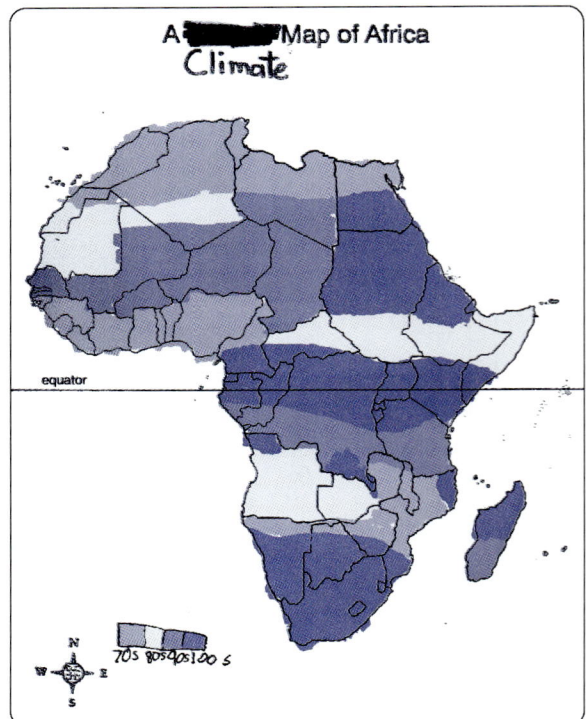

FIGURE 10.6   *Richard's Map of Africa*

will do it for him because they want a better grade. To allow for fairness in grading, Ms. Golden asks oral questions of students regarding the project they developed and gives differential grades according to each student's understanding of the material.

Ms. Golden feels that Richard needs more support at home. He is always punished and seems to have just given up. Richard's father lays ceramic tile on ships. Richard's mother works as a cashier and has commented that she has never read an entire book. Ms. Golden talks to Richard's mother about once a week, mostly about Richard not getting his homework in and continuously losing it. Recently, Richard's mother said that Richard was just diagnosed as having severe astigmatism. It's difficult to know how much this condition has affected his performance since no one knows how long Richard has had it. Ms. Golden feels that Richard would benefit from consistent tutoring.

The maps of Africa were part of a unit for which students had several assignments they could choose from to gain the total twenty points possible. Richard chose to make a map showing the climate of Africa (see Figure 10.6). His representation looks somewhat random, thus Ms. Golden raised a question about the source of the information. For the entire project Richard received eight out of twenty points. Another class project was to develop a notebook of geographic terms with definitions,

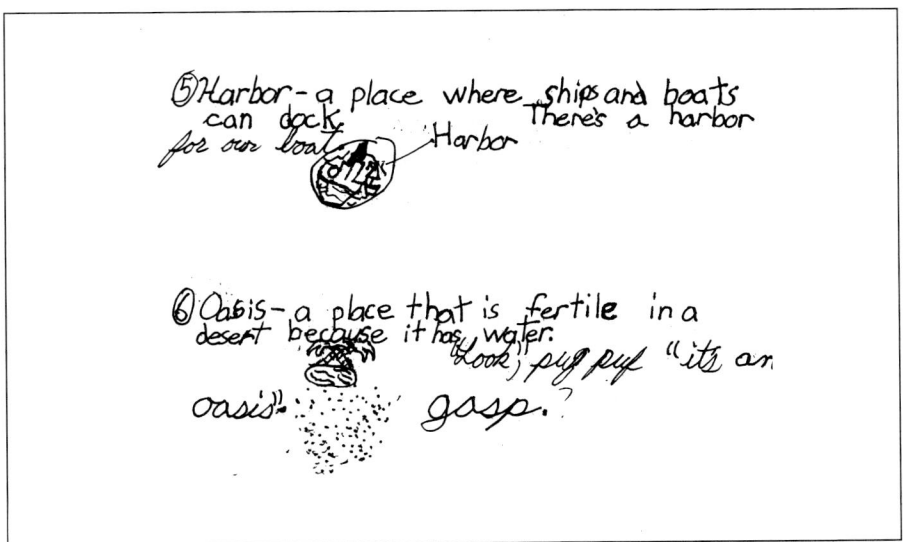

FIGURE 10.7   *A Sample from Richard's Notebook of Geographic Terms*

illustrations, and complete sentences using the terms accurately (see Figure 10.7). Richard completed the assignment, receiving a B. In contrast to more polished work, Richard could improve by reducing spelling errors, enhancing illustrations, and developing more descriptive sentences.

On Richard's test (see Figure 10.8) on Europe, he scored an 86 percent, which suggests that he may have put more time and effort into his studies. Another contributing factor that may have helped Richard was the development of an activity wheel that was produced in small groups. Each group designed a wheel for twenty European countries, which included factual information about climate, neighboring countries, major cities, imports/exports, government, language, money, food, landforms, and waterways. The groups exchanged wheels for studying purposes. Figure 10.9 shows a model wheel of Luxembourg. Activities such as these, which reinforce information in more creative ways, assist students who may have difficulty studying traditional print materials such as worksheets, class notes, or textbooks.

We see evidence of erratic performance from Richard's homework assignments. The assignment that asked students to investigate questions about Japan, North, and South Korea reveals that Richard took the assignment seriously (see Figure 10.10). The assignment that asked students to compare and contrast the United States and China demonstrates that Richard did not put much effort into his homework (see Figure 10.11).

Given limited support in the home and Richard's lack of motivation, you can sense the frustration that Ms. Golden feels in working with a student who is not working to his potential. It is obvious from the notes on Richard's papers that Ms. Golden looks for ways to give positive encouragement. Not accepting lame excuses, Ms. Golden is careful to ignore acts of helplessness. She encourages Richard

NAME_

DATE_

O

Write the letter of the correct answer in the blank provided. (4 points each)

A 1. Which of the following are the major rivers located in the heartland of
Europe?
A. The Danube and Rhine rivers
B. The Danube and Mississippi rivers
C. The Rhine and Nile Rivers
D. The Nile and Amazon Rivers

D 2. The tall, rugged mountains that separate the heartland countries from Italy, and
whose tallest peak is Mont Blanc, are the_____.
A. Pyrenees
B. Jura
C. Ardennes
D. Alps

A 3. Fertile soils and a mild climate make extensive farming possible in the _____
A. North European Plain
B. Alps
C. Ardennes
D. North European Plain and Alps

A 4. While wheat is France's leading crop, France is well-known for its_____
A. grapes
B. corn
C. flowers
D. rice

D 5. Belgium's population is divided into Dutch-speaking Flemings and French-
speaking _____.
A. Slavs
B. Lemmings
C. Zuider Zees
D. Walloons

D 6. Amsterdam, the capital of the Netherlands, is well-known for _____.
A. cocoa
B. chocolate candy
C. cutting diamonds
D. all of the above

FIGURE 10.8 *Richard's Test on Europe*

to accept responsibility and forge ahead, and she makes specific recommendations
for ways to improve. Based on the work samples and anecdotal information presented by Ms. Golden, how would you respond if working with Richard?

Sharon is a B/C student who gives 110 percent. She earned an A during the last
grading period and worked very hard to get it. Sharon's extracurricular interest is
horseback riding, and she occasionally brings in newspaper articles to share information about her competitions. Sharon's parents are very supportive; her father is an
archaeologist and her mother is a beautician.

Ms. Golden says that Sharon is sweet, quiet, attentive, and generally focused,
one who most likely would like to be getting A/B grades rather than B/C. During

FIGURE 10.9 *Model Wheel of Luxembourg*

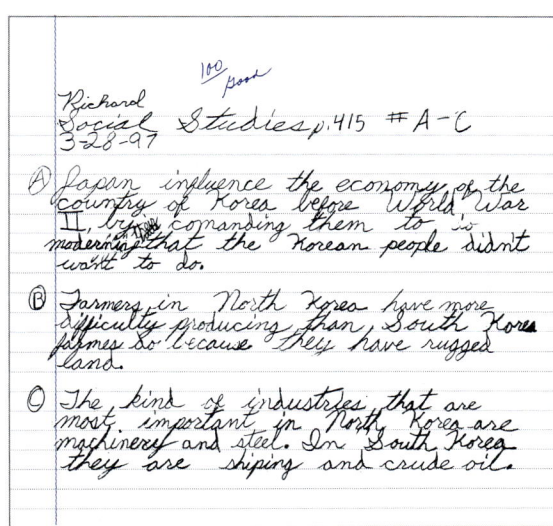

FIGURE 10.10 *Richard's Homework Assignment on Japan and North and South Korea*

large-group instruction Sharon will not raise her hand unless she is fairly certain that she has the right answer. She is not one whom you can draw out by taking her thinking to another level "on the spot." In small groups, Sharon needs structure and a clear sense of what is expected. She adapts to the group and likes to please. If the group

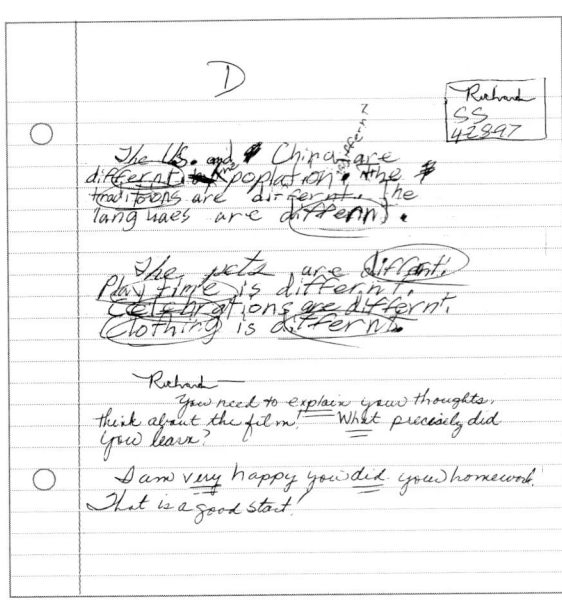

FIGURE 10.11   *Richard's Homework Contrasting the United States and China*

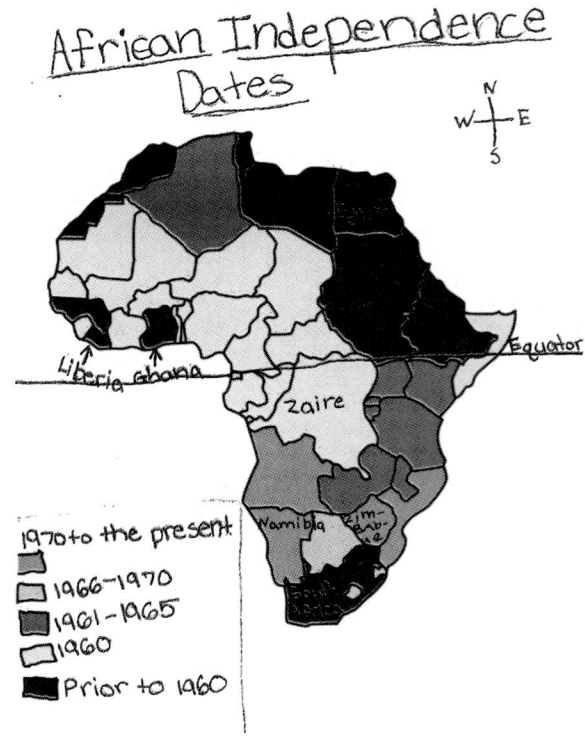

FIGURE 10.12   *Sharon's Map of Africa*

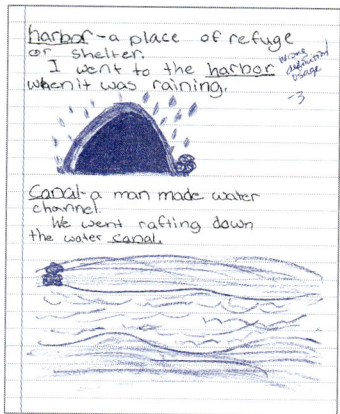

FIGURE 10.13   *A Sample from Sharon's Notebook on Geography Terms*

needs her to be a leader she will; if there is someone more aggressive, then she will do what she is asked to do.

Sharon's map of Africa depicts the dates of independence for each nation (see Figure 10.12). For the overall project she earned the full credit of twenty points for an A. On her geography terms booklet, she also earned an A with only five points deducted for incorrect usage of terms. Figure 10.13 illustrates her work.

On the test of Japan, North Korea and South Korea, Sharon scored an 83 percent, receiving a B (see Figure 10.14). Her performances on homework assignments are somewhat erratic, where the designated areas of improvement are the need to provide more details when asked specific questions (see Figure 10.15) and to summarize information when asked for main ideas or themes (see Figure 10.16).

With Sharon's perseverance, yet some tentativeness when it comes to expressing ideas, what approaches would you take as her teacher? Again, we have seen Ms. Golden's support for Sharon's efforts as well as encouragement to reach for higher levels of performance. What about the observation that Ms. Golden made with regard to traditional roles that girls have assumed in class (e.g., wanting to please). Not taking risks in classroom discussions, which characterizes Sharon, is another pattern often observed with girls. Yet, as we saw with Richard, he also "clams up" when called on, so risk-taking with regard to classroom discussions is not unique to gender in the case of these two students.

Trey is at the top in terms of his academic level in the class. According to Ms. Golden, he is very bright, everything comes easily, and nothing is the result of exceptional effort. He participates with seventh graders for math and a special enrichment program for students who have been identified as gifted (e.g., scoring in the 90th percentile on standardized tests). He tends to be silly at times; he could be a leader, but he's not there yet because he is not sure of himself. He will still follow the more popular student. He is a higher-level thinker and often has things figured out while others are still thinking about the problem.

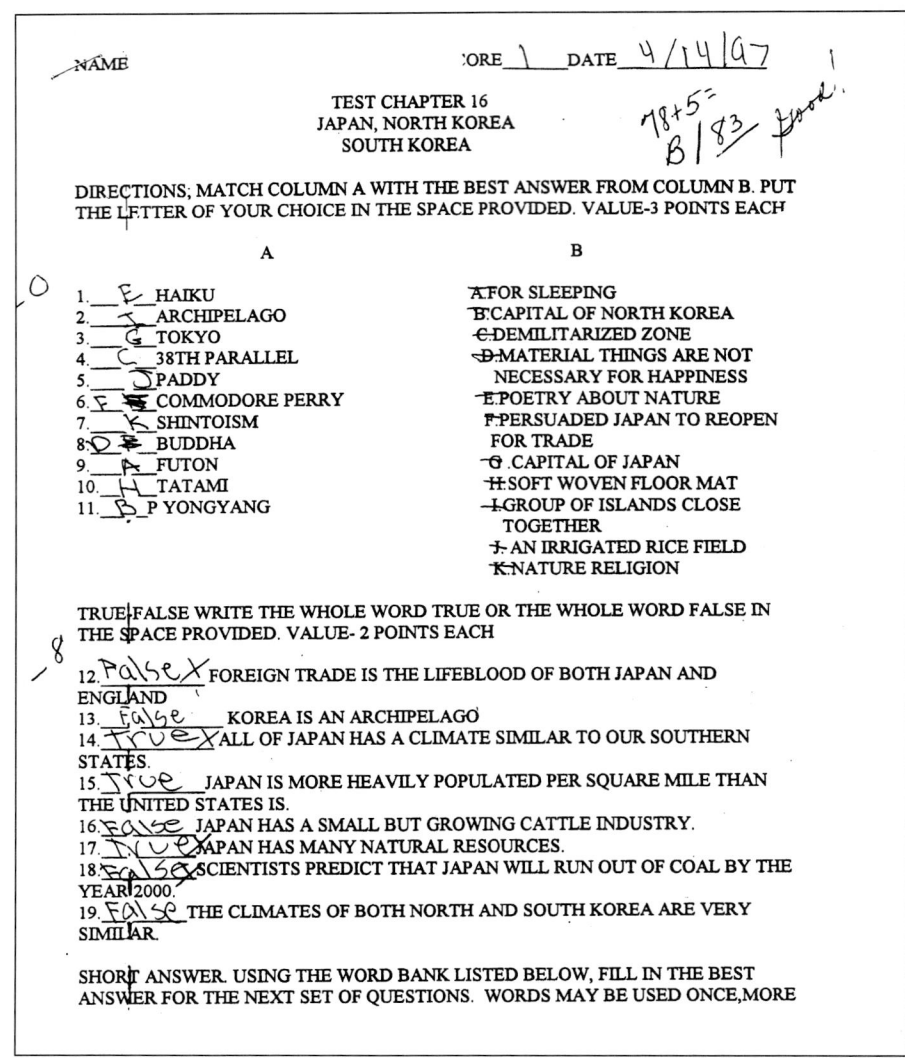

FIGURE 10.14   *Sharon's Test on Japan and North and South Korea*

During large-group instruction, Trey readily participates. He gets very excited when he is thinking on the higher levels of Bloom's Taxonomy, e.g., synthesis and analysis. Information at the knowledge level is almost mundane to him. Trey is a field-independent learner; he will go above and beyond. For example, he will take part of a group project and do it on his own so that he can take it to his level of challenge. Not only does Trey have high expectations but his parents do as well. At times, Ms. Golden feels that they demand a lot. The contact with parents has been minimal, and Ms. Golden feels that the parents can be somewhat aloof. Ms. Golden said that

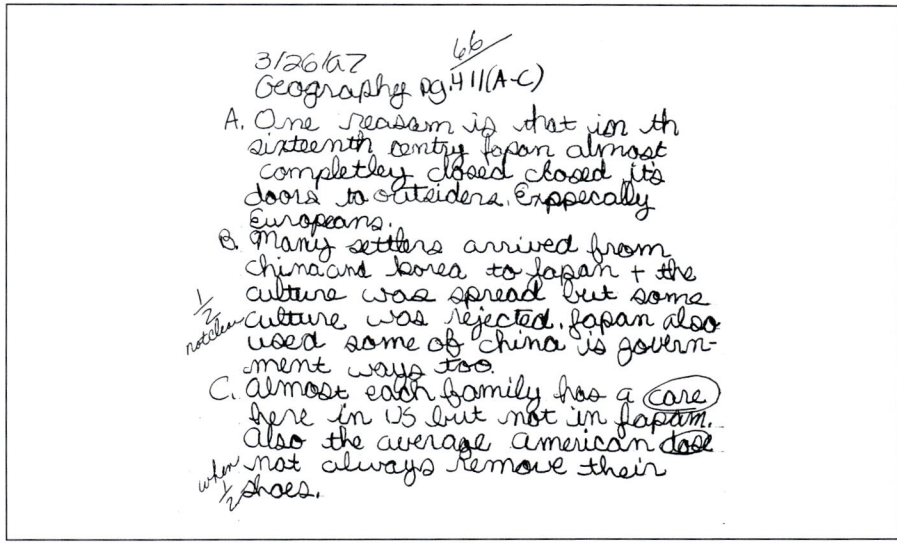

FIGURE 10.15   *Sharon's Homework Contrasting the United States and Asia*

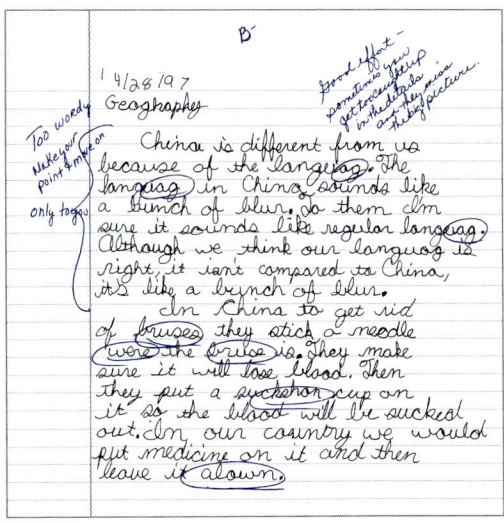

FIGURE 10.16   *Sharon's Homework Contrasting the United States and China*

the mother works as a bookkeeper or insurance clerk in a cardiologist's office. Trey's father owns a restaurant. Recently, the mother was quite supportive, however. When Trey broke his collarbone and Ms. Golden looked out for him and provided extra assistance, his mother sent flowers and a thank you note.

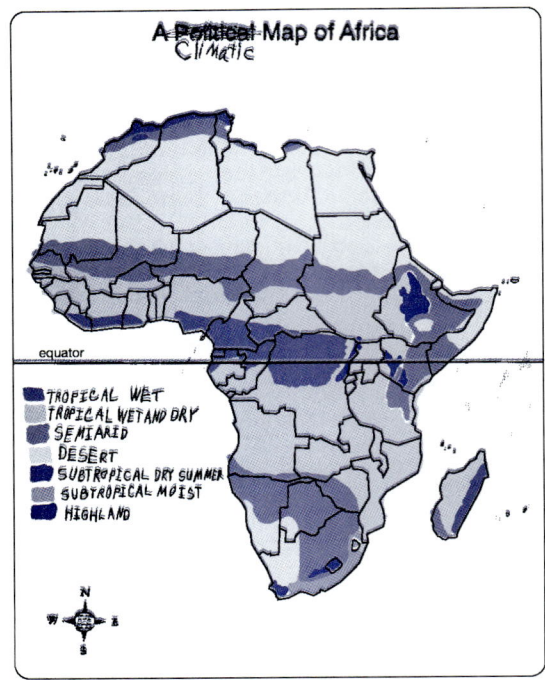

FIGURE 10.17   *Trey's Map of Africa*

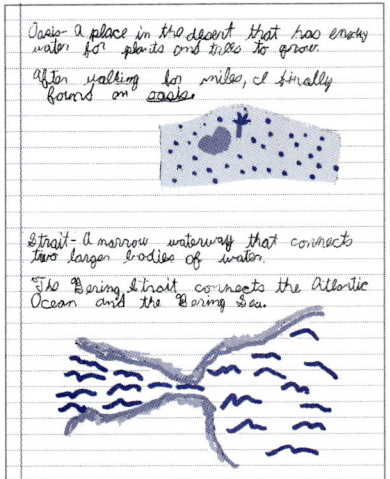

FIGURE 10.18   *A Sample from Trey's Notebook of Geographic Terms*

+5   105   Wonderful!

DATE

Write the letter of the correct answer in the blank provided. (4 points each)

__A__ 1. Which of the following are the major rivers located in the heartland of
        Europe?
        A. The Danube and Rhine rivers
        B. The Danube and Mississippi rivers
        C. The Rhine and Nile Rivers
        D. The Nile and Amazon Rivers

__D__ 2. The tall, rugged mountains that separate the heartland countries from Italy, and
        whose tallest peak is Mont Blanc, are the_____.
        A. Pyrenees
        B. Jura
        C. Ardennes
        D. Alps

__A__ 3. Fertile soils and a mild climate make extensive farming possible in the _____.
        A. North European Plain
        B. Alps
        C. Ardennes
        D. North European Plain and Alps

__A__ 4. While wheat is France's leading crop, France is well-known for its_____.
        A. grapes
        B. corn
        C. flowers
        D. rice

__D__ 5. Belgium's population is divided into Dutch-speaking Flemings and French-
        speaking _____.
        A. Slavs
        B. Lemmings
        C. Zuider Zees
        D. Walloons

__D__ 6. Amsterdam, the capital of the Netherlands, is well-known for _____.
        A. cocoa
        B. chocolate candy
        C. cutting diamonds
        D. all of the above

FIGURE 10.19   *Trey's Test on Europe*

Trey chose to make a climatic map of Africa. His work is accurate, legible, and neat (see Figure 10.17). He received the full twenty points credit for the project. His booklet of geographic terms also reflects care in preparation, thoroughness, and sentences that reflect clarity of understanding (see Figure 10.18). The test on Europe, shown in Figure 10.19, is error-free and includes five bonus points. Homework assignments are consistently well developed, as shown in Figure 10.20,

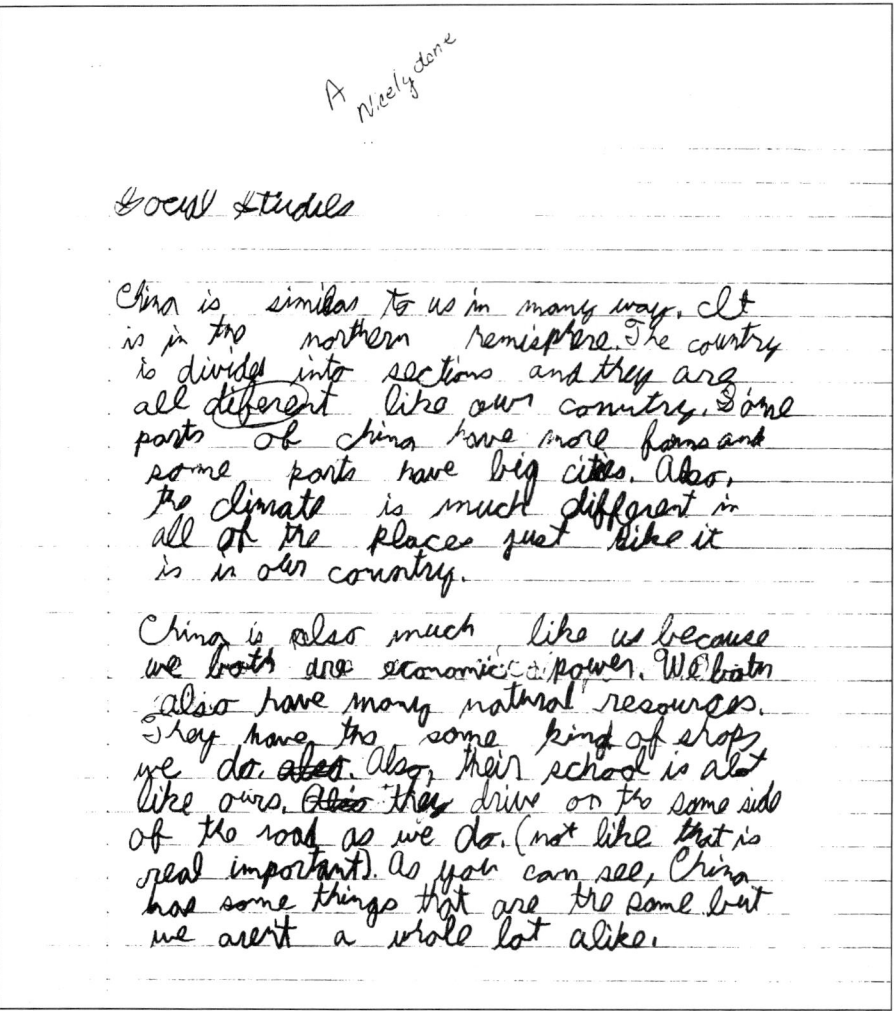

FIGURE 10.20   *Trey's Homework Contrasting the United States and China*

with the exception of the one shown in Figure 10.21 where Trey had not para-phrased his article for current events.

Given Trey's high ability and achievement, what would you do to keep him challenged academically and socially? Working with gifted students keeps teachers on their toes, often designing ways to adjust the pace and the depth of the lessons. You can see that Ms. Golden is aware of the structure of lessons that enable students such as Trey to work in heterogeneous groups, yet have opportunities to progress at a faster rate and in greater depth. Can you think of other teaching strategies that may be useful?

C

a large part of this is copied straight from the article.

Current event
11/14/[?]

Mine Rescuers find bodies survivors.

Rescuers looking for 60 people trapped in a gold mine found five of them. Two of them were dead but the other three survived. They got trapped by a powerful earthquake that rattled southern Peru.

Mine rescuers find bodies, survivors

NAZCA, Peru — Rescuers looking for up to 60 miners trapped in a gold mine found two bodies and three survivors Wednesday, and said they believed others remained trapped by a powerful earthquake that rattled southern Peru.

Army patrols set out Wednesday morning for the Huanca mine, 480 miles southeast of Lima, which caved in during Tuesday's magnitude-6.4 quake.

Eleven people have been confirmed dead and 560 were injured, civil defense Gen. Julio Alcocer said.

FIGURE 10.21   *Trey's Homework on Paraphrasing Current Events*

✦ INTERNET LINKS

INTERNET LINKS

Research on Evaluation and Testing

http://cresst96.cse.ucla.edu/

National Center for Research on Evaluation, Standards, and Student Testing

This organization conducts research on topics related to K–12 testing. This site offers reports on testing and evaluation, the organizations newsletters, overheads, Web links, sample assessments, and four sample rubrics. Two examples of the sample assessments are: fifth-grade European history, and eighth-grade Civil War. The site also features a parents' page that displays articles on testing, Web links, and regional education labs that are all geared toward a parents' interest in educational assessment.

Internet Links

Testing and Evaluation

http://www.natd.org/

National Association of Test Directors (NATD)

This site provides a wealth of information about testing from a different view. NATD gives information about district-level assessment policies, regulations, and testing schedules, the Code of Fair Testing Practices in Education, the Code of Professional, Responsibilities in Educational Measurement, and other topics. NATD also lists links to other sites about assessment and evaluation research and has an interesting section of articles entitled Assessment in the News.

Internet Links

Alternative Assessment

http://www.nejesc.k12.us/alta.html

Alternative Assessment Grant

This site is about "using alternative assessment procedures within a problem-solving model to improve educational decision making and student outcomes." The site analyzes four variables: student, curricula, instructional, and environmental. Within those variables, the following critical educational factors are addressed: Ecobehavioral Assessment Systems Software, The Instructional Environment System-II, Curriculum-Based Assessment, Curricula Analysis, Instructional Consultation, and Early Screening Project. Just to give an example of what you might find, under Curriculum-Based Assessment are related research references, training materials, evaluation tools, case studies, and a section titled "Etc."

Summary

Evaluation procedures have improved a great deal since the days when I was an elementary teacher. Conscientious teachers typically provided varying kinds of feedback to students and utilized formative evaluation techniques. Standardized tests and teacher-constructed tests and quizzes were the norm for summative evaluation, but the criteria for designing the teacher-constructed tests varied tremendously from one teacher to another. A major difference today is the impact of national, state, and school standards. Greater effort is devoted to aligning national, state, and school standards with individual teacher objectives and assessments. In schools where this alignment process is supported by administrative leaders, teachers are more likely to feel that their professional judgment is valued and respected. When national and state standards are viewed as the only curriculum content, teachers often feel deprived of their expertise in analyzing how such standards should be addressed, supported, supplemented, and modified where appropriate. Since the 1990s was a period when the standards movements were gaining momentum, the new millennium will no doubt see continued refinement of the process. In the end, a generally agreed upon curriculum is very useful in guiding teachers toward accountability. However, these general guidelines should allow for individual creativity and professional expertise when making decisions about individual and regional needs of students.

The *Self in the World* orientation has been reinforced by the various suggestions for student evaluation. Recalling how identity is shaped by one's interpretations of feedback given by others as well as self-assessments, the teacher's role in providing feedback about a student's performance is quite powerful. The willingness to receive and respect teachers' judgments is influenced to a great extent by the thoroughness and organization that teachers put into their evaluation techniques. As this chapter has indicated, evaluation should be an ongoing process involving formative and summative evaluation strategies. In addition, the process should be shared among students, teachers, peers, and parents. When the process is ongoing and open, assessment techniques are demystified and guesswork removed. The desired result is a dedicated teacher who is helping students find their way in the world with direction and guidance.

PROFESSIONAL DISCUSSIONS AND FIELD EXPERIENCES

Professional Discussions

1. As a future teacher it is important to discuss social studies assessment in the context of the elementary and middle school curriculum. It is not unusual for social studies to be taught on alternating weeks with science. When compared with the amount of time devoted to math and language arts, science and social studies lag behind. As a class, imagine that you are on a schoolwide committee that has been asked to examine this disparity. What would the committee recommend regarding whether or not to increase the amount of time devoted to social studies?

2. Stedman (1997) reviewed evidence from major international assessments spanning the past two decades. He found high school math and science performances poor, with an average rating for geography. In his article, "International Achievement Differences: An Assessment of a New Perspective," Stedman points out that government responses such as Goals 2000, which has called for the United States to be first in the world in math and science achievement, prompts the question, "If we must strive to be first in something, why not history and literature or the quality of educational resources provided to children?" Do you think this debate reflects the educational climate where you live? Discuss Stedman's question in light of international assessments and their impact on elementary and middle schools. How should social studies curriculum and instruction fit into these overarching goals?

Field Experiences

1. When parent-teacher conferences are scheduled, ask if it would be possible to sit in on several. Try to select conferences that would provide you with a range of

issues addressed by the teacher with parents. For example, keeping in mind the case studies in this chapter, consider a range of abilities and backgrounds. Did you and the teacher gain new information about the student? Was there anything in the manner and personality of the parents or guardians that gave you greater insight into the students' performances or attitudes? How was the tone of the conference? Do you feel it was productive? In what ways, or why not? Did both the teacher and the parents or guardians leave with a clearer understanding of future realistic goals for the student? Was there anything you might have done differently if you were conducting the conference? If so, what?

2. Select a social studies topic that is being taught in the grade level where you are observing. Ask the teacher to share his or her means of formative and summative evaluation for that topic. Compare the authentic assessments developed by the teacher with the standards and assessments offered by your state (if available). Next, identify alignment with national standards. Is there overlap and reinforcement? In what ways are they aligned? In what ways do they deviate from one another? Where possible, compare the alignment with standardized tests for the same topic. How would you characterize the knowledge, skills, and attitudes that are assessed by the various evaluation instruments? What are the strengths and weaknesses of each? How has this exercise influenced the way you think about valuation and accountability?

REFERENCES

Airasian, P. (1994). *Classroom assessment.* New York: McGraw-Hill.

Alleman, J., & Brophy, J. (1998). Assessment in a social constructivist classroom. *Social Education, 62* (1), 32–34.

Alternative Assessment Database. Available online: cresst96.cse.ucla.edu/database.htm.

Association for Supervision and Curriculum Development. (1996). *Communicating student learning.* Alexandria, VA: Association for Supervision and Curriculum Development.

Association for Supervision and Curriculum Development. (1991). *Expanding student assessment.* Alexandria, VA: Association for Supervision and Curriculum Development.

Borg, W. R., & Gall, M. D. (1963). *Educational research: An introduction* (2nd ed.). New York: David McKay.

Ellis, A. K. (1995). *Teaching and learning elementary social studies* (5th ed.). Boston: Allyn & Bacon.

ERIC Clearinghouse on Assessment and Evaluation. Available online: ericae.net/main.htm

Gronlund, N. E. (1971). *Measurement and evaluation in teaching* (2nd ed.). New York: Macmillan.

Gronlund, N. E. (1998). *Assessment of student achievement* (6th ed.). Boston: Allyn & Bacon.

Herman, J., Aschbacher, P. R., & Winters, L. (1992). *A practical guide to alternative assessment.* Alexandria, VA: Association for Supervision and Curriculum Development.

Huck, S. W., Cormier, W. H., & Bounds, W. G. (1974). *Reading statistics and research.* New York: Harper & Row.

Isaac, S., & Michael, W. B. (1971). *Handbook in research and evaluation.* San Diego: Knapp.

Jarolimek, J. (1990). *Social studies in elementary education.* New York: Macmillan.

Johnson, N., & Rose, L. M. (1996, November). *Portfolios: Clarifying, constructing, and enhancing—An administrator's guide.* Lancaster, PA: Technomic.

Marzano, R., Pickering, D., & McTighe, J. (1994). *Assessing student outcomes.* Alexandria, VA: Association for Supervision and Curriculum Development.

Payne, D. (1992). *Measuring and evaluating educational outcomes.* New York: Macmillan.

Ross, E. W. (1996). The role of portfolio evaluation in social studies teacher education: How evaluation practices shape learning experiences. *Social Education, 60* (3), 162–166.

Stedman, L. C. (1997). International achievement differences: An assessment of a new perspective. *Educational Researcher, 26* (3), 4–15.

U.S. Department of Education. (1994). *Geography framework for the 1994 National Assessment of Educational Progress.* Washington, DC: National Assessment Governing Board.

U.S. Department of Education. (1994). *U.S. history framework for the 1994 National Assessment of Educational Progress.* Washington, DC: Author.

Williams, P. L., Lazer, S., Reese, C. M., & Carr, P. (1995, November). *NAEP 1994 U.S. history: A first look: Findings from the national assessment of educational progress.* Washington, DC: Department of Education Office of Education Research and Improvement.

Worthen, B., Borg, W. R., & White, K. R. (1993). *Measurement and evaluation in the schools.* New York: Longman.

PART III

PUTTING IT ALL TOGETHER

Unit Development

Throughout Part I and Part II, model lessons illustrate specific teaching strategies and social science disciplines. Although individual lessons are quite common in teaching, there are times when thematic units are prepared to provide great depth and breadth in an area of study. Chapters 11 and 12 teach you how to design curriculum units and provide sample resource and teaching units. Chapter 11 presents literature-based social studies resource units designed by students like you who created the units as part of a teacher preparation course. Chapter 12 presents a humanities unit *Artforms,* which was designed and field-tested with fourth- through ninth-grade students enrolled in a summer program. The units may initially seem overwhelming, but once preservice teachers have been through the process that follows they feel confident that they can tackle curriculum development.

© Bob Daemmrich/The Image Works

CHAPTER 11

DEVELOPING CURRICULUM UNITS

Chapter Outline

Unit Format

    Components of Units

    A Systematic Approach for Preparing Instructional Units

Interdisciplinary and Discipline-Focused Teaching Units

Literature-Based Social Studies Resource Units

❖ Primary Application: Folktales and Fairytales Around the World

❖ Primary Application: Farm Animals

❖ Intermediate Application: A Sense of Place

❖ Intermediate Application: Survival

❖ Intermediate Application: Women and Girls in Literature

❖ Middle School Application: From West Africa to Slavery

Literature Across Scope and Sequence

❖ Internet Links

Summary

Resources: Teacher and Student Materials

References

CHAPTER OBJECTIVES

No doubt by this stage in thinking about social studies you are probably enthusiastic about the range of possibilities for instruction. But the depth versus coverage dilemma may also be a concern. How will you prioritize curricula? How will you balance your interests with institutional expectations? What format will you follow when developing a curriculum unit? Upon completion of this chapter you will be able to:

1. List the important components of teaching and resource units.
2. Identify characteristics of interdisciplinary and discipline-focused teaching units.
3. Examine six resource units and analyze how preservice teachers integrate literature into social studies curricula.

One of the most rewarding aspects of teaching is the creative energy generated from developing curriculum units. When researching a topic, teachers find a wealth of information and enjoy exploring the resources that are available. The difficult part is narrowing the findings to a manageable unit, which may take the form of a resource unit or a teaching unit. A *resource* unit is a compilation of materials that is pertinent to a topic.

Typically, the teacher adds to the unit each year and modifies how it is presented. Broad units might be entitled *Transportation, Exploration, Community Helpers,* or *The Civil War.* The *teaching* unit takes the gathering of resources one step further by translating the materials into daily lesson plans. It too is modified from year to year, but it reflects more refinement. More focused teaching unit topics are *The Contributions of Thomas Jefferson, The California Goldrush,* or *How a Letter Reaches Its Destination.*

Curriculum development is an ongoing process within schools. Teaching units are most popular in social studies, science, and language arts where natural themes emerge. The thematic approach provides cohesion to a series of lessons and allows for greater depth and focus than isolated lessons. The many factors in the following list influence the decision-making process about which topics should be developed:

Teacher interests and experiences
Community and parental resources
School or district guidelines
Textbook adoption
State standards
National standards
Student needs
Grant opportunities
Recommendations from professional organizations

Once the topics are selected, the work itself might originate from several sources. Occasionally curriculum coordinators budget money for teachers to develop units during their summer months or over the course of the school year. Grants are another source of collaboration and whoever writes and receives the grant may develop the requested materials. Teachers and other professionals may be hired as consultants by local and/or state agencies for curriculum development. Museums and the private sector also have educators who assist with educational programming. Most of curriculum development, however, takes place on a daily basis by classroom teachers as a part of their ongoing responsibilities. Decisions about what and how to teach are daily challenges and few teachers have the time to write detailed lesson plans that can be translated into written teaching units. Teaching units are provided in Chapter 12 and Appendix B. Literature resource units are provided in this chapter to demonstrate ways to integrate social studies and language arts. Before specific illustrations, however, let's examine unit format.

✦ UNIT FORMAT

Teachers develop their own preferred style for curriculum development. However, regardless of format and order of presentation there are fundamental components. The following checklist provides useful guidelines.

Components of Units
Section I: Laying the Foundation

____ Grade level, topic, and authors are listed on title page

____ Rationale addresses significance and purpose of unit

____ Linkages are made to national and state standards

____ Long-term goals are listed

____ Content outline provided

Section II: Daily Lesson Plans

____ Objectives listed for each day's lesson

____ Objectives behaviorally stated when appropriate

____ Key concepts and/or new vocabulary listed; definitions explicitly provided

____ Introduction provides appropriate lead-in to content focus

____ Content is focused; evidence that objectives are addressed

____ Content reflects children's intellectual and interest stages of development

____ Key questions included for discussion

____ Activities are consistent with goals and objectives

____ Closure is provided to reinforce objectives or provide culminating experience

____ Includes formative and summative methods that assess pupils' achievement

____ Required materials are listed on daily lesson plans

____ Bibliography of teacher and student resources included at end of unit

____ Background information is thorough and well researched; that is, it:
specifies a particular time period ___
provides global, national and/or local context ___
cites experiences of individuals ___
addresses ethnicity, gender, or class ___

____ Student handouts and worksheets are included for each day

____ Lessons are manageable within the allotted time framework

____ Includes adaptations for individual needs, for example, race, class, disabilities, gender, exceptionalities, language, and religion

____ Extensions provided

Section III: General Criteria

____ Appears to be educationally sound

____ Format consistent among lessons

____ Variation in instructional strategies is apparent

____ Unit reflects initiative in conducting research, obtaining references, guidance, assistance, supplementary materials, and so on

____ Continuity between lessons is apparent

____ Good balance between skills/content; active/passive roles; direct/indirect instruction

How to begin! Once you begin researching a particular topic, your ideas will expand in many directions simultaneously. But the time to make decisions about narrowing the focus is on you in no time at all. The staff at the Racine Title III educational service center in Racine, Wisconsin, developed *A Systematic Approach to Be Used in Preparing Instructional Units.* An adaptation of their earlier version follows. As the title implies, it is a way to make the open and creative process of curriculum development both manageable and practical.

A Systematic Approach for Preparing Instructional Units

Adapted from: Racine Title III Staff, 2230 Northwestern Avenue, Racine, WI 53404. This worksheet represents a process or procedure that can be used in planning a unit.

First Phase: Organizing the Unit

Step I
    Name of Unit _____
Step II: Unit Objectives
    A. Identify the significance and importance of the unit
        1. _____
        2. _____
    B. Ultimate Outcomes
        1. Knowledge or information to be learned
            a. _____
            b. _____
        2. Attitudes to be developed
            a. _____
            b. _____
        3. Skills to be taught
            a. _____
            b. _____
Step III: Planning for Concepts to Be Covered in Unit
    A. Identify all concepts that could be taught in unit (brainstorm)

1. _____	5. _____	9. _____
2. _____	6. _____	10. _____
3. _____	7. _____	11. _____
4. _____	8. _____	12. _____

    B. Select concepts to be taught and list in sequence

1. _____	4. _____	7. _____
2. _____	5. _____	8. _____
3. _____	6. _____	9. _____

    C. Make time allocation for each concept/topic

Day 1 _____	Day 6 _____
Day 2 _____	Day 7 _____
Day 3 _____	Day 8 _____
Day 4 _____	Day 9 _____
Day 5 _____	Day 10 _____

Second Phase: Organizing a Unit

Step I
  Name of Unit Selected _____
Step II: State *Broad* Learning Objectives to Be Achieved with Unit
  A. _____
  B. _____
Step III: Follow This Task Analysis Sequence
  A. Identify major ideas to be stressed
    1. _____
    2. _____
    3. _____
  B. Skills to be taught
    1. _____
    2. _____
    3. _____
    4. _____
  C. Attitudes to be developed
    1. _____
    2. _____
    3. _____
  D. Are there any prerequisites for students that must be considered?
    1. _____
    2. _____
    3. _____
Step IV: State *Learning Objectives* in Performance Terms (Behaviorally stated)
  A. _____
  B. _____
  C. _____
  D. _____
Step V: Strategies to Be Employed for Learning
  A. Students could *read*
    1. _____
    2. _____
    3. _____
    4. _____
    5. _____
    6. _____
  B. Students can *investigate*
    1. _____
    2. _____
    3. _____
    4. _____
    5. _____
    6. _____

    C. Students could *listen* to

       1. _____

       2. _____

       3. _____

       4. _____

       5. _____

       6. _____

    D. Students might *construct*

       1. _____

       2. _____

       3. _____

       4. _____

       5. _____

       6. _____

    E. Students may *write*

       1. _____

       2. _____

       3. _____

       4. _____

       5. _____

       6. _____

    F. Students should *discuss*

       1. _____

       2. _____

       3. _____

       4. _____

       5. _____

       6. _____

Step VI: *Methodology*—Which learning experiences are *most effectively* provided in

    A. Large group?

    B. Small group?

    C. Individual instruction?

    D. Through counseling?

> *Note:* Identify methodology selected by unit or by team by placing LG, SG, II, or CS in front of each learning experience listed under Step V, A.

Step VII: What *Pretesting* Could or Should Be Done Before Students Start the Unit?
- Diagnostic tests can cut down considerably on the need for pretests.

Step VIII: What *Posttesting* Will Be Used?
- A combination of essay and objective tests are desirable.
- Authentic assessment

Third Phase:

Division of Labor (when unit is developed by a group) Unit or team members are assigned to various tasks and roles to plan and prepare unit as follows:

    A. Plan large-group activities

    B. Plan small-group activities

   C. Plan individualized activities
      1. Consider exceptionalities
      2. Consider cultural expectations
      3. Consider thinking skills
      4. Consider learning styles
      5. Other
   D. Write behavioral objectives
   E. Prepare pretest and/or posttest
   F. Other tasks

Fourth Phase:

Unit or Team Members *Present Plans* and Suggestions to Whole Unit or Team for Suggestions and Modifications.

Fifth Phase:

Unit or Team Makes *Staff Assignments* for Implementation.

Sixth Phase:

Unit or Team Formally *Evaluates* Their Successes and Failures in Presenting the Unit in Order to Improve Their Effectiveness During the Next Unit, and for Improving This Specific Unit Next Year.

❖ INTERDISCIPLINARY AND DISCIPLINE-FOCUSED TEACHING UNITS

Two teaching units are provided as models for you—*Artforms* and *Congressional Elections*. The *Artforms* unit in Chapter 12 is an interdisciplinary unit, which incorporates psychology, sociology, economics, anthropology, political science, and the humanities. Table 11.1 indicates how this is accomplished.

TABLE 11.1

Interdisciplinary Aspects of Artforms Unit

Psychology, Sociology, Economics, and Political Science	**Anthropology and the Humanities**
Each lesson featured a specific artform, and whenever possible, an artist whose art reflected that specific style. Biographical sketches were provided emphasizing the following psychosocial aspects of creative development: personal characteristics, early development, arts and nature, economic influences, and art as political and social expression.	The Artforms unit was also cross-cultural, which added an anthropological feature. Since art was the theme bridging cultures and historical periods, the unit had strong humanities elements. Lessons addressed the ancient universal mandala symbol, folk art, fish printing, illustrated manuscripts, impressionism and postimpressionism.

The middle school unit on congressional elections by Michael Buhl (Appendix B) is an example of a discipline-focused unit. Political science concepts include congressional districts, minority-majority districts, debate, and political issues. Discipline-focused units allow the teacher to provide greater investigation into the conceptual understanding of a specific discipline. Additional examples of discipline-based units are Powhatan Kinship Patterns (anthropology), Entrepreneurship (economics), Genealogy and Oral History (sociology), and Cardinal Directions (geography).

✧ LITERATURE-BASED SOCIAL STUDIES RESOURCE UNITS

Educational trends toward interdisciplinary teaching have sparked interest in combining literature and social studies topics. Several factors have influenced this enhancement. Social historians have paid greater attention to human interest stories than in the past. Educators emphasize that history as a story well told can revitalize the traditionally dry expository approach of social studies texts. Selected textbook publishers have responded and now include literary passages. See, for example, the excerpt

© John Berry/The Image Works

from McGraw-Hill's second-grade text *People Together* (2001, pp. 66, 69) featured on pages 348 and 349. Children can read Arthur Dorros' book *This Is My House,* a story about children around the world and the shelters in which they live. Children's literature and trade books have expanded the genres of historical fiction, fantasy, biography, fiction, nonfiction, and contemporary realistic fiction, thus creating more social studies linkages.

Joy Hakim is one who has demonstrated great perseverance in trying to publish children's history books that tell a story. Through her career as a journalist she quickly learned to appreciate the importance of holding the reader's attention. The series *A History of U.S.* (1994) illustrates the art of weaving history, literature, and human interest stories into social studies. But don't be intimidated by not having a journalism background—you too can begin this process! In the sample units that follow, you will see how preservice teachers developed literature units for integration into social studies lessons.

Excerpts of six resource units are presented to demonstrate how preservice teachers can integrate literature into the social studies curriculum. Linkages to national social studies, history, geography, and civics and government standards are provided. Units for the primary students include *Folktales and Fairytales Around the World* and *Farm Animals.* Intermediate units are tied to the themes of *A Sense of Place, Survival,* and *Women and Girls in Literature.* An upper elementary unit presents *From West Africa to Slavery* through literature and social studies.

Primary Application: Folktales and Fairytales Around the World

Ryan Whipple's unit, "Fairytales and Folktales Around the World," gives students opportunities to learn that people throughout the globe have common concerns. Through this unit, a teacher can address the moral of the stories and how individual hopes, fears, strengths, and weaknesses are expressed in other cultures. Children learn how role expectations are taught throughout the world through unique traditions.

National Standards
The following standards reinforce the salient aspects of the core literature selected for integration with social studies.

National Council for the Social Studies/Global Connection
Social studies programs should include experiences that provide for the study of global connections and interdependence, so that the learner can (a) explore ways that language, art, music, belief systems, and other cultural elements may facilitate global understanding or lead to misunderstanding. (1994, p. 70)

National History Standards/Historical Comprehension
Listen to or read historical stories, myths, legends, and narratives imaginatively by developing warranted suggestions of the probable motives, hopes, fears, strengths, and weaknesses of the individuals involved. (1994, p. 21)

Following is a matrix of themes identified by Ryan to integrate the core literature (see Table 11.2). The themes allow the teacher to compare and contrast selections, thus providing more cohesiveness to the unit. Learning to weave the stories together becomes

from

THIS IS MY HOUSE

Written and illustrated by Arthur Dorros

66

*What's in
a yurt*

AY-neh MIH-nee GER

This is my house.

Our tent in the mountains has a door. A
floor and carpets keep us off the cold ground.
We can carry our tent, called a *yurt,*
when we move.

MONGOLIA

69

T A B L E   1 1 . 2

Folktales and Fairytales Around the World

By Ryan Whipple

	Themes						
Book	**Animal Personification**	**Escape**	**Trickery/ Deceit**	**Smartness**	**Disobedience**	**Number 3**	**Forest**
Hansel and Gretel		*	*	*			*
Goldilocks and the Three Bears	*	*			*	*	*
The Three Little Wolves and the Big, Bad Pig	*	*	*	*		*	
Little Red Cap	*	*	*		*		*

a rudimentary step toward literary analysis. The table is followed by brief synopses of the core literature. Selected discussion questions are provided to demonstrate how Ryan encourages students to compare and contrast events in the core literature.

Folktales and Fairytales Core Literature

Lesser, R. (1984). *Hansel and Gretel.* New York: P. G. Putnam's Sons.
Main Characters: Hansel, Gretel, Father, Mother
Setting: Forest

Plot: Hansel and Gretel's mother convinces their father to leave them in the forest, since the family is poor and has no food for the children. Hansel and Gretel become lost despite their efforts to leave a trail back to the house. They arrive at the house of a witch and must outsmart her in order to survive.

Marshall, J. (1988). *Goldilocks and the three bears.* New York: Dial Books for
    Young Readers.
Main Characters: Goldilocks, Papa Bear, Mama Bear, Baby Bear
Setting: Forest

Plot: Goldilocks ventures into the forest that she has been told not to enter. She enters the house of the three bears and helps herself to their porridge, sits in their chairs, and lies down in their beds. She falls asleep in Baby Bear's bed and is awakened by the return of the bear family. She must escape from the house to get away from the angry bears.

Trivias, E. (1993). *The three little wolves and the big, bad pig.* New York: Margaret
    K. McElderry Books.
Main Characters: Three wolves, wolves' mother, pig, flamingo, kangaroo, beaver,
    rhinoceros
Setting: Rural town

Plot: The wolves' mother instructs them to watch out for the big, bad pig as they leave
home. The wolves build three different types of houses, all of which the pig destroys.
As the wolves make their third near escape, they decide to build a fourth house made
of flowers. Although this is not a sturdy home, the pig is mesmerized by the scent of
the flowers, and he realizes how mean he has been. The wolves befriend the pig, and
the four live happily ever after in the wolves' house.

Crawford, E. D. (1983). *Little red cap.* New York: William Morrow and Company.
Main Characters: Little Red Cap, Little Red Cap's mother, Little Red Cap's
    grandmother, wolf, hunter
Setting: Forest

Plot: Little Red Cap ventures to her grandmother's house in the forest to bring her
a basket of cookies and some wine. Despite her mother's warnings, Little Red Cap
tarries in the forest, and at the suggestion of the wolf, picks a bouquet of flowers
for her sick grandmother. The wolf reaches the grandmother's house first, eats the
grandmother, and awaits Little Red Cap's arrival. As Little Red Cap does not recognize the wolf disguised as her grandmother, she moves too close to him and is
also eaten. A passing hunter, suspicious of the loud snoring coming from the cot-
tage, stops to check on the old woman and saves her and Little Red Cap from the
wolf's stomach.

Discussion Questions

1. Were Goldilocks and Little Red Cap disobedient for the same reasons? What
   was different about how they disobeyed their mothers?
2. Why is the setting in *Little Red Cap, Goldilocks and the Three Bears,* and
   Hansel and Gretel important? How might these stories have been different if
   they took place somewhere other than the forest?
3. How are the animals in *The Three Little Wolves and the Big, Bad Pig* and
   Goldilocks and the Three Bears unrealistic? What do they do that real animals
   do not?
4. How many times can you find the number "3" in *Goldilocks and the Three
   Bears* and *The Three Little Wolves and the Big, Bad Pig?*
5. Goldilocks, Little Red Cap, Hansel and Gretel, and the three wolves all
   escaped from trouble or danger at the end of the stories. What was different
   about how the characters made their escapes?
6. The three wolves and Hansel and Gretel were all smart characters. How did
   their cleverness help them?
7. Why did Hansel and Gretel and the three wolves use tricks in the stories?
   Give examples of some of the tricks they used.
8. What was different about why the wolf used tricks in *Little Red Cap,* and the
   reason that Hansel and Gretel used tricks?

9. What do all four of these stories have in common that makes them all folktales or fairytales?
10. What was your favorite tale? Why?
11. What did you learn about right and wrong in each of the books?

Ryan integrated chronological order (social studies) and sequencing (language arts) by asking the children to draw a picture of beginning, middle, and ending events that took place in *Goldilocks and the Three Bears.* In addition to the core literature to spark children's interest in events around the world and how other children learn right from wrong, Ryan Whipple identified related stories that could be used in setting up a Folktale/Fairytale Learning Center in the classroom. Her bibliography is listed at the end of this chapter.

Primary Application: Farm Animals

Meagan Heaslip's literature selections make daily farm events come alive. She has chosen books ranging from imaginary fantasy to realistic relationships among family members who share the responsibilities of farm life. Activities incorporate music, art, and diary analysis. Social studies texts often emphasize the rural nature of farm life and the route that products follow to processing plants, to grocery stores, and finally to the kitchen table. Meagan's core literature highlights the human element of farm life. Primary students can better relate to the music, care of animals, and daily life of a 12-year-old. Along with the "challenges and difficulties" cited in the following national standard, children will learn what attracts farmers to their way of life. Table 11.3 presents the themes identified by Meagan, followed by the core literature. When discussing *Farm Boy's Year* with the children, Ms. Heaslip asks questions to encourage character development. The questions that follow the core literature summaries probe for understanding the influence of the community and close friends. In addition to the core books, Ms. Heaslip developed a bibliography of additional resources to extend the children's interests.

National Standards

National History Standards
Students should be able to describe the challenges and difficulties encountered by people in a pioneer farming community such as those found in the old Northwest (e.g., Ohio), the prairies, the Southwest (e.g., Santa Fe), eastern Canada (e.g., Quebec), and the Far West (e.g., Salt Lake City). (1994, p. 38)

Farm Animals Core Literature

Traditional Folk Song. (1988). *The farmer in the dell.* Scholastic, Inc.
Main Characters: The farmer, his wife, their child, the nurse, the dog, the cat, the mouse, and the cheese
Setting: Traditional country farm

Plot: "The Farmer in the Dell" is the best known of the many singing games that originated in the Middle Ages. It was a functional part of social life, in which young people could declare preferences for each other within the safe, formal framework of the

TABLE 11.3

Farm Animals Literature Unit

By Meagan Heaslip

Themes

Book	Friends	Music/ Dancing	Family	Dreams	Hard Work	Shared Responsibility
The Day the Goose got Loose	*		*	*		*
Farm Boy's Year	*		*		*	*
A Treeful of Pigs	*		*		*	*
Barn Dance		*	*	*		
Farmer in the Dell	*	*	*			

circle-dance game. The story/song is filled with rhymes and simple vocabulary that allow for young students to read the verses as they sing.

McPhail, D. M. (1992). *Farm boy's year*. New York: Atheneum.
Main Characters: Farm Boy; his friend Joey Parsons; his mother and father; his
    teacher, Miss Gould
Setting: Traditional New England farm, late 1800s

Plot: Tells the story of the life of a 12-year-old boy through his diary entries. We see snapshots of his life through his eyes, month by month, throughout the year. Whether sledding on March's Hill, gathering sap for maple sugar, skipping school to go fishing, or haying with his father in July, it is a life that combines hard work and play.

Martin, B., Jr., & Archambault, J. (1986). *Barn dance*. New York: Henry Holt.
Main Characters: A skinny kid, an old hound dog, a scarecrow, and all the barn
    animals
Setting: Traditional American farm

Plot: Late at night, a young boy is beckoned from his bedroom by voices coming from the barn. As he gets closer, he hears the sweet sounds of a country fiddler and the rhythmic thumping of dancing feet. He enters the barn and finds there really is magic in the air. The authors have a marvelous ear for dialect and are able to perfectly capture the bouncing cadence of a square dance caller.

Character Development

1. Does the community play an important role in Farm Boy's life? How can you tell?
2. What personal traits does Farm Boy's mother see as important? How do you know?

TABLE 11.4

A Sense of Place

By Kimberly Parker

Themes

Book	Growing Up	Danger	Bravery	Trust	Companionship	Determination
The Phantom Tollbooth	*	*	*	*	*	*
A Wrinkle in Time	*	*	*	*	*	*
The Wizard of Oz	*	*	*	*	*	*
The Hobbit	*	*	*	*	*	*

3. What personal traits are important to Farm Boy's father? How do you know?
4. Who is Farm Boy's best friend? How do you know?
5. How does Farm Boy feel about school? Why do you think he feels this way?
6. How does Farm Boy spend his "free time" when he is not working on the farm? Is this similar to the way you spend your free time?
7. What are the different jobs/responsibilities Farm Boy has around the farm? Do you think he enjoys this work?
8. Does family (immediate and extended) play an important role in Farm Boy's life? How do you know?
9. Does Farm Boy change in any way from January to December?
10. Would you like to trade places with Farm Boy for one year? Why or why not?

Intermediate Application: A Sense of Place

The idea for literature relevant to a "sense of place" resulted from the fact that the class Kimberly Parker worked with was studying cities around the world. She wanted to make the interdisciplinary unit in the form of a trip, with student passports to the cities of New York City, San Francisco, Mexico City, Nairobi, Tokyo, and Moscow. One of the goals was that students would appreciate the unique features of each culture and the similarity of people everywhere. The core books Kimberly selected feature fantasy and lend themselves to the common themes of bravery, determination, growing up, and companionship (see Table 11.4). Another feature of this resource unit is the emphasis on writing in a variety of styles: journal, narrative, skit, and imaginary.

National Standards

National Council for the Social Studies/People, Places, and Environments
Social studies programs should include experiences that provide for the study of people, places, and environments, so that the learner can examine the interaction of

human beings and their physical environment, the use of land, building of cities, and ecosystem changes in selected locales and regions. (1994, p. 54)

Sense of Place Core Literature

Juster, N. (1961). *The phantom toll booth.* New York: Random House.

Main Characters: Milo (young boy and hero of the story), Tock (a watchdog and faithful companion of Milo), Humbug (a talkative, boastful bug and companion of Milo), King Azaz (King of Dictionopolis), Mathemagician (King of Digitopolis)

Setting: Present day in magical and mysterious world known as The Lands Beyond

Plot: A young boy, Milo, finds a toy tollbooth in his bedroom one day, pays the fare, and becomes caught up in an adventure in The Lands Beyond. He discovers that the world of knowledge—of words, numbers, music, and colors—can be exciting and that anything is possible if you put your mind to it.

L'Engle, M. (1962). *A wrinkle in time.* New York: Dell.

Main Characters: Meg Murry (a young teenager and heroine of the story), Charles Wallace (Meg's extremely intelligent 5-year-old brother), Calvin O'Keefe (a friend of Meg and Charles who accompanies them on the journey), Mr. Murry (Meg and Charles' father who has been working for the government on tesseracts before disappearing)

Setting: Present day in outerspace on the planet of Camazotz

Plot: Meg Murry, her younger brother Charles Wallace, and Calvin O'Keefe become involved in a dangerous search for Meg's father, who disappeared while working on a secret space project for the government.

Baum, L. F. (1982). *The wizard of Oz.* New York: Holt, Rinehart & Winston.

Main Characters: Dorothy (a young girl and heroine of the story who is lost in Oz and searching for a way back to Kansas), Toto (Dorothy's dog), Scarecrow (a friend of Dorothy's in search of a brain), Tin Man (a friend of Dorothy's in search of a heart), Lion (a friend of Dorothy's in search of courage)

Setting: Present day, over the rainbow in the magical land of Oz

Plot: A tornado swoops Dorothy and Toto in their farmhouse into the land of Oz, where they meet up with the Scarecrow, the Tin Man, the Lion, the Munchkins, the good witch and the wicked witch. As each comrade searches for his or her need, they encounter adventure and danger on the way to Emerald City.

Tolkien, J. R. R. (1966). *The hobbit.* Boston: Houghton Mifflin.

Main Characters: Bilbo Baggins (a hobbit and hero who joins a band of dwarves in a quest for justice), Gandalf (the great wizard who recruits Bilbo), Thorin (leader of the dwarves), Old Smaug (the terrible dragon)

Setting: Long, long ago during an era of Middle Earth when elves, wizards, goblins, dragons, and hobbits lived

Plot: The mundane life of Hobbit Bilbo Baggins is interrupted when he is recruited for a journey to slay a dragon. Many dangers await Bilbo and test his courage and determination.

Writing Activities

1.   Although each story takes place in a different setting, each main character faces a similar challenge testing his or her bravery and determination. Choose one of the stories and an especially dangerous part of the story. Become the main character and write a narrative of what you might have felt and thought in this scene. Were you at all scared? What made you go on? How did you feel?

2.   Similar to *Around the World in Eighty Days* by John Burningham, plan an itinerary for a trip to at least eight different places in the world. Keep journal responses as John Burningham did, noting your travel arrangements (plane and train departure times), hotels you stayed at, what you did in each place, the people you met, and when you had to leave. Conclude the entries by returning to the place you departed from. You may include pictures of what you saw if you'd like.

3.   Plan a short skit of a scene from one of the books. This skit will be an advertisement to encourage others to read the story. You will need to focus on the setting and the people in the story—is the setting eerie, faraway, tropical, nighttime, and so on? What are the people like? Friendly, shy, brutal, human in appearance, frightening, and so on? Groups of three to four students can work together and brainstorm ideas for a skit full of detail and then present it for the class.

4.   Sometimes we go on a journey and discover something we've had all along. Milo discovered that knowledge, which was all around him to begin with, is exciting and interesting. Dorothy discovered that home is the most wonderful place to be. Bilbo discovered he was a courageous hobbit all along, and Meg discovered love can conquer evil. But without their adventures, these characters may never have made these discoveries. Choose one of the stories and imagine what would have happened to these main characters if they had not gone on their adventure. What would the life of Bilbo, Meg, Milo, or Dorothy have been like? Choose one and write a different version of the story.

To offer students a greater selection of books on the various countries studied, Ms. Parker created a bibliography of books based on the countries in which the featured cities are located, for example, United States, Mexico, Africa, Japan, and Russia. See the bibliography at the end of the chapter.

Intermediate Application: Survival

Adventure and excitement appeal to the imaginations of intermediate students. Paul Cinoa's unit for fifth graders takes students to wilderness drama in Canada, Alaska, and islands in the Caribbean and off the coast of California. Overcoming obstacles, danger, loneliness, friendship with animals, and determination are just a few of the subthemes of survival. From a social studies perspective the core literature Paul selected helps students identify with explorers who charted new territory as well as individuals who for various reasons may have been separated from family and loved ones (see Table 11.5). Paul had an opportunity to teach parts of his unit. Some of his reflections and self-evaluation about the effectiveness of lessons are included in his description of writing activities.

TABLE 11.5

Survival
By Paul Cinoa

Themes

Book	Loneliness	Fear	Danger	Growing Up	Friendship	Friendship with Animals	Prejudice	Bravery	Positive Attitudes	Overcoming Obstacles	Death	Determination
The River		*	*	*	*			*	*	*		*
Dogsong	*	*	*	*	*	*	*	*	*	*	*	*
The Cay	*	*	*	*	*	*	*	*	*	*	*	*
Island of the Blue Dolphins	*	*	*	*	*	*		*	*	*	*	*

National Standards

National Council for the Social Studies/Culture

Social studies programs should include experiences that provide for the study of culture and cultural diversity, so that the learner can explain why individuals and groups respond differently to their physical and social environments and/or changes to them on the basis of shared assumptions, values, and beliefs. (1994, p. 79)

National Council for the Social Studies/Science, Technology, and Society

Social studies programs should include experiences that provide for the study of relationships among science, technology, and society, so that the learner can show through specific examples how science and technology have changed people's perceptions of the social and natural world, such as their relationship to the land, animal life, family life, and economic needs, wants, and security. (1994, p. 99)

Survival Core Literature

Paulsen, G. (1991). *The river.* New York: Dell.
Main Characters: Brian Robeson (15 years old), Derek Holtzer (government
     psychologist), Brian's mother
Setting: Canadian wilderness; summer; present

Plot: Two years earlier, Brian Robeson was stranded in the Canadian wilderness for fifty-four days. Now a government psychologist wants to accompany him back into the wilderness so that he can learn "firsthand" about survival. However, he is hit by lightning and Brian must travel down a river to get him medical attention.

Paulsen, G. (1985). *Dogsong.* New York: Bradbury Press.
Main Characters: Russel Susskit (14 years old), Russel's father, Oogruk (old
     Eskimo man), Nancy (Eskimo girl/woman), The Dogs (Oogruk's five dogs)
Setting: Alaskan wilderness; present

Plot: Russel is dissatisfied with modern living in his Eskimo village. He wants to know about the Eskimos of the past. His father is unable to help him and sends him to Oogruk, an old Eskimo man. He informs Russel that to learn about the old ways he must take a journey through the Alaskan wilderness. He must struggle to survive. Only then will he find the answers to his questions about life and growing up.

Taylor, T. (1969). *The cay.* New York: Doubleday.
Main Characters: Phillip Enright (11 years old), Grace Enright (Phillip's mom),
     Phillip Enright (Phillip's father), Timothy (West Indian black man), Henrik
     (Phillip's friend)
Setting: A small Caribbean Island during World War II

Plot: Phillip and his parents live off the coast of Venezuela. His father is working for an American company during World War II. One day he and his mother decide to return to America and their ship is destroyed by a German submarine. Phillip and Timothy, a crew member on the ship, drift to safety on a lifeboat to a small island. Phillip is blinded and relies on Timothy, a black man, to survive, thus facing prejudice of which he had been unaware.

O'Dell. S. (1960). *Island of the blue dolphins.* Boston: Houghton Mifflin.
Main Characters: Karana (young girl), Ulape (Karana's older sister), Wintscha
    (Aleut girl), Ramo (Karana's younger brother), Rontu (Karana's dog)
Setting: Small island off the coast of California; early 1800s

Plot: Karana and her family live on San Nicholas Island and are members of the Gha-las-at Tribe. The tribe decides to move to a new island, but Karana and her brother are left behind. Her brother is killed by wild dogs, and she must survive on the island for eighteen years. The story describes her struggles with nature and her friendships with the animals on the island.

Writing Activities

I. **Book Review:** *The River* (Persuasive writing assignment)
It is very important for students to learn how to be persuasive writers. One way for students to get this practice would be to have them write a book review about *The River.* To complete this assignment, the students should use the writing process that is in their language arts textbook (*World of Language,* Silver, Burdett & Ginn, 1990). The five stages include prewriting, writing, revising, proofreading, and publishing. For this assignment, a book review is defined as the writer's opinion about a book.

Students will state their opinion or opinions of the book and then use information from *The River* to support their opinion in order to persuade someone to read or not to read the book. To get the students motivated for this assignment, I will tell them that the fifth-grade class next door, Mrs. Moran's class, will be reading *The River* in a few weeks. This assignment is an opportunity for them to tell her class something about the book. Further, this assignment will tie in nicely with other material that Mr. Abrams is presenting to the class during language arts. Persuasive writing is highlighted in this material and it fits nicely with this writing assignment.

Since I have already completed this writing assignment with the class as part of this social studies literature unit, I want to take a moment to evaluate the lessons. Overall, I think the students did a good job on their reviews. However, I learned a lot and I realized how great a challenge it is to work with students on writing projects. All twenty students in the class are at a different place. Some students had difficulty brainstorming but had no problem writing. Others could not even write a good topic sentence. Still others had difficulty with spelling and punctuation. And the list goes on. In conclusion, I think that a book review is an excellent way to give students practice in persuasive writing but I have realized that it takes a lot of time. In the future I will need to spend more than four lessons on this assignment. However, that is all the time that we could fit into the already very busy class schedule.

II. **"Where Is Russel Now?":** *Dogsong* (Creative writing assignment)
In this book, Russel ventures out into the Alaskan Wilderness to try and find answers to many questions about life. By the end of the book, Russel has had many of his questions answered. In this writing assignment the students will describe what type of life they think Russel has chosen to lead. They will be asked to write

about Russel's life and about what they think that he is doing. Some important things for them to think about before they begin writing are his Eskimo village, his father, and his relationship with Nancy. Ultimately, students will be answering the question, "Where do you think Russel might be now?"

This is a good exercise for students because they will need to rely on the story for clues and also to help support their ideas. It provides them with an excellent opportunity to be creative and to share some of their thoughts about Russel's life. It might also be helpful to introduce this writing assignment as an opportunity for students to write the next chapter of the book *Dogsong.* Another way to look at it might be to explain to students that they are going to write about what Russel is doing two or three years after the book was written. They will be providing an update on Russel based on their own thoughts, opinions, and ideas.

III. **Interview/News Story:** *The Cay* (Expository writing assignment)
This assignment will require students to assume that they are newspaper reporters writing a story on Phillip's ordeal on the island. As reporters who cover the war, they will have an opportunity to interview Phillip when he returns and they will write a story for their newspaper.

To begin with, the students will prepare interview questions that they would want to ask Phillip. They will then pair up with another student and ask them the questions. This student will answer the questions based on the information that they have from the book. Students will then take this information from their interview and write a newspaper story, with a headline, describing Phillip's ordeal and explain to the readers what happened to him. As reporters, they will also need to include a picture and caption with their story. The students can draw a picture or look for a picture from a magazine that they think is appropriate.

After students have written their news story, they will have an opportunity to read it to the class. Finally, we will post the news stories and pictures on a class bulletin board.

IV. **Journal:** *Island of the Blue Dolphins* (Conveying feelings)
The students will keep a daily journal of the book. After each chapter, the students will be required to write a two-paragraph journal entry as if they were the main character, Karana. They need to imagine that they were on the island and were keeping a journal about what had happened to them. What the students put in the journal is up to them. Some of the things that will be suggested to them and that we will talk about as a class will include the following: the important things that they did on that day; feelings of loneliness; feelings of fear and hunger; how they spent their time each day; high points and low points of living on the island.

This activity will hopefully help the students understand fully some of the feelings, hardships, and struggles that Karana had to face while on the island. Having them "believe" that they are Karana will require them to think about what they would do if they were ever in a similar situation. It gives them an opportunity to express their feelings and thoughts about this difficult ordeal. I will let the students know that this assignment will not be graded on the content but on whether they complete the assignment successfully.

© Elizabeth Crews

Intermediate Application: Women and Girls in Literature

Kara Gallagher selected books that portrayed strong female characters. Her core book selections for fifth graders include historical fiction, fantasy, futurism, and contemporary realistic fiction (see Table 11.6). The female characters demonstrate bravery, perseverance, and social and political astuteness as they respond to life's challenges. Kara selected a character web to show how Eleanor Roosevelt changed and grew throughout her life. The web highlights important events and people in Roosevelt's life. In a classroom situation, the initial categories of Early Life, Adulthood, and After Franklin's Death are provided while students volunteer extensions. Ms. Gallagher's bibliography of women (listed at the end of this chapter) is organized around topics of interest for students: biographies/autobiographies (science; art and literature; history; sports; politics, sociology) and fiction (fantasy; science fiction; historical fiction; realistic fiction).

TABLE 11.6

Women and Girls in Literature

By Kara Gallagher

Themes

Book	Perseverance and Bravery	Change	Evils of Man	Cooperation	Survival	Strong Female Characters	Growing Up	The Natural World	Importance of Literature	Relationships	Physical Disabilities	Death and Violence
The Green Book	*	*		*	*	*	*		*			
Eleanor Roosevelt: A Life of Discovery	*	*			*	*	*			*	*	
Run with the Wind	*	*	*	*	*	*	*	*		*	*	*
Julie of the Wolves	*	*	*	*	*	*	*	*		*	*	*

National Standards

National Standards for Civics and Government/Foundations of the American Political System

Students should be able to describe historical and contemporary efforts to reduce discrepancies between ideals and the reality of American public life, e.g., abolition, suffrage, civil rights, and environmental protection movements. (1994, p. 60)

Core Literature on Women and Girls in Literature

Freedman, R. (1993). *Eleanor Roosevelt: A life of discovery.* New York: Scholastic.
Setting: The book begins with Eleanor Roosevelt's childhood in the late 1800s and chronicles her life until her death on November 7, 1962.

Paton Walsh, J. (1982). *The green book.* New York: Farrar, Straus & Giroux.
Main Characters: Pattie (youngest child), Sarah (Pattie's older sister), Joe (Sarah and Pattie's big brother), Father
Setting: In the future after the destruction of earth on the planet Shine

Plot: Survival on Shine depends on cultivating edible food. When it appears that the wheat crop has turned into a lethal crystalline grain, everyone begins to lose hope. Sarah and Pattie, however, refuse to give up.

McCaugren, T. (1983). *Run with the wind.* Dublin: Wolfhound Press.
Main Characters: Black Tip (leader), Vickey (Black Tip's mate), Old Sage Brush (wise old fox, She-la's father), Fang (male fox), She-la (Skulking Dog's mate), Hop-along (handicapped mate), Skulking Dog (male fox), Sinnead (female fox)
Setting: Current day in the Land of Sinna, south of Dublin along the River Liffey

Plot: Black Tip and his friends are searching for the secret of survival, spurred on by the wisdom of Old Sage Brush and the strength and compassion of Vickey.

George, J. C. (1972). *Julie of the wolves.* New York: Harper & Row.
Main Characters: Julie/Miyax, Amaroq (wise wolf leader), Kapu (the young wolf "prince"), Jello (the outcast wolf), Kapugen (Julie's father)
Setting: Present time in the northern tundra of Alaska

Plot: Miyax has run away from her husband's home and is headed for San Francisco to live with her pen pal. The journey is longer than she had anticipated, and she survives on the tundra by befriending a pack of wolves and remembering the Eskimo ways that her father had taught her.

Middle School Application: From West Africa to Slavery

Elaine Dawson selected a variety of time periods and literary interpretations of slavery with the goal of demonstrating harsh realities to upper elementary students. Life on a slave ship, gaining freedom from dishonest masters, learning to understand ancestral slavery, and fighting for an education and freedom were themes of the core literature (see Table 11.7). All books included the themes of prejudice, separation,

Character Webs of Eleanor Roosevelt

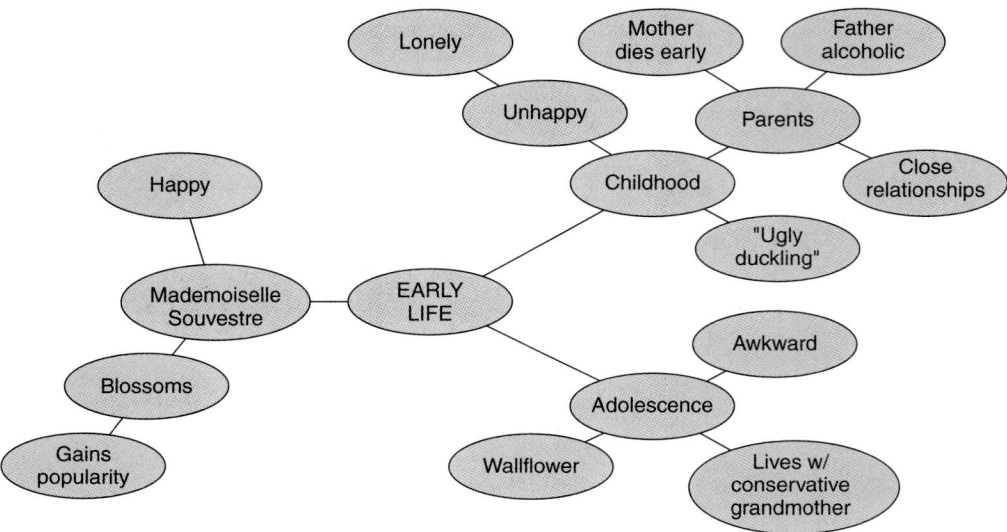

FIGURE 11.1 *Character Web—Eleanor Roosevelt: Early Life*

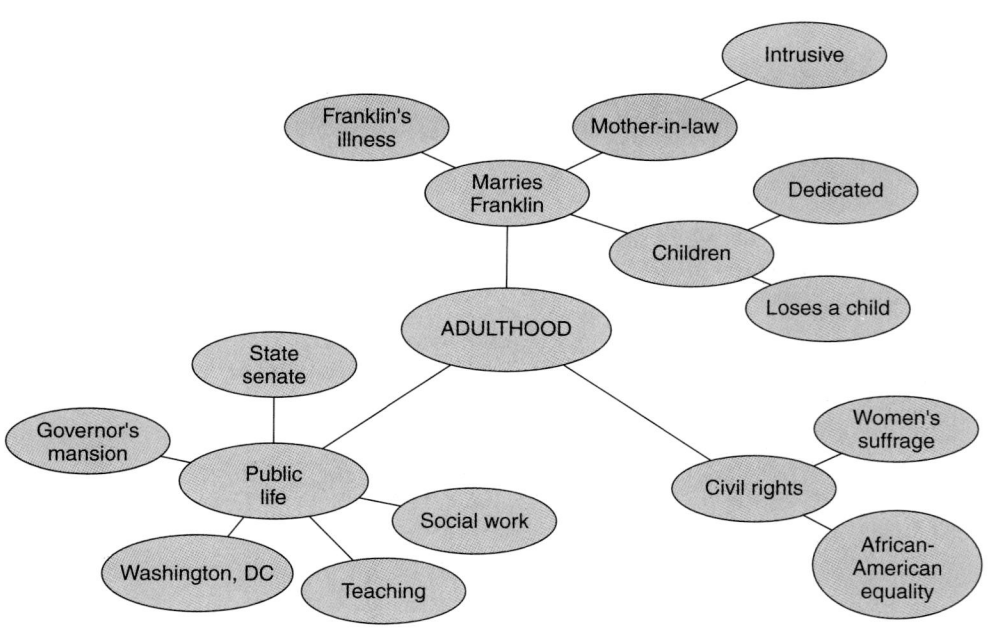

FIGURE 11.2 *Character Web—Eleanor Roosevelt: Adulthood*

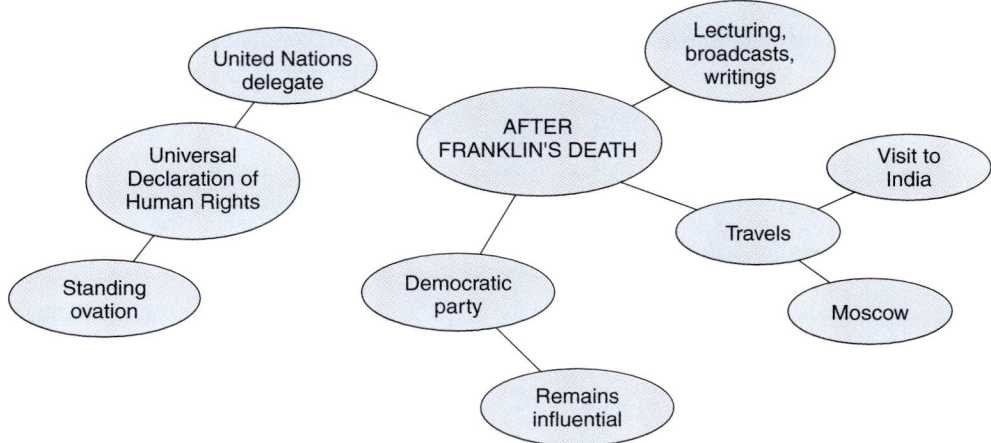

FIGURE 11.3   *Character Web—Eleanor Roosevelt: After Franklin's Death*

growing up, danger, violence, and bravery. Elaine's writing activities provide opportunities to write an autobiographical narrative, persuasive letter, reflections on freedom, and a news story. To provide students with greater information about the culture in which Africans lived prior to their capture, she divided the bibliography into books on slavery and books on life in West Africa.

National Standards

National Standards for U.S. History

Students should be able to demonstrate understanding of the abolitionist movement by analyzing the changing ideas about race and nationality, and assessing the influence of proslavery and antislavery ideologies. (1994, p. 114)

Slavery Core Literature

Fox, P. (1973). *The slave dancer.* New York: Dell.
Main Characters: Jesse Bollier (13 years old), Captain Cawthorne (captain of *The Moonlight*), Nicholas, Spark (mate of *The Moonlight*), Clay Purvis, Claudius Sharkey, Ben Stout (crew), Ras (young boy slave)
Setting: Slave ship, *The Moonlight,* 1840

Plot: Jessie Bollier was kidnapped and dumped aboard *The Moonlight,* a slave ship. He was forced to play his fife so the slaves could "dance" to keep their bodies strong and profitable. After four months of fear, calculated torture, and hazardous sailing with a degraded crew, Jessie experienced the horror of seeing the slaves thrown overboard in the shark-filled waters of Cuba. Jessie and Ras survived the wreck of *The Moonlight.* After a short stay with Daniel, an escaped slave, Ras is led north and Jessie returns home.

T A B L E 1 1 . 7

From West Africa to Slavery

By Elaine Dawson

Themes

Book	Prejudice	Separation	Growing Up	Danger	Running Away/Being Lost	Death, Murder, or Violence	Bravery
Slave Dancer	*	*	*	*	*	*	*
A Girl Called Boy	*	*	*	*	*	*	*
Samuel's Choice	*	*	*	*		*	*
Jump Ship to Freedom	*	*	*	*	*	*	*

Berleth, R. (1990). *Samuel's choice.* New York: Albert Whitman.
Main Characters: Samuel (a slave in New York), Sana Williams (a slave), Toby (a slave), Issac van Ditmas (a rich farmer who owned Samuel, Sana, and Toby), Major Mordecai Gist (commander of Maryland soldiers)
Setting: New York, 1776

Plot: A slave in New York, Samuel feels no connection to the American Revolution, and he doubts it will free him. However, he becomes involved when he uses his master's boat to row soldiers to safety—a daring choice. Then he is chosen to tow a rope across the Hudson to help Washington's army escape. When Samuel's master is arrested for helping the British, Samuel becomes a free man.

Hurmence, B. (1850s). *A girl called boy.* New York: Clarion Books.
Main Characters: Blanche Overtha Yancy (Boy for short)
Setting: Mountains of North Carolina

Plot: Blanche Overtha Yancy (Boy for short) has a special reason for disliking her name. It's a traditional one in her family and Boy wants no part of any tradition that links her with her slave ancestors. To Boy, a pampered and self-centered 11-year-old, their bondage was a sign of weakness. She is sure nobody could have made her a slave. But one day while on a family outing, Boy gets lost in the mountain wilderness of North Carolina. Confused and frightened, she stumbles onto a remote cabin and meets a pair of menacing strangers who hold her captive. Soon she realizes that she is back in the 1850s amid slave catchers and plantation owners. As Boy struggles to return to her own time, she makes some startling discoveries about slavery—and about herself. Her compelling story is based on the oral histories and plantation records of actual slaves.

Collier, J. L., & Collier, C. (1981). *Jump ship to freedom.* New York: Delacorte Press.
Main Character: Daniel Arabus, a 14-year-old slave
Setting: Stratford, Connecticut, 1787

Plot: Young Daniel Arabus and his mother, slaves in Captain Iver's house in Stratford, Connecticut, should be free. Daniel's father had served in the Revolution and was entitled to his freedom. He had earned $600 in Continental notes with which to buy freedom for his family. Anxious to buy freedom for himself and his mother, Daniel escapes from a dishonest master and tries to find help in cashing in his father's notes.

Pickney, A. D. (1994). *Dear Benjamin Banneker.* San Diego: Harcourt Brace.
Main Characters: Benjamin Banneker, Thomas Jefferson
Setting: Maryland and Washington, DC, 1771

Plot: Born a free man, Benjamin Banneker was one of the few blacks of his day, slave or free, to receive an education. All the Southern states and some in the North had passed laws making it illegal to teach blacks. Even in the North, there was a strong sentiment against educating African-Americans because it was believed that literacy would encourage their militancy and resistance to authority. Banneker became an inventor, surveyor, mathematician, and astronomer. Nevertheless, he suffered from the general perception of the time that blacks were intellectually inferior. In 1787 Thomas Jefferson had published his notes on the state of Virginia in which he expressed the opinion that blacks were inferior to whites in reason and in imagination. Banneker called for the abolition of slavery and for a more enlightened attitude toward blacks.

Writing Activities

1. *Writing an autobiographical narrative.* Select an experience that brought about a change in your life and write about it. Be sure to include actions, observations, thoughts, feelings, and conversations in enough detail to allow readers to feel they are a part of your experience.

   If you like, think about a time when you had to leave the comfort and security of home to go to a new place and meet strangers. How did you feel? What did you expect? Were there any surprises? If so, were they negative or positive? What did you learn from the experience? Share writing with a classmate.

2. *Writing a persuasive letter.* Bring up some national, local, or school issues and elicit students views on them. If possible, contrast their views with those held by elected officials. Ask students if they have ever felt like writing their congressional representative, local town council person, or school principal to try to change that individual's position on an issue. Emphasize that letting one's views be known is an important part of living in a democracy. Have them select the issue they feel most strongly about and write a letter asking for the support of an official who might help.

3. *Writing about freedom.* After his ordeal, Samuel (*Samuel's Choice*) understands the meaning of freedom. In their journals, students can write about what freedom means to them.

4. *Writing a news story.* In *Slave Dancer, The Moonlight* sank in the Gulf of Mexico. Compose a news story about this event. Many news stories include the *5W-How* questions in the lead. Answer each of these questions, using the information in the story. Who? What? When? Where? Why? How? Combine these facts into one or two sentences for your lead, which will give a summary of the action.

❖ Literature Across Scope and Sequence

Literature units are creative designs for interdisciplinary curriculum development. The topics are well suited to both literature and social studies. In addition to these resource units, a guide is included in Appendix C that lists books that are relevant to traditional scope and sequence patterns. That is, books are grouped according to the expanding horizons approach followed by most textbook series. As you can see from the list, however, the selections can be used for a variety of grade levels. Vicky Pettigo, a librarian at Rawls Byrd Elementary School, and Ames Morton, a graduate student at the College of William and Mary, both in Williamsburg, Virginia, collaborated on the development of the bibliography.

❖ Internet Links

Internet links provide tremendous resources for teachers. The Children's Literature Web Guide offers Newbery and Caldecott winners, best books of the preceding year, teaching ideas, authors on the Web, and many more guidelines (http://www.acs.ucalgary.ca/~dkbrown/). The Children's Literature Nook is another site that enables teachers and parents to supplement their current reading programs (http://www.geocities.com/Heartland/Estates/4967/index.html).

Internet Links

Children's Literature

http://www.carr.org/read/

The Reading Corner

This site is "a great place to find books." The Reading Corner is organized by the following book categories: Caldecott, Newbery, State Awards, fiction, nonfiction, new books, picture books, YA, and the author corner. Once a category has been selected, the books within that category are listed alphabetically by author, with a brief synopsis of the book. The author corner is also interesting because it provides links to other sites about authors.

INTERNET LINKS

Reading Lists

http://www.2.wcoil.com/~ellerbee/childlit.html

Database of Award-Winning Children's Literature

This site will help teachers or parents to develop a reading list that is tailored to specific needs or interests. Simply by choosing the options that best suit the topic, such as age of the reader, setting, historical period, genre, and so on, it has never been easier to create a book list for children. Not only is it fun, but the list can be downloaded and used for class, or changed at any time to accommodate a new topic.

INTERNET LINKS

Authors' and Children's Literature Activities

http://www.simonsayskids.com/kids/

Simon Says Kids.com . . . The Coolest Books on the Planet

This site is excellent for involving students in literature. It has pages about book series that are popular with children, games related to literature, quizzes on the books, and activities. Some of the pages relate to books such as: Blues Clues, Rug Rats, and Alice. The site also features Find a Book to locate hundreds of titles by topic. The Teachers Lounge provides guides to children's books that can be printed, with discussion questions and activities. And last, but not least, Meet the Brains allows children to learn about their favorite authors and other books they may have written.

SUMMARY

Units that incorporate literature into the social studies curriculum create many advantages. When teaching, preservice teachers often recall that their social studies classes were somewhat dull, with too much emphasis on names and dates. Bringing in children's literature with biographies and historical fiction that make history come alive is a wonderful way to spark children's enthusiasm. With units such as those presented in this chapter, a variety of genres, including poetry, fantasy, and fiction, can be tied in as student interest carries over into the language arts curriculum. The two content areas can work hand in hand. Primary teachers often spotlight the importance of teaching children to read as a reason to relegate social studies to shorter time periods. The goal to increase literacy does not have to be seen as competing with the social studies curriculum. Reading tied to the content areas of science and social studies is a way to pursue multiple objectives simultaneously.

The *Self in the World* theme has been illustrated through literature-based social studies units. As demonstrated by the units, students are transported across time and space to all parts of the world to face the challenges shared by the human spirit. To mention just a few, literature selections included Germany, Mexico, West Africa, Japan, Russia, Canada, United States, Cuba, and Ireland. The literature provided teachers with wonderful opportunities to help children address developmental issues such as social responsibility, friendship, family relationships, dreams, work, bravery, prejudice, growing up, and survival. With so many talented authors and illustrators of children's books producing by leaps and bounds, the opportunities for interdisciplinary social studies units are limitless.

RESOURCES: TEACHER AND STUDENT MATERIALS

Bibliography for Ryan Whipple's *Folktale* Unit

Andersen, H. C. (1963). *The wild swans.* New York: Charles Scribner's Sons.
Andersen, H. C. (1982). *The emperor's nightingale.* New York: Shocken Books.
Asbjornsen, P. (1957). *The three billy goats gruff.* New York: Harcourt Brace.
Baxter, R. (1979). *The frog prince.* New Jersey: Troll Associates.
Biro, V. (1989). *Jack and the beanstalk.* Oxford: Oxford University Press.
Birrer, C. (1983). *The shoemaker and the elves.* New York: Lothrop, Lee & Shepard Books.
Black, A. (1973). *The woman of the wood: A tale from old Russia.* New York: Holt, Rinehart & Winston.
Cooper, S. (1986). *The Selkie girl.* New York: Margaret K. Elderberry Book.
DeGerez, T. (1986). *Louhi, witch of north farm.* New York: Viking Kestrel.
Elkin, B. (1957). *Six foolish fishermen.* Chicago: Children's Press.
Galdone, P. (1972). *The three bears.* New York: Clarion Books.
Galdone, P. (1975). *The gingerbread boy.* New York: Clarion Books.
Galdone, P. (1982). *Hansel and Gretel.* New York: McGraw-Hill.
Hautzig, D. (1989). *The pied piper of Hamlin.* New York: Random House.
Hillert, M. (1981). *The cookie house.* Chicago: Follett.
Hillert, M. (1981). *The little cookie.* Cleveland: Modern Curriculum Press.
Hong, L. T. (1993). *Two of everything.* Morton Grove, IL: A. Whitman.
Hooks, W. (1987). *Moss gown.* New York: Clarion Books.
Hooks, W. (1989). *The three little pigs and the fox.* New York: Macmillan.
Hutton, W. (1985). *Beauty and the beast.* New York: Atheneum.
Hyman, T. (1983). *Little red riding hood.* New York: Holiday House.
Marshall, J. (1987). *Red riding hood.* New York: Dial Books for Young Readers.
Marshall, J. (1987). *The three little pigs.* New York: Dial Books for Young Readers.
Marshall, J. (1988). *Goldilocks and the three bears.* New York: Dial Books for Young Readers.
Marshall, J. (1990). *Hansel and Gretel.* New York: Dial Books for Young Readers.
Mayer, M. (1980). *East of the sun and west of the moon.* New York: Four Winds Press.
Myers, B. (1985). *Sidney Rella and the glass sneaker.* New York: Macmillan.
Osborne, M. P. (1987). *Beauty and the beast.* New York: Scholastic.
Paterson, K. (1992). *The king's equal.* New York: HarperCollins.
Rockwell, A. (1975). *The three bears and other stories.* London: Hamish Hamilton.
Tolhurst, M. (1990). *Somebody and the three Blairs.* New York: Orchard Books.
Trivias, E. (1993). *The three little wolves and the big, bad pig.* New York: Macmillan.
Tudor, T. (1969). *The Tasha Tudor book of fairy tales.* New York: Platt & Monk.

Watson, R. (1989). *Tom Thumb.* San Diego: Harcourt Brace.

Zelinsky, P. (1984). *Hansel and Gretel.* New York: G. P. Putnam's Sons.

Zwerger, L. (1983). *Little red cap.* New York: William Morrow.

Bibliography for Meagan Heaslip's *Farm* Unit

JUVENILE FICTION

Anholt, C. (1988). *Chaos at cold custard farm.* New York: Oxford University Press.

Avi. (1994). *The barn.* New York: Orchard Books.

Aylesworth, J. (1994). *My son John.* New York: Henry Holt.

Barber, A. (1993). *Gemma and the baby chick.* New York: Scholastic Hardcover.

Baynton, M. (1987). *Fifty gets the picture.* New York: Crown.

Blanchard, A. (1989). *The naughty lamb.* New York: Dial Books for Young Readers.

Brown, M. W. (1989). *Big red barn.* New York: Harper & Row.

Brown, R. (1985). *The big sneeze.* New York: Lothrop, Lee & Shepard.

Buchanan, D. L. (1992). *The falcon's wing.* New York: Orchard Books.

Burton, M. R. (1982). *Aaron awoke: An alphabet story.* New York: Harper & Row.

Casey, M. (1994). *Over the water.* New York: Holt, Rinehart.

Casey, P. (1988). *Quack, quack.* New York: Lothrop, Lee & Shepard.

Coulter, H. N. (1993). *Uncle Chuck's truck.* New York/Toronto: Bradbury Press; Maxwell Macmillan Canada; Maxwell Macmillan International.

Curran, E. (1985). *Hello, farm animals.* Mahwah, NJ: Troll Associates.

DeFelice, C. C. (1984). *Mule eggs.* New York: Orchard Books.

DeMuth, P. (1991). *The ornery morning.* New York: Dutton Children's Books.

Domanska, J. (1985). *Busy Monday morning.* New York: Greenwillow Books.

Dragonwagon, C. (1984). *Jemima remembers.* New York: Macmillan.

Dunrea, O. (1983). *Eddy B., pigboy.* New York: Atheneum.

Edwards, M. (1991). *Chicken man.* New York: Lothrop, Lee & Shepard.

Ehrlich, A. (1992). *Parents in the pigpen, pigs in the tub.* New York: Dial Books for Young Readers.

Ehrlich, A. (1994). *Maggie and Silky and Joe.* New York: Viking.

Ernst, L. C. (1984). *The prize pig surprise.* New York: Lothrop, Lee & Shepard.

Ericsson, J. A. (1993). *No milk!* New York: Tambourine Books.

Fakih, K. O. (1994). *High on the hog.* New York: Farrar Straus & Giroux.

Fleischman, P. (1983). *The animal hedge.* New York: Dutton.

Frascino, E. (1988). *Nanny Noony and the magic spell.* New York: Pippin Press.

Gaeddert, L. B. (1994). *Breaking free.* New York: Atheneum.

Gammell, S. (1981). *Once upon MacDonald's farm.* New York: Four Winds Press.

Gibson, B. (1991). *The story of Little Quack.* Boston: Joy Street.

Greene, C. (1982). *Hinny Winny Bunco.* New York: Harper & Row.

Griffith, H. V. (1987). *Grandaddy's place.* New York: Greenwillow Books.

Harold, J. N. (1993). *Harvey Potter's balloon farm.* New York: Lothrop, Lee & Shepard.

Harris, K. M. (1988). *The wonderful hay tumble.* New York: Morrow.

Harrison, D. L. (1994). *When cows come home.* Honesdale, PA: Boyds Mills Press.

Hass, J. (1994). *Mowing.* New York: Greenwillow Books.

Holmes, E. T. (1977). *Amy's goose.* New York: Crowell.

Johnston, T. (1992). *The promise.* New York: Harper & Row.

Kaufman, J. (1994). *Milk rock.* New York: Henry Holt.

Kinsey-Warnock, N. (1991). *The night the bells rang.* New York: Cobblehill Books.

Kinsey-Warnock, N. (1993). *When spring comes.* New York: Dutton Children's Books.

King-Smith, D. (1982). *Pigs might fly: A novel.* New York: Viking Press.

King-Smith, D. (1987). *Cuckoobush farm.* New York: Greenwillow Books.

King-Smith, D. (1987). *Farmer Bungle forgets.* New York: Atheneum.

Kunhardt, E. (1990). *Which pig would you choose?* New York: Greenwillow Books.

Kwitz, M. D. (1992). *Little Chick's friend, Duckling.* New York: HarperCollins.

Laird, E. (1991). *The day the ducks went skating.* New York: Tambourine Books.

Laird, E. (1991). *The day Veronica was nosy.* New York: Tambourine Press.

Levin, B. (1994). *Starshine and sunglow.* New York: Greenwillow Books.

Lindbergh, R. (1989). *Benjamin's barn.* New York: Dial Books for Young Readers.

Lindbergh, R. (1990). *The day the goose got loose.* New York: Dial Books for Young Readers.

Lionni, L. (1988). *Six crows.* New York: Knopf.

Lobel, A. (1979). *A treeful of pigs.* New York: Greenwillow Books.

Locker, T. (1988). *Family farm.* New York: Dial Books for Young Readers.

Luttrell, I. (1992). *Be nice to Marilyn.* New York/Toronto: Atheneum; Maxwell Macmillan Canada; Maxwell Macmillan International.

Martin, B., Jr. (1986). *Barn dance!* New York: Henry Holt.

McConnachie, B. (1992). *Elmer and the chickens vs. the big league.* New York: Crown.

McGee, M. (1991). *The quiet farmer.* New York/Toronto: Atheneum; Collier Macmillan Canada; Macmillan International.

McGuire, L. (1981). *This farm is a mess.* New York: Parents Magazine.

McPhail, D. M. (1985). *Farm morning.* San Diego: Harcourt Brace.

McPhail, D. M. (1992). *Farm boy's year.* New York/Toronto: Atheneum; Collier Macmillan Canada; Maxwell Macmillan International Pub. Group.

Miller, J. (1983). *The farm alphabet book.* Englewood Cliffs, NJ: Prentice-Hall.

Morris, L. L. (1991). *Morning milking.* Saxonville, MA: Picture Book Studio.

Noble, T. H. (1984). *Apple tree christmas.* New York: Dial Books for Young Readers.

Nordqvist, S. (1985). *Pancake pie.* New York: Morrow.

Nordqvist, S. (1988). *The fox hunt.* New York: Morrow Junior Books.

Paterson, K. (1991). *The smallest cow in the world.* New York: HarperCollins.

Pellowski, A. (1981). *Stairstep Farm: Anna Rosa's story.* New York: Philomel Books.

Pellowski, A. (1981). *Willow Wind Farm: Betsy's story.* New York: Philomel Books.

Pellowski, A. (1982). *Winding Valley Farm: Annie's story.* New York: Philomel Books.

Pellowski, A. (1983). *Betsy's up-and-down year.* New York: Philomel Books.

Pinkney, G. (1992). *Back home.* New York: Dial Books for Young Readers.

Pizer, A. (1989). *Charlie the puppy.* Minneapolis: Carolrhoda.

Pizer, A. (1989). *Hattie the goat.* Minneapolis: Carolrhoda.

Pizer, A. (1989). *Percy the duck.* Minneapolis: Carolrhoda.

Pizer, A. (1989). *Penelope pig.* Minneapolis: Carolrhoda.

Proulx, A. (1992). *Postcards.* New York: Simon & Schuster.

Pryor, B. (1991). *Greenbrook farm.* New York: Simon & Schuster Books for Young Readers.

Purdy, C. (1987). *Least of all.* New York: M. K. McElderry Books.

Rae, M. M. (1988). *The farmer in the dell.* New York: Viking Kestrel.

Richardson, A. (1980). *Still more stories from grandma's attic.* Elgin, IL: Chariot Books.

Sneed, B. (1992). *Lucky Russell.* New York: Putnam.

Steele, M. Q. (1984). *The crow and Mrs. Gaddy.* New York: Greenwillow Books.

Stevens, K. (1983). *Molly McCullough and Tom the rogue.* New York: Crowell.

Tafuri, N. (1994). *This is the farmer.* New York: Greenwillow Books.

Thomas, J. R. (1989). *The princess in the pigpen.* New York: Clarion Books.

Tresselt, A. (1991). *Wake up farm!* New York: Lothrop, Lee & Shepard.

Waddell, M. (1992). *Farmer duck.* Cambridge, MA: Candlewick Press.

Wahl, R. (1972). *What will you do today, little Russell?* New York: Putnam.

Wolff, A. (1985). *Only the cat saw.* New York: Dodd, Mead.

Worthington, P. (1985). *Teddy bear farmer.* New York: Viking Kestrel.

Yolen, J. (1977). *The giant's farm.* New York: Seabury Press.

Yolen, J. (1993). *Honkers.* Boston: Little, Brown.

JUVENILE NONFICTION—SCIENCE/ZOOLOGY

Freedman, R. (1981). *Farm babies.* New York: Holiday House.

Gemming, E. (1974). *Born in the barn: Farm animals and their young.* New York: Coward, McCann & Geoghegan.

Moscow, H. (1979). *Domestic descendants: based on the television series Wild, Wild World of Animals.* New York: Time-Life Films.

Paladino, C. (1991). *Our vanishing farm animals: Saving America's rare breeds.* Boston: Joy Street Books.

Patent, D. H. (1984). *Farm animals.* New York: Holiday House.

Pringle, L. P. (1983). *Feral: Tame animals gone wild.* New York: Macmillan.

Windsor, M. (1984). *Baby farm animals.* Washington, DC: National Geographic Society.

JUVENILE NONFICTION—SOCIAL STUDIES

Anderson, J. (1989). *The American family farm.* San Diego: Harcourt Brace.

Fradin, D. (1983). *Farming.* Chicago: Children's Press.

Gibbons, G. (1988). *Farming.* New York: Holiday House.

Graff, N. (1989). *The strength of the hills: A portrait of a family farm.* Boston: Little, Brown.

Goodall, J. S. (1989). *The story of a farm.* New York: M. K. McElderry Books.

McFarland, C. (1990). *Cows in the parlor: A visit to a dairy farm.* New York: Atheneum.

Pistorius, A. (1990). *Cutting hill: A chronicle of a family farm.* New York: Knopf.

Bibliography for Kimberly Parker's *A Sense of Place* Unit

PICTURE BOOKS—ALL AGES

Africa:

Grifalconi, A. (1986). *The village of round and square houses.* Boston: Little, Brown.

Japan:

Baker, K. (1989). *The magic fan.* San Diego: Harcourt Brace.

Friedman, I. R. (1984). *How my parents learned to eat.* Boston: Houghton Mifflin.

Johnston, T. (1990). *The badger and the magic fan: A Japanese folktale.* New York: G. P. Putnam's.

Mexico:

Lewis, T. P. (1971). *Hill of fire.* New York: Harper & Row.

Russia:

Marshak, S. (1989). *The pup grew up!* New York: Henry Holt.

Silverman, M. (1984). *Anna and the seven swans.* New York: William Morrow.

World:

Burningham, J. (1972). *Around the world in eighty days.* London: Jonathan Cape.

JUVENILE BOOKS—GRADES 2–8

Africa:

Naidoo, B. (1985). *Journey to Jo'berg: A South African story.* New York: J. B. Lippincott.

Japan:

Coerr, E. (1977). *Sadako and the thousand paper cranes.* New York: Dell.

Maruki, T. (1980). *Hiroshima no pika.* New York: Lothrop, Lee & Shepard.

Mexico:

DeGerez, T. (1984). *My song is a piece of jade: Poems of ancient Mexico in English and Spanish.* Boston: Little, Brown.

Lifton, B. J. (1976). *Jaguar, my twin.* New York: Atheneum.

Titus, E. (1976). *Basil in Mexico.* New York: McGraw-Hill.

Walker, A. (1974). *Langston Hughes, American poet.* New York: Crowell.

New York:

Adams, L. (1983). *Alice and the boa constrictor.* Boston: Houghton Mifflin.

Averill, E. (1972). *Captains of the city street: A story of a cat club.* New York: Harper & Row.

Farber, N. (1977). *Six impossible things before breakfast.* Reading, MA: Addison-Wesley.

Hilibok, B. (1981). *Silent dancer.* New York: Messner.

Hurwitz, J. (1976). *Busybody Nora.* New York: Morrow.

Irving, W. (1990). *The legend of sleepy hollow.* Mankato, MN: Creative Education.

Konigsburg, E. L. (1967). *From the mixed-up files of Mrs. Basil E. Frankweiler.* New York: Atheneum.

Levinson, R. (1987). *Dinnie Abbie sister-R-R!* New York: Bradbury Press.

Lord, A. V. (1984). *Today's special: Z. A. P. and Zoe.* New York: London: Macmillan, Collier Macmillan.

Selden, G. (1960). *The cricket in Times Square.* New York: Ariel books.

Shub, E. (1986). *Cutlass in the snow.* New York: Greenwillow Books.

Taylor, S. (1951). *All-of-a-kind family.* Chicago: Follett Publishing.

Tobias, T. (1975). *Arthur Mitchell.* New York: Crowell.

Wojciechowska, M. (1969). *Hey, what's wrong with this one?* New York: Harper & Row.

Russia:

Price, S. (1987). *The ghost drum: A cat's tale.* New York: Farrar Straus & Giroux.

Titiev, E. (1976). *How the moolah was taught a lesson and other tales from Russia.* New York: Dial Press.

San Francisco:

Cameron, E. (1973). *The court of the stone children.* New York: Dutton.

Ewing, K. (1980). *Things won't be the same.* New York: Harcourt Brace.

Sachs, M. (1990). *At the sound of the beep.* New York: Dutton Children's Books.

Uchida, Y. (1971). *Journey to Topaz: A story of the Japanese-American evacuation.* New York: Scribner.

Imaginary Setting:

Asimov, J. (1988). *The package in hyperspace.* New York: Walker & Company.

Baum, L. F. (1982). *The wizard of Oz.* New York: Holt, Rinehart.

Cole, J. (1990). *The magic school bus, Lost in the solar system.* New York: Scholastic.

Juster, N. (1961). *The phantom toll booth.* New York: Random House.

L'Engle, M. (1962). *A wrinkle in time.* New York: Dell.

Lewis, C. S. (1950). *The lion, the witch, and the wardrobe.* New York: Macmillan.

MacGregor, E. (1983). *Miss Pickerell and the blue whales.* New York: McGraw-Hill.

Tolkien, J. R. R. (1966). *The hobbit.* Boston: Houghton Mifflin Company.

World:

Verne, J. (1978). *Around the world in eighty days.* London: Octopus.

YOUNG ADULT BOOKS BY DISCIPLINE—GRADES 9–12

History:

Kammen, M. G. (1975). *Colonial New York.* New York: Scribner.

Mathematics:
Haskins, J. (1987). *Count your way through Japan.* Minneapolis: Carolrhoda Books.
Haskins, J. (1989). *Count your way through Mexico.* Minneapolis: Carolrhoda Books.

Science:
Yoshida, T. (1989). *Young lions.* New York: Philomel Books.

Bibliography for Paul Cinoa's *Survival* Unit
JUVENILE BOOKS—GRADES 2–8

Aaron, C. (1973). *An American ghost.* New York: Harcourt Brace.
Aiken, J. (1983). *Bridle the wind.* New York: Delacorte Press.
Alcock, G. (1986). *Dooley's lion.* Owings Mills, MD: Stemmer House.
Archer, M. (1978). *The young boys gone.* New York: Walker & Company.
Baillie, A. (1992). *Adrift.* New York: Viking Press.
Bodecker, N. M. (1981). *Quimble wood.* New York: Atheneum.
Chambers, J. (1979). *Fritizi's winter.* New York: Atheneum.
Christopher, J. (1977). *Empty world.* New York: Dutton.
Christopher, M. (1974). *Stranded.* Boston: Little, Brown.
Clark, M. T. (1973). *If the earth falls in.* New York: Seabury Press.
Clifford, E. (1977). *The curse of the moonraker.* Boston: Houghton Mifflin.
Cohen, P. (1970). *Morena.* New York: Atheneum.
Collins, D. R. (1983). *The golden circle.* Nashville, Tenn.: Winston-Derek.
Cooper, C. (1985). *Earthchange.* Minneapolis: Lerner Publications.
Defoe, D. (1981). *Robinson Crusoe.* New York: Penguin Books.
De Roo, A. (1980). *Scrub fire.* New York: Atheneum.
Dixon, F. (1980). *The Hardy boys handbook.* New York: Wanderer Books.
East, B. (1979). *Danger in the air.* Mankato, MN: Crestwood House.
East, B. (1979). *Desperate search.* Mankato, MN: Crestwood House.
East, B. (1979). *Forty days lost.* Mankato, MN: Crestwood House.
East, B. (1979). *Found alive.* Mankato, MN: Crestwood House.
East, B. (1979). *Mistaken journey.* Mankato, MN: Crestwood House.
East, B. (1979). *Trapped in devil's hole.* Mankato, MN: Crestwood House.
Eckert, A. (1971). *Incident at Hawk's Hill.* Boston: Little, Brown.
Fleming, Susan. (1978). *Trapped on the golden flyer.* Philadelphia: Westminster Press.
Freedman, R. (1987). *Indian chiefs.* New York: Holiday House.
George, J. C. (1972). *Julie of the wolves.* New York: Harper & Row.
George, J. C. (1979). *River rats, Inc.* New York: Dutton.
Gunning, T. (1984). *Amazing escapes.* New York: Dodd, Mead.
Haller, D. R. (1982). *Not just any ring.* New York: Knopf, distributed by Random House.
Hallman, R. (1986). *Panic five.* New York: Dodd, Mead.
Hammer, C. (1987). *Wrong-way ragsdale.* New York: Farrar Straus & Giroux.
Hamre, L. (1973). *Operation Arctic.* New York: Atheneum.
Hill, K. (1990). *Toughboy and sister.* New York: M. K. McElderry Books.
Houston, J. A. (1977). *Frozen fire: A tale of courage.* New York: Atheneum.
Houston, J. A. (1981). *Long claws: An Arctic adventure.* New York: Atheneum.
Johnson, A. (1981). *Finders keepers.* New York: Four Winds Press.
Landsman, S. (1986) *Castaways on Chimp Island.* New York: Atheneum.
Leigh, B. (1977). *The far side of fear.* New York: Viking Press.
Liptack, K. (1990). *North American Indian survival skills.* New York: F. Watts.
Mayhar, A. (1985). *Medicine walk.* New York: Atheneum.
Mayne, W. (1993). *Low tide.* New York: Delacorte.

Mazer, H. (1973). *Snow bound.* New York: Delacorte Press.

Mazer, H. (1986). *The cave under the city.* New York: T. Y. Crowell.

McClung, R. (1990). *Hugh Glass, mountain man.* New York: Morrow Junior.

Mc Neer, M. (1957). *Armed with courage.* New York: Abingdon Press.

Mikaelsen, B. (1991). *Rescue Josh McGuire.* New York: Hyperion Books for Children.

Milton, H. (1979). *Mayday! mayday!* New York: F. Watts.

Milton, H. H. (1980). *The brats and Mr. Jack.* New York: Beaufort Books.

Moeri, L. (1981). *Save Queen of Sheba.* New York: E. P. Dutton.

Moeri, L. (1984). *Downwind.* New York: Dutton.

Niemark, P. (1981). *Survival.* Chicago: Children's Press.

O'Dell, S. (1960). *Island of the blue dolphins.* Boston: Houghton Mifflin.

O'Dell, S. (1980). *Sarah Bishop.* Boston: Houghton Mifflin.

Paulsen, G. (1989). *The voyage of the frog.* New York: Orchard Books.

Paulsen, G. (1994). *Father water, mother woods.* New York: Delacorte Press.

Phleger, M. (1963). *Pilot down, presumed dead.* New York: Harper & Row.

Politzer, A. (1974). *My journals and sketchbooks.* New York: Harcourt Brace.

Roth, A. (1974). *The iceberg hermit.* New York: Four Winds Press.

Roth, D. (1981). *River runaways.* Boston: Houghton Mifflin.

Skurzynski, G. (1982). *Lost in the devil's desert.* New York: Lothrop, Lee & Shepard.

Speare, E. (1983). *The sign of the beaver.* New York: Dell.

Sperry, A. (1940). *Call it courage.* New York: Macmillan.

Steig, W. (1976). *Abel's island.* New York: Farrar Straus & Giroux.

Sullivan, M. (1982). *Earthquake 2099.* New York: Lodestar Books.

Todd, J. M. (1978). *A child's Swiss Family Robinson.* New York: Hart Publishing.

Voight, C. (1981). *Homecoming.* New York: Atheneum.

Walter, D. (1978). *Great adventures.* London: Macdonald Educational for Marks and Spencer Ltd.

Whitefeather, W. (1990). *Outdoor survival handbook for kids.* Tucson: Harbinger House.

Williams, G. (1977). *True escape and survival stories.* New York: F. Watts.

Wyss, J. D. (1968). *The Swiss Family Robinson.* Chicago: Children's Press.

Yolen, H. (1981). *The boy who spoke chimp.* New York: Knopf, distributed by Random House.

JUVENILE CASSETTES—GRADES 2–8

George, J. C. (1993). *Julie of the wolves.* Prince Frederick, MD: Recorded Books.

O'Dell, S. (1992). *Island of the blue dolphins.* Prince Frederick, MD: Recorded Books.

Paulsen, G. (1989). *The voyage of the frog.* Prince Frederick, MD: Recorded Books.

Sperry, A. (1994). *Call it courage.* Prince Frederick, MD: Recorded Books.

Bibliography for Kara Gallagher's *Women and Girls in Literature* Unit
Biographies/Autobiographies

1. SCIENCE/SCIENCE RELATED TOPICS

Billings, C. (1989). *Grace Hopper: Naval admiral and computer pioneer.* Hillside, NJ: Enslow Publishers.

Baker, R. (1960). *America's first woman astronaut.* New York: Julian Messner.

Dash, J. (1991). *The triumph of discovery: Women scientists who won the Nobel Prize.* Englewood Cliffs, NJ: Silver Burdett Press.

Davis, B. (1972). *Amelia Earhart.* New York: G. P. Putnam's Sons.

Fisher, L. E. (1994). *Marie Curie.* New York: Macmillan.

McGovern, A. (1978). *Shark lady: True adventures of Eugenie Clark.* New York: Four Winds Press.

Pflaum, R. (1993). *Marie Curie and her daughter Irene.* Minneapolis, MN: Lerner Publications.

2. ART AND LITERATURE

Biracree, T. (1955). *Grandma Moses.* New York: Chelsea House Publications.

Gherman, B. (1986). *Georgia O'Keefe: The wideness and wonder of her world.* New York: Atheneum.

Guzetti, B. (1994). *A family called Brontë.* New York: Dillon Press.

Jones, J. A. (1993). *Frida Kahlo.* Vero Beach, FL: Rourke Publications.

Shuker, N. (1990). *Maya Angelou.* Englewood Cliffs, NJ: Silver Burdett Press.

Wilder, L. I. (1962). *On the way home.* New York: Harper & Row.

3. HISTORY

Amdur, R. (1993). *Anne Frank.* New York: Chelsea House Publishers.

Bacon, M. (1974). *I speak for my slave sister, the life of Abbey Kelley Foster.* New York: Thema Cromwell Co.

Buckmaster, H. (1966). *Women who shaped history.* New York: Crowell-Collier Press.

Coil, S. M. (1993). *Harriet Beecher Stowe.* New York: Franklin Watts.

DePaw, L. G. (1975). *Founding mothers: Women of America in the revolutionary era.* Boston: Houghton Mifflin Co.

Hoobler, D. (1988). *Cleopatra.* New York: Chelsea House Publishers.

Hoople, C. (1978). *As I saw it: Women who lived the American adventure.* New York: Dial Press.

Leitner, I. (1992). *The big lie.* New York: Scholastic.

Peterson, H. S. (1971). *Susan B. Anthony: Pioneer in women's rights.* Champaign, IL: Garrard Publishing.

4. SPORTS

Goldstein, M. (1994). *Jackie Joyner Kersee: Super-woman.* Minneapolis, MN: Lerner Publications.

Knudson, R. R. (1988). *Racing against the world.* New York: Penguin Group.

5. POLITICS/SOCIOLOGY

Brin, R. F. (1977). *Contributions of women: Social reform.* Minneapolis, MN: Dillon Press.

Currimbhoy, N. (1985). *Indira Gandhi.* New York: F. Watts.

Freeman, R. (1993). *Eleanor Roosevelt: A life of discovery.* New York: Scholastic.

Haskins, J. (1975). *Fighting Shirley Chisolm.* New York: The Dial Press.

Levinson, N. S. (1986). *I left my lamp: Emma Lazarus and the Statue of Liberty.* New York: Lodestary Books.

Morin, I. (1994). *Women of the U.S. Congress.* Minneapolis, MN: The Oliver Press.

Patrick, D. (1991). *Coretta Scott King.* New York: F. Watts.

Roberts, J. (1994). *Ruth Bader Ginsberg.* Brookfield: The Millbrook Press.

Weidt, M. N. (1991). *Stateswoman to the world: A story about Eleanor Roosevelt.* Minneapolis: Carolrhoda.

6. MISCELLANEOUS

Fitzgerald, E. D. (1958). *Althea Gibson: I always wanted to be somebody.* New York: Harper & Row.

Ilginfritz, E. (1991). *Anne Hutchinson.* New York: Chelsea House Publishers.

Kronstadt, J. (1990). *Florence Sabin.* New York: Chelsea House Publishers.

Plowden, M. (1993). *Famous firsts of black women.* Gretna: Pelican Publishing.

Tibble, A. (1958). *Helen Keller.* New York: G. P. Putnam's Sons.

Topalian, E. (1984). *Margaret Sanger.* New York: F. Watts.
Turner, R. M. (1994). *Dorothea Lange.* Boston: Little, Brown.

Fiction

1. FANTASY

McCaughren, T. (1985). *Run with the wind.* Dublin: Wolfhound Press.
White, E. B. (1952). *Charlotte's web.* New York: HarperCollins.

2. SCIENCE FICTION

Paton Walsh, J. (1982). *The green book.* New York: Farrar Straus & Giroux.

3. HISTORICAL FICTION

Lowry, L. (1989). *Number the stars.* New York: Dell.
MacLachlan, P. (1985). *Sarah, plain and tall.* New York: HarperCollins.

4. REALISTIC FICTION

Choi, S. N. (1994). *Gathering of pearls.* Boston: Houghton Mifflin.
Dugan, B. (1994). *Good-bye, hello.* New York: Greenwillow Books.
Fritz, J. (1982). *Homesick.* New York: G. P. Putnam's Sons.
George, J. C. (1972). *Julie of the wolves.* New York: HarperCollins.
Namioka, L. (1994). *April and the dragon lady.* New York: Harcourt Brace.
O'Dell, S. (1960). *Island of the blue dolphins.* New York: Dell.
Sigal, A. (1981). *Upon the head of the goat.* New York: Farrar Straus & Giroux.
Voigt, C. (1983). *Dicey's song.* New York: Atheneum.

Bibliography for Elaine Dawson's Unit From West Africa to Slavery

Juvenile Books—Slavery, Grades 2–8

Anderson, J. (1988). *A Williamsburg household.* New York: Clarion Books.
Collier, J. L. (1983). *War comes to Willie Freeman.* New York: Delacorte.
Collier, J. L. (1984). *Who is Carrie?* New York: Delacorte.
Conley, K. (1989). *Benjamin Banneker.* New York: Chelsea House.
Clark, M. G. (1980). *Freedom crossing.* New York: Scholastic.
Davis, B. (1976). *Black heros of the American Revolution.* New York: Chelsea House.
Fagan, Y. (Ed.). (1987). *Incidents in the life of a slave girl written by herself by Harriet Jacobs.* Cambridge, MA: Harvard University Press.
Hamilton, V. (1985). *The people could fly: American Black folktales.* New York: Knopf.
Hamilton, V. (1993). *Many thousand gone: African Americans from slavery to freedom.* New York: Knopf.
Hine, D. C. (1989). *Blacks in American history.* New Jersey: Globe Book Company.
Katz, W. L. (1990). *Breaking the chains: African-American slave resistance.* New York: Atheneum.
Lester, J. (1968). *To be a slave.* New York: Dial Press.
O'Dell, S. (1989). *My name is not Angelica.* Boston: Houghton Mifflin.
Meltzer, M. (1980). *All times, all peoples: A world history of slavery.* New York: Harper & Row.
Nolen, B. (1972). *Africa is thunder and wonder.* New York: Charles Schribner's Sons.
Pelz, R. (1990). *Black heros of the wild west.* Seattle, WA: Open Hand.
Snuicker, B. (1977). *Run away to freedom.* New York: Harper & Row.
Walvin, J. (1983). *Slavery and the slave trade.* Jackson: University Press of Mississippi.
Winter, J. (1988). *Follow the drinking gourd.* New York: Knopf.

Juvenile Books on Life in West Africa

Arkhurst, J. C. (1992). *The adventures of spider: West African folk tales.* Boston: Little, Brown.
Gerson, M. (1985). *Why the sky is far away.* Boston: Little, Brown.
Grey, E. (1989). *A country far away.* New York: Orchard Books.

Grifalconi, A. (1986). *Darkness and the butterfly.* Boston: Little, Brown.

Grifalconi, A. (1986). *The village of round and square houses.* Boston: Little, Brown.

Haley, G. E. (1989). *A story a story.* New York: Atheneum.

Hardema, V. (1992). *Why mosquitos buzz in people's ears: A West African tale.* New York: Penguin Group.

Spears, R. (Ed.). (1991). *West African folk tales.* Collected and Translated by Jack Berry. Evanston, IL: Northwestern University Press.

Steptoe, J. (1987). *Mufaro's beautiful daughters: An African tale.* New York: Lothrop, Lee & Shepard.

Teacher Resources

Bontempts, A. (1969). *Great slave narratives.* Boston: Beacon Press.

Courlander and Herzog. (1986). *The cowtail switch and other West African stories.* New York: Henry Holt.

Davis, D. B. (1966). *The problem of slavery in western culture.* Ithaca: Cornell University Press.

Davis, D. B. (1986). *Slavery in the colonial Chesapeake.* Williamsburg, VA: Colonial Williamsburg Foundation.

Ferguson, L. (1986). *Archeology and early African America.* Washington and London: Smithsonian Institution Press.

Jefferson, T. (1825). *Notes on the State of Virginia.* Philadelphia: H. C. Carey & I. Lea.

Jordon, W. (1968). *White over black.* Chapel Hill: University of North Carolina Press.

Meltzer, M. (1972). *Slavery II: From Renaissance to today.* Chicago: Crowles Book Company.

Miller, R. (Ed.). (1990). *Dear master. Letters of a slave family.* Athens: University of Georgia Press.

Morgan, E. S. (1975). *American slavery, American freedom.* New York: W. W. Norton.

Pinckard, Dr. G. (1971). "Notes on the West Indies." In *Black voyage eyewitness accounts of the Atlantic slave trade.* Boston: Little, Brown.

Redford, D. S. (1988). *Somerset homecoming.* New York: Doubleday.

Sobel, M. (1987). *The world they made together.* Princeton: Princeton University Press.

Spears, R. (Ed.) (1991). *West African folk tales.* Collected and Translated by Jack Berry. Evanston, IL: Northwestern University Press.

Tate, T. W. (1965). *The negro in Eighteenth-Century Williamsburg.* Charlottseville: The University Press of Virginia.

REFERENCES

Armento, B. J. et al. (1991). *America will be.* New York: Houghton Mifflin.

Atwell, N. (1987). *In the middle: Writing, reading and learning with adolescents.* Portsmouth, NH: Boyton/Cook Publishers.

Banks, J. A., Beyer, B. K., Contreras, G., Craven, J., Gladson-Billings, G., McFarland, M. A., & Parker, W. C. (2001). *People together: Adventures in time and place,* second grade text. New York: McGraw-Hill School Division.

Berleth, R. (1990). *Samuel's choice.* New York: Albert Whitman & Company.

Brown, D. K. (1998). The Children's Literature Web Guide. Available online: www.acs.-ucalgary.ca/~dkbrown/

Burke, E. M. (1986). *Early childhood literature: For love of child and book.* Boston: Allyn & Bacon.

Collier, J. L., & Collier, C. (1981). *Jump ship to freedom.* New York: Delacorte Press.

Ewing, K. (1999). The Africanization of an American classroom in Hong Kong: the power of literature. *English Journal, 89* (2), 83–86.

Expectations of excellence: Curriculum standards for social studies. (1994). Washington, DC: National Council for the Social Studies.

Fox, P. (1973). *The slave dancer.* New York: Dell.

Glazer, J. I. (1991). *Literature for young children* (3rd ed.). New York: Merrill.

Gray, B. G., Toth, M. D., & Ragno, N. N. (1990). *World of language.* Morristown, NJ: Silver, Burdett & Ginn.

Hakim, J. (1994). *A history of US: War, terrible war.* New York: D.C. Health.

Heller, M. F. (1995). *Reading-writing connections: From theory to practice.* New York: Longman.

Hurmence, B. (1850s). *A girl called boy.* New York: Clarion Books.

Moore, J. N. (1997). *Interpreting young adult literature.* Portsmouth, NH: Heineman.

Monson, D. L. (Ed.). (1985). *Adventuring with books: A book list for pre-k–grade 6.* Urbana, IL: National Council of Teachers of English.

National standards for civics and government. (1994). Calabasas, CA: The Center for Civic Education.

National standards for history. (1994). Los Angeles, CA: National Center for History in the Schools.

Norton, D. E. (1991). *Through the eyes of a child: An introduction to children's literature* (3rd ed.). New York: Merrill.

Norton, D. E. (1992). *The impact of literature-based reading.* New York: Merrill.

Osburg, B. (1999). Building a new generation of democratic citizens through literature. *English Journal, 89* (2), 111–118.

Pappas, C. C., Kiefer, B. Z., & Levstik, L. S. (1995). *An integrated language perspective in the elementary school: Theory into action* (2nd ed.). New York: Longman.

Pickeny, A. D. (1994). *Dear Benjamin Banneker.* San Diego, CA: Harcourt Brace.

Schiller, L. (1999). Making American literature in middle school. *English Journal, 89* (2), 98–104.

Smith, C. (Ed.). (1991). *Daily life: A sourcebook on Colonial America.* Brookfield, CT: The Millbrook Press.

Strickland, D. S. et al. (1990). *HBJ language grade 4 teacher edition.* (1990). San Diego/Chicago/Dallas: Harcourt Brace.

The Children's Literature Nook. (August 6, 1998). Available online: www.geocities.com/-Heartland/Estates/4967/index.html.

Wepner, S. T., & Feeley, J. T. (1993). *Moving forward with literature: Basals, books, and beyond.* New York: Merrill.

CHAPTER 12

ARTFORMS

A Humanities Teaching Unit for Intermediate Students

Coauthored with Ann McEachron

Chapter Outline

CHAPTER OBJECTIVES

Artistic expression is everywhere. We are surrounded by creative works in buildings, technology, clothing, furnishings, and websites! The urge to create is human. Do you know your preferences for creative expression? Perhaps you are musically inclined, like ceramics, writing, or contemplating the nature of the world. Perhaps your preference in one of the humanities makes you feel less confident in other areas. In this chapter, you will learn how to develop art curriculum even if you don't consider yourself artistic. The Artforms unit format can be adapted to other humanities themes. Upon completion of this chapter you will be able to:

1. Identify ways to develop humanities themes across time and space via a conceptual approach.
2. Engage students in artistic activities as they learn about the cultural context of artistic expression.
3. Represent artistic expression in a global context.

✦ THE HUMANITIES

The humanities encompass the disciplines of music, religion, literature, art, and philosophy. During the fourteenth century, the humanities emerged as *studia humanitatis* (philology, languages, ancient literature) in opposition to medieval scholasticism. In this context, "the humanist was the person who studied the ancients in a new spirit free of dogmatic prejudices; the key features of that spirit were intellectual curiosity, sympathy, the free exercise of critical reason and the appreciation of human values (truth, beauty, glory) for their own sake" (Vidal-Naquet, 1987, p. 146). Humanism put the human being in the center of the universe.

A key distinction between classroom lessons that emphasize the humanities and traditional social studies lessons is an emphasis on human values *for their own sake*. Traditional social studies lessons emphasize historical events and are written in an expository style. More recently, social studies educators have incorporated literature, music, art, diaries, and oral histories as a means to *humanize* historical analyses. Curriculum developers have incorporated human interest stories to supplement historical descriptions. The humanities teaching unit in this chapter places the study of humans in the forefront in the tradition of the earliest humanists. By so doing, the artistic expression of others becomes a catalyst for elementary and middle school students to express their own human values and appreciation for truth, beauty, and glory. This does not mean, however, that historical events and other traditional social studies approaches are ignored. On the contrary, the historical context for each of the featured artforms is presented to enhance the relationship of the individual to culture.

In *Artforms,* artistic expression is the point of departure for history, biography, cross-cultural study, and human rights. Some of the artforms have survived anonymously over the centuries, and others can be traced to specific artists. The unit emphasizes the human urge to create and the factors that support and inhibit individual and collective expression. The artforms represent cultures around the world thereby providing a global perspective. Another important feature of *Artforms* is its child-centered approach. After exposure to others' works of art, students are encouraged to express themselves by experimenting with a variety of artforms, music, and literature. By consulting "The Incredible Art Department" through the Internet, teachers and students can access endless creative suggestions for further artistic expression (http://www.artswire.org/kenroar/index.html).

✦ ARTFORMS[1]

Table of Contents

Content Outline

Style	Period/Culture	Featured Artist(s)
Nonobjective/Abstract	20th Century/American Contemporary	Masterfield
Abstract/Cubism	Post Impressionist/Modern	Picasso
Universal Language in Music and Art	Universal	McEachron and Lee Baska (Musician)
Triptychs/Illustrated Manuscripts	Early Medieval	Monks
Impressionism	France and United States	Monet/Cassatt
American Folk Art	17th–20th Centuries	Ringgold
Fantasy Beasts	17th–20th Centuries	Russian/European
Mandalas	Navajo Indians/ Tibetan Monks	Navajos/Monks
Gyotaku	Japanese	Japanese
Abstract/Naturalism	American Southwest	O'Keeffe

---

[1]"Artforms" was created through a partnership between Ann McEachron, watercolor artist, and Gail McEachron, professor and author.

Rationale

Art represents the act of creation. Educators have recognized the importance of providing elementary and middle school students with opportunities for creative expression, arguing that cognitive and emotional development is enhanced. Appendix A shows both the National Standards for the Social Studies and the National Standards for Art Education that are relevant for this unit. Unfortunately, systematic presentation of the arts is limited to one class of music and one class of art per week in most schools. With only weekly meetings, music and art teachers have difficulty implementing in-depth units that require concentrated periods of time. *Artforms* is a humanities unit designed for classroom teachers and special summer programs. The course allows teachers and students to explore art in a historical context for a period of approximately twenty hours of instruction.

In a traditional elementary or middle school classroom, *Artforms* would fit logically into the social studies curriculum because the unit emphasizes the ways in which individuals have shaped and been shaped by history. Yet, there are several naturally integrated educational experiences with music and science as well. The most enjoyable part of *Artforms* from a teaching standpoint is that it is activity centered. Students know that each day they will be given an opportunity to create their own "masterpiece" after studying the contributions of famous artists. Knowing this enhances the significance and sense of purpose to the information that is presented, because students will immediately create the artform. In this way, that which is learned becomes personally integrated.

The interdisciplinary course is designed with four major goals in mind: personal, historical, creative and conceptual.

Goals

Personal. Students will appreciate their own capabilities and preferences for artforms. (Affective Domain)

Historical. Students will reiterate the contributions of selected artists and important events in their lives given the time periods in which they lived. (Cognitive Domain)

Creative. Students will create ten different artforms. (Artistic/Psychomotor Domain)

Conceptual. Students will analyze the social foundations of artistic ability. (Cognitive Domain)

Conceptual Themes

I. Social Foundations of Artistic Ability
   A. Personal Characteristics
      1. Perseverance
      2. Strong convictions
      3. Urge to create
   B. Early Development
      1. Support
      2. Obstacles
      3. Family roles

    C. Arts and Nature
       1. Nature
       2. People
       3. Abstract/Nonobjective
    D. Economic Issues
       1. Class
       2. Starving artist syndrome
       3. Patrons
    E. Art As Political and Social Expression
       1. Political protest
       2. Artists' professional organizations
       3. Ethnic heritage
II. Featured Artists
    A. Georges Braque
    B. Mary Cassatt
    C. Maxine Masterfield
    D. Claude Monet
    E. Georgia O'Keeffe
    F. Pablo Picasso
    G. Faith Ringgold

TIME LINE OF FEATURED ARTISTS

1825	1840	1855	1870	1885	1900	1915	1930	1945	1960	1975	1990	2005
Claude Monet 1840–1926												
Mary Cassatt 1844–1924												
Pablo Picasso 1881–1973												
Georges Braque 1882–1963												
Georgia O'Keefe 1887–1986												
Maxine Masterfield (circa) 1934–present												
Faith Ringgold 1930–present												

Model Lesson:
Daily Lesson Plans

Day One

Topic: Nonobjective/Abstract   **Time:** 2 Hours

Purpose: Students will gain an appreciation for the creative strength of individuals who sought to be original.

Generalizations:

Art—Nonconformist artists follow their own vision, life experiences, hopes, and energies.

Social studies—Originality often goes unnoticed or is criticized when it doesn't conform to traditional standards.

Concepts:

Art—nonobjective; abstract; solar painting
Social studies—nonconformity; conformity

Objectives:

Knowledge:
1. Students will compare and contrast nonobjective and abstract art.
2. Students will describe Maxine Masterfield based on the five social foundations of artistic ability.

Application:
3. Students will create a solar painting.
4. Students will construct a portfolio.

Procedure:

Introduction: Since it is the first day of class, introductions will be made with instructors and students sharing information about themselves. Overview of course and orientation to art supplies will be given. Administer pretest. The same instrument can be used as a posttest at the end of the unit to demonstrate what students have learned.

Content Focus: Provide definitions of nonobjective and abstract art, showing illustrations from books. After giving a few examples, show students pictures and ask them to categorize based on the two categories. A biographical sketch of Maxine Masterfield will be given, showing cards and pictures of her work. See background information for details and definitions of concepts. Write definitions of concepts on board or flip chart. Emphasize generalizations previously stated.

Demonstration and Activity: Demonstrate technique for making solar painting.
1. Line cardboard box with plastic.
2. Crinkle plastic wrap and put in bottom.
3. Lay a sheet of rice paper in box.
4. Arrange objects on top of rice paper.
5. Squirt top with three to five different colors of ink.
6. Lay a second sheet of rice paper on top. Add lace, gauze, or plastic on top.
7. Set in sun to dry or leave overnight so that all liquid from ink will evaporate.
8. Carefully remove rice paper sheets. Press with iron if necessary.

Take students outside to collect objects that will create different textures (e.g., rocks, twigs, shells). Provide students with additional objects (e.g., paper clips, metal shapes). Students then are ready to create their own solar paintings.

Closure: Ask students to recall information about the life of Maxine Masterfield, re-iterating the social foundations of artistic ability; for example, personal characteristics, early development, arts and nature, economic issues, art as political and social expression. Ask students to identify whether pictures in books are examples of abstract art, nonobjective art, and so on.

Extension:

Teacher demonstrates construction of portfolio, which students will use to store their artwork throughout the unit. Students then construct their own.

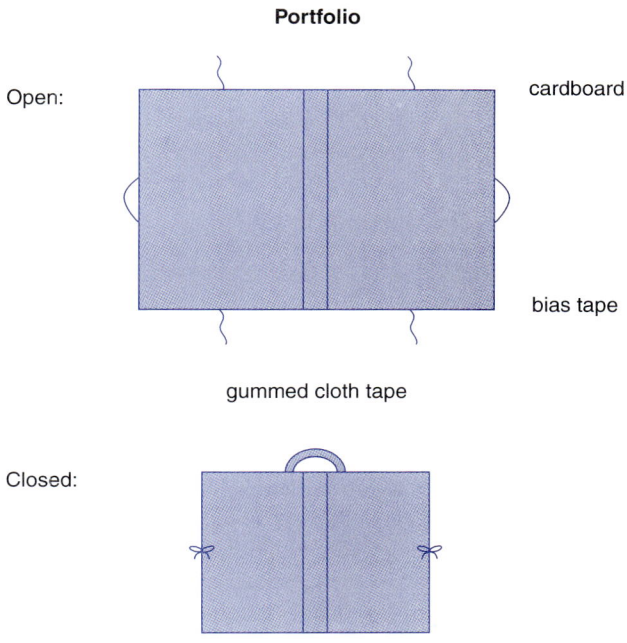

Portfolio

Open: cardboard

                                                                         bias tape

gummed cloth tape

Closed:

Evaluation:

Formative: pretest; listening skills; following directions; creation of solar painting and portfolio

Summative: solar painting; portfolio

Background Information:

NONOBJECTIVE/ABSTRACT

Nonobjective art depicts color, shape, and form but does not include subject matter. It is art that depends on design and color to please the eye. The viewer can use his/her imagination to project images into the nonobjective art, images that are not necessarily those intended by the artist. There are times when the viewer experiences an emotional response based on the art.

Abstract paintings can have subject matter that may or may not be recognizable. Abstract works of art range from highly distorted images to images that look realistic with slight abstractions. The distorted images sometimes create dissonance for the viewer, but at the same time, by abstracting an image and leaving a lot to the imagination, it holds the viewer's interest longer.

Some of the twentieth-century contemporary painters who are well known for their nonobjective and/or abstract art include: Pablo Picasso, Piet Mondrian, Paul Klee, Jackson Pollack, Paul Jenkins, Jasper Johns, Charles Demuth, and Roy Lichtenstein. They all created paintings that were easily remembered because they were different and stayed in your mind.

In contemporary art, whether it is in the form of paintings, sculpture, ceramic designs, advertising logos, or music, the purpose is to move viewers or listeners to remember what they saw or heard. "Contemporary" means happening, existing, living, or coming into being during the same period of time. Contemporary art is art being produced and having the characteristics of the present, of today. Additional words describing contemporary art include: *modern, new-fashioned, present-day, up-to-date, up-to-the-minute, progressive, innovative,* and *forward-looking.*

Maxine Masterfield is an abstract naturalist painter who lives in Florida and is experimenting with water media materials such as inks and watercolor, using a free-spirited approach. She uses unusual tools such as combs, rollers, squeeze bottles and needle-type points, wax paper, leaves, stones, shells, salt, plastic wrap, and paraffin wax. She lets her feelings about forms in nature, such as rocks, mountains, trees, water, leaves, flowers, or clouds, influence her compositions.

As a result of this experimentation, Ms. Masterfield has developed the "solar" painting method—using watercolor and inks poured onto smooth paper, letting the sun evaporate the liquid. The results are exciting and unusual. Her paintings are nonobjective naturalism because she gets her inspiration from nature. Her style is not an imitation of someone else's; she is constantly trying new ideas.

Contemporary painters of today have two choices of style: conformity and nonconformity. Conformity requires clinging to the security of whatever style you were taught in the beginning, following someone else's style, sticking to rigid rules. This is a beginning but can stunt artistic growth. Nonconformity is trusting that the only thing one has to express is one's own vision, life experiences, hopes, desires, and energies. In art it is uniqueness that makes a work different and stand out from the rest. Maxine Masterfield encourages her students to follow their own star, an important sentiment that fosters creativity. Encourage students to feel free to express themselves in innovative or traditional ways throughout the duration of the unit and to be aware of their surroundings in ways that give them insight into how people shape society and how society influences people.

Materials and Resources:

Books: Masterfield (1984, 1990)

Solar painting supplies: cardboard boxes, plastic liners, clips, metal, ink, rice paper, pipette, lace gauze, plastic

Portfolio supplies: matboard or cardboard, gummed cloth tape, bias tape

Note: On the second day, students enjoy taking apart their solar paintings and looking for interesting patterns, textures, and shapes. Be sure they do this carefully so as not to tear the rice paper. One of our students asked an excellent question: "What if I see a shape in the picture but no one else sees it? Would it be nonobjective or abstract?" We then had an interesting discussion about the way in which people view art differently. In some cases one painting might be abstract to one person and nonobjective to another, depending on whether or not objects are seen.

Name _____

Art Appreciation

1. Do you think creativity is something one is born with, is developed throughout one's lifetime, or is some combination of both? Explain your answer.

2. Do you think that you are creative? If so, in what way? If not, why not?

3. Can you remember when you became interested in art? If so, describe when or how.

4. Describe art classes you have had other than in school.

5. Is there an artist and/or particular style of art that you admire or prefer? Please explain.

6. When studying an artist, do you think that it is possible to appreciate his or her artform if you do not like the way he or she led his/her life? Explain.

Art History

7. Name three necessary ingredients in a solar painting.

8. Describe a nonobjective painting.

9. What do you call a painting that shows several sides of an object?

10. Name one of Picasso's painting periods.

11. Name a word used by both musicians and artists when referring to a composition.

12. What color in a painting would describe a soft soothing melody?

13. Name two artforms used in the medieval period.

14. How were books made before the printing press was invented? Who made them?

15. What were the artists called who first started painting the effects of sunlight and shadows out of doors?

16. Name one of the artists in the period in question number 9 and describe his/her brush strokes.

17. Who was the American who was invited to join the French Impressionist group? What was the main subject matter of her painting?

18. Name the artform that contains symbols and geometric shapes that can have meaning in *your personal* life.

19. In what country did gyotaku originate?

20. Name one purpose of fish printing.

21. Name a contemporary artist who combined the artform of quiltmaking with her painting.

22. What is a triptych and how was it used?

23. Why was it necessary for monks to copy manuscripts?

24. What is the difference between abstract and nonobjective art?

25. Name an artist who often painted abstract scenes and skulls in the Southwest.

26. In what way did Mary Cassatt use her art to stage a political protest?

27. What are some of life's challenges addressed through folktales and fantasy?

28. What artform did the Russian artist Fabergé create?

29. What is the significance of a universal system of symbols?

30. How were mandalas used by the Navajo Indians?

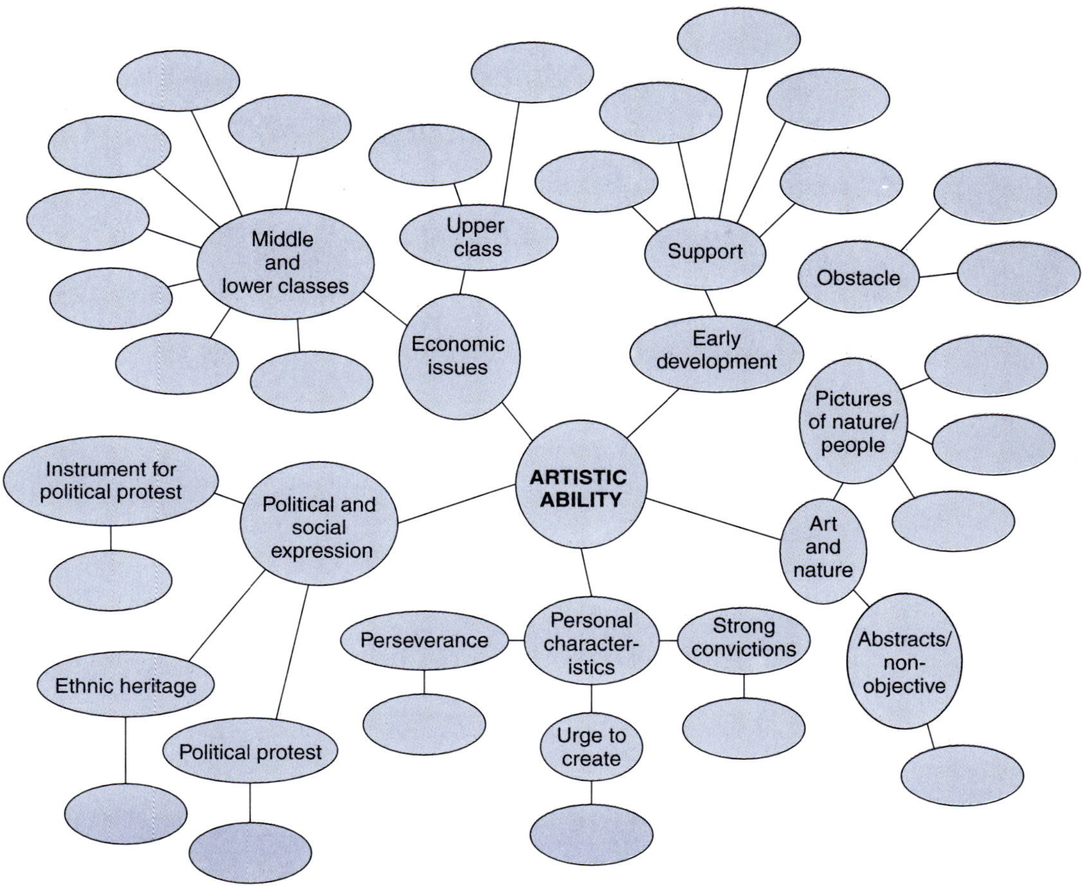

FIGURE 12.1 ***Social Foundations of Artistic Ability***

MODEL LESSON: DAILY LESSON PLANS

DAY TWO

Topic: Abstract/Cubism **Time:** 2 Hours

Purpose:

Students will view art as a form of freedom of expression, like music, literature, and the press.

Generalizations:

Art—Abstract paintings can have objects that may or may not be recognizable. Cubism attempts to display several surfaces of an object simultaneously and by fragmenting the form of depicted objects.

Social studies—Art can be a personal expression of a political event; it then becomes a political statement. Countries that support freedom of expression protect the rights of people to express themselves in art.

Concepts:

Art—abstract; cubism
Social studies—political/personal art; art as political statement

Objectives:

Knowledge:

1. Students will listen to a biographical sketch of Picasso.
2. Students will define cubism.
3. Students will describe Pablo Picasso based on the five social foundations of artistic ability.
4. Students will identify art as a form of freedom of expression.

Application:

5. Students will create a cubist painting.

Procedure:

Introduction: Read the First Amendment to the Constitution. The first ten amendments, known as the Bill of Rights, were ratified in 1791. Then discuss the meaning of the terms and the implications of the amendment for free expression in art. Talk about the similarity of laws in France and Spain where the featured artist of the day, Pablo Picasso, lived.

> Amendment 1: Freedom of religion, speech, and the press; rights of assembly and petition Congress shall make no law respecting an establishment of religion, or prohibiting the free exercise thereof; or abridging the freedom of speech or of the press; or the right of the people peaceably to assemble, and to petition the government for a redress of grievances.

Content Focus: Give a biographical sketch of Pablo Picasso, providing pictures of the various phases of his art. See Background Information for details.

Demonstration and Activity: Display a variety of blocks and objects that create unusual cubist forms. Draw them in their flat form on chalkboard; then draw them depicting cubist forms. Make a display of various objects that would be appropriate for a cubist painting (e.g., tabletop with tablecloth, guitar, vase, etc.). Students sketch the cubist forms they would like to paint on tracing paper. Students transfer drawing to paper, then paint.

Closure: Ask students to recall information about the life of Pablo Picasso, reiterating the social foundations of artistic ability. Ask students to define cubism; ask students to recall what the First Amendment of the Constitution guarantees, stating the implications for artistic expression.

Evaluation:

Formative: listening skills, following directions, creation of cubist sketch and painting, responses to questions

Summative: cubist sketch and painting

Background Information:

CUBISM

The years 1907 to 1914 perhaps marked the most influential and complete artistic revolution since the Renaissance—the Cubist movement. Led by the Spanish artist Pablo Picasso and the French artist Georges Braque, the Cubists reexamined the Renaissance concept of pictorial space and transformed subject matter by rendering it as a series of geometric planes. Picasso's landmark *Les Desmoiselles d' Avignon* (1907) depicts this new cubist pictorial space with an unfixed point of view and partial picture abstraction. Other influential Cubists of the time were Juan Gris of Spain and Fernard Leger of France.

Early Cubism was heavily influenced by Cezanne and the arbitrary use of color as seen in the fauve exhibition in 1905. Furthermore, forms of African sculpture, in particular mask sculpture, were incorporated into early cubist works. Most Cubists chose still life as their principal subject, often using such commonplace subject items as tabletops, musical instruments, and bottles.

Picasso and Braque, working closely together at times, progressed toward complete subject/pictorial space integration via complete abstraction. In Braque's *Violin and Palette* (1909–10), he achieves this integration, ushering in *analytical cubism.* Later, the movement would branch into *synthetic cubism,* where pictorial subjects often combined with newspaper, text, and real items to form collage-like works such as Picasso's *Still Life with Chair Caning* (1911–12) and others.

Materials and Resources:
Books: Golding (1988); Janson (1970); Lepscky (1984); Mullins (1968); Venezia
       (1988); Zurcher (1988)
Supplies for Cubist painting: Guitar, vase, round paper weight, tablecloth; paper,
       watercolor pigments, water, brushes, transfer (carbon) paper, tracing paper,
       pencils

Extensions:
Ask students to research the two kinds of cubist painting—analytic cubism and synthetic cubism. Analytic cubism refers to the way artists break down, or analyze, and then reassemble observed forms. Synthetic cubism combines, or synthesizes, imaginative elements into new figurative forms. Students can report to class, showing pictures to illustrate the two kinds. Or ask students to research the controversy over Robert Maplethorpe's art and the implications of interpreting the First Amendment.

TIME LINE OF PABLO RUIZ PICASSO'S LIFE
1881   Pablo born in Malaga, Spain
1889   Entered school and hated it
1891   Moved to Corunna on the coast of Spain; was allowed to study in the art
        school where his father taught
1895   Don Jose realized that his son was a better painter than he was and gave his
        paints and brushes to Pablo, age 14
1900   Went to Paris at age 19 and was influenced by French artists

	Blue Period; his paintings weren't selling; near starvation; Gertrude Stein offered a large price for several of his canvases; his poverty was over
1907	Transition of cubist period; one of the most important periods in modern art; for years people had tried to paint things to make them look real; Picasso changed the tradition
1911	People called Pablo's pictures with objects glued to them "collages"; French word for glue is *colle*
1914	Picasso painted richly colored still lifes of bottles, glasses, and guitars
1918	Married ballerina Olga Khoklova
1919	Picasso combined realism and cubism in his paintings
1921	Paul Picasso born
1923	Inspired by Russian ballet dancers; painted them frequently
1937	Bought estate in Boisgeloup, not far from Paris; now had plenty of room to paint and sculpt in clay and plaster
	After hearing about German bombing, he made hundreds of drawings of wounded people and animals
1939	As war between France and Germany became more alarming, portraits of friends became more twisted
1947	Modeled figures of clay
1951	Potters of Valluris gave Picasso a 70th birthday party
1973	Picasso died at age 92 in France

Model Lesson: Daily Lesson Plans

Day Three

Topic: Universal Language in Music and Art   **Time:** 2 Hours

Purpose: Students will identify the common language between music and art.

Generalizations:
Art/music—Musicians and artists "speak" a common language.
Social studies—Music and art are universal forms of expression.

Concepts:
Art—line, color, shape, texture
Music—melody, rhythm, harmony, mood
Both—composition, dominant theme, subdominant theme
Social studies—universal language

Objectives:
Knowledge:
1. Students will identify the design elements that an artist considers when composing an artform (e.g., line, color, texture, shape, movement, pattern, scale).

2. Students will identify the elements that a musician considers when composing music (e.g., melody, rhythm, harmony, mood, repetition, sequence, tone, movements).

3. Students will state that compositions in music and art consist of a dominant theme with a subdominant theme.

Application:

4. Given a series of slides of paintings, students will identify dominant and subdominant themes, mood, color, balance, pattern, and repetition with variation.

5. Given a saxophone solo, students will respond to the music by painting their reactions on a large sheet of paper.

6. Given a flute solo, students will respond to the music by painting in various squares depicting moods.

7. Students will paint a picture in response to music.

Procedure:

Introduction: Discuss the universal nature of music and art, stressing that people throughout the world express their feelings and moods through music and art. Music and art are also representative of the cultural context from which they originate. Even though music and art share common themes (e.g., harmony, theme, mood), the specific form of expression is created by the uniqueness of the composer/artist and the influence of the culture in which he or she lives.

Content Focus: Identify the common elements in music and art. Refer to Background Information for details. Write different lines on board to represent a variety of moods (e.g., long flowing, wavy, short, choppy, pointed). Show slides of various paintings, identifying color contrast/harmony, dominant and subdominant themes, as well as other details listed in Background Information. Ask students to identify the various elements in subsequent slides of paintings. (Slides of paintings can be rented from the National Gallery of Art free of charge. See bibliography.)

Demonstration and Activity: Students are given large sheets of paper and a crayon. After introducing musician, he/she plays while the students react to the music by drawing on their paper. Students have large grocery sacks on heads so that they will concentrate on the music and their own perceptions without looking at their friends' papers! Students then take off grocery sacks and compare their reactions. During the next phase of the lesson, students are given a sheet of paper that has squares depicting various moods. The musician plays the flute, emphasizing a variety of moods, and the students draw in the squares that most closely resemble the mood that they are feeling. Not all students will respond in the same way. Students then compare their work briefly, selecting an inspiration from their notes for further development. For the remainder of the period, music is played (audiotape or synthesizer) while students paint freely to the music, developing previous sketches or starting anew.

Closure: Ask students to state some of the common elements in music and art. Each student is called on to offer at least one common element. Students are asked what is meant by the term "universal." Students share their painting, describing elements they consider when composing the paintings (e.g., mood, line, color, contrast, movement, texture, repetition, etc.).

Extensions:

Play music representing different regions of the world (e.g., African, South American, Middle Eastern). If available, display instruments representative of the various regions (e.g., drums, maracas, sitar). Locate regions on world map. Show pictures of artforms representative of these same regions. Ask students to research the evolution of various art and music traditions in a particular country or region of the world.

Evaluation:

Formative: listening skills; following directions; responses to music; answers to questions

Summative: mood drawings; painting

Background Information:

SIGHTS AND SOUNDS

Musicians and artists "speak" a common language. Art and music have the capacity to awaken our imaginations, to take us on a journey, to change our mood, and to stir our emotions. Artists use line, color, texture, and shape in compositions. They consider form, pattern, scale, gesture, unity, and contrast. The organization of different elements is the problem of design, such as proportion, rhythm, balance, repetition, harmony, and sequence, among others. Unity, contrast, dominance, proportion, rhythm, balance, repetition with variation, and harmony are the principles of successful art.

Paintings need to be held together by dominance with variety and can reflect a peaceful, tranquil state or may be arranged through contrast for a dramatic exciting mood. Line work can be very expressive and imitate the sound of notes played on instruments. *The Flute Player* by Judith Layster illustrates dominant and subdominant themes in art. The dominant theme is the boy playing the flute. The subdominant theme is the display of musical instruments in the background. (Dominant and subdominant themes can be identified from most paintings available to the instructor.)

Likewise, in music we think of a piece as harmonious or dissonant through the arrangement of its structure. Musicians consider such terms as melody, rhythm, harmony, or mood. Compositions consist of a dominant theme (the main melody) with a subdominant theme repeated with variations on those themes. Arrangements can create emotional responses depending on the tempo, the tone, and the movements in their design.

It is also possible for an artist to express feelings with paint and brushes in response to listening to music. Creativity is enhanced by the stimulation of a variety of musical sounds. Natural sounds in the environment can be inspirational such as ocean waves, water cascading over rocks, rain and wind, singing birds, and many others. Many artists paint while listening to music. It puts them in a state of mind conducive to creativity.

Materials and Resources:

Guest musician/instruments, slides, projector, screen, audiotape or synthesizer, tape player, blank paper, grocery sacks, paper with squares indicating various moods, crayons, watercolor pigments, palettes, brushes, water. For extension, books, pictures, maps, instruments.

Model Lesson:
Daily Lesson Plans

Day Four

Topic: Triptychs/Illustrated Manuscripts   **Time:** 2 Hours

Purpose:
Students will differentiate between medieval art and Renaissance art, stating the importance of the rise of the humanities.

Generalizations:
Art—Medieval art contains brilliant, deep, strong, and intense colors mostly
        expressed in the forms of stained glass, mosaics, and enamels.
Social studies—Art in the medieval period was inspired by religion and supported
        by religious institutions in Europe and what is now called the Middle East.

Concepts:
Art—Illuminated manuscripts, mosaics, altarpieces
Social studies—Religious art; secular art; humanities

Objectives:
Knowledge:
  1. Students will describe art in the medieval period (e.g., mosaics, altarpieces,
     triptychs, diptychs, stained glass, and manuscript illumination).
  2. Students will explain the relationship between art and religion in the medieval
     period.
  3. Students will contrast medieval art to art that flourished during the Renaissance,
     characterizing the growth of the humanities.

Application:
  4. Students will create an altarpiece and manuscript illumination, for example,
     decorated letter.

Procedure:
Introduction: Teacher explains the role of art during the medieval period, A.D. 350–
A.D. 1400, emphasizing the influence of religion and religious institutions.

Content Focus: With supplementary resources (see Bibliography and Background
Information) teacher explains triptychs, diptychs, mosaics, altarpieces, stained
glass, and manuscript illumination, providing illustrations. Show a map of Europe
and the Middle East during the medieval period, pointing out places when referred
to, for example, Spain, Germany, Italy, Jerusalem. Discuss Petrarch and the rise of
the humanities.

Demonstration and Activity: Teacher demonstrates how to paint an altarpiece and cut
it out. Copies of altarpieces or books are distributed to students so that they can get
ideas for the details. Students create, cut out and fold altarpiece so that it will stand
up. Teacher demonstrates decorated letter and margins. Provide models of cinquains.
Students write phrase or cinquains to go with decorated letter and margins. Students
draw, then paint.

Closure: Students share either their altarpiece or letter, with prose. Ask students to recall examples of art created during the Medieval Period and explain the rise of the humanities.

Evaluation:

Formative: listening skills; following directions; creation of altarpiece and letter, closure

Summative: altarpiece, decorated letters, decorated margins, and prose

Background Information:

MANUSCRIPT ILLUMINATION AND ALTARPIECES

Art of the medieval period, A.D. 350–A.D. 1400, contained brilliant, deep, strong, and intense colors mostly expressed in the forms of stained glass, mosaics, and enamels. These rich colors were used in the field of manuscript illumination (today we say book illustration) and altarpieces in the shape of triptychs (three panels). Medieval art encompasses the Imperial, Carolingian, Ottonian, Byzantine, and ultimately the Romanesque styles.

BOOK COVERS AND MANUSCRIPTS

Before Gutenberg of Germany developed movable type for printed books in 1450, books were handwritten. Monks living in church monasteries copied manuscripts of the Gospels and were the artists who created beautiful Carolingian script writing (today called Roman script), as well as decorative illustrated pages. Emperor Charlemagne (King Charles I of the new Roman Empire) in Aachen, Germany, sponsored the collecting and copying of ancient Roman literature to preserve the classics. A book of Gospels presented to Emperor Charlemagne had large initials, sometimes filling a whole page, consisting of elegant, foliate (leafy) scrolls, interlaced in silver and gold against intensely bright blue, green, and purple backgrounds.

The Gospel Book of Otto III, produced probably about A.D. 900, now in the Cathedral Treasury at Aachen, refers to St. Augustine's commentary on Psalm 90—the "imperial" Psalm par excellence—and illustrates a loftier concept of government by Divine Right. Emperor Otto combined the rule of emperor and the pope, stating the emperor was Christ on earth. The covers of these books were sometimes carved ivory, or gold plates covered with pearls and precious stones, or bright enamels on sheets of copper. Enamels are created with a translucent glaze over intensely colored metal.

STAINED-GLASS WINDOWS

Theophilus in the twelfth century knew recipes for colored glass that went back before his time, which were secrets from the late Roman glass makers of the Rhineland

(Germany). Small pieces of stained glass were arranged between strips of lead to form pictures and patterns, which were then placed as windows in cathedrals. Notre Dame Cathedral, Paris, built A.D. 1163–1250 has the famous Rose Window. Another rose window is in the Chartres Cathedral, France, built in A.D. 1180.

MOSAICS

Mosaic decoration was used after the rise of Islam, with Byzantine assistance, in the Dome of the Rock at Jerusalem in A.D. 691. The entire scheme of decoration reflects that of Solomon's Temple. The Ark of the Covenant was the sole decoration in the earliest Jewish Bibles dating from the tenth century. These were influenced by the early Spanish Jewish Bibles. Mosaic decoration at Germany-des-Pres represents a form of iconoclast art largely Jewish in inspiration (ninth century).

TRIPTYCH AND DIPTYCH PAINTINGS

The altars of cathedrals built during this period were furnished with artifacts and religious relics brought from Rome. Some altarpieces were painted on three panels of gold-leafed wood and called triptychs. The center panel was larger and the "wings" were made to fold over the center to close it. The images painted on these altarpieces were in small sections. Angels, monks, the Crucifixion, evangelists, symbols of the sun and moon, crowns, scenes from the Book of Genesis, saints, and apostles were painted to form part of the design.

Gospel manuscripts, about A.D. 1000, presented to the Emperor Otto III lavishly illustrated scenes telling religious stories. When divided in two parts, half the scene on one page, half on another, the architectural framework was called a diptych. Today the triptych and diptych formats are used for paintings showing a wide view of one scene or three different compositions, all relating to each other.

THE HUMANITIES

In A.D. 1046 the power of the Church increased and overcame the secular authority. The medieval period gradually ended and by the fourteenth century the Renaissance (rebirth) began. Readiness to question traditional beliefs and practices was characteristic of the Renaissance. The origin of this "New Age" labeled a "rebirth" can be traced back to the 1330s in the writings of the Italian poet Petrarch, the first of the great Renaissance men. Humanism, to Petrarch, meant a belief in the importance of what we call "the humanities" or "humane letters" (rather than the study of Divine letters or Scriptures); that is, the pursuit of learning in languages, literature, history, and philosophy for its own end, in a secular rather than religious framework.

Materials and Resources:

Books: Beckwith (1964); Janson (1970); Kidson (1967)
Medieval art painting supplies: copies of examples, watercolor pigments, palettes, paper, painting boards, water containers, scissors

MODEL LESSON: DAILY LESSON PLANS

DAY FIVE

Topic: Impressionism   **Time:** 2 Hours

Purpose:
Students will identify impressionistic art as a form of innovative expression that altered the art world.

Generalizations:
Art—Impressionist artists paint what they see, not what is imagined, remembered, or invented.

Social studies—Innovative expression requires a break from tradition.

Concepts:
Art—impressionism; "en plein air"

Social studies—innovative expression

Objectives:
Knowledge:
1. Students will give the characteristics of impressionistic art.
2. Students will describe Claude Monet or Mary Cassatt based on the five social foundations of artistic ability.
3. Students will compare and contrast the lives of previously studied artists with Monet.

Application:
4. Students will paint an Impressionist painting "en plein air."

Procedure:
Introduction: Create a context for the evolution of Impressionism by showing students pictures of art that was acclaimed by the Salon prior to 1865.

Content Focus: Using illustrations from books, give a biographical sketch of Claude Monet (if male) or Mary Cassett (if female). Recount events of life by dressing up as character and acting in first person. See Background Information for details and definitions of concepts and generalizations. After asking students to explain the social foundations of Monet's or Cassatt's artistic ability, ask them to compare and contrast the lives of previously studied artists (e.g., Masterfield and Picasso).

Demonstration and Activity: Take students to a location that includes water, flowers, and trees, if possible. A bridge would be a nice addition to simulate Monet's Japanese bridge in Giverny. Demonstrate Impressionist painting. Paint is applied to the canvas in small touches; strokes of color laid side by side or overlapping, like a patchwork, rather than large flat washes of color. Students then paint.

Closure: One at a time, ask students to hold up their paintings; point out positive features on each one (e.g., reflections picked up in water, different shades of green, shadows, etc.). Ask students to summarize the characteristics of impressionistic art.

Evaluation:

Formative: listening skills; following directions; creation of Impressionist painting.

Summative: Impressionist painting.

Background Information:

IMPRESSIONISM

Impressionists were a group of painters who worked outdoors and painted what they saw in nature between the years 1865 and 1890. Their method of painting was to first look directly at their subject, then paint exactly what they saw. Impressionism is paint applied to the canvas in small touches; strokes of color are laid side by side or overlapping, like a patchwork, rather than large flat washes of color. The subject must be seen, not imagined, remembered, or invented; seen as a whole without recomposing or changing. The artists paint the actual world they live in—the scenes, people, and landscapes they know. Color is closely observed, especially the colors in shade and shadows and the effects of sunlight on trees, water, all things in nature as well as sunlight cast on people, their clothes, and surroundings.

Impressionism is loosely defined as any picture of everyday life painted with reference to outdoor light, or with a broken touch.

> When you go out to paint, try to forget what objects you have in front of you, a tree, a field . . . merely think, here is a little square of blue, here is an oblong of pink, here a streak of yellow, and paint it just as it looks to you, the exact color and shape, until it gives your own naive impression of the scene." (Claude Monet)

Around the turn of the century, the Impressionists would exhibit their paintings just as they were painted "en plein air" (outdoors in the open air) without finishing them in their studios. This created a lot of controversy because the artists using traditional methods, such as glazing with thin layers of paint, thought these new paintings looked like unfinished sketches. The originators of this new approach of handling the pigments with freshness and rich pure color were Claude Monet, Auguste Renoir, Alfred Sisley, and Camille Pissaro. Other artists at that time who painted in the Impressionist style were Paul Cezanne, Edouard Manet, and Pierre Auguste Degas; however, their work included traditional studio painting as well.

Claude Monet forged his own unique artistic style that expressed his challenge to the traditional art of the period. In 1874 he organized the first Impressionist exhibition that included such painters as Pissaro, Renoir, Degas, and Sisley. He also participated in three other independent shows throughout the decade, reinforcing his independence and confidence in his art. Monet's art reflected the changing social conditions occurring in France during the middle to late 1800s. He chose his subjects to paint from the everyday scenes he saw around him. He captured the progress of French industrialization in *The Train, The Path through the Vineyard,* and countless other paintings that included scenes of factories and other more modern elements.

Monet stood to paint all his life until extreme old age. He never said that a picture was finished. He was in the habit of leaving the edges of canvases unpainted and they were often not filled in until he came to sign the picture. He had great physical vigor and appetite for work, but also suffered from extreme depression about his painting and destroyed more of his own work than any other of the great nineteenth-century painters.

Monet had the habit of working in series, showing the same subject under various conditions of light and atmosphere. Poplars, cathedrals, and water lilies were painted only when the light was exactly right, "until the sunlight left a certain leaf"—then he took out the next canvas and worked on that. In that way he was not tempted to overwork or alter an individual canvas because the others were waiting their turn.

One of Monet's major early works, *Women in the Garden/Femmes au Jardin,* over eight feet tall, was painted entirely out of doors. To reach the top of the canvas he had a trench dug in the garden so the canvas could be lowered by a system of pulleys. Obviously it was not possible to paint on this size canvas with the small brush stroke, *le petit tache.* Vigorous strokes were applied solidly, with directness and simplicity of touch.

The paint quality in another of Monet's great large-scale works, painted toward the end of his life, the *Water Lilies/Nympheas,* is totally different. The paint is dragged, scumbled, or loaded onto the canvas with careless virtuosity; touch after touch is superimposed; sometimes long brush strokes over dry paint in such a way as to pick up new color on the raised surface of the dry impasto, giving a broken, crumbled appearance.

TIME LINE OF CLAUDE MONET'S LIFE*

1840   Born in Paris on November 14
1846   Moves to LeHavre with parents
1859   Travels to Paris to study painting
1867   Monet and Camille's son, Jean, is born
1870   Monet and Camille get married
1877   Earnest Hochede flees to Belgium; Jean-Pierre is born
1878   Monet, Camille, Alice, and the children rent a summer house in Vetheuil; Michel is born
1879   Camille dies; Alice takes care of eight children
1883   Monet rents the house at Giverny
1890   Monet can finally afford to buy the house
1891   Ernest Hochede dies and is buried in Giverny
1892   Alice and Monet get married
1893   Monet buys the land for the lily pond
1897   Blanche and Jean get married
1900   Theodore Butler remarries
1908   Monet's sight becomes worse
1911   Alice dies on May 19
1914   Jean dies. World War I begins
1916   The large studio is ready; Monet begins to work on the water lilies
1921   Monet's sight becomes worse
1923   Monet is operated on for cataracts
1926   The water lily paintings are finished; Monet dies on December 5

*Bjork & Anderson, 1985, p. 53

Born in 1844, Mary Cassatt lived during a time when it was unusual for women to think and speak strongly about issues. Despite these social expectations, Cassatt was a strong, opinionated, and intelligent person. She earned a reputation as an artist who painted for herself rather than to please the public. In 1877 she accepted an invitation to display her work with Edgar Degas and a group of independent painters who were dedicated to expressing themselves through their art without being confined by external boundaries. Later this group became known as Impressionists.

Although she spent the majority of her life in France, she never fully integrated into French society or the artistic circles there. She preferred a few close friends to many and often had trouble maintaining friendships because she easily offended others with her strong opinions. Perhaps Mary Cassatt's independent disposition contributed to her success in breaking away from traditional role expectations for women.

TIME LINE OF MARY CASSATT'S LIFE

1844	Mary Cassatt is born in Allegheny City, Pennsylvania, on May 22
1851–1855	Cassatt and family live in Europe
1860	Cassatt enrolls in Pennsylvania Academy of Fine Arts
1866	Cassatt moves to Paris; studies painting
1870	Cassatt returns to America
1871	Travels to Chicago where much of her work is destroyed by Great Chicago fire
	Returns to Europe and settles in Parma, Italy
1872	Travels in Spain
1874	Moves to Paris
1877	Accepts Edgar Degas's invitation to join the Impressionists
1879	Cassatt's first exhibition with the Impressionists
1880	First of mother/child paintings
1882	Lydia Cassatt, Mary's sister, dies
	Cassatt boycotts Impressionists in response to their refusal to include several newcomers
1886	Final Impressionist show
1891	Cassatt's first solo exhibition
1894	Cassatt buys home in countryside—"Chateau de Beaufresne"
1895	Katherine Cassatt, Mary's mother, dies
1898	Extended visit to the United States begins
1901	Travels through Italy and Spain
1904	Named to French Legion of Honor
1908–1909	Revisits the United States and becomes active in Women's Suffrage Movement
1910–1911	Cassatt travels in Egypt
	Gardner Cassatt, Mary's brother, dies; Mary's health begins to deteriorate
1915	Cassatt ends her work due to failing eyesight
1926	Dies at age 82 at Chateau de Beaufresne on June 14

Materials and Resources:

Books: Bjork & Anderson (1985); Mount (1966)

Impressionist painting supplies: watercolor pigments, palettes, paper, painting
        boards, rags, water containers, brushes.

Subject for painting: Outdoor scene, preferably with pond, lake, stream,
        or river.

MODEL LESSON: DAILY LESSON PLANS

DAY SIX

Topic: American Folk Art   **Time:** 2 Hours

Purpose:

Students will recognize quiltmaking as a long-standing artform that has been adapted
to a variety of cultural contexts and social issues.

Generalizations:

Art—Quilts express life experiences and ideas of the artist.

Social studies—Quiltmaking can result in social statements that bind people
        together.

Concepts:

Art—quilting

Social studies—ethnic heritage; social unity

Objectives:

Knowledge:

1. Students will recall the meaning of quilts in historical and contemporary
   contexts.
2. Students will listen to *Tar Beach,* an autobiographical account of the quiltmaker
   Faith Ringgold.

Application:

3. Students will create quilt patterns and transfer them to computer applications.

Procedure:

Introduction: Display several quilts and books with pictures of quilt patterns.
Point out the variation in design as well as the meanings of the patterns.

Content Focus: With books as props, present the history of quiltmaking as outlined
in Background Information. To bring discussion up-to-date, show video of AIDS
quilt and emphasize how quiltmaking has provided a means for people to come together in their fight for freedom (e.g., Underground Railroad) or their need to grieve
the loss of loved ones (AIDS quilt). Show students the June 1993 issue of the *Quilt-
ers Newsletter Magazine,* which features an article by Marie Shirer, "Kids Make
Quilts, Too!" Point out that the students who made quilts created designs that had per-

sonal meaning. Read *Tar Beach,* which chronicles Faith Ringgold's life and the personal meaning that she puts into her quilts.

Demonstration and Activity: Demonstrate geometric quilt designs with the use of a compass and ruler on an 8½ × 11 sheet of paper. Talk about the primary patterns and the secondary patterns that emerge in the corners if four sheets of the same pattern are put together. Ask students to create their own design; color; then put on computer. Aldus Super Paint, Escher Sketch, and MacPaint are computer programs that work well for this activity. Geometric designs lend themselves well to computer applications. However, if students would prefer to create more abstract images or landscapes, for example, encourage their creativity. Even though a total quilt image may not be able to be depicted on a computer screen as readily, the exercise of creating other images may lead to larger representations if lessons on scale are provided.

Closure: Ask students to name quiltmakers and describe the events in their lives that influenced their designs. Ask students to outline the social foundations of artistic ability with regard to Faith Ringgold. Ask students to explain how quilts served as a means to unite people.

Extensions:

Create a class quilt by having students collectively decide on a theme and design. Quilt could be made from fabric, on computer, or with squares made out of paper.

Evaluation:

Formative: listening skills; following directions; use of compass

Summative: quilt designs

Background Information:

QUILTS

Quilts have been created by generations of American women since homes were first established in the seventeenth century; however, Americans didn't invent quilting. There is evidence that quilting was done in ancient Greece, India, and China. By the eleventh century, quilting had spread throughout Europe. When colonists arrived in the Western Hemisphere, they brought along not only quilts as family heirlooms, but quilting techniques. The oldest quilt in America is a McCord quilt dated 1726. It wasn't until the late eighteenth century that needlework achieved hobby status, yet even then it was never just a creative outlet, it was a woman's occupation.

With the gradually increasing quality of life, imported cloth arriving more frequently, and goods becoming cheaper, piecing and block-style quilting started in America in the mid-1700s. Pioneers traveled inland carrying printed textiles in specially designed wagons with flaps on the sides to protect and display the bolts of cloth. The country women in small towns and villages, where few patterns existed and materials were limited, depended on their memories and imaginations for original designs, using pleasing combinations of lines, masses, and colors.

To appreciate quilts, it is necessary to understand their connection to the lives of their makers. Quilts are much more than just bed covering providing warmth and comfort. A quiltmaker can display her or his talents with color, original designs, needlework skills, and expression of life experiences and ideas. Some of the

© Bob Daemmrich/Stock Boston

early-nineteenth-century quilt patterns are representative of our country's history and the pioneers who lived it. These patterns depict settling the wilderness, as well as the tragedy of a country divided by the Civil War. Block patterns with historical significance include: Underground Railroad, Lincoln's Platform, Sherman's March, Union, Log Cabin, Women's Christian Temperance Union, Centennial, Our Country, Lewis and Clark, Dolly Madison Star, Clays Choice, Yankee Puzzle, Navajo, and Rail Fence.

Women who traveled west in covered wagons took quilts along, made them on the trail ride, and continued to sew them while getting settled in their new surroundings. Quilts were treasures on the journeys to offer peace, security, and cultural identity when travelers were faced with exhaustion, isolation, illness, and death in the unknown territories. Women shared this coveted aspect of their lives by exchanging quilt patterns and fabrics.

Quilts were used as decorative items in covered wagons and tents, creating a homelike setting. They lined the walls of wagons to insulate against cold weather and served as privacy barriers to wall off sleeping and dressing areas. Quilts were used as money and traded for much needed supplies. One quilt could pay to travel through the Barlow Toll Road on Mount Hood in Oregon, part of the Oregon Trail. They were traded for horses, canoes, and food on the wagon trails to the West.

Quilting bees date from colonial days and are another purely American tradition that continues to the present. Bees were different in colonial and pioneer days. During these periods, quilting bees were family and community events involving women, men, boys, and girls. Guests arrived early, admired the quilt top, and set to work attaching it to the quilt frame. They spent the rest of the day talking and quilting. Husbands and boyfriends were invited to supper and they came in their Sunday-best clothes. After supper, everyone stayed for talk, games, and dancing. Bees were also part of courtship. One superstition was for young men and women to hold the completed quilts while a cat was placed in the center. Whoever the cat jumped over to get off the quilt would be the next of the group to get married. Sometimes a betrothed man might design a quilt for his bride-to-be to make for their new home. Usually a quilting bee consisted of eight women, two on each side of the quilt, their heads bent over the job, talking and sharing details of their lives. They would work in shifts, alternating between quilting and preparing the evening meal until the stitching was completed.

Today's quilt guilds and clubs are the natural evolution of the colonial quilting bee. They further education on techniques, share patterns and fabrics, talk, laugh, and gather together in social context. But rarely does the group meet to finish another member's quilt unless it is a fund-raising project.

The Great Depression saw many quilts made from the printed cloth of feed bags, flour sacks, and inexpensive cottons. Some Depression-era quilts were used to pay debts in lieu of cash—some even to meet tithing pledges at church. This was the era of Sunbonnet Sue, Scotty Dogs, Airplanes, Double Wedding Ring, Grandmother's Fan, and Dresden Plate. Factory-made blankets were not in general use until the late 1800s and early 1900s.

As a nation, we have been slow to recognize and appreciate our ancestors' great accomplishments in the decorative arts. It wasn't until 1924, with the opening of the American Wing at the Metropolitan Museum of Art in New York, that major display space in a museum was given to collections of textiles such as quilts.

The art of quilting today is very advanced and sophisticated. It also is great fun and lets one be very creative. The quilting guilds have national juried exhibits with many categories to enter, such as: pictorial, abstract, traditional, wall-hangings, hand-pieced, wearable art, appliqué, machine quilted, and geometrics to name a few. The AIDS quilt is also an example of ways in which community spirit is captured through quiltmaking.

Materials and Resources:
Books: Ringgold, F. (1991, 1992). *Common threads: Stories from the quilt*
     (Friedman & Epstein, 1989) [video].
Quiltmaking supplies: compasses, rulers, markers, computer, computer software:
     Aldus Super Paint 3.0, Silicon Beach Software Inc.; Escher Sketch 1.4;
     MacPaint 2.0, Claris Corporation.

Extension:
"Geometry Through Art," on the Internet, is another way to access and create visual art through the use of technology (http://forum.swarthmore.edu/~sarah/shapiro/).

Model Lesson: Daily Lesson Plans

Day Seven

Topic: Russian Art and Juvenile Literature   **Time:** 2 Hours

Purpose:
Students will gain an appreciation for Russian works of art.

Generalizations:
Art—Artistic imagination can create fantasy beasts and inspire literature.
Social studies—A culture's folklore often survives temporary political regimes.

Concepts:
Art—fantasy beasts
Social studies—freedom of expression

Objectives:
Knowledge:
1. Students will identify Russian artforms, naming one Russian artist.

Application:
2. Students will write a folktale featuring a fantasy beast of their own creation.

Procedure:
Introduction: Ask students if they can recall recent events in Russia. Review perestroika and show maps of the Soviet Union and Russia before and after 1989.

Content Focus: Provide a brief history of Russian art, showing pictures featuring Fabergé's eggs and other Russian works of art. See Background Information. Show elaborately illustrated Russian folktales, which typically include Baba Yaga. The *Time-Life* books are a great source for inspirational models of fantasy beasts. Discuss the importance of preserving works of art and literature as a means of preserving the history of one's culture. Emphasize the importance of having the freedom to express oneself through art, music, literature, and religion. Freedom of expression allows one to create new images of the world both realistic and imaginary. Encourage students to think about designing their own fantasy beast and story explaining its role. Review some of the themes in folktales such as: good triumphs over evil; unselfish love conquers; justice triumphs; kindness, diligence, and hard work bring rewards. Additional themes include: explanations for natural disasters, sibling rivalry, accomplishing challenging feats, and trickery. Motifs in folktales include supernatural beings; extraordinary animals; magical objects, powers, and transformations.

Demonstration and Activity: Students create fantasy beasts using pencil first, then watercolor. For homework or during another class period, students write stories featuring fantasy beasts.

Closure (Next Day): Students share stories and pictures of fantasy beasts with peers and/or parents.

Evaluation:

Formative: listening skills, following directions, creation of fantasy beasts

Summative: fantasy beast and stories

Background Information:

THE ARTS OF RUSSIA

After World War I when Russia became a communist nation, the arts were suppressed. Most of the art was government controlled. Then, during the World War II, the national art treasures were hidden away for protection; at that time, many freedoms of expression such as art, literature, and religion were banned.

Today, with the new political changes in the countries of the former Soviet Union, a wave of renewal through "perestroika" (peaceful coexistence) has aroused the complex network of Russian republics. The process of learning new forms of organizing social, political, economic, and cultural life is ongoing. Art teachers can study and teach about other artists besides Russians, and study schools of painting other than realism.

After a recent visit to Russia, the Citizen Ambassador People-to-People group shared reports from professional Russian colleagues and counterparts in the arts and humanities. People from the various republics discussed "changes in the curriculum at both school and university levels, . . . intellectual freedom heretofore never experienced by many teachers; [how] . . . ingenious methods by which Communist-banned library materials and visual artifacts, now accessible to the public, were secretly preserved for decades."[1] Now, not only artists but everyone will benefit from the open exchange of ideas and cultural arts between new Soviet nations and other countries.

The Hermitage, the national museum in St. Petersburg, Russia, was formerly a winter palace for the czars. It was Catherine the Great, the last reigning czarina, who began an impressive collection of master works in 1764. However, she considered her possessions only for herself and her court. Not until 1850 were any visitors allowed, the only exceptions being a few art lovers, foreign visitors, and teachers and students of the Academy of Arts.

In 1778, Catherine the Great commissioned artist Christopher Unterberger to copy the Vatican Paintings by Raphael, the celebrated *Loggias.* It took ten years before the canvasses were mounted in the new building at the Hermitage. This was a significant event in the cultural life of Russian society at the time, 1788.

After the October Revolution of 1917, Lenin's Council of Peoples' Commissars issued a decree protecting art and antique relics. Huge private collections were nationalized and brought to the Hermitage. Today, the museum collection consists of three million pieces in 353 rooms occupying five buildings. The six departments are Prehistoric Culture, Art of Classical Antiquity, Art of the Peoples of the East, Western European Art, Russian Culture, and Numismatics (coins and medals).

---

[1]Correspondence to Dr. Victor Herbert, Superintendent of Phoenix Union High School District, from Catherine R. Gira, President, Delegation Leader, Citizen Ambassador People-to-People, Frostburg State University, Maryland, November 20, 1992.

The Department of Russian Culture traces Russian artistic development over fifteen hundred years, from the sixth to twentieth century. Russian fresco paintings were uncovered on the walls of the Church of the Intercession in Pskov dating back to the mid–fourteenth century. Examples of fifteenth-century applied arts include needlework and engraved gold and silver items. New entries come from archaeological excavations, which began in 1948, as well as folk art. Folk art includes household items executed with great care and artistry, such as portable lanterns, drinking vessels, tin and copper utensils, caskets, and printed calicos. Icons, pottery, wood carvings, and folk costumes are included.

Unique to Russia is the technique produced by seventeenth-century craftsmen of Solvychegodsk: various silver and copper bowls, goblets, and bottles entirely covered with vivid ornamentation in painted enamel. Russian scientist Mikhail Lomonosov (1711–1765), invented a new method of coloring glass with a richness of color not seen before. He also founded Moscow University in 1755. Another process unique to Russian craftsmen is nielloed silver—a process to decorate the surface of silver.

The second half of the nineteenth century and early twentieth is represented by the works of whole families of well-known masters such as Fabergé, using semi-precious stones from the Urals and Siberia and colored enamels. The Tula craftsmen produced a decorative effect in their wares by combining silver, polished to a mirror sheen, with gilt bronze. Often they covered their articles with hundreds of cut steel "heads" faceted like diamonds and polished to resemble sparkling gems. Many works of Russian art have been exhibited in museums of France, Japan, Finland, the United States, and Germany.

FANTASY BEASTS

While art appreciation has experienced political ups and downs throughout Russia's history, children's literature has perhaps followed a more stable path. Baba Yaga and other fantasy characters inspire young and old.

The creation of the "fantasy beast" is exciting and motivating for most students. Students should be allowed sufficient time to fabricate the beasts' physical appearance, special powers, personality, history, language, and name before having to place it in the context of a story or specific role. Students develop a sense of ownership as they alter and add characteristics to their magical being.

Through such in-depth character development, students are allowed freedom to express themselves in a unique and inspiring manner. Most children are fascinated with the world of the supernatural. The imaginary world is full of curiosities and questions that students may answer using their interpretative creativity. The creation of the fantasy beasts serves as a springboard for creative writing, drama, and music activities incorporating themes common to folktales around the world. Having poured so much of oneself into the development of the beast, stories become more personal, more detailed, and, in a sense, more real.

Materials and Resources:

Books: *The Enchanted World of Magical Beasts* (1985) Time-Life Books, vol. 7.
          Alexandria, VA.
Supplies: pencils, watercolors

Extensions:

Students can share their stories with children in the primary grades either orally or through the creation of a puppet show, turning their fantasy beast into a puppet with accompanying characters.

MODEL LESSON: DAILY LESSON PLANS

DAY EIGHT

Topic: Mandalas   **Time:** 2 Hours

Purpose:

Students will recognize the importance of symbols as a means of transmitting culture.

Generalizations:

Art—The mandala is a universal symbol of integration, harmony, and
      transformation.

Social studies—Many cultures create folklore that places their way of life in the
      center of the universe.

Concepts:

Art—mandala

Social studies—universal symbols

Objectives:

Knowledge:

  1. Students will describe mandalas from a variety of cultures.

Application:

  2. Students will create their own mandala.

Procedure:

Introduction: On overhead projector provide students with traditional symbols that were placed on shingles to signify activities within certain buildings. For example, a shoemaker would have a picture of a shoe, and blacksmith might have a horseshoe, and a hat might signify a millinery store. Divide students into groups and provide them with more contemporary symbols, asking if they can identify their meaning.

Content Focus: Define a mandala as a universal symbol of integration, harmony, and transformation. Provide several examples from a variety of cultures, explaining the significance for each culture. See Background Information.

Demonstration and Activity: Demonstrate how to make a mandala. On a 12″ × 12″ sheet of paper, draw a circle with a compass (or trace around a cardboard circle). Create geometric spaces by superimposing triangles and other shapes. Tell students that each space can include a symbol of something in their life that has personal meaning. Favorite activities, events, celebrations, and accomplishments are just some of the sources for symbols. In addition to symbols that may be obvious to an observer, students can create a symbol that has meaning to the creator only and that no one else will understand. Emphasize that the mandala is a means of defining one's identity and expressing future goals and aspirations; hence, the mandala can also represent transformation. Students then create mandalas.

Closure: Students share their mandalas explaining self-selected symbols. Close by saying that the mandala activity is something that can be repeated by individuals in any cultural context. The form may vary, but the act of defining one's identity in relation to others is a universal process.

Evaluation:
Formative: listening skills, following directions, creating mandala

Summative: mandalas

Background Information:
The mandala is a universal symbol of integration, harmony, and transformation. No two mandalas are ever the same, for each represents a unique integration of worship, knowledge, and beauty. In ancient artforms they are called "Sun Wheels." They appear in rock engravings that date back to the neolithic epoch before the wheel was invented. *Mandala* is the Sanskrit (Hindu language in India) word for circle, a circle that is designed with symbols so it has meaning and order. Mandalas can be drawn, painted, danced, or shaped into three-dimensional form. In a very elaborate Buddhist mandala, for example, there is the deity (God) in the center as the power source. The outside images would be the high ideals or goals to strive for to live an honorable life.

Many cultures create folklore that places their way of life in the center of the cosmos. The Chinese used to say that China was Kingdom of the Center, and the Aztecs had a similar saying. The Navajo Indians in America conduct healing ceremonies through sand paintings that are mandalas on the ground. The sand painting must be circled by the patient before entering. The person to be treated moves into the mandala as a way of moving into a symbol of power. He or she becomes the center on which the healing power is focused. A Navajo sand painting also can show the history of Navajo beliefs, such as the story of Coyote, who stole fire from the Gods and gave it to humans.

The use of mandalas for meditation and healing is also used in Tibet. Tibetan monks practice sand painting, drawing cosmic images (moon, sun, and stars) to represent spiritual powers that influence their lives. It helps to center their thinking on God and brings order to their daily living. The symbols used are imagined to have spiritual powers. These powers inspire them to accomplish perfection in what they do and reach total harmony and renewal of the soul.

The circle is used in designs of buildings (domes), gardens (paths and plantings), plans of cities (Washington, D.C., Paris, and Rome), calendar stones of the Aztecs, Indian shields, and wedding rings as circular symbols of marriage. The word *sym-bol* means two things put together.

The mandala motif generally symbolizes a natural wholeness. The round table is a well-known symbol of wholeness and plays a role in mythology, such as King Arthur's round table, which itself is an image derived from the Last Supper. (The original depiction of the Last Supper was a round table; da Vinci painted his interpretation of the Last Supper lengthwise.) Abstract mandalas also appear in European Christian art. Some of the best examples are the rose windows in cathedrals. These are representations of the Self of humankind transposed onto the cosmic plane. Notre Dame in Paris and Chartres Cathedral have stained-glass rose windows in the form of mandalas.

In the visual art of India and the Far East, the four- or eight-rayed circle is the usual pattern of the religious images that serve as instruments of meditation. Some are purely geometrical in design and are called yantras. In addition to the circle, a very common yantra is formed by two interpenetrating triangles (one pointing up, the other down). It expresses the union of opposites—the union of the soul with God—or the wholeness of the psyche or Self. In the Zen sect the circle represents enlightenment and symbolizes human perfection.

To set the creative stage for student inspiration, tell them: You are the center of your own life. When working out a mandala try to organize your personal circle showing different value systems in your life. Draw a circle, then think of your life—your values, your interests, the goals you are reaching for, the things that bring you happiness. Then compose them and try to find a central theme. What is the central most thought, activity, or influence in your life. This is a discipline for pulling all those scattered aspects of your life together, bringing order to your experiences, finding a focus and orienting yourself to it, coordinating your thoughts and actions. The symbols you use can be personal and have meaning only to you. Your symbols, therefore, should be your own designs.

Materials and Resources:
Supplies for making mandalas: compasses or cardboard circle for tracing; watercolors, or markers; rulers

---

MODEL LESSON: DAILY LESSON PLANS

DAY NINE

Topic: Gyotaku   **Time:** 2 Hours

Purpose:
Students will recognize gyotaku as an Asian artform that has functional origins.

Generalizations:
Social studies—The function of artforms is dependent on their cultural context.
Science—Fins and scales enable fish to survive in water.

Concepts:
Art—gyotaku (fish printing)
Social studies—economic value
Science—fish anatomy

Objectives:
Knowledge:
1. Students will explain the Asia origins of gyotaku.
2. Students will explain the functions of fish fins and scales.

Application:
3. Students will create fish print (gyotaku).

Procedure:
Introduction: Hold up fish print and ask students if they know where fish printing originated. After telling them the answer (if no one knows), ask students to explain the original purpose of fish printing.

Content Focus: Explain the history of fish printing. Show several examples of gyotaku from books. Explain the function of the fins and scales of a fish. See Background Information.

Demonstration and Activity: Demonstrate gyotaku technique.
1. Wearing gloves, wash fish with detergent to remove mucus. Dry with paper towels.
2. Place the fish on the foam board and put it in the foil-covered box. Put paper towels under the fish to absorb any fluids. Spread out the fins, put small pieces of foam board underneath them, and pin in position.
3. Paint the fish with 2 or 3 different colored inks, brush strokes going with the scales, starting at the mouth, jaw and eye region. Move toward the tail. Do the fins and tail last since they dry the fastest.
4. Spray rice paper with a fine mist to make it pliable.
5. Press paper on fish with fingers starting with mouth, jaw and eye region, moving slowly to tail, pressing top and bottom alternately. This will imprint the scales and fins. Do this only once to avoid double images.
6. Gently pull paper off from head to tail.
7. Hang to dry. Re-create the eye with watercolor and a fine brush.

To make a shadow print on the same sheet of paper, cut a template of the fish and tape it over the first image. Then reposition the paper and print a second time, immediately after the first printing.

The fish then can be repainted with other colors and another print can be printed from the same fish on a new piece of rice paper.

Closure: Ask students to recall the origins of gyotaku. Ask them to share their fish prints and explain the functions of fish fins and scales.

Evaluation:
Formative: listening skills; following directions; fish printing technique

Summative: fish prints

Background Information:
Gyotaku is the Japanese word for "fish rubbing," a procedure by which the features and details of a fish are reproduced on paper by rubbing and dabbing. Gyotaku originated in Japan and has been practiced there for more than two hundred years. Fish printing in Japan is a highly refined artform. There are rules for placement, composition, color, and even for the printer's signature. The Japanese fish printer is bound to

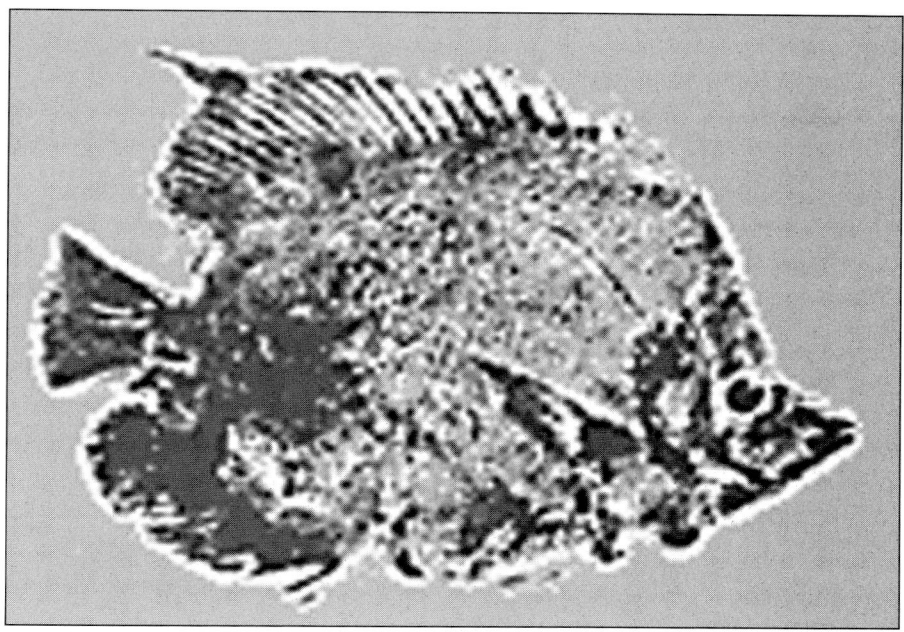

© Waikiki Aquarium

centuries of tradition that have set the standards for the art. In the West, however, it is called nature printing and no traditions have been set. It is treated as a new artform and artists are using new materials and techniques, creating images that combine the best of both nature and art.

The difference between the Japanese indirect method and the Western direct method is that in Japan a thin wet paper is molded to the fish first. When dry, ink is applied to the paper in a dabbing motion with silk-covered pieces of cotton called "tampos." Then the paper is pulled off. In the West, the ink or watercolor is painted directly on the fish first, then the misted paper is placed on the fish and pressed with the fingers to transfer the ink, then gently peeled off. This direct method is a result of nature printing techniques that have developed in Europe over the last five centuries.

There are many reasons to print fish besides an innovative art medium. Fish printing is used by a biologist to reproduce in detail the external features of a fish specimen. To a fisherman, a print is evidence of a record catch or an alternative to taxidermy. Schoolteachers use it as a fun way to introduce students to fish anatomy and the creative process.

A fish print has all the elements found in other two-dimensional art—composition and balance, illusion of depth and volume, color and shading, and the interplay of color and shape. A good print must have clean sharp margins without distortion of the anatomical parts, good relief and detail reproduction and a lack of stain from fluids or blood.

Handmade Japanese paper with long fibers is best for this process because it has strength when wet and will conform to the shape of the fish. Large-scaled, rough-featured fish such as perch and sole, in good condition with no gaff marks and all the scales intact and no damage to the fins, should be used. Other selections could include bass, rock fish, salmon, and trout. Marine creatures such as shrimp, crab, lobster, octopus, starfish, seaweeds, coral, and shells also can be printed.

Watercolors, water-soluble inks, and the slower-drying oil-based inks are used for the painting process.

Materials and Resources:

Fish printing supplies: a gutted fish in perfect condition, at room temperature (suggested types: perch, sole, bass, or rockfish; small bluegills are nice); inks, water-soluble, such as Pelikan, Rotring, Higgins; bristle brushes, soft brushes, and a small fine-tipped brush for painting eyes; plastic gloves, dish detergent, paper towels, Sumi-E sketch paper (rice paper), clothespins for hanging print to dry; spray bottle, scissors, round-head pins, cardboard box (low sided) lined with foil, foam board used to mount fish, and several smaller pieces of foam board to position under the fins and tail.

Extensions:

Gyotaku designs can be made on T-shirts as well.

MODEL LESSON: DAILY LESSON PLANS

DAY TEN

Topic: Abstract/Naturalism   **Time:** 2 Hours

Purpose:

Students will appreciate abstract art as an artform that emits different reactions for different people.

Generalizations:

Art—Abstract art can be interpreted differently by the artist and the viewer.
Social studies—An artist's urge to create follows a lifelong journey.

Concepts:

Art—abstract
Social studies—biography

Objectives:

Knowledge:
1. Students will identify the characteristics of abstract art.
2. Students will identify the social foundations of artistic ability with regard to Georgia O'Keeffe.

Application:
3. Students will create an abstract painting, large floral painting, or a painting of a cow's skull.

Procedure:

Introduction: Teacher comes in dressed as Georgia O'Keeffe, all in black with black hat and white scarf, carrying a stick. Biographical sketch could be done as a monologue. However, since, by this time, students will have pursued the social foundations of artistic ability with several other artists, the teacher may instead ask students to ask questions about her life with the prompt: I know that you have been studying other artists besides me; what would you like to know about the events in my life that have influenced my artistic expression?

Content Focus: Provide biographical sketch of Georgia O'Keeffe. See Background Information. Use art books to show examples of abstract art, large florals, and cow's skulls.

Demonstration and Activity: Bring in flowers, for example, petunias for students to examine in detail. Demonstrate the painting technique of making very large flowers. Provide other examples of O'Keeffe's work through pictures in books. If possible, bring in cow's skull! Students create their own painting.

Closure: Ask students to share their artwork. Ask students to define abstract art and the differential effect it has for the artist and the viewer. Ask students to recount the social foundations of artistic ability with regard to Georgia O'Keeffe.

Evaluation:

Formative: listening skills; following directions; creation of abstract, floral, or skull painting

Summative: painting

Background Information:

Georgia O'Keefe, even to this day, remains somewhat a mystery. She was a private woman who preferred to keep to herself, despite the fact that she made bold statements with her artwork. In fact, the first display of her work was done without her permission. Alfred Stieglitz, a photographer, was shown some of O'Keeffe's drawings by a mutual friend, Anita Pollitzer. After seeing the drawings, Stieglitz took it upon himself to display the drawings in his art gallery, 291, without asking the artist's permission. Infuriated, O'Keeffe demanded that Stieglitz take the works off display and return them to her. His reply to her reflected a familiar attitude at the time: "The work of an artist was the offspring of its creator, whose rights to it were usurped the moment it was created" (Hogrele, p. 65).

Constantly analyzed and critiqued by the art world, O'Keeffe remained an individual who lived a unique life. She spoke through her art, which allowed her the freedom of expression that she avoided verbally.

GEORGIA O'KEEFFE

1887	Born on a farm outside Sun Prairie, Wisconsin; second of seven children; independent thinker
1898	Georgia and her sisters took private drawing and painting lessons
1900	By the age of 13, Georgia knew she wanted to be a painter
1902	Moved to Williamsburg, Virginia; attended Chatham Episcopal Institute (between Danville and Lynchburg); won the Chatham art prize

1905	During college years, attended Art Institute of Chicago and Art Students' League in New York City
1909	Inspired by Alon Bement at the University of Virginia when he told students to "fill a space in a beautiful way" (quoting his teacher Dow)
1912	Worked as an art supervisor and teacher in Amarillo, Texas, to earn money so she could study art with Arthur Wesley Dow (Bement's teacher), a Professor at Columbia University Teachers College in New York City
1915	Art teacher at a Methodist women's college in South Carolina; knew this would be an opportunity to examine her own work Sent her work to friend Anita Pollitzer for her comments; Anita showed paintings to Alfred Stieglitz, a famous photographer in New York City; Stieglitz hung her drawings in his gallery without her permission
1916	Teacher and head of art department at West Texas State Normal School in Canyon, Texas; inspired by the wide open spaces, vast plains, and sunsets
1918	Returned to New York City and fell in love with Stieglitz
1924	Married (moved into skyscraper); liked to go to Lake George (alone or with Stieglitz)
1929	Visited New Mexico and fell in love with the desert; paintings in next ten years were unprecedented in the history of art
1932	Had a nervous breakdown
1946	A few years after Stieglitz died, Georgia returned to New Mexico and painted until she was nearly blind
1986	Died at the age of 98

Materials and Resources:

Books: Callaway & Arrowsmith (1989); Castro (1985); Robinson (1989)
Painting supplies: watercolors; watercolor paper; brushes; flowers

---

✦ INTERNET LINKS

INTERNET LINKS

Artists

http://metalab.unc.edu/louvre/paint/auth/

Webmuseum, Paris

This site provides an extensive resource on artists and their paintings. The sketches, short biographies about the artists, are arranged alphabetically, beginning with Pieter Aertsen and ending with Joseph Wright. In between, you can find all the old favorites, including Sandro Botticelli, Paul Cezanne, and Edgar Degas. Within each of the sketches are a few of the paintings done by each artist, listing the period of the work, the type, medium, and where it is now located.

INTERNET LINKS

Art History

http://www.best.com~natalew/index.html

Renaissance Art

This site was developed by Natale Williams as a resource for art history. The site discusses styles and movements and is organized in several manners: artist index or period, style, or medium. A sampling of the periods covered in this site includes: Italian Renaissance, baroque, and realism. Williams also includes Art 101, art facts, art history notes, and time lines of history in the art field. This site is a good source for any art buff or a novice who is interested in learning more.

INTERNET LINKS

Interactive Art

http://www.kn.pacbell.com/wired/art2/

Eyes on Art (A Learning to Look Curriculum)

Eyes on Art is a curriculum enhancer, online. This site provides ways for students to expand their knowledge in a fun manner. There are quizzes about art; Artspeak 101 explains the definitions associated with art, No Fear O' Eras develops an understanding of the elements of a style or era, and You Choose lets the students pick their favorite works of art and create a gallery. Each section along the way asks the students to explain how a painting makes them feel, and develops opinions on art. This is a very good source.

SUMMARY

To the artist Sally Warner (1989), the process of making art is natural to children. Warner hopes that parents and educators will view art as something that is for every child and not an activity that should be left to the experts. Hopefully this chapter has inspired you to take that first step, that is, if you are artistically timid, and attempt some of these lessons in your own classroom. You will see the benefits immediately! Once the creative works of young people are displayed, your room will feel lighter and more spontaneous. Once you have worked out the distribution and care of materials, you will find that there will be relatively few discipline problems because students will be thoroughly engaged. Soon you will be convinced that the arts are a significant part of the elementary classroom, and an ongoing search for humanities links to the social studies will no doubt ensue.

Schwartz (1986) underscores the importance of art as a building block to cognitive development:

> If we develop the building blocks of visual perception, visual spatial organization, and visual discrimination by learning to draw, our brains cannot help but transfer these skills to such tasks as mathematics, which is at its base the organization of objects in space, or to reading and spelling, which require visual attention to detail as well as pattern and organization in space, as the eye sweeps across the line of print and down to the next line. (pp. xvi–xvii)

In addition to the intellectual development described by Schwartz, an appreciation for the beauty in the world and social awareness are enhanced. The *Self in the World* orientation is reinforced by the artforms selected for this unit in several ways. Children are given an opportunity to explore the artforms created by artists throughout the world—Japan, Russia, France, Spain, Italy and the United States, to mention a few. In addition, they are encouraged to appreciate the fact that many of the artists created new artforms not popular during the time periods in which they lived. Highlighting the artists' perseverance for innovation gives children the courage to be unique.

Best wishes as you pursue a career in teaching. In the artistic spirit of being unique, don't be afraid to make mistakes as you try to innovate. As a fellow educator once said, "If you don't make mistakes, you probably aren't doing anything interesting!" Social studies is about people who strive to make a difference in the world. Good luck as you make a difference in the lives of your students and strive to become a master teacher.

References

Arnason, H. H. (1990). *History of modern art.* Englewood Cliffs, NJ: Prentice-Hall.

Batt, M. (1988). *The complete guide to creative watercolor.* Fort Lauderdale, FL: Creative Art.

Beckwith, J. (1964). *Early medieval art.* New York: Praeger.

Bjork, C., & Anderson, L. (1985). *Linnea in Monet's garden.* New York: Farrar Straus & Giroux.

Boyle, R. (1983). *American impressionism.* New York: Little, Brown.

Brookes, M. (1986). *Drawing with children.* New York: St. Martin's.

Cain, M. (1989). *Mary Cassatt.* New York: Chelsea House.

Callaway, N., & Arrowsmith, A. (Eds.). (1989). *Georgia O'Keeffe: One hundred flowers 1989 engagement calendar.* New York: Knopf.

Campbell, J., & Moyers, B. (1988). *The power of myth.* New York: Doubleday.

Castro, J. G. (1985). *The art and life of Georgia O'Keeffe.* New York: Crown.

Chadwick, W. (1992). *Women, art, and society.* London: Thames & Hudson.

Chicago, J. (1997). *Beyond the flower: The autobiography of a feminist artist.* New York: Penguin Books.

Cogniat, R. (1978). *Sisley.* New York: Crown.

Coskey, E. (1973). *Easter eggs for everyone.* Nashville, TN: Abingdon.

Cross, M. B. (1993). *Treasurer in the trunk.* Nashville, TN: Rutledge Hill.

Dorson, R. M. (Ed.). (1975). *Folktales told around the world.* Chicago: University of Chicago Press.

Fewkes, J. W. (1973). *Designs on prehistoric Hopi pottery.* New York: Dover.

Fogel, J. A., & Stevens, R. L. (1996). The Safford, Arizona, murals of Seymour Fogel: A study in artistic controversy. *Social Education, 60* (5), 287–291.

Fortmer, H. (1990, November/December). Direct fish printing. *Inksmith,* 7–11.

Friedman, J. (Producer), & Epstein, R. (Director). (1989). *Common threads: Stories from the quilt* [Video]. New York: Telling Pictures, Inc., & Couturie Co.

Golding, J. (1988). *Cubism: A history and analysis.* Cambridge, MA: Harvard University Press.

Gordon, D. (1991). *Patches of glory, an American sampler.* Tucson, AZ: First Star.

Greenbacker, L., & Barach, K. (1992). *Quilts: Identification and price guide.* New York: Avon.

Groth, J. L., & Albert, M. (1997). Arts alive in the development of historical thinking. *Social Education, 61* (1), 42–44.

Hale, N. (1987). *Mary Cassatt.* Reading, MA: Addison-Wesley.

Harris, A. S., & Nochlin, L. (1977). *Women artists: 1550–1950.* New York: Knopf.

Heller, N. (1987). *Women artists.* New York: Abbeville Press.

Hogrele, J. (1992). *O'Keeffe: The life of an American legend.* New York: Bantam Books.

Isaak, J. A. (1996). *Feminism and contemporary art: The revolutionary power of women's laughter.* New York: Routledge.

Janson, H. W. (1970). *History of art.* New York: Abrams.

Jung, C. (1972). *Mandala symbolism.* Princeton, NJ: Princeton University Press.

Jung, C. (1988). *Man and his symbols.* New York: Doubleday.

Kidson, P. (1967). *The Medieval world.* New York: McGraw-Hill.

Lepscky, I. (1984). *Pablo Picasso.* New York: Barron's Educational Series.

Leyster, J. (1987). The flute player. In N. Heller, *Women artists.* (p. 45). New York: Abbeville.

Manion, M. M., & Vines, V. F. (1984). *Illuminated manuscripts, medieval and Renaissance.* New York: Thames & Hudson.

Masterfield, M. (1984). *Painting the spirit of nature.* New York: Watson-Guptill.

Masterfield, M. (1990). *In harmony with nature.* New York: Watson-Guptill.

Matthews, N. M. (1994). *Mary Cassatt—A life.* New York: Villard.

Matthews, N. M. (Ed.). (1984). *Cassatt and her circle: Selected letters.* New York: Abbeville Press.

May, R. (1975). *The courage to create.* New York: Norton.

McCall, A. (1998). Hmong Paj Ntaub: Using textile arts to teach young children about cultures. *Social Education, 62* (5), 294–296.

Meyer, S. E. (1990). *Mary Cassatt.* New York: Abrams.

Mount, C. (1966). *Monet.* New York: Simon & Schuster.

Mullins, E. (1968). *The art of Georges Braque.* New York: Abrams.

Piotrovsky, B. (1987). *The Hermitage.* Leningrad: Auror Art.

Raboff, E. (1969). *Pablo Picasso.* New York: Gemini-Smith.

Richardson, J. (1991). *A life of Picasso. Volume I, 1881–1906.* New York: Random House.

Ringgold, F. (1991). *Tar beach.* New York: Crown.

Ringgold, F. (1992). *Aunt Harriet's underground railroad in the sky.* New York: Crown.

Ripley, E. (1959). *Picasso.* New York: Lippincott.

Robinson, R. (1989). *Georgia O'Keeffe.* New York: Harper & Row.

Rosenthal, C. L. (1991). *The art world at your fingertips.* Scottsdale, AZ: J/C Ranch.

Safford, C. L., & Bishop, R. (1985). *America's quilts and coverlets.* New York: Bonanza.

Scheader, C. (1977). *Mary Cassatt.* Chicago: Children's Press.

Schwartz, G. (1986). A note to scientists, educators, and parents. In M. Brookes, *Drawing with children.* (pp. xv–xvii). New York: St. Martin's Press.

Shirer, M. (1993). Kids make quilts too! *Quilter's Newsletter Magazine, 25* (5), 20.

Sills, L. (1989). *Inspirations: Stories about women artists.* Niles, IL: Whitman.

Soltow, W. A. (1993). *Designing your own quilts.* Radnor, PA: Chilton.

Stevens, R. L., & Fogel, J. A. (1998). The depression in the south: Seymour Fogel's images of African Americans. *Social Education, 62* (2), 80–83.

The Incredible Art Department. Available online: www.artswire.org/kenroar/index.html

Time-Life Books. (1985). *The enchanted world of magical beasts* vol. 7. Alexandria, VA.

Tucker, P. H. (1982). *Monet at Argenteuil.* New Haven: Yale University Press.

Venezia, M. (1988). *Picasso.* Chicago: Children's Press.

Vidal-Naquet, P. (Ed.). (1987). *The Harper atlas of world history.* New York: Harper & Row.

Warner, S. (1989). *Encouraging the artist in your child (even if you can't draw).* New York: St. Martin's Press.

Willard, C. (1971). *Famous modern artists.* New York: Chanticleer Press, Platt and Munk.

Wiser, W. (1991). *The great good place: American expatriate women in Paris.* New York: W. W. Norton.

Zurcher, B. (1988). *Georges Braque: Life and work.* New York: Rizzoli.

APPENDIX A
National Standards

APPENDIX OUTLINE

THE NATIONAL HISTORY STANDARDS
History for Grades K–4

Standard 1. Chronological Thinking
A. Distinguish between past, present, and future time.
B. Identify in historical narratives the temporal structure of a historical narrative or story.
C. Establish temporal order in constructing their [students'] own historical narratives.
D. Measure and calculate calendar time.
E. Interpret data presented in time lines.
F. Create time lines.
G. Explain change and continuity over time.

Standard 2. Historical Comprehension
A. Reconstruct the literal meaning of a historical passage.
B. Identify the central question(s) the historical narrative addresses.
C. Read historical narratives imaginatively.
D. Evidence historical perspectives.
E. Draw upon the data in historical maps.
F. Draw upon visual and mathematical data presented in graphics.
G. Draw upon the visual data presented in photographs, paintings, cartoons, and architectural drawings.

Standard 3. Historical Analysis and Interpretation
A. Formulate questions to focus their inquiry or analysis.
B. Identify the author or source of the historical document or narrative.
C. Compare and contrast differing sets of ideas, values, personalities, behaviors, and institutions.
D. Analyze historical fiction.
E. Distinguish between fact and fiction.
F. Compare different stories about a historical figure, era, or event.
G. Analyze illustrations in historical stories.
H. Consider multiple perspectives.
I. Explain causes in analyzing historical actions.
J. Challenge arguments of historical inevitability.
K. Hypothesize influences of the past.

Standard 4. Historical Research Capabilities
A. Formulate historical questions.
B. Obtain historical data.
C. Interrogate historical data.
D. Marshall needed knowledge of the time and place, and construct a story, explanation, or historical narrative.

Standard 5. Historical Issues—Analysis and Decision Making
A. Identify issues and problems in the past.
B. Compare the interests and values of the various people involved.
C. Suggest alternative choices for addressing the problem.
D. Evaluate alternative courses of action.
E. Prepare a position or course of action on an issue.
F. Evaluate the consequences of a decision.

United States and World History 5–12

Standard 1. Chronological Thinking
A. Distinguish between past, present, and future time.
B. Identify in historical narratives the temporal structure of a historical narrative or story.
C. Establish temporal order in constructing historical narratives of their own.

D. Measure and calculate calendar time.

E. Interpret data presented in time lines.

F. Reconstruct patterns of historical succession and duration.

G. Compare alternative models for periodization.

Standard 2. Historical Comprehension

A. Reconstruct the literal meaning of a historical passage.

B. Identify the central question(s) the historical narrative addresses.

C. Read historical narratives imaginatively.

D. Evidence historical perspectives.

E. Draw upon data in historical maps.

F. Utilize visual and mathematical data presented in charts, tables, pie and bar graphs, flowcharts, Venn diagrams, and other graphic organizers.

G. Draw upon visual, literary, and musical sources.

Standard 3. Historical Analysis and Interpretation

A. Identify the author or source of the historical document or narrative.

B. Compare and contrast differing sets of ideas, values, personalities, behaviors, and institution.

C. Differentiate between historical facts and historical interpretations.

D. Consider multiple perspectives.

E. Analyze cause-and-effect relationships and multiple causation, including the importance of the individual, the influence of ideas, and the role of chance.

F. Challenge arguments of historical inevitability.

G. Compare competing historical narratives.

H. Hold interpretations of history as tentative.

I. Evaluate major debates among historians.

J. Hypothesize the influence of the past.

Standard 4. Historical Research Capabilities

A. Formulate historical questions.

B. Obtain historical data.

C. Interrogate historical data.

D. Identify the gaps in the available records, marshall contextual knowledge and perspectives of the time and place, and construct a sound historical interpretation.

Standard 5. Historical Issues—Analysis and Decision Making

A. Identify issues and problems in the past.

B. Marshall evidence of antecedent circumstances and contemporary factors contributing to problems and alternative courses of action.

C. Identify relevant historical antecedents.

D. Evaluate alternative courses of action.

E. Formulate a position or course of action on an issue.

F. Evaluate the implementation of a decision.

NATIONAL SOCIAL STUDIES STANDARDS

Time, Continuity, and Change

Early Grades

a. demonstrate an understanding that different people may describe the same event or situation in diverse ways, citing reasons for the differences in views;

b. demonstrate an ability to use correctly vocabulary associated with time such as past, present, future, and long ago; read and construct simple time lines; identify examples of change; and recognize examples or cause-and-effect relationships;

c. compare and contrast different stories or accounts about past events, people, places, or situations, identifying how they contribute to our understanding of the past;

d. identify the use of various sources for reconstructing the past, such as documents, letters, diaries, maps, textbooks, photos, and others;

e. demonstrate an understanding that people in different times and places view the world differently;

f. use knowledge of facts and concepts drawn from history, along with elements of historical inquiry, to inform decision making about and action taking on public issues.

Middle Grades

a. demonstrate an understanding that different scholars may describe the same event or situation in different ways but must provide reasons or evidence for their views;

b. identify and use key concepts such as chronology, causality, change, conflict, and complexity to explain, analyze, and show connections among patterns of historical change and continuity;

c. identify and describe selected historical periods and patterns of change within and across culture, such as the rise of civilizations, the development of transportation systems, the growth and breakdown of colonial systems, and others;

d. identify and use processes important to reconstructing and reinterpreting the past, such as using a variety of sources; providing, validating, and weighing evidence for claims; checking credibility of sources; and searching for causality;

e. develop critical sensitivities such as empathy and skepticism regarding attitudes, values, and behaviors of people in different historical contexts;

f. use knowledge of facts and concepts drawn from history, along with methods of historical inquiry, to inform decision making about and action taking on public issues.

Individuals, Groups, and Institutions

Early Grades

a. identify roles as learned behavior patterns in group situations such as student, family member, peer play group member, or club members;

b. give examples of and explain group and institutional influences such as religious beliefs, laws, and peer pressure, or people, events, and elements of culture;

c. identify examples of institutions and describe the interactions of people with institutions;

Middle Grades

a. demonstrate an understanding of concepts such as role, status, and social class in describing the interactions of individuals and social groups;

b. analyze group and institutional influences on people, events, and elements of culture;

c. describe the various forms institutions take and the interactions of people with institutions;

Early Grades	**Middle Grades**
d. identify and describe examples of tensions between and among individuals, groups, or institutions, and how belonging to more than one group can cause internal conflicts;	d. identify and analyze examples of tensions between expressions of individuality and group or institutional efforts to promote social conformity;
e. identify and describe examples of tensions between an individual's beliefs and government policies and laws;	e. identify and describe examples of tensions between belief systems and government policies and laws;
f. give examples of the role of institutions in furthering both continuity and change;	f. describe the role of institutions in furthering both continuity and change;
g. show how groups and institutions work to meet individual needs and promote the common good, and identify examples of where they fail to do so.	g. apply knowledge of how groups and institutions work to meet individual needs and promote the common good.

NATIONAL GEOGRAPHY STANDARDS

The 1994 National Geography Standards evolved over a decade. This evolution is described in Appendix A of *Geography for Life,* the National Geography Standards. In 1984, *Guidelines for Geographic Education, K–12* were published by the Joint Committee on Geographic Education, establishing the following five themes for geography teaching:

Location: Position on the Earth's Surface

Place: Physical and Human Characteristics

Relationships Within Places: Humans and Environments

Movement: Humans Interacting on the Earth

Regions: How They Form and Change

The themes offered a manageable way to organize geography concepts in the social studies curriculum, and as a result, state agencies, local school districts, and commercial textbook publishers readily incorporated the themes into various curriculum development projects. Since 1984, the geography community has utilized these themes in preparing the *Geography Assessment Framework for the 1994 National Assessment of Educational Progress* (NAEP) as well as the 1994 National Standards, which expanded the number of themes to six. Following is a summary of the National Geography Standards from *Geography for Life* (1994):

The World in Spatial Terms

Geography studies the relationships between people, places, and environments by mapping information about them into a spatial context. The geographically informed person knows and understands:

1. How to use maps and other geographic representations, tools, and technologies to acquire, process, and report information from a spatial perspective.
2. How to use mental maps to organize information about people, places, and environments in a spatial context.
3. How to analyze the spatial organization of people, places, and environment on Earth's surface.

Places and Regions

The identities and lives of individuals and people are rooted in particular places and in those human constructs called regions. The geographically informed person knows and understands:

1. The physical and human characteristics of places.
2. That people create regions to interpret Earth's complexity.
3. How culture and experience influence people's perceptions of places and regions.

Physical Systems

Physical processes shape Earth's surface and interact with plant and animal life to create, sustain, and modify the ecosystems. The geographically informed person knows and understands:

1. The physical processes that shape the patterns of Earth's surface.
2. The characteristics and spatial distribution of ecosystems on Earth's surface.

Human Systems

People are central to geography in that human activities help shape Earth's surface, human settlements and structures are part of Earth's surface, and humans compete for control of Earth's surface. The geographically informed person knows and understands:

1. The characteristics, distribution, and migration of human populations on Earth's surface.
2. The characteristics, distribution, and complexity of Earth's cultural mosaics.
3. The patterns and networks of economic interdependence on Earth's surface.
4. The processes, patterns, and functions of human settlement.
5. How the forces of cooperation and conflict among people influence the division and control of Earth's surface.

Environment and Society

The physical environment is modified by human activities, largely as a consequence of the ways in which human societies value and use Earth's natural resources, and human activities are also influenced by Earth's physical features and processes. The geographically informed person knows and understands:

1. How human actions modify the physical environment.
2. How physical systems affect human systems.
3. The changes that occur in the meaning, use, distribution, and importance of resources.

The Uses of Geography

Knowledge of geography enables people to develop an understanding of the relationships between people, places, and environments over time—that is, of Earth as it was, is, and might be. The geographically informed person knows and understands:

1. How to apply geography to interpret the past.
2. How to apply geography to interpret the present and plan for the future.

National Social Studies Standards
People, Places, and Environments

Early Grades	Middle Grades
Early Grades	**Middle Grades**

Early Grades

a. construct and use mental maps of locales, regions, and the world that demonstrate understanding of relative location, direction, size, and shape;

b. interpret, use, and distinguish various representations of the earth, such as maps, globes, and photographs;

c. use appropriate resources, data sources, and geographic tools such as atlases, databases, grid systems, charts, graphs, and maps to generate, manipulate, and interpret information;

d. estimate distance and calculate scale;

e. locate and distinguish among varying landforms and geographic features, such as mountains, plateaus, islands, and oceans;

f. describe and speculate about physical system changes, such as seasons, climate and weather, and the water cycle;

g. describe how people create places that reflect ideas, personality, culture, and wants and needs as they design homes, playgrounds, classrooms, and the like;

h. examine the interaction of human beings and their physical environment, the use of land, building of cities, and ecosystem changes in selected locales and regions;

i. explore ways that the earth's physical features have changed over time in the local region and beyond and how these changes may be connected to one another;

j. observe and speculate about social and economic effects of environmental changes and crises resulting from phenomena such as floods, storms, and drought;

k. consider existing uses and propose and evaluate alternative uses of resources and land in home, school, community, the region, and beyond.

Middle Grades

a. elaborate mental maps of locales, regions, and the world that demonstrate understanding of relative location, direction, size, and shape;

b. create, interpret, use, and distinguish various representations of the earth, such as maps, globes, and photographs;

c. use appropriate resources, data sources, and geographic tools such as aerial photographs, satellites images, geographic information systems (GIS), map projections, and cartography to generate, manipulate, and interpret information such as atlases, databases, grid systems, charts, graphs, and maps;

d. estimate distance, calculate scale, and distinguish other geographic relationships such as population density and spatial distribution patterns;

e. locate and describe varying landforms and geographic features, such as mountains, plateaus, islands, rain forests, deserts, and oceans, and explain their relationships within the ecosystem;

f. describe physical system changes such as seasons, climate and weather, and the water cycle and identify geographic patterns associated with them;

g. describe how people create places that reflect cultural values and ideals as they build neighborhoods, parks, shopping centers, and the like;

h. examine, interpret, and analyze physical and cultural patterns and their interactions, such as land use, settlement patterns, cultural transmission of customs and ideas, and ecosystem changes;

i. describe ways that historical events have been influenced by, and have influenced, physical and human geographic factors in local, regional, national, and global settings;

j. observe and speculate about social and economic effects of environmental changes and crises resulting from phenomena such as floods, storms, and drought;

k. propose, compare, and evaluate alternative uses of land and resources in communities, regions, nations, and the world.

Production, Distribution, and Consumption

Early Grades	Middle Grades
a. give examples that show how scarcity and choice govern our economic decisions;	a. give and explain examples of ways that economic systems structure choices about how goods and services are to be produced and distributed;
b. distinguish between needs and wants;	b. describe the role that supply and demand, prices, incentives, and profits play in determining what is produced and distributed in a competitive market system;
c. identify examples of private and public goods and services;	c. explain the difference between private and public goods and services;
d. give examples of the various institutions that make up economic systems such as families, workers, banks, labor unions, government agencies, small businesses, and large corporations;	d. describe a range of examples of the various institutions that make up economic systems such as households, business firms, banks, government agencies, labor unions, and corporations;
e. describe how we depend upon workers with specialized jobs and the ways in which they contribute to the production and exchange of goods and services;	e. describe the role of specialization and exchange in the economic process;
f. describe the influence of incentives, values, traditions, and habits on economic decisions;	f. explain and illustrate how values and beliefs influence different economic decisions;
g. explain and demonstrate the role of money in everyday life;	g. explain and illustrate how values and beliefs influence different economic decisions;
h. describe the relationship of price to supply and demand;	h. compare basic economic systems according to who determines what is produced, distributed, and consumed;
i. use economic concepts such as supply, demand, and price to help explain events in the community and nation;	i. use economic concepts to help explain historical and current developments and issues in local, national, or global contexts.
j. apply knowledge of economic concepts in developing a response to a current local economic issue, such as how to reduce the flow of trash into a rapidly filling landfill.	

Science, Technology, and Society

a. identify and describe examples in which science and technology have changed the lives of people, such as in homemaking, child care, work, transportation, and communication;	a. examine and describe the influence of culture on scientific and technological choices and advancement, such as in transportation, medicine, and warfare;
b. identify and describe examples in which science and technology have led to changes in the physical environment, such as the building of dams and levees, offshore oil drilling, medicine from rain forests, and loss of rain forests due to extraction of resources or alternative uses;	b. show through specific examples how science and technology have changed people's perceptions of the social and natural world, such as in their relationship to the land, animal life, family life, and economic needs, wants, and security;

c. describe instances in which changes in values, beliefs, and attitudes have resulted from new scientific and technological knowledge, such as conservation of resources and awareness of chemicals harmful to life and the environment;

d. identify examples of laws and policies that govern scientific and technological applications, such as the Endangered Species Act and environmental protection policies;

e. suggest ways to monitor science and technology in order to protect the physical environment, individual rights, and the common good.

c. describe examples in which values, beliefs, and attitudes have been influenced by new scientific and technological knowledge, such as the invention of the printing press, conceptions of the universe, applications of atomic energy, and genetic discoveries;

d. explain the need for laws and policies to govern scientific and technological applications, such as in the safety and well-being of workers and consumers and the regulation of utilities, radio, and television;

e. seek reasonable and ethical solutions to problems that arise when scientific advancements and social norms or values come into conflict.

NATIONAL CONTENT STANDARDS IN ECONOMICS

Content Standard 1

Students will understand that: Productive resources are limited. Therefore, people cannot have all the goods and services they want; as a result, they must choose some things and give up others.

Students will be able to use this knowledge to: Identify what they gain and what they give up when they make choices.

Content Standard 2

Students will understand that: Effective decision making requires comparing the additional costs of alternatives with the additional benefits. Most choices involve doing a little more or a little less of something; few choices are all-or-nothing decisions.

Students will be able to use this knowledge to: Make effective decisions as consumers, producers, savers, investors, and citizens.

Content Standard 3

Students will understand that: Different methods can be used to allocate goods and services. People, acting individually or collectively through government, must choose which methods to use to allocate different kinds of goods and services.

Students will be able to use this knowledge to: Evaluate different methods of allocating goods and services by comparing the benefits and costs of each method.

Content Standard 4

Students will understand that: People respond predictably to positive and negative incentives.

Students will be able to use this knowledge to: Identify incentives that affect people's behavior and explain how incentives affect their own behavior.

Content Standard 5

Students will understand that: Voluntary exchange occurs when all participating parties expect gain. This is true for trade among individuals or organizations within a nation, and among individuals or organizations in other nations.

Students will be able to use this knowledge to: Negotiate exchanges and identify the gains to themselves and others. Compare the benefits of costs of policies that alter trade barriers between nations, such as tariffs or quotas.

Content Standard 6

Students will understand that: When individuals, regions, and nations specialize in what they can produce at the lowest cost and then trade with others, both production and consumption increase.

Students will be able to use this knowledge to: Explain how they can benefit themselves and others by developing special skills and strengths.

Content Standard 7

Students will understand that: Markets exist when buyers and sellers interact. This interaction determines market prices and thereby allocates scarce goods and services.

Students will be able to use this knowledge to: Identify markets in which they have participated as a buyer and a seller and describe how the interaction of all buyers and sellers influences prices. Also, predict how prices change when there is either a shortage or surplus of the product available.

Content Standard 8

Students will understand that: Prices send signals and provide incentives to buyers and sellers. When supply or demand changes, market prices adjust, affecting incentives.

Students will be able to use this knowledge to: Predict how prices change when the number of buyers or sellers in a market changes, and explain how the incentives facing individual buyers and sellers are affected.

Content Standard 9

Students will understand that: Competition among sellers lowers costs and prices and encourages producers to produce more of what consumers are willing and able to buy. Competition among buyers increases prices and allocates goods and services to those people who are willing and able to pay the most for them.

Students will be able to use this knowledge to: Explain how changes in the level of competition in different markets can affect price and output levels.

Content Standard 10

Students will understand that: Institutions evolve in market economies to help individuals and groups accomplish their goals. Banks, labor unions, corporations, legal systems, and not-for-profit organizations are examples of important institutions. A different kind of institution, clearly defined and well-enforced property rights, is essential to a market economy.

Students will be able to use this knowledge to: Describe the roles of various economic institutions.

Content Standard 11

Students will understand that: Money makes it easier to trade, borrow, save, invest, and compare the value of goods and services.

Students will be able to use this knowledge to: Explain how their lives would be more difficult in a world with no money or in a world where money sharply lost its value.

Content Standard 12

Students will understand that: Interest rates, adjusted for inflation, rise and fall to balance the amount saved with the amount borrowed, thus affecting the allocation of scarce resources between present and future uses.

Students will be able to use this knowledge to: Explain situations in which they pay or receive interest, and explain how they would react to changes in interest rates if they were making or receiving interest payments.

Content Standard 13

Students will understand that: Income for most people is determined by the market value of the productive resources they sell. What workers earn depends, primarily, on the market value of what they produce and how productive they are.

Students will be able to use this knowledge to: Predict future earnings based on their current plans for education, training, and career options.

Content Standard 14

Students will understand that: Entrepreneurs are people who take the risks of organizing productive resources to make goods and services. Profit is an important incentive that leads entrepreneurs to accept the risk of business failure.

Students will be able to use this knowledge to: Identify the risks, returns and other characteristics of entrepreneurship that bear on its attractiveness as a career.

Content Standard 15

Students will understand that: Investment in factories, machinery, new technology, and the health, education, and training of people can raise future standards of living.

Students will be able to use this knowledge to: Predict the consequences of investment decisions made by individuals, businesses, and governments.

Content Standard 16

Students will understand that: There is an economic role for government to play in a market economy whenever the benefits of a government policy outweigh its costs. Governments often provide for national defense, address environmental concerns, define and protect property rights, and attempt to make markets more competitive. Most government policies also redistribute income.

Students will be able to use this knowledge to: Identify and evaluate the benefits and costs of alternative public policies, and assess who enjoys the benefits and who bears the costs.

Content Standard 17

Students will understand that: Costs of government policies sometimes exceed benefits. This may occur because of incentives facing voters, government officials, and government employees, because of actions by special interest groups that can impose costs on the general public, or because social goals other than economic deficiency are being pursued.

Students will be able to use this knowledge to: Identify some public policies that may cost more than the benefits they generate, and assess who enjoys the benefits and who bears the costs. Explain why the policies exist.

Content Standard 18

Students will understand that: A nation's overall levels of income, employment, and prices are determined by the interaction of spending and production decisions made by all households, firms, government agencies, and others in the economy.

Students will be able to use this knowledge to: Interpret media reports about current economic conditions and explain how these conditions can influence decisions made by consumers, producers, and government policymakers.

Content Standard 19

Students will understand that: Unemployment imposes costs on individuals and nations. Unexpected inflation imposes costs on many people and benefits some others because it arbitrarily redistributes purchasing power. Inflation can reduce the rate of growth of national living standards, because individuals and organizations use resources to protect themselves against the uncertainty of future prices.

Students will be able to use this knowledge to: Make informed decisions by anticipating the consequences of inflation and unemployment.

Content Standard 20

Students will understand that: Federal government budgetary policy and the Federal Reserve System's monetary policy influence the overall levels of employment, output, and prices.

Students will be able to use this knowledge to: Anticipate the impact of the federal government's and the Federal Reserve System's macroeconomic policy decisions on themselves and others.

National Council for the Social Studies Standards

Culture

Early Grades	Middle Grades
a. explore and describe similarities and differences in the ways groups, societies, and culture address similar human needs and concerns;	a. compare similarities and differences in the ways groups, societies, and cultures meet human needs and concerns;
b. give examples of how experiences may be interpreted differently by people from diverse cultural perspectives and frames of reference;	b. explain how information and experiences may be interpreted by people from diverse cultural perspectives and frames of reference;
c. describe ways in which language, stories, folktales, music, and artistic creations serve as expressions of culture and influence behavior of people living in a particular culture;	c. explain and give examples of how language, literature, the arts, architecture, other artifacts, traditions, beliefs, values, and behaviors contribute to the development and transmission of culture;
d. compare ways in which people from different cultures think about and deal with their physical environment and social conditions;	d. explain why individuals and groups respond differently to their physical and social environments and/or changes to them on the basis of shared assumptions, values, and beliefs;
e. give examples and describe the importance of cultural unity and diversity within and across groups.	e. articulate the implications of cultural diversity, as well as cohesion, within and across groups.

Individual Development and Identity

a. describe personal changes over time, such as those related to physical development and personal interests;	a. related personal changes to social, cultural, and historical contexts;
b. describe personal connections to place—especially place as associated with immediate surroundings;	b. describe personal connections to place—as associated with community, nation, and world;
c. describe the unique features of one's nuclear and extended families;	c. describe the ways family, gender, ethnicity, nationality, and institutional affiliations contribute to personal identity;
d. show how learning and physical development affect behavior;	d. relate such factors as physical endowment and capabilities, learning, motivation, personality, perception, and behavior to individual development;
e. identify and describe ways family, groups, and community influence the individual's daily life and personal choices;	e. identify and describe ways regional, ethnic, and national cultures influence individuals' daily lives;
f. explore factors that contribute to one's personal identity such as interests, capabilities, and perceptions;	f. identify and describe the influence of perception, attitudes, values, and beliefs on personal identity;
g. analyze a particular event to identify reasons individuals might respond to it in different ways;	g. identify and interpret examples of stereotyping, conformity, and altruism;
h. work independently and cooperatively to accomplish goals.	h. work independently and cooperatively to accomplish goals.

Global Connections

Early Grades	**Middle Grades**
a. explore ways that language, art, music, belief systems, and other cultural elements may facilitate global understanding or lead to misunderstanding;	a. describe instances in which language, art, music, belief systems, and other cultural elements can facilitate global understanding or cause misunderstanding;
b. give examples of conflict, cooperation, and interdependence among individuals, groups, and nations;	b. analyze examples of conflict, cooperation, and interdependence among groups, societies, and nations;
c. examine the effects of changing technologies on the global community;	c. describe and analyze the effects of changing technologies on the global community;
d. explore causes, consequences, and possible solutions to persistent, contemporary, and emerging global issues, such as pollution and endangered species;	d. explore the causes, consequences, and possible solutions to persistent, contemporary, and emerging global issues, such as health, security, resource allocation, economic development, and environmental quality;
e. examine the relationships and tensions between personal wants and needs and various global concerns, such as use of imported oil, land use, and environmental protection;	e. describe and explain the relationships and tensions between national sovereignty and global interests, in such matters as territory, natural resources, trade, use of technology, and welfare of people;
f. investigate concerns, issues, standards, and conflicts related to universal human rights, such as the treatment of children, religious groups, and effects of war.	f. demonstrate understanding of concerns, standards, issues, and conflicts related to universal human rights;
	g. identify and describe the roles of international and multinational organizations.

National Social Studies Standards (1994)

Power, Authority, and Governance

a. examine the rights and responsibilities of the individual in relation to his or her social group, such as family, peer group, and school class;	a. examine persistent issues involving the rights, roles, and status of the individual in relation to the general welfare;
b. explain the purpose of government;	b. describe the purpose of government and how its powers are acquired, used, and justified;
c. give examples of how government does or does not provide for needs and wants of people, establish order and security, and manage conflict;	c. analyze and explain ideas and governmental mechanisms to meet needs and wants of citizens, regulate territory, manage conflict, and establish order and security;
d. recognize how groups and organizations encourage unity and deal with diversity to maintain order and security;	d. describe the ways nations and organizations respond to forces of unity and diversity affecting order and security;
e. distinguish among local, state, and national government and identify representative leaders at these levels such as mayor, governor, and president;	e. identify and describe the basic features of the political system in the United States, and identify representative leaders from various levels and branches of government;

Early Grades

f. identify and describe factors that contribute to cooperation and cause disputes within and among groups and nations;

g. explore the role of technology in communications, transportation, information-processing, weapons development, or other areas as it contributes to or helps resolve conflicts;

h. recognize and give examples of the tensions between the wants and needs of individuals and groups, and concepts such as fairness, equity, and justice.

Middle Grades

f. explain conditions, actions, and motivations that contribute to conflict and cooperation within and among nations;

g. describe and analyze the role of technology in communications, transportation, information-processing, weapons development, or other areas as it contributes to or helps resolve conflicts;

h. explain and apply concepts such as power, role, status, justice, and influence to the examination of persistent issues and social problems;

i. give examples and explain how governments attempt to achieve their state ideals at home and abroad.

Civic Ideals and Practices

a. identify key ideals of the United States' democratic republican form of government, such as individual human dignity, liberty, justice, equality, and the rule of law, and discuss their application in specific situations;

b. identify examples of rights and responsibilities of citizens;

c. locate, access, organize, and apply information about an issue of public concern from multiple points of view;

d. identify and practice selected forms of civic discussion and participation consistent with the ideals of citizens in a democratic republic;

e. explain actions citizens can take to influence public policy decisions;

f. recognize that a variety of formal and informal actors influence and shape public policy;

g. examine the influence of public opinion on personal decision making and government policy on public issues;

h. explain how public policies and citizen behaviors may or may not reflect the state ideals of a democratic republican form of government;

i. describe how public policies are used to address issues of public concern;

j. recognize and interpret how the "common good" can be strengthened through various forms of citizen action.

a. examine the origins and continuing influence of key ideals of the democratic republican form of government, such as individual human dignity, liberty, justice, equality, and the rule of law;

b. identify and interpret sources and examples of the rights and responsibilities of citizens;

c. locate, access, analyze, organize, and apply information about selected public issues—recognizing and explaining multiple points of view;

d. practice forms of civic discussion and participation consistent with the ideals of citizens in a democratic republic;

e. explain and analyze various forms of citizen action that influence public policy decisions;

f. identify and explain the roles of formal and informal political actors in influencing and shaping public policy and decision making;

g. analyze the influence of diverse forms of public opinion on the development of public policy and decision making;

h. analyze the effectiveness of selected public policies and citizen behaviors in realizing the stated ideals of a democratic republican form of government;

i. explain the relationship between policy statements and action plans used to address issues of public concern;

j. examine strategies designed to strengthen the "common good," which consider a range of options for citizen action.

National Social Studies Standards

Culture

Early Grades	Middle Grades
b. give examples of how experiences may be interpreted differently by people from diverse cultural perspectives and frames of reference;	b. show how information and experiences may be interpreted by people from diverse cultural perspectives and frames of reference;
c. describe ways in which language, stories, folktales, music, and artistic creations as expressions of culture influence behavior of people living in a particular culture;	c. show how language, literature, the arts, architecture, other artifacts, traditions, beliefs, values, and behavior contribute to the development and transmission of culture;
d. compare ways in which people from different cultures think about and deal with their physical environment and social conditions;	d. explain why individuals and groups respond differently to their physical and social environments and/or changes to them on the basis of shared assumptions, values, and beliefs;
e. give examples and describe the importance of cultural unity and diversity within and across groups.	e. articulate the implications of cultural diversity, as well as cohesion, within and across groups.

Time, Continuity, and Change

b. demonstrate an ability to use correctly vocabulary associated with time such as past, present, future, long ago; read and construct simple time lines; identify examples of change; and recognize examples of cause-and-effect relationships;	b. identify and use key concepts such as chronology, causality, change, conflict, and complexity to explain, analyze, and show connections among patterns of historical change and continuity;
c. compare and contrast different stories or accounts about past events, people, places, or situations identifying how they contribute to our understanding of the past.	c. identify and describe selected historical periods or patterns of change within and across cultures such as the rise of civilizations, the development of transportation systems, the growth and breakdown of the colonial systems and others.

People, Places, and Environment

b. interpret, use, and distinguish various representations of the earth, such as maps, globes, and photographs;	b. create, interpret, use and distinguish various representations of the earth, such as maps, globes, and photographs;

Individual Development and Identity

a. describe personal changes over time such as those related to physical development and personal interests;	a. relate personal changes to social, cultural, and historical contexts;
b. describe personal connections to place—especially place as associated with immediate surroundings;	b. describe personal connections to place—as associated with community, nation, and world;
c. describe the unique features of one's nuclear and extended families;	c. describe the ways family, gender, ethnicity, nationality, and institutional affiliations contribute to personal identity;

Early Grades	**Middle Grades**
d. show how learning and physical development affect behavior;	d. relate such factors as physical endowment and capabilities, learning, motivation, personality, perception, and behavior to individual development;
e. identify and describe ways family, groups, and community influence the individual's daily life and personal choices;	e. identify and describe ways regional, ethnic, and national cultures influence individuals' daily life;
f. explore factors that contribute to one's personal identity such as interests, capabilities, and perceptions.	f. identify and describe the influence of perceptions, attitudes, values, and beliefs on personal identity.

Individuals, Groups, and Institutions

d. identify and describe examples of tensions between and among individuals, groups or institutions, and how belonging to more than one group can cause tensions.	d. identify and analyze examples of tensions between expressions of individuality and group or institutional efforts to promote social conformity.

Power, Authority, and Governance

a. examine the rights and responsibilities of the individual in relation to his/her social group such as family, peer group, school class;	a. examine persisting issues involving the rights, role, and status of the individual in relation to the general welfare;
c. give examples of how government does or does not provide for needs and wants of people, establish order and security and manage conflict.	c. analyze and explain ideas and governmental mechanisms to meet needs and wants of citizens, regulate territory, manage conflict, and establish order and security.

Production, Distribution, and Consumption

	b. explain and illustrate how different values and beliefs influence different economic decisions;
f. describe the influence of incentives, values, traditions, and habits on economic decisions.	f. describe the role that supply and demand, prices, incentives, and profits play in determining what is produced and distributed in a competitive market system.

Science, Technology, and Society

	b. show through specific examples how science and technology have changed people's perceptions of the social and natural world such as in their relationship to the land or animal life, family life, economic needs, wants and security.

Global Connections

a. explore ways language, art, music, belief systems, and other cultural elements can facilitate global understanding and cause misunderstandings.	a. describe instances where language, art, music, beliefs and other cultural elements can facilitate global understanding, and cause misunderstandings.

Civic Ideals and Practices

a. identify key ideals of the United States' democratic republican form of government such as liberty, justice, equality, the rule of law, and discuss their application in specific situations.

a. examine the origins and continuing influence of key ideals of the democratic republican form of government such as liberty, justice, equality, the rule of law, and individual human dignity.

NATIONAL STANDARDS FOR ART EDUCATION

Understanding and Applying Media, Techniques, and Processes

Early Grades

c. use different media, techniques, and processes to communicate ideas, experiences, and stories;

d. use art materials and tools in a safe and responsible manner.

Middle Grades

c. use different media, techniques, and processes to communicate ideas, experiences, and stories;

d. use art materials and tools in a safe and responsible manner.

Using Knowledge of Structures and Functions

c. use visual structures and functions of art to communicate ideas.

c. select and use the qualities of structures and functions of art to improve communication of their ideas.

Choosing and Evaluating a Range of Subject Matter, Symbols, and Ideas

a. explore and understand prospective content for works of art;

a. integrate visual, spatial, and temporal concepts with content to communicate intended meaning in their artworks;

b. select and use subject matter, symbols, and ideas to communicate meaning.

b. use subjects, themes, and symbols that demonstrate knowledge of contexts, values, and aesthetics that communicate intended meaning in artworks.

Understanding the Visual Arts in Relation to History and Cultures

a. know that the visual arts have both a history and specific relationships to various cultures;

b. identify specific works of art as belonging to particular cultures, times, and places;

c. demonstrate how history, culture, and the visual arts can influence each other in making and studying works of art.

a. know and compare the characteristics of artworks in various eras and cultures;

b. describe and place a variety of art objects in historical and cultural contexts;

c. analyze, describe, and demonstrate how factors of time and place (such as climate, resources, ideas, and technology) influence visual characteristics that give meaning and value to a work of art.

Reflecting upon and Assessing the Characteristics and Merits of Their Work and the Work of Others

b. describe how people's experiences influence the development of specific artworks;

b. analyze contemporary and historic meanings in specific artworks through cultural and aesthetic inquiry;

Early Grades	**Middle Grades**
c. understand there are different responses to specific artworks.	c. describe and compare a variety of individual responses to their own artworks and to artworks from various eras and cultures.

Making Connections Between Visual Arts and Other Disciplines

a. understand and use similarities and differences between characteristics of the visual arts and other arts disciplines;

b. identify connections between the visual arts and other disciplines in the curriculum.

a. compare the characteristics or works in two or more artforms that share similar subject matter, historical periods, or cultural context;

b. describe ways in which the principles and subject matter of other disciplines taught in the school are interrelated with the visual arts.

References

Center for Civic Education. (1994). *National standards for civics and government.* Calabasas, CA: Center for Civic Education.

Consortium of National Arts Education Associations. (1994). *National standards for arts education.* Reston, VA: Music Educators National Conference.

Geography Education Standards Project. (1994). *Geography for life: National geography standards 1994.* Washington, DC: National Geographic Research & Exploration.

National Center for History in the Schools. (1996). *National standards for history for grades K–4: Expanding children's world in time and space.* Los Angeles, CA: National Center for History in the Schools.

National Center for History in the Schools. (1996). *National standards for United States history: Exploring the American experience (5–12).* Los Angeles, CA: National Center for History in the Schools.

National Center for History in the Schools. (1996). *National standards for world history: Exploring the paths to the present (5–12).* Los Angeles, CA: National Center for History in the Schools.

National Council for the Social Studies. (1994). *Expectations of excellence: Curriculum standards for social studies.* Washington, DC: National Council for the Social Studies.

National Council on Economic Education. (1997). *Voluntary national content standards in economics.* New York: National Council on Economic Education.

APPENDIX B
Middle School Curriculum Applications

CHINA: FROM THE PAST TO THE PRESENT

The following lesson was prepared by Paul Cinoa as a part of a ten-day unit. Paul was enrolled in a social studies methods course, which preceded his student teaching semester. Some of the information for the unit came from interviews with his brother's fiancée who emigrated from China in 1994. The lesson is a good model for presenting conflicting accounts of an historical event, as well as demonstrating how someone with no teaching experience can weave personal interests into curriculum development.

MODEL LESSON:
CHINA: FROM THE PAST TO THE PRESENT

By Paul Cinoa

Level: Middle School   **Time:** 1 Hour

Topic: Tiananmen Square, June 1989

Purpose:
To have students generate questions and hypotheses about the social and political ramifications of events in Tiananmen Square in June 1989.

Concepts:

Tiananmen Square, Beijing Massacre

Objectives:

1. Students will formulate questions and hypotheses about the incidents that occurred at Tiananmen Square by reading personal accounts of people who were there.
2. Students will gather information from sources supplied by the teacher in order to assist in answering their questions and hypotheses.
3. Students will share their questions, hypotheses, and comments of the personal accounts in a large group discussion.

Procedure:

Introduction: Begin the lesson by talking about all of the conflicts that are occurring around the world in places such as Bosnia, Haiti, and the Middle East. Explain to students that at any given time in history, conflicts occur in different countries. Explain that it is difficult to understand these incidents of conflict and violence, but in today's class we are going to look at an incident that happened in China in 1989. It is a difficult issue to sort out and one that is still being discussed today. It was a conflict that occurred in Tiananmen Square in Beijing, China. Beijing is the capital of China and Tiananmen Square is a large area with buildings, museums, and gardens.

Content Focus: Break the class into groups of four students. Explain to the students that you will be handing out some excerpts from individual personal accounts of this conflict that occurred in Tiananmen Square. Their task is to generate three questions that arise when reading these personal accounts and three hypotheses of why they think this conflict occurred. Someone should act as a recorder. Each group will get the same personal accounts to read. Hand out the worksheet that the recorder can use to put down the information (see worksheet that follows).

After twenty minutes, call the whole class back together. Have each group share its questions and hypotheses and write them on the board. To keep all of the groups active, have one group give a question and then move to another group. Once all of the questions have been recorded on the board, have the groups share their hypotheses of why they think a conflict occurred.

After the groups have shared all of their information, tell them that it was important that they generated their own questions because these are the things that they felt were the most important or compelling to them as they read the personal accounts. Ask students what resources they could use to find some answers. Next, to assist them in looking for some answers to their questions and hypotheses, supply them with a number of resource materials. Give the students copies of American and Chinese newspaper articles of the incident as well as information from magazines. Further, supply the students with excerpts from books to help them look for answers.

Closure: Explain to students that they will not have adequate time today to address all of their questions, but they should pick one of their questions and research it to try to find an answer to it. Let them know that they will have an opportunity in future classes to use these resources and others to find answers to their many questions. Mention to the students that while they are researching answers to their questions and hypotheses they may develop new questions and hypotheses. Tell them that this is okay, and it is an important part of the process of inquiry and research. Let the students know that even today, many people are still generating questions and answers to what occurred in Tiananmen Square in June 1989. Close by letting the students know that they have done an excellent job of dealing with a difficult topic and commend them for their hard work. Ask for their comments about this lesson and ask if they think this is a good way to study events that happen around the world.

Evaluation:

Formative: Listening skills, small-group participation, following directions, large-group participation, questions, hypotheses.

Summative: Group activity worksheet that includes questions and hypotheses.

Materials and Resources:

Personal accounts; worksheet; books, magazines, and newspapers for student use.
Beijing Review. (1989, June 12–25), p. 9.
Beijing Review. (1989, June 26–July 2), pp. 15–19.
Des Forges, R. V. (1993). *Chinese democracy and the crisis of 1989.* Albany: State
    University of New York Press.
Free China Review. (1989, August), pp. 5–10.
Hook, B. *The Cambridge encyclopedia of China.* Cambridge: Cambridge University Press.
Jiang, J., & Qin Zhou. (1989). *June Four: A chronicle of the Chinese democratic uprising.*
    Fayetteville: The University of Arkansas Press.
Kwan, M. D. (1990). *Broken portraits: Encounters with Chinese students.* San Francisco:
    China Books & Periodicals.
Lin, N. (1992). *The struggle for Tiananmen.* London: Praeger.
Mu, Y., & Thompson, M. V. (1989). *Crisis at Tiananmen: Reform and reality in modern
    China.* San Francisco: China Books & Periodicals.
Salisbury, H. E. (1989). *Tiananmen diary: Thirteen days in June.* Boston: Little, Brown.
Yu, M. C., & Harrison, J. F. (1990). *Voices from Tiananmen Square.* New York: Black Rose
    Books.

Background Information: (also see personal accounts and handouts.)

The events that led up to Tiananmen Square are extremely complicated. Prodemocracy groups have been organizing for years. Students will be provided with personal accounts of the events that began occurring in Tiananmen Square on May 13, 1989, which led to the Beijing massacre on June 2–4. Following is a brief time line for the teacher to use.

May 13	A prodemocracy group goes to Tiananmen Square and about a thousand students begin a hunger strike.
May 18	Li Peng, the leader of China meets with the students.
May 19	Zhao Aiyan goes to Tiananmen Square to express sympathy to the students.
May 20	State Council declares martial law in Beijing. Students and others begin to erect barricades in Tiananmen Square.
May 25	A prodemocracy demonstration with one hundred thousand workers and students takes place. They want Li Peng to resign and he refuses.
June 2	Three people are killed by a police jeep in Beijing and the government says that it was an accident.
June 3	Crowds of students prevent soldiers from entering Tiananmen Square by placing more barriers. The government says that students are attacking soldiers.

June 3 & 4	The Beijing massacre occurs. Soldiers of the People's Liberation Army and the police move to clear the square of all demonstrators. The first real violence occurs at about 10 p.m. and continues for over fourteen hours. Deaths run between two thousand and three thousand. By the afternoon of June 4, the soldiers again have control of the square.
June 5	The government declares victory against the students and their rebellion.
June 9	Deng Xiaoping and other leaders go on television and praise the military in their role in bringing peace. They pledge that the handful of students who started the riots never threatened the CCP or the People's Republic of China.

PERSONAL ACCOUNT

I am a 20-year-old student at Qinghua University. Last night I sat on the steps of the Monument to the People's Heroes and witnessed the whole incident in which the army shot the students and the citizens.

Some of my schoolmates were shot dead. My clothes are still stained with their blood. As an eyewitness and survivor, I disclose what I saw during the massacre to all kind and peace-loving people.

In truth, we knew that the army would actively suppress us yesterday afternoon. A person called on us at 4:00 p.m. and told us that the army would use violence to clear everybody from the Square. After we were told this we discussed the matter urgently. We decided to adopt some measures to alleviate the conflict and to avoid great bloodshed.

At that time we had twenty-three guns and some bombs, which were obtained from the army during the conflict that occurred in the previous two days. The Autonomous Students Union of Beijing Universities (ASUBU) decided to give these back to the army to demonstrate our principle of "Promoting Democracy by Non-Violence." Last night we contacted the army under the Tiananmen Well. An officer replied that they could not accept the weapons by order of senior-ranking officials. Following that, the students destroyed these weapons at 1:00 a.m. because the situation had turned critical, and these weapons might have been used as "evidence" of killing soldiers.

ASUBU announced that the situation was getting worse. Since bloodshed could not be avoided, some students and citizens had to leave the Square. But there were forty to fifty thousand students and a hundred thousand citizens who decided to remain behind. I also remained.

The atmosphere was very tense. The students had never experienced anything like this. They were certainly frightened, but they were fully prepared psychologically, their minds were firm, and many students thought that the soldiers would not open fire. Anyway, we were encouraged by a noble feeling that it was worthwhile to sacrifice ourselves for democracy and development in China.

After midnight, when two armored vehicles sped through the two sides of the Square, the situation became much more serious. The loudspeakers of the army repeated an announcement that we should leave. Many soldiers in battledress invaded the Square from the surrounding streets. In the darkness, machine guns were set at the top of the Historical Museum.

All of the students were forced to retreat to the area around the Monument of the People's Heroes. I remember that one-third were girls, and the rest were boys. Students from Beijing's higher educational institutions made up 30 percent, the rest being students from other provinces or cities.

At 4:00 a.m. the lights in the Square were extinguished. Again we were told to evacuate the Square. My heart pounded, as if it were saying: the time has come, the time has come. At that moment, some people who joined the hunger strike, including Hou Dejian (a popular songwriter), negotiated with the army. They agreed that the students could leave peacefully. However, when the students prepared to leave, the lights in the Square were turned on. Some red flares exploded in the sky at 4:40 a.m. I saw that many soldiers had occupied the area in front of the Square. A large group of them ran out from the eastern door of the Hall of People. They wore uniforms, helmets and gas masks, and carried guns. (At 6:00 p.m. on June 3, we had spoken with a regiment of soldiers outside the western door of the Hall. They had said that they were only a supporting regiment, and that later there would be an army from Sichuan that would deal with the students directly. Their spokesman guaranteed that they would not shoot. Therefore, the soldiers who now came out were in all probability from Sichuan).

When these soldiers appeared they assembled in a row ten or so machine guns, in front of the Monument. The gunmen all crouched down on the ground with their guns pointing toward the Monument. When this was done, many soldiers and armed police, carrying flashlights, rubber clubs, whips, and various weapons, rushed toward the passive students. They attacked violently, forcing the students to separate into two groups and move upward on the Monument. I saw forty to fifty students with blood on their faces. Just at that moment, many armored vehicles and soldiers moved forward. These vehicles totally surrounded us, only leaving a gap in the direction of the Museum.

The soldiers and armed police who followed us up to the third level of the Monument destroyed all our broadcasting equipment, printing machines, and everything else. They then hit the students and forced them to go down. We did not move, but held our hands tightly, singing the *Internationale* and shouting, "The People's Army would not hurt people." But the attack was so violent that we were eventually forced to move down.

When we reached the ground, the machine guns opened fire. Some soldiers knelt down to shoot, and their bullets just flew over our heads. But others aimed low, and their bullets hit the chests and heads of the students. We had to go up the Monument again, then the machine guns stopped firing. But the soldiers there forced us down again. Once again we were shot by the machine guns.

Meanwhile, some workers and citizens dashed toward the soldiers brandishing bottles and clubs. Then the ASUBU ordered us to retreat outward from the Square. The time was a little before 5:00 a.m. Students then began to rush toward the spaces between the armored vehicles. These were closed by other vehicles. Moreover, more than thirty armored vehicles were driven at people. Some students were run over. The flagpoles were destroyed in this way. Thus the whole Square was in a state of chaos. I couldn't believe that the students were so brave. They rushed the vehicles. Many were killed. Others stepped over the dead bodies and ran forward again. At last there was a gap, and something like three thousand students dashed out, reaching the Historical Museum. Only a little more than one thousand of these were to survive.

There were many citizens there. Together we tried to go north, but there was gunfire. So we went toward the Qianmen Gate at the south end of the Square. I was running and crying. There was a mass of students running out under gunfire. Many people fell down. When we reached Qianmen, soldiers rushed toward us from the Jewellery Market (Zhubao Shi). They carried large clubs and hit us fiercely. Many people fought with the soldiers, which allowed us to run toward the Beijing Railway Station. The soldiers chased us from behind.

Source: Yu, Mok Chiu, & Harrison, J. F. (1990). *Voices from Tiananmen Square.* New York: Black Rose Books.

[Additional personal accounts can be obtained from the resources listed in the bibliography of this lesson plan.]

The Tiananmen Square lesson offers an international context to explore important social studies concepts such as protest, human rights, stability, power, social process, leadership, and government. United States and World History standards addressed by this lesson include: (1, B); (2, B, C); (3, B, J); (4, A) (see Appendix A). The NCSS standards for *Time, Continuity, and Change* relevant to this lesson are: (b) and (e); for *Power, Authority, and Governance:* (a), (b), (c), (d), (f), (h), and (i) (see Appendix A).

List three questions that you have after reading the personal accounts.

List three hypotheses of why this incident occurred.

INTERNET LINKS

This middle school lesson explored several important social studies concepts including human rights and government.

The broader topic of China is often covered in many primary and secondary units or lesson plans. Gathering information and resources on the Internet can make this task easier and more fun!

INTERNET LINKS

General Teacher Resource

http://www.neat-schoolhouse.org

Awesome Library

This is an excellent resource for the education community. It provides information for principals, teachers, nurses, counselors, parents, and students on topics such as assessment, standards, alcohol and drugs, and school improvement. This site also does an excellent job of organizing resources in the different content areas: math, science, art, technology, language arts, health, physical education, and social studies. When exploring the social studies page, two sites appear that would be extremely useful in teaching a unit or lesson on China.

INTERNET LINKS

Ancient China

http://members.aol.com/Donnclass/Chinalife.html

Daily Life in Ancient China

This site is very good at providing a mix of factual information with lesson plans and activities. The information provided focuses on the daily life of farmers, merchants, warriors, and nobles in four different Chinese dynasties. Information regarding Confucianism, Taoism, and Buddhism is also presented as well as links to Ancient Chinese fables. The lesson plans and activities included on this site, either directly or through links, are diversified and engaging. They include titles such as Mrs. Donn's Taoism and Winnie the Pooh lesson idea, Chinese Celebrations, Chinese Dialect Exercises, Chinese Proverbs, Writing Throughout History, Chinese Kite History, and Chinese Inventions. Several units, project ideas, and curriculum guides are included: Imperial Tombs Curriculum Guide, China projects, Ming China Unit, and 6th Grade China Unit.

INTERNET LINKS

Modern China

http://www.kn.pacbell.com/wired/China/index.html

Six Paths to China

This site complements the previously described site very well by providing a more modern look at China. It accomplishes this by outlining six different ways to explore China: hotlist, scrapbook, treasure hunt, subject sampler, intro webquest, and full webquest.

The hotlist is just as its name implies—a collection of Internet sites on China. This organization and listing of related Internet links is probably the best feature of this site in that the sites listed provide extensive information and lesson plan ideas. However, some of the other features are useful as they are more interactive and student centered.

The multimedia scrapbook is an activity designed for students. Directions are provided on how to make a scrapbook on China by downloading images and text. (Internet links are provided from which the information and images can be downloaded.)

The treasure hunt is designed for students to gain knowledge of China's past and present by answering a series of questions. Answers to these questions can be located by exploring different Internet sites that have been provided. This is advantageous for students as they are learning how to "surf the Net" for educational purposes.

The subject sampler provides activities for students such as copying a Chinese proverb they like and then writing a modern American version that shares the same meaning. Likewise, the intro webquest and full webquest are also activities for students, but they go a step further and promote higher-order thinking and collaboration.

NORTH AMERICAN FREE TRADE AGREEMENT

The following lesson on the North American Free Trade Agreement (NAFTA) was prepared by Kara Gallagher and Katie Flaherty who were enrolled in a teacher preparation program. The debate format developed by Kara Gallagher served as the foundation from which Katie developed the national issue into a lesson for middle school students. The lesson also illustrates how state standards can be incorporated along with national standards.

MODEL LESSON: NORTH AMERICAN FREE TRADE AGREEMENT

By Katie Flaherty

Level: Seventh–Eighth Grade   **Time:** 3 Hours, 3 Days

National Standards:
Science, Technology, and Environment

b. show through specific examples how science and technology have changed people's perceptions of the social and natural world, such as in their relationship to the land, animal life, family life, and economic needs, wants, and security

Virginia Social Studies Standards of Learning:

* The student will demonstrate the ability to use reference sources.
* The student will interpret graphic information with particular emphasis on interpreting maps.
* The student will analyze mass media. Emphasis will be placed on current, local, state, national, and international issues with stress being placed on interpreting facts, distinguishing relationships, cause and effect, differentiating between fact and opinion, and evaluating for accuracy. Sources should include TV, newspapers, radio, magazines, and eyewitness accounts.
* The student will demonstrate an understanding of the increasing interdependence of Virginia and the United States within the international community.
* The student will participate effectively in group activities.

Concepts: import, export, tariff

Objectives:

1. Students will interpret product maps and export/import maps.
2. Students will look up the tariffs currently imposed on imports and exports and demand statistics for particular products using reference materials.
3. Students will use mass media to describe the purpose and policy impact of NAFTA.

Procedure:

Introduction: Ask student to name something they own that came from another country. State that it is unusual that one particular country is able to produce all the goods and services it needs. Instead, countries usually trade with each other. State that today's lesson will examine such exchanges in North America.

Content Focus: Introduce product maps showing what is produced in the United States, Canada, and Mexico and import/export maps that graphically represent products imported and exported in each country. Explain tariffs and why they are imposed on products imported/exported to and from countries.

Developmental Activities: Divide class into six groups. Have each group investigate two products produced in one country and also in the other two countries involved in NAFTA. Do any patterns appear? Does one country produce a surplus of one product that another country has a shortage of? Can one country produce a particular product at a lower rate than another country? Encourage the students to discuss these topics within their groups. Have a reporter from each group share major points of group discussion with the class.

Introduce the North American Free Trade Agreement to the class. Inquire if any of the students have heard about NAFTA. Allow students to share their knowledge of NAFTA. Round out the explanation of NAFTA. Explain what it is designed to accomplish. See Background Information.

Discuss the impact of NAFTA on a variety of people. How would it be perceived by a poor farmer in Mexico? A businessman/woman who owned a factory in the United States? A government official in Canada? Call on a variety of students.

Have class return to original groups. Distribute the NAFTA debate by Kara Gallagher. Assign three groups a Pro NAFTA approach and the remaining three a Con NAFTA approach. Each group in the Pro and Con categories will identify a more specific viewpoint from which to analyze NAFTA (e.g., government official, worker, or business owner). Each student should locate three brief articles supporting their position and bring them to class. Review use of periodicals, *New York Times Index,* and other newspaper indexes.

Have class discuss their articles within their groups. Each group should focus on formulating an argument for or against NAFTA. Responses should be summarized on the following "Pro/Con NAFTA" worksheet. Encourage groups to anticipate their opponents' arguments and to address them in their remarks.

Have the class participate in a mock debate. Each group should elect a representative to present their argument. Have class vote to determine which side "won" the debate. Discuss with class the importance of stating a position clearly and logically to be able to persuade and influence others. What is the point of a debate?

Closure: Review the concepts introduced: import, export, tariff. Review the differential impact of NAFTA on the three groups presented: worker, government official, business owner. Discuss impact of NAFTA on the three countries involved: the United States, Canada, and Mexico. Ask: How much money is estimated to be involved with NAFTA being enacted? What do you think will happen to NAFTA and the three countries in the future?

Evaluation:

Formative: Small groups: Observe to determine level of participation of each group member.

Summative: Individual: Collect and check articles researched and summarized by each student.

Background Information:

The main goal of the North American Free Trade Agreement, or NAFTA, is to lower trade and investment barriers between the United States, Mexico, and Canada. The main components of NAFTA address: tariffs, investment, rules of origin, health and environment, safeguards, services, intellectual property, and side agreements.

NAFTA eliminates all tariffs on goods produced and sold in North America. Although some of the tariffs were eliminated immediately with the passing of NAFTA, others will be phased out over ten years. Each country has interest in protecting specific products and, therefore, the same product may be treated differently for tariff purposes depending on which country produces it. This is especially true for import-sensitive products—for example, it will take fifteen years to phase out U.S. tariffs on glassware, footwear, and ceramic tile. Import-sensitive products are those products that will be most affected by a relaxing of the trade barriers; most likely because the cost to produce them in another country is less than it is in the United States.

Regarding investment, NAFTA guarantees national treatment toward foreign investors, which means that each country pledges to treat investors from other countries as favorably under its laws as it does its own investors. This treatment will prevent governments from imposing special requirements on foreign investors such as forcing foreign investors to purchase parts for a product from a local manufacturer rather than from a manufacturer in the foreign investor's home country.

NAFTA also includes rules that will deter countries outside of the pact from reaping benefits from the agreement. In other words, France could not ship products to the United States, have minor modifications made to the products, and then have the same products sent to Mexico under the provisions of NAFTA. This prevents outside countries from deriving benefits from the open market created by NAFTA between the United States, Canada, and Mexico.

Health and environmental issues have been a big concern in the debate over NAFTA. The agreement obligates the three countries to work toward common standards to protect the food supply and the environment, but it does not lay out specific requirements. NAFTA allows each individual country to decide what level of protection is appropriate.

A "snapback" provision (a provision that allows the original tariffs that existed prior to NAFTA to be reimposed for a period of time) is included in the agreement as a last resort safeguard. Tariffs can be reimposed temporarily to protect domestic industries of imports if a particular product floods the market of any of the countries. This provision was written into the agreement to protect the countries; however, it is intended only to be used in a worst case scenario.

The United States gained an advantage with NAFTA by convincing Mexico to open up its market for services from the United States including banking, telecommunications, transportation, and government procurement. Some restrictions on market share would remain in place until the year 2000 on U.S. and Canadian banks and securities firms operating in Mexico.

Three side agreements were signed by the United States, Canada, and Mexico. The NAFTA side agreements address issues of environmental cleanup and enforcement, labor rights, and protections against a rapid increase in imports. The side agreements established a Commission for Environmental Cooperation and a Commission for Labor Cooperation. These commissions include representatives from each country and are responsible for monitoring compliance with labor and environmental laws in each country.

A year after NAFTA was put into effect, there is still little agreement as to the impact it has had on trade between the United States, Canada, and Mexico. It is hard to get a clear picture of the agreement because of the emotional arguments centered around NAFTA and because of the selective media coverage focused on the subject. Proponents and opponents alike bolster their arguments regarding the impact of NAFTA by picking and choosing selective facts that don't represent the whole story. This has created a great deal of confusion about what the agreement actually does. Most debates over NAFTA have focused on trade between the United States and Mexico and have all but ignored Canada. The agreement was designed to have a long-term impact on trade; a short-term analysis will not present a clear picture.

The NAFTA debate included in this chapter reflects some of the complexities surrounding economic factors that influence the way of life in the United States as well as throughout the globe.

DEBATE FORUM: THE NORTH AMERICAN FREE TRADE AGREEMENT

BY KARA GALLAGHER

BACKGROUND INFORMATION:

According to Dr. Steven Globerman, professor of economics at Simon Fraser University, the North American Free Trade Agreement (NAFTA), is a process by which Mexico, the United States, and Canada have agreed to cooperate over certain aspects of their trade policy (Globerman & Walker, 1993). Dr. Globerman goes on to state that the parties involved agreed to these conditions in order to enjoy the advantages of transnational trade free of protectionism.

Stelios Loizides in his publication, *The North American Free Trade Agreement,* sponsored by the Conference Board of Canada, states that "the NAFTA . . . will create the largest free-trade zone in the world, with a single market of more than 360 million people and a combined output of U.S. $7.5 trillion. The pact, expected to take effect on January 1, 1994, will eliminate virtually all tariffs and trade barriers among the three partners over a minimum of ten years, with the exception of tariffs for certain sensitive items that will be phased out over a period of up to 15 years" (Loizides & Rheaume, 1993). In addition, Mexico, the United States, and Canada have agreed to keep current protectionist measures against non–North American trading partners in place.

PRO NAFTA

NAFTA is an economically sensible move considering the nature of trade in the North American region. Steven Globerman, cited earlier, explains that an argument in favor of NAFTA is that North America is a natural market for the United States. Canada and Mexico are already the first and third trading partners of the United States. Mario Bognanna cautions against shunning NAFTA in light of the worldwide movement toward free trade regions. He states that promoting worldwide competitiveness is a concern as the European Union and the Pacific Rim are moving toward the formation of regional trading blocs" (Bognanna & Ready, 1993). If the United States chooses to retain protectionist trading policies, it may eventually be locked out of the free trade movement.

NAFTA has accelerated U.S. exports to Mexico. This fact is supported by Sarah Anderson in her article appearing in *The New York Times.* She states that "in 1994, U.S. exports to Mexico jumped twenty percent over those of 1993, and many companies have enjoyed benefits (Anderson & Cavanagh, 1995, p. A25)."

Provisions under NAFTA make it more cost effective for American businesses to open operations in Mexico. As a direct result, American companies are enjoying the advantages of being closer to other southern markets. Robert Keatingly demonstrates this point in his article, "Reaping the Benefits": "for Bennett X-Ray Technologies, Mexico's proximity to other Latin American nations has led to further sales. When the company showed its wares at a Mexico City trade fair, a Panamanian buyer ordered six machines. Says Mr. Muzzy, 'He probably never would have visited a Chicago fair (Keatingly, 1994, p. R4).' "

NAFTA has translated into economic growth for Canada. Clyde Farnsworth states that "exports have brought much needed job growth . . . the export surge has made Canada—a country of 28 million people that must export to survive—the fastest growing of the seven leading industrial countries (1995, F12)." Given the lucrative trade relationship the U.S. shares with Canada, prosperity for Canada will most certainly have positive effects in the United States.

Con NAFTA

The Mexican nation is extremely poor. Delai Baer, in a text entitled, *The NAFTA Debate: Grappling with Unconventional Trade Issues,* cites the following statistic: "about 40% of the Mexican population still lives in conditions of absolute poverty" (Baer & Weintraub, 1994, p. 163). With the population possessing little disposable income, it is unlikely that the United States will find a profitable market for consumer goods.

Although NAFTA requires the respective governments to place environmental considerations above business interests, according to Paul Sherman, evidence shows that the Mexican government is allowing industry to circumvent environmental regulations: "Some Mexicans, including many businesspeople, say the urgent need to restart the economy, weakened by the devaluation of the peso, should take priority over Mexico's environmental agenda, despite the country's pledges to tighten enforcement of environment laws under NAFTA" (1995, p. A14). Such attitudes are jeopardizing the breeding grounds of endangered whales and have caused the deaths of 40,000 North American migratory birds (DePalma, 1995, p. A14).

Proponents of NAFTA claim that liberalizing trade will decrease Mexican unemployment *and* as a result decrease illegal immigration. The numbers tell a different story: "Hinojosa and Robinson estimate that the elimination of protection for corn will lead to the emigration of 800,000 Mexicans to the United States (Globerman & Walker, 1993, p. 11)."

As the United States sinks more assets into the Mexican market, it opens itself up to a plethora of financial vulnerabilities. Allen Myerson writes, "Many companies have coordinated their North American operations so closely that labor unrest in Mexico resulting from the peso's plunges led to production shutdowns far to the north," and that "as Mexico suffers a slump expected to turn last year's American trade surplus with Mexico into a large deficit, the United States economy is likely to suffer job losses of tens, perhaps hundreds of thousands" (1995, p. D1).

Contrary to expectations of lower market prices, the influx of Mexican produce has forced American farmers to accept substantial losses while the consumer continues to pay the same prices. Sarah Anderson explains in her article, "NAFTA's Unhappy Anniversary": "Imports of cheaper tomatoes into the U.S. have increased 25% since NAFTA took effect, while the prices U.S. producers received last year for their crops were only one half of 1993 prices according to the Institute for Agriculture and Trade Policy. Meanwhile, prices for tomatoes at the supermarket have stayed about the same" (Anderson & Cavanaugh, 1995, p. A25).

REFERENCES

Anderson, S., & Cavanagh, J. (1995, February 7). NAFTA's unhappy anniversary. *The New York Times,* p. A25.

Baer, M. D., & Weintraub, S. (1994). *The NAFTA debate: Grappling with unconventional trade issues.* Boulder, CO: Reinner.

Bognanna, M., & Ready, K. J. (1993). *The North American Free Trade Agreement: Labor, industry, and government perspectives.* Westport, CT: Quorum.

DePalma, A. (1995, June 8). Deaths of birds in Mexico lake test trade pact. *The New York Times,* p. A4.

Farnsworth, C. (1995, February 12). In Canada, doubts fade quickly about trade accord. *The New York Times,* p. F12.

Globerman, S., & Walker, M. (1993). *Assessing NAFTA: A trinational analysis.* Vancouver: The Fraser Institute.

Keatingly, R. (1994, October 28). Reaping the benefits. *The Wall Street Journal,* p. R4.

Loizides, S., & Rheaume, G. (1993). *The North American Free Trade Agreement: Implications for Canada.* Ottowa: The Conference Board of Canada.

Myerson, A. (1995, February 14). Strategies on Mexico cast aside. *The New York Times,* p. D1.

Sherman, P. (1995, April 27). The friends of the whales fight a salt factory. *The New York Times,* p. A4.

Materials and Resources:

Cloud, D. S. (1993, October 16). Sound and fury over NAFTA overshadows the debate. *Congressional Quarterly Weekly Reports, 51* (41), 2791–2796.

McWilliams, G. (1993, November 22). A GOP stronghold says: Pipe down, Ross. *Business Week, 3347,* 38.

Mexico starts again. (1995, August 26). *The Economist, 336* (7929), 11–12.

Mexico: The long haul. (1995, August 26). *The Economist, 336* (7929), 17–19.

Mitchell, C. (1995, January 1). Life after NAFTA. *The Atlanta Journal and the Atlanta Constitution,* p. R/01.

Morris, S. E. (1993). *Using and understanding maps: Industry of the world.* New York: Chelsea.

NAFTA and U.S. Economic Policy. (1995). *Congressional Record,* January 11.

Samuelson, R. J. (1993, November 22). The isolationist illusion. *Newsweek,* p. 30.

The slings and arrows of outrageous fortune. (1993, October 30). *The Economist, 329* (7835), 25–26.

Standards of Learning for Virginia Public Schools. (1995). Richmond, VA: Board of Education, Commonwealth of Virginia.

By using a debate format for analysis, middle school students learn many geographic, economic, and global principles in this NAFTA lesson. For the NCSS standards for *Science, Technology and the Environment,* (b) is addressed. For *Production, Distribution and Consumption* the following are addressed: (a), (b), (i). For *Global Connections* (b), (d), (e), and (g) are addressed. The National Geography Standards addressed include: *Human Systems* (5) and *Environment and Society* (1), (2), (3). As you can see, the selection of complex topics or issues lend themselves more easily to interdisciplinary approaches.

✦ INTERNET LINKS

To supplement the middle school lesson on NAFTA it may be of interest to explore the NAFTA homepage.

INTERNET LINKS

NAFTA

http://www.itaiep.doc.gov/nafta/nafta2.htm

The NAFTA Homepage

Although the information contained on this site may be too complex for the average middle school student, it is a good place for teachers to look for information pertaining to this issue and this lesson.

G R O U P   W O R K S H E E T

Names: _____

_____

_____

_____

NAFTA Debate Worksheet

Perspective: Government Official

Business Owner

Worker

Please circle the perspective from which your group is debating NAFTA.

Pro Arguments	**Con Arguments**
1.	1.
2.	2.
3.	3.
4.	4.

ALBERTA CLARDY: ELDERLY IDENTITY IN A YOUTH CULTURE

Biographies are a great way to appreciate the lives and accomplishments of others, whether they are famous people or a next-door neighbor. Young people can take the role of a social scientist and researching the life of a member of the family or a member of the community. In the lesson that follows the author utilized research from her great-grandmother's diaries to investigate roles of the elderly. To contrast stereotypes of the elderly in an American culture that places so much emphasis on youth, physical appearance, and media imagery, the lesson demonstrates the vitality and active lifestyle of a woman from ages 76 to 85. Students are encouraged to reflect on their own images of and experiences with elderly people.

MODEL LESSON: ALBERTA CLARDY: ELDERLY IDENTITY IN A YOUTH CULTURE

Level: Seventh   **Time:** 2 Hours

Topic: The Elderly in American Culture

Standards:

National Council for the Social Studies Standards:
Individual Development and Identity

c.   Describe the ways family, gender, ethnicity, nationality, and institutional affiliation contribute to personal identity
g.   Identify and interpret examples of stereotyping, conformity, and altruism

Objectives:

1. Students will make inferences about an elderly person's identity by analyzing Alberta Clardy's diary entries.
2. Students will analyze stereotypical thinking about the elderly, reflecting on their own views in relation to the influence of popular culture that emphasizes youth.

Procedure:

Introduction: Tell students to imagine that they are winding up their day and that they routinely make diary entries. Ask them to make a diary entry. For those who are willing to share, ask them to volunteer the nature of the activities or sentiments they recorded and why. Say that diaries can tell a lot about a person's life and the way one brings order and understanding to it. Today's lesson will give them insight into the life of Alberta Clardy. They will be able to compare the nature of their diary entries with hers.

Content Focus: Show students the excerpt from Alberta Clardy's diary from the week of May 3 to May 8, 1957. Don't tell students the year it was recorded or the age of Alberta. Ask students to describe Alberta Clardy, what she does, and how old she is. Most likely they will describe Alberta Clardy as someone younger than her actual age, someone who is active with family and community. After exchanging ideas, tell students that they will be making inferences about the life of Alberta Clardy during her elderly years when she was 76 to 85 years of age. Ask students what they would like to know about Alberta Clardy. Generate student questions and record on board. Possible questions are:

1. Meaningful Activities. What kinds of activities did Alberta Clardy do with her husband, family, friends?
2. Change over the Life Span. How did her activities change over the course of ten years?
3. Feelings. Which events were characterized by positive or negative associations?
4. Work. What role did Alberta Clardy's work play in her life and how did it change over the years?

Provide background information about Alberta Clardy's life up until the time the diaries were written. See Background Information. The diary entries are coded on the basis of several categories of interaction with people and the community: husband, family, friends, community, work, and regional and international events. In addition, the entries were evaluated for emotional content and coded, using positive ($+$), negative ($-$), and neutral (0) categories. Go through 1957 so that they understand how to use the codes. See the Model Code Analysis.

In groups, provide students with the 1957 diary excerpts. Discuss the entries with some of the codes completed, which will enable students to make inferences. Ask them to record their inferences for the remaining blanks based on information in the diary (see the following worksheet). Share responses. Provide pie chart of all years' activities so the selected week can be compared with the ten-year pattern. After discussing summaries of group work, return to questions generated in the beginning by students.

Closure: Ask students to reflect on their views of the elderly. Ask them to contrast their views with descriptive words they might use to describe Alberta Clardy. Did views reinforce or contrast with stereotypes of the elderly? Ask students if they can give other examples of positive images or experiences they have had with the elderly. Close by asking students to think about how American culture contributes to stereotypical roles for the elderly. Point out that according to Cowgill and Holmes (1972) the elderly living in industrialized countries express greater dissatisfaction with their lives than do the elderly in nonindustrialized countries. Issues such as mandatory retirement, popular culture's emphasis on youth, misinformation, health care, ignorance about physical conditions, and the perpetuation of stereotypes all contribute to this cultural phenomena (Gutman, 1994).

Evaluation:

Formative: Students' questions; cooperation during group activities.

Summative: Recorded list of inferences.

Materials and Resources:

Data from Alberta Clardy's diary; books:

Cowgill, D. O., & Holmes, L. D. (Eds.). (1972). *Aging and modernization.* New York: Appleton-Century-Crofts.

Gutman, D. (1994). *Reclaimed powers: Men and women in later life.* Evanston, IL: Northwestern University Press.

Background Information:

Alberta Louise Chadwick Clardy was born in Rockdale, England, August 26, 1880, and lived in Castleton, England, until she was about 5 years old. She then came to the United States with her father, James Chadwick, mother, Mary Gregson Chadwick, and sister, Alice, who was 10 years old. The family first settled in Duluth, Minnesota, before moving to Glendora, California.

When Alberta was 16 she met William Giles Clardy who was 26. They married in 1897 and later had two children, Edwin James Clardy, born May 16, 1898, and Edith Rose Clardy, born October 15, 1899. The photo on page 464 shows Alberta, William, Edwin and Edith around 1906. In the school photo taken in Los Angeles around 1904, Edwin is fourth from the left on the bottom row. During the time in which the enclosed diary excerpts were written, Alberta and William had seven grandchildren and eighteen great-grandchildren. The excerpts represent activities for the week May 3 to May 9, 1957. Following is an explanation of the relationships of family members mentioned. Others named were friends.

Dad—husband, William Giles Clardy (died in 1959)
Ed and Margaret—son and daughter-in-law
Winny—cousin
Edith and Ed—daughter and son-in-law
Bill and Mary—grandson and his wife
Milt—grandson
Genevieve—granddaughter (Edwin James's daughter)
Marjorie and Linda—granddaughter and great-granddaughter
Loves—daughter's married name and their children

National Council for the Social Studies standards for *Individual Development and Identity* (c) and (g) reinforce the importance of cultural traditions while cautioning against stereotyping. Concepts from psychology and anthropology that can be stressed include: change, family, custom, habit, interdependence, labor, mobility, needs, norms, and welfare.

Edwin Clardy, bottom row, fourth from left, around 1904 in a Los Angeles, California Elementary School

The Clardy family around 1906; left to right, Edith Clardy, Alberta Clardy, William Giles Clardy, and Edwin Clardy

MODEL CODE ANALYSIS: 1957

Date	Description	Code	Activity	Feelings
5/3/57	Watered	12B		
5/3/57	Mowed lawns all in	12B		
5/4/57	Did yard work	12B	Yard Work	Neutral
5/6/57	Worked in yard	12B		
5/7/57	Worked in yard some more	12B		
5/8/57	Worked in yard	12B		
5/4/57	Cleaned house	13B		
5/6/57	Washed	13B	Cleaning	Neutral
5/7/57	Washed	13B		
5/3/57	Checks came, went to bank	14B	Shopping/bank	Neutral
	Shopped, paid bills			
5/8/57	Shopped	14B		
5/4/57	Ed & Margaret came in p.m.	22B	Family visits	Neutral
5/9/57	Winny phoned. Alice coming,			
	she arrived 6:30 p.m.	22B		
5/8/57	Got card & $10 from Ed & Margaret	25B	Receiving gifts	Neutral
5/4/57	Dad miserable	26C	Husband's health	Negative
5/5/57	Dad raved all nite	26C		
5/5/57	Nice day	51A	Weather	Positive
5/5/57	Went to Pasadena/cafeteria, then to	52B	Outings	Neutral
	Brookside Park			

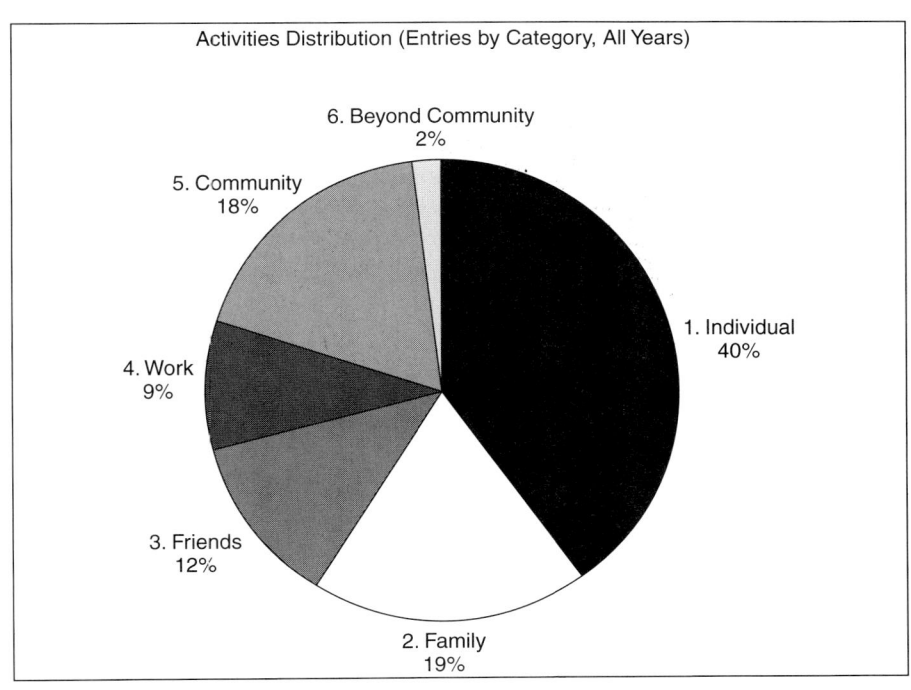

Activities Distribution (Entries by Category, All Years)

6. Beyond Community 2%

5. Community 18%

4. Work 9%

3. Friends 12%

2. Family 19%

1. Individual 40%

CODE FOR DESCRIPTION OF ACTIVITIES

Feelings: A = + (positive)   B = 0 (neutral)   C = − (negative)

1. Individual
   - 11 Cooking
   - 12 Yard work
   - 13 Cleaning
   - 14 Shopping/bank
   - 15 Self feelings; staying home; phoning
   - 16 Description of intent/report
   - 17 Health care (hair appts., dr. appts., glasses, funeral, license)
   - 18 Maintenance (Law work done by others, cleaners, car, appliances, fixing, etc.)
2. Family
   - 21 Go to visit family
   - 22 Family comes to visit
   - 23 Description of health/activities
   - 24 Celebrations, funerals, birthdays, weddings, etc.
   - 25 Giving/receiving gifts
   - 26 Husband's health or activity
3. Friends
   - 31 Go to visit friends
   - 32 Friends come to visit/phoned
   - 33 Description of health/activities
   - 34 Celebrations, funerals, birthdays, weddings, etc.
   - 35 Giving/receiving gifts
4. Work
   - 41 Sewing; selling fruit
5. Community
   - 51 Weather
   - 52 Going on outings
   - 53 Church
   - 54 Events, activities, clubs, Needlework Guild, Old Timers
   - 55 Ethnic activities/references
6. State/Regional
   - 61 Outings
7. National
   - 71 National news/events/holidays
8. International
   - 81 International news/events

G R O U P   W O R K S H E E T

Inferences Generated from Alberta Clardy's Diary

Individual (Codes 11–18):

Family (Codes 21–26):

Friends (Codes 31–35):

Work (Code 41):

Community (Codes 51–55):

State/Regional (Code 61):

National (Code 71):

International (Code 81):

Congressional Elections

Mickey Buhl prepared the following unit as a part of course fulfillments while taking an elementary social studies class. As a preservice student he was able to pursue his interest in politics while conducting the research for the unit. Eventually Mickey's first teaching assignment was in a middle school and he was able to incorporate many of the following lessons when teaching.

Model Lesson: Congressional Elections

A Social Studies Unit for Eighth Grade Students

By Michael Buhl

Rationale

The purpose of this unit is to increase students' knowledge of the American political system. It seeks to improve student's appreciation and understanding of the Congress and the political process by focusing on the politics of congressional elections. The unit is not a thorough examination of Congress or congressional elections; rather, it focuses on several topics that illustrate the political nature of the body and the election process. The unit is designed to supplement a traditional examination of the structure of the federal government, the division of power between the three branches, and the relationship between the federal government and the people.

Why try to improve students' political awareness? Democracy means government by the people. Democracy works only with civic participation; the people must be educated about government in order to govern. The United States is the foundation of democracy throughout the world. However, voting patterns and other statistics on civic awareness show a disturbing trend of reduced involvement in government, and public cynicism about government is very high. To reverse these trends, students must be educated about the governmental process, and the role they play in it. This unit is designed to do exactly that. It presents students with a view of how the political process works and the roles different actors and various forces play in determining political and governmental outcomes.

Long-Term Goals

Personal   Students will be prepared to participate in government by learning their role as citizens and voters within the political system.
Students will be able to analyze, evaluate, and discuss sensitive political issues, such as race, in a mature manner.

Conceptual   Students will be better able to understand the American political system, the political process, and their relationship with government, and will be better able to understand political events that occur around them.
Students will understand differences between the political parties and among candidates, thus being able to evaluate politicians and political statements.

Linkage to National Social Studies Standards

Individuals, Groups, and Institutions

Apply knowledge of how groups and institutions work to meet individual needs and promote the common good.

Analyze group and institutional influences on people, events, and elements of culture.

Describe the various forms institutions take and their interactions with people.

Describe the role of institutions in furthering both continuity and change.

Identify and analyze examples of tensions between expressions of individuality and group or institutional efforts to promote social conformity.

Power, Authority, and Governance

Describe the powers of government and how its powers are acquired, used, and justified.

Identify and describe the features of the U.S. political system, and identify representative leaders from various levels and branches of government.

Explain and apply concepts such as power, role, status, justice, and influence to the examination of persistent issues and social problems.

Civic Ideals and Practices

Examine the origins and continuing influence of key ideals of the democratic republican form of government such as liberty, justice, equality, the rule of law, and individual human dignity.

Practice forms of civic discussion and participation consistent with the ideals of citizens in a democratic republic.

Analyze the effectiveness of selected public policies and citizen behaviors in realizing the stated ideals of a democratic republican form of government.

Culture

Explain why individuals and groups respond differently to their physical and social environments and/or changes to them on the basis of shared assumptions, values, and beliefs.

Articulate the implications of cultural diversity, as well as cohesion, within and across groups.

Linkage to the Virginia Standards of Learning for the Eighth Grade

8.1   The student will identify rights, responsibilities, and duties of individual citizens as listed in Virginia and United States historical documents.

8.2   The student will demonstrate a basic understanding of the American legal, political, and economic system.

8.4   The student will identify the structure and function of local, state, and federal government.

8.5   The student will identify basic concepts of American and other political and economic systems.

8.6   The student will recognize the values, traditions, and/or attitudes of various cultural/ethnic groups in America.

8.7   The student will participate effectively in group activities.

8.9   The student will interpret and analyze political maps.

8.10   The student will use a variety of sources and approaches in research.

CONTENT OUTLINE

	Lesson Title	**Activity**	**Learning Area Focus**	**Type**
Lesson 1	The Drawing of Congressional District Maps	Interpreting congressional district maps	Understanding political divisions Map interpretation skills	Map and Globe
Lesson 2 must be preceded by viewing a videotape on the struggle for black voting rights				
Lesson 2	Minority-Majority Districts	Small-group and full-class discussion of race and politics	Appreciation of and ability to address sensitive issues Critical thinking skills	Thinking Skills
Lesson 3 must be preceded by a lesson outlining basic differences between Republicans and Democrats				
Lesson 3	The Political Spectrum	Small-group activity to frame critical questions about political issues to ask political candidates	Understanding political positions Participation in group activities	Direct Instruction/ Small Group
Lesson 4	Debate	The Debate, Robb vs. North	The nature of political debate Asking questions to get information in formal setting	Bio sketch (adapted)
Lesson 5	The Political Candidate	Class analysis of critical issues affecting voters' perception of candidates	Awareness of the relationship between the public and government Higher-level thinking skills/questioning strategies	Inquiry

BIBLIOGRAPHY

This unit was constructed primarily from my personal knowledge and experience accumulated while completing an undergraduate degree in political science and economics at the University of North Carolina, a master's degree in Public Policy at the University of California at Berkeley, and while working in the Congress for the Congressional Budget Office. In addition, I consulted these sources for general and specific information.

Birnbaum, J. H., & Murray, A. S. (1987). *Showdown at Gucci Gulch: Lawmakers, lobbyists, and the unlikely triumph of tax reform.* New York: Vintage.

Congressional Yellow Book. (1992). Washington, DC: Government Printing Office.

de Toqueville, Alexis. (1945). *Democracy in America.* New York: Vintage Books.

Hyde, A. C. (1992). *Government budgeting: Theory, process, and politics.* Pacific Grove, CA: Brooks/Cole.

O'Conner, K., & Sabato, L. J. (1993). *American government: Roots and reform.* New York: Macmillan.

Reiter, H. L. (1993). *Parties and elections in corporate America.* New York: Longman.

Wayne, S. J. (1992). *The road to the White House 1992, The politics of presidential elections.* New York: St. Martin's Press.

Wildavsky, A. (1992). *The new politics of the budgetary process.* New York: HarperCollins.

Wilson, J. Q. (1989). *Bureaucracy: What government agencies do and why they do it.* New York: Basic Books.

P R E T E S T / P O S T T E S T

Name _____

Fill in the Blank

1. Congress is made up of two bodies, the _____ and the _____ ___ _____ .
2. Each Senator represents the entire state. Each member of the House represents one _____ _____ .
3. After each census state legislatures redraw the boundaries of congressional districts. This process is called _____ .
4. A political _____ is when two candidates face each other on a stage in front of an audience of voters to argue the issues of a campaign.
5. On the political spectrum, from left to right, Democrats are considered to be on the _____ .
6. The two major political parties in the United States are the _____ and the _____ .

True/False (Circle T for true, F for false.)

1. Congressional districts are permanent and never change shape.   T   F
2. Each state has the same number of congressional districts.   T   F
3. An important reason people vote for political candidates is because the candidate looks good on television.   T   F
4. About 11 percent of the population of the United States is black. Less than 11 percent of the members of Congress are black.   T   F
5. One of the factors that affects how congressional districts are drawn is a desire by political parties to maximize the number of their party's candidates who are elected.   T   F
6. The Supreme Court has required states to create minority-majority districts (Districts where the majority of the voters are of the same minority group.)   T   F

Multiple Choice (Circle the correct answer.)

1. Politicians argue over how much the government should do to take care of the poor and less fortunate. Which type of politician would be most in favor of the government doing *a lot* to take care of the poor?
   a. A conservative Republican   c. A conservative Democrat
   b. A liberal Democrat   d. A liberal Republican

2. When the Constitution was first written, only white men were guaranteed the right to vote. After the Civil War African-Americans were granted the right to vote, but discriminatory laws in the South prevented most blacks from voting until the 1950s and 1960s. The movement that helped bring about equal voting rights for blacks is called
   a. The Women's Suffrage movement   c. The Civil Rights movement
   b. The Black Equality movement   d. The 1950s movement

3. About 6,600,000 people live in the state of Virginia. Virginia has 11 congressional districts. About how many people live in each congressional district?
   a. 10 million   c. 4,000,000
   b. 20,000   d. 600,000

4. The Voting Rights Act of 1965 was designed to improve and succeeded in improving the voting rights for which group of Americans?
   a. African-Americans
   b. Women
   c. Northern conservatives
   d. Irish Americans

5. Whether someone is registered as a Republican or Democrat or some other party is called that person's
   a. Political or party affiliation
   b. Title
   c. Representation
   d. Nickname

6. Members of congress refer to the people in their districts (the people they represent) as their
   a. "Little darlings"
   b. Sons and daughters
   c. Constituents
   d. Employees

Short Answer (Answer in *complete sentences.* Use the space provided.)

1. State two reasons why we would want states to create congressional districts where the majority of the voters are black.

2. Choose *one* of the following political issues.

   Issues: Gun Control   Government programs to help the poor
              Family Values   Military intervention

   Briefly describe the stand that the following politicians might take on the issue you choose.

   Liberal Democrat:

   Liberal Republican:

   Conservative Democrat:

   Conservative Republican:

MODEL LESSON: DRAWING CONGRESSIONAL DISTRICT MAPS

DAY ONE

Topic: A Map Lesson for Eighth-Grade Social Studies

Purpose:

1. Teach students to gather specific information from complex maps.
2. Teach students how political factors influence the way congressional districts are drawn.
3. Improve students' understanding of representative democracy.

Objectives:

1. The class will watch the teacher create congressional districts on a specially designed map of the state of Arizona according to the political affiliation of different regions.
2. In small groups, students will interpret the maps of the congressional districts, and will answer specific questions from the maps.

Concepts/Vocabulary: congressional districts, constituents, redistricting, political affiliation

Procedure:

Introduction: Review previous material on congressional districts. (5 minutes)

A.   Congress—Structure. Set the stage by reminding students what we have studied (and what today's lesson will relate to). We've studied the two houses of Congress, how many members are in each, and how members are elected to each body. Reinforce that Congress is the heart of our representative democracy.

B.   Congressional Districts. Review how each state is divided into congressional districts; that each district sends one person to the House of Representatives; that each district has the same number of *constituents* (define); and that after the 1990 census each district on average contained 573,394 constituents.

Content Focus: Present information on redistricting. (Lecture) (10–15 minutes)

A.   Redistricting. Describe *redistricting* by addressing the following questions:
   What is redistricting?
   • The redrawing of congressional district boundaries.
   When does redistricting occur?
   • Every ten years after the census is taken.
   How does the census affect the House of Representatives?
   • It tells us the population of different areas.
   Why must we redistrict?
   • To maintain equal representation.
   Who controls where the lines are drawn?
   • State legislatures redraw boundaries.

B. How does political affiliation affect redistricting? Discuss in detail how *political af-filiation* (Democrat or Republican) affects how district lines are redrawn.
1. *Constitutional forces:* maintain equal representation.
2. *Political forces:* maximize number of representatives from a political party.

Map Drawing, Modeling Exercise: Draw Congressional District maps. (10 minutes)

A. Present color-coded map. Show the overhead of the specially color-coded map of Arizona. Explain the coding and the parameters.
1. *Color-coding:* Pink = Democrat, Blue = Republican.
2. *Counties:* Show them which lines divide the counties.
3. *Population:* Each county has 200,000 people.
4. *District:* Ask students: *About how many constituents are there in a congressional district?* (600,000)
Each district will contain three counties. There will be six districts.

B. Map drawing. The teacher pretends to be the state legislature and draws congressional district boundaries on the specially color-coded map of Arizona. Draw two maps.
1. First, pretend to be a Democrat—maximize the number of Democrats who would be elected.
2. Second, pretend to be a Republican—maximize the number of Republicans who would be elected.

The teacher draws the boundaries on the overhead version of the color-coded map. While drawing the boundaries, show how each district contains three counties, but do not explain why you group certain counties together. *The primary purpose of the map-drawing exercise is to familiarize the students with the map to facilitate their map-interpretation activity.*

Map-Interpretation Activity: (15–20 minutes)

A. Democrat or Republican Groups. Divide students into groups of four or five. Give each group a copy of one of the two maps the teacher just produced. Each group will have either the Republican map or the Democrat map.

B. Analyze maps. Each group will analyze its map and answer the questions on the worksheet.

Closure: (5 minutes)

Exercise:
Review how different the Democrat and Republican maps looked. Discuss the impact political affiliation played on the outcome of the maps.

Discuss the ways that redrawing districts is much more complicated in real life: population not evenly spread across and among counties; need for minority districts; strong pressure to keep incumbents safe; a states loss (or gain) of districts.

Overall Lesson:
Review what we learned.

1. Redistricting is the redrawing of congressional districts.
2. Drawing of district lines is an extremely political process.

Evaluation:

Formative: Did students remember basic information about congressional districts? Completion of worksheet and map-interpretation activity.

Summative: Unitwide assignments.

Assignment #1: Each student must pick one congressional district outside of Virginia (or whatever the home state is). Student must go to the library and consult the following sources listed to answer the following questions:

1. Which state, which district? Provide a map of the district—photocopies are acceptable.
2. Who is the current representative?
3. Which political party?
4. What is the population of the district (all should be about the same)?
5. A brief (2–3 paragraphs) discussion about the district. A student could explore any or several of the following:
   * the political orientation of the district over time
   * the economic base of the district
   * whether it is urban or rural
   * what ethnic groups are present in the district
   * any other topic of interest related to the district

Sources:

1. The Congressional Yellow Book
2. Congressional Districts in the 1990s
3. Congressional Districts in the 1980s (will provide a historical comparison for question 5)
4. America Votes 20—1990
5. Ask the librarian for other sources.

Assignment #2: In a short paper (less than one page), tell me what happened to Montana as a result of redistricting in 1992. What questions does the Montana case raise about equal representation?

Be sure to explain "redistricting" and "equal representation" as part of your answer.

Background Information:

Each state is divided into *congressional districts*. Each district contains about the same number of people (members of Congress refer to the people in their districts as *constituents*). Each district sends one representative to the House of Representatives; thus, each member of the House represents an equal number of constituents.

The census tells us where people have moved from and to. To maintain equal representation, the principle of one person–one vote, congressional district boundaries must be redrawn to account for population shifts. This process is called *redistricting*.

The redistricting process is extremely political. *Political affiliation*—that is, alignment with either the Democratic Party or the Republican Party—is one key factor that affects redistricting. Each side seeks to maximize the number of representatives from that party by analyzing maps showing the voting patterns of different regions within the state and drawing boundaries accordingly.

Many other factors also affect redistricting: (1) the party that controls the state legislature may be different from the party of the state's congressional representatives; (2) incumbents in Congress, regardless of party, are very influential in state legislatures, thus incumbency is protected; (3) recent court interpretations of the Voting Rights Act of 1965 require states to draw districts that are predominantly of one ethnic minority—particularly black districts in southern states; (4) the loss of a district (due to reduced population relative to other states) requires pitting incumbents against one another.

Materials and Resources:
1. Overhead map of color-coded map of Arizona
2. Paper copies of color-coded map—Democrat and Republican versions
3. Map-interpretation worksheet

Extensions:
From the lecture, math is essential to dividing a state into districts and maintaining equal representation. During the map-interpretation activity, students must use math to answer many of the questions.

Analyze the color-coded map of Arizona and answer these questions:

1. How many congressional districts are there?

2. How many Democrats would you expect to be elected?

3. How many Republicans would you expect to be elected?

4. How many constituents are in each district?

5. What is the total population of the state?

6. Which party do you think controlled the Arizona state legislature that drew your map?

7. How would the map be different if the other party had controlled the Arizona state legislature?

MODEL LESSON: MINORITY-MAJORITY CONGRESSIONAL DISTRICTS

DAY TWO

Topic: A Thinking Skills Lesson for Eighth-Grade Social Studies

Purpose:

1. To explore the phenomenon of underrepresentation of minority groups in American politics.
2. To *analyze* and *evaluate* information about a sensitive public policy issue.

Objectives:

Knowledge:

1. Students will watch a videotape from the *Eyes on the Prize* series depicting the struggle for black voting rights in the South. (*The previous day*).
2. In small groups students will list and discuss their reaction to the creation of congressional districts in which a majority of the electorate is black.
3. Students will present their reactions/opinions to the class.

Affective: Students will discuss sensitive issues in mature, responsible manner.

Procedure:

Introduction: Remind students about the video. (3 minutes) The previous day, the class will view a segment on the fight for black voting rights from the *Eyes on the Prize* series about the civil rights movement.

Introduce today's lesson by simply reminding students of the basic content of the video.

Content Focus: Present background knowledge on the Voting Rights Act of 1965 and the creation of minority-majority congressional districts. (Lecture) (15 minutes)

1. Minority groups have always been *underrepresented* in Congress and in other electoral bodies, partly due to restricted voting rights. That means the percentage of representatives in Congress who are black or Hispanic is much lower than the percentage of the population that is black or Hispanic. Basically, minorities don't get elected very often.
2. In response to the activism of people like Martin Luther King, Jr., and others involved in the civil rights movement, which highlighted the great injustices being committed against blacks in the South, the federal government passed the *Voting Rights Act of 1965*.
   I. Guaranteed the same voting rights to all citizens, regardless of race, gender, or ethnicity.
   II. Required states that had a history of segregation to remedy the past discrimination.
      A. Federal government oversees the states' plans.
      B. Has led to the creation of *minority-majority congressional districts,* in which the majority of the constituents is black.

C. Present maps of NC 1st and 12th districts and LA 4th district. Present the basic issues in the controversy over the districts, all of which are in court. *(Simply raise the questions; don't try to answer them. You just want to get the kids thinking about the issue.)*

   1. Strange maps skew notion of representation. What do the people within those districts have in common? Shouldn't districts be regional so that the area has common interests?
   2. Do blacks only vote for black candidates and whites for white candidates? Is this a safe assumption to make?
   3. The strange districts probably result in more black members of Congress by concentrating black voting strength in certain districts. But doing so dilutes black voting strength in other districts, which severely limits the voice of the black constituents.

Group Discussion: Divide class into groups of about four students each.
   1. Give each group a worksheet outlining basic questions that minority-majority districts raise. Have each group write down their reactions and opinions.
   2. Have one student from each group present the groups opinions to the entire class.
   3. Synthesize all of the groups' reactions into two or three general opinions and involve the entire class in a discussion to evaluate the issue.

Closure: (5 minutes) Summarize the issue, point out that personal opinions on issues like this can vary and that no opinion is right. Each person has the right to his or her opinion, and rather than dispute someone else's opinion, we must respect it and should seek to understand it.

Hand out copies of William Raspberry's column from the *Washington Post* discussing the court cases involving the districts presented. Highlight important passages.

Evaluation:

Formative: Did the students participate in the group discussion and the class discussion? Did their comments and questions reflect "higher" levels of thought, or just the reciting of factual information?

Summative: Each student shall summarize their personal reactions and opinions to the videotape, the information presented in class, and the group and class discussions. The summary can be in whatever form the student desires (subject to prior teacher approval)— a one-page written summary, a poster, a poem, a song, a cartoon, and so on.

Background Information:

Minorities have traditionally been underrepresented in Congress and other electoral bodies. This is partly due to the intentional restriction of minorities' voting rights, particularly against blacks in the South. The *Eyes on the Prize* series is a wonderful documentary of the civil rights movement that will present the background knowledge necessary for the students to think more deeply about the issue of minority voting rights.

The Voting Rights Act of 1965 guaranteed the same voting rights to all citizens, regardless of race, gender, or ethnicity. It was passed in response to the activism of the civil rights movement. The law requires states that had a history of segregation to remedy the past discrimination. Recently federal courts have interpreted that to mean that states had to draw congressional districts in which blacks were a majority.

Bizarre-looking districts have resulted, and the issue is back in court. The proper way to redress discrimination against blacks, and to increase black (and other minorities) voting power is extremely unclear, as Raspberry's column points out.

Many sensitive issues are involved. On the one hand, creating black-majority districts probably has resulted in more blacks being elected to Congress than would have occurred otherwise. However, there are costs. Namely, pooling black voters into a few districts reduces their number and influence in other districts. So representatives in other districts may be more focused on courting white voters than they would be if their district contained a larger number of blacks. Furthermore, creating districts to elect black representatives polarizes politics along racial lines even more than is already the case. Black political equality may best be served at the point when black representatives are elected from districts with a majority of white voters.

Materials and Resources:

Videotape, *Eyes on the Prize*—voting rights.
Overhead transparency of the NC 1st & 12th districts, and LA 4th district
Discussion Guide
Copies of the newspaper column, William Raspberry, *Washington Post,* October 1994

D I S C U S S I O N   G U I D E

Minority/Majority Districts

Write down your reactions and opinions to the following issues. You do not have to answer the questions specifically, just write down your group's opinions. *Honor each person's opinion.*

Should we create minority-majority congressional districts? Why?

Should we assume that people want to vote for a candidate of the same race as them? Why?

Do the bizarrely shaped districts conform to your notion of representation? Why?

 MODEL LESSON: THE POLITICAL SPECTRUM

DAY THREE

Topic: A Teacher-Directed Lesson for Eighth-Grade Social Studies

Purpose:

1. To introduce students to the range of political positions along the political spectrum.
2. To introduce students to the complexity of political issues.

Concepts: political spectrum, "left," "right"

Objectives:

1. In small groups, students will discuss issues of national significance and their ramifications.
2. Students will generate questions about specific issues to ask political candidates.

Procedure:

Introduction: Review yesterday's lesson, preview next two days. (3–5 minutes)

Yesterday, we studied the basic differences between the Republicans and the Democrats.

Today, we will look at differences in political opinion in more detail by studying a wider range of positions along the political spectrum. Also, we will prepare for tomorrow's debate by framing questions about specific issues to ask the candidates.

Tomorrow, two visitors will play the roles of Chuck Robb and Oliver North, Virginia's Democratic and Republican candidates for the U.S. Senate, in a mock political debate.

Content Focus: Introduce political platforms. (15–20 minutes)

1. Define the *political spectrum:* (lecture—draw and label the spectrum as follows while lecturing)

   <_____>

   The positions people take on the political issues spectrum ranges from "left" to "right." Republicans are generally considered to be on the right. This is the conservative side of the spectrum. Democrats are considered to be on the left side, which is the liberal side of the spectrum.

   The more conservative your position, the further along the *right* side of the spectrum you are. The more liberal you are, the further to the *left* you are on the spectrum.

2. Describe how politicians range all along the political spectrum. All Democrats and all Republicans are not the same. Introduce distinctions between conservative/liberal Republicans and conservative/liberal Democrats based on the view of the role of government in providing for the less fortunate.

   Conservative Republican: Ex. Oliver North/George Allen/Jesse Helms.

   The government should be as small as possible. This means lower taxes, fewer income support programs, and less income redistribution. The poor are on their own like everyone else. The unfettered private marketplace will provide for people better than government can.

Liberal Republican: Ex. Bob Michel/Lowell Weicker. Government role should be minimized, but present. Government must support the poor through some type of redistributive income support programs, but government should not get in the way of the private sector because economic growth is still the best way to provide for all people.

Conservative Democrat: Ex. Chuck Robb/Bill Clinton (the candidate, at least). Close to Liberal Republicans. Government should be involved, must provide support for the poor, but should reduce its role. Conservative Democrats do not distrust private business as true liberals do; they, like liberal Republicans, embrace business as the best source of growth. Unlike liberal Republicans, they believe that government can and should play a role in both regulating and stimulating business growth.

Liberal Democrat: Ex. Pat Schroeder/Ted Kennedy/Mario Cuomo. Liberal Democrats favor strong government support for the less fortunate through redistributive policies. They believe that relatively high taxes on the well off are necessary to provide adequate support for those unable to provide for themselves.

3. Stress that many factors determine what stand individual candidates take on any given issue. Which political party they are with tells you a lot, but individual differences can place candidates anywhere along the spectrum.

Group Activity: Frame questions for tomorrow's debate. (25 minutes)

1. Hand out Political Debate Topic Sheet. (One to each student.)
2. Divide students into six groups (of about four students each). Assign each group one of the topics on the topic sheet. Visit each group to answer questions about the topic. *(Stress to them that it's not important that they understand the topic thoroughly. Encourage them to generate questions based on the explanation and what they already know.)*
3. Each group discusses the topic and writes down at least three questions they might ask a political candidate to find out where he or she stands on the issue. (15 minutes)
4. The teacher goes over each group's questions and writes them on the board. Each student writes the questions in the spaces provided on the topic sheet. (10 minutes)

Closure: Prepare for tomorrow's debate. (3–5 minutes)
Describe the process for the political debate. Explain that the Democrat will champion a platform along the liberal lines discussed today, and the Republican will back a more conservative platform.

Evaluation:

Formative: Did the students participate in the group discussion? Were they able to generate questions about the topics?

Background Information:

Party affiliation tells you a lot about where a candidate stands on many issues. Indeed, being a Democrat or Republican is the most telling label in politics; the entire political system in the United States is framed around this bipartisan identification. However, not all Democrats and Republicans are the same. Members of both parties have very different views on many issues. The *political spectrum* defines the entire range of political stands, ranging from the very liberal far *left* to the ultraconservative far *right*.

Candidates from each party can be said to be conservative or liberal. That designation refers to their relative position within their party, as all Democrats are generally considered to be to the left of center and all Republicans to the right. Thus, a conservative Democrat is usually considered to be to the left of a liberal Republican.

Voters must look at a lot of information to determine where a candidate stands on any given issue. Party affiliation is the biggest clue, but how liberal or conservative the candidate is within the party also matters. Also, the candidate's individual preferences will affect how he or she feels about any specific issue.

Even though a candidate takes stands on individual issues, and to gain a deep appreciation for that candidate's position a voter must do quite a bit of research, the basic distinction of conservative/liberal Democrat or conservative/liberal Republican usually will give the voter a very good summary of where the candidate stands on issues generally. Thus, understanding that distinction will help citizens be informed voters.

Materials and Resources:

Political Debate Topic Sheets

POLITICAL DEBATE TOPIC SHEET

Several key issues are described in the following. The class will frame questions to ask about each topic. During the debate, you do not have to ask only the questions on this sheet. *You are encouraged to ask questions about any topic of interest.*

GUN CONTROL

Violent crime involving guns has increased alarmingly. Many people have proposed limiting people's right to own and carry guns as a way to reduce violent crime. Should the government restrict private citizens' right to own guns?

POSSIBLE QUESTIONS:

THE DEFICIT

The federal government spends more money than it raises in taxes each year. The difference is called the deficit. (This is similar to you or your parents spending more money than you or your family makes each year.) To reduce the deficit, the government must either raise taxes or cut spending. Both options have negative consequences. Should the government raise taxes, reduce spending, or allow the deficit to continue?

POSSIBLE QUESTIONS:

CRIME

Controlling crime is one of the jobs government has to do to protect its citizens. Everyone wants to reduce crime, but no one knows the best way to do so. Democrats and Republicans have different ideas on how to reduce crime. Should criminals be put in jail longer? Should the government focus more on programs to try to prevent crime, such as drug addiction treatment programs?

POSSIBLE QUESTIONS:

EDUCATION

Educating the youth of America is vital for our nation's future. Many people feel that our public school system is failing today's students. In particular, many people feel that schools in poor inner-city neighborhoods are much worse than other schools. What can the government do to improve education? Should more of an effort be made to improve the schools in inner cities? How?

POSSIBLE QUESTIONS:

FAMILY VALUES

Many people feel that Americans' moral principals are not as strong as they used to be. These people cite the large number of divorces, increasing violent crime, an increasing number of unmarried women having children, and teenage sexual activity as examples of America's moral decline. Should government try to improve American's values? What can government do to affect people's values?

POSSIBLE QUESTIONS:

MILITARY INTERVENTION

When two foreign countries or two groups within the same country go to war, many people may be killed and peace in that region is threatened. At those times, many people call for the United States to send its military forces to stop the war or fight for one side in the war. The Persian Gulf War against Iraq and the U.S. actions in Haiti are examples. Should the United States become involved in foreign conflicts even if there is no direct threat to the United States? Should we do so only to protect our interests, or should we send military forces to save other people's lives and to promote peace in general?

POSSIBLE QUESTIONS:

MODEL LESSON: A POLITICAL DEBATE

DAY FOUR

Topic: A Lesson on Debate for Eighth-Grade Social Studies

Purpose:
1. To introduce students to the nature of political debate and political argument.
2. To introduce students to being involved in civic concerns and activities such as elections.

Concepts: political debate

Objectives:
Students will question candidates about their positions on specific issues during a mock political debate between a prominent Democratic and a prominent Republican politician.

Procedure:
Introduction: Prepare students for the debate. (5–10 minutes)
Explain the format of the upcoming political debate:

a. Two candidates for the U.S. Senate in 1994 were Oliver North and Chuck Robb from Virginia. Each, played by an adult, will debate the issues with the teacher moderating.
b. Candidates will briefly present their platforms.
c. Students will ask questions of the candidates. Questions can be from the Topic Sheet or any issue of interest to the student.
d. Encourage students to ask follow-up questions if the candidates did not answer their first question or if the answer raised another question.

Content Focus: The debate. (35–40 minutes)

1. Teacher moderates, introduces the two candidates (dressed in suits if possible).
2. Candidates present their platforms in terms of basic beliefs and specific issues. (Less than 5 minutes each)

3. Moderator asks one question, then students ask questions of the candidates until the time is up. (Teacher/moderator keeps time—stop question/answer session after thirty minutes.)

Closure: Summary (5 minutes)
Each candidate has two minutes to summarize his platform.

Evaluation:

Formative: Did students listen attentively to the debate? Did students participate by asking questions? Did students ask follow-up questions after a candidate's response to their first query?

Summative: Students will complete a three-step assignment.
a. Each student will specify where along the political spectrum each candidate lies.
b. Each student will summarize what they think of each candidate. What did you like and dislike about each one?
c. Each student will write about two points made by the candidates. The student will summarize the position of the candidate and state whether the student agrees or disagrees and why.

Background Information:

Political debates are a traditional means for candidates in an election to present their views on various issues. Debates provide voters with an especially good opportunity to compare the two candidates' platforms, since both candidates must respond to questions posed either by moderators or the public. This is in contrast to other means of campaign publicity, such as television commercials, where the candidate completely controls what information is relayed to the voters. Thus, political debates are a wonderful way for voters to inform themselves about candidates and to prepare themselves to vote. The chart that follows outlines the two candidates' positions on the issues the class has prepared.

Materials:

Political Debate Topic Sheets for the students. (Developed by the class in previous lesson.) Two adult volunteers.

> Possibilities for volunteers: the principal and assistant principal; other teachers; parents; local politicians. The teacher should consult with the volunteers to share and discuss the platform they must present.

POLITICAL POSITIONS FOR NORTH AND ROBB

Issue:	Oliver North	Chuck Robb
Gun Control	North favors no government restriction on people's right to own guns. North is supported by the NRA and is a very conservative Republican.	Robb supports some government restrictions on gun ownership. He voted for the ban on assault weapons but does not favor strict restrictions, partly because Virginia as a state is anti-gun control.

The Deficit	North advocates massive government tax cuts and proposes to reduce the size of government (i.e., reduce government spending). However, as with most "tax-cutters" he is not specific on how he proposes to reduce spending. Thus, he does not take a strong position on reducing the deficit—he ignores it.	Robb is a moderate to conservative Democrat. As such, he proposes reducing government spending and the deficit. He voted for President Clinton's deficit-reducing budget bill last year and thus can claim credit for fighting the deficit. However, as with most politicians, his deficit-cutting fervor is limited.
Crime	North takes the conservative Republican line of getting tough on criminals. This means longer sentences, more prisons, and support for the death penalty.	Robb also wants to get tough on crime, but Democrats tend to attack crime from less of a "cowboys and Indians" point of view. He proposes more money for police, tighter gun control, and other measures.
Education	North favors a radical restructuring of education—calling for school choice. That means he wants the government to give parents vouchers that they can spend to send their children to the school of their choice—public or private, thereby creating a competitive marketplace in which public schools must compete for students.	Robb is against school choice. He, like most Democrats, wants to protect public education and strengthen it with more resources.
Family Values	One of North's biggest campaign issues is a return to "family values." Strongly supported by the Religious Right, North advocates government promoting religious and other values. This manifests itself in his strong support for school prayer, and welfare restrictions for unmarried women.	Robb and the Democrats want to keep religion out of government, and government out of the values business. They see school prayer as a violation of the separation of church and state. Robb too wants to reform the welfare system but does not couch his policies in terms of family values.
Military Intervention	Republicans in general tend to favor military intervention to protect U.S. interests, and not for humanitarian ventures. North is famous for his role in the Iran-Contra affair, a scandal partly from the illegal support of military regimes in Central America. He can be considered to strongly support U.S. military action to further our national goals.	Democrats tend to be more wary of using military intervention to further U.S. goals. Conversely, they are perceived to be more willing than Republicans to support military intervention for humanitarian purposes (Somalia, Haiti). Robb, who distinguishes himself little as an individual, except through sex scandals, can be considered a middle-of-the-road Democrat.

MODEL LESSON:
THE POLITICAL CANDIDATE

DAY FIVE

Topic: An Inquiry Lesson for Eighth-Grade Social Studies

Purpose:

1. To understand a candidate's combination of image and substance in a political campaign.
2. To develop the students' analytical abilities to ask and explore questions about unknown topics.

Concepts: public image, television advertising, campaign finance

Objectives:

1. Students will list factors and develop hypotheses about why people vote the way they do.
2. Students will conduct interviews to test their hypotheses.

Procedure:

Introduction: Recap yesterday's debate. (10 minutes)

Review yesterday's debate through class discussion/question and answer process. Choose students to:

1. Label each candidate (liberal/conservative Democrat/Republican).
2. Position each candidate on the political spectrum.
3. Summarize their position on at least three of the issues on the Topic Sheet.

Content Focus: Generate hypotheses about why people vote the way they do. (25 minutes)

1. Ask five different students to give three reasons why they voted for the candidate they did. In keeping with the sense of privacy accorded to a person's voting habits, request that the students do not tell you the name of the candidate they chose, just three reasons why they voted for that candidate. (Do not force students to give their summary; make it voluntary.)

   Write the reasons on the board in no particular order. Simply write what the student says; for example, "I liked his position on gun control" or "He spoke very well" or "I liked his tie."

   Do not qualify or judge any of the reasons.

2. Create a chart on the board outlining the factors that influenced why students voted the way they did. I have in mind something like this:

Policy Reasons	Voter's Personal Reasons	Candidate's Personal Characteristics
Liked stand on one issue	My mother votes for Democrats	He spoke well
Agreed with general platform	My friend told me this candidate was the best	He looked capable and confident
Etc.	Etc.	Etc.

However, do not dictate even the headings on the chart. Ask the students to look at the reasons listed on the board from the five students, and have them see if they can make any generalizations about the statements. Draw a chart and suggest headings if they have problems, but leave open other columns to add new headings. Have the students copy down the chart as it is created so they can take it home.

After generating statements from the students' experience with the debate, ask the students to go beyond the reasons listed on the board and have them theorize about reasons people might vote for candidates in real life. Accept all reasons; shape them only so far as to focus the language.

3. Instructional Input. If the students do not list it, add the following reason to the list: A candidate's *public image* (definition: the image or picture of the candidate that the campaign tries to create in the public's eye. Campaigns want to paint the candidate in as favorable a light as possible).
   a. Describe the nature of political image making in campaigns.
   b. Stress the importance of *television advertising* as the principal tool to shape a candidate's image. (Unlike a debate, television gives the campaign total control over what messages and image is seen by voters.)
   c. State that television ads are extremely expensive, and thus state how money is extremely important. In fact *campaign finance issues* (definition: paying for or financing the campaign) dominate a campaign. The candidate with the most money wins a very high percentage of the time. This is because advertising and the public image shaping that it allows is extremely effective, and you need money to advertise.

Closure: Discuss Interview Process. (15 minutes)

1. How do we test our theories? How do we find out whether the factors that we think affect people's voting behavior really are important?
   We will do a survey. Each student will conduct three to five interviews with adults who voted in any recent election. The election could have been for President of the United States, the U.S. Senate or U.S. House of Representatives, the governor, the state legislature, a local political race, a election for officers at work or in some other civic organization, or any other election.
2. Model an interview by simply interviewing one student and filling out an interview guide.
3. Pass out interview guides. Students should take five interview sheets and a copy of the chart we constructed in class.

Evaluation:

Formative: Students participation in the class generation of a chart explaining voting behavior.

Summative: Each student will complete five interviews. In addition, each student will compare and contrast the chart we created in class and what they found out from their interviews.

Background Information:

People vote the way they do for many reasons. Academic theories on voting behavior abound. For the purposes of this class, however, we want only to understand the relationship between what some describe as "substance versus image." Substance means a candidate's general political platform and his or her stands on specific policy issues. The debate we held in class illustrates the traditional relationship between the voter and the candidate. The candidates present their general political stances, voters ask them questions to elicit their views on pertinent public issues, and the candidates respond with substantive answers outlining their positions.

This model highlights the importance of policy issues in an election. However, as important, if not more so, is the public's perception of the candidate as a person, his or her *public image*. Modern campaigns carefully cultivate a candidate's public image through carefully scripted releases of information. Increasingly the mode of transmission of campaign information is through *television advertising*. Television has become the dominant medium for getting a candidate's message across. Because the television allows the candidate (and the campaign managers) to control exactly what is seen and heard, campaign information often centers more on image building than on discussing policy issues. Another concern in the modern campaign is *campaign finance*. Television ads are very expensive, but effective. Thus, fund-raising is of enormous concern in any campaign. Past election data show that the candidate with the most money wins a very high percentage of the time (around 90 percent; from Federal Election Commission data on the 1988, 1990, and 1992 elections that I examined thoroughly while working at CBO on campaign finance reform legislation.)

Materials and Resources:

Interview Guides (lots of them—five per student)

I N T E R V I E W   G U I D E

Name of Person Being Interviewed _____

Name of Interviewer _____

In the last election in which you voted:

1. What are the top three reasons you voted for the candidate you did?

2. Did you vote for a candidate from the same party that you had voted for during the last election in which you voted?

3. Did you vote for the same candidate that your boss recommended?

4. Did you vote for the same candidate that your husband/wife voted for?

5. Did you vote for the same candidate that your mother voted for?

6. Did you vote for the same candidate that your father voted for?

7. Did you see advertisements for any of the candidates? Where (TV, billboards, bumper stickers, newspapers, magazines, radio)?

8. Where did you get most of your information about the candidates (TV ads, other ads, talking to friends/family/colleagues, televised or live debates, pamphlets or other promotional literature)?

9. Did you receive more information about the candidate you voted for than his or her opponent?

10. If you did receive more information about the candidate you voted for than his or her opponent, how did it affect your impression of both candidates?

11. Describe the personal characteristics of the candidate you voted for (as you perceived them at the time of the election).

12. Describe the personal characteristics of the candidate you did not vote for (as you perceived them at the time of the election).

13. Was the candidate you voted for a better speaker than his or her opponent?

Students should add at least two questions that they think are critical to assessing why this person voted the way he or she did.

APPENDIX C
Incorporating Literature in the Social Studies

To assist you in preparing social studies lessons that incorporate literature, the following literature selections have been included. They are organized on the basis of familiar topics tied to social studies curricula and represent both K–3 and 4–8 grade-level divisions. In addition, you may want to consult the following general Children's Literature Selection Guides as well as the specific linkages to social studies listed in the journals *Social Education* and *Social Studies and the Young Learner*.

CHILDREN'S LITERATURE SELECTION GUIDES

Adamson, L. A. (1994). *Recreating the past: A guide to American and world historical fiction for children and young adults.* Westport, CT: Greenwood Press.

Aronson, M., Galbo, K., Schulz, A. R., & Shawkey, J. (1996). Time traveling with children's literature. *Social Studies & the Young Learner, 9* (1), P1–P8.

Atwell, N. (1987). *In the middle: Writing, reading and learning with adolescents.* Portsmouth, NH: Boyton/Cook.

Banks, D. N. (1998). From Hiroshima to Homer Simpson: Using literature to confront the impact of nuclear energy. *Social Education, 62* (4), 196–200.

Barr, C. (Ed.). (1998). *From biography to history: Best books for children's entertainment and education.* New Providence, NJ: R. R. Bowker.

Barr, C. (Ed.). (1999). *Reading in a series: A selection guide to books for children.* New Providence, NJ: R. R. Bowker.

Burke, E. M. (1986). *Early childhood literature: For love of child and book.* Boston: Allyn & Bacon.

Brown, D. K. (1998). The Children's Literature Web Guide. Available online: www.acs.-ucalgary.ca/~dkbrown/

Colburn, C. (1994). *What do children read next?: A reader's guide to fiction for children.* Detroit: Gale Research.

Cordier, M. H., & Perez-Stable, M. A. (1996). Latino connections. *Social Studies and the Young Learner, 9* (1), 20–22.

Donavin, D. P. (Ed.). (1992). *American library association the best of the best for children: Books, software, magazines. Videos, audio, toys.* New York: Random House.

Freeman, J. (1990). *Books kids will sit still for: The complete read-aloud guide* (2nd ed.). New York: R. R. Bowker.

Freeman, J. (1995). *More books kids will sit still for: A read-aloud guide.* New Providence, NJ: R. R. Bowker.

Gillespie, J. T. (Ed.). (1998). *Best books for children: Preschool through grade 6* (6th ed.). New Providence, NJ: R. R. Bowker.

Glazer, J. I. (1991). *Literature for young children* (3rd ed.). New York: Merrill.

Heller, M. F. (1995). *Reading-writing connections: From theory to practice.* New York: Longman.

Hicks, S. J. (1996). Promoting civic competence using children's trade books. *Social Education, 60* (4), 216–219.

Jensen, J. M., & Roser, N. L. (1993). *Adventuring with books: A booklist for pre-K–grade 6* (10th ed.). Urbana, IL: National Council of Teachers of English.

Kim, C. Y., & Garcia, J. (1996). Diversity and trade books. *Social Education, 60* (4), 208–211.

Lima, C. W., & Lima, J. A. (1998). *A to zoo: Subject access to children's picture books* (5th ed.). New Providence, NJ: R. R. Bowker.

Maxim, G. (1998). Writing poetry in the elementary social studies classroom. *Social Education, 62* (4), 207–211.

Miller-Lachman, L. (1992). *Our family, our friends, our world: An annotated guide to significant multicultural books for children and teenagers.* New Providence, NJ: R. R. Bowker.

Monson, D. L. (Ed.). (1985). *Adventuring with books: A booklist for pre-k–grade 6.* Urbana, IL: National Council of Teachers of English.

National Council for the Social Studies. (1996). 1996 notable children's trade books in the field of social studies. *Social Education, 60* (4), S1–S15.

National Council for the Social Studies. (1999). Carter G. Woodson book awards. *Social Education, 63* (4), 225–227.

National Council for the Social Studies. (1994). Notable children's trade books. *Social Education, 58* (4).

National Council for the Social Studies. (1999). Notable social studies trade books for young people 1999. *Social Education, 63* (4), S1–S15.

National Council for the Social Studies. (1998). Notable children's trade books in the field of social studies 1998. *Social Education, 62* (4), S1–S15.

National Council for the Social Studies. (1996). The 1995 Carter G. Woodson book awards. *Social Education, 60* (4), 221–222.

Norton, D. E. (1991). *Through the eyes of a child: An introduction to children's literature* (3rd ed.). New York: Merrill.

Norton, D. E. (1992). *The impact of literature-based reading.* New York: Merrill.

Nourie, B. L., & Hull, S. L. (1996). The concept of garden in children's learning and literature. *Social Studies and the Young Learner, 9* (1), 17–19.

Odean, K. (1997). *Great books for girls: More than 600 books to inspire today's girls and tomorrow's women.* New York: Ballantine Books.

Odean, K. (1998). *Great books for boys: More than 600 books for boys 2 to 14.* New York: Ballantine Books.

Spencer, P., & Ansell, J. (1997). *What do children read next?: A reader's guide to fiction for children, volume 2.* Detroit: Gale Research.

Stange, T. V., & Wyant, S. L. (1999). The great American prairie: An integrated fifth grade unit. *Social Education, 63* (4), 216–219.

The Children's Literature Nook. (1998, August 6). Available online: www.geocities.com/-Heartland/Estates/4967/index.html.

Tomlinson, C. M. (Ed.). (1998). *Children's books from other countries.* Lanham, MD: The Scarecrow Press.

Wepner, S. T., & Feeley, J. T. (1993). *Moving forward with literature: Basals, books, and beyond.* New York: Merrill.

Zarnowski, M., & Gallagher, A. F. (Ed.). (1998). *Children's literature and social studies: Selecting and using notable books in the classroom.* Washington, DC: National Council for the Social Studies.

Family

Books for Children Grades K–3

Ackerman, K. (1988). *Song and dance man.* New York: Knopf. Caldecott Medal.

Bailey, D. (1990). *Facts about families.* Austin, TX: Steck-Vaughn.

Blaine, M. (1984). *The terrible thing that happened at our house.* New York: Macmillan.

Carlstrom, N. W. (1990). *Grandpappy.* Boston, MA: Little, Brown.

Children of the world—series. (1990). Milwaukee, WI: Gareth Stevens Children's Books.

Cooper, M. (1993). *I got a family.* Jacksonville, IL: Permabound. NCSS-CBC Notable Children's Trade Book in the Field of Social Studies.

The family series. (1987). Chicago, IL: Children's Press (includes *Children, Grandparents, Parents, Teenagers*)

Flournoy, V. (1985). *The patchwork quilt.* New York: Dial Books for Young Readers.

Girard, L. W. (1987). *At daddy's on Saturdays.* New York: A. Whitman.

Goble, P. (1989). *Beyond the ridge.* New York: Bradbury Press.

Grifalconi, A. (1986). *The village of round and square houses.* Boston, MA: Little, Brown. Caldecott Honor, ALA Notable Book.

Hazen, B. S. (1992). *Even if I did something awful.* New York: Macmillan.

Hest, A. (1988). *The mommy exchange.* New York: Macmillan.

Hines, A. G. (1986). *Daddy makes the best spaghetti.* New York: Clarion.

Hulbert, J., & Kantor, S. (1990). *Armando asked "why"?* Milwaukee, WI: Raintree.

Kalman, B. (1986). *Family days.* New York: Crabtree.

Kimmelman, L. (1990). *Me and Nana.* New York: Harper and Row.

Lewin, H. (1983). *Jafta's father.* Minneapolis, MN: Carolrhoda (Also available *Jafta's mother, Jafta and the wedding, Jafta—the journey, Jafta—the town, Jafta—the homecoming*). All Reading Rainbow Books and NCSS-CBC Notable Trade Books in the Field of Social Studies.

Polacco, P. (1988). *The keeping quilt.* New York: Simon & Schuster Books for Young Readers.

Ransom, C. (1993). *We're growing together.* Jacksonville, IL: Perma-Bound.

Rosenberg, M. B. (1984). *Being adopted.* New York: Lothrop, Lee & Shepard.

Rylant, C. (1986). *The relatives came.* New York: Bradbury. Caldecott Honor.

Schick, E. (1976). *Neighborhood knight.* New York: Greenwillow (available also *Peggy's new brother, Rainy Sunday*).

Steptoe, J. (1980). *Daddy is a monster sometimes.* Philadelphia: Lippincott. Featured in Reading Rainbow.

Steptoe, J. (1987). *Mufaro's beautiful daughters.* New York: Lothrop, Lee & Shepard. Caldecott Honor.

Super, G. (1991). *What is a family?* MD: Twenty-First Century.

Super, G. (1991). *What kind of family do you have?* MD: Twenty-First Century.

Super, G. (1992). *Family traditions.* Frederick, MD: Twenty-First Century.

Tedesco, D. (1993). *Do you know how much I love you?* New York: Bradbury Press.

Thomas, A. D. (1991). *Life in the ghetto.* Kansas City, MO: Landmark Editions.

Williams, S. A. (1992). *Working cotton.* San Diego: HBJ. Caldecott Honor.

Williams, V. B. (1984). *Music, music for everyone.* New York: Greenwillow.

Williams, V. B. (1990). *More more more said the baby.* New York: Greenwillow. Caldecott Honor.

Yolen, J. (1987). *Owl moon.* New York: Philomel. Caldecott Medal.

Zolotow, C. (1966). *Big sister and little sister.* New York: Harper & Row. (Also *William's doll* [1972]).

Zolotow, C. (1969). *Some things go together.* New York: Crowell.

Books for Children Grades 4–8

Blume, J. (1972). *Tales of a fourth grade nothing.* New York: E. P Dutton (Also *Superfudge* [1980], *Fudge-a-mania* [1990], *Starring Sally J. Freedman as herself* [1977] and *Are you there, God? It's me, Margaret* [1970]).

Brooks, B. (1992). *What hearts.* New York: HarpersCollins. Newbery Honor.

Byars, B. (1970). *The summer of the swans.* New York: Viking Kestrel. Newbery Award.

Cleary, B. (1955). *Beezus and Ramona.* Jacksonville, IL: Permabound (Also *Ramona the brave* [1975], *Ramona and her father* [1977], *Ramona and her mother* [1979], *Ramona Quimby, age 8* [1981], *Ramona forever* [1984] and *Ramona the pest* [1968]).

Delton, J. (1989). *Angel's mother's baby.* Boston: Houghton Mifflin (Also *Angel's Mother's boyfriend* [1986] and *Angel's mother's wedding* [1987]).

Hermes, P. (1982). *You shouldn't have to say good-bye.* New York: HBJ.

Hopkins, L. B. (1993). *Mama and her boys.* Jacksonville, IL: Permabound.

Jenness, A. (1993). *Families: a celebration of diversity, commitment and love.* Boston: Houghton Mifflin.

Lowry, L. (1985). *Anastasia on her own.* California: Cornerstone Books (Also *Anastasia again* [1981], *Us and Uncle Fraud* [1984]).

MacLachlan, P. (1985). *Sarah, plain and tall.* New York: Harper & Row. Newbery Medal.

Mathis, S. B. (1975). *The hundred penny box.* New York: Viking. Newbery Honor.

Mazer, N. F. (1987). *After the rain.* New York: William Morrow & Co. Newbery Honor. (Also *My name is Danita* [1991]).

Miles, M. (1971). *Annie and the old one.* Boston, MA: Little, Brown. Newbery Honor.

Paterson, K. (1978). *The great Gilly Hopkins.* New York: Harper & Row. Newbery Honor.

Paterson, K. (1980). *Jacob have I loved.* New York: Harper LB. Newbery Award.

Patrick, D. (1993). *Family celebrations.* New York: Silver Moon Press.

Paulsen, G. (1987). *Hatchet.* New York: Bradbury. Newbery Honor.

Pullman, P. (1992). *Broken bridge.* New York: Knopf.

Rosenberg, M. B. (1992). *Living with a single parent.* New York: Bradbury.

Rylant, C. (1993). *Missing May.* New York: Orchard. Newbery Medal.

Salat, C. (1993). *Living in secret.* New York: Bantam Books.

Slepian, J. (1993). *Back to before.* New York: Philomel.

Thomas, J. R. (1988). *Saying good-bye to Grandma.* Jacksonville, IL: Permabound. ALA Notable Book and a NCSS-CBC Notable Children's Trade Book in the Field of Social Studies.

Voigt, C. (1982). *Dicey's song.* New York: Atheneum. Newbery Medal.

Wallace-Brodeur, R. (1992). *Godmother tree.* New York: HarperCollins.

Friends
Books for Children Grades K–3

Aliki. (1982). *We are best friends.* New York: Greenwillow LB.

Anglund, J. W. (1958). *A friend is someone who likes you.* New York: HBJ.

Anzaldua, G. (1993). *Friends From the Other Side (Amigos Del Otro Lado).* Jacksonville, IL: Perma-Bound.

Baldwin, A. N. (1973). *A friend in the park.* New York: Four Winds.

Buckley, K. (1989). *Love notes.* Niles, IL: Albert Whitman.

Carlstrom, N. W. (1990). *Blow me a kiss, Miss Lilly.* New York: Harper & Row.

Choi, S. N. (1993). *Halmoni and the picnic.* Boston: Houghton Mifflin.

Conta, M. M., & Reardon, M. (1974). *Feelings between friends.* Milwaukee, WI: Raintree.

Dantzer-Rosenthal, M. (1986). *Some things are different, some things are the same*. Niles, IL: Albert Whitman.

DePaolo, P. (1992). *Rosie and the yellow ribbon*. Boston: Little, Brown.

Everett, L. (1988). *Amigo means friend*. Jacksonville, IL: Perma-Bound.

Grimes, N. (1994). *Meet Danitra Brown*. New York: Lothrop, Lee & Shepard.

Hilton, N. (1993). *Andrew Jessup*. New York: Ticknor & Fields.

Hutchins, P. (1993). *My best friend*. Jacksonville, IL: Perma-Bound.

James, R. (1994). *Sadie*. Jacksonville, IL: Perma-Bound.

Joosse, B. M. (1988). *Better with two*. New York: Harper & Row.

Kellogg, S. (1986). *Best friends*. New York: Dial LB.

Komaiko, Leah. (1987). *Annie Bananie*. New York: Harper & Row. IRA-CBC Children's Choice for 1988.

Kudlinski, K. V. (1993). *Pearl Harbor is burning: A story of World War II*. New York: Viking.

Levi, D. H. (1989). *A very special friend*. Washington, DC: Kendall Green.

Mayer, M. (1989). *This is my friend*. New York: Golden Book.

Nones, E. J. (1993). *Caleb's friend*. New York: Farrar Straus & Giroux.

Perrine, M. (1970). *Nannabah's friend*. Jacksonville, IL: Perma-Bound.

Russo, M. (1992). *Alex is my friend*. New York: Greenwillow LB.

Schulz, C. M. (1964). *I need all the friends I can get*. San Francisco, CA: Determined Productions.

Shannon, G. (1994). *Seeds*. Boston: Houghton Mifflin.

Smith, J. L. (1984). *Kid next door and other headaches*. New York: Harper & Row.

Surat, M. M. (1983). *Angel child, dragon child*. Milwaukee, WI: Raintree.

Viorst, J. (1974). *Rosie and Michael*. New York: Atheneum.

York, C. B. (1994). *Key to the playhouse*. New York: Scholastic.

Zolotow, C. (1973). *Janey*. New York: Harper LB. (Also *My friend John* [1968]).

Books for Children Grades 4–8

Aamundsend, N. R. (1990). *Two short and one long*. Boston: Houghton Mifflin.

Adler, C. S. (1990). *Always and forever friends*. New York: Avon paper.

Banks, J. T. (1993). *Project wheels*. Boston: Houghton Mifflin.

Brooks, B. (1984). *The moves make the man*. New York: Harper & Row.

Carrick, C. (1987). *Some friend!* Boston: Houghton Mifflin.

Derman, M. (1981). *The friendstone*. New York: Dial.

Girion, B. (1990). *Indian summer*. New York: Scholastic.

Greene, C. (1988). *The Jenny summer*. New York: Harper LB.

Haas, D. (1988). *New friends*. New York: Scholastic.

Hansen, J. (1980). *The gift giver*. Boston: Houghton Mifflin.

Hansen, J. (1986). *Yellow bird and me*. Boston: Houghton Mifflin.

Hermes, P. (1984). *Friends are like that*. New York: Harcourt.

Hill, D. (1994). *See ya', Simon*. New York: Dutton Children's Books.

Konigsburg, E. L. (1967). *Jennifer, Hecate, MacBeth, William McKinley, and me, Elizabeth*. New York: Antheneum. Newbery Honor.

Lowry, L. (1989). *Number the stars*. New York: Dell. Newbery Medal.

Neville, E. (1963). *It's like this, Cat*. New York: Harper & Row. Newbery Medal.

Norment, L. (1994). *Once upon a time in junior high*. Jacksonville, IL: Perma-Bound.

Paterson, K. (1977). *Bridge to Terabithia*. New York: Harper LB. Newbery Medal.

Peck, R. N. (1974). *Soup*. New York: Knopf.

Reit, A. (1992). *Promise you won't tell*. New York: Dell paper.

Sirof, H. (1993). *Because she's my friend*. New York: Atheneum.

Snyder, Z. K. (1990). *Libby on Wednesday.* New York: Delacorte Press. ALA Best Book for Young Adults.

Tate, J. (1972). *Wild boy.* New York: Harper & Row.

Wilson, N. H. (1994). *Bringing Nettie back.* New York: Macmillan.

Wirths, C. G., & Kruhm-Bowman, M. (1993). *Your circle of friends.* New York: Twenty-First Century.

Woodson, J. (1993). *Between Madison and Palmetto.* New York: Delacorte Press.

SCHOOL
Books for Children Grades K–3

Allard, H. (1985). *Miss Nelson has a field day.* New York: Houghton Mifflin. (Also *Miss Nelson is missing* [1977]).

Aseltine, L. (1988). *First grade can wait.* Niles, IL: Whitman.

Baer, E. (1990). *This is the way we go to school.* New York: Scholastic.

Breinburg, P. (1974). *Shawn goes to school.* New York: Harper LB.

Bunting, E. (1992). *Our teacher's having a baby.* New York: Clarion.

Cleary, B. (1990). *Muggie Maggie.* New York: Morrow Junior Books.

Cohen, M. (1980). *First grade takes a test.* Jacksonville, IL: Perma-Bound.

Cohen, M. (1980). *No good in art.* New York: Greenwillow.

Conford, E. (1993). *Can do, Jenny Archer.* Boston: Springboard Books.

Dakos, K. (1993). *Don't read this book whatever you do.* New York: Four Winds.

Delton, J. (1979). *The new girl at school.* New York: Dutton.

Duey, K. (1992). *Mr. Stump Guss is a third grader.* Jacksonville, IL: Perma-Bound.

Ehrlich, F. (1992). *A class play with Ms. Vanilla.* New York: Viking.

Giff, P. R. (1980). *Next year I'll be special.* New York: Dutton.

Giff, P. R. (1980). *Today was a terrible day.* New York: Viking.

Gilson, J. (1991). *Itchy Richard.* New York: Clarion Books.

Howe, J. (1986). *When you go to kindergarten.* New York: Knopf.

Hurwitz, J. (1987). *Class clown.* New York: Morrow.

Kalman, B. (1985). *I like school.* New York: Crabtree.

Lawlor, L. (1988). *How to survive third grade.* Niles, IL: Whitman.

Levine, E. (1989). *I hate English!* New York: Scholastic.

McGovern, Ann. (1993). *Drop everything, it's d.e.a.r. time!* New York: Scholastic.

McKenzie, E. K. (1990). *Stargone John.* New York: Henry Holt.

Oxenbury, H. (1993). *First day of school.* Jacksonville, IL: Perma-Bound.

Rabe, B. (1981). *Balancing girl.* New York: Dutton. Child Study Association Book of the Year.

Rockwell, A. (1981). *When we grow up.* New York: Dutton.

Schwartz, A. (1988). *Annabelle Swift, kindergartner.* New York: Orchard.

Tate, E. (1992). *Front porch stories at the one room school.* New York: Bantam.

Tester, S. R. (1979). *We laughed a lot, my first day of school.* Chicago: Children's Press.

Whittman, S. (1982). *The wonderful Mrs. Trumbly.* New York: Harper.

Yashima, T. (1955). *Crow boy.* New York: Viking. Caldecott Honor.

Books for Children Grades 4–8

Asch, F. (1994). *Hands around Lincoln school.* New York: Scholastic.

Auch, M. J. (1989). *Glass slippers give you blisters.* New York: Holiday.

Butterworth, W. E. (1982). *Moose, the thing and me.* Boston: Houghton Mifflin.

Carlson, N. S. (1965). *The empty schoolhouse.* New York: Harper LB.

Caudill, R. (1966). *Did you carry the flag today, Charlie?* New York: Henry Holt.

Cooper, I. (1987). *The winning of Miss Lynn Ryan.* New York: Morrow.
Dahl, R. (1988). *Matilda.* New York: Viking.
Danziger, P. (1974). *The cat ate my gymsuit.* New York: Delacorte Press.
DeClements, B. (1985). *Sixth grade can really kill you.* New York: Scholastic.
Estes, E. (1944). *The hundred dresses.* New York: Harcourt.
Gilson, J. (1988). *Double dog dare.* New York: Lothrop, Lee & Shepard.
Guy, R. (1993). *Ups and downs of Carl Davis III.* New York: Delacorte Press.
Kaherdian, D. (1993). *Asking the river.* New York: Orchard Books.
Korman, G. (1982). *The war with Mr. Wizzle.* New York: Scholastic.
Martin, A. M. (1984). *Stage fright.* New York: Scholastic.
Miles, B. (1980). *Maudie and me and the dirty book.* New York: Knopf.
Shaw, J. (1986). *Kirsten learns a lesson: A school story.* Madison, WI: Pleasant Co.
Siskind, L. (1992). *Hopscotch tree.* Jacksonville, IL: Perma-Bound.
St. Antoine, S. (1992). *Dress code mess.* New York: Bantam.
Tolan, S. S. (1993). *Save Halloween!* New York: Morrow Junior Book.
Wirths, C. G., & Bowman-Kruhm, M. (1993). *Your new school.* Jacksonville, IL: Permabound.

Neighborhood and Community
Books for Children Grades K–3

Anno, M. (1986). *All in a day.* New York: Putnam LB.
Arnold, C. (1982). *What is a community?* New York: Franklin Watts.
Baylor, B. (1983). *The best town in the world.* New York: Macmillan.
Burton, V. L. (1978). *The little house.* Boston: Houghton Mifflin. Caldecott Medal.
Butterworth, N. (1992). *Busy people.* Cambridge, MA: Candlewick.
Dorros, A. (1992). *This is my house.* New York: Scholastic.
Garland, M. (1989). *My cousin Katie.* New York: Harper LB.
Greenfield, E. (1991). *Night on neighborhood street.* New York: Dial LB.
Grejniec, M. (1993). *Look.* New York: North-South Books.
Grossman, P. (1991). *The night ones.* New York: Harcourt.
Hazen, B. S. (1992). *Mommy's office.* New York: Macmillan.
Hellen, N. (1988). *The bus stop.* New York: Orchard.
Isadora, R. (1992). *City seen from a to z.* New York: Greenwillow.
Johnson, A. (1992). *The leaving morning.* New York: Orchard.
Jonas, A. (1983). *Round trip.* New York: Greenwillow. A Reading Rainbow, ALA Notable Book. Winner of New York Times Best Illustrated book.
Komaiko, L. (1990). *My perfect neighborhood.* New York: Harper & Row.
Levison, R. (1992). *Country dawn to dusk.* New York: Dutton LB.
Rius, M. (1986). *Let's discover the countryside.* Woodbury, NY: Barron's. (Also *Let's Discover the city*).
Rosen, M. J. (Ed.). (1992). *Home.* New York: Harper LB.
Showers, P. (1993). *Listening walk.* New York: Crowell.
Spier, P. (1980). *People.* New York: Doubleday LB.

Books for Children Grades 4–8

Atkins, S. B. (1993). *Voices from the field: children of migrant farm workers tell their stories.* Boston: Joy Street Books.
Carey, H. H., & Hanka, D. (1983). *How to use your community as a resource.* New York: Watts.
Kalman, B. (1990). *Visiting a village.* Toronto: Crabtree.

Krull, K. (1993). *City within a city: how kids live in New York's Chinatown.* New York: Lodestar Books.

Soto, G. (1992). *Neighborhood odes.* San Diego: HBJ.

STATE AND REGIONS

Southern States

Aylesworth, T. G., & Aylesworth, V. L. (1988). *Atlantic: District of Columbia, Virginia, West Virginia.* Chelsea. (Also *Lower Atlantic: North Carolina, South Carolina, The South: Alabama, Florida, Mississippi, The Southeast: Georgia, Kentucky, Tennessee.*)

Berger, G. (1984). *The Southeast States.* New York: Watts LB.

Griffith, H. V. (1986). *Georgia music.* New York: Greenwillow.

Rom, C. S. (1988). *Everglades.* Makato, MN: Crestwood.

Southwest

Ashabranner, B. (1989). *Born to the land: An American portrait.* New York: Putnam.

Aylesworth, T. G., & Aylesworth, V. L. (1988). *The Southwest: Colorado, New Mexico, Texas.* Chelsea. (Also *The West: Arizona, Nevada, Utah.*)

Carpenter, A. (1979). *Arizona.* Chicago Childrens LB. (Also *New Mexico, Oklahoma, Texas.*)

Phillips, B. L., & Phillips, B. (1987). *Texas.* New York: Watts.

Woods, G., & Woods, H. (1984). *The South Central States.* New York: Watts LB.

Midwestern States

Aylesworth, T. G., & Aylesworth, V. L. (1988). *Eastern Great Lakes: Indiana, Michigan, Ohio.* Chelsea. (Also *The Great Plains: Montana, Nebraska, North Dakota, South Dakota, Wyoming, South Central: Arkansas, Kansas, Louisiana, Missouri, Oklahoma, Western Great Lakes: Illinois, Iowa, Minnesota, Wisconsin.*)

Jacobson, D. (1984). *The North Central States.* New York: Watts LB.

Pfeiffer, C. (1989). *Chicago.* Minneapolis, MN: Dillon.

Siebert, D. (1989). *Heartland.* New York: Crowell.

Western States

Fradin, D. B. (1980). *Wyoming in words and pictures.* Chicago: Children's Press. (Also *Colorado in words and pictures, Idaho in words and pictures, Montana in words and pictures, Nevada in words and pictures* and *Utah in words and pictures.*)

Mell, J. (1988). *Grand Canyon.* Mankato, MN: Crestwood.

Skurzynski, G. (1984). *Caught in the moving mountains.* New York: Lothrop, Lee & Shepard.

Taylor, L. B., & Taylor, C. L. (1984). *The Rocky Mountain states.* New York: Watts LB.

Northeastern States

Adams, B. J. (1988). *New York City.* Minneapolis, MN: Dillon.

Aylesworth, T. G., & Aylesworth, V. L. (1988). *Mid-Atlantic: Delaware, Maryland, Pennsylvania.* New York: Chelsea. (Also *Northern New England, Southern New England* and *Upper Atlantic New Jersey.*)

Coerr, E. (1986). *Lady with a torch: How the Statue of Liberty was born.* New York: Harper LB.

Gilfond, H. (1984). *The Northeast States.* New York: Watts LB.

Krementz, J. (1987). *A visit to Washington D.C.* New York: Scholastic.
Monke, I. (1989). *Boston.* Minneapolis, MN: Dillon.
Munro, R. (1987). *The inside-outside book of Washington D.C.* New York: Dutton.

Pacific States

Aylesworth, T. G., & Aylesworth, V. L. (1987). *The Pacific: California, Hawaii.* New York: Chelsea.
Bauer, H. (1982). *Hawaii: The aloha state.* Honolulu, HI: Bess Press.
Carpenter, A. (1978). *California.* Chicago: Children's Press. (*Alaska, Hawaii, Oregon, Washington*)
Dunnahoo, T. (1987). *Alaska.* New York: Watts.
Feeney, S. (1985). *Hawaii is a rainbow.* Honolulu: University of Hawaii Press.
Haddock, P. (1989). *San Francisco.* Minneapolis, MN: Dillon.
Lawson, D. (1984). *The Pacific States.* New York: Watts LB.
Radlauer, R. (1984). *Yosemite National Park.* Chicago: Children's Press.

Nation and Western Hemisphere
Books for Children Grades K–3

Adoff, A. (1988). *Flamboyan.* New York: HBJ.
Andrews, J. (1986). *Very last first time.* New York: Atheneum.
Anno, M. (1983). *Anno's U.S.A.* New York: Philomel.
Ashrose, C. (1993). *Very first Americans.* Jacksonville, IL: Perma-Bound.
Blumberg, R. (1993). *Bloomers!* New York: Bradbury.
Cameron, A. (1988). *The most beautiful place in the world.* New York: Knopf.
Carter, W. E. (1983). *South America.* New York: Watts LB.
Cherry, L. (1990). *A great Kapok tree: A tale of the Amazon rain forest.* New York: HBJ.
Cohn, A. L. (1993). *From sea to shining sea.* New York: Scholastic.
Colman, W. (1987). *Constitution.* Jacksonville, IL: Perma-Bound.
Deacre, L. (1989). *Arroz con leche: Popular songs and rhymes from Latin America.* New York: Scholastic.
George, D. V. (1986). *South America.* Chicago: Children's Press.
Harrison, T. (1977). *Children of the Yukon.* Toronto, Ontario: Tundra.
Haskins, J. (1989). *Count your way through Mexico.* Minneapolis, MN: Carolrhoda.
Kuklin, S. (1992). *How my family lives in America.* New York: Bradbury.
Levine, E. (1993). *If your name was changed at Ellis Island.* New York: Scholastic.
Medearis, A. S. (1993). *Our people.* New York: Atheneum.
Moak, A. (1984). *A big city abc.* Toronto, Ontario: Tundra.
Vineberg, E. (1987). *Grandmother came from Dworitz: A Jewish love story.* Toronto, Ontario: Tundra.

Books for Children Grades 4–8

Adams, F. (1986). *El Salvador: Beauty among the ashes.* Minneapolis, MN: Dillon.
Brickenden, J. (1989). *Canada.* New York: Watts LB.
Carlson, L. M., & Ventura, C. L. (1990). *Where angels glide at dawn: New stories from Latin America.* New York: J. B. Lippincott.
Carpenter, A. (1979). *Far-flung America.* Chicago: Children's Press.
Casagrande, L. B., & Johnson, S. A. (1986). *Focus on Mexico: Modern life in an ancient land.* Minneapolis, MN: Lerner.
Catalano, J. (1988). *The Mexican Americans.* New York: Chelsea House.

Holbrook, S. (1983). *Canada's kids.* New York: Atheneum.

Harrison, T. (1993). *O Canada.* New York: Ticknor & Fields.

Irizarry, C. (1987). *Passport to Mexico.* New York: Watts.

Jacobsen, P. O., & Kristensen, P. S. (1986). *A family in Central America.* New York: Bookwright.

Knight, M. B. (1993). *Who belongs here? An American story.* Gardiner, ME: Tilbury House.

Markun, P. M. (1983). *Central America and Panama.* New York: Watts LB.

McKissack, P., & McKissack, F. (1994). *African-American inventors.* Brookfield, CT: Millbrook Press.

McKissack, P., & McKissack, F. (1994). *African-American scientists.* Brookfield, CT: Millbrook Press.

Nixon, J. L. (1993). *Land of promise.* New York: Bantam.

Nixon, J. L. (1994). *Land of dreams.* New York: Delacorte Press.

Reef, C. (1994). *Black fighting men: A proud history.* New York: Twenty-First Century.

Swanson, J. (1983). *The spice of America.* Minneapolis, MN: Carolrhoda.

Wade, H. (1988). *Afro-bets book of black heroes from A to Z.* Jacksonville, IL: Perma-Bound.

Westridge Young Writers Workshop. (1992). *Kids explore America's hispanic heritage.* Jacksonville, IL: Perma-Bound.

WORLD AND EASTERN HEMISPHERE
Books for Children Grades K–3

Africa

Aardema, V. (1984). *Oh, Kojo! How could you! An Ashanti tale.* New York: Dial LB.

Brian, A. (1986). *Lion and the ostrich chicks and other African folktales.* New York: Macmillan.

George, D. V. (1986). *Africa.* Chicago: Children's Press.

Jacobsen, P. O., & Kristensen, P. S. (1985). *A family in West Africa.* New York: Watts.

Lye, K. (1986). *Take a trip to Ethiopia.* New York: Watts. (Also *Take a trip to Kenya, Take a trip to Egypt, Take a trip to Morocco, Take a trip to Zimbabwe, Take a trip to Nigeria.*)

McKenna, N. D. (1986). *A Zulu family.* Minneapolis, MN: Lerner.

Musgrove, M. (1976). *Ashanti to Zulu: African traditions.* New York: Dial LB. Caldecott Medal.

Shachtman, T. (1981). *Growing up Masai.* New York: Macmillan.

Books for Children Grades 4–8

Africa

Barker, C. (1985). *A family in Nigeria.* Minneapolis, MN: Lerner.

Chaisson, J. (1987). *African Journey.* New York: Macmillan.

Evans, M. (1988). *South Africa.* New York: Gloucester.

Griffin, M. (1988). *A family in Kenya.* Minneapolis, MN: Lerner.

Kristensen, P., & Cameron, F. (1987). *We live in Egypt.* New York: Watts LB.

MacClintock, D. (1984). *African Images.* New York: Macmillan.

McCulla, P. E. (1988). *Tanzania.* New York: Chelsea.

Ngubane, H. (1987). *Zulus of Southern Africa.* Vero Beach, FL: Rourke.

Pitcher, D. (1981). *Tokoloshi: African folk tales retold.* Millbrae, CA: Celestial Arts.

Serwadda, W. M. (1974). *Songs and stories from Uganda.* New York: Harper LB.

Timberlake, L. (1986). *Famine in Africa.* New York: Gloucester.

Books for Children Grades K–3

Asia

Bang, M. (1984). *Dawn.* New York: Morrow.

Bannerman, H. (1923). *The story of little black Sambo.* New York: Lippincott.

Brown, M. (1961). *Once a mouse: A fable cut in wood.* New York: Scribner's.

Coerr, E. (1993). *Sadako.* New York: Putnam.

Garland, S. (1993). *The lotus seed.* San Diego: Harcourt.

Handforth, T. (1938). *Mei Li.* New York: Doubleday.

Keller, H. (1994). *Grandfather's dream.* New York: Greenwillow.

Mosel, A. (1968). *Tikki Tikki Tembo.* New York: Holt.

Mosel, A. (1972). *The funny little woman.* New York: Dutton.

Otsuka, Y. (1969). *Suho and the white horse: A legend of Mongolia.* Indianapolis: Bobbs-Merrill.

Say, A. (1993). *Grandfather's journey.* Boston: Houghton Mifflin.

Yashima, T. (1955). *Crow boy.* New York: Viking.

Yolen, J. (1967). *The emperor and the kite.* Cleveland, OH: World.

Books for Children Grades 4–8

Asia

Carlson, D. (1970). *Warlord of the Genji.* New York: Atheneum.

Dickson, P. (1979). *Tulku.* New York: Dutton.

Eaton, J. (1950). *Ghandi: Fighter without a sword.* New York: Morrow.

Edmonds, I. G. (1971). *The possible impossible of Ikkuyu the wise.* Macrae Smith.

Fritz, J. (1982). *Homesick: My own story.* New York: Putnam's.

Gaer, J. (1954). *The adventures of Rama.* Boston: Little, Brown.

Linevski, A. (1973). *An old tale carved out of stone.* New York: Crown.

Muhlenweg, F. (1952). *Big Tiger and Christian.* New York: Pantheon.

Paterson, K. (1975). *The master puppeteer.* New York: Crowell.

Seeger, E. (1967). *The five sons of king Pandu: The story of the Mahabharata.* New York: Scott.

Yep, L. (1975). *Dragonwings.* New York: Harper.

Books for Children Grades K–3

Australia and the Pacific Islands

Baker, J. (1995). *The story of Rosy Dock.* New York: Greenwillow.

Parker, K. (1966). *Australian legendary tales.* New York: Viking.

Books for Children Grades 4–8

Australia and the Pacific Islands

Berry, E. (1968). *The magic of banana and other Polynesian tales.* Day.

Maralngura, N. (1976). *Tales from the spirit time,* IN: Indiana University Press.

Park, R. (1982). *Playing Beatie Bow.* New York: Atheneum.

Perkins, C. M. (1972). *The sound of boomerangs.* New York: Atheneum.

Southall, I. (1966). *Ash road.* New York: St. Martin's Press.

Southall, I. (1971). *Josh.* New York: Macmillan.

Wrightson, P. (1968). *A racecourse for Andy.* San Diego: Harcourt.

Wrightson, P. (1974). *The nargun and the stars.* New York: Atheneum.

Books for Children Grades K–3

The Middle East

Singer, I. B. (1967). *Mazel and Shlimazel.* New York: Farrar, Straus & Giroux.

Travers, P. L. (1980). *Two pairs of shoes.* New York: Viking.

Walker, B. (1967). *Watermelons, walnuts, and the wisdom of Allah and other tales of the Hoca.* New York: Parents' Magazine.

Books for Children Grades 4–8

The Middle East

Cottrell, L. (1960). *Land of the pharaohs.* Cleveland, OH: World.

Davis, R., & Ashabrunner, B. (1960). *Ten thousand desert swords: The epic story of a great Bedouin tribe.* Boston: Little, Brown.

Dickson, P. (1973). *The dancing bear.* Boston: Atlantic/Little, Brown.

Downing, C. (1965). *Tales of the Hodja.* New York: Doubleday.

Ensor, D. (1962). *The adventures of Hatim Tai.* Walck.

Harris, R. (1970). *The moon in the cloud.* New York: Macmillan.

Kherdian, D. (1979). *The road from home: The story of an Armenian girl.* New York: Greenwillow.

Moorehead, A. (1966). *No room in the ark.* New York: Harper.

Newlon, C. (1977). *The Middle East, and Why.* New York: Dodd, Mead.

Picard, B. L. (1972). *Tales of ancient Persia.* New York: Oxford University Press.

Name Index

Subject Index